A Companion to Ayn Rand

Blackwell Companions to Philosophy

This outstanding student reference series offers a comprehensive and authoritative survey of philosophy as a whole. Written by today's leading philosophers, each volume provides lucid and engaging coverage of the key figures, terms, topics, and problems of the field. Taken together, the volumes provide the ideal basis for course use, representing an unparalleled work of reference for students and specialists alike.

Already published in the series:

A Companion to Ayn Rand

Edited by

Allan Gotthelf and Gregory Salmieri

WILEY Blackwell

In the pages that follow, you will read a great deal about a heroism that consists in loving one's life and living it fully. This book is dedicated to the memory of two of its authors who were such heroes – men who, throughout their lives, projected a profound benevolence and love of this world; and who, during their battles with cancer, often served as a comfort and an inspiration to the friends who sought to comfort them.

To John David Lewis (1955–2012), a consummate fighter for his values.

And to Allan Gotthelf (1942–2013), whose spirit and wisdom have informed every page of this Companion, *both through his own editorial work and through his influence on those of us who live on – his coeditor, especially.*

Contents

CONTENTS

Notes on Contributors

Harry Binswanger, who was an associate of Ayn Rand in her final years, teaches philosophy at the Objectivist Academic Center of the Ayn Rand Institute. He has taught, and lectured on, esthetics at Pratt Institute and elsewhere and has taught philosophy at Hunter College (City University of New York) and the University of Texas at Austin. He edited *The Ayn Rand Lexicon* (Penguin, 1986) and coedited (with Leonard Peikoff) the expanded second edition of Rand's *Introduction to Objectivist Epistemology* (Penguin, 1990). He is the author of *The Biological Basis of Teleological Concepts* (ARI Press, 1990) and *How We Know: Epistemology on an Objectivist Foundation* (TOF Publications, 2014).

Tore Boeckmann is an independent scholar of Romanticism in art. He has lectured and written extensively on Ayn Rand's novels and literary esthetics, and he edited for publication her guide to literature, *The Art of Fiction* (Plume, 2000). His most significant recent work includes an essay on the painter Caspar David Friedrich; his most delightful work includes an essay on the literary origins of Rand's flamboyant playboy hero Francisco d'Anconia in Robert Mayhew (ed.), *Essays on Ayn Rand's* Atlas Shrugged (Lexington Books, 2009). He is currently writing a book on Romanticism from Victor Hugo to Ayn Rand.

Onkar Ghate is a senior fellow at the Ayn Rand Institute, where he specializes in philosophy. He teaches in the Institute's Objectivist Academic Center and serves as a writer, media spokesman, and senior editor for the Institute. He publishes both scholarly and popular articles on Rand's fiction and philosophy. Recent essays include "*Atlas Shrugged*: America's Second Declaration of Independence," in Debi Ghate and Richard E. Ralston (eds.), *Why Businessmen Need Philosophy* (New American Library, 2nd edition, 2011) and "The Plight of Leo Kovalensky," in *Essays on Ayn Rand's* We the Living (Lexington Books, 2nd edition, 2012). His current research focuses on religion and morality and the separation of church and state.

Allan Gotthelf (1942–2013) was, at the time of his death, Anthem Foundation Distinguished Fellow for Research and Teaching in Philosophy at Rutgers University and Professor Emeritus of Philosophy at The College of New Jersey. From 2003 to 2012 he was Visiting Professor of History and Philosophy of Science at the University of Pittsburgh, where he held an Anthem Fellowship for the Study of Objectivism. He was a founding member of the Ayn Rand Society and served as chair of its steering committee (from 1990 until his death) and as the primary editor of the Society's *Philosophical Studies* series. He is the author of *On Ayn Rand*

(Wadsworth, 2000), and of many articles on Aristotle, 15 of which are collected in his *Teleology, First Principles, and Scientific Method in Aristotle's Biology* (Oxford University Press, 2012).

Lester H. Hunt is Professor of Philosophy at the University of Wisconsin, Madison. He has also taught at Carnegie-Mellon University, the University of Pittsburgh, and Johns Hopkins University. He is the author of *Nietzsche and the Origins of Virtue* (Routledge, 1990), *Character and Culture* (Rowman & Littlefield, 1997), and *Anarchy, State, and Utopia: An Advanced Guide* (Wiley-Blackwell, 2015) and is editor of two books of original essays: *Grade Inflation: Academic Standards in Higher Education* (SUNY, 2008) and (with Noel Carroll) *Philosophy in the Twilight Zone* (Wiley-Blackwell, 2009). He has also written several dozen scholarly articles on ethics, social and political philosophy, the presentation of philosophical ideas in literature and film, and problems in the history of philosophy.

John David Lewis (1955–2012), after a 25-year career in business, changed direction and earned a PhD in Classics at the University of Cambridge in 2001. At the time of his death, in 2012, he was Visiting Associate Professor in the Philosophy, Politics, and Economics Program at Duke University and Adjunct Associate Professor of Business at the University of North Carolina at Chapel Hill. He published three books, *Solon the Thinker: Political Thought in Archaic Athens* (Bristol Classics, 2006), *Early Greek Lawgivers* (Bloomsbury Academic, 2007), and *Nothing Less than Victory: Decisive Wars and the Lessons of History* (Princeton University Press, 2010), and many articles and reviews in academic journals and the public press.

James G. Lennox is Professor of History and Philosophy of Science at the University of Pittsburgh. He was one of the founding members of the Ayn Rand Society, and is currently co-chair of the Society's steering committee and coeditor of its *Philosophical Studies* series. He is author of *Aristotle's Philosophy of Biology* (Cambridge University Press, 2001) and *Aristotle on the Parts of Animals I–IV* (Oxford University Press, 2001), and coeditor of *Philosophical Issues in Aristotle's Biology* (Cambridge University Press, 1987), *Concepts, Theories, and Rationality in the Biological Sciences* (University of Pittsburgh Press, 1995) and *Being, Nature, and Life in Aristotle: Essays in Honor of Allan Gotthelf* (Cambridge University Press, 2010). Currently he is working on a book on Aristotle's norms of inquiry and collaborating on a translation and commentary of Aristotle's *Meteorology IV*.

Shoshana Milgram is Associate Professor of English at Virginia Tech, where she has taught since earning her PhD in Comparative Literature from Stanford University. She has published articles on nineteenth- and twentieth-century writers in French, Russian, and English/American literatures, including Victor Hugo, George Sand, Chekhov, Dostoevsky, Tolstoi, Victoria Cross, George Eliot, John Fowles, W.S. Gilbert, Ursula K. LeGuin, Nabokov, Herbert Spencer, Steinbeck, E.L. Voynich, and Ayn Rand. She has also published articles on "Capitalism," "Cinema," and "Leader" in J.C. Seigneuret's *Dictionary of Literary Themes and Motifs*, as well as introductions to editions of Hugo's *Toilers of the Sea* and *The Man Who Laughs* and Nevil Shute's *The Seafarers*. She is at work on a book-length study of Ayn Rand's life from birth to 1957.

Fred D. Miller, Jr. is Research Professor at the Center for the Philosophy of Freedom at the University of Arizona and Emeritus Professor of Philosophy and Executive Director of the Social Philosophy and Policy Center at Bowling Green State University. He is author of *Nature, Justice, and Rights in Aristotle's Politics* (Oxford University Press, 1995) and coeditor of *A Companion to Aristotle's Politics* (Blackwell, 1995), *Freedom, Reason, and the Polis: Essays in Ancient Greek Political*

Philosophy (Cambridge University Press, 2007), *A History of the Philosophy of Law from the Ancient Greeks to the Scholastics* (Springer, 2007), and *Reason and Analysis in Ancient Greek Philosophy* (Springer, 2012). He is also Executive Editor of *Social Philosophy & Policy*. He is currently preparing a translation of Aristotle's *De Anima* and *Parva Naturalia* for Oxford University Press.

Adam Mossoff is Professor of Law at George Mason University School of Law and a co-founder of and Director of Academic Programs at the Center for the Protection of Intellectual Property at Mason Law. He has published numerous book chapters, essays, and journal articles on topics in patent law, property law, legal history, and legal philosophy, including "Saving Locke from Marx: The Labor Theory of Value in Intellectual Property Theory" (*Social Philosophy and Policy*, 29(2), 2012). He has testified before the Senate and House on patent legislation, and he is a frequent speaker at professional and academic conferences, as well as at the PTO, the DOJ, the National Academy of Sciences, and the Smithsonian Institution, on topics in intellectual property policy.

Jason G. Rheins is Assistant Professor of Philosophy at Loyola University Chicago. He was a Visiting Assistant Professor at the University of North Carolina, Chapel Hill, and has held teaching positions at St. John's University, Swarthmore College, and the University of Pennsylvania, where he received his PhD in Philosophy in 2010 with a dissertation on Plato's theology and its place within his ontology and natural philosophy. He has published articles on topics in the philosophy of science and Ancient Greek philosophy. His current research focuses on metaphysical issues related to the cosmology and theology of Plato, Aristotle, and their successors.

Gregory Salmieri holds a fellowship in philosophy at the Anthem Foundation and teaches at Rutgers University. He received his PhD in philosophy from the University of Pittsburgh in 2008, and subsequently held teaching and research positions at the University of North Carolina, Chapel Hill (2008–2012) and at Boston University (2012–2014). He has published on issues in Aristotle's epistemology and ethics and on Rand's philosophy and novels. He is co-chair of the Ayn Rand Society's Steering Committee, and coeditor of its *Philosophical Studies* series. He is also the editor of a forthcoming multi-author volume on Aristotle's epistemology.

Tara Smith is Professor of Philosophy at the University of Texas at Austin, where she holds the BB&T Chair for the Study of Objectivism and is the Anthem Foundation Fellow. She is the author of *Judicial Review in an Objective Legal System* (Cambridge University Press, 2015), *Ayn Rand's Normative Ethics: The Virtuous Egoist* (Cambridge University Press, 2006), *Viable Values: A Study of Life as the Root and Reward of Morality* (Rowman & Littlefield, 2000), and *Moral Rights and Political Freedom* (Rowman & Littlefield, 1995), as well as numerous articles in moral, legal, and political philosophy.

Darryl Wright is Professor of Philosophy at Harvey Mudd College (The Claremont Colleges). He works in the areas of moral and political philosophy and has published several articles on Ayn Rand's ethical thought as well as articles on G.E. Moore and F.H. Bradley. Recent publications include "Evaluative Concepts and Objective Values: Rand on Moral Objectivity" (*Social Philosophy and Policy*, 25(1), 2008) and "Reasoning About Ends: Life as a Value in Ayn Rand's Ethics," in A. Gotthelf and J.G. Lennox (eds.), *Metaethics, Egoism, and Virtue: Studies in Ayn Rand's Normative Theory* (University of Pittsburgh Press, 2011). He is currently writing a book on Ayn Rand's ethics and its relation to contemporary (meta)ethical theories.

Acknowledgments

Work on this book began in December of 2006 when Allan Gotthelf and I first discussed the possibility of a companion-style volume on Ayn Rand. He was my teacher and dear friend, and his death in 2013, after a 15-year battle with prostate cancer, was a loss to the philosophy profession and a profound loss to me personally. Our collaboration on this project was one of the great joys of my life, and I wish he could have lived to see its completion. Now that the work is finished, I can find no better way to express my gratitude to Allan than by repeating the words of a friend to whom he introduced me 17 years ago: οὕτω δ᾽ ἔοικε καὶ τοῖς φιλοσοφίας κοινωνήσασιν· οὐ γὰρ πρὸς χρήμαθ᾽ ἡ ἀξία μετρεῖται, τιμή τ᾽ ἰσόρροπος οὐκ ἂν γένοιτο, ἀλλ᾽ ἴσως ἱκανόν, καθάπερ καὶ πρὸς θεοὺς καὶ πρὸς γονεῖς, τὸ ἐνδεχόμενον (Aristotle, *Nicomachean Ethics* 1164b2–6).

There are many others who deserve thanks for their role in making this book possible. First, I trust that I speak for all the contributors to this *Companion* when I acknowledge the great debt we owe to Leonard Peikoff, who has been a teacher to all of us (whether in person or through his books and recorded courses). The many citations to him throughout this book are testament to this debt. Moreover, as the executor of Rand's estate he is responsible for making available the many posthumously published and archival materials that have enriched all of our understanding of Rand's thought and life.

This brings me to the subject of the Ayn Rand Archives. Thank you to Mike Berliner, Jeff Britting, and Jenniffer Woodson for building and maintaining the Archives, for making it available to us, and for all of your help navigating it over the years. The Ayn Rand Institute, of which the Archives is a department, has been responsible for a host of programs and events over the past 30 years that contributed immeasurably to the work and intellectual development of many of the contributing authors (myself included).

The last decade of Allan's life was a period of great productivity made possible by the support of the Anthem Foundation for Objectivist Scholarship, which has also supported my research since 2008. I would like to acknowledge three people at Anthem in particular. John McCaskey, who founded Anthem and was its first president, created the fellowship that brought Allan to the University of Pittsburgh in 2003 (when I was a graduate student there) and put him in a position to organize workshops and conferences that raised the scholarly level of work on Rand immeasurably. John was also instrumental in placing me in my first job in 2008, and he has been a source of professional advice in the years since. Debi Ghate, Anthem's president 2009–2013, was a constant supporter of my and Allan's careers and an able executive in difficult times. The same is true of Yaron Brook, the executive director of the Ayn Rand Institute, who also serves as the chairman of Anthem's board of directors and who took over as president when Debi left.

Thank you also to Jim Lennox, for being an excellent doctoral advisor, for his role in bringing Allan to Pittsburgh, for being a vital part of the intellectual community there, and for his continuing support and advice in countless matters big and small.

Our editors at Wiley Blackwell, several of whom have come and gone while we were working on this book, have displayed supernatural patience. I am grateful to all, but I'd like to thank especially Nick Bellorini, with whom we signed our contract in 2008, and Deirdre Ilkson, who proposed incorporating the book into the Blackwell Companions to Philosophy series. Thanks also to Fiona Screen, who shepherded this book through the production process, and to our two copyeditors, Michael Coultas and Anna Oxbury. All three have been a consistent pleasure to work with, despite my frustrating habit of introducing changes (and lengthening chapters) long after submission of the manuscript. Michael and I made most of the decisions concerning formatting and style together, and he copyedited more than half of the book before unexpectedly passing away. We did not meet in person, but his emails revealed him to be a kind and thoughtful man who loved his work and took pride in doing it well. Anna, working with remarkable speed, both maintained the high standard Michael had set and finished the copyediting in time to meet our production schedule.

I would like to acknowledge several friends and colleagues to whom Allan and I turned for advice either about individual chapters or the design of the book as a whole: Geoff Sayre-McCord, James Brazell, Mary Ann Sures, and Shoshana Milgram. Mike Mazza, in his capacity as a research assistant, checked most of the quotes in the book and made many helpful suggestions about the content of various chapters. Three other friends – Matt Bateman, Ben Bayer, and Onkar Ghate – took on significant editorial work, each on a different chapter, during a period when Allan's health prevented him from working and I was overwhelmed. They have my deep gratitude both for their friendship and for their excellent work.

Thank you to all of the contributors to this volume both for bearing with our sometimes demanding editorial style, and for their patience with the many delays on the road to publication.

Finally, I'd like to thank my wife, Karen, both for her help with this project (which took many forms) and for everything she's brought to my life. And I'd like to thank Cass Love and her husband Ron for all of their help with this project, for their friendship, and for the unique role they played in Allan's life.

Gregory Salmieri

A Note on Abbreviations and References

Rand's own works and certain others that we have identified as "quasi-primary sources" are listed in the annotated bibliography at the end of this volume and cited in the text by the abbreviations indicated below. The numbers after the abbreviations indicate where they can be found in the bibliography.

In some cases, where a passage exists in two sources, we cite it to both separated by a slash. In such cases, the quoted material (if any) is as it appears in the first of the two citations. This format is used (among other times) when quoting from the original archival sources of material by Rand that has been posthumously published in an edited form.

Citations to works by figures in the history of philosophy are given in the standard formats used by scholars of those figures: Bekker numbers for Aristotle, Academy numbers for Kant, and so on. Other works are cited in the author/date format; bibliographic information for these works can be found in the references at the end of each chapter. Multiple works by an author from the same calendar year are distinguished by letters, and these references are standardized throughout the volume; so, for example, Allan Gotthelf's essay on "Dagny's Final Choice" is referenced as Gotthelf 2009b even in chapters that do not also make reference to Gotthelf 2009a.

Answers	*Ayn Rand Answers: The Best of Her Q&A.* #46.
Anthem	Revised edition of *Anthem.* #3.
Anthem38	1938 edition of *Anthem.* #3.
AOF	*The Art of Fiction: A Guide for Writers and Readers.* #44.
AON	*The Art of Nonfiction: A Guide for Writers and Readers.* #45.
ARL	*The Ayn Rand Letter.* #18.
Atlas	*Atlas Shrugged.* #5.
Biographical Interviews	Biographical interviews of Ayn Rand conducted by Barbara and Nathaniel Branden in 1960–1961. #49.
Column	*The Ayn Rand Column.* #14.
CUI	*Capitalism: The Unknown Ideal.* #8.
Early	*The Early Ayn Rand.* #36.
Fountainhead	*The Fountainhead.* #4.
FTNI	*For The New Intellectual: The Philosophy of Ayn Rand.* #6.

HOP1	Leonard Peikoff. *Founders of Western Philosophy: Thales to Hume.* #32.
HOP2	Leonard Peikoff. *Modern Philosophy: Kant to the Present.* #33.
Ideal	*Ideal: The Novel and the Play.* #39.
ITOE	*Introduction to Objectivist Epistemology.* #9.
Journals	*Journals of Ayn Rand.* #42.
Letters	*Letters of Ayn Rand.* #41.
Marginalia	*Ayn Rand's Marginalia: Her Critical Comments on the Writings of over 20 Authors.* #40.
OPAR	Leonard Peikoff. *Objectivism: The Philosophy of Ayn Rand.* #52.
Papers	The Ayn Rand Papers, a collection of the Ayn Rand Archives. #48.
Parallels	Leonard Peikoff. *The Ominous Parallels: The End of Freedom in America.* #35.
Playboy Interview	Ayn Rand's interview in *Playboy Magazine.* #23.
Plays	*Three Plays.* #37.
PWNI	*Philosophy: Who Needs It.* #12.
RM	*The Romantic Manifesto: A Philosophy of Literature.* #10.
ROTP	*Return of the Primitive: The Anti-Industrial Revolution.* #15.
Russian Writings	*Russian Writings on Hollywood.* #43.
Speaking	*Objectively Speaking: Ayn Rand Interviewed.* #47.
TIA	*The Intellectual Activist.* #19.
TO	*The Objectivist.* #17.
TOF	*The Objectivist Forum.* #20.
TON	*The Objectivist Newsletter.* #16.
TPO	Leonard Peikoff. *The Philosophy of Objectivism.* #34.
Unconquered	*The Unconquered* with another, earlier adaptation of *We the Living.* #38.
VAR	Nathaniel Branden. *The Vision of Ayn Rand: The Basic Principles of Objectivism.* #51.
VOR	*The Voice of Reason.* #13.
VOS	*The Virtue of Selfishness: A New Concept of Egoism.* #7.
WIAR	Nathaniel Branden. *Who Is Ayn Rand?* #31.
Workshops	Transcript of the Objectivist Workshops. #50.
WTL	Revised edition of *We the Living.* #1.
WTL36	1936 edition of *We the Living.* #1.

Part I

Context

1

An Introduction to the Study of Ayn Rand

GREGORY SALMIERI

"Ayn Rand ... is among the most outspoken – and important – intellectual voices in America today," wrote *Playboy Magazine* in 1964. "She is the author of what is perhaps the most fiercely damned and admired best seller of the decade, *Atlas Shrugged.*" The magazine goes on to describe the novel's impressive sales ("more than 1,200,000 copies since its publication six years ago"), the discussion groups and debate it spawned on college campuses, and the thousands of people who subscribed to Rand's *Objectivist Newsletter* or attended lecture courses on her philosophy.

> That any novel should set off such a chain reaction is unusual; that *Atlas Shrugged* has done so is as-tonishing. For the book, a panoramic novel about what happens when the "men of the mind" go on strike, is 1,168 pages long. It is filled with lengthy, sometimes complex philosophical passages; and it is brimming with as many explosively unpopular ideas as Ayn Rand herself. Despite this success, the literary establishment considers her an outsider. Almost to a man, critics have either ignored or denounced the book. She is an exile among philosophers, too, although *Atlas* is as much a work of philosophy as it is a novel. Liberals glower at the very mention of her name; but conservatives, too, swallow hard when she begins to speak. For Ayn Rand, whether anyone likes it or not, is *sui generis*: indubitably, irrevocably, intransigently individual. (*Playboy Interview* 35)

Over 50 years later, and 33 years after her death, Rand remains one of the most important intellectual voices in our culture. In the last six years alone (2009 through 2014) *Atlas* has sold 2.25 million copies – one million more than in the six years immediately after its publication. In total, more than 30 million copies of Rand's books have been sold.[1] Her ideas are as radical today as they were during her lifetime. And there remains a pronounced disconnect between the inspiration (both esthetic and intellectual) that so many readers take from her books and the dismissive or scornful response that these same books still often meet in academia.

In the political arena, liberals still despise and mock her, as do many leaders of the Christian right, neo-conservative, and libertarian movements. Yet Rand's influence is always evident wherever one finds morally self-confident opposition to regulation, taxes, or entitlements, and wherever one sees celebrations of business and the free market. Thus, sales of Rand's books

A Companion to Ayn Rand, First Edition. Edited by Allan Gotthelf and Gregory Salmieri.
© 2016 John Wiley & Sons, Ltd. Published 2016 by John Wiley & Sons, Ltd.

soared to record levels in 2008 and 2009 as Americans struggled to make sense of the financial crisis, and slogans referencing John Galt (the hero of *Atlas*) were ubiquitous at the early "Tea Party" protests against the interventionist measures by which the Bush and Obama administrations responded to the crisis. Rand has been frequently referenced in American political discourse since, both by those who cite her as an inspiration and by commentators who attribute many of the nation's ills to Rand's influence.[2] But references to Rand, on both sides, are usually superficial. They are attempts to evoke or to smear – but not to engage with – that strand in the American consciousness which resonates to Rand's distinctive vision of what a human life can and should be.

She described this vision as "the concept of man as a heroic being, with his own happiness as the moral purpose of his life, with productive achievement as his noblest activity, and reason as his only absolute" (*Atlas* 1070).[3] Rand viewed "man" as a "heroic being" in the sense that she thought that human nature sets a demanding ideal that each individual can and should achieve in his own life and character (though few people do achieve it). This ideal is the fit object of the emotion of reverence, and Rand sometimes speaks of "worshiping" it or the people (real or fictional) who embody it. This ideal – the life proper to a human being – is egoistic in the sense that an individual leading such a life is dedicated as a matter of moral principle to his own happiness. Happiness, for Rand, is not mere pleasure or desire-satisfaction. It is that state of "non-contradictory joy" (*Atlas* 1022) that is the concomitant of achieving what one has rationally identified as objectively good. A heroic human being is committed to the fullest use of his reason; and he uses it to conceive ambitious, life-sustaining goals, and to achieve them via productive activity. All the aspects of this vision and Rand's arguments for them are discussed in detail in later chapters. So are other aspects of her thought, including the view that, because such a life requires the political freedom to live by one's own judgment, laissez-faire capitalism is the only moral social system. It is enough for now to note that this vision evokes intense reactions in many people: some are inspired; others, revolted; some find it profound; others, juvenile.

Rand used the phrase "sense of life" to designate the aspect of a person's or a culture's psychology that generates the differing emotional reactions we have to artworks and (especially) to the view of the world and of humanity that they project. A sense of life is an implicit worldview – a "pre-conceptual metaphysics" that is experienced as a "constant, basic emotion" and expressed in a person's "widest goals or smallest gestures" ("Philosophy and Sense of Life" *RM* 8, 18, 22).[4] Part of maturing, Rand held, is translating one's sense of life into conscious convictions, which one can rationally evaluate; correct, if necessary; and then consistently implement. Adopting this terminology, then, we can say that, for better or for worse, Rand's vision holds a deep and enduring appeal for something in "the American sense of life" – or, at least, for a sense of life that is shared by many Americans and that contributes to the character of the nation. If so, then engagement with her works and thought is a crucial means by which scholars can help America to understand itself, and by which they can help the many people, in every country, who find Rand inspiring or repugnant to understand one another.[5]

Taking Rand Seriously

The scholarly study of Rand's works was postponed by two generations of academics who found her vision appalling and thought or hoped that she was a passing fad, and that their students' attraction to her was a youthful indiscretion. These hopes have been dashed. Decades after her death, Rand's appeal and influence cannot be denied; and very often something of her heroic vision of man remains even in the souls of readers who "outgrow" her and resign themselves (sadly or smugly) to a world in which they believe the kind of life she projects is impossible or vicious.

Happily, these facts are beginning to be recognized. Rand's novels have, perhaps grudgingly, been admitted to the literary canon. They are seldom discussed in journals, but one increasingly finds *Anthem* and *The Fountainhead* taught in high school English courses or listed on summer reading lists, and *Atlas Shrugged* has begun to appear in university syllabi. Objectivism, as Rand called her philosophical system, may still be regarded as a curiosity by most philosophy professors, but her defense of egoism is now often covered in ethics textbooks, excerpts from her essays are widely anthologized, and there are entries on Rand in the two major encyclopedias of philosophy.[6] Moreover, there is a small but growing number of scholars and advocates of Objectivism within the philosophy departments of America's colleges and universities.[7]

Indeed, the last decade saw a boom in quality Rand scholarship. Among the highlights are Tara Smith's (2006) *Ayn Rand's Normative Ethics*, Robert Mayhew's (2004, 2005a, 2007, 2009, 2012a) edited collections of essays on each of Rand's novels, and the first two volumes of the Ayn Rand Society's *Philosophical Studies* series: *Metaethics, Egoism, and Virtue* (2011) and *Concepts and Their Role in Knowledge* (2013), both edited by Allan Gotthelf and James Lennox. Since its founding in 1987, the Society (of which I am co-secretary) holds sessions on Rand's ideas at meetings of the American Philosophical Association. There have been 30 such meetings, collectively involving 48 panelists who represent 41 academic departments from institutions on three continents.[8] Some of these panelists are advocates for Objectivism; many are not; but all are participating in the stimulating exchange of ideas that occurs whenever philosophers take Rand's works seriously.

Turning from scholarly to popular books, two biographies of Rand were published in 2009, by Jennifer Burns and Anne C. Heller. Burns's book, especially, is less informative than one might hope about Rand's ideas and intellectual development; and both authors, in what seem to be attempts to create what they regard as a satisfying narrative about Rand's later life, emphasize the painful episodes and underplay the bright points; but each biography is a significant improvement over any previously available book-length treatment of Rand's life.[9] There is also Gary Weiss's (2012) *Ayn Rand Nation*, which, though not very deep and rife with inaccuracies, clearly recognizes the need for sustained reflection by leftists about the nature of Rand's ideas and the source of their appeal.[10] Weiss is trying to combat Rand's influence, but there have also been several recent books put out by major publishing houses that expound some of Rand's ideas sympathetically for a popular audience: Donald Luskin and Andrew Greta's (2011) *I Am John Galt: Today's Heroic Innovators Building the World and the Villainous Parasites Destroying It*, Yaron Brook and Don Watkins's (2012) *Free Market Revolution: How Ayn Rand's Ideas Can End Big Government*, and Peter Schwartz's (2015) *In Defense of Selfishness: Why the Code of Sacrifice Is Unjust and Destructive*.

There are other books that could be named as well, but this list is sufficient to illustrate a growing recognition – both within academia and without, in several disciplines, and across the ideological spectrum – that Ayn Rand should be taken seriously.

To take an author seriously means to read her, not with an eye toward confirming one's prejudices (whether favorable or unfavorable), but simply with an eye to understanding what she thinks and why. If one finds her approach unfamiliar and difficult, it means working to overcome that. If one finds what she says implausible or unmotivated, it means taking the time to consider why it seems otherwise to her and to the readers who find her convincing – and it means giving thought to the question of whether it is you or she who is mistaken. By the same token, if she strikes you as obviously correct with respect to an issue where you know many people find her views counterintuitive, it means working to identify the premises that you share with her and not with them, and then figuring out how to determine whether those premises are true.

This approach is especially important in the case of Rand, because she is (as *Playboy* put it) "brimming" with "explosively unpopular ideas." In particular, she maintained that our society is unjust in deep and pervasive ways, and that at the heart of this corruption are the moral ideals by which we are taught to live our lives, and on which we are taught to base our self-esteem. Rand is thus a *radical* critic of society. In this respect she is analogous to other radical thinkers of various stripes – nineteenth-century abolitionists, twentieth-century Marxists, and those who inveigh against what they see as the inherent racism, sexism, or imperialism of Western culture.

As with many such thinkers, Rand's writing often has a confrontational character. For example, she explains, in the introduction to *The Virtue of Selfishness*, that she gave the work the title she did "For the reason that makes you afraid of it" (*VOS* vii). The title *is* frightening. It challenges our fundamental moral beliefs – beliefs that are central to all of our goals, to our sense of self-esteem. It takes courage and a commitment to introspective honesty to consider challenges to such beliefs. When one's sense of self-worth is threatened, there is always a temptation to seize upon any convenient rationalization for rejecting the challenge (and the challenger) rather than taking the time, and putting forth the effort, required to understand and evaluate it. On the other hand, if one feels alienated from or unappreciated by one's fellow human beings, a radical criticism of one's society can serve as a rationalization for these feelings and a weapon with which one can lash out against others. Whether one finds Rand appealing or repugnant, the sorts of issues that she raises are fraught with temptations for intellectual dishonesty, and one will find no shortage of facile reasons to dismiss or embrace her ideas too quickly.

Readers who resist these temptations, and approach Rand seriously, will, I think, find her to be a powerfully unconventional artist and a philosopher of great breadth and subtlety. They may also come to see her, as I do, as the discoverer of some profound and empowering truths. But it is not my aim here to argue for this evaluation of Rand, nor is that the purpose of any of the chapters in this book. All of the contributing authors are professional intellectuals who have made mastering Rand's works and philosophy a significant part of their careers, despite working in fields where she is too seldom taken seriously and where a perceived interest in her can be a professional liability. It stands to reason that we would all be great admirers of her, and two of us (Allan Gotthelf and Harry Binswanger) counted her as a mentor and a personal friend. In other contexts, many of us have written as defenders of her philosophy, but our purpose throughout this book is to serve, not as advocates, but as guides. This is something that Allan Gotthelf and I, in our capacity as editors, stressed throughout the editorial process, from our initial invitations to the contributors, to our (often extensive) feedback on drafts.

The consistent aim of the book is to facilitate the study of Rand's works and thought by identifying Rand's key theses and methods and her reasons for them, by tracing the role that these theses and methods play in her thought, by showing the evidence in her texts for all of our interpretive conclusions, and by drawing illuminating comparisons between Rand and other thinkers. Of course, there are many occasions when the contributing authors (myself included) have found that this end is best served by raising and/or responding to objections to Rand's positions, but such arguments are presented here only as means to clarification. We hope that the book will be useful to critics and admirers of Rand alike, and that it will thereby help to increase the intellectual sophistication and scholarly rigor of the discourse about her both within the academy and in the culture at large.

Some Challenging Features of Rand's Ideas and Writings

Reading Rand seriously, as opposed to merely reacting passively to her writings, is demanding intellectual work. This is true to some extent of all authors, but there are several features of Rand's corpus and of her position in the culture that make it particularly difficult in her case.

Scholars and students of philosophy trained in analytic departments (as were most of the contributors to this volume) may find that Rand's philosophical essays read as though they come from an alien tradition. She addresses recognizable philosophical issues, but they are framed differently; the context and values she assumes are unfamiliar, as are her methods of argument and analysis. In all these respects, reading Rand is like reading a figure from a different philosophical school (or a different period in the history of philosophy). However, she is not only an outsider to the specific tradition of analytic philosophy; she is (as *Playboy* put it) *sui generis*. Rather than working within an established school of thought, Rand's essays are addressed either to a general audience or (more often) to the audience that she herself created. Most of her non-fiction was written for her own periodicals, and it sometimes presumes familiarity with her novels and with the ideas expounded in earlier issues.

When Rand does engage with the intellectual traditions of her time, she does so as an outsider – often a hostile one. In this respect, she is like such early modern intellectuals as Bacon, Descartes, Locke, and Spinoza. The comparison I am making is not to the intellectual stature of these thinkers, but to their relation to the intellectual establishment of their day. When they wrote, the universities were dominated by Scholasticism, an entrenched intellectual tradition with an established vocabulary, shared assumptions, an institutional structure, conventions of discourse, and a credentialing method. Rather than developing and presenting their ideas within this structure, the early modern intellectuals struck out on their own. They found their own audience and often explained their ideas in ways that made little reference to the establishment. When they did discuss Scholasticism it was in broadsides that the scholastics must have thought missed the nuances of their arguments and trivialized the differences between their positions (e.g., the differences between Scotists and Thomists). Likewise, Rand's often contemptuous remarks about the academic philosophy of the mid-twentieth century did not win her many friends in the philosophy departments of the time. However, 50 years later, most academic philosophers do not have much more regard for the positions Rand dismissed (e.g., logical positivism and flagrant subjectivism about ethical principles) than she did in the 1960s.[11]

The philosophers with reference to whom Rand situates herself are not her contemporaries in the academy, but world historical figures – chiefly, Plato, Aristotle, and Kant. And, rather than engaging in minute scholarship of these thinkers, she speaks of them as they most often spoke of one another – in essentialized sketches. (See James Lennox's discussion of Rand's take on the history of philosophy, Chapter 13, below.)

Like these world historical philosophers, Rand aimed to be *systematic*. Objectivism (as she called her philosophy) comprises five branches: metaphysics, epistemology, ethics, political theory, and esthetics. It also includes theses that we might describe as belonging to philosophical psychology, the philosophy of economics, and the philosophy of history. In many essays, Rand used this system as a framework within which to interpret the events of her time, and to recommend courses of political action and cultural activism.

There is a definite hierarchical structure to her thinking. At the base of this system is the metaphysical conviction that Rand called "The Primacy of Existence" – the thesis "that the universe exists independent of consciousness (of *any* consciousness), that things are what they are, that they possess a specific nature, an *identity*. The epistemological corollary is the axiom that consciousness is the faculty of perceiving that which exists" ("The Metaphysical Versus the Man-Made" *PWNI* 32). (See Jason Rheins's discussion in Chapter 11, below.) The distinctively human form of consciousness is reason, which enables us to understand the world and to guide our actions by means of a system of concepts that are formed, ultimately, on the basis of sense-perception. Unlike sense-perception, which Rand regarded as a direct, inerrant, and automatic awareness of external objects, reason is volitional and (consequently) fallible. Because of this, human beings need epistemology, the "science devoted to the discovery of the proper methods of acquiring and validating knowledge" (*ITOE* 36). The centerpiece of Rand's epistemology is her theory of concept-formation. In Chapter 12, I examine this theory, and explain the role that Rand thought her theory (and epistemology as a whole) played in enabling human beings to achieve objectivity in their thinking. This thinking includes, importantly, the reasoning by which we validate moral principles and by which each of us conceives and pursues personal values. Thus Rand's ethics rests on her epistemology and metaphysics.

In ethics, Rand articulates the essential values that constitute "man's life" (the moral ideal we discussed earlier); she argues that these values are based in the requirements of human survival, and she shows how they form a standard by reference to which an individual can form and pursue rational goals. These issues are the subjects of the chapters that make up Part II of this volume. Part III concerns her social theory – especially her endorsement of capitalism as the ideal social system. I indicated earlier how this endorsement follows from her ethics.

In esthetics, Rand's aim is to identify the essence of art and the human need that it serves. Doing so makes possible objective standards by which art can be evaluated. The function of art, she maintains, is to enable a human being to experience concretely his (or another's) sense of life. Rand explores the epistemological function of a sense of life, and its nature as a psychological phenomenon. A sense of life is a body of implicit metaphysical convictions, and Rand defines the school of art to which she belongs by identifying its core metaphysical conviction: "Romanticism is a category of art based on the recognition of the principle that man possesses the faculty of volition" ("What Is Romanticism?" *RM* 91).

Rand is a systematic philosopher in the sense that her thinking has a self-conscious, wide-ranging, and complex logical structure; but she did not present her philosophy systematically. There are theoretical essays on foundational issues in different branches of philosophy, but no architectonic presentation of the whole, and key concepts or theses are sometimes introduced in unexpected places. For example, it is in an essay on capitalism that Rand first expresses her view that there are three broad theories of the relationship between human consciousness and existence ("What Is Capitalism?" *CUI* 13–16; for discussion, see below 67–68, 228–232, 290–292, 446–447). This tendency to discuss fundamental philosophical issues as they arise in the course of addressing other subjects is fairly common among systematic thinkers, and it is part of why many of us find such thinkers – and Rand, in particular – so stimulating. What may seem at first to be a delimited treatment of some discrete phenomenon, suddenly opens up into a discussion of a fundamental question bearing on all of human life; one is exposed to new possibilities and new ways of thinking; and, perhaps most importantly, one becomes attuned to the many, often non-obvious ways in which philosophy bears on one's life, and one learns to dig deeper and to cast a wider net in one's own thinking. Nonetheless, this feature of Rand's writing poses challenges to students and scholars, especially when first approaching her corpus.

Rand did speak sometimes of her intention to write "a detailed, systematic, presentation in a philosophical treatise" (*FTNI* vii), but she never did so. After her death, her student Leonard Peikoff did write such a treatise – *Objectivism: The Philosophy of Ayn Rand* (*OPAR*) – based upon a lecture course he delivered that Rand endorsed as "the only *authorized* presentation of the entire theoretical structure of Objectivism, i.e., the only one that I know of my own knowledge to be fully accurate" ("A Last Survey" *ARL* 4(3) 387). Because of its origins in this course, and because of Peikoff's close intellectual relationship with Rand over the course of 30 years, *OPAR* can be seen as a quasi-primary source for Objectivism – a sort of extension or supplement to Rand's corpus. It is not an exercise in exegesis of Rand's own writings (though it does often refer to them), but a presentation of her philosophic system as Peikoff learned it from Rand. *OPAR* is an impressive work of philosophy in its own right, and an invaluable aid to interpreting Rand. You will find it referenced very frequently in the chapters below.

Rand's own most comprehensive presentation of Objectivism can be found in her last novel, *Atlas Shrugged*. The novel contains several speeches, which can be read as philosophical essays in their own right, and which were reprinted (along with excerpts from her other novels) in her first non-fiction book, *For the New Intellectual* (*FTNI*). Of these speeches, the largest is Galt's radio address (*Atlas* 1009–1068). It covers a startling range of topics from all the fields of philosophy, and Rand's introduction to it in *FTNI* reads simply "This is the philosophy of Objectivism" (130). You will find many quotations from this speech in the chapters that follow.[12]

Though the speeches from Rand's novels can be read as philosophical essays, they are best read in the context of the novels, as summations of ideas that have been demonstrated by the prior events through which the characters have lived. Each novel is a work of philosophy, not only or primarily because it contains philosophical speeches, but in the very construction of the plot. In each novel, philosophical premises figure into the characters' motivations, and the central conflict is resolved when reflecting on earlier events leads one or more of the characters to correct a mistaken premise or grasp a new principle.[13] One can think of the novels as, in effect, elaborate thought experiments, the results of which are summarized by the speeches.

We find a complex, iterative version of this construction in *Atlas Shrugged*. As the story progresses, certain of the protagonists (and, with them, observant readers) identify in increasingly abstract terms the events of the story, their own motives, and the motives of the other characters. At each stage in this process, the identifications become deeper, and this enables the protagonists to understand more fully and on a larger scale what is happening in their world and what causal role they themselves are playing. This new understanding enables them to act in new ways that lead (among other things) to new discoveries and deeper understanding. Galt's speech occurs at the culmination of this process.

Philosophical engagement with Rand's novels as works of literature is intellectually rewarding in its own right and is a vital means to understanding her philosophy. The novels are, therefore, frequently discussed in many of the chapters that make up this volume.

Though Rand's novels are works of philosophy in the sense I have been discussing, she did not intend them as pedagogical devices. They are intended, rather, as art – as the profound esthetic experiences that so many readers have found them to be. Rand was emphatic on this point – see "The Goal of My Writing" (*RM* 163). But the philosophical sophistication of her characterization and plots poses a challenge to readers interested in studying her novels as works of literature. It is not the only challenge. I have met many people to whom Rand's novels are a guilty pleasure – guilty, because, although they respond to them esthetically, they think that they are poorly written. Often they think this (usually without conviction) because they are judging the novels by parochial and inapplicable standards – for example, whether the dialogue is realistic (as though anyone actually spoke in iambic pentameter, like Hamlet, or in incisive witticisms, like Algernon Moncrieff). It is not always obvious which standards are applicable when judging a piece of literature, nor how to understand our own responses to it. It can help to know something about an author's literary aims and methods – especially when they are outside of the contemporary mainstream. On this issue, I direct readers to Tore Boeckmann's Chapter 17 on Romanticism, the literary school with which Rand identified.

Historians, political scientists, and other readers interested in Rand's analyses of the concrete political and cultural events of her time, will also need to contend with her positions on a wide range of philosophical issues and with the historical narrative in light of which she interpreted contemporary events. Since a person's actions are caused primarily by his ideas, Rand reasoned, so too a culture's thinking – its philosophy – is the dominant cause of its history. Thus the principal actors in Rand's historical narrative are philosophers. She held that, over the course of generations, the ideas of a period's prominent philosophers diffuse out through cultural products and institutions, eventually shaping the public's daily life and sense of life.

Rand saw many of the developments of the fourteenth through nineteenth centuries as the results of the Aristotelianism that had come into the mainstream of European thought through the work of Thomas Aquinas. Though Aristotle's philosophy was "far from perfect" (*Papers* 031_04x_005_001/*Journals* 692), Rand thought it contained the essentials of a rational metaphysics and epistemology: the world we perceive is real and populated by entities with determinate natures that we can come to understand by means of a rational process that begins with sense perception and culminates in a systematic knowledge in universal and essentialized terms.[14] The Aristotelian emphasis on observation, logical rigor, and causal explanation made possible the Renaissance in art and the scientific revolution. A growing respect for reason and an appreciation of life on earth led people to value the freedom that reason and the pursuit of happiness require. In the seventeenth century, John Locke identified the rights that (in Rand's terms) "define and sanction" this freedom; and, in the eighteenth century, these rights were implemented in the American Declaration of Independence and Constitution. There were important contradictions in the American form of government – worst of all, the toleration of slavery in the South – but America's distinguishing feature was an explicit (if compromised) commitment to rights. The resulting social system, capitalism, made it possible for the businessmen of the nineteenth century to use the growing scientific knowledge in new and innovative ways to "fill men's physical needs and expand the comfort of men's existence" (*FTNI* 27).

> The creative energy, the abundance, the wealth, the rising standard of living for *every* level of the population were such that the nineteenth century looks like a fiction-Utopia, like a blinding burst of sunlight in the drab progression of most of human history. If life on earth is one's standard of value, then the nineteenth century moved mankind forward more than all the other centuries combined. ("Faith and Force" *PWNI* 89)

Thus Rand thought that the period held forth the promise of a future ideal society – one that would implement the principle of individual rights fully and consistently. But this ideal was not to come.

While the practical consequences of Aristotelianism were reaching men's daily existence, its theoretical influence was long since gone: philosophy, since the Renaissance, had been retrogressing overwhelmingly to the mysticism of Plato. Thus the historically unprecedented events of the nineteenth century – the Industrial Revolution, the child-prodigy speed in the growth of science, the skyrocketing standard of living, the liberated torrent of human energy – were left without intellectual direction or evaluation. The nineteenth century was guided, not by an Aristotelian philosophy, but by *an Aristotelian sense of life*. (And, like a brilliantly violent adolescent who fails to translate his sense of life into conscious terms, it burned itself out, choked by the blind confusions of its own overpowering energy.) ("What Is Romanticism?" *RM* 95)

Rand thought that all of the prominent philosophers of the seventeenth and eighteenth centuries contributed (in most cases, unwittingly) to this retrogression into mysticism, but she identified the key figure as Immanuel Kant. As Rand understood it, Kant's philosophy is an attack on all the essentials of a rational way of life; his epistemology undercuts human beings' confidence in reason, and his ethics pits morality against self-interest. She regarded all of the prominent philosophies of the nineteenth and twentieth centuries as minor variations on Kant's, and she thought this pervasive Kantianism stunted the newly formed sciences of esthetics and economics, thereby preventing some of the achievements of the nineteenth century from being properly identified or defended. The nineteenth century's great esthetic achievement, Romantic art, was supplanted first by Naturalism and then by increasingly unintelligible and ugly modern art. Capitalism also gave way in the twentieth century, and much of Europe descended into dictatorship. The descent was slower in America, which had a more deeply Aristotelian sense of life, but Rand saw signs that the country was moving in the same direction. Objectivism is the philosophy she thought was needed to reverse this trend: a more consistent Aristotelianism that exposes the fallacies of Kantianism and provides the guidance needed to achieve the future promised by the nineteenth century.

Rand's view of and relation to Aristotle, Kant, and other historical philosophers is discussed in many of the chapters below, in connection with her positions on various philosophical issues (see the entries for these thinkers in the index). Chapter 13 by James Lennox is an overview of her take on the history of philosophy and its influence; and, in Chapter 15, John Lewis and I discuss the use Rand made of this historical perspective in interpreting the events and trends of her own time.

We have discussed some of the reasons for studying Rand, some of the challenges involved, and some of the ways in which the chapters of this book will address those challenges. I would like to discuss now a few features of Rand's corpus and her life that should be borne in mind when studying her.

Rand's Works and Related Sources

The Fountainhead, published in 1943, is the book that made Rand's reputation as a novelist. Prior to it, she had published one other novel, *We the Living* (in 1936) and a novella, *Anthem* (in 1938). She had also written a successful Broadway play, *Night of January 16th* (which premiered in 1935), and a number of plays and short stories that would not be performed or published until later in her life or, in some cases, after her death.

Rand seems to have regarded *The Fountainhead* as her first mature work of fiction. She later wrote that, in the period prior to *The Fountainhead*, she sometimes "felt that my means were inadequate to my purpose, and that I had not said what I wanted to say as well as I wished" (*WTL* ix). Accordingly, she produced revised versions of *Anthem* (in 1946) and *We the Living* (in 1959). (A detailed account of these revisions can be found in Mayhew 2012b and 2005b.) By contrast, in later editions of *The Fountainhead*, she "left the text untouched" because "I want it to stand as written" – this despite the fact that she thought there was a minor semantic error in the novel and one misleading statement, both of which she explained in her introduction to the 25th anniversary edition (*Fountainhead* x–xi).

If *The Fountainhead* marks Rand's maturity as a novelist, it is *Atlas Shrugged*, published in 1957, that marks her maturity as a philosopher. In her afterword to the novel, she wrote that she has "held the same philosophy I now hold, for as far back as I can remember" and that, though she "learned a great deal through the years and expanded my knowledge of details, of specific issues, of definitions, of applications," she "never had to change any of my fundamentals" (*Atlas* 1070). This is the same afterword in which she writes that her philosophy is "in essence, the concept of man as a heroic being, with his own happiness as the moral purpose of his life, with productive achievement as his noblest activity, and reason as his only absolute." Indeed nascent forms of all the ideas she names in that quote are prominent in the posthumously published notes and short stories from the 1920s that are her earliest surviving writings in English (*Early* 3–146, *Journals* 4–48). What we do not find in these early materials – or even in *The Fountainhead* – is the philosophical system whose outline I sketched above. Much of the content of her ethics is explicit from the beginning (though formulations and emphases change), but it is only in the period between *The Fountainhead* and *Atlas Shrugged* that she worked out her view of reason and of volition (or "free will"), and these ideas enabled her to integrate her thoughts into a system and remove some important ambiguities.[15]

In particular, the idea that reason is a volitional faculty led her to the conviction that an individual's values and moral character derive from his choices – fundamentally, from the choice between engaging one's reason in order to grasp reality and subverting one's consciousness in order to indulge a contradiction. In Rand's mature system, the fundamental virtue is rationality, and it consists in choosing the first of these alternatives – in volitionally recognizing the primacy of existence. In *The Fountainhead*, she had treated independence as the primary virtue; and it is left ambiguous in much of her work prior to *Atlas* whether all of the morally significant differences she sees among people are matters of choice. The centrality of reason and volition to Rand's system explains her choice to name it "Objectivism"; for to be "objective" is (as Peikoff aptly formulates Rand's view) "volitionally to adhere to reality by following certain rules of method, a method based on facts *and* appropriate to man's form of cognition" (*OPAR* 117).

Most of Rand's significant philosophical ideas are explicit in *Atlas* (though not always in the same terminology in which Rand would later express them in her non-fiction). Of those that are not present, the most significant is Rand's theory of concepts, which did not appear in print until 1966, but the core of this theory was formed in the years between *The Fountainhead* and *Atlas*, when she was systematizing her thought.[16] After *Atlas*, the system was essentially complete, and such ideas as she added (e.g., probably, some of her esthetic theories, the concepts of certain fallacies, and some of her classifications of philosophical theories) took their place within an existing structure.

Atlas was Rand's last novel. Her later work is all non-fiction, most of it talks or essays. In these later works, she elaborates on her philosophical system and uses it as a framework from which to comment on contemporary events. These works are also informed by the historical narrative discussed earlier, which seems to have been formulated while she was writing *Atlas*, or very shortly thereafter. It is clearly in evidence in some of her speeches and essays from the late 1950s and early 1960s.[17]

I indicated earlier that most of Rand's non-fiction first appeared in publications she edited, which were addressed to the audience she had created by her novels. These periodicals also contained articles by some of Rand's students and associates, and she included some such pieces in her books. She endorsed all the articles published in her periodicals as expressions of Objectivism; thus they provide definitive evidence of her positions. The same is true for certain other works, all of which are listed in section I of the "Annotated Bibliography of Primary and Quasi-Primary Sources" at the end of this volume.

Among Rand's students whose works she endorsed, two warrant special mention. Nathaniel Branden was the coeditor with Rand of *The Objectivist Newsletter* (*TON*) and then (until May, 1968) *The Objectivist* (*TO*). He was also the president of the Nathaniel Branden Institute (NBI), an organization endorsed by Rand that put on lectures about Objectivism. Branden's articles in the periodicals and his book *Who Is Ayn Rand?* (also endorsed by Rand) are important parts of the Objectivist corpus and are referenced frequently in this volume. His *Basic Principles of Objectivism* lecture course, first given in 1958, was the first extended non-fiction treatment of Rand's philosophy available to the general public.[18] Branden would later release a recorded version of this course and a book transcript of it, but the precise relation of the available material to the course Rand authorized is uncertain (see Annotated Bibliography, entry #51).

Branden and Rand had a close personal and professional relationship that came to a bitter end in 1968, when she learned that he had been deceiving and manipulating her for four years.[19] Branden's subsequent public accounts of this episode are not all consistent with one another, or with the accounts by Barbara Branden (with whom Rand also broke over her role in the same events), or with Rand's private notes concerning the episode.[20] In the decades that followed, Nathaniel Branden gained acclaim as a popular psychologist, and he continued to periodically write or lecture on Rand and her philosophy. In my opinion, his writings pertaining to Rand after their break routinely misrepresent Rand's views and (especially) their relation to his own.[21]

The second of Rand's students who warrants special mention is Leonard Peikoff. We discussed him briefly earlier in connection with his 1976 course on Objectivism and his book *Objectivism: The Philosophy of Ayn Rand*. Rand endorsed numerous lecture courses that he gave during her life, and her introduction to his first book, *The Ominous Parallels* (published shortly after her death), describes it as "the first book by an Objectivist philosopher other than myself." After Rand's death, Peikoff continued to lecture and write on a wide range of topics, always drawing on an Objectivist foundation, and he founded the Ayn Rand Institute (ARI), the largest organization devoted to promoting Rand's ideas in the world today.[22] As Rand's heir and the executor of her estate, he established ARI's Ayn Rand Archives (a resource that has been invaluable in the research for this volume) and he has overseen the posthumous publication of a great deal of material by Rand, including notes, letters, marginalia, early stories, and edited transcripts of courses and workshops. (See section II of the Annotated Bibliography.)

When an author's estate first publishes material that was not written for publication or that the author did not think was finished, the material is almost always edited with an eye to making its literary or intellectual value maximally accessible, rather than with an eye to the needs of scholars, and there is never any shortage of critics to allege that the public is being misled and that the author is being distorted, exploited, or otherwise misused.[23] Rand's case is no exception.[24] Though there are editorial decisions in some of her posthumously published volumes that I wish had been made differently, all these books serve their purpose well, and the material they contain richly deserves to be read. Much of it is cited in the chapters that follow. However, none of these books can be viewed as an authoritative source for Rand's views, because little of the material they contain was composed with the care she used when writing for publication, and all of it has been edited by other hands.[25] Our contributing authors have used this material advisedly and have consulted the original sources whenever possible. I encourage future scholars to follow the same policy, and to view these books as means to become acquainted with materials that they may need to later examine in their original forms.

Organization of the *Companion*

As with most reference works, the chapters in this volume are written so that they can be read independently, with none presupposing any other. However, my coeditor and I have made the authors aware of material in other chapters that bears on their topics, and we have encouraged extensive cross-referencing. It is our hope that readers will dive in to the chapter on whichever topic interests them most, and that the cross-references will help them to discover and explore the many (sometimes non-obvious) connections between the different departments of Rand's thought.

This said, we have had to put the chapters in a sequence, and we have chosen the one that we think takes the reader on the most natural path through the subject matter. As will be clear from the table of contents, the book is divided into six parts. The first, which comprises the present Chapter 1 and Shoshana Milgram's Chapter 2 on Rand's life and works, aims to provide a broad context for the study of Rand's works.

Part II deals with Rand's view of ethics and human nature. Though ethics is not the field that Rand considered fundamental, it forms the most natural entry point into the study of Rand, because the issue of values and their place in human life was never far from her thinking, and her views on this subject bear directly on everything she wrote – from her earliest notes for stories, to her novels, to her most abstract essays in metaphysics or epistemology and her analyses of political events. The part begins with Chapter 3 in which I trace central themes in Rand's thought on values as these themes develop from her early story notes to her mature theory. Chapter 4, by Allan Gotthelf, covers the core of Rand's ethics, and Chapter 5, by Onkar Ghate, discusses her view of character and related issues pertaining to moral psychology. Rand's egoism is a subordinate theme in all of these chapters; I focus on it directly in Chapter 6.

Part III concerns Rand's view of society. It opens with Chapter 7 in which Darryl Wright explores the principles on which Rand thinks that a properly human society is based, including especially the principle of individual rights. Rand held that capitalism is the only moral political system, because it is the only one that protects individual rights. This view, and Rand's political philosophy more generally, is discussed by Fred Miller and Adam Mossoff in Chapter 8. Among the topics Miller and Mossoff cover is Rand's view that the protection of rights requires a government to implement a system of objective laws governing the use of retaliatory force. In Chapter 9, Tara Smith looks in more detail at Rand's view of objective law and at her criticisms of some laws that she regarded as non-objective. The section on society closes with Chapter 10 by Onkar Ghate discussing Rand's distinctive philosophical perspective on the operations of markets and her view that economic freedom is a corollary of intellectual freedom.

14

Part IV concerns the two fundamental branches of Rand's philosophical system. Jason Rheins discusses her metaphysics in Chapter 11, and I cover her epistemology in Chapter 12. Both chapters emphasize the ways that these foundational aspects of Rand's thought relate to the ethical and political issues discussed in earlier chapters.

The subject of Part V is the history of philosophy and its influence on culture and history. In Chapter 13, James Lennox discusses Rand's approach to the history of philosophy and her view of the figures she considered most important. Friedrich Nietzsche is not one of those figures, but Rand read a great deal of him as a young adult, and he loomed large in her mind as she began to work out her own views in ethics. Lester Hunt discusses her evolving relationship to Nietzsche in Chapter 14. Chapter 15, by John Lewis and me, is a study of Rand's extensive writing on the events of her own time and the philosophical ideas that she identified as causes of these events.

Part VI addresses Rand's view of art, both as a theorist and as a literary artist. In Chapter 16, Harry Binswanger covers her theory of art generally. Tore Boeckmann, in Chapter 17, discusses Rand's view of Romantic literature and how this view is embodied in her own novels.

The book closes with a brief "coda" in which Allan Gotthelf and I examine two theses that Allan liked to call "hallmarks of Objectivism." One is Rand's view, discussed above, of man as a "heroic being." The other is what she called "the benevolent universe premise" – the idea that the universe is hospitable to human achievement, such that a person who lives morally can expect to live happily. We show how these two "hallmarks" follow from the more technical aspects of Rand's philosophy covered in the earlier chapters. Because the hallmarks constitute much of the sense of life projected by Rand's novels, the coda underscores the connection between this more technical material and the issues with which I began this introduction. For it is the conviction that what Rand envisions is possible and proper that evokes such strong reactions (positive and negative) in so many readers, and this is what has made Rand (to paraphrase *Playboy*) the most fiercely damned and admired author of our time.

Notes

1 Thank you to Richard Ralston at the Ayn Rand Institute for sharing these sales figures. The figures include all sales of English-language editions of Rand's books (including e-books and the more than 3.6 million books purchased by the Ayn Rand Institute as part of its "Free Books for Teachers" program), but the figures do not include foreign-language editions. There have been at least 100 translations of Rand's works into at least 26 languages.

2 Examples of this left-wing take include: Weiss 2012, Gage 2012, Krugman 2012, McMurry 2014, Levine 2014.

3 The word "man" as used in this formulation – and as Rand often uses it – is meant to subsume all members of the human species, regardless of their sex. Such generic uses of "man" and of masculine pronouns have fallen out of favor in recent decades on the grounds that they reinforce the view that the adult male is the paradigm case of a human being and that women are derivative or special cases (see Miller and Swift 1976, Moulton 1981, Warren 1986, and Little 1996). I doubt this would have persuaded Rand. She held that men and women are equal morally and intellectually, but she thought that regarding the adult male as the primary representative of the human species is part of healthy human sexual psychology, especially female sexual psychology. (See 395 n. 83 in this volume and the sources cited there.)

The contributors to this volume usually retain Rand's gendered language when commenting directly on passages in which she uses such language, since to do otherwise would be confusing. In other contexts, each contributor has adopted whatever policies with regard to gendered language he or she thinks best. For my part, when writing as sole author of a chapter, I refer to persons of unspecified gender by the pronoun of the gender opposite to that of whoever else is most discussed in the immediate context. This policy has the advantage of using the pronoun's gender as an aid to disambiguation. (Since Rand is the dominant subject of this book, this policy has most often led to the choice of masculine pronouns.)

4 Rand is not the first person to use this phrase. It occurs in the title of Miguel de Unamuno's *Tragic Sense of Life*, and a Google Books search reveals that it can be found in many nineteenth-century authors, often in discussions of religion. I do not know where Rand first encountered the phrase or whether she coined it independently of the earlier usages. She writes of a "sense of living" in notes from 1928 (*Journals* 28), enclosing the phrase in quotes. Her earliest use of "sense of life" that I know of is in an outline for *Atlas*, dated August 24, 1946 (*Papers* 158_02B_002_002/*Journals* 532), and the word "life" is enclosed in quotes (which the editor of *Journals* omitted); this indicates that she didn't yet regard the phrase as a unit. In a letter dated September 30, 1946 (*Papers* 102_21A_018_001), Frank Lloyd Wright asks Rand whether she has read Unamuno's book. She replies, in a letter dated October 10 (*Papers* 102_21A_019_002/*Letters* 117), that she has not, "but I shall get it and read it." The sentence before Wright's question about Unamuno reads "*Anthem* is very clean and clear." So likely the question was prompted by something in *Anthem* (perhaps 101–102) that reminded him of Unamuno.

5 For Rand's own view of the "American sense of life" and her relation to it, see "Don't Let It Go" (*ARL* 1(4) 16). And see my and John Lewis's discussion below, 385–386. On the concept of sense of life, more generally, see Onkar Ghate's discussion, 118–123. On its role in responses to art, see Harry Binswanger, 417–418.

6 Among the textbooks and anthologies that include material by or about Rand are: Rachels 1986, Feinburg and Shafer-Landau 1999, Presbey, Struhl, and Olsen 2000, Pojman 2004, Boss 2005, Lawhead 2006, Palmer 2006, Solomon 2008, Pojman and Vaughn 2012, Bowie, Michaels, and Solomon 2007, Vaughn 2012, Wilkens 2011, and Clark and Allison 2015. To my knowledge the first ethics textbook to include discussion of her views was John Hospers's (1961) *Human Conduct*; Rand and Hospers were carrying on a correspondence at the time, her side of which can be found in *Letters* 502–563. Entries on Rand in prominent philosophical reference works include the oddly inept piece by Chandran Kukathas (1998) in the *Routledge Encyclopedia of Philosophy* (among other gross errors, he describes *The Virtue of Selfishness* as a novel), Stephen Hicks's (2006) entry in the *Internet Encyclopedia of Philosophy*, and Badhwar and Long's (2012) entry in the *Stanford Encyclopedia of Philosophy*.

7 Rand introduced the term "Objectivism" as a name for her philosophy in the late 1950s, "a time when my philosophy was beginning to be known and some people were starting to refer to themselves as 'Randists'"; she recognized the need for some such term, but objected to derivative uses of her name ("To the Readers of the Objectivist Forum" *TOF* 1(1) 1). More generally, Rand disapproved of coining nouns for ideologies or movements from the names of living people, because she thought it led to a focus on personalities rather than on the contents of the ideas (*Speaking* 27). But Rand did intend the term to represent her specific system of ideas rather than as a term for a more generic ideological orientation (as is the case with "existentialism" or "pragmatism"). For this reason, she always capitalized the "O" in "Objectivism." We follow Rand in this usage.

8 My coeditor, Allan Gotthelf, served as secretary of the society (or, briefly, co-secretary) from 1990 until his death in 2013. My current co-secretary, James Lennox, is also a contributor to this volume, as are three of the other four current members of the society's Steering Committee.

9 Burns's (2009) biography was based on her PhD dissertation (University of California, Berkeley, Department of History, 2005), and it purports to be a study of "Ayn Rand and the American Right," but I treat is as a popular biography because it contains much about Rand's personal life and comparatively little about her ideas and intellectual development. The book is particularly disappointing in its account of Rand's relation to other thinkers who are (or are perceived to be) on the "right." The chronology Burns provides of Rand's interactions with prominent conservatives of the 1940s and 1950s is useful and usually accurate (though see 391, n. 42, below). However, with only a few exceptions, she says little about the intellectual content of these interactions. Moreover, Burns ignores the bulk of what Rand wrote about politics after the 1964 presidential election. For example, she implies falsely that Rand said nothing significant about the Johnson administration (227), she does not mention Rand's discussions of the Nixon shock and Watergate, and, incredibly, she says nothing at all

about the 1972 presidential election (except as regards the activities of the Libertarian Party), even though Rand wrote extensively about this election and regarded McGovern's defeat as a significant turning point for the nation. As John Lewis and I show below (363–366, 379–380), Rand's views of these events and others form a definite narrative about the course down which America was traveling. Surely part of the story of "Ayn Rand and the American Right" is how Rand's narrative relates to that of prominent conservative and libertarian thinkers, but Burns leaves readers in the dark not just about this relation, but about the fact that there is anything to relate. She is at her best when tracing Rand's influence on several social and political movements that arose in the 1970s (see 247–278), including the budding libertarian movement. But here, too, her account is undermined by her inattention to Rand's political writings from the period. Most notably, Burns writes that the newly formed Libertarian Party, "unlike Rand," "offered a positive program for the future" (269). Perhaps this is how members of the Party interpreted the matter, but two of Rand's articles from the first six months of the Party's existence (January to June of 1972) are calls to action on behalf of specific policies that she argued were both politically achievable and necessary to reorient the country toward freedom. (For details, see 377, below.) If the Libertarians did not regard Rand as having a program for action, this reflects a substantive disagreement between them and Rand about what constitutes genuine and viable pro-liberty political action. Thus, where Burns paints a picture of a dispirited woman whose erstwhile followers have had to look elsewhere in search of leadership, the reality is that there were two conflicting views of political activism based in differing ideas. (In fact, there were more than two, since the libertarian movement was not unified in support of the Party.)

10 Here are some examples of inaccuracies or misleading statements: Weiss (2012, 25) writes that "*Atlas* and *Fountainhead* make it easy to love individualism and no-government capitalism." But Rand wasn't for "no-government capitalism"; she was a fierce critic of anarchism. (See, in this volume, 193–194 and 381–382). Among the ways in which Weiss says the novels do this is by showing a world in which "poverty and unemployment are a distant, alien presence. The only member of the underclass Dagny encounters [in *Atlas Shrugged*] is a railroad hobo who turns out to be an Objectivist with a lead on Galt." Presumably, Weiss is referring to Dagny's encounter with Jeff Allen (*Atlas* 656–672), though it is mysterious why he calls him an Objectivist; however, this is hardly Dagny's only encounter with someone who is desperately poor and devoid of hope. Weiss ignores her conversations with the dejected patrons of a slum diner (176–178), her visit to Starnesville and the impression its grinding poverty makes on her (283–286), her visit to Gerald Starnes's "flophouse" (321–322), and her experience with the mob at Wyatt Junction before the last run on the John Galt Line (519–521). The novel contains many other descriptions of poverty. So does *The Fountainhead* and, especially, *We the Living*. These scenes may not emphasize the issues that Weiss thinks are most significant, but that is no excuse for his writing as though the scenes do not exist.

Or again, Weiss (2012, 61–63) paints it as a hypocrisy that Rand, who opposed Medicare, enrolled in the program in 1976. But, of course, whether one thinks a program should exist and how one should deal with it once it does exist are distinct issues; and, ten years prior to enrolling, Rand wrote an essay explaining why opponents of the welfare state should claim whatever benefits are due them under the programs they oppose ("The Question of Scholarships" *VOR*). Weiss ignores her stated position and quotes, *as though it were Rand's reason for enrolling in Medicare*, the opinion of an associate with whom she disagreed. The associate, Evva Pryor, worked for Rand's attorney and was authorized to handle certain financial matters for Rand, including dealing with government benefits; the two became friends, but neither their friendship nor Pryor's authorization to handle the relevant financial matters implies that Rand agreed with Pryor's reasons for thinking that Rand should accept Medicare and Social Security payments, nor does Pryor say that Rand agreed with these reasons. (The material Weiss relies on from Pryor can be found in McConnell 2010, 520–521.)

There are also many inaccuracies pertaining to the Objectivist movement. For example, Weiss (2012, 201) writes that between 1968 (when Nathaniel Branden debated Albert Ellis) and 2011 (when ARI began a series of debates with speakers from Demos) no "leading Objectivist debated anyone of stature from the political mainstream." In fact, during those years, Leonard Peikoff, Harry Binswanger, John Ridpath, and other prominent Objectivist intellectuals engaged in many debates, and their opponents included academics, journalists, and politicians, such as Bogdan Denitch (sociology, CUNY), Christopher Hitchens (then a writer for *The Nation*), John Judis (*The New Republic*), Randall Kennedy (Harvard Law), Robert Lekachman (economics, CUNY), and Bob Rae (who became Premier of Ontario shortly after his debate with Ridpath). These opponents are, if not part of the mainstream, no further from it than are Ellis and Demos. (My information on these debates comes largely from Binswanger, but I have seen or heard recordings of several myself.) Weiss's claim serves his narrative about an odd and insular movement, but it is simply untrue.

11 For some of her views on the philosophers of her times, see, in the present volume 75, 254, 278, 297, 299, 304 n. 34, 331, and 397 n. 93.

12 On Galt's speech as a whole, including its structure and its role in the novel, see Ghate 2009b and Gotthelf 2009a.

13 I discuss this process in detail in the cases of *Anthem* (see Salmieri 2005) and *Atlas Shrugged* (2009b; cf. Ghate 2009a). In the case of *We the Living*, Andrei comes to grasp the evil of totalitarianism largely by witnessing its effects on Kira, the woman he loves (see Smith 2012, 364–370). In *The Fountainhead*, Roark is able to successfully defend himself at his second trial (whereas he was not able to at his first) because he has come to grasp in essential terms the difference between "creators" and "second-handers"; Dominique is ready to stand by Roark's side at the end of the novel because, through her observation of Roark's life and (especially) Wynand's, she has grasped the impotence of second-handers and the ability of creators to succeed in the world; and Wynand closes the *Banner* (which was the chief organ of the opposition to Roark) after he learns this same lesson when Roark is acquitted. (On these points, see Ghate 2007.)

14 See Lennox's discussion of Rand's view of Aristotle, 334–337, below. For her presentation of this historical progression, see *FTNI*. For a more detailed account, endorsed by her, of the figures in the history of philosophy discussed there, see Peikoff, *HOP1* and *HOP2*.

15 On these issues, see Wright 2009, and my discussion below, 63–68.

16 Rand said that she first formed the theory in the 1940s (*ITOE* 307), and the central idea that concepts are formed by an act of "measurement omission" is attributed to Rand in a 1952 term paper (*Papers* 020_01K_003) by her (then) friend Barbara Weidman (later, Barbara Branden).

17 On the relevant published works, see my and John Lewis's discussion below, 355–357. Judging by some of Rand's notes (*Papers* 47_26x), this narrative seems to have informed a number of talks she gave in 1958, but (to my knowledge) no copies of these talks survive.

18 It was not, however, the first course on the philosophy. Leonard Peikoff had given an informal course in 1954 that covered metaphysics, epistemology, and ethics. See Sures and Sures 2001, 21–22.

19 Because Branden's deceptions concerned a romantic relationship he was having, and because he and Rand had also been romantically involved, Rand's anger at Branden is often trivialized as the response of a "woman scorned" (see B. Branden [1986, 356], N. Branden [1989, 404], and Levine 2014). This is a peculiarly amoral interpretation of the events. By all accounts, including Nathaniel Branden's (1989) own, he not only concealed this affair from Rand, but engaged in countless hours of discussion with her in which he deliberately misrepresented the facts of his life and the state of his psychology, all in order to maintain a professional and social relationship with Rand that he thought she would not grant him if she knew the truth. Moreover, by all accounts, Rand not only loved Branden, she (perhaps naively) believed him to be personally committed to the virtues that they both espoused – virtues that included honesty, integrity, and justice. On this basis, she promoted him as a psychologist and a teacher of her moral philosophy. In so doing, she staked much of her own reputation on his character, and she directed thousands of trusting admirers in his direction (including the woman with whom Branden carried on his affair and her husband) who then became his clients or students. What sort of person would not be incensed to discover that someone whom she had promoted in this way was capable of pervasive and sustained dishonesty? And what sort of person, having discovered this, would not feel obligated to publicly and emphatically withdraw her endorsement?

20 Nathaniel Branden wrote a memoir (1989) of his relationship with Rand, and Barbara Branden wrote a biography (1986) of her. The latter book is filled with psychological speculation that seems to be aimed at making sense of her own relationship with Rand. Both Brandens have discussed the circumstances of their relationship and break with Rand in several other forums. Valliant 2005

documents the inconsistencies among the Brandens' several accounts. His book is of special value because it contains Rand's notes pertaining to her discussions with the Brandens in the period leading up to the revelation of Branden's affair. In addition to being the only contemporaneous evidence concerning the episode, these notes provide interesting insight into Rand's view of psychology and how she applied it to a very difficult situation in her personal life. However, Valliant's book is marred by his grandiose speculations about Nathaniel Branden's psychology (e.g., 382–384).

21 Here are a few brief examples, all from "The Benefits and Hazards of the Philosophy of Ayn Rand" (*VAR*). As evidence that Rand's philosophy encourages repression, he points to examples of heroic characters suppressing unpleasant emotions or feeling isolated from others, and he promotes some of his later books as offering advice on how to overcome this tendency. However, in *Atlas Shrugged*, the suppression Branden calls attention to is portrayed, not as a healthy way of functioning, but as an error that admirable people often make in difficult circumstances. The heroes who make this error are shown to suffer for it, and they learn to correct it by the end of the novel (see Salmieri 2009b on Dagny and Rearden's progression in this respect). In the same piece, he warns that too many Objectivists disown their authentic emotions in an attempt to live up to abstract moral principles that they have accepted as duties, and again he recommends books in which he advises students not to approach morality in this way. He neglects to mention that this is a problem that Rand herself had pointed out in his own psychology and that she struggled to help him with during the very conversations in which he was deceiving her (see Valliant 2005, 205–206, 299–301). In both of these (related) cases, Branden directs Rand's own (uncredited) criticisms against a straw man that he presents as her view. In other cases, he disguises the differences between Rand's view and his own. For example, though he claims to agree with Rand's view of free will, he writes that: "We are, all of us, organisms trying to survive. We are, all of us, organisms trying in our own ways to use our abilities and capacities to satisfy our needs" (*VAR* 549). But the essence of Rand's view of free will is that this is not the case. (See below, 64–65, 110.) Rand's villains are not trying to survive, and neither, argues Rand, is anyone in the moment of committing an immoral (as opposed to merely mistaken) action. Branden goes on to say that, when people fail to take actions conducive to their survival, it is due to mistakes. In essence, he is denying the distinction that Rand draws between errors of knowledge and moral breaches; and, given that this distinction is closely allied with the view of free will he has just contradicted, it makes sense for him to deny this as well. But it is not a clear and open statement of how he differs with Rand on a fundamental principle – nor does one find any such open statements in Branden's later writing about Rand. He gives the impression of amending something peripheral to Rand's philosophy or objecting to something idiosyncratic to her personality, when he is in fact differing in fundamentals.

22 Two of our contributing authors (Harry Binswanger and Tara Smith) sit on ARI's board of directors; one (Onkar Ghate) is a senior fellow there, and many other contributors (myself included) sometimes teach or consult for ARI or otherwise participate in its programs.

23 Two examples, one from the world of literature and the other from philosophy, should suffice to illustrate this phenomenon. See Trogdon 2013 on the controversies concerning the posthumous publication of novels and other materials by Ernest Hemingway. See Stern 1996 and Toynton 1997 on the editing by Ludwig Wittgenstein's trustees of material from his *Nachlass*.

24 Critics of the editing of Rand's posthumously published books include Sciabarra 1998, Burns 2009, 291–293, and Campbell 2011. Their descriptions of the changes made are (in those cases where I have checked) accurate, but I disagree with their assessment of the editing, and I think that the moralistic tone taken in some of these critical pieces is a result of dropping the context of the purpose of the books, the task with which Rand entrusted Peikoff as her literary executor, and the general nature of posthumously published works. Readers who want a sense of the changes made can now compare the quotes from archival materials in this volume with the published versions of that material (which are indicated in the references). I discuss some of these posthumous books individually in section II of the Annotated Bibliography.

25 *Letters of Ayn Rand* is a partial exception on both counts: Rand took great care with her correspondence, and the editing in that book is limited to omitting material that is unlikely to be of general interest.

References

Badhwar, Neera, and Roderick Long. 2012. "Ayn Rand." *Stanford Encyclopedia of Philosophy*, http://plato.stanford.edu/entries/ayn-rand/ (accessed May 22, 2015).

Boss, Judith A. 2005. *Analyzing Moral Issues*, 3rd edition. New York, NY: McGraw-Hill.

Bowie, G. Lee, Meredith W. Michaels, and Robert C. Solomon. 2007. *Twenty Questions: An Introduction to Philosophy*, 6th edition. Belmont, CA: Thompson Wadsworth.

Branden, Barbara. 1986. *The Passion of Ayn Rand*. Garden City, NY: Doubleday.

Branden, Nathaniel. 1989. *Judgment Day: My Years with Ayn Rand*. New York, NY: Avon Books.

Brook, Yaron, and Don Watkins. 2012. *Free Market Revolution: How Ayn Rand's Ideas Can End Big Government*. New York, NY: Palgrave Macmillan.

Burns, Jennifer. 2009. *Goddess of the Market: Ayn Rand and the American Right*. Oxford: Oxford University Press.

Campbell, Robert. 2011. "The Rewriting of Ayn Rand's Spoken Answers." *Journal of Ayn Rand Studies*, 11(1).

Clark, Henry C., and Eric Allison. 2015. *Economic Morality: Ancient to Modern Readings*. Lanham, MD: Lexington Books.

Feinburg, Joel, and Russ Shafer-Landau. 1999. *Reason and Responsibility: Readings in Some Basic Problems of Philosophy*, 10th edition. Belmont, CA: Wadsworth.

Gage, Beverly. 2012. "Why Is There No Liberal Ayn Rand?" *Slate.com*, http://www.slate.com/articles/news_and_politics/history/2012/08/paul_ryan_and_ayn_rand_why_don_t_america_liberals_have_their_own_canon_of_writers_and_thinkers_.single.html (accessed May 22, 2015).

Ghate, Onkar. 2007. "The Basic Motivation of the Creators and the Masses in *The Fountainhead*." In Mayhew 2007.

Ghate, Onkar. 2009a. "The Part and Chapter Headings of *Atlas Shrugged*." In Mayhew 2009.

Ghate, Onkar. 2009b. "The Role of Galt's Speech in *Atlas Shrugged*." In Mayhew 2009.

Gotthelf, Alan. 2009a. "Galt's Speech in Five Sentences (and Forty Questions)." In Mayhew 2009.

Gotthelf, Allan, ed., and James G. Lennox, assoc. ed. 2011. *Metaethics, Egoism, and Virtue: Studies in Ayn Rand's Normative Theory*. Ayn Rand Philosophical Studies, vol. 1. Pittsburgh, PA: University of Pittsburgh Press.

Gotthelf, Allan, ed., and James G. Lennox, assoc. ed. 2013. *Concepts and Their Role in Knowledge: Reflections on Objectivist Epistemology*. Ayn Rand Philosophical Studies, vol. 2. Pittsburgh, PA: University of Pittsburgh Press.

Heller, Anne C. 2009. *Ayn Rand and the World She Made*. New York, NY: Doubleday.

Hicks, Steven. 2006. "Ayn Rand." *Internet Encyclopedia of Philosophy*. http://www.iep.utm.edu/rand/ (accessed May 22, 2015).

Hospers, John. 1961. *Human Conduct: An Introduction to the Problems of Ethics*. New York, NY: Harcourt, Brace & World.

Krugman, Paul. 2012. "Disdain for Workers." *New York Times*, September 20, http://www.nytimes.com/2012/09/21/opinion/krugman-disdain-for-workers.html (accessed May 22, 2015).

Kukathas, Chandran. 1998. "Rand, Ayn." In *Routledge Encyclopedia of Philosophy*, edited by Edward Craig. New York, NY: Routledge.

Lawhead, William F. 2006. *The Philosophical Journey: An Interactive Approach*, 3rd edition. New York, NY: McGraw-Hill.

Levine, Bruce. 2014. "One Nation Under Galt: How Ayn Rand's Toxic Philosophy Permanently Transformed America." *Salon.com*, http://www.salon.com/2014/12/15/one_nation_under_galt_how_ayn_rands_toxic_philosophy_permanently_transformed_america_partner/ (accessed May 22, 2015).

Little, Margaret Olivia. 1996. "Why a feminist approach to bioethics?" *Kennedy Institute of Ethics Journal*, 6(1).

Luskin, Donald, and Andrew Greta. 2011. *I Am John Galt: Today's Heroic Innovators Building the World and the Villainous Parasites Destroying It*. Hoboken, NJ: John Wiley & Sons, Inc.

Mayhew, Robert, ed. 2004. *Essays on Ayn Rand's* We the Living. Lanham, MD: Lexington Books.

Mayhew, Robert, ed. 2005a. *Essays on Ayn Rand's* Anthem. Lanham, MD: Lexington Books.

Mayhew, Robert. 2005b. "*Anthem* '38 and '46." In Mayhew 2005a.

Mayhew, Robert, ed. 2007. *Essays on Ayn Rand's* The Fountainhead. Lanham, MD: Lexington Books.

Mayhew, Robert, ed. 2009. *Essays on Ayn Rand's* Atlas Shrugged. Lanham, MD: Lexington Books.

Mayhew, Robert, ed. 2012a. *Essays on Ayn Rand's* We the Living, 2nd edition. Lanham, MD: Lexington Books.

Mayhew, Robert. 2012b. "*We the Living* '36 and '59." In Mayhew 2012a.

McConnell, Scott. 2010. *100 Voices: An Oral History of Ayn Rand*. New York, NY: New American Library.

McMurry, Evan. 2014. "The Stunning Weirdness of Ayn Rand: Why Her Newfound Popularity Makes No Sense." *Salon.com*, http://www.salon.com/2014/10/06/the_stunning_weirdness_of_ayn_rand_why_her_newfound_popularity_makes_no_sense_partner/ (accessed May 22, 2015).

Miller, Casey and Swift, Kate. 1976. *Words and Women*. Garden City, NY: Anchor Press/Doubleday.

Moulton, Janice. 1981. "The Myth of the Neutral 'Man'." In *Sexist Language: A Modern Philosophical Analysis*, edited by Mary Vetterling-Braggin, 100–116. Totowa, NJ: Littlefield, Adams.

Palmer, Donald. 2006. *Why It's Hard to Be Good: An Introduction to Ethical Theory*. New York, NY: McGraw-Hill.

Pojman, Louis. 2004. *The Moral Life: An Introductory Reader in Ethic and Literature*, 2nd edition. New York, NY: Oxford University Press.

Pojman, Louis P., and Lewis Vaughn. 2012. *Philosophy: The Quest for Truth*, 8th edition. New York, NY: Oxford University Press.

Presbey, Gail M., Karsten J. Struhl, and Richard E. Olsen. 2000. *The Philosophical Quest: A Cross-Cultural Reader*, 2nd edition. New York, NY: McGraw-Hill.

Rachels, James. 1986. *The Elements of Moral Philosophy*. New York, NY: McGraw-Hill.

Salmieri, Gregory. 2005. "Prometheus' Discovery: Individualism and the Meaning of the Concept 'I' in *Anthem*." In Mayhew 2005a.

Salmieri, Gregory. 2009b. "Discovering Atlantis: *Atlas Shrugged*'s Demonstration of a New Moral Philosophy." In Mayhew 2009.

Sciabarra, Chris Matthew. 1998. "Bowdlerizing Ayn Rand." *Liberty*, September.

Schwartz, Peter. 2015. *In Defense of Selfishness: Why the Code of Self-Sacrifice Is Unjust and Destructive*. New York, NY: Palgrave Macmillan.

Smith, Tara. 2006. *Ayn Rand's Normative Ethics: The Virtuous Egoist*. Cambridge: Cambridge University Press.

Smith, Tara. 2012. "Forbidding Life to Those Still Living." In Mayhew 2012a, 370–364.

Solomon, Robert C. 2008. *Introducing Philosophy: A Text with Integrated Readings*, 9th edition. New York, NY: Oxford University Press.

Stern, David G. 1996. "The Availability of Wittgenstein's Philosophy." In *The Cambridge Companion to Wittgenstein*, edited by Hans D. Sluga and David G. Stern. Cambridge: Cambridge University Press.

Sures, Mary Ann, and Charles Sures. 2001. *Facets of Ayn Rand*. Marina Del Rey, CA: ARI Press.

Toynton, Evelyn. 1997. "The Wittgenstein Controversy." *The Atlantic Magazine*, June, http://www.theatlantic.com/magazine/archive/1997/06/the-wittgenstein-controversy/376881/ (accessed May 22, 2015).

Trogdon, Robert W. 2013. "Posthumous Publications." In *Ernest Hemingway in Context*, edited by Debra A. Moddelmog and Suzanne delGizzo. Cambridge: Cambridge University Press.

Valliant, James S. 2005. *The Passion of Ayn Rand's Critics: The Case Against the Brandens*. Dallas, TX: Durban House.

Vaughn, Lewis. 2012. *Great Philosophical Arguments: An Introduction to Philosophy*. New York, NY: Oxford University Press.

Warren, Virginia L. 1986. "Guidelines for Non-Sexist Use of Language." *Proceedings and Addresses of the American Philosophical Association*, 59(3).

Weiss, Gary. 2012. *Ayn Rand Nation*. New York, NY: St. Martin's Griffin.

Wilkens, Steve. 2011. *Beyond Bumper Sticker Ethics: An Introduction to Theories of Right and Wrong*. Downers Grove, IL: Intervarsity Press.

Wright, Darryl. 2009. "Ayn Rand's Ethics: From *The Fountainhead* to *Atlas Shrugged*." In Mayhew 2009.

2

The Life of Ayn Rand

Writing, Reading, and Related Life Events

SHOSHANA MILGRAM

> The motive and purpose of my writing is *the projection of an ideal man*.
> Ayn Rand, 1963 ("The Goal of My Writing" *RM* 155)

To project the human ideal in fiction, Ayn Rand had to become both a novelist and a philosopher. She had to develop, in literature, the relevant skills of narrative and style, and also to identify, in reality, the nature and requirements of human goodness. Her career as a writer of fiction, accordingly, was preceded and accompanied by her work on the system of philosophic thought she ultimately called "Objectivism" ("Preface" *FTNI* vii–viii).

Her life, she said, was "single-tracked," "consciously devoted to a conscious purpose" (1945, "Letter to Readers of *The Fountainhead*" *Letters* 670). In *The Fountainhead* (1943), Howard Roark is similarly focused and dedicated: "The only thing that matters, my goal, my reward, my beginning, my end is the work itself. My work done my way" (*Fountainhead* 606). My purpose in this chapter is to introduce her writing by showing how the chosen actions of "a life consciously devoted to a conscious purpose" were integrated with the texts she crafted, in both fiction and non-fiction – a body of work that is the subject of the articles in this volume.[1]

Leaving Russia (1905–1926)

For the first 12 years of Rand's life, her family's circumstances were more than comfortable. Her father, Zinovy Zakharovich Rozenbaum (1869–1939), was a successful pharmacist; after establishing his business in St Petersburg, he had married Anna Borisovna Kaplan (1880–1941) in 1904; Alisa Rozenbaum (as Rand was then called), was born less than a year later, on February 2, 1905, with two sisters following in 1907 and 1909.[2]

The most important year of Rand's youth was 1914: at the age of nine, she decided to be a writer. She had been writing stories for several years at this point. One night, in a London hotel room, when she was entertaining her sisters by inventing a story about the chorus girls she had

A Companion to Ayn Rand, First Edition. Edited by Allan Gotthelf and Gregory Salmieri.
© 2016 John Wiley & Sons, Ltd. Published 2016 by John Wiley & Sons, Ltd.

seen on a theatrical poster, she realized that this task of devising interesting narratives about human lives was a writer's life work – and the very career she wanted. Earlier that year, she had discovered her first literary image of a hero in Maurice Champagne's *La Vallée Mystérieuse*, a serialized adventure novel about British officers in India, which she read in a French children's magazine that her mother had ordered for her.[3] The protagonist, Cyrus Paltons, was courageous and competent, principled and ruthless, untiring and unconquered. Decades later, Rand remembered vividly his valiant actions and proud demeanor, the defiance in his voice, the illustrations by René Giffey of his face and form, and the love she herself felt for this hero.[4]

Alisa Rozenbaum developed strong value judgments; for example, she vastly preferred French literature, which she read at home, to the Russian classics, which she studied at school. Having seen from her home (in what was now called Petrograd) the first shots of the February Revolution, she became interested in current politics, reading newspapers secretly and against her mother's wishes. She wrote novels about the heroic adventures of brave girls (e.g., a young British girl who saves her nation from the Germans). At 12 she began to keep a journal of her convictions and her reasons for holding them. "I began to ask myself the why of the ideas that I believed," seeking to integrate her ideas, rather than "arguing on single points or single issues." "Thinking in principle" (as she called this practice) had an impact on her fiction-writing: she "began to project a story by a different method," working to integrate the events and characters of any story she was writing with a broad, abstract theme.

The Bolshevik Revolution in October, 1917, gave her "the sense of total chaos … something brutal and incomprehensible." One day the brutality came home. Soldiers marched in and shut down her father's pharmacy business, sealing it off from the family's apartment on the same floor. In the fall of 1918, the family left Petrograd for the Crimea, which was in the hands of the White Army.

She continued to write in her journal and to read widely. Literary discoveries from this period include Walter Scott (whose *Ivanhoe* she read in translation just prior to the Revolution), Edmond Rostand, and Victor Hugo. Decades later, she would describe Rostand's *Cyrano de Bergerac* as "without a doubt the greatest play in world literature" (*Answers* 196),[5] and Hugo remained the novelist she most admired. She loved Hugo for the grandeur of his worldview, the seriousness of his characters, and the integration in his plots of narrative and theme.[6] Required school reading included Dostoevsky (whose moral fervor she relished in spite of her disagreement with the specific morality he dramatized), Tolstoy (whose *Anna Karenina* she deplored as an attack on the possibility of achieving joy in life), and Nikolai Chernyshevsky's *What Is to Be Done?* (a novel that promoted, under the name of "rational egoism," utilitarianism and socialism).[7] She also read such English writers as H.G. Wells and Arthur Conan Doyle.

The family returned to Petrograd in the summer of 1921, and Alisa Rozenbaum entered the University of Petrograd in the Historical/Pedagogical Faculty, majoring in history (with the Middle Ages as her area of specialization). Her three-year program included many history courses (including the histories of Greece, Rome, and the Crusades), as well as courses in biology, French, and logic, along with required Soviet courses on such topics as "Historical Materialism."[8]

Her favorite class from the first year was a full-year course in ancient philosophy, focused on Plato and Aristotle.[9] She was attracted to Aristotle's emphasis on reason and this world, and came to see him as a potential intellectual source and, in effect, an ally.[10]

During the same year, she first heard the name of another potential philosophical ally: Friedrich Nietzsche. One of her cousins told her that she should read Nietzsche: "He has

23

anticipated you. He has said all the things you're saying." Curious, she first read *Thus Spake Zarathustra*, and then read everything by Nietzsche that had been translated into Russian. She discovered some points of contact (his celebration of human greatness) and some significant disparities (his hostility to reason and his conflation of power over nature with power over other people). She originally placed a quotation from Nietzsche at the head of her manuscript for *The Fountainhead*, and selected additional Nietzsche quotations for each of the four parts of the novel. In her introduction to the 25th anniversary edition of *The Fountainhead*, she explained that she decided against any Nietzschean epigraphs because of her "profound disagreement" with his philosophy, but she added that "as a poet, he projects at times (not consistently) a magnificent feeling for man's greatness" (*Fountainhead* xii). An echo of Nietzsche the poet can be found in John Galt's references to "the hero in your soul" (*Atlas* 1060, 1069).[11]

Rand's university studies were completed under extraordinarily difficult conditions, including a purge in her third year that led to her temporary expulsion, followed by a reluctant readmission. She nourished her spirit by attending performances of operettas by Kalman, Millöcker, Offenbach, and Lehar (often seeing her favorites many times), by reading the works of Schiller and other writers she admired, and by seeking out foreign films.[12] She also worked on her own writing, creating some characters and plot ideas that would find their way into her mature works.[13]

After receiving her degree, she began a two-year program in the State Institute for Cinematography. The free passes to movie theatres provided by the school enabled her to see many foreign films, in which she found "an ideal, right here on earth, and the kind of men and women that I could like."[14] Also during these years, she discovered the inventive, optimistic fiction of the American writer O. Henry, who was being translated into Russian for the first time.

While at the Institute, she wrote two pamphlets on film: the 16-page "Pola Negri" (about a passionate and unconventional Polish actress) was published anonymously in 1925, and the 64-page *Gollivud: Amerikanskij Kino-Gorod* [Hollywood: American Movie-City] was published the following year under the name "A. Rozenbaum."[15]

Rand had always hated Russia, and it was becoming increasingly clear to her that the kind of heroes she wanted to portray and the stories she wanted to tell would not be permitted there. So when relatives in Chicago invited her to visit, she left for the United States to make a new life for herself under a new name (though her official reason for the trip was to study movie-making). Henceforth, although her legal name in English was "Alice Rosenbaum" (or, later, "Alice O'Connor"), she was known, personally and professionally, as "Ayn Rand."[16]

Early Career as an American Writer (1926–1936)

Ayn Rand landed in New York City in February of 1926 (having traveled by way of Riga, Berlin, and Paris), and made her way to Chicago, where she spent six months writing her first fiction in English and attending 135 movies (many of them at the New Lyric Theatre, owned by her relatives) (*Russian Writings* 137–154, 190–202). In September she arrived in Hollywood with a letter of introduction to the DeMille Studio. She had praised his romanticism in her *Hollywood: Movie-City*, where she contrasted his approach with the naturalism of D.W. Griffith. She applied to be a junior screenwriter, thinking that her limited command of English would be sufficient for the silent screen. Walking out of the studio after a discouraging interview, she encountered DeMille in person. He invited her to the set of *The King of Kings*, and soon hired her, first as an extra and then as a junior screenwriter (a job she held until DeMille closed his independent studio in 1928). Though few of her contributions were used in the actual films, and she received no screen credits, she learned several principles of storytelling from her conversations with DeMille.

At this time, she was especially interested in reading American fiction, both to practice her English and thus become more familiar with American culture, and to find books that she could send to her mother, who was translating English novels into Russian. A favorite from this period was Sinclair Lewis (whose *Mantrap* her mother was the first to translate into Russian).

The most personally important consequence of her time in DeMille's studio was meeting Charles Francis O'Connor (1897–1979), known as "Frank," who had a small part in *The King of Kings*. For Rand, it was love at first sight; although they lost touch after the end of the film shoot, they found each other again at a Hollywood Library a few months later, and began an enduring romantic relationship, marrying in 1929. He was, she said, her first reader and, in his unbending integrity, the model for all of her heroes. In the early years of their marriage, he moved from bit parts in *Cimarron* (1931) and *Three on a Match* (1932) to a featured speaking role in *As Husbands Go* (1934). During their first residence in New York (1934–1943), he acted in summer stock and as a Broadway understudy, and, in lean times, worked in a cigar store. During their second residence in California (1944–1951, after the publication of Rand's first commercially successful novel), he managed the ranch surrounding the Richard Neutra house they had bought in Chatsworth (a real-estate purchase he had researched and recommended). During the years after they returned to New York, he developed an interest and skill in painting. The cover of the 25th anniversary edition of *The Fountainhead* features one of his paintings.

Rand's family had supported in every way her move to America, and she hoped they would be able to follow her. During her early time in Hollywood, she corresponded with them extensively.[17] Her sisters had recently married and could not come, but she worked strenuously to rescue her parents, filing documents and even purchasing ocean liner tickets – with no success. Permission to travel was denied. It was dangerous, she believed, for her parents to receive letters from America; the correspondence, on both sides, came to an end.

Her first career milestone in the United States occurred on September 2, 1932, when she sold "Red Pawn" and "Treason," two screen treatments set in Russia, to Universal Pictures.[18] She had been working for several years as manager of the wardrobe office department at RKO: the sale allowed her to quit this job and devote all of her time to writing.

She had worked to develop her writing skills by composing short stories, which she did not attempt to publish, and she considered several different ideas for her first American novel.[19] One of these, "The Little Street," had as its theme the antagonism between the spiritual ugliness of the contemporary world and the spiritual splendor of a lone defiant man (*Journals* 23–47).[20] Another possibility was based on an idea she had had in Russia: a science-fiction adventure, set on an airship lost in space, in which communist villains beg the hero-scientist to take control after their actions have endangered the ship. She chose instead a subject that was personally closer. *We the Living* (originally entitled "Airtight") is the story of three university students in 1920s Soviet Russia, whose lives and deaths dramatize the conflict between the individual and the collective. Kira Argounova, a fiercely independent engineering student, becomes the mistress of Andrei Taganov, an idealistic young Communist, in order to obtain funds to save the life of her lover, Leo Kovalensky, a defiant but embittered son of an aristocrat, by sending him to a tuberculosis sanitarium. Andrei comes to understand the value of individual lives through his love for Kira – a process that reaches its climax when he discovers her motive for her affair with him. The novel was published by Macmillan in March of 1936.[21] In 1959, Random House published a new edition, revised by Ayn Rand, with an introduction by her.[22]

While attempting to complete and sell her novel, Rand also worked on smaller projects. One of these was a three-act courtroom drama, suggested by the suicide of Ivar Kreuger (1880–1932), the Swedish "Match King," after the exposure of his financial fraud. Her play – originally entitled "Penthouse Legend," first produced in California as *Woman on Trial*, and later performed on Broadway and worldwide as *Night of January 16th* – featured a gimmick: a jury chosen from audience volunteers was seated on the stage, and, at the conclusion, they rendered a verdict in a murder trial. The presence of an on-stage jury makes salient that the limited physical evidence must be interpreted by each of us in the light of his own view of what is possible and desirable for human beings.

The play had a moderate success in Hollywood, in October 1934, under the direction of E.E. Clive and was optioned for production on Broadway by Al Woods (who had produced *The Trial of Mary Dugan*, the play that had led Rand to consider writing a courtroom drama). Rand and O'Connor moved to New York. For a year, while waiting for the play to open and seeking a publisher for her novel, Rand worked as a paid reader and a writer of synopses, first for RKO, then also for MGM. Woods not only delayed the opening for nearly a year (for financial reasons), but also diluted the value conflict at the heart of the play by adding melodramatic devices and formulaic comedy.[23]

Then, after interminable delays, Rand experienced acclaim and success. *Night of January 16th* opened in September 1935, and ran through March 1936 – when Macmillan published *We the Living*. Ticket sales for the play were good. The novel was widely reviewed, and led to a flurry of speaking engagements, in which Rand explained the factual basis of her fictional account of the misery of life in collectivist Russia.[24] As the author of a Broadway play and a new novel, she herself became a news story: O.O. McIntyre commented, in a nationally syndicated column, that she had "proved that America is a land of opportunity. ... Imagine her scoring such a success in Soviet Russia!" ("New York Day by Day," June 8, 1936).

The Fountainhead: The Creation of Her First Ideal Man (1936–1943)

Ayn Rand's next major project was *The Fountainhead* (originally entitled "Second-Hand Lives"). The hero, Howard Roark, is a man of independent mind – a modern architect pitted against the forces of conformity and tradition.[25] Roark comes into conflict with three characters who are variations of "second-handedness": Peter Keating (an architect who borrows ideas from other architects and is similarly dependent in all his values), Ellsworth Toohey (a critic and organizer, who advocates self-sacrifice and seeks political power), and Gail Wynand (a newspaper magnate, who has sacrificed his first-hand values in order to achieve power over the mob). Roark is in conflict also with Dominique Francon; the two are in love, and she admires his artistic ability and nobility of character, but believes that he will be inevitably destroyed because the world is dominated by second-handers. The novel ends with Roark's spiritual and existential triumph.

More than eight years passed between Rand's first notes for the novel in December of 1935 and its publication in 1943. For the first two and a half years she worked primarily on smaller projects while acquiring the background to write knowledgeably about architecture. The writing itself began on June 26, 1938, and continued until December of 1940, by which time she had a draft of the first third of the novel. At that point she put the novel aside for about a year, during which time she became involved in political activism and, after parting company with her agent, Ann Watkins, attempted on her own to find a publisher. She resumed work on the novel in December of 1941, after signing a contract with Bobbs-Merrill, and completed the manuscript by the end of 1942.

Between 1935 and 1938 Rand made extensive notes for the novel and researched it by reading widely about architecture and working as a filing clerk in the office of architect Ely Jacques Kahn (her purpose known only to him).[26] In the hope of earning money to finance her work on the novel, she also worked on shorter projects, including three plays: *Ideal* (adapted from an episodic novella she had written in the early 1930s) and *Think Twice*, neither of which were produced, and a stage adaptation of *We the Living*, entitled *The Unconquered*.[27] A more successful short-term project was the novella *Anthem* (originally entitled "Ego") about the meaning and glory of the ego. It was composed in the summer of 1937, based on an idea from her youth in Russia for a play set in a future world from which the word "I" had disappeared. *Anthem* tells the story of a man, Equality 7-2521, living in a collectivist and primitive culture, who rediscovers individualism in the course of reinventing the light bulb, and, at the novel's climax rediscovers the concept "I." The novella was published in 1938 by Cassell, the British publisher of *We the Living*. Rand revised the novella in 1946 for publication in the United States by Pamphleteers (it was later published in cloth by Caxton in 1953).[28]

Also during the mid-1930s, she read about politics and economics, including works of non-fiction like Carl Snyder's *Capitalism the Creator* and fiction such as Sinclair Lewis's *It Can't Happen Here* (1935). "By that time," she said, "I was very interested in the state of American politics. I was beginning to see that they were really wrecking this country." She subscribed to the *American Mercury*, and watched every issue of the *New York Times Book Review* for any new books advocating capitalism. She wrote letters to the editor, worked in Wendell Willkie's 1940 presidential campaign (as organizer of an "intellectual ammunition bureau"), and participated in several question-and-answer programs a day in a Union Square theatre.[29] Willkie's campaign was a rallying point for individualists, and after he lost the election (in her view, because he failed to defend individualism), she tried (with writer Channing Pollock) to start a pro-individualist organization, writing its statement of principles, an action plan, and publicity material. Three of her political writings – "To All Innocent Fifth Columnists," "The Individualist Manifesto," and "The Individualist Credo" – were intended for wide circulation. Though her political thought would mature throughout the 1940s, its essence, which she would later call the "trader principle" (*Letters* 498; cf. *Atlas* 276, 961, 1022–1023) is already present in her statement in "The Individualist Credo" (May 5, 1941) that "men must deal with one another as equals, in voluntary, unregulated exchange – not mutual slaves."[30]

She was, at this time, not working systematically on *The Fountainhead*. There is a break in the dates she wrote on each chapter of her manuscript; although she typically spent no more than a month or two on a given chapter, there are no dates between December 11, 1940 and December 18, 1941. Although financial concerns and political activism contributed to the delay, another factor was her discouragement with the culture. Against that discouragement, she had a powerful defender: her husband. In her introduction to the 1968 edition of *The Fountainhead*, she wrote that he "saved" the book, one night, by talking to her for hours and convincing her "of why one cannot give up the world to those one despises." He was, then and enduringly, an ally and a support. Reflecting privately on his character, years later, she commented: "he has never failed to project an unbreached self-esteem, in major, fundamental issues and situations."[31] The "secret of Frank's unbreached self-esteem" was his holding "as an *automatic absolute*, that one's own life must be lived by one's own judgment and mind and intelligence," an "inability to accept anything on blind faith, without first-hand understanding, even from those one respects and admires." She dedicated the novel to him because, as she wrote on the original dedication page, he was "less guilty of second-handedness" than anyone else she knew.

In 1941, Rand became friends with Isabel Paterson, a novelist, reviewer, and columnist for the *New York Herald Tribune*, who took a personal interest in Rand, when the latter tried (unsuccessfully) to recruit her for Pollock's individualist organization (the group for which Rand had written "The Individualist Manifesto" and "The Individualist Credo"). The two talked and corresponded for years about history, politics, literature, and philosophy. The surviving correspondence, mostly from 1944–1949 (when Rand was living in California), indicates the range, depth, pleasure, and contentiousness of their interactions.[32] The friendship was especially strong when they were living in New York, working, respectively, on *The Fountainhead* and *The God of the Machine*, both published in 1943. Rand eventually gave her friend a copy of *The Fountainhead*, inscribing it with the sentence Howard Roark wrote to Gail Wynand: "You have been the one encounter in my life that can never be repeated."[33]

Rand wrote the final two-thirds of *The Fountainhead* in little more than one year. After reaching Part Two, Chapter 7, and taking nearly a year's break, she received a contract to write the rest. Her book, after being rejected by 12 publishers, was accepted at Bobbs-Merrill, when a new editor, Archibald Ogden staked his job on its merit. In early December 1941, Rand signed a contract to submit a full manuscript by the end of 1942: "I spent the last and final year writing steadily, literally day and night; once I wrote for thirty hours at a stretch, without sleep, stopping only to get some food. It was the most enjoyable year of my life" (1945, "To the Readers of *The Fountainhead*" *Letters* 672).

Published on April 15, 1943, *The Fountainhead* gradually began to rise on the best-seller lists, due in large part to word of mouth. In order to increase intelligent readership and focus attention on the novel's theme, Rand agreed to write a non-fiction "sequel," to be published by Bobbs-Merrill as "The Moral Basis of Individualism," and planned a national lecture tour.[34] When Warner Brothers, on October 12, 1943, met her asking price of $50,000 for the film rights to the novel, she accepted the offer, and the O'Connors soon left for California. She believed that the movie would advertise the book; she hoped that, through her work on the screenplay, she would be able to protect the integrity of her theme. She was right, on both counts. The film's production was delayed; it was not released until 1949.[35] Though it was not a fully satisfactory artistic achievement, the film – produced by Henry Blanke, starring Gary Cooper, Patricia Neal, and Raymond Massey – brought publicity to the novel, and restored it to the best-seller lists. Ayn Rand, moreover, had seen to it, by strenuous efforts, that Roark's courtroom speech was shot exactly as written.

Atlas Shrugged: The Mind on Strike (1943–1957)

The money from the movie rights to *The Fountainhead* bought Ayn Rand time to begin her next novel, *Atlas Shrugged*, the theme of which was "the role of the mind in man's existence – and, as corollary, the demonstration of a new moral philosophy: the morality of rational self-interest" (*FTNI* 97). The novel is set in a decaying world from which the men of achievement are mysteriously vanishing. Although these story elements and others derive from a novel she had projected as a teenager in Russia, the central premise came to her in the year after she completed

The Fountainhead. When Isabel Paterson told her that she had a duty to present her ideas to the world, she objected to the notion of such an unchosen obligation, and asked: What if I went on strike? What if all the men of the mind went on strike?[36]

Whereas the theme of *The Fountainhead* was "individualism versus collectivism, not in politics but in man's soul," "The Strike" (as *Atlas Shrugged* was initially called) was designed to dramatize the conflict between individualism and collectivism within the political/economic realm. She expected the book to require no new philosophical ideas, to be significantly shorter than *The Fountainhead*, and to take only a few years to write. The novel was ultimately half as long again as *The Fountainhead*, took approximately twice as long to complete, and not only formulated a new code of morality, but did so in relation to a complete philosophical system.

Within the novel, the author of this system is John Galt, an inventor-philosopher who initiates a strike of the "men of the mind" against the world's moral code. Although Galt, Rand's ultimate projection of the ideal man, is the cause of the novel's key events, he is not seen until the third and final part of the book, at which point the secret of the strike is revealed. The novel follows the last remaining "scabs," railroad executive Dagny Taggart and steel magnate Henry Rearden, as they struggle to sustain their businesses, to understand the world's state, and to resolve personal conflicts that result from their ignorance or tolerance of aspects of the moral code of self-sacrifice.

After she completed the preliminary screenplay for *The Fountainhead*, in May 1944, Rand was in demand as a screen writer, and Hal Wallis (who had produced *Casablanca*) hired her on the terms she requested (six months of work for his studio, six months for her own writing). During her half-year stints of studio work for Hal Wallis, she worked on a number of films, including *Love Letters* (1945), which received four Oscar nominations, and "Top Secret," an unproduced screenplay about the development of the atomic bomb. She received credit for her contribution to *You Came Along*, based on an original story by Robert Smith; she contributed, without credit, to additional films.[37]

During Rand's first break from Wallis's studio, in 1945, she continued to work on "The Moral Basis of Individualism" and to read philosophy, including B.A.G. Fuller's *A History of Philosophy* and *The Basic Works of Aristotle* (edited by Richard McKeon). She abandoned her non-fiction project when she realized that it would be "totally useless to present a morality without a metaphysics and epistemology," but many of the ideas intended for the work found expression in *Atlas Shrugged*.[38]

Most of the pre-writing for *Atlas* took place between April and August of 1946. During this period she made notes, sometimes in the form of substantial essays, on philosophical issues and on the novel's theme, characters, and plot.[39] In the course of her extensive research, she recorded observations based on her reading (and interviews and site visits) regarding railroads and steel, the facts of industry and geography. In successive outlines, she tied together the events, the philosophy, and the facts.

The period of the late 1940s was also a high point of Ayn Rand's political activism. It included meetings and correspondence with Leonard Read (founder of the Foundation for Economic Education) and Rose Wilder Lane.[40] Rand was also active in the American Writers Association and the Motion Picture Alliance for the Preservation of American Ideals. For the latter's publication (*The Vigil*), she wrote "Screen Guide for Americans" and "Textbook of Americanism."[41] In 1947, she was invited to testify to the House Committee on Un-American Activities, which was investigating the penetration of Communist ideas into contemporary films. She was prepared to denounce such current and popular films as *The Best Years of Our Lives*, which, by implication, promoted anti-capitalist ideas within an American setting. She was, however, asked only about *Song of Russia*, a meaningless comedy "that wouldn't fool anybody and had failed very badly at the box office anyway."[42]

In 1950, she met Nathan Blumenthal (later Nathaniel Branden), a psychology student at UCLA and admirer of *The Fountainhead* who would play a significant role in her life. Over the next year and a half, he visited Rand's home often, usually accompanied by Barbara Weidman, a fellow *Fountainhead* admirer and UCLA student, to discuss Rand's ideas and to read the new novel as it was being written.[43] The two students would marry in February 1953, with Rand and her husband as matron of honor and best man.

In the summer of 1951, Blumenthal and Weidman left California for New York City, to study at New York University (he completing his BA in psychology, she beginning her MA in philosophy). Rand and her husband followed in October 1951, after she completed "Atlantis" (the first chapter in the last section of *Atlas Shrugged*). As Rand continued to work steadily on the book, completing five of the remaining chapters over the next 20 months, Blumenthal and Weidman gathered a group of their friends and relatives, all admirers of *The Fountainhead*, to join them in discussing ideas and reading the draft of the new novel. The group came to be called the "Class of '43" (for the year of *The Fountainhead*'s publication), or, ironically, "the Collective." The members included Leonard Peikoff, Weidman's cousin, whom she had introduced to Rand in Los Angeles and who was now studying philosophy at NYU, and Alan Greenspan. Peikoff would go on to work closely with Rand, eventually becoming her heir and later writing a comprehensive presentation of her philosophy.[44]

Rand also socialized with older friends, including Henry Hazlitt (a prolific writer of pro-capitalist books and columns, whose wife, Frances Kanes, had been the assistant head of Paramount's reading department in New York, and Rand's boss). Hazlitt had introduced Rand, on one of her earlier trips to New York, to economist Ludwig von Mises, whose work had interested her for many years, and whom she saw occasionally on her return to New York.[45] She was also visited several times by Murray Rothbard, a young free-market economist, who had been introduced to her by 1952 and who would later figure prominently in the libertarian movement; he brought several of his younger friends, also defenders of the free market, including George Reisman and Robert Hessen, both of whom became long-time friends of Rand's and contributed essays to her publications.[46]

In the fall of 1954, there was a significant development in Rand's personal life: her relationship with Nathaniel Branden became one of romantic love. She considered him her ideal reader, regarded him as a genius and an innovator in psychology, and had spent many hours each week, over several years, in intellectual companionship with him. The romance was intended to remain private (a secret known only to the two and their spouses); the fact of a romance is clear, but the details are not well documented.[47]

From July 1953 through October 13, 1955, Rand worked in near seclusion on Galt's Speech. Within the context of the novel, the purpose of the speech was to explain the reason for the strike and to address all minds that might respond to those reasons; within the context of Rand's system of thought, the function of the speech was to serve as an outline of her philosophy, including the exposition of a new morality.[48]

When she completed it, she began the process of selecting a publisher, ultimately choosing Random House.[49] The novel was finished on March 20, 1957, and published on October 10 of that year.

Objectivism: A Philosophy for Living on Earth (1957–1982)

Despite mostly vicious reviews that mocked her writing and misrepresented her ideas, *Atlas Shrugged* became a best-seller.[50] She would, however, never go on to publish any new fiction. Why not? Partly because, as she said, she believed that she had achieved her full goal as a novelist and could not create a hero superior to Galt.

But the time after the publication of *Atlas Shrugged* was difficult for her, psychologically. One reason was the nature of the reviews. She expected opposition; she did not expect the degree of misunderstanding, or the mockery. She saw the caliber of the reviews as a symptom of the state of the culture, which was evidently worse than she had thought – she who had just completed a novel about the end of the world. Another reason was that she did not have an immediate career goal – she who said that there was nothing important to be said about her other than her work. She had written a book that achieved everything she wanted to achieve. She believed she could create no hero superior to John Galt. She did not have in mind any specific writing project that was as personally important as *Atlas Shrugged*, or as intellectually ambitious.

What, then, did she do? Within a month, she began making notes for another novel (tentatively titled "To Lorne Dieterling"), on the theme of maintaining one's ambition and love of life in an unappreciative culture; she referred to it as her novel about unrequited love.[51] On June 8, 1958, she began to make notes for a projected non-fiction book, "Objectivism: A Philosophy for Living on Earth," and she soon began to accept invitations to lecture, speaking at major universities and over the radio. She would work to support and defend the novel that had been misjudged and misunderstood, and also to crusade for reason (her top value, she said, ever since she could remember). She became aware of "the magnitude of what had to be done in epistemology," of the urgency of the need for fundamental philosophical and cultural change. At this time, she said:

> I read a few of those modern philosophy essays that Nathan gave me, and all the questions that Leonard [Peikoff] was bringing home. And my conversations with Leonard. I began to see that what I took as almost self-evident, was not self-evident at all. ... Leonard began to realize the importance of my statement that "existence is identity," and he explained to me in what sense no philosopher had claimed it, not in this form. I had thought of it as what I said in Galt's speech, that it's merely clarification of Aristotle. I began to realize in what way it isn't. And it was *that* that was the turning point in my decision. I knew then that I could not write another novel for a long time. (*Biographical Interviews* 622–623)

As she began to write non-fiction – about core philosophical issues and their applications in human life – she experienced the "wonderful feeling" of "taking on a big assignment."

In 1961, Random House published her first non-fiction book, *For the New Intellectual: The Philosophy of Ayn Rand*. It contains the main philosophic passages from her novels and a long title essay (based in part on her recent lectures), which dramatically analyzes the development, and possible future, of Western culture.

On March 26, 1961, Ayn Rand appeared for the first time at the Ford Hall Forum in Boston, a venue to which she returned 18 more times (with her last appearance in 1981). She regarded it as "the only lecture organization in the country that takes ideas seriously as a matter of policy; it presents speakers of every viewpoint, treats them with scrupulous objectivity, and attracts audiences who have active minds."[52] She was invited to contribute a weekly column to the *Los Angeles Times*, and was interviewed frequently on radio and television and in print.[53]

In January 1958, Nathaniel Branden had begun a 20-lecture series on "Basic Principles of Objectivism." From an early brochure:

> The lectures are not given to convert antagonists. They are addressed exclusively to readers of Miss Rand's works, who are in agreement with the essentials of the philosophy presented in these books, and seek an amplification and further study of this philosophy.

The enterprise, later known as the Nathaniel Branden Institute or NBI, expanded its activities, with subsidiary companies (NBI Press, NBI Book Service, NBI Art Reproductions). In the 1960s, the Institute (of which Barbara Branden served as Executive Vice-President) held public readings of Ayn Rand's plays, a series of social evenings, and several seasons of film screenings. Courses by the Brandens, Peikoff, Greenspan, and others were offered live in New York and by tape transcription elsewhere. Rand participated frequently in the question periods for the "Basic Principles" course and was closely involved in its development.[54] In later versions of the course, Rand delivered some of the lectures, including two on "The Esthetics of Literature" that she wrote for the course in 1963 (*Papers* 109_31x, 32x, 33x, 34x), and the lecture on epistemology, of which she prepared a revised version in 1967 (*Papers* 109_30x).[55] She also authorized the Brandens' book *Who Is Ayn Rand?*, published in hardcover by Random House, and consisting of three essays by Nathaniel Branden (dealing with Ayn Rand's literary method, the "moral revolution" of *Atlas Shrugged*, and the implication of the Objectivist ethics for psychotherapy), followed by a biographical sketch by Barbara Branden, based on 19 interviews conducted in 1960 and 1961.[56]

Together, Rand and Nathaniel Branden launched *The Objectivist Newsletter*, in 1962. She described its purpose as "the application of the philosophy of Objectivism to the issues and problems of today's culture – more specifically, with that intermediary level of intellectual concern which lies between philosophical abstractions and the journalistic concretes of day-to-day existence." The publication was intended for those not necessarily in agreement but "strongly interested in and sympathetic to Objectivism, and who want to know more about it and about its practical and cultural application." "Contributors will often remind their readers of the common frame of reference, of the basic ideas of Objectivism, but we are not announcing them for the first time to an audience who is not familiar with them."[57]

The Objectivist Newsletter (1962–1965), generally four or six pages in length, included new articles, book reviews, an "Intellectual Ammunition Department" answering questions about Objectivism and its applications, and an "Objectivist Calendar" of upcoming events. At first almost all the articles were by Rand and Nathaniel Branden, but in time other writers (from the Collective and beyond it) began to contribute. In January of 1966, the publication expanded to a magazine format of approximately 16 pages and was renamed *The Objectivist* (1966–1971).

To provide guidance for prospective contributors to these periodicals, Rand offered a private course in non-fiction writing, first in 1961 and again in 1969.[58] Most of the articles had the benefit of several drafts with much editorial input; in some cases, the edited draft of a manuscript contains paragraphs or full pages in Ayn Rand's handwriting.[59] Because the periodicals were intended to represent the philosophy of Objectivism, she was committed to making everything within them fully professional, accurate, and representative of her philosophy.

In addition to the "Collective" and other students of Objectivism, Rand's contacts during the 1960s included John Hospers and several other professors of philosophy (e.g., Martin Lean).[60] She read and reviewed Harold Fleming's *The Thousand Commandments: A History of the Antitrust*

Laws and Lowell Mason's *The Language of Dissent*; both writers became friends, as did Mickey Spillane, a new favorite whose thrillers she admired for their moral passion and vivid style.[61]

She read the *New York Times* regularly and carefully, annotating articles with impassioned marginal comments. She read, and sometimes reread, works of non-fiction that she judged relevant to her work, such as Wilhelm Windelband's *A History of Philosophy* and Stanley Rothman and Charles Mosman's *Computers and Society*.[62] She revisited favorite classic fiction, writing an introduction to Victor Hugo's *Ninety-Three* (*Quatrevingt-treize*) at the invitation of Bantam Books, and introductions to NBI Press editions of Hugo's *The Man Who Laughs* and Samuel Merwin and Henry K. Webster's *Calumet "K"* (Rand's favorite novel, to which she had been introduced by DeMille).

She decided to collect her published articles in a form more permanent than periodicals. She initially planned a book focused on the Kennedy administration, with the title "The Fascist New Frontier," to be published by Random House. When the publishers objected to some of the content (e.g., the title essay and "J.F.K., High Class Beatnik"), in what she maintained was a violation of their agreement, she began a publishing relationship with New American Library.[63] Some of the topical articles were removed in favor of more theoretical pieces, and the initially proposed book became two separate books: *The Virtue of Selfishness: A New Concept of Egoism* (published first as a Signet paperback in December 1964, and then in hardcover in 1965) and *Capitalism: The Unknown Ideal* (published by NAL in hardcover in 1966 and subsequently in an expanded Signet paperback in 1967).

In her introduction, Rand describes *The Virtue of Selfishness* as "not a systematic discussion of ethics, but rather a series of essays on those ethical subjects that needed clarification, in today's context, or that had been most confused by altruism's influence" (*VOS* xii). It consists of 11 articles by Rand and five by Nathaniel Branden, many of which had appeared in *The Objectivist Newsletter*. She described *Capitalism: The Unknown Ideal* as a "nonfiction footnote to *Atlas Shrugged*," intended to identify the nature of capitalism and to illustrate the political implications of the novel's theme, the role of the mind in man's existence. *Capitalism: The Unknown Ideal* is twice the length of its predecessor, but similar in format, including pieces by Nathaniel Branden, Alan Greenspan, and Robert Hessen.

Her next two books were based on sustained sequences of articles for *The Objectivist*. The first of these, "Introduction to Objectivist Epistemology" (July 1966–February 1967), fulfilled a promise she made in *For the New Intellectual* to present a "new theory of the nature, source, and validation of concepts." It was subsequently published as a small volume by *The Objectivist* in 1967, and in a trade edition by New American Library in 1979.[64]

Her next book, *The Romantic Manifesto: A Philosophy of Literature* was published first in hardcover in 1969 (by World Press), and then in an expanded (Signet) paperback edition in 1971 (with one new essay, "Art and Cognition"). It discusses the purpose and nature of art in general and the nature of literature in particular, going on to analyze and champion the Romantic school of literature. She also addresses the psychological aspects of both artistic creation and the esthetic response, as well as specific artworks. Some of the material in the book was first presented in a private course on fiction-writing that Rand gave in 1958; an edited version of much of the remaining course content has been published as *The Art of Fiction: A Guide to Writers and Readers*, ed. Tore Boeckmann (New York: Plume, 2000).

By the time of the publication of *The Romantic Manifesto*, however, there had been a major upheaval in Ayn Rand's personal life, NBI had closed, and she had become sole editor of *The Objectivist*. During the years of NBI's expansion, Nathaniel Branden and Barbara Branden had

33

separated and divorced; they continued to work together on NBI business, and each maintained a personal relationship with Rand, but these relations became increasingly strained. Rand observed that Nathaniel Branden had failed to revise his "Basic Principles of Objectivism" lectures (much of the material for which had already appeared in print) or to write his share of new articles for *The Objectivist*.[65] In private meetings, he described personal problems that constituted obstacles to his work and to his relationship with Rand.[66]

In July 1968, she ended their personal relationship after receiving from him a letter she deemed offensive.[67] She did not, however, end their business relationship, and she continued to promote his career.[68] She broke with him completely in August 1968, when she learned that he had been conducting for several years a secret romantic relationship, which was germane to the personal issues he had been discussing with her, and that much of what he had said in these discussions had been untrue. Shortly afterward, she also ended her personal and business relationships with Barbara Branden.[69]

Her anthology, *The New Left: The Anti-Industrial Revolution* (1971), focused on the increasing advocacy of irrationalism and primitivism on the political left, as manifested in such developments as environmentalism, the student rebellion, and progressive education.[70] She continued editing *The Objectivist*, writing on topics ranging from the space program to the importance of sensory experience in concept-formation, until 1971, when she closed it and launched *The Ayn Rand Letter*, a shorter, bi-weekly publication geared to a wider audience, presenting her philosophical commentary on current events, trends, and ideas. Because of health problems and her unwillingness to comment on a culture she found increasingly repugnant, she closed the publication in 1976.[71]

Also that year, she participated in many of the question periods for a 12-lecture course by Leonard Peikoff on "The Philosophy of Objectivism," which she endorsed as "the only *authorized* presentation of the entire theoretical structure of Objectivism, i.e., the only one I know of my own knowledge to be fully accurate" ("A Last Survey" ARL 4(3) 387). The course would become the basis for his 1991 book *Objectivism: The Philosophy of Ayn Rand* (OPAR). At the time, Peikoff (who had completed his PhD in 1964 and taught at Hunter College, the University of Denver, and Brooklyn Polytechnic Institute) was working on *The Ominous Parallels: The End of Freedom in America*, a study of the evil ideas underlying Nazism, and the evidence of these evil ideas in the United States. She made extensive comments on the drafts of several chapters of his book, and parts of the work-in-progress were published in *The Objectivist* and *The Ayn Rand Letter*. His book was published in 1982, with an introduction by Rand.

In 1980 she became a "philosophical consultant" to a new bimonthly publication, *The Objectivist Forum*, edited by Harry Binswanger, who had received his PhD in philosophy from Columbia in 1973 and had, with Rand's approval, taught a course on Objectivism at the New School for Social Research. (Peikoff was the publication's consulting editor.) Although her involvement was not as direct as had been the case with her own magazines, she provided input into the selection of topics and authors, and her own work appeared in it.[72]

Philosophy: Who Needs It, the last book she planned, dealt with the relation of philosophy to life. It collected several of the essays she had published in *The Ayn Rand Letter*, with the addition of "Faith and Force: Destroyers of the Modern World," a speech she had delivered at Yale in 1960, which had previously been published only in pamphlet form and in *Vital Speeches of the Day*. The title essay, "Philosophy: Who Needs It," had been delivered in a major address at West Point, in 1974. She made a preliminary selection of the essays to be included, and discussed the list with Leonard Peikoff, who made the final editorial decisions and brought the book to press in 1982 after her death. (Peikoff later collected other, non-anthologized essays in *The Voice of Reason: Essays in Objectivist Thought*.)[73]

She delivered her final speech, "The Sanction of the Victims," to the National Conference on Monetary Reform in New Orleans (November 21, 1981). She told her audience of 3,000 businessmen that they were the genuine heroes of the world, although they were perpetually denounced, despised, and blamed. She told them that they should stop supporting an intellectual establishment that taught hatred of reason, hatred of the individual, hatred of success. She also told them about her new and current adventure: she was writing a screenplay for *Atlas Shrugged*, which she intended to produce herself.[74] Her journey to New Orleans, however, worsened her congestive heart disorder, and she died in New York City on March 6, 1982.

The Fountainhead and *Atlas Shrugged* end with the hero's living triumph: Roark is building his greatest architectural achievement, and Galt has carried out a moral revolution and is prepared to build the world anew. Ayn Rand, too, had fulfilled her great artistic project, and had defined the philosophy that lay behind it. As she wrote in "The Goal of My Writing," at a time when she had completed her work in fiction and published her first non-fiction book:

> The motive and purpose of my writing can best be summed up by saying that if a dedication page were to precede the total of my work, it would read: To the glory of Man.
> And if anyone should ask me what it is that I have said to the glory of Man, I will answer only by paraphrasing Howard Roark. I will hold up a copy of *Atlas Shrugged* and say: "The explanation rests." (*RM* 165–166)[75]

She is alluding to Howard Roark in *The Fountainhead*, who defended himself at a court trial concerning the merits of one of his buildings. As his sole defense, he held up photographs of the structure: his work done his way. Her life – "a life consciously devoted to a conscious purpose" – had achieved her purpose of defining and celebrating the ideal man.

Appendix: Concerning Biographical Sources

In this chapter I draw on research I have done, much of it in the Ayn Rand Archives (a division of the Ayn Rand Institute), toward a book-length study. I have also worked with archival holdings in several other libraries. I thank my extraordinary editors for helping me shape this chapter. At their direction, my focus here is to set briefly the biographical context for the composition of Rand's key fictional and philosophical texts; in my book, I will supply abundant information about additional important aspects of her colorful and heroic life, as well as fuller accounts of my sources and my detective work in following clues that have led to the facts.

For the facts of Ayn Rand's life, I have relied whenever possible on primary sources, including contemporary written documents and an extensive series of biographical interviews conducted by Barbara Branden in 1960–1961 in preparation for a biographical project (*Biographical Interviews*). The source for information about Rand's childhood, unless otherwise indicated, is this series of biographical interviews, which are also the source for any quotations from Rand that are otherwise unidentified. Cassette copies of the original reel-to-reel tapes are available in the Ayn Rand Archives, where I consulted them.

These interviews (over 300,000 words in length) are a uniquely valuable resource. Considering the amount of information conveyed and the time that had passed since many of the events, Ayn Rand's specific observations and her recall are impressive, and her memory lapses or uncertainties (regarding, say, years or names) are few and minor. The interviews were done for the immediate purpose of the "Biographical Essay" sketch published in 1962 (*WIAR* 149–239), and for a more long-term purpose of a longer biography to be written in the future.

The longer biography that Branden eventually produced (B. Branden 1986) is one of four full-length books on Rand that contain substantial biographical material. The others are: N. Branden 1989 (and 1999), Heller 2009, and Burns 2009. I have consulted all four works, but have not relied on them as sources of information, and I have found each to contain claims that are unsupported or contradicted by the available primary sources.

Barbara Branden's book does not supply documentation for many of its assertions, and states that much of the information is based on memory and on the aforementioned interviews with Rand. But Branden significantly distorts the contents of these interviews, and this casts doubt upon her use of sources I was not able to check. Her "Biographical Essay" had included few extensive direct quotations (i.e., words within quotation marks) from Ayn Rand; the rendering of Rand's words was faithful to the meaning, but not always verbatim. The essay also used some of Rand's phrases (e.g., "a three-year jail sentence," describing her employment in RKO's wardrobe) without enclosing them in quotations or attributing them to her. In *The Passion of Ayn Rand*, Barbara Branden used much more of the material from the biographical interviews. This time, she continued her practice of borrowing Rand's language or observations without clear attribution, and did so more frequently. She also presented many more lengthy direct quotations (or what appear to be direct quotations) than she had in the essay. Significant discrepancies are clear from a comparison of the statements attributed to Ayn Rand in this book with the statements she makes on the tapes. Here is one example. In the biographical interview of May 3, 1961, Ayn Rand said (speaking to Barbara Branden):

> As to the three of you, that is, yourself, Nathan, and Leonard, I expect world-shaking achievements. Whether the world shakes immediately or not is a different issue, but *we* will know that it will eventually. I do expect "miracles," I say that in quotes. But I mean what anyone else would consider miracles. That I knew from the beginning. I could not have, from the beginning, said what I expect from Leonard, beyond the mind. Now I know we can expect a really brilliant career. As far as you're concerned career-wise ...[and she goes on to compliment Barbara Branden and Nathaniel Branden]. (*Biographical Interviews* 633–653)

In *The Passion of Ayn Rand* (255), Ayn Rand is quoted as saying: "Of you, Barbara, and of Nathan, I expect world-shaking achievements. I do expect miracles. As far as you're concerned, Barbara, career-wise ..." (and the passage continues with the compliment to Barbara).

Rand's actual statement includes material that is omitted from *The Passion of Ayn Rand*. Rand had been realistic: she said that the effect of the achievements might not be immediate. Even in speech, moreover, she insisted on dispelling the suggestion of the supernatural in the word "miracle." And her list of those from whom she expected greatness originally contained three people, not two; *The Passion of Ayn Rand* omits one of the names, and also the compliment to him. In the introduction to the book, Barbara Branden states that all quotations of Ayn Rand, unless otherwise specified, come from her own first-hand experience: "I have edited such comments only for clarity." In this case (and others) the editing has distorted Rand's comments. Jennifer Burns (2009, 295) notes Branden's rewriting of Rand's interviews.

Comparison of the 1986 book with the interviews (and with available documents) raises serious questions about the accuracy of the book and its use of the materials. The discrepancies I found when checking this book against sources I could inspect constitute a serious reason to doubt the credibility of this source regarding alleged information (e.g., statements made in private) for which there are no sources to inspect.

Inspection of the biographical interviews reveals problems with Nathaniel Branden's books as well. He has taken statements made by Ayn Rand during the interviews and inserted them verbatim into scenes (complete with conversational exchanges and reactions) that he appears to invent. For example, he describes vividly the events of an evening in the Spring of 1956 when, he says, Rand told the Collective about her decision, as a child on vacation in London, to become a writer (Branden 1999, 167–168, cf. the more detailed account in N. Branden 1989, 195–197). After telling the story, Branden claims, Rand asked him to accompany her into the kitchen, where they embraced and she told him that there was no reason their affair could not go on forever (1999, 171–172; 1989, 199–200). However, this event could not have taken place as described. On the recording of a biographical interview conducted on December 19, 1960, Nathaniel Branden can clearly be heard expressing surprise that she had ever been in London, when she relates the story his memoir claims she shared with the Collective four years earlier. His book, moreover, gives him undue credit. For example, he states that, in August of 1961 "I proposed to Ayn that together we create an intellectual newsletter" (1999, 255; 1988, 291), but it is clear from an interview recorded on August 25, 1961, that "two years ago" she had discussed with him "the kind of magazine I someday would like to have if it is possible," and had proposed "The New Intellectual" as the tentative title "that I would like for such a magazine," because the magazine would provide "what it is that people need to be men of action *and* intellectuals."

Heller's book has much new material, but the sources it cites do not always support her assertions. Two examples will suffice: Heller states that Ayn Rand depicted a "heroine named 'Thunder' (Rpom)" (20), but there is no Russian word "rpom," and Heller's cited source, Binswanger 1993, makes no reference to the names of any of the heroines of the novels Rand wrote as a child; neither do the biographical interviews, which were Binswanger's source (and to which Heller says she "enjoyed unprecedented access" [2009, xiv]). (As to the source of this error, Binswanger quotes Rand's description of her early heroines as "slender," which sounds a bit like "thunder"; and "rpom" looks a bit like the Cyrillic spelling of "grom," which is the actual Russian word for thunder. It appears that Heller misheard Binswanger and then supplied and mistransliterated the Russian word.) A second example of Heller's carelessness with sources concerns the claim that Isabel Paterson's Monday-night circle compared themselves to "an earlier group of literary wits led by Dorothy Parker, Heywood Broun, and Alexander Woollcott that met at the Algonquin Hotel" (135). Heller cites John Chamberlain's *A Life with the Printed Word* for the observation, but that book does not discuss the Monday-night sessions at all (neither on "p. 55," which Heller cites, nor elsewhere). Heller's actual source is probably Britting, who describes Paterson's friends as "parallel to the Algonquin Round Table" (2004, 57) without saying, as Heller does (without support), that Paterson's friends themselves made the comparison. Heller also misrepresents some of Rand's writings. For example, she says that "The Ethics of Emergencies" (*VOS*) "warns against defining national emergencies too broadly or, worse, making them permanent, so that everyone is expected to sacrifice his liberties all the time" (322); in fact, that article deals exclusively with individual moral choices, and says nothing about national emergencies or government policy.

Burns, who supplies substantial useful information, gives undue credence to sources such as B. Branden's biography, which Burns deems "marred by serious inaccuracies," including the "debunked story that Rand named herself after her typewriter"(2009, 295). There are other problems. For example, Burns states, regarding Isabel Paterson's disastrous visit to Ayn Rand in California (see note 33): "It was the last time the two women would meet" (131). Rand, writes Burns, "could no longer retain respect for Paterson, downgrading her to a second-rate novelist rather than an important thinker" (132). But Rand did in fact meet with Paterson in New York, in 1961, to provide feedback and advice about Paterson's unpublished novel "Joyous Gard" (*Biographical Interviews* 524–526). Moreover, Rand's opinion of Paterson's work did not change when their personal relationship ended; she had always admired Paterson's political writing (and, as Burns notes, continued to recommend it), and she had never expressed admiration for Paterson's fiction. The errors here promote the false view that Ayn Rand allowed her judgment of someone's character (or her experience of someone's behavior) to affect her assessment of that person's work.

Notes

1 See the Appendix to this chapter for the sources I have consulted.
2 Although the conventional English equivalent of the Russian "Rozenbaum" is "Rosenbaum," I have chosen here to use a strict transliteration of the Russian of her last name, as "Alisa" is a strict transliteration of her original first name.
3 The novel was translated into English by Bill Bucko as *The Mysterious Valley* (Lafayette, CO: The Atlantean Press, 1994), and published with an introduction by Harry Binswanger and the original illustrations by René Giffey. For information about Maurice Champagne, René Giffey, and the original serialization, see Bucko 2009.
4 For a discussion of Cyrus Paltons in relation to Ayn Rand's fictional characters, see Milgram 2007b, esp. 177–183.
5 For some of her comments on Rostand, see WKCR Interview on "*Cyrano de Bergerac*"(*Speaking* 117) and "Vandalism" (*Column*).
6 For her comments on Hugo, see "Introduction to *Ninety-Three*" (*RM*) and *AOF* 34–35, 98–104. On Rand's relation to these authors, see also Milgram 2012b, 2007b (esp. 183–195); and Tore Boeckmann, Chapter 17, below.
7 In the biographical interviews, she comments at length on Dostoevsky and Tolstoy. See *RM* 30, 33, and 107 for some of her public comments on Dostoevsky. For her most extensive public discussion of Tolstoy's *Anna Karenina*, see *Speaking* 101–109. Although detailed information about the curriculum in her secondary school is not available, it is likely that Chernyshevsky's *Chto delat'?* [What Is to Be Done?] was required reading, since it "was continuously studied in Soviet schools" (Lonergan 1998, 227). Rand's work is sometimes likened to his, but the similarities are superficial at best. The "rational egoism" he advocates is a psychological rather than a moral theory, and he was not an individualist: his novel presents a socialist utopia, and his "rational" fictional characters seek to achieve the greatest happiness of all concerned, with no special regard for their own happiness.
8 The standard text for this last was Nikolai Ivanovich Bukharin's *Theory of Historical Materialism: Popular Textbook of Marxist Sociology* [Teorija istoricheskogo materializma: populjarnij uchebnik Marksistskoj sotsiologii]. Her description of her college textbook, in the biographical interviews, corresponds well with the content and approach of Bukharin, to whom, moreover, she refers disparagingly in her account in *WTL* of the education of Kira Argounova (188, 404).
9 The textbook, which she described as "a very detailed study of Plato and Aristotle," was most likely *Lektsii po drevnejf ilosofii* [Lectures in Ancient Philosophy] (St Petersburg: University of St Petersburg, 1911–1912) by Aleksandr Ivanovich Vvedenskij, [also transliterated Vvedensky] (1856–1925). (Wilhelm Windelband's *History of Ancient Philosophy* is recommended, within its pages, as a supplement to the textbook.) Vvedenskij, who was the chair of the department, probably also taught the course (as he often did). Rand later remembered the teacher as having been Nikolaj Onufrevich Losskij [also transliterated Lossky] (1870–1965), but this is likely a confusion, since the description Rand gave of the teacher's career, age, appearance, demeanor, and scholarly expertise is more consistent with its having been Vvedenskij. On these points see Milgram 2012a, esp. 92–94. Chris Matthew

Sciabarra, who believes that Losskij was a formative influence on Rand, comments on my observations about Losskij and Vvedenskij (Sciabarra 2013, 393–399), but he continues to maintain, without resolving the discrepancies between Rand's description and Losskij, that she was probably correct to name him as the teacher.

10 See James Lennox's discussion in Chapter 13, 334–337.

11 The phrase "hero in thy soul" can be found on page 27 of Thomas Common's (2011) translation of *Thus Spake Zarathustra* as part of a passage that Rand had considered for an epigraph to Part III of *The Fountainhead*. On these epigraphs and the relation between Nietzsche and *Fountainhead*, see Milgram 2007a, esp. 13–17. On Rand and Nietzsche more generally, see also Mayhew 2012b, 209–241; Mayhew 2005b, 28–54; and Lester Hunt's Chapter 14 in the present volume.

12 Her movie diary (*Russian Writings* 109–214), which begins in 1922 with D.W. Griffith's *Intolerance*, had 170 entries by the time she left Russia at the beginning of 1926. For conditions at the university in the early 1920s, see Sorokin 1950.

13 See Milgram 2005b, 119 and 2009, 55–56.

14 Her favorites were Fritz Lang's *Siegfried* (1924), Joe May's *Das Indische Grabmal* [The Indian Tomb] (1921, screenplay by Thea von Harbou and Fritz Lang from a novel by Thea von Harbou), and Maurice Tourneur's *Isle of Lost Ships* (1923, from a novel by Crittenden Marriott). For additional information about her film studies and interests, see Milgram 2012a, esp. 99–105.

15 Translations of both pamphlets, along with facsimiles in the original Russian, are available in *Russian Writings*.

16 On her choice of this name, see Britting 2004, 33. Although her sister Nora's early letters make clear that Rand chose the name "Rand" before leaving Russia and that she chose the last name before she determined on the first name ("Lil" was one alternative she considered, instead of "Ayn"), the reasons for her name choice have thus far remained unknown. Although she described her name as an abbreviation of her Russian name (and one that retained the initials) and stated that the "Ayn" was borrowed from a Finnish name, she did not state publicly why she had chosen this particular abbreviation, or who "Ayna" was. She chose the name "Rand" before there were any "Remington-Rand" typewriters; hence the typewriter is not the source of the name. Nor was "Ayn" a family nickname; her family's letters refer to her as "Alisa," "Alyonochka," (the diminutive of "Alyona," a Russian equivalent of the name "Alisa"), and "Dact" (for the pterodactyl in Arthur Conan Doyle's *The Lost World*). The letters "ay" in Russian represent the sound "au" in "Rozenbaum"; this may, however, be a mere coincidence, as is the resemblance of "Ayn," as pronounced, to the German word "ein" (meaning: one) or the resemblance of "Rand" to the protagonist of Ibsen's *Brand* ("No compromise! No half measures!") or to "Prince Ayan," the name of the character played by Conrad Veidt, then her favorite actor, in the film *The Indian Tomb*. It is possible, too, that the full name "Ayn Rand" may represent a phrase or unit (much like "Mark Twain," which referred to a measurement of water depth) that had meaning to her, although, if so, it was a meaning that remained private.

17 The Ayn Rand Archives have over 900 letters from the Rozenbaums to Ayn Rand; her part of the family correspondence, however, has been lost. From their part of the correspondence (most of it from her mother and her sister Nora), it is clear that they followed with great admiration and curiosity her stay in Chicago, her work with DeMille, and her relationship with Frank O'Connor. Some of the correspondence concerns practical matters, e.g., the repayment of the loan she received from her Chicago relatives or, later, her sending money to her parents. An especially interesting part of the correspondence deals with her family's reactions to *Night of January 16th* (see below, 26); her father and Nora judged Karen to be not guilty; her mother and sister Natasha disagreed.

18 An edited version of *Red Pawn* has been published in *Early*. The original versions are in the Ayn Rand Papers.

19 Five of her early short stories (written in Chicago and in Hollywood) – "The Husband I Bought," "Good Copy," "Her Second Career," "Escort," and "The Night King" – have been published posthumously in *Early*.

20 On the place of "The Little Street" in her early thought, see David Harriman's introduction to her undated notes (*Journals* 20–23) and Ghate 2007, 244; and in the present volume, Lester Hunt, Chapter

14, 344, and Gregory Salmieri, Chapter 3, 68 n. 1. The springboard for "The Little Street" was the public response to the murder trial of William Edward Hickman, much as the springboard for *Night of January 16th*, a few years later, was the suicide of Ivar Kreuger, a Swedish financier. In neither case was her projected fictional character based on the personal qualities of the real-life figure.

21 It took some time to find a publisher, even with the help of H.L. Mencken and of Gouverneur Morris, a successful Hollywood writer of screenplays and fiction. Many were unwilling to publish an anti-Soviet novel.

22 For the differences between the first and second edition, see Mayhew 2012b. For the novel's publication history, see Ralston 2012. *We the Living* was also published by Cassell, in England, in September 1936, with a few brief cuts of sexual content.

23 A bowdlerized version of the play was published for amateur productions, as *Night of January 16th: A Comedy-Drama in Three Acts* by Ayn Rand, edited by Nathaniel Edward Reeid (New York: David McKay, 1936). Rand's definitive edition of the play was published in hardcover (New York: World, 1968) and is now available in *Three Plays*. It includes an introduction in which she describes the play's history.

24 Autobiographical elements in *We the Living* included her experiences of poverty and propaganda (in the university and in the culture); several characters, moreover, were inspired in part by individuals she had known. See McConnell 2012, Federman 2012, and Lewis 2012.

25 Roark's architectural style and career path were analogous in some respects to those of Frank Lloyd Wright; Rand greatly admired his work, though not his philosophy or personal character. For information about her knowledge of Wright's work and her eventual interactions with him, see Berliner 2007. This well-documented article corrects errors in many published accounts of the Rand–Wright relationship.

26 Rand's voluminous notebooks, published in part in *Journals* chs. 4–6, contain dated and undated notes from 1935 to 1942. See Milgram 2007a.

27 *Ideal* and *Think Twice* were published posthumously, and can be found in *The Early Ayn Rand* and *Three Plays*. The play *Ideal* has also been published in 2015 in conjunction with a novella-version. There are multiple drafts of both. For the production history of *The Unconquered*, which closed on Broadway after six performances, see Britting 2012; for two versions of *The Unconquered*, see *The Unconquered*: With Another, Earlier Edition of *We the Living*, edited by Robert Mayhew (New York: Palgrave Macmillan, 2014). The holdings of the Ayn Rand Papers (Ayn Rand Archives) contain multiple drafts of these plays.

28 For the publication history, see Ralston 2005 and Milgram 2005a. For information about other works in dystopian fiction (including *We* by Evgeny Zamyatin), some of which Rand knew, see Milgram 2005b.

29 Gloria Swanson later commented: "Of all the guest speakers who came to talk there and share the podium with me, the most memorable by far was Ayn Rand, who had a fascinating mind and held audiences hypnotized" (1980, 461–462).

30 "To All Innocent Fifth Columnists" has been published in *Journals* 345–355. For drafts and correspondence regarding her political writing at this time, see *Papers* 029_90A, 030_90B, 030_90C, 146_PO1, 146_PO1, 146_PO2, 146_PO3, and 146_PO4. See also Britting 2005.

31 "Note on: unbreached self-esteem" (July 14, 1968), *Papers* 035_21F.

32 The extant copies of letters on both sides of the correspondence are available at both the Ayn Rand Archives and the Isabel Paterson Papers at the Herbert Hoover Memorial Library (West Branch, Iowa). Rand's letters are printed in Chapter 5 of *Letters*. Paterson's letters are more frequent; especially in the year after Rand moved to California, Paterson offered much unsolicited advice such as that Rand should not take her prescribed Benzedrine or waste her time engaging in political activism or responding to fan letters. But much of their correspondence reflected their mutual interests in political ideas. Rand spoke at length about her relationship with Paterson in the 1960–1961 biographical interviews.

33 The sentence quoted in the inscription appears in *The Fountainhead* (693). Sadly, the inscription took on a new significance, when, like Roark and Wynand, the two friends were friends no longer. According to Rand, Paterson, during a visit in 1948, insulted friends whom Rand had invited to meet her,

and Rand learned that Paterson had refused to review *The Fountainhead* because she had a negative opinion of the book. Although Rand was later to praise, in print, *The God of the Machine* (*TON* 3(10)), and Paterson was later to condemn as "inexcusable" the publication of Whittaker Chambers's review of *Atlas Shrugged* in *National Review*, the personal relationship was irretrievably broken. They met one more time, in New York, when Paterson sought Rand's advice and help regarding an unpublished novel, *Joyous Gard*. Rand's notes on the novel are in *Papers* 033_15x. For Paterson's response to the Chambers review, see her letter (undated, but evidently January, 1958) to Muriel Hall (Isabel Paterson Papers). For much more information about Paterson, see Cox 2004. An important primary source for Rand's ultimate assessment of Paterson's work is a 13-page handwritten document (undated, but written between 1961 and 1964) containing her comments on *The God of the Machine*, which she reread with a view to republishing it (*Papers* 035_22x).

34 She worked on this book in New York in 1943 and in California in 1944–1945. For notes and multiple drafts, see *Papers* 032_11A, 032_11B, 032_11C, 032_11D, 032_12A, 032_12B, 033_13A, 033_13B, 033_14A, and 033_14B. Some of the material appears, edited, in *Journals* ch. 8.

35 She wrote the first screen treatment, prepared the initial full script and the final screenplay, and served on the set as consultant, coaching Gary Cooper, for example, on the presentation of Roark's trial speech. The Ayn Rand Archives contain multiple versions of the scripts; in the biographical interviews, she comments on the many discussions about the language and filming of Roark's courtroom speech. For information about the adaptation process, including scripts by other writers, see Britting 2007. For information about versions of the screenplay and the circumstances of the delay, see Britting 2007.

36 Although Ayn Rand did not publicly identify her interlocutor, Rand refers to "The Strike" in a letter (October 10, 1943) to Paterson (*Letters* 174). For information about her early projected novel about the disappearance of men of achievement, see Milgram 2009, esp. 55–56.

37 Some of her notes for *Top Secret* appear, edited, in *Journals* ch. 9. Scripts, notes, and correspondence regarding her film work are available at the Ayn Rand Archives and the Margaret Herrick Library (Academy of Motion Picture Arts and Sciences) in Beverly Hills, CA. Her unproduced (and unpublished) screenplays for Hal Wallis included adaptations of Mabel Seeley's *The Crying Sisters* and Maria Luisa Bombal's *House of Mist*.

38 See Darryl Wright's analysis of Rand's early notes for *Atlas Shrugged*, and of the role of her work on "The Moral Basis of Individualism" in the development of her ethical theory, in Wright 2009, 253–257.

39 Among the important ideas that she developed in this period, she named "the sanction of the victim" (see Chapter 4, below, 95), "the issue of man being a volitional consciousness" (Chapter 5, 107–112), the "death premise" (Chapter 3, 64–65), "the reification of the zero" (Chapter 3, 70 n. 23, Chapter 6, 144, and Chapter 11, 266 n. 6), "the issue of space and time not being infinite" (Chapter 11, 252–253), "the role of the law of identity as the bridge between metaphysics and epistemology" (Chapter 11, 250–251 and Chapter 12, 291), and her "theory of universals" (Chapter 12, 289–291).

40 Both sides of the correspondence with Leonard Read are available in the Ayn Rand Archives. Both sides of the correspondence with Rose Wilder Lane are available at the Ayn Rand Archives and in the Rose Wilder Lane Papers at the Herbert Hoover Memorial Library (West Branch, Iowa). Burns (2009, 139) quotes Lane's correspondence with Jasper Crane about Rand, without the omissions made in the previous publication of the correspondence in MacBride 1973.

41 "Screen Guide for Americans" is reprinted in *Journals*, and "Textbook of Americanism" has been reprinted in *Column*.

42 Her testimony, along with edited versions of her notes on several films and the issues involved in the HUAC investigation, can be found in *Journals*. See also Mayhew 2005c and Lewis and Salmieri's discussion, below, 354–355.

43 For their early correspondence with Rand, see *Papers* 019_01A, 019_01B, 019_01C, 019_01D, 019_01E, 019_01F, 019_01G, and 020_01H.

44 *Objectivism: The Philosophy of Ayn Rand* (*OPAR*), on which see Chapter 1, above, 9. Alan Greenspan became prominent as the Chair of the Council of Economic Advisors (1974–1977) and as the

Chairman of the Federal Reserve (1987–2006). The other members of the original "Collective" included Allan Blumenthal (Nathaniel's cousin), Joan Mitchell (Barbara's friend, later Joan Mitchell Blumenthal), Elayne Kalberman (Nathaniel's sister) and her husband Harry Kalberman, and Mary Ann Rukavina (later Sures), a friend of Joan Mitchell.

45 Rand and Mises remained in touch into the 1970s. Mises praised *Atlas Shrugged* on its publication, and four of Mises's books were reviewed under her auspices in *TON* 1(1), 1(5), 1(9),and *TO* 9(8), and an additional four titles are included in *CUI*'s bibliography of recommended readings. Excerpts from her comments on several of his books can be found in *Marginalia* 105–144. On Rand's view of Mises, including her philosophical disagreements with him, see Onkar Ghate's discussion, below, 237–238.

46 The Murray Rothbard Papers at the Ludwig von Mises Institute (Auburn, Alabama) contain much relevant information, including Rothbard's early letter to Isaac Don Levine (November 12, 1947) stating his high regard for *Anthem* and *The Fountainhead*, as well as later letters in which he expressed disagreements and criticisms. Rothbard initially praised *Atlas* in a long (and personal) letter to Rand (October 3, 1957), and championed it publicly in letters to editors of many periodicals. But in July 1958, he ended his association with the "Collective" in the wake of allegations by Nathaniel Branden that he failed to cite key ideas from Rand and others in a draft of a conference paper. Rothbard's subsequent writings are consistently negative about Rand, her work, her admirers, and his experiences with them. (There has not yet been a full account of the documentation controversy – one that considers not only the correspondence and the published version of the article, but also the original and successive drafts of the paper, which I examined in the Murray Rothbard Papers.) For Rand's view of anarchism and the libertarian movement, see below, Chapter 8, 193–194 and Chapter 15, 381–382.

47 The Brandens' subsequent accounts of these events cannot be relied on (see Chapter 1, above, 13, 19 n. 21). See my Appendix for problems with the memoirs written decades later by the Brandens. Rand did not prepare a written chronology of the early stage of the romantic relationship. However, her practice inscription (Ayn Rand Archives) for the copy of *Atlas Shrugged* that she later gave to Branden indicates that the date September 13, 1954 (which corresponds with the Brandens' accounts of the acknowledgment of romantic emotions between Rand and Nathaniel Branden), was an important emotional milestone on her journey to the decision to dedicate *Atlas Shrugged* "to Frank O'Connor and Nathaniel Branden."

48 On the nature of the speech and its role in the novel, see Ghate 2009b and Gotthelf 2009a.

49 For the history of her selection of a publisher, see Ralston 2009.

50 See Berliner 2009.

51 Her notes for "To Lorne Dieterling," as well as the contract, are in the Ayn Rand Archives; an edited version of the notes appears in *Journals* 704–716.

52 *Objectivist Calendar* 2, 2, May 1977. (This 1–2 page newsletter, initiated upon the close of *ARL* and edited by Rand's secretary, Barbara Weiss, was a continuation of the column under the same name that had appeared in *ARL* and her prior publications.)

53 For the edited texts of some of the interviews on radio and television, see *Speaking*. For her *Los Angeles Times* columns June 17–December 16, 1962, see *Column*.

54 Her involvement is clear from an undated five-page manuscript, entirely in her handwriting, entitled "(The start of Social Metaphysics) (Discards from NB's Lecture 8)" and written in the style of a lecture (*Papers* 034_20C_007).

55 There are indications in Rand's day calendar that she occasionally delivered the lectures on other topics as well.

56 On these interviews, and the Brandens' use of them, see my Appendix.

57 "Editorial Memo Re: The Objectivist Newsletter" (July 22, 1961) with handwritten revisions by Ayn Rand and "Policy and Purpose of the Objectivist Newsletter" (July 26, 1961) (*Papers*, 060_17x).

58 An edited transcript of the 1969 course has been published as *The Art of Non-Fiction: A Guide for Writers and Readers*, ed. Robert Mayhew (New York: Plume, 2001) [*AON*].

59 The Ayn Rand Archives contain Ayn Rand's handwritten revisions for 13 articles and reviews written by other writers and published in *TO* (as well as for other articles that were ultimately not published). See *Papers* 014_01A, 014_01B, 014_02x, 014_013x, 014_04x, 014_05x, 014_06x, 014_07x,

014_08x, 014_09x, 014_10A, 014_10B, 015_10C, 015_10D, 015_10E, 015_13x, 015_14x, 016_16A, and 061_15D.

60 Hospers and Rand corresponded at length on philosophical subjects. Both sides of the correspondence are in the Ayn Rand Papers; her side has been published in *Letters* ch. 7. As she wrote in her letter of March 31, 1961 (*Letters* 307–308), a paragraph in "For the New Intellectual" (directed to "the best of today's intellectuals") was "specifically and personally dedicated" to him. Their friendship ended after he served as commentator for her invited lecture on "Art as Sense of Life" at the annual meeting of the American Society for Aesthetics at Harvard on October 26, 1962. There is no audio or video recording of this event, and no transcript of what he said in his commentary. Her brief, handwritten notes on that commentary indicate that at least some of his remarks were antagonistic, which she did not expect and had no reason to expect, given their many cordial and challenging conversations about philosophy and art. For example, she writes, in quotation marks, that he said "sense of life is irrelevant" – which, given that her topic was "Art as Sense of Life," appears to be a substantial objection regarding a topic that they had already discussed many times (*Papers* 110_36x_004).

61 Rand's reviews of Fleming's book and Mason's can be found, respectively, in *TON* 1(4) and 2(8). For her opinion of Spillane's writing, see *TON* 1(10) and 3(10), *RM* 33–34, 86–88, 103, 127, and *AOF* 132–134, 158. Regarding their friendship, see *Letters* 589–590, 600–601 and McConnell 2010, 232–239.

62 Copies of her notes on these and other books can be found in the marginalia collection of the Ayn Rand Archives. Edited versions of her notes on some books were published in *Marginalia*.

63 See her long letter of October 30, 1962 to Bennett Cerf (*Letters* 617–621). On Rand's view of Kennedy, see Lewis and Salmieri's discussion, below, 359–361.

64 In 1990, Dutton published an expanded second edition (edited by Harry Binswanger and Leonard Peikoff) which includes, as an appendix, material taken from a transcript of workshops Rand held on the treatise in 1969–1970 for professors and graduate students of philosophy (and other subjects). The 1979 and 1990 editions also include an essay by Peikoff on "The Analytic-Synthetic Dichotomy," which was first published in *TO* 6(5–9). In the biographical interviews, Rand spoke of having been convinced by Peikoff of the need for a book on her epistemology/new theory of concepts. Allan Gotthelf, a 1975 Columbia University PhD, associated with the movement in New York since 1962 (and coeditor of the present volume), recalls Rand telling him in 1967 that, along with Peikoff's earlier urging, it was a similar case he, Gotthelf, made to her, in 1963, that led to the decision to publish it at the time she did; in an inscription dated August 13, 1967, in his copy of the early book form of the series, she wrote: "To Allan Gotthelf – / – The book you had asked me for many years ago – /With best wishes for its full use – /Ayn Rand." For the circumstances of his conversation with Rand, see McConnell 2010, 340.

65 Rand and Branden had agreed to contribute equally to the publication; the number of his contributions, however, had been declining. In 1962, for example, they contributed approximately an equal number of articles (13 from him, 14 from her, not counting the reprinting of her columns from the *Los Angeles Times*); in 1966, by contrast, she contributed to every monthly issue, sometimes twice (for a total of 14), whereas he missed three months (resulting in a total of 9 articles).

66 Her 1967–1968 notes (see my next note) are her contemporary written record of her impressions of his statements. She also records her attempts to help him understand and resolve his problems.

67 There is incomplete documentary information about the course of the romantic relationship between Rand and Branden. At some point, Rand wrote in her personal notes, they had made a "Platonic decision" (quotation marks in the original), which signaled a change in their relationship. Her notes from 1967–1968 are in the Ayn Rand Archives; an edited version was published in Part Two of Valliant 2005. Her comments regarding his July letter appear in her notes. The letter itself, however, is not in the Ayn Rand Archives.

68 For example, on August 2, 1968, she turned down a lecture invitation from the New York State Psychiatric Institute, and suggested him as an alternative, describing him as "a psychologist who has done a great deal of original and important work in applying the principles of my philosophy to the field of psychology, psychiatry and mental health" (*Papers* 041_01B).

69 For Rand's public statement of the reasons for her actions, see "To Whom It May Concern" *TO* 7(5), which was published in September 1968. In October 1968, Nathaniel Branden and Barbara Branden mailed to the NBI mailing list the statements they had written in response: "In Answer to Ayn Rand" (in two parts, one written by each of them).

70 A second edition was published in 1975, with one additional article ("The Age of Envy"). An expanded edition was published posthumously, under the editorship of Peter Schwartz (on whom, see below, note 72), as *Return of the Primitive: The Anti-Industrial Revolution* (New York: Plume 1999) [*ROTP*].

71 Her health problems included a diagnosis of lung cancer and subsequent surgery; the removal of the cancer was followed by a long, painful convalescence. In addition, her husband suffered from atherosclerosis; he was repeatedly hospitalized, and needed constant care when at home. His death in 1979, she said, was the loss of her top value. Personal stresses included a difficult, and short-lived, reunion with her surviving sister, Nora.

72 In the first issue of the publication (February 1980), she stated that she approved of it, but that it was "not the official voice of Objectivism." Instead, "this magazine is a *forum* for students of Objectivism to discuss their ideas, each speaking only for himself." In her final speech, "The Sanction of the Victim" (published in *VOR*), she quoted from articles in *The Objectivist Forum* and in another new Objectivist publication, *The Intellectual Activist*, edited by Peter Schwartz. Schwartz was a Syracuse University graduate in journalism. He subsequently served as chairman of the board of The Ayn Rand Institute. Harry Binswanger subsequently published *The Ayn Rand Lexicon* and serves on the board of The Ayn Rand Institute. He is also a contributing author to this volume.

73 As her heir, Leonard Peikoff was entrusted with her papers and manuscripts. In addition to these two anthologies, he oversaw the publication of edited versions of her letters, journals, marginalia, courses, and unpublished fiction.

74 Earlier plans to adapt the novel had included a film to be produced by Albert Ruddy and a television mini-series to be produced by Michael Jaffe (for which Sterling Silliphant wrote a script). Correspondence about these projects can be found at the Ayn Rand Archives. For information about Ayn Rand's own plan and screenplay, see Britting 2009. In April 2011, the film *Atlas Shrugged, Part I* was released. Directed by Paul Johansson from a script by the producer John Aglialoro and Brian Patrick O'Toole, it dealt with the events in the first part of the novel. The film *Atlas Shrugged, Part 2: The Strike* was shot in 2012 with an entirely new cast; it was released in October of that year. Directed by John Putch from a script by Duke Sandefur, Brian Patrick O'Toole, and Duncan Scott, it dealt with the second part of the novel. *Atlas Shrugged, Part 3: Who Is John Galt?* was released in September 2014, with a script by J. James Manera (who also directed), Harmon Kaslow, and John Aglialoro.

75 The essay was originally published in 1963.

References

Berliner, Michael S. 2007. "Howard Roark and Frank Lloyd Wright." In Mayhew 2007.

Berliner, Michael S. 2009. "The *Atlas Shrugged* Reviews." In Mayhew 2009.

Binswanger, Harry 1993. "Ayn Rand's Life: Highlights and Sidelights." Lecture. Recording available at https://estore.aynrand.org/p/206 (accessed May 22, 2015).

Branden, Barbara. 1986. *The Passion of Ayn Rand*. New York, NY: Doubleday.

Branden, Nathaniel. 1989. *Judgment Day: My Years With Ayn Rand*. Boston, MA: Houghton Mifflin.

Branden, Nathaniel. 1999. *My Years With Ayn Rand*. San Francisco, CA: Jossey-Bass.

Britting, Jeff. 2004. *Ayn Rand*. New York, NY: Overlook Duckworth.

Britting, Jeff. 2005. "*Anthem* and 'The Individualist Manifesto'." In Mayhew 2005a.

Britting, Jeff. 2007. "Adapting *The Fountainhead* to Film." In Mayhew 2007.

Britting, Jeff. 2009. "Adapting *Atlas Shrugged* to Film." In Mayhew 2009.

Britting, Jeff. 2012. "Adapting *We the Living*." In Mayhew 2012a.

Bucko, Bill. 2009. *Ayn Rand's French Children's Magazines*. Irvine, CA: Ayn Rand Institute Press.

Burns, Jennifer. 2009. *Goddess of the Market: Ayn Rand and the American Right*. Oxford: Oxford University Press.

Cox, Stephen. 2004. *The Woman and the Dynamo: Isabel Paterson and the Idea of America*. New Brunswick, NJ: Transaction Publishers.

Federman, Dina. 2012. "*We the Living* and the Rosenbaum Family Letters." In Mayhew 2012a.

Ghate, Onkar. 2007. "The Basic Motivation of the Creators and the Masses in *The Fountainhead*." In Mayhew 2007.

Ghate, Onkar. 2009b. "The Role of Galt's Speech in *Atlas Shrugged*." In Mayhew 2009.

Gotthelf, Alan. 2009a. "Galt's Speech in Five Sentences (and Forty Questions)." In Mayhew 2009.

Heller, Anne C. 2009. *Ayn Rand and the World She Made*. New York, NY: Doubleday.

Lewis, John David. 2012. "Kira's Family." In Mayhew 2012.

Lonergan, Jennifer. 1998. "Nikolai Gavrilovich Chernyshevskii." In *Reference Guide to Russian Literature*, edited by Neil Cornwell. Chicago, IL: Fitzroy Dearborn.

MacBride, Roger Lea, ed. 1973. *The Lady and the Tycoon: The Best of Letters between Rose Wilder Lane and Jasper Crane*. Caldwell, ID: Caxton.

Mayhew, Robert, ed. 2005a. *Essays on Ayn Rand's* Anthem. Lanham, MD: Lexington Books.

Mayhew, Robert. 2005b. "*Anthem*: '38 and '46." In Mayhew 2005a.

Mayhew, Robert. 2005c. *Ayn Rand and Song of Russia: Communism and Anti-Communism in 1940s Hollywood*. Lanham, MD: Rowman and Littlefield.

Mayhew, Robert, ed. 2007. *Essays on Ayn Rand's* The Fountainhead. Lanham, MD: Lexington Books.

Mayhew, Robert, ed. 2009. *Essays on Ayn Rand's* Atlas Shrugged. Lanham, MD: Lexington Books.

Mayhew, Robert, ed. 2012a. *Essays on Ayn Rand's* We the Living, 2nd edition. Lanham, MD: Lexington Books.

Mayhew, Robert. 2012b. "*We the Living*: '36 and '59." In Mayhew 2012a.

McConnell, Scott. 2010. *100 Voices: An Oral History of Ayn Rand*. New York, NY: New American Library.

McConnell, Scott. 2012. "Parallel Lives: Models and Inspirations for Characters in *We the Living*." In Mayhew 2012a.

Milgram, Shoshana. 2005a. "*Anthem* in Manuscript: Finding the Words." In Mayhew 2005a.

Milgram, Shoshana. 2005b. "*Anthem* in the Context of Related Literary Works: 'We are not like our brothers.'" In Mayhew 2005a.

Milgram, Shoshana. 2007a. "*The Fountainhead* from Notebook to Novel: The Composition of Ayn Rand's First Ideal Man." In Mayhew 2007.

Milgram, Shoshana. 2007b. "Three Inspirations for the Ideal Man: Cyrus Paltons, Enjolras, and Cyrano de Bergerac." In Mayhew 2007.

Milgram, Shoshana. 2009. "Who Was John Galt?: The Creation of Ayn Rand's Ultimate Ideal Man." In Mayhew 2009.

Milgram, Shoshana. 2012a. "The Education of Kira Argounova and Leo Kovalensky." In Mayhew 2012a.

Milgram, Shoshana. 2012b. "*We the Living* and Victor Hugo: Ayn Rand's First Novel and the Novelist She Ranked First." In Mayhew 2012a.

Nietzsche, Frederich. 1911. *Thus Spake Zarathustra*, translated by Thomas Common. New York, NY: Macmillan.

Ralston, Richard. 2005. "Publishing *Anthem*." In Mayhew 2005a.

Ralston, Richard. 2009. "Publishing *Atlas Shrugged*." In Mayhew 2009.

Ralston, Richard. 2012. "Publishing *We the Living*." In Mayhew 2012a.

Sciabarra, Chris Matthew. 2013. *Ayn Rand: The Russian Radical*, 2nd edition. University Park, PA: Penn State University Press.

Sorokin, Pitirim. 1950. *Leaves from a Russian Diary, and Thirty Years After*. Boston, MA: Beacon Press.

Swanson, Gloria. 1980. *Swanson on Swanson*. New York, NY: Random House.

Valliant, James S. 2005. *The Passion of Ayn Rand's Critics: The Case against the Brandens*. Dallas, TX: Durban House.

Wright, Darryl. 2009. "Ayn Rand's Ethics: From *The Fountainhead* to *Atlas Shrugged*." In Mayhew 2009.

Part II

Ethics and Human Nature

3

The Act of Valuing (and the Objectivity of Values)

GREGORY SALMIERI

Your soul has a single basic function – the act of valuing. "Yes" or "No," "I wish" or "I do not wish."
Fountainhead 564, cf. 539

In this chapter, I trace a significant strand in Rand's intellectual development, showing how an idea that figures prominently in her early vision of a hero develops into the central concept for which she named her mature philosophy. Along the way, I introduce a number of the distinctive theses and concepts that will be explored in subsequent chapters of this *Companion*.

The idea which will be our focus is expressed by Howard Roark in the passage that serves as the epigraph to this chapter: "the act of valuing," he says, is the soul's "basic function." The idea of valuing as an activity of the soul or mind can be found in many of Rand's published works and it occurs frequently in the notes she made while planning her novels. Often, this idea is paired with the concern that many people do not perform this activity at all, or else do so only inconsistently. More than any other feature, what distinguishes Rand's heroes is that they are valuers on a grand scale, and central to her own intellectual development was sustained reflection on what it is to value and on the alternative between valuing and its absence.

Living and Valuing in *The Little Street* and *We the Living*

Rand's earliest surviving reference to valuing as an activity occurs in notes she made in 1928 for a novel that she intended to call *The Little Street*. She describes the protagonist she envisioned as wanting "to *live* every second" and "being unable to *exist* as other men do" (*Journals* 28, cf. 25).[1] The notes associate *living* with being active, feeling strong emotions (especially exaltation), and being unwilling to spend one's days working at a job one does not love. Rand writes that her protagonist "wants *all* of his life to be high, supreme, full of meaning." By contrast, too many people – those who merely exist – "lack [the capacity for] *reverence* and '*taking things seriously*'."[2]

> They do not hold anything to be very serious or profound. There is nothing that is sacred or immensely important to them. There is nothing – no idea, object, work, or person – that can inspire them with a profound, intense, and all-absorbing passion that reaches to the roots of their souls.

A Companion to Ayn Rand, First Edition. Edited by Allan Gotthelf and Gregory Salmieri.
© 2016 John Wiley & Sons, Ltd. Published 2016 by John Wiley & Sons, Ltd.

> They do not know how to value or desire. They cannot give themselves entirely to anything. There is nothing absolute about them. They take all things lightly, easily, pleasantly – almost indifferently, in that they can have it or not, they do not claim it as their absolute necessity. (*Journals* 28)[3]

The sort of person who does not "know how to value or desire" also "does not know how to believe anything," "has never believed consistently and does not know how to be true to any idea or ideal." He is "illogical" and unable to "connect together the things [he] observes." As a result, his existence is "a chaos of inconsistent ideas, actions, and feelings that can't be put together." (*Journals* 24)

We can see from this that Rand regarded valuing as a *rational* process – one that involves the logical (non-contradictory) integration of observations.[4] The notes do not tell us much about the nature of this process, but we can infer that it involves ensuring that one's values are consistent with one another and that one's actions are consistent with one's values. Consistency among one's values is needed, because if a person's values pull him in opposite directions, he will not be able to give himself *entirely* to anyone of them. The need for integrity – for consistency between one's values and one's actions – was evidently very salient for Rand during this period, for the *Little Street* notes are filled with discussions about the hypocrisy of the non-valuing characters (and, indeed, of mankind in general). Presumably her view was that only a person of integrity – someone who is actively and consistently pursuing values – can experience the all-consuming passions that she associates with living. The role she envisions for reason seems to go beyond merely harmonizing one's desires and calculating the means to them; it seems to also play a role in generating our desires. This is suggested by the following passage:

> A perfect, clear understanding also means *a feeling*. It isn't enough to realize a thing is true. The realization must be so clear that one feels this truth. For men act on feelings, not on thoughts. Every thought should be part of yourself, your body, your nature, and every part of your nature should be a thought. Every feeling – a thought, every thought – a feeling. (*Journals* 24)

Whatever the details, it is clear that Rand thought that there is some cognitive process that makes it possible for a human being to invest himself in a value and to experience a range of attendant emotions. Performing this process, being so invested, and feeling and acting on intense emotions seems to be what Rand means by "living" as opposed to merely "existing."[5]

Rand soon abandoned the *Little Street* project, but many of the ideas from these notes can be found in her first novel, *We the Living* (published 10 years after the notes were made). The word "living" in the title is clearly intended in the special sense we have been discussing. We can see this in a statement made by the heroine, Kira Argounova, at the novel's climax:

> Now look at me! Take a good look! I was born and I knew I was alive and I knew what I wanted. What do you think is living in me? Why do you think I'm alive? Because I have a stomach and eat and digest the food? Because I breathe and work and produce more food to digest? Or because I know what I want, and that something which knows how to want – isn't that life itself? (*WTL36* 496/*WTL* 385)

We can see all the features Rand associates with *living* in Kira's character. "She was ready for her future, a future of the hardest work. She was to be an engineer" (*WTL36* 43/*WTL* 34–35). When Kira made this determination, in childhood, her thought had been "quiet and reverent," and she regarded her future as "consecrated." She has learned the "profound joy of life" from gay operetta songs which she invested with "a solemn reverence." Her "highest reverence" (*WTL36* 445/*WTL* 345) is Leo Kovalensky, her lover, whose life and soul she struggles tirelessly to preserve despite impossible circumstances created by the Soviet dictatorship under which they live. Leo, defeated near the end of the novel, remarks that she has "never outgrown that tendency to be so serious about everything" (*WTL36* 445–446/*WTL* 345). In her last moments, she thinks of the life "to which she had been faithful her every living hour" and "would not betray now by stopping while she was still living, a life she could serve still, by walking, by walking forward a little longer, just a little longer." "Life, undefeated," she concludes, "existed and could exist" (*WTL36* 568–570/*WTL* 442–443).[6]

The use of religious words like "reverence" to describe Kira's attitude toward her life is significant. It is a theme of both the *Little Street* notes and *We the Living* that accepting religious (and otherwise impracticable) ideals undermines one's ability to value. In the notes, Rand describes "Morals (as connected with religion)" as

> the real reason for all hypocrisy. The wrecking of man by teaching him ideals that are contrary to his nature; ideals he has to accept as his highest ambition, even though they are organically hateful and repulsive to him. And when he can't doubt them, he doubts himself. He becomes low, sinful, imperfect in his own eyes; he does not aspire to anything high, when he knows that the high is inaccessible and alien to him. Humanity's morals and ideals, its ideology, are the greatest of its crimes. ("Unselfishness" first of all.) (*Journals* 25, cf. 37)

Given the context, the fact that Rand lists "ideals" along with "morals" at the end, makes it clear that this passage is not a criticism of morality as such, but of "humanity's morals" – that is, of the generally accepted morality that Rand would go on to criticize and offer an alternative to in her later works. What is her criticism of it at this early stage? Recall her view that someone who clearly understands something will have an associated feeling. Here she discusses what happens when a person attempts to accept an irrational ideal that cannot be understood and is contrary to human nature – for example, the ideal of chastity or of selflessness. Not only will the person not be able to experience the feeling and motivation that comes from understanding, the ideal will necessarily contradict feelings that he does have – for example, his sexual desires, or the desire for happiness more generally. If he does not reject the ideal, he will come to see himself as unworthy and unable to achieve ideals at all, and so he will become a non-valuing hypocrite. Rand would continue to make this criticism of religion and altruism throughout her career.[7] The effect of a good man's damning his sexual desires, in particular, is a major subordinate theme in *Atlas Shrugged*.[8]

We find a related criticism of religion in *We the Living*. A "favorite question" of Kira's is whether people believe in God; "if they say they do – then, I know they don't believe in life."

> Because, you see, God – whatever anyone chooses to call God – is one's highest conception of the highest possible. And whoever places his highest conception above his own possibility thinks very little of himself and his life. It's a rare gift, you know, to feel reverence for your own life and to want the best, the greatest, the highest possible, here, now, for your very own. To imagine a heaven and then not to dream of it, but to demand it. (*WTL36* 129/*WTL* 101)

Here the focus is not on any inner conflict engendered by religion; Kira's point is that someone whose ideals are not realizable in his own life will not be capable of committing to his own life and to the values that can be realized in it. We find variations of this criticism in

51

Atlas Shrugged. John Galt says that anyone who does not work to give values "expression in material form" is a "cheap little hypocrite" whose "existence is unrelated to his convictions" (*Atlas* 1029). Similarly, Dagny Taggart reflects disapprovingly on the emotion "others claimed to feel at the sight of the stars – stars safely distant by millions of years and thus imposing no obligation to act, but serving as the tinsel of futility." Looking out the window of an airplane she realized that she felt this emotion instead for "the sight of electric bulbs lighting the streets of a town. It was this earth below that had been the height she had wanted to reach" – "her goal, her beacon, the aspiration drawing her upon her upward course" (691). Dagny's attitude toward the electric lights, and toward the industrial civilization that they represent, is what Rand considers genuine reverence: the attitude one has toward a profound and extremely demanding value to which one gives oneself entirely. It requires great effort to keep the lights lit, and Dagny has spent her life in such effort.[9] By contrast, Rand thinks, a claimed reverence for something that cannot be achieved – and, therefore, toward which one can take no *action* – is a cause of, and rationalization for, non-valuing.[10] In *We the Living* we see religion playing this role in the life of Kira's sister, Lydia.

To some extent Lydia represents merely existing, as opposed to valuing, but the novel's clearest representative of mere existence is Citizen Ivan Ivanov, whose life is narrated briefly in the final chapter (*WTL36* 562–564/*WTL* 437–439). He acts only on sordid and transient desires, none of which he feels deeply. He serves in the Red Army but is indifferent to Communist ideology (he attends church with equal indifference), and when he is wounded and expects to die, "he stared dully at the wall, for it did not make any difference." After recovering, he marries "a servant girl with round cheeks and round breasts, because he had gotten her in trouble," and he settles into a domestic life that he thinks of as "happy," but when he is "transferred to the border patrol" there is no sign that he is pained to leave his family behind, or that he expends any effort or thought to avoid doing so.

Ivan Ivanov represents one of two broad categories of non-valuers that are contrasted with the heroes in Rand's fiction. His non-valuing takes the form of bovine passivity. He pursues no goals beyond the range of the immediate moment. The other type of non-valuer does pursue goals, but in a manner essentially different from the heroes. In *We The Living*, Pavel Syerov, Comrade Sonia, Victor Dunaev, and Karp Morozov are examples of this second type. All are scheming and ambitious, but in a limited and thoughtless way. The first three are members of the Communist Party, but they are motivated not by a deep belief in the cause, but by petty power-lust and by resentment of others; Morozov is a grafter and black market merchant. Though such characters are existentially more active than Ivanov, they are shown to be no more spiritually active. Their motives, though less short-range, are no less crude and obvious, and these characters are not shown to feel deeply for anything.

Among the characters in the novel, Kira is unique in her ability to maintain and act on her commitment to her values despite the most oppressive circumstances, but she is not the only valuer. Among the others are: Leo (already mentioned), Andrei Taganov, Stepan Timoshenko Sascha, and Irina. Taganov and Timoshenko are significant because they represent a central theme in Rand's thinking that is not yet present in the *Little Street* notes: that it is only insofar as a person is a valuer that he is efficacious.[11] At the beginning of the novel, Timoshenko and especially Taganov are idealistic Communists – valuers, who are genuinely and deeply committed to their cause. The novel makes clear that it is the activities of such men that made the Bolshevik Revolution possible and brought to power a system that (as Kira puts it) "forbade life to the living" (*WTL36* 496/*WTL* 385). Both *The Little Street* and *We the Living* are set in nightmare environments where the valuers are sacrificed to placate the petty resentments and short-range desires of those who do not know how to value. But, unlike the *Little Street* notes, *We the Living* makes it clear that this environment was created by mistaken valuers. The horror of a world in which the *living* are sacrificed on the altar of the merely existing is not inherent in human nature or the nature of the universe. It is the result of errors made by some people of the sort who are victimized by such societies, and such errors can be prevented or corrected. The realization of this fact by a central character is crucial to the plot resolution of both *The Fountainhead* and *Atlas Shrugged*. (On this point see Chapter 18, below, 457–458.)

A final theme, present already in *We the Living* (but not in the *Little Street* notes), is that *living* requires freedom. We can see why in what Kira says immediately after identifying her life itself with that thing in her that "knows how to want."

> And who – in this damned, endless universe – who can tell me why I should live for anything but for that which I want? Who can answer that in human sounds that speak for human reason? ... But you've tried to tell us what we should want. You came as a solemn army to bring a new life to men. You tore that life you knew nothing about, quivering, out of their very guts and you told them what it had to be. You took their every hour, every minute, every nerve, every thought in the farthest corners of their souls, and you told them what it had to be. You came and you forbade life to the living. You've driven us all into an iron cellar and you've closed all doors, and you've locked us airtight, airtight till the blood vessels of our spirits burst! Then you stare and wonder what it's doing to us. Well, then, look! All of you who have eyes left – look! (*WTL36* 496/*WTL* 385)

Kira's charge against the Communist system under which she has been forced to live is that it removes the conditions needed for the psychological activity of valuing. By depriving the people of choice, the Communists have asphyxiated their souls.

What then do we know from *We the Living* and the *Little Street* notes about this activity of valuing itself? It is what makes human beings efficacious and enables them to make serious commitments and experience profound emotions; it involves reasoning, and in particular, choosing consistent values that are both demanding and achievable in this world; it is undermined by ideologies that propound unattainable ideals; and it requires freedom. However, we do not see much of the mechanics of the valuing process. For that we will need to turn to *The Fountainhead*.

The Fountainhead on the Activity of Valuing

The Fountainhead shows that the spiritual activity that Rand sees as the essence of human life is incompatible with a primary orientation toward other people.[12] The novel contrasts people who perform the function of valuing for themselves with those who "live second-hand" (633). The former type is epitomized by "the great creators – the thinkers, the artists, the scientists, the inventors" (710), among whom is the novel's hero, Howard Roark; but members of this type can be found in any legitimate profession and at any level of natural ability. This is illustrated by the fact that Roark is able to find "my kind of people" in all walks of life (157). Consider, for example, the jurors that he selects for his second trial: "There were two executives of industrial concerns, two engineers, a mathematician, a truck driver, a bricklayer, an electrician, a gardener and three factory workers" (707). What all these people have in common is that they are "men of self-sufficient ego" (636) and "unborrowed vision"

(710) – that is, they perform for themselves the process of valuing, which Rand thinks is the essence of human life.

This is what the second-hander does not do. Instead, he is moved as an after-effect of the functioning of other people. This point is dramatically illustrated by Dominique Francon, who, for a time, makes herself into an artificially clear example of a second-hander by acceding to every wish of those around her. In a conversation with Dominique, Peter Keating describes the effect:

> "You've never said, not once, what you thought. Not about anything. You've never expressed a desire. Not of any kind … You're not real. You're only a body … You understand what death is? When a body can't move any more, when it has no … no will, no meaning. You understand? Nothing. The absolute nothing. Well, your body moves – but that's all. The other, the thing inside you, your – oh, don't misunderstand me, I'm not talking religion, but there's no other word for it, so I'll say: your soul – your soul doesn't exist. No will, no meaning. There's no real you any more."
> "What's the real me?" she asked. For the first time, she looked attentive; not compassionate; but, at least, attentive.
> "What's the real anyone?" he said, encouraged. "It's not just the body. It's … It's the soul … It's – you. The thing inside you."
> "The thing that thinks and values and makes decisions?"
> "Yes! Yes, that's it. And the thing that feels. You've – you've given it up …
> "So there are two things that one can't give up: One's thoughts and one's desires?"
> "Yes! Oh, you do understand! So you see, you're like a corpse to everybody around you. A kind of walking death … You're not here. You've never been here. If you'd tell me that the curtains in this room are ghastly and if you'd rip them off and put up some you like – something of you would be real, here, in this room. But you never have. You've never told the cook what dessert you liked for dinner. You're not here, Dominique. You're not alive. Where's your I?" (425)

The second-hander is the person who lacks an "I." The novel introduces us to several varieties of such people. First there are minor characters who (like Ivan Ivanov in *We the Living*) are almost entirely passive. For example, "Renée Slottern," who "sat curled up on a footstool, munching peanuts. Once in a while she reached up to the crystal dish on a side table and took another. She exhibited no further exertion" (581). At one point she is described as feeling "a vapid wonder about how it felt to have a man one really wanted and how one went about wanting" (582). Unlike Renée, most of the novel's second-handers are outwardly very busy. Keating (like Victor Dunaev in *We the Living*) is an ambitious social climber who holds no genuine values. He seeks only to advance a career that he chose for its prestige. Ellsworth Toohey (like Pavel Syerov, though more so) is animated by fear of and resentment toward the valuers. Despite their busyness, all of these characters are spiritually passive. They do not engage in the processes of thinking or valuing on matters of any scale or depth, and so they do not have thoughts or desires of their own, and their orientation in life derives from the mental functioning of others. The final example of a second-hander is Gail Wynand, a tragic figure analogous to Taganov. Roark says of Wynand that he "was not born to be a second-hander," meaning that, unlike the other second-handers mentioned, he does have thoughts and forms values of his own, and consequently, he is able to feel strong passions. However, he dedicates his life to achieving and maintaining power over non-valuing people by catering to their superficial and second-hand desires. He believes, in the beginning at least, that this power will enable him to protect his values against these people, whom he sees as a threat, but in fact his policy gives them power over him by making their petty and vicious motives the central determinant of his life.[13]

Through the depictions of Roark and Keating, *The Fountainhead* shows us in more detail than do Rand's earlier works the nature of the mental activity that differentiates those who live from those who merely exist. Roark and Keating are both architects, and one area in which we see the difference between valuing and its absence is their different approaches to their work. Keating designs buildings by using well-codified methods to adapt the designs of earlier buildings to different sites and purposes. It is a relatively mechanical process. And when it is completed, he has little conviction about the resulting designs.

> When the drawings were ready, he stood looking at them uncertainly. Were he to be told that this was the best or the ugliest house in the world, he would agree with either. He was not sure. He had to be sure. (63)
>
> He felt nothing but immense uncertainty when his sketches were ready and the delicate perspective of a white marble edifice lay, neatly finished, before him ... It looked good ... it might be good ... he was not sure. (171)

In both of these cases, Keating is highly motivated to evaluate his designs and is trying to do so, but he finds that he *cannot*. He does not *know how to value*. This inability is not due to stupidity or ignorance of architecture, for Keating is intelligent and well educated in the field. Indeed, he can often notice problems with other people's designs. But observe how he does so:

> When he glanced at his [colleague's] plans again, he noticed the flaws glaring at him from the masterpiece. It was the floor of a private residence, and he noted the twisted hallways that sliced great hunks of space for no apparent reason, the long, rectangular sausages of rooms doomed to darkness. Jesus, he thought, they'd have flunked me for this in the first term. (28)
>
> Keating thought that four of the windows faced four mammoth granite columns. (31)

In those cases where Keating is able to confidently judge a design, it is by applying some simple rule: rooms ought to be light; windows ought to have a view; hallways ought to be straight. Presumably he has a repertoire of such rules that enables him to recognize typical architectural failings. When he does not notice some such rule being violated, he cannot confidently form any opinion about a building's merits, and since the rules pertain only to *typical* situations, they cannot guide him in the creation of anything original. Moreover, each of the rules stands in Keating's mind as an injunction imposed by the professors who would have "flunked" him for violating it. Because of this, the judgments he makes on the basis of these rules are not really his own; they are merely dutiful applications of other people's standards.

Roark, by contrast, says: "I set my own standards. I inherit nothing." (13)

> Here are my rules: what can be done with one substance must never be done with another. No two materials are alike. No two sites on earth are alike. No two buildings have the same purpose. The purpose, the site, the material determine the shape. Nothing can be reasonable or beautiful unless it's made by one central idea, and the idea sets every detail. A building is alive, like a man. Its integrity is to follow its own truth, its one single theme, and to serve its own single purpose. A man doesn't borrow pieces of his body. A building doesn't borrow hunks of its soul. Its maker gives it the soul and every wall, window and stairway to express it. (12)

Rather than being limited to such narrow and discrete issues as what shape specific sorts of rooms should be or how much light they should have, Roark's rules deal with the fundamental question of how a building's shape should be determined. Because of this, Roark has distinctive criticisms of buildings that none of the professors would flunk: in one of the first scenes, he tells the Dean of his school what's "rotten" about the *Parthenon* – "Yes, God damn it, the Parthenon!" (12). More importantly, Roark's rules enable him to conceive of and to wholeheartedly endorse radically bold new designs: "The buildings were not Classical, they were not Gothic, they were not Renaissance. They were only Howard Roark" (7).

What makes these rules Roark's *own?* How is it that when he applies them to make (or to judge) a particular architectural decision, he is independently performing the act of valuing, whereas, when Keating applies the rules he has learned, he is merely functioning second-hand? The answer is not that Roark was the first to think of the rules: Henry Cameron, whom Roark seeks out as a mentor, knew and was implementing them before Roark was born, and Roark has much to learn from Cameron about how to implement them consistently (33–34, 38). Moreover, Roark does not regard the rules as defining an idiosyncratic style of his own. He regards them as objective esthetic standards, and at points in the novel he tries (sometimes successfully) to teach others that they are *true* (12, 160–164, 195–196).

Roark's rules are his own because of the relation in which they stand to the mental processes that he performs as an individual. This is true in two respects. First, though Roark was not the first to think of these rules, he did the thinking needed to understand them and the facts that give rise to them. Consequently, they stand in his mind as knowledge, rather than as edicts accepted on the authority of others; and, when he makes decisions by applying the rules, he is acting wholly on his own judgment. Second, whereas Keating proceeds by rote, Roark's rules demand a great deal of original thought at each stage. He must first *understand* the relevant architectural problem by *identifying* the proposed building's function and location and the nature of the available materials, then he must *conceive* some central idea as a specific solution to this problem, and then *select* every detail of the building in accordance with this central idea, thereby *integrating* the building into a harmonious whole.[14]

For example, the problem raised by the proposed Cortlandt Homes project is: "How to design a decent modern unit that could rent for fifteen dollars a month" (598). To complete the statement of the problem we would need to add the location, Astoria (because different designs might be required to accomplish this end in different climates), and a host of facts about the materials available in 1937 (when this part of the novel is set). Solving such a problem requires, first, grasping a complex array of causal relationships involving the site, the function, and the available materials and, then, thinking creatively. In this case, Roark needs to identify the various factors that normally make housing costly (e.g., the demolition necessary to make repairs) and he needs to grasp how the nature of the existing building materials allows them to be used in various ways that might minimize cost (e.g., that plastic can be injection molded into shapes of certain sorts). Here is Roark's solution to this problem – the central idea of his design for Cortlandt:

> six [concrete] buildings, fifteen stories high, each made in the shape of an irregular star with [triangular] arms [containing modular apartments with prefabricated plastic and light metal components] extending from a central shaft [containing elevators, stairways, and utilities]. (613)

Once Roark conceives a central idea for a building, he embraces it as a value (says "Yes" to it as a solution to the architectural problem), and it becomes the standard of value by which he selects and judges every detail of the building. The description of Cortlandt indicates how its details are selected in accordance with Roark's central idea:

The ceilings were pre-cast; the inner walls were of plastic tile that required no painting or plastering; all pipes and wires were laid out in metal ducts at the edge of the floors, to be opened and replaced, when necessary, without costly demolition; the kitchens and bathrooms were prefabricated as complete units; the inner partitions were of light metal that could be folded into the walls to provide one large room or pulled out to divide it ... (613)

Selecting each of these details required an original act of thought. Because the central idea for Cortlandt is original, there are no ready-made methods to implement the idea – no earlier designs to copy. This is not to say that Roark cannot make use of knowledge he has gained from other buildings. Of course he does, but he cannot rely (as Keating does) on already established patterns or habits of thought or action. Any methods or features suggested to him by his knowledge of past buildings cannot simply be followed, they must be *judged* in accordance with Cortlandt's central idea, and since the central idea is new, applicable features or methods from earlier buildings cannot just be superficially adapted to it; they would need to be fundamentally reconceived. Fresh thinking is required at every step.

The thinking required by Roark's rules at every step in the design process is not automatic, and it is not something that anyone automatically knows how to do. It must be learned. By the time we meet Roark, he is 22 and has worked "in the building trades since childhood" (13, 14). We are given every indication that he has spent all of these years constantly thinking and learning about how buildings are designed and constructed, about the reasons behind this, and about how buildings might be designed better. But Roark still has a great deal to learn. We can see this in Cameron's criticisms of one of Roark's early drawings:

It's a crime. Look ... at that. What in Christ's name was your idea? What possessed you to indent that plan here? Did you just want to make it pretty, because you had to patch something together? Who do you think you are? Guy Francon, God help you? ... Look at this building, you fool! You get an idea like this and you don't know what to do with it! You stumble on a magnificent thing and you have to ruin it! Do you know how much you've got to learn?" (38)

At this point in the story, Roark doesn't know how to determine whether his idea for a certain building calls for indenting a certain plan. He has no reason for indenting it or for the alternative and so relies on a generalized sense of "what looks pretty" without understanding what makes an indented plan pretty and, therefore, whether one will add or detract from this building. Setting all the details in accordance with one's central idea is a skill that Roark must learn, and even after learning it, it takes effort to apply it to each new design, because in each case he is working with a new central idea, and cannot rely on patterns or habits of thought that he automatized on earlier buildings.[15]

I do not mean to imply that deliberate effort is needed at every moment in such a process. A central idea may occur to one in a flash of inspiration, but only if one has learned the method and done the thinking required to grasp the architectural problem.[16] Similarly, once one has committed to the central idea, one may sometimes be able to recognize immediately some of its implications for narrower issues. The more adept one is at the process, the more often this will happen, but the fact remains that architecture, as Roark practices it, is a demanding intellectual discipline that has to be learned, and cannot be performed mindlessly by rote.

This process epitomizes valuing as Rand understood it. Every architectural element that Roark selects – including, first, his central idea and, then, subordinate design elements – becomes one of his values: he acts to bring it into reality; it serves as a standard by which he judges and selects subordinate values; and he feels joy when he achieves it. Because Keating does not perform this process, he designs only *secondhand*. His designs are not his own but aftereffects of the work of the earlier architects whose buildings he copied and whose rules he obediently and joylessly follows.

As an intellectual process that must be learned, Roark's approach to architecture illustrates what Rand means by *knowing how to value*. One must know how to intelligently select and judge specific values in accordance with a central value (as Roark selects the details of each building in accordance with its central idea) and know how to conceive of and commit to a central value in a context that is determined by a set of needs and resources.

This is the activity that Rand identifies with *living* for a human being. It is an activity that a person of self-sufficient ego performs not only in architecture or any other specific domain, but across the whole of his life. To the extent that one fails to do this, one leads a second-hand life. Such lives are, like Keating's buildings, senseless collections of elements borrowed from others. When criticizing such buildings, Roark often stresses their lack of the sort of integration that is characteristic of living things:

> Now take a human body. Why wouldn't you like to see a human body with a curling tail with a crest of ostrich feathers at the end? And with ears shaped like acanthus leaves? It would be ornamental, you know, instead of the stark, bare ugliness we have now. Well, why don't you like the idea? Because it would be useless and pointless. Because the beauty of the human body is that it hasn't a single muscle which doesn't serve its purpose ... (132; cf. 163, and 606)

Roark's own buildings, by contrast, have the integrated character of the human body, and he analogizes their integration also to moral integrity, which (as we saw earlier) was central to Rand's conception of living as opposed to merely existing.

> He explained why an honest building, like an honest man, had to be of one piece and one faith; what constituted the life source, the idea in any existing thing or creature, and why – if one smallest part committed treason to that idea – the thing or the creature was dead; and why the good, the high and the noble on earth was only that which kept its integrity. (195)

Putting these passages together, then, we have a three-way analogy between the integration in virtue of which an organism is alive, the moral virtue of integrity, and the integration of a building. We have seen some indication of how the last two of these three are the product of the mental activity of valuing. I turn now to the issue of what it means to engage in this process, not just in a specific field, but in one's life as a whole.

The Fountainhead on Work as the Meaning of Life

Just as each of Roark's buildings is integrated around a central idea, so his life is integrated around a central purpose that he has conceived for himself and committed to. This purpose is summed up by the inscription on the door to his office: "Howard Roark, Architect" (129). Cameron comments that the inscription "doesn't say much ... But it's like those mottoes men carved over the entrance of a castle and died for" (129). Roark has chosen the work he wants to do and set his standards for it, and a life centered around this work is his ultimate value: "The only thing that matters, my goal, my reward, my beginning, my end is the work itself. My work done my way" (24, 579).

All of Roark's other values are means to or components of a life integrated around this central purpose, and it sets the standard by which he judges other things as good or bad for him. Thus, in a pivotal scene, he sees refusing the commission for the Manhattan Bank building as a selfish act, because the money and fame he might acquire from the commission cannot be of any value to him if acquired by violating the architectural principles that define the work which is his central purpose (196).

Of course a life integrated around a career includes values that are not means to or components of one's work. Most notably, Roark loves Dominique and Wynand. But his love for these individuals is nonetheless an expression of his central purpose. Each of his buildings too includes elements that are not means to or parts of its central idea, but they are not chosen at random, but as "an emphasis of the principle that makes [the building] stand" (132). He exercises similar selectivity in choosing his relationships: "He responded only to the essence of a man: to his creative capacity" (317). As a result, his relationships are an emphasis of the principle by which he lives and works.[17]

The central idea of each of Roark's buildings is unique, but in integrating the building around such an idea, he is following architectural principles that he thinks are applicable to all buildings. Likewise, Roark's life has a unique central purpose, but in organizing his life around such a purpose, he is following ethical principles that apply to all human beings.

The principle most stressed in *The Fountainhead* is integrity. We've seen that Roark thinks that integrity is possible for both buildings and human beings, and that it is rare in both cases. To achieve this integrity in architecture, one must know what considerations are and are not genuine parts of the architectural problem to which a building's central idea is the solution. For example, the fact that Roark's client Austin Heller needs a large and accessible study in his house qualifies (133), but the Manhattan Bank board's preference for a classical façade does not (194–195). The felt need for a classical façade on an office building is the result of a failure to architecturally value properly – specifically, it is the result of bowing to the opinions of others and a slothful preference for familiar features, even in contexts where those features would be senseless. What considerations, then, are valid for determining the course of one's life?

First, of course, as in architecture, Roark holds that it is wrong to let one's life course be determined by other people. Roark's is the "code of the creator" and the creator, he says, "is not concerned with [other people] in any primary matter"; a creator may, of course, trade with or work for other people, but he will not let his life "depend *primarily* upon other men," as does "the gangster, the altruist and the dictator."

> A man thinks and works alone. A man cannot rob, exploit or rule – alone. Robbery, exploitation and ruling presuppose victims. They imply dependence. They are the province of the second-hander.
> Rulers of men are not [egoists]. They create nothing. They exist entirely through the persons of others. Their goal is in their subjects, in the activity of enslaving. They are as dependent as the beggar, the social worker and the bandit. The form of dependence does not matter. (714)[18]

We can see from these passages that Roark thinks that, to be independent, one must produce the values one needs, rather than depending on others for them. Fundamentally, to be independent is to be creative, and the central concern of a creator – the thing around which he builds his life – is work. Roark expresses this point dramatically in an exchange with Wynand.

> Roark got up, reached out, tore a thick branch off a tree, held it in both hands, one fist closed at each end; then, his wrists and knuckles tensed against the resistance, he bent the branch slowly

59

into an arc. "Now I can make what I want of it: a bow, a spear, a cane, a railing. That's the meaning of life ... Your work." He tossed the branch aside. "The material the earth offers you and what you make of it ..." (577)[19]

Notice that all the items Roark says that he might make of the branch have a role in sustaining human life. Later in the novel Roark says that "The code of the creator is built on the needs of the reasoning mind which allows man to survive" (713). Clearly, then, when Roark speaks of work, he means not just any activity that might keep one busy, but *productive work*. In a later essay, Rand describes production as "the application of reason to the problem of survival" ("What is Capitalism?" *CUI* 17).

At least as early as the *Little Street* notes, Rand held that living consists in valuing – in a certain activity of the soul that makes one's life meaningful to one. By connecting meaning to work and work to survival as he does, Roark strengthens the connection between *living* (as opposed to merely existing) and living in the biological sense (in which it is opposed to dying). It is by the spiritual activity of living (i.e., of valuing) that human beings literally survive. This is an idea that Rand develops in much greater depth in *Atlas Shrugged* and "The Objectivist Ethics" (*VOS*). In these works and others, she discusses values such as art, philosophy, self-esteem, and love, arguing that our need for them is tied "to man's survival – not to his physical survival, but to that on which his physical survival depends: to the preservation and survival of his consciousness" ("The Psycho-Epistemology of Art" *RM* 5).[20]

Recall that Kira had insisted that she was alive, not because "I breathe and work and produce more food to digest," but "because I know what I want" – where this latter is associated with profound spiritual values such as her love of Leo. Is Roark reversing this order by putting work at the center of life? Certainly not. Consider how he describes his motivation in building:

> You see, I'm never concerned with my clients, only with their architectural requirements. I consider these as part of my building's theme and problem, as my building's material – just as I consider bricks and steel. Bricks and steel are not my motive. Neither are the clients. Both are only the means of my work. (*Fountainhead* 604)

Just as Roark has clients in order to build, so too he eats in order to build, rather than the reverse. The clients' architectural needs provide part of the *context* for Roark's work, but it is the work itself, not the satisfaction of these needs, that is his central purpose. Similarly, the biological needs that make it necessary for human beings to work provide part of the context in which Roark has defined a productive career, but it is the career, not the satisfaction of the biological needs, that is his purpose. That there is a client with a need for a building and that human beings have survival requirements are both essential to the work Roark does: it would not be architectural work if it didn't fulfill an architectural need, and it would not be productive work at all if it did not play a role in fulfilling some biological need. But it is the work and not the need-fulfillment that Roark loves and around which he has integrated his life.

A life, as Rand conceives of it, is its own goal; and a person's "work is the primary" constituent of his life.[21] As Roark points out early in the novel, most of one's life is spent working (13). Moreover, one is most alive when one is at work. Kira had said that life itself is "that something which knows how to want"; Roark adds that productive work is *making what one wants* out of the material offered by the earth. In this way productive work epitomizes the very process in which Rand thinks life consists. Consider how she describes the relation between work and values in *Atlas Shrugged*:

> [P]roductive work is the process by which man's consciousness controls his existence, a constant process of acquiring knowledge and shaping matter to fit one's purpose, of translating an idea into physical form, of remaking the earth in the image of one's values. (*Atlas* 1020)

It is especially clear how Roark's work consists in remaking the earth in the image of his values. His job is to order granite cut to make walls, and trees split into rafters (*Fountainhead* 4), and he chose this work precisely to change "the shape of things on this earth" (39). Other productive endeavors also consist in reshaping materials in the image of one's values. For example, Austin Heller, in writing his column, shapes ink on paper into the form of words which express ideas that he wants to convey, and a good janitor transforms a dirty building into the kind of environment he values.

To the extent that a man does not "know how to want," he has no values in the shape of which to remake the earth, no ideas to translate into physical form. To the extent that he produces anything at all, he does so second-hand by repeating "in uncritical stupor a routine he has learned from others" (*Atlas* 1020). If his motions bring him any returns, it is only because of the prior functioning of other men, who authored the routines he apes and valued the results they lead to.

Productive work is not just a consequence of valuing, it is its implementation. As we discussed above (in connection with the issue of religious ideals), Rand held that a professed value that one does not work to bring into existence is not really a value at all.[22] Conversely, only people who do work to bring their values into existence are genuine valuers – only they experience the intense emotions Rand associated with "valuing" and "living" (as opposed to merely existing). In *The Fountainhead*, Heller describes Roark's attitude toward his work as a "combination of holy sacrament, Indian torture and sexual ecstasy" (*Fountainhead* 257), and we can see this in Roark's bearing, earlier in the novel, as he walks through the skeleton of the half-completed Heller House:

> There were moments when something rose within him, not a thought nor a feeling, but a wave of some physical violence, and then he wanted to stop, to lean back, to feel the reality of his person heightened by the frame of steel that rose dimly about the bright, outstanding existence of his body as its center. He did not stop. He went on calmly. But his hands betrayed what he wanted to hide. His hands reached out, ran slowly down the beams and joints. The workers in the house had noticed it. They said: "That guy's in love with the thing. He can't keep his hands off." (130; cf. 4, 15, 96–97, 315, 608)

Though Roark's intensity is exceptional, Rand thought that one can find sparks of the same kind of joy in anyone who loves his work. Because such people spend their days conceiving goals and pursuing them in action, they experience a deep satisfaction in the work itself, and they feel a sense of personal achievement when they complete a given project or advance to a new level of work.

By contrast, non-valuing people find no pleasure in their work, whether they are janitors or celebrated architects. Guy Francon is uninterested in building: his Frink National Bank Building "was the last structure [he] ever designed; its prestige spared him the bother from then on" (33). Keating does not answer, when, after looking at his sketches for his first house, Roark asks if he enjoys "doing this sort of thing" (64), but it is clear from the narration that he did not enjoy designing it. "Looking down at a blank sheet of paper" on which he was about to draft the house, he felt "cold and empty": "It had never been quite real to him before that this was the thing actually expected of him – to fill a sheet of paper, to create something on a sheet of paper." And "He hated every piece of stone on the face of the earth. He hated himself for having chosen to be an architect" (62–63).

There is nothing to enjoy about the kind of work Keating and Francon do. It consists in tedious copying of structures that they do not appreciate, in accordance with rules whose purpose they do not understand. In essence, they work only for "more food to digest" and for other goals that are unrelated to the work itself. Keating is motivated primarily by a desire for prestige, and Francon shows more concern for an antique snuffbox than for the affairs of his office (79). The lives of such people are joyless routines that provide them the means to seek some shred of pleasure on the weekends. This attitude is represented by a group that Roark observes during his visits to the Heller House construction site.

> An open car drove by, fleeing into the country. The car was overfilled with people bound for a picnic. There was a jumble of bright sweaters, and scarfs fluttering in the wind; a jumble of voices shrieking without purpose over the roar of the motor, and overstressed hiccoughs of laughter; a girl sat sidewise, her legs flung over the side of the car; she wore a man's straw hat slipping down to her nose and she yanked savagely at the strings of a ukulele, ejecting raucous sounds, yelling "Hey!" These people were enjoying a day of their existence; they were shrieking to the sky their release from the work and the burdens of the days behind them; they had worked and carried the burdens in order to reach a goal – and this was the goal. (131)

A picnic can be a reinvigorating way to spend an afternoon, bright colors can be festive, and playing an instrument can be a rewarding avocation. Notice, however, that this car is "fleeing" to the country, that the revelers see this picnic as a "release" from "a burden," and that their laughter is overstressed. When a person has no interest in the activity that occupies his days, he can only view leisure activities as an escape. Such activities are enjoyable as a rest in the context of a life devoted to some satisfying work, but when one tries to live for them, whatever pleasure one finds will necessarily be affected and hollow. Someone who selects and pursues values only in self-contained episodes on the weekends will have a commensurately shallow emotional life. Only insofar as a person's life is an integrated process of reshaping the world in the image of his values will he experience his life as meaningful.

A good life, then, according to Roark, is one focused on creative work, pursued independently and with integrity. It is a life of valuing, and of valuing oneself as a valuer. And as we have seen, valuing is a *rational* activity. Thus, Roark celebrates the mind at the novel's climax:

> Man cannot survive except through his mind. He comes on earth unarmed. His brain is his only weapon. Animals obtain food by force. Man has no claws, no fangs, no horns, no great strength of muscle. He must plant his food or hunt it. To plant, he needs a process of thought. To hunt, he needs weapons, and to make weapons – a process of thought. From this simplest necessity to the highest religious abstraction, from the wheel to the skyscraper, everything we are and everything we have comes from a single attribute of man – the function of his reasoning mind. (711)

"The function of man's reasoning mind" is the theme of *Atlas Shrugged*. More exactly, Rand formulated the theme as follows: "The role of the mind in man's existence" (*FTNI* 88,

CUI ix). *Atlas* illustrates dramatically how the mind is both the *productive faculty* (i.e., the source of "everything we have") and the *valuing faculty* (i.e., "the source of everything we are" – of the values that define an individual's character and shape the course of his life). Let us turn to it now.

The Choice to Live and the Objectivity of Values in *Atlas Shrugged* and Later Works

Atlas Shrugged contains Rand's first presentation of her mature philosophy. This includes her moral theory and her view of character, which are the subjects of the next two chapters, respectively. In what remains of the present chapter, I discuss how certain key aspects of these theories are developments of the earlier ideas we have been considering.

From Rand's first notes, we found the idea that, for a human being, living consists in valuing. One way we can formulate this is to say that the spiritual activity that is present in Kira and missing from Ivan Ivanov is analogous to the vital processes that are present in a living plant or animal and absent from a dead one. *Atlas* makes it clear that this is more than just an analogy. "Life," says John Galt, "is a process of self-sustaining and-self-generated action." Every non-human organism is programmed by its nature to act in just those ways that will bring about certain items and conditions without which it could not survive. For the organism to survive means for it to remain in existence and to continue acting in the relevant ways. The items or conditions that the organism brings about by acting in these ways are its values – "'value' is that which one acts to gain and keep" (*Atlas* 1012).

The phenomenon of values only arises in the context of life. A value is something that an organism pursues as part of its process of sustaining itself, and each species has some faculty or mechanism by which it selects what values to pursue by the standard of what serves its life. For example: "A plant must feed itself in order to live; the sunlight, the water, the chemicals it needs are the values its nature has set it to pursue; its life is the standard of value directing its actions" (1013). Similarly, a non-human animal acts by the guidance of its senses and pleasure–pain mechanism, and these are geared to lead it to the values (food, shelter, etc.) that an animal of its species requires.

The mechanisms or faculties by which non-human organisms direct their actions toward values are automatic. Because of this, each non-human organism can only survive in a delimited range of circumstances, but when it is in the relevant circumstances, it will invariably take the actions its survival requires. Human beings are different. The faculty by which we direct our action is *reason*, and it enables us to discover new ways to survive in new circumstances, but there are no circumstances in which reason automatically and invariably guides a person to the actions his survival requires.

> The key to what you so recklessly call "human nature," the open secret you live with, yet dread to name, is the fact that *man is a being of volitional consciousness*. Reason does not work automatically; thinking is not a mechanical process; the connections of logic are not made by instinct. The function of your stomach, lungs or heart is automatic; the function of your mind is not. In any hour and issue of your life, you are free to think or to evade that effort. But you are not free to escape from your nature, from the fact that *reason* is your means of survival – so that for *you*, who are a human being, the question "to be or not to be" is the question "to think or not to think."
>
> A being of volitional consciousness has no automatic course of behavior. (1012)

The *choice to think* is the basic act of valuing. In engaging one's mind, one embraces the world and one brings oneself into existence as a thinking being. Reason is the faculty by which human beings discover our needs, circumstances, and abilities (including the fact that reason is our means of survival and that our lives depend on our own actions) and by which we project values. A person who consistently chooses to think will form specific, life-sustaining values and integrate them into a self-sustaining life that he loves. By making this manner of functioning explicit, Galt's morality enables such a person to value his life with full and self-conscious consistency. Thus Galt describes himself as having "taught men how life is to be loved" (960).

Since the choice to think is the basic act of valuing, a person who chooses to evade the effort of thinking (to whatever extent he evades this effort) will not value anything – not even his own life:

> [E]ven man's desire to live is not automatic: your secret evil today is that *that* is the desire you do not hold. Your fear of death is not a love of life and will not give you the knowledge needed to keep it. (1013, cf. 107–118)

It follows that the inveterate evader has no values; this is not to say, however, that he lacks motives altogether. Galt describes such people as motivated by fear. More generally, Rand thought, they experience the negative sensations (such as thirst and hunger) that are signals of unmet physical needs and the negative emotions (such as chronic fear and self-doubt) that signal unmet psychological needs. Needs of both sorts form part of the context for the process of valuing. But unlike the valuer, who sees satisfying these needs as a part of and means to achieving his own life and happiness, evaders merely "seek escape from pain" (1024). In Rand's view, these forms of motivation are fundamentally different.[23]

Where the evader seeks only to eliminate a negative, the valuer seeks to achieve a positive: "[A]chieving life is not the equivalent of avoiding death. Joy is not 'the absence of pain'" (1024). And whereas the evader acts blindly and short-range, seeking only the cessation of the current unpleasant feeling, the valuer recognizes that "joy is the goal of existence, and joy is not to be stumbled upon" (931), but requires a sustained, rational course of action. In evading the need for thought, a person is effectively regarding reality and the demands it places on him as an imposition to be avoided, and this is the attitude an evader takes toward his life. Rand held that the psychological effect of sustained and pervasive evasion is a holistic hatred of reality and a resentment of successful, happy people. The evader hates reality for not allowing him to exist unperturbed without effort, and he resents successful, happy people because they stand as a reproach to him. Rand illustrates the full development of this psychology through the character of James Taggart, who in a pivotal scene is forced to confront a long-evaded truth about himself:

> He was suddenly seeing the motive that had directed all the actions of his life ... [I]t was the lust to destroy whatever was living, for the sake of whatever was not. It was the urge to defy reality by the destruction of every living value, for the sake of proving to himself that he could exist in defiance of reality and would never have to be bound by any solid, immutable facts. (1145)

This is Rand's mature conception of evil. Her villains are not just non-living, but "anti-life" (864–908). There are anticipations of this view in her earlier work. She described the villain she envisioned for *The Little Street* as, "a small soul choked with a poisonous ambition to dominate and crush everybody and everything"; he is "the kind that says: 'I know that I am inferior and therefore I don't want to let anything superior exist'" (*Journals* 31). This description applies also to Pavel Syerov (in *We The Living*) and Ellsworth Toohey (in *The Fountainhead*). However it is not until *Atlas* that we find Rand's full theory of this sort of motivation.[24]

As Galt's morality articulates the process of valuing (and enables a person to make it a self-conscious policy), Rand thought that mysticism and altruism articulate the ideas implicit in an anti-valuing mentality. At root, she held, these doctrines are rationalizations for evil; and, when they are put into practice, rational people who love their lives are sacrificed to enable the thoughtless, joyless evil of the worst evaders. *Atlas Shrugged* is set in a society (like that of *The Little Street* or the USSR of *We the Living*) that is animated by these vicious ideas. The spiritual and material poverty that is their inevitable consequence is intensified by Galt, who calls a strike of "the men of the mind" against the anti-life society (*Atlas* 1010). Rather than allowing themselves to be sacrificed in order to maintain this evil society, Galt and his strikers withdraw, precipitating its collapse, so that they can rebuild a proper society based on a recognition of the role of the mind in man's existence. The novel follows Dagny Taggart and Hank Rearden, who are the last two "scabs" to join Galt's strike. They do so when they come to understand how, by participating in the society, they are enabling the destruction of their own values.

For Dagny, in particular, the key realization is that the villains do not value their own lives. Until she sees this, she believes that, when the circumstances become dire enough, everyone will recognize the consequences of their life-defeating ideas and reverse course:

> I cannot believe that men can refuse to see, that they can remain blind and deaf to us forever, when the truth is ours and their lives depend on accepting it. They still love their lives – and *that* is the uncorrupted remnant of their minds. So long as men desire to live, I cannot lose my battle. (807)

In the novel's final chapters, Dagny realizes that many of the people around her exist in a "permanent state" of "inanimate indifference," with "no purpose and no passion": "This was the state of a non-valuing soul; those who chose it – she wondered – did they want to live?" (1109). In effect, what she is grasping is that many people are non-entities, like Ivan Ivanov (in *We the Living*) or Renée Slottern (in *The Fountainhead*). Seeing this, she begins to feel a strange indifference for such people and to regard them as "not living or human" (1109). But her real breakthrough comes later, when she grasps the motivation of the truly anti-life characters, like her brother James. She observes that he and his cronies are driven to torture and kill Galt, even though they know that their own lives depend on his survival.[25]

> Moved by the panic of their nameless emotions, they had fought against reality all their lives – and now they had reached a moment when at last they felt at home. They did not have to know why they felt it, they who had chosen never to know what they felt – they merely experienced a sense of recognition, since *this* was what they had been seeking, *this* was the kind of reality that had been implied in all of their feelings, their actions, their desires, their choices, their dreams. This was the nature and the method of the rebellion against existence and of the undefined quest for an unnamed Nirvana. They did not want to live; they wanted *him* to die. (1135)

When she sees how the villains' basic motivation is different from her own, Dagny grasps something important about the role of the mind in values as such. As Darryl Wright formulates the point: "one's need for, and thus one's potential receptiveness to, morality depends on a basic choice to live" (Wright 2009, 266). This was a view Rand herself came to in the period between *The Fountainhead* and *Atlas Shrugged*.

65

During part of that time, she worked on an aborted treatise called *The Moral Basis for Individualism* in which she tried to ground morality on the axiom that "Man exists and must survive as man" (*Papers* 032_12A_002_21/*Journals* 255). By contrast, in *Atlas*, Galt says that his morality is "contained in a single axiom: existence exists – and in a single choice: to live" (*Atlas* 1018). There are two crucial differences between these formulations. First, the axiom in *Atlas* has grown much wider than the axiom in *The Moral Basis*; it pertains not just to human beings and their survival, but to all of existence. Jason Rheins discusses the existence axiom in Chapter 11, below (see also my discussion at 300); for our present purposes, it is enough to say that the axiom is meant to stand for the sum of factual knowledge – including knowledge of the material and spiritual requirements of human survival. The second difference between *The Moral Basis*'s axiom and Galt's is that the *Moral Basis* treats it as a fundamental *fact* that one's survival as a human being is desirable, but Galt takes valuing one's life to be a *choice*. It is only insofar as a person chooses to live that any facts (or the sum of all facts) can make anything good for him, or any course of action right.

The choice to live is the choice to think, which we earlier identified as the basic act of valuing, for it is by choosing to think that one embraces reality and brings oneself fully to life as a human being in the moment, and it is by thinking that one learns how to sustain a human life and that one conceives of and pursues the specific values that constitute one's own life.

This idea that morality rests on such a choice has been much discussed in the secondary literature on Rand.[26] Some have worried that it makes morality subjective or arbitrary, and that it leaves the most evil people outside of the scope of moral evaluation. Rand did not see it in this way.

Though James Taggart's failure to choose to live does place him beyond the reach of moral guidance, it does not change the fact that his chosen actions are contrary to morality (that is, to the code of values a person needs to follow in order to live); nor does it change the fact that he has, by his own choice, become an enemy of life. Therefore, those who do value their lives must judge him as evil and treat him accordingly. (On this point, see Allan Gotthelf's discussion of the virtue of justice, in the next chapter, 95–96.) On Rand's view, life-haters like Taggart can and must be morally condemned, but their evil cannot be understood as a violation of an *obligation* to live, for Rand held that there are no such categorical obligations or duties. Rather she shared the view that Philippa Foot nicely expressed in the title of a (1972) paper: "Morality as a System of Hypothetical Imperatives."[27]

Here is how Rand (writing in 1970) formulates the point:

> The proper approach to ethics, the start from a metaphysically clean slate, untainted by any touch of Kantianism, can best be illustrated by the following story. In answer to a man who was telling her that she's *got to* do something or other, a wise old Negro woman said: "Mister, there's nothing I've *got to* do except die."
>
> Life or death is man's only fundamental alternative. To live is his basic act of choice. If he chooses to live, a rational ethics will tell him what principles of action are required to implement his choice. If he does not choose to live, nature will take its course.
>
> Reality confronts man with a great many "musts," but all of them are conditional; the formula of realistic necessity is: "You must, if –" and the "if" stands for man's choice: " – if you want to achieve a certain goal." You must eat, if you want to survive. You must work, if you want to eat. You must think, if you want to work. You must look at reality, if you want to think – if you want to know what to do – if you want to know what goals to choose – if you want to know how to achieve them. ("Causality versus Duty" *PWNI* 133, cf. *Atlas* 1015)

For Rand, as for Foot, morality's grip on a person depends on his holding a value that not all people hold. In particular, for Rand, it depends on his valuing his life. This value is not one among a set of alternative values that someone might hold, for (as we have seen) Rand held that the phenomenon of valuing only arises in the context of an organism's pursuit of its life as its ultimate value.[28] At whatever times and to whatever extent a person is not engaged in this pursuit, he can have no values at all, and can act only in the joyless, destructive manner of James Taggart.

The connection between rationality and the choice to live puts us in a position to see why Rand does not think that the role of this choice in valuing makes values (or morality) subjective. It also brings us to the final step in the progression that I have been tracing in this chapter: the relation between Rand's early idea that valuing is a rational activity and her conception of *objectivity*.

I discuss objectivity at length in Chapter 12, below. (See especially 274 and 290–292). Here I provide only a brief sketch. Rand thinks of objectivity (in the relevant sense) not as the ontological status of existing independently of the mind, but as an attribute of certain, chosen mental processes and states – the attribute of methodically corresponding to mind-independent facts. This is the sense in which we use the word "objective," when we speak of "objective grading" or "objective reporting." In such uses, "objectivity" names a quality of one's thinking. Peikoff (elaborating on Rand's view) describes this quality as follows: "To be 'objective' in one's conceptual activities is volitionally to adhere to reality by following certain rules of method, a method based on facts *and* appropriate to man's form of cognition" (*OPAR* 117). Valuing, for Rand, is a conceptual activity that can and must be performed by just such a fact-based method. It is in this sense that Rand thinks that values are objective. She describes herself as holding an "objective theory of the good":

> The *objective* theory holds that the good is neither an attribute of "things in themselves" nor of man's emotional states, but an *evaluation* of the facts of reality by man's consciousness according to a rational standard of value. (Rational, in this context, means: derived from the facts of reality and validated by a process of reason.) The objective theory holds *that the good is an aspect of reality in relation to* man – and that it must be discovered, not invented, by man. Fundamental to an objective theory of values is the question: Of value to whom and for what? An objective theory does not permit context-dropping or "concept-stealing"; it does not permit the separation of "value" from "purpose," of the good from beneficiaries, and of man's actions from reason. ("What is Capitalism?" *CUI* 14)[29]

She distinguishes this theory from two other "schools of thought on the nature of the good": "the intrinsic theory" and "the subjective theory."

> The *intrinsic theory* holds that the good is inherent in certain things or actions as such, regardless of their context and consequences, regardless of any benefit or injury they may cause to the actors and subjects involved. It is a theory that divorces the concept of "good" from beneficiaries, and the concept of "value" from valuer and purpose – claiming that the good is good in, by, and of itself.
>
> The subjectivist theory holds that the good bears no relation to the facts of reality, that it is the product of a man's consciousness, created by his feelings, desires, "intuitions," or whims, and that it is merely an "arbitrary postulate" or an "emotional commitment."
>
> The intrinsic theory holds that the good resides in some sort of reality, independent of man's consciousness; the subjectivist theory holds that the good resides in man's consciousness, independent of reality. (*CUI* 13–14)

We can see here the full development of a view the germ of which was present already in Rand's early notes. Rather than thinking of objects or states of affairs as being intrinsically valuable, independent of anyone's attitude toward them, the young Rand viewed values as the objects of a mental or spiritual activity that she called *valuing*. The activity involves intense desire and she sometimes simply describes it as "wanting," but there are indications even in her early notes that this is not an arbitrary or subjective commitment or response that one can have in any which way to any random objects. Valuing is a process that must be performed consistently and holistically, and that enables one to give oneself entirely to one's values. This process is incompatible with the attempt to live for other people and it is undermined by attempts to perform it on supernatural or otherwise unattainable objects. From the beginning, Rand understood it as a *rational* activity that a person must know how to perform. As she matured, she thought more deeply and more articulately about the nature of this process and the knowledge required to perform it fully and consistently. The result, in *Atlas Shrugged* and her subsequent essays, is a philosophical system built around a distinctive conception of objectivity.

Acknowledgment

Some of the ideas in this chapter were first presented as a talk, and then as a lecture course in 2008 (Salmieri 2008b). Thank you to those audiences and to Gena Gorlin, Maryah Haidery, and Karen Salmieri for feedback on the chapter itself.

Notes

1 For reasons that I will come to presently, this character, Danny Renahan, has been much discussed. He is often described as the "hero" of *The Little Street* and parallels are drawn between him and the heroes of Rand's completed novels. David Harriman, in his introduction to the *Little Street* notes (*Journals* 26), does use the term "hero" to refer to Renahan, but it is misleading. Rand never herself refers to him as a hero; and, though she intends him as an admirable character, he is not the sort of character that she would call a hero. She reserves that term for characters that realize the human ideal and are victorious spiritually, if not existentially. Renahan, by contrast, is someone with great potential, who is destroyed by a hostile society. In this respect, he is like Leo Kovalevsky in *We the Living*, but a closer parallel is Steven Mallory, in *The Fountainhead*, prior to his meeting with Roark.

   Rand's notes concerning Renahan have been the subject of many critical (and, often, oddly gloating) articles (e.g., Ames 2010, Sapp 2011, and Prescott 2013), because she based aspects of his character and story on that of William Edward Hickman, who was then standing trial for murdering and dismembering a 12-year old girl. Here is how Rand describes the relationship between Renahan and Hickman, whom she describes as "a purposeless monster": "The model for the boy is Hickman. Very far from him, of course. The outside of Hickman, but not the inside. Much deeper and much more. A Hickman with a purpose. And without the degeneracy. It is more exact to say that the model is not Hickman, but what Hickman suggested to me." (*Journals* 27) She recognized that even the positive traits she saw in the real Hickman were likely her own invention: "I am afraid that I idealize Hickman and that he might not be this at all. In fact, he probably isn't" (*Journals* 39). However, it remains troubling to think that anyone (much less an author and moralist who has inspired millions) would see anything admirable in such a monster. This is especially so, since some of the traits of "the outside Hickman" Rand mentions read like symptoms of sociopathy. (The fad of ascribing this condition to people with whose politics one disagrees partially explains the profusion of enthusiastic articles and web-posts about the Rand–Hickman connection.)

It has been pointed out in Rand's defense that she was only 23 years old when she wrote these notes, that she was living through a difficult period, and that her fascination with Hickman is of a piece with the Nietzschean strand in her early thought (Burns 2009, 24–25; Heller 2009, 70–71.) (On Rand's evolving view of Nietzsche, see Lester Hunt's Chapter 14, below.) These points are well taken, but more relevant, I think, is that Rand was an aspiring *novelist* who was on the lookout for maximally dramatic characters and conflicts. Flamboyant criminals often capture the public's attention and it is easy (and common) to imagine in them virtues that they do not really possess. If one's aim is to understand the facts of the case, or to identify what the episode really reveals about human nature, then this tendency to romanticize must be fought, but Rand's primary aim in these notes (and at this stage of her life) was to develop ideas for literary works with grand conflicts and philosophical themes. Thus, instead of trying to temper her tendency to idealize, she deliberately indulged it. After writing that Hickman was probably not at all as she imagined, she continues: "But it does not make any difference. If he isn't, he *could* be, and that's enough. The reaction of society would be the same, if not worse, toward the Hickman I have in mind. This case showed me how society can wreck an exceptional being, and then murder him for being the wreck that it itself has created. This will be the story of the boy in my book." (*Journals* 39) Given her aims, the actual Hickman and his character and motives didn't much matter to her; what mattered is that reflecting on his case prompted her to imagine a certain sort of person who *could* exist and to project the conflict he *would* face with the rest of society. (On the esthetic significance of whether a character could exist and would be treated in the relevant ways, see Tore Boeckmann's discussion, below 433–434 and 444.)

2 The notes for *The Little Street*, written in what seems to have been a particularly bleak period for Rand, attribute this non-living mentality to "most people." The distance between what she saw as the human potential and what she observed of the people around her (and the causes of this distance), remained an issue in Rand's thinking throughout her life, but the mature Rand did not hold that *most* people entirely lack the capacity for reverence or taking things seriously – certainly she did not hold that most *young* people lack it or that anyone lacks it *innately*. However, she thought that the dominant ideas and cultural and institutions were poisonous to this capacity, with the result that most people's abilities to value are underdeveloped or stunted in various ways. We can already see the idea that certain beliefs, institutions, and cultures are poisonous to valuing throughout the notes for *The Little Street*. For Rand's development on these issues, see Ghate 2007 and Wright 2005, 198–202; for her view of character development, see Chapter 5, below; and for her view of twentieth-century culture, see Chapter 15.

3 The interpolation "the capacity for" is in *Journals*. The original manuscripts for these notes are not in the Ayn Rand Archives and are missing.

4 Rand would later define logic as "the art of non-contradictory identification" (*Atlas* 1016). See, below, 251 and 300.

5 Earlier Romantic writers also distinguish "living" from "existing." Extolling the ideals provided by art, Victor Hugo (who was Rand's favorite novelist) writes: "It is by the real that we exist; it is by the real that we live" (Hugo 1864 256). Living, he says, distinguishes human beings from animals, and he associates it with understanding, ambition, judgment, self-worth, and conscience. Oscar Wilde (on whom see *AOF* 167, *Speaking* 136, 134–35) writes: "To live is the rarest thing in the world. Most people exist, that is all" (Wilde 1909 19). He associates living with "the full expression of a personality"—something that has been realized only in art, but that he hopes socialism will make possible in action. (See also, Burnett 1907, 60.) I do not know whether Rand was aware of these passages.

6 On Kira's reverence, see Mayhew 2012c, 308–312.

7 See: *Atlas* 1030, 1032–1034, 1052–1054; 1056–1060; "Faith and Force: The Destroyers of the Modern World" *PWNI* 92.

8 For discussion, see Salmieri 2009a, 236–242, 2009b 403–420.

9 The comparison between the lights and the stars is poignant in the novel, because it comes at a point when Dagny has come to think that it is impossible to keep industrial civilization from being destroyed – and, more generally, has come to question her conviction that values are achievable. For discussion, see my 2009b, 420–436.

10 For discussion, see Salmieri 2009a, 244–246.

11 It is largely the absence of this idea that accounts for the bleakness and bitterness of the *Little Street* notes as compared with all of Rand's other fiction. Her earlier stories and notes have a benevolent tone more in keeping with her mature fiction, but they do not deal with the evils that she addressed both in the *Little Street* notes and in her mature fiction.

12 Rand formulated the novel's theme as follows: "individualism *versus* collectivism, not in politics, but in man's soul; the psychological motivations and the basic premises that produce the character of an individualist or a collectivist" (*FTNI* 73).

13 For discussion of Wynand's error, see Ghate 2007, 260–267. See also, Lester Hunt's discussion, below, 346.

14 The role played in Roark's architecture by a central idea is analogous to the role that Rand thinks is played by plot in Romantic literature. See Tore Boeckmann's discussion of Romanticism and values in Chapter 17, below.

15 Later in life Rand made this point explicitly in connection with her own inability to automatize the writing of *The Ayn Rand Letter*: "I had hoped that I could learn to write the *Letter* fast enough to be able to combine it with working on a book. I have tried it. It took me four years to convince myself that it cannot be done or, at least, that I cannot do it. I thought that it was merely a matter of automatizing the process of writing an article." "For me, every article has to involve some new identification, big or small, not only new to my readers, but new to me. I cannot bear merely to repeat myself ... This is why I was unable to automatize the process of writing an article. What I was asking of myself was a contradiction: one automatizes the known, one cannot automatize the new" ("A Last Survey" *ARL* 6(2) 382). On the respective roles of automatization and volitional work in different aspects of thinking, see, in this volume 115, 123, 125, 288, and 305 n. 46.

16 In *Atlas* 215–216 Rearden, in such a flash of inspiration, conceives of the central idea for a bridge that would solve an engineering problem that he had grappled with years earlier.

17 On Rand's view of love and friendship, see, in this volume 88–89 and 135–136.

18 In the novel, Roark says "egotist," rather than "egoist." Rand later referred to this as "a minor error," which she did not correct in subsequent printings because she wanted to let the text of the novel stand as written (vii). She did correct it, however, in the version of Roark's speech reproduced in *For the New Intellectual* (81).

19 The setting in which Roark says that work is the meaning of life is significant, because it suggests that his point is meant to apply in some way to all forms of life: "They sat down on a fallen tree trunk, they saw the structure in the distance through the stems of the brushwood. The stems were dry and naked, but there was a quality of spring in the cheerful insolence of their upward thrust, the stirring of a self-assertive purpose" (576). Like Roark, the brushwood stems are reshaping the material provided by nature in the form of their values, specifically into the form of their mature bodies. The difference, of course, is that the stems are not literally purposeful. The mature form toward which they are developing is not a conscious value, but a genetically programmed end.

20 For discussion, see, in this volume 86, 88, 117, 321, 408, and 413. See also Wright 2005.

21 On this issue, see Allan Gotthelf's discussion, below 77 and 81, of the relation between the means to and constituents of life.

22 On this point, see Ghate's (2007, 253–297) discussion of Wynand and Dominique.

23 On these two forms of motivation, which Rand and her associates sometimes called "motivation by fear" and "by love," see *OPAR* 338–339 and Branden "Pseudo-Self-Esteem" *TON* 3(5–6). Rand recognized that there are those who would deny this distinction and claim that "there's only pain and the absence of pain, only pain and the zero, when one feels nothing" (*Atlas* 931, cf. 1024). She saw this position as an expression of a non-valuing mentality and rejected it contemptuously as "zero worship" or "nirvana worship." As the second of these names indicates, this position is associated with Hinduism and Buddhism. It also had some notable advocates in the history of Western Philosophy – including (arguably) Epicurus (see his *Letter to Menoeceus*) and (certainly) Schopenhauer (see his *Studies in Pessimism*). (Peikoff discusses this view in these two philosophers, respectively, in *HOP1* 6(00:30:32–00:31:48) and *HOP2* 5(00:21:20–00:29:00) [cf. *Parallels* 51].) Variants of this same

view have been advocated under various names by thinkers in several fields dealing with human motivation. In *Marginalia* 108–109, Rand remarks on its role in von Mises's theory of "Praxeology."

24 Onkar Ghate briefly discusses psychology of evil in Chapter 5, below (110 and 125–126). He has a
fuller discussion in Ghate 2012.

25 In Salmieri 2009b (446–448), I discuss in greater detail the steps by which Dagny comes to this realization about the villains.

26 See Peikoff *OPAR* 241–249; Gotthelf 1990; Smith 2000, 97–111; Rasmussen 2002, 2006, 2007a,
2007b; Smith 2008; Wright 2011a (esp. 29–32); Moen 2012; and Kelley 2015.

27 Foot, of course, is drawing heavily on Anscombe 1958, which was published around the same time
as *Atlas*. There are several significant parallels between Rand and Anscombe that are worth exploring
in further depth. For some brief leads on this issue, See 99, n. 14.

28 Rand's position that one commits to certain moral norms by the very act that commits one to holding values at all invites comparison to neo-Kantian "constitutivist" theories where a commitment to
norms is partially constitutive of agency. See, e.g., Korsgaard 2008 and Velleman 2009. For another
take on (what amount to) the same issues with which Rand's view might be fruitfully compared, see
Bratman 2007. I regret that I do not have the space or time to pursue any of these comparisons here.

29 On "concept stealing" and "package dealing," see below 297–299.

References

Ames, Mark. 2013. "Ayn Rand, Hugely Popular Author and Inspiration to Right-Wing Leaders, Was a
Big Admirer of Serial Killer." *Alternet*. Available at http://www.alternet.org/story/145819/ayn_rand,_
hugely_popular_author_and_inspiration_to_right-wing_leaders,_was_a_big_admirer_of_serial_
killer (accessed June 29, 2015).

Anscombe, G.E.M. 1958. "Modern Moral Philosophy." *Philosophy*, 33 1–19.

Bratman, Michael E. 2007. *Structures of Agency*. New York, NY: Oxford University Press.

Burnett, Francis Hodgeson. 1907. *The Shuttle*. New York, NY: Grosset & Dunlap.

Burns, Jennifer. 2009. *Goddess of the Market: Ayn Rand and the American Right*. Oxford: Oxford University
Press.

Foot, Philippa. 1972. "Morality as a System of Hypothetical Imperatives." *The Philosophical Review*, 81(3).

Ghate, Onkar. 2007. "The Basic Motivation of the Creators and the Masses in *The Fountainhead*." In *Essays
on Ayn Rand's* The Fountainhead, edited by Robert Mayhew. Lanham, MD: Lexington Books.

Ghate, Onkar. 2012. "The Death Premise in *We the Living* and *Atlas Shrugged*." In Mayhew 2012a.

Gotthelf, Allan. 1990. "The Choice to Value." Paper presented at the 1990 meeting of the Ayn Rand Society. First published in Gotthelf and Lennox 2011.

Gotthelf, Allan, ed., and James G. Lennox, assoc. ed. 2011. *Metaethics, Egoism and Virtue: Studies in Ayn
Rand's Normative Theory*. Ayn Rand Society Philosophical Studies, vol. 1. Pittsburgh, PA: University of
Pittsburgh Press.

Heller, Anne C. 2009. *Ayn Rand and the World She Made*. New York, NY: Doubleday.

Hugo, Victor. 1864. *William Shakespear*. United Kingdom: Hurst and Blackett.

Kelley, David. 2015. "Happiness or Life, or Both: Reply to Ole Martin Moen." *Reason Papers* 37(1).

Korsgaard, Christine M. 2008. *The Constitution of Agency: Essays on Practical Reason and Moral Psychology*.
New York, NY: Oxford University Press.

Mayhew, Robert, ed. 2005a. *Essays on Ayn Rand's* Anthem. Lanham, MD: Lexington Books.

Mayhew, Robert, ed. 2009. *Essays on Ayn Rand's* Atlas Shrugged. Lanham, MD: Lexington Books.

Mayhew, Robert, ed. 2012a. *Essays on Ayn Rand's* We the Living, 2nd edition. Lanham, MD: Lexington Books.

Mayhew, Robert, 2012c. "Kira Argounava Laughed: Humor and Joy in *We the Living*." In Mayhew 2012a.

Moen, Ole Martin. 2012. "Is Life the Ultimate Value? A Reassessment of Ayn Rand's Ethics." *Reason Papers*
34(2).

Paul, Ellen Frankel, Fred Miller Jr., Jeffrey Paul, eds. 2008. *Objectivism, Subjectivism, and Relativism in Ethics.* Cambridge: Cambridge University Press.

Prescott, Michael. 2013. "Romancing the Stone-Cold Killer: Ayn Rand and William Hickman." Online article, available at: http://michaelprescott.freeservers.com/romancing-the-stone-cold.html (accessed June 29, 2015).

Rasmussen, Douglas B. 2002. "Rand on Obligation and Value." *Journal of Ayn Rand Studies,* 4(1).

Rasmussen, Douglas B. 2006. "Regarding Choice and the Foundation of Morality: Reflections on Rand's Ethics." *Journal of Ayn Rand Studies,* 7(2).

Rasmussen, Douglas B. 2007a. "The Aristotelian Significance of the Section Titles of *Atlas Shrugged*: A Brief Consideration of Rand's View of Logic and Reality." In Atlas Shrugged: *A Philosophical and Literary Companion,* edited by Edward M. Younkins. Aldershot, UK: Ashgate.

Rasmussen, Douglas B. 2007b. "Rand's Metaethics: Rejoinder to Hartford." *Journal of Ayn Rand Studies,* 8(2).

Salmieri, Gregory. 2008b. *Ayn Rand's Conception of Valuing.* Lecture series, available at: https://estore.aynrand.org/p/442 (accessed June 29, 2015).

Salmieri, Gregory. 2009a. "*Atlas Shrugged* on the Role of the Mind in Man's Existence." In Mayhew 2009.

Salmieri, Gregory. 2009b. "Discovering Atlantis: *Atlas Shrugged's* Demonstration of a New Moral Philosophy." In Mayhew 2009.

Sapp, Eric. 2011. "Why Democrats Must Read Ayn Rand" *The Huffington Post.* Available at: http://www.huffingtonpost.com/eric-sapp/ayn-rand-democrats_b_855797.html (accessed June 29, 2015).

Smith, Tara. 2000. *Viable Values: A Study of Life as The Root and Reward of Morality.* Lanham, MD: Rowman & Littlefield.

Smith, Tara. 2008. "The Importance of the Subject in Objective Morality: Distinguishing Objective from Intrinsic Value." In *Objectivism, Subjectivism, and Relativism in Ethics,* edited by Ellen Frankel Paul, Fred Miller Jr., and Jeffrey Paul. Cambridge: Cambridge University Press.

Velleman, David. 2009. *How We Get Along.* Cambridge: Cambridge University Press.

Wilde, Oscar. 1909. *The Soul of Man Under Socialism.* London: Arthur L. Humphreys.

Wright, Darryl. 2005. "Needs of the *Psyche* in Ayn Rand's Early Ethical Thought." In *Essays on Ayn Rand's Anthem,* edited by Robert Mayhew. Lanham, MD: Lexington Books.

Wright, Darryl. 2009. "Ayn Rand's Ethics: From *The Fountainhead* to *Atlas Shrugged*." In Mayhew 2009.

Wright, Darryl. 2011a. "Reasoning about Ends: Life as a Value in Ayn Rand's Ethics." In Gotthelf and Lennox 2011.

4

The Morality of Life

ALLAN GOTTHELF
(completed by Gregory Salmieri)[1]

> To live, man must hold three things as the supreme and ruling values of his life: Reason – Purpose –
> Self-esteem. *Reason*, as his only tool of knowledge – *Purpose*, as his choice of the happiness which
> that tool must proceed to achieve – *Self-esteem*, as his inviolate certainty that his mind is competent
> to think and his person is worthy of happiness, which means: is worthy of living. These three values
> imply and require all of man's virtues, and all his virtues pertain to the relation of existence and
> consciousness: rationality, independence, integrity, honesty, justice, productiveness, pride.
>
> *Atlas* 1018

In 1959, some two years after the publication of *Atlas Shrugged*, an interviewer asked Ayn Rand
to "capsulize" her philosophy. She began by saying that it "is based on the idea that reality is an
objective absolute, that reason is man's means of perceiving it and that man needs a rational
morality. I am primarily the creator of a new code of morality" (*Speaking* 169). The centrality of
this new code of morality to the novel is indicated by Rand's later statement that "the demonstration of a new moral philosophy" is "corollary" to *Atlas*'s theme (*FTNI* 97). In a radio speech
delivered in part III of the novel, John Galt explains to a world on the brink of destruction why
a new morality is needed:

> Your moral code has reached its climax, the blind alley at the end of its course. And if you wish to
> go on living, what you now need is not to *return* to morality – you who have never known any – but
> to *discover* it. (*Atlas* 1011)

The passage from later in that broadcast that serves as this chapter's epigraph eloquently
summarizes the *content* (and some of the *foundation*) of this new morality, which Galt twice calls
"the Morality of Life" (*Atlas* 1051, 1069; cf. 1014). This epigraph will serve as a guide to much
of what we explore in this chapter, but I would like us to begin by considering the way in which
Rand offers us a *new concept of morality* – a new view of what morality is.[2] This will lead us to
Rand's view of why human beings need values. We will then explore Rand's view that "man's
life" is "the standard of value" and look at each value that Galt (in our epigraph) describes
as "supreme and ruling" and, then, at the range of other values that Rand thinks man's life

---

requires. In discussing the supreme and ruling values we will consider the three virtues that correspond to them: rationality, productiveness, and pride. Once we have considered the other values life requires, we will consider Rand's view of virtue in general and then look at the four remaining virtues she identifies. We will close by examining Rand's view of heroism, which is closely connected with her ethics.

Throughout, we will make frequent reference to Galt's broadcast, which includes Rand's first systematic exposition of her mature moral philosophy, and to *Atlas Shrugged* more generally. We will also rely heavily on "The Objectivist Ethics," a 1961 talk which is the first chapter of *The Virtue of Selfishness*. Other important sources for her ethical theory include the other essays in that anthology (especially "The Ethics of Emergencies" and "The 'Conflicts' of Men's Interests") and "Causality Versus Duty" (*PWNI*).

A New Concept of Morality

Immediately after his statement that men need to discover morality, Galt elaborates:

> You have heard no concepts of morality but the mystical or the social. You have been taught that morality is a code of behavior imposed on you by whim, the whim of a supernatural power or the whim of society, to serve God's purpose or your neighbor's welfare, to please an authority beyond the grave or else next door – but not to serve *your* life or pleasure. Your pleasure, you have been taught, is to be found in immorality, your interests would best be served by evil, and any moral code must be designed not *for* you, but *against* you, not to further your life, but to drain it. (*Atlas* 1011)

Here Rand's new concept of morality is contrasted with familiar concepts according to which morality is an imposition on an individual that demands that he forgo his own interests as a sacrifice, whether to other people or to God.[3] Amidst the many advocates of this "morality of sacrifice," Galt tells us, "no one came to say that your life belongs to you and that the good is to live it" (*Atlas* 1012). Part of what is new in Rand's approach to morality, then, is that she sees it as essentially *for the benefit of* the agent – as *furthering his own life*. Indeed, Rand identifies the "new moral philosophy" *Atlas* demonstrates as "the morality of rational-self-interest" and her collection of essays on ethics is titled *The Virtue of Selfishness: A New Concept of Egoism*.

This may seem puzzling in two respects. First, since Rand is not the first thinker to have endorsed some form of ethical egoism, someone might wonder what she is claiming to be *new* about her concept. Second, most philosophers (including most egoists) since Kant have denied that any form of egoism is a moral philosophy; instead they view it as endorsing either a non-moral "prudence" or an immoral *subjectivism* according to which the good is determined by one's desires. We will want to get clearer on why Rand thinks what she is offering is a concept *of morality*.

Morality, on the (now standard) Kantian view, is understood as something that *constrains* an individual's pursuit of his interests. These interests are typically identified with what Rand would call *whims*. She defines a whim as "a desire experienced by a person who does not know and does not care to discover its cause" ("The Objectivist Ethics" *VOS* 14). But, Rand held, acting on such unexamined motives is self-destructive, so one's actual interests (as opposed to what happens to interest one at the moment) are *objective* – that is, based on fact.[4] Identifying and achieving what is good for one requires discovering and adhering to the rich and complex code of values, virtues, and principles that Galt outlines in our epigraph. Rand's concept of egoism, then, is distinctive in that she conceives of self-interest as objective and as requiring such a code.[5]

"A code of values accepted by choice," Galt tells us, "is a code of morality" (*Atlas* 1013). Elsewhere, Rand defines morality as "a code of values to guide ... the choices and actions that determine the purpose and the course of [man's] life" (*VOS* 13).[6] By this definition both Rand's egoism and conventional moral theories qualify as moralities, and it is easy to see points of contact between "morality" so defined and the way in which that term is used by other philosophers: because an agent's morality sets the purpose and course of his life, it serves as a *demanding standard* to which he must live up *by choice* in *all* of his actions, even when doing so is difficult and he may be tempted to do otherwise. Rand stresses the demanding character of morality in several passages in *Atlas* that challenge conventional thinking about what and who is truly moral.

For example, a disillusioned bum who bemoans mankind's vulgar devotion to industry and wealth tells Dagny Taggart that morality is: "judgment to distinguish right and wrong, vision to see the truth, courage to act upon it, dedication to that which is good, integrity to stand by the good at any price. But where," he asks, "does one find it?" (*Atlas* 177) These qualities are all conspicuously illustrated by Dagny and Hank Rearden in their battle to build a railroad line out of Rearden's innovative new alloy. And in the scene immediately following Dagny's encounter with the bum, Rearden courageously refuses to be intimidated or bribed into retracting the metal. He gives as his reasons that the metal is *his*, that it is *good*, and that the charges against it are *false* (*Atlas* 178–182). Later in the novel, Francisco d'Anconia also speaks of "the courage of acting on your own judgment" when he explains why Rearden's manner of running his mills shows him to be "one of last moral men left to the world" (*Atlas* 454, 451).

We can capture the commonality between Rand's view of the moral and the conventional view by saying that moral action is to be contrasted with "whim-worship" – the practice of acting on one's whims.[7] With this in mind, recall Galt's claim that his audience has "been taught that morality is a code of behavior imposed on you by whim, the whim of a supernatural power or the whim of society." The only alternative to whim-worship offered by the conventional (mystical and social) concepts of morality is bowing to the dictates of some authority. But Rand argues that these dictates are themselves whims, because there is no intelligible explanation of why the (divine or social) authority demands what it does or why anyone is obliged to obey it. This point applies straightforwardly to divine command ethics and to secular forms of it that simply substitute society for God, but it applies also to any morality that demands that one subordinate one's interests to any concept of "value" (or "good") that is "unrelated to, underived from and unsupported by any facts of reality."[8] Rand thought that this is true of all previous moral theories: rather than offering an *objective* morality that would be a genuine alternative to whim-worship, the history of moral philosophy has been a dispute about whose whims should take precedence.

> Faith – instinct – intuition – revelation – feeling – taste – urge – wish – *whim*. Today, as in the past, most philosophers agree that the ultimate standard of ethics is *whim* (they call it "arbitrary postulate" or "subjective choice" or "emotional commitment") – and the battle is only over the question of *whose* whim: one's own or society's or the dictator's or God's. Whatever else they may disagree about, today's moralists agree that ethics is a *subjective* issue and that the three things barred from its field are: reason – mind – reality. (*VOS* 15)[9]

When Galt tells his audience that they need to *discover* morality, he means not only that they need to learn the content of the correct moral code, but also that they need discover *why human beings need to act one way rather than another*. What they need to learn is the answer to the question: "*Why* does man need a code of values?" In "The Objectivist Ethics," Rand writes that this question "has to be answered, as a precondition of any attempt to define, to judge or to accept any specific system of ethics." "Let me stress this. The first question is not: What particular code of values should man accept? The first question is: Does man need values at all – and why?" (*VOS* 14).

Why Man Needs a Code of Values

Rand's view that man's life is the standard of value follows from her distinctive answer to the question of whether and why man needs values at all. Her answer begins by considering the context that is presupposed by the concept "value."

> "Value" is that which one acts to gain and/or keep. The concept "value" is not a primary; it presupposes an answer to the question: of value to *whom* and for *what*? It presupposes an entity capable of acting to achieve a goal in the face of an alternative. Where no alternative exists, no goals and no values are possible. (*VOS* 16)

A *value*, as opposed to a mere wish, is something that one is prepared (under appropriate conditions) to *act* for. Goal-directed action presupposes an entity that is capable of that action and that faces an alternative. The entity needn't be conscious of the alternative, but it must *face* it, in the sense that there will be different outcomes for the entity depending on whether or not it secures the value. The outcome that depends on securing the value is the "for *what*" that Rand mentions in the passage quoted above, and the entity is the "to *whom*."

One value may make a difference to the achievement of some further value, so that the alternative the entity faces in pursuing the first value is whether it will achieve the second, but then achieving this second value also must make some difference to the entity. It may be valuable as a means to achieve yet another value, but this sequence cannot continue without end; it must terminate in an *ultimate value* – a "final goal or end to which all lesser goals are the means" and which "sets the standard by which all lesser goals are *evaluated*" (*VOS* 17). This ultimate value must correspond to a *fundamental alternative*.

> There is only one fundamental alternative in the universe: existence or non-existence – and it pertains to a single class of entities: to living organisms. The existence of inanimate matter is unconditional, the existence of life is not: it depends on a specific course of action. Matter is indestructible, it changes its forms, but it cannot cease to exist. It is only a living organism that faces a constant alternative: the issue of life or death. Life is a process of self-sustaining and self-generated action. If an organism fails in that action, it dies; its chemical elements remain, but its life goes out of existence. It is only the concept of "Life" that makes the concept of "Value" possible. It is only to a living entity that things can be good or evil. (*Atlas* 1012–1013, quoted at *VOS* 16)

One can, of course, speak of inanimate objects going out of existence – for example, of a rock crumbling into sand. When asked about such changes, Rand treated them as examples of matter merely changing form. She likened it to a corpse decomposing into its elements, and she regarded this transformation as essentially different from what happens when a human being dies, leaving a corpse behind.[10] In the latter case, "that attribute of a human being which is life does go out of existence totally" (*Workshops* 289).[11] At least part of the difference, as Rand saw it, is that, unlike a rock or a corpse, "an organism is integrated as a whole"; and, as a whole, the organism has distinctive capacities and engages in the distinctive actions, all of which go wholly out of existence when it dies.[12]

Not only *can* an organism go out of existence (in the absolute sense that Rand thinks is inapplicable to inanimate objects), it *will* go quickly out of existence, unless it takes a certain definite course of action. There is nothing that a stone can or must do in order to remain a stone; if no external force intervenes, it will remain unaltered forever. But a living thing's survival is conditional: it will not continue to exist unless it continually acts in the ways necessary to secure certain values. It is this *conditional character of life*, Rand argues, that gives rise to an organism's *need* to act one way rather than another, and thus to such concepts as "need," "should," "ought," and "good" and "evil." To reinforce the point that these concepts apply only to living things because only they face the alternative of life or death, Rand asks readers "to imagine an immortal, indestructible robot, an entity which moves and acts, but which cannot be affected by anything, which cannot be changed in any respect, which cannot be damaged, injured, or destroyed." Because the robot "would have nothing to gain or to lose," she argues, "it could not regard anything as *for* or *against* it" (*VOS* 16).[13]

"An organism's life," writes Rand, "is its *standard of value*: that which furthers its life is the *good*, that which threatens it is the *evil*" (*VOS* 17). And, in this way, "the fact that a living entity *is*, determines what it *ought* to do." It *should* do that which its nature requires it to do *if* it is to continue to exist (*VOS* 18).[14]

The specific values that an organism needs to survive and the actions it must take to secure them depends on its specific nature – on the *type* of organism it is. For a plant to survive, for example, it needs certain nutrients that it attains by absorbing them from the soil. But "animals would not be able to survive by attempting the method of plants, by rejecting locomotion and waiting for the soil to feed them" (*VOS* 25). Likewise (as we will discuss in detail later) human beings cannot survive "by attempting the method of animals," that is, by acting irrationally on the perceptions and desires of the immediate moment and dealing with others by force rather than persuasion. As in the case of every other species, there is a specific *human* way in which a human being must function if he is to survive. And to function in this way is what it means for a human being to live.

Rand characterized life as "a process of self-sustaining and self-generated action."[15] The content of a goal-directed process is determined by the means needed to reach the goal. In the case of life, the goal is for the organism to sustain itself – that is, to remain in existence as the living thing that it is. Life is a process the goal of which is to carry on performing that very process. The specific process will be different in the case of different species, and for each species, the fundamental means to its life necessarily *constitute* the life of that species. In the case of man, the values and actions that are the fundamental requirements for human survival themselves define what life is for man.

Life, as Rand understands it, is a full-time activity: *all* of an organism's actions must contribute directly or indirectly to sustaining itself: "Since life requires a specific course of action, any other course will destroy it" (*Atlas* 1014).[16] Her point, of course, is not that a single action not aimed at life will necessarily (or even usually) result in death. However, by squandering time, energy, and other resources that may be needed for life-sustaining goals, any action that does not aim at life imperils it and lessens the range of circumstances in which the organism will be able to survive.

The conditional character of life, including the fact that living is a full-time job, establishes an organism's life as its ultimate value: "Metaphysically, *life* is the only phenomenon that is an end in itself: a value gained and kept by a constant process of action" (*VOS* 18). In other words, life is the only thing which, by its nature, requires that all action be consistently directed toward it; thus it is the only thing that qualifies as an "ultimate value." Life is, as Harry Binswanger puts it, "a process of action which, if successful, results in its own continuation. Life is the goal of life – which is another way of saying that life is an end in itself" (Binswanger 1992, 99).

The basic fact at the root of the existence of values is the fact that the existence of any living thing requires that it take a specific course of action, with all of its actions and goals selected by the standard of its life. With the exception of human beings, every organism automatically acts on such a standard. Human beings' actions are determined by the faculty of reason, which does not function automatically. Consequently, man "has no automatic course of behavior," and so "needs a code of values to guide his actions" (*Atlas* 1012).

> Man has been called a rational being, but rationality is a matter of choice – and the alternative his nature offers him is: rational being or suicidal animal. Man has to be man – by choice; he has to hold his life as a value – by choice: he has to learn to sustain it – by choice; he has to discover the values it requires and practice his virtues – by choice.
> A code of values accepted by choice is a code of morality. (*Atlas* 1013)

Human beings need morality, on Rand's view, to fulfill a function that in other species is fulfilled by automatic (psychological or physiological) mechanisms: the function of selecting all the organism's goals and actions by the standard of what sustains its life.

Man's Life as the Standard of Value

Rand sees the standard of moral value as following directly from the reason human beings need morality. She describes this standard as "man's life" or "man's survival *qua* man." Here is how she elaborates on it in Galt's speech:

> Man's life, as required by his nature, is not the life of a mindless brute, of a looting thug or a mooching mystic, but the life of a thinking being – not life by means of force or fraud, but life by means of achievement – not survival at any price, since there's only one price that pays for man's survival: reason. (*Atlas* 1014)

What Rand means by "man's life" is neither bare survival nor longevity *per se*. Man's life is a specific kind of life, central to which is rationally discovering and producing the values one's survival requires. Someone who survives, instead, by "looting" or "mooching" is not leading man's life, no matter how long he may manage to survive in this manner.

Some readers have concluded from this that what Rand means by "man's life" or "survival *qua* man" is some particular way of life which is not required for survival, but which Rand thinks is somehow more proper or appropriate for human beings than alternative ways of living.[17] We might express this interpretation by saying that the standard of her morality is really "survival *qua* John Galt" – that is, living in the specific way exemplified by Rand's heroes and codified in "The Objectivist Ethics" and Galt's speech.

If this interpretation were correct, it would entirely undermine Rand's moral philosophy. She claims that the principles put forward by earlier ethicists are subjective because they are all (in one manner or another) assumed without proof. The standard of man's life is supposed to be objective because it is derived from the facts that give rise to the phenomenon of values. This derivation requires that the word "life" (or "survival") in the standard be understood literally, in terms of the alternative between existence and non-existence. If it is instead understood to mean surviving *qua* John Galt, then Rand would be guilty of an elementary equivocation, and the content of her standard would be left without validation.[18] By Rand's lights, the standard would be subjective – reflecting not facts of reality, but her personal preference for (or approval of) a life like Galt's.

The structure of Rand's argument makes it clear that she intended the standard of value to include only content that could be derived from the requirements of man's literal survival, and we can see evidence of this intent in the first of the two elaborations she gives in the passage quoted above. She differentiates "man's life" from "survival at any price," not by claiming that man's life is something over and above his survival, but by saying that "there is only one price that pays for man's survival: reason."

To understand Rand's position we must see why she thinks that rationality (along with all the virtues she thinks it entails) is a requirement for literal survival, and how she can think that this is compatible with the obvious fact that many people do survive (some of them, for a long time) despite acting very irrationally.

Consider the analogous case of health. Health is the physical condition of an organism that maximizes its ability to survive in the widest range of contexts across the lifespan of an organism of its species.[19] Thus the standard of human health is the requirements of human survival. This is perfectly consistent with the fact that there are many unhealthy people who are alive, and that some of them have outlived many healthy ones.

A living organism is a highly integrated, delicately balanced set of components each of which must function in a manner conducive to the optimal functioning of every other part of the whole. Any malfunction of any part throws the entire system into danger – into a state in which there is a specific threat to its survival. A person may remain alive for a long time in such a condition, but this does not change the fact that his life is in danger because his ability to function in the widest range of circumstances is impaired. For example, a person with severe lung disease might be kept alive on a respirator; but, unlike a healthy person, his life is at the mercy of a power outage, and he would not be able to survive at all, if he lived at a time or in a place without modern technology.

Moreover, though the patient in this example is not dead, he also is not living fully and successfully. He is not fully engaging in "a process of self-sustaining and self-generated action." He is alive in that many of his organs and biological systems continue to play their role in sustaining his life, but he is not performing the process of respiration (or, at least, he is not performing it in a self-generated way), and this process is a vital part of self-sustenance. In this respect, we might say that, though the patient is alive, he is not "living the life of an air-breathing animal" or that he is not "surviving *qua* air-breather." In saying this, we are not appealing to any standard or value apart from (or more demanding than) literal survival. We simply mean that the nature of certain animals, including human beings, is that breathing air is a crucial part of how they survive. This remains true even though there are circumstances in which such animals can be kept alive for a long time, while their respiratory systems are not functioning.[20]

We should understand Rand's statements about "man's life," "survival *qua* man," and "the life proper to man" in this same way. She thinks that, by being irrational (either in a single instance or as a general policy), a person constricts the range of circumstances in which he will be able to function, thereby jeopardizing his survival. If an irrational person manages to survive for long, it is only because of the rationality of others who are keeping him alive, much as the respirator does in the case of the patient with lung disease. Like the diseased man, the irrational man is failing to perform a crucial part of the process by which a human being sustains himself; and so, to the extent that he is irrational, his ability to survive is constricted.

Rand held that the sort of life she calls "man's life" is the only life that ensures a human being's survival across a human lifespan, so far as this is up to one's choice. To the extent that a person deviates from this standard, he puts his life in jeopardy and leaves his continued survival to chance.

> "Man's survival *qua* man" means the terms, methods, conditions and goals required for the survival of a rational being through the whole of his lifespan – in all those aspects of existence which are open to his choice. (*VOS* 26)

Rand's reference to the human lifespan is significant. No organism lives forever, and the ultimate value for Rand is not to approximate immortality by remaining in existence for as long as one can. Rather the ultimate value is *one's own life*, which means some specific, chosen constellation of activities and values – a constellation of the sort that can sustain a human being across a human lifespan. The function of morality, and of the standard "man's life," is to guide one in choosing such a life for oneself by defining the types of values needed to sustain a human being.

> The Objectivist ethics holds man's life as the *standard* of value – and *his own life* as the ethical *purpose* of every individual man.
>
> The difference between "standard" and "purpose" in this context is as follows: a "standard" is an abstract principle that serves as a measurement or gauge to guide a man's choices in the achievement of a concrete, specific purpose. "That which is required for the survival of man *qua* man" is an abstract principle that applies to every individual man. The task of applying this principle to a concrete, specific purpose – the purpose of living a life proper to a rational being – belongs to every individual man, and the life he has to live is his own.
>
> Man must choose his actions, values and goals by the standard of that which is proper to man – in order to achieve, maintain, fulfill and enjoy that ultimate value, that end in itself, which is his own life. (*VOS* 27)

Notice that Rand includes *enjoying* one's life as part of morality's goal. Similarly, she sometimes writes of "the achievement of his own happiness" as "man's highest moral purpose" (*Atlas* 1014, *VOS* 30). Though life and happiness are not identical, Rand does not think that they constitute distinct purposes, for the same reason that she would not view life and health as distinct goals. To pursue life at all is to pursue all the values needed to live fully and successfully (rather than in some partial and precarious manner). Happiness in Rand's view is "the successful state of life"; she defines it as "that state of consciousness which proceeds from the achievement of one's values" (*Atlas* 1014, *VOS* 31). It is "a state of non-contradictory joy" experienced by someone who is successfully performing the process by which a human being survives (*Atlas* 1022).[21] Therefore:

> The maintenance of life and the pursuit of happiness are not two separate issues. To hold one's own life as one's ultimate value, and one's own happiness as one's highest purpose are two aspects of the same achievement. Existentially, the activity of pursuing rational goals is the activity of maintaining one's life; psychologically, its result, reward and concomitant is an emotional state of happiness. It is by experiencing happiness that one lives one's life, in any hour, year or the whole of it.

And when one experiences the kind of pure happiness that is an end in itself—the kind that makes one think: "This is worth living for"—what one is greeting and affirming in emotional terms is the metaphysical fact that *life* is an end in itself. (*VOS* 32)

Since the fundamental means by which a life is sustained are themselves part of that life, Rand thinks that, in addition to being the *means* to life and happiness, the values and virtues of the Objectivist ethics are also essential *constituents* of a successful and happy life. This is why, in "The Objectivist Ethics," Rand describes "the three cardinal values" of reason, purpose, and self-esteem as "the *means to* and the *realization of* one's ultimate value, one's own life" (*VOS* 27, emphasis added).[22] There is an important sense, then, in which these values are part of the ultimate end, which is one's life. However, we miss the essence of Rand's ethics if we forget that these virtues and values have the place they do in a successful human life only because each plays a crucial role in enabling a human being to survive. It is by showing this in the case of each value and virtue that Rand establishes her moral code.

The Value of Reason and the Virtue of Rationality

Rand's view of reason is discussed at length by Gregory Salmieri in Chapter 12 below, so my treatment will be comparatively brief. Reason (or "the mind") is the faculty responsible for thinking. It is a uniquely human faculty, which can be distinguished from the cognitive faculties of sensation, perception, and memory. These are the faculties by which other animals guide their actions, but for human beings they serve as the source of the data on which thinking is based. Rand also distinguishes reason from emotions, which are not "tools of cognition," but "automatic results of man's value judgments integrated by his subconscious" (*VOS* 32, 27). We have already touched on one crucial way in which Rand thinks reason is unlike any of these other faculties: whereas they are all automatic, reason is volitional. The process of thinking needs to be initiated, sustained, and directed by choice. Thus Rand describes man as *"a being of volitional consciousness"* (*Atlas* 1012).[23]

Rand explains in the "The Objectivist Ethics" that "consciousness – for those living organisms which possess it – is the basic means of survival." Of course, she recognizes that there are many physiological processes that an animal must perform in order to be conscious, but she holds that there is a more important respect in which these processes depend on consciousness: consciousness is the faculty that directs the animal toward all the values (food, shelter, etc.) that it needs to survive and thus to continue performing the various physiological processes that are part of its survival. In the case of human beings it is reason specifically that plays this role.

For man, the basic means of survival is *reason*. Man cannot survive, as animals do, by the guidance of mere percepts. A sensation of hunger will tell him that he needs food (if he has learned to identify it as "hunger"), but it will not tell him how to obtain his food and it will not tell him what food is good for him or poisonous. He cannot provide for his simplest physical needs without a process of thought. He needs a process of thought to discover how to plant and grow his food or how to make weapons for hunting. His percepts might lead him to a cave, if one is available – but to build the simplest shelter, he needs a process of thought. No percepts and no "instincts" will tell him how to light a fire, how to weave cloth, how to forge tools, how to make a wheel, how to make an airplane, how to perform an appendectomy, how to produce an electric light bulb or an electronic tube or a cyclotron or a box of matches. Yet his life depends on such knowledge – and only a volitional act of his consciousness, a process of thought, can provide it. (*VOS* 22–23)[24]

Here Rand focuses on reason's role in identifying and producing values, such as food, clothing, shelter, and medicine, which are directly needed for a physical survival. As we will see, Rand also argues that such values as self-esteem, art, and friendship are necessary for human survival, and that they can only be achieved through reason. As Howard Roark puts the point in *The Fountainhead*, "from [the] simplest necessity to the highest religious abstraction, from the wheel to the skyscraper, everything we are and everything we have comes from a single attribute of man – the function of his reasoning mind" (711).

To hold reason as a value means to choose consistently to think – to make and maintain a "commitment to reason, not in sporadic fits or on selected issues or in special emergencies, but as a permanent way of life" (*VOS* 29). This is the core of *rationality*, which Rand identifies as "man's basic virtue" and the "source of his other virtues."

> The virtue of *Rationality* means the recognition and acceptance of reason as one's only source of knowledge, one's only judge of values and one's only guide to action. It means one's total commitment to a state of full, conscious awareness, to the maintenance of a full mental focus in all issues, in all choices, in all of one's waking hours. It means a commitment to the fullest perception of reality within one's power and to the constant, active expansion of one's perception, *i.e.*, of one's knowledge. It means a commitment to the reality of one's own existence, *i.e.*, to the principle that all of one's goals, values and actions take place in reality and, therefore, that one must never place any value or consideration whatsoever above one's perception of reality. It means a commitment to the principle that all of one's convictions, values, goals, desires and actions must be based on, derived from, chosen and validated by a process of thought – as precise and scrupulous a process of thought, directed by as ruthlessly strict an application of logic, as one's fullest capacity permits. (*VOS* 28)

When Rand says that rationality requires being "in full mental focus" in "all one's waking hours," she does not mean that a person must be constantly engaged in difficult thinking. Her point is that he must be mentally present: aware of his situation, of what he is doing, and why he is doing it. He must be unwilling to settle for vagueness or inconsistency on these issues, or to act on motives that he does not understand. And (as Leonard Peikoff puts it) he must be "alert to the possibility that a process of cognition may be required of him at any time" (*OPAR* 58).

A person who is in focus is committed to "the fullest perception of reality" and an "active expansion" of his knowledge. This does not mean that he makes it a priority in every moment to discover the answer to every question he can come up with. But it does mean that he is not content to stagnate at his present level of knowledge; he values new knowledge because he recognizes that (as Tara Smith puts it) "[t]he wider and deeper a person's knowledge, the better position he will be in to steer his life successfully" (2006, 66).

As a central part of this commitment to expand one's knowledge, Rand stresses the need to *integrate* one's findings without contradiction into an ever-widening sum. A crucial aspect of this process is "discovering *causal connections*." A rational person sees causes and effects not as discrete existents but as necessarily connected parts of a whole, and this perspective informs his desires and actions.

> [Rationality] means that one must never desire effects without causes, and that one must never enact a cause without assuming full responsibility for its effects – that one must never act like a zombie, *i.e.*, without knowing one's own purposes and motives – that one must never make any decisions, form any convictions or seek any values out of context, *i.e.*, apart from or against the total, integrated sum of one's knowledge – and, above all, that one must never seek to get away with contradictions. (*VOS* 28, cf. "The 'Conflicts' of Men's Interests" *VOS* 57–63)

The alternative to the state of focus required by rationality is to "drift in a semiconscious daze, merely reacting to any chance stimulus of the immediate moment, at the mercy of [one's] undirected sensory-perceptual mechanism and of any random, associational connections it might happen to make." When someone is "drifting," his mental state approximates that of an animal's "since he experiences sensations and perceptions," without engaging in the process of thought. This level of awareness is sufficient to guide other animals in the actions they need to take to survive, but it is insufficient for a human being, so such a person "may be said to be conscious in a subhuman sense of the word" ("The Objectivist Ethics" *VOS* 22, cf. *FTNI* 8–9).

The "basic vice," which is contrary to the virtue of rationality, is the act of "evasion" or "blanking out" – that is, "unfocusing your mind and inducing an inner fog to escape the responsibility of judgment" (*Atlas* 1017, cf. *VOS* 22–24). To evade is to turn off one's mind and induce a state of drift in order to avoid facing an uncomfortable fact. Rand thinks that it is only through evasion that a chronic state of drift can be maintained. Peikoff explains: "If a drifter in a given situation apprehends (dimly or clearly) the need to initiate a thought process, yet refuses to do so, the refusal involves an evasion (he is evading the fact that thought is necessary)" (*OPAR* 61).

Evasion amounts to elevating a whim over one's perception of reality. Galt dramatically describes the consequence of such a choice:

> Whenever you committed the evil of refusing to think and to see, of exempting from the absolute of reality some one small wish of yours, whenever you chose to say: Let me withdraw from the judgment of reason the cookies I stole, or the existence of God, let me have my one irrational whim and I will be a man of reason about all else – *that* was the act of subverting your consciousness, the act of corrupting your mind. Your mind then became a fixed jury who takes orders from a secret underworld, whose verdict distorts the evidence to fit an absolute it dares not touch – and a censored reality is the result, a splintered reality where the bits you chose to see are floating among the chasms of those you didn't, held together by that embalming fluid of the mind which is an emotion exempted from thought. (*Atlas* 1037)

We can appreciate from this passage why Rand thinks that the commitment to reason must be absolute. Even a single evasion perverts one's entire consciousness so long as it goes uncorrected, because it serves to *disintegrate* reality into discrete "bits," rather than integrating one's knowledge into a non-contradictory sum, as rationality requires. Galt says that the "links" that evaders "try to drown" are the very "causal connections" that inform a rational person's desires and actions.

Part of valuing reason is valuing the freedom required to develop one's mind and to act on its judgment. This is the ultimate source in Rand's philosophy of the rights that are at the basis of her political theory (and are discussed at length in Part III of this volume). Someone who appreciates the role of the mind in human life, will value not only his own freedom but also that of others, because he will see each individual's mind as a potential source of tremendous values, which he will realize depend on the individual's freedom. *Atlas Shrugged* dramatizes the value of reason by showing the disintegration of a society that is deserted by the "men of the mind" because it fails to recognize these facts. At the beginning of the novel we see a society that has already become poor both financially and spiritually: shops are closed even on the most prosperous streets, and beggars are everywhere; what art remains is vapid, and there are few achievements to admire. As more thinkers disappear, so does technology: people are left at the mercy of storms and other weather events that they used not to notice; others die in catastrophes caused when the remaining machines are used by people who do not (and do not care to) understand them. In time, the society is reduced to the back- and spirit-breaking labor of a pre-industrial existence.[25] By contrast, the life of the strikers in their valley hideaway illustrates physical and spiritual prosperity that are the rewards of an unbreached rationality.

Purpose and Productiveness

Rand held that reason pertains not only to calculating the means to values, but also to defining and choosing one's values.[26] We have already considered the reasoning by which she establishes that life is the ultimate value. It is also by a rational process that she thinks that a person conceives of and directs himself toward the specific constellation of values that constitute his own life and happiness. This brings us to the second of her cardinal values: *purpose*. Galt describes it as man's "choice of the happiness which [his reason] must proceed to achieve" (*Atlas* 1018).

To value purpose is to be purpose*ful* – to define and pursue purposes in all aspects of one's life. Purposefulness is a hallmark of Rand's heroes. For example: as a child, Francisco d'Anconia "could always name the purpose of his every random moment" and would neither "stand still" nor "move aimlessly." He asks "What for?" about "any activity proposed to him and nothing would make him act, if he found no valid answer" (*Atlas* 94). As he gets older, Francisco's answers to this question are increasingly given in terms of the central purpose of running d'Anconia Copper, and he shows increasing awareness of the moral significance of this choice (*Atlas* 94–99). Dagny Taggart worships purposefulness; her thoughts about it underscore the role of a central purpose in organizing a person's life, and they indicate the relation between purpose and morality. Reflecting on the engines in the locomotive on the first run of the John Galt Line, she thinks that they are "a moral code cast in steel" and embody "the power of a living mind – the power of thought and choice and purpose." "Every part of the motors was an embodied answer to 'Why?' and 'What for?' – like the steps of a life-course chosen by the sort of mind she worshipped" (*Atlas* 245–246; cf. 87, 730–731).

To maintain a purpose one must *work* to achieve it, and this is the virtue of *Productiveness*. Galt describes it as

> your recognition of the fact that you choose to live – that productive work is the process by which man's consciousness controls his existence, a constant process of acquiring knowledge and shaping matter to fit one's purpose, of translating an idea into physical form, of remaking the earth in the image of one's values. (*Atlas* 1020)

"Production is the application of reason to the problem of survival" ("What Is Capitalism?" *CUI* 8), and just as the virtue of rationality demands that one seek to continually expand one's knowledge, the virtue of productiveness requires a person to regard "his work as constant progress, as a constant upward motion from one achievement to another, higher one, driven by the constant expansion of his mind, his knowledge, his ability, his creative ingenuity, never stopping to stagnate on any level" ("From My Future File" *ARL* 3(26) 373). Since productive work is the activity by which one achieves values, to resign oneself to working below one's potential is to renounce the pursuit of some of the (spiritual and material) values that one's survival may require. Rational beings can identify an ever-wider range of such values, and can develop ever more efficient means to achieve them. In a division of labor society, they can specialize, and trade with others. This is a continuous and demanding process, which must take a dominant role in one's life.[27] Thus Rand regarded "productive work" as "the central *purpose* of a rational man's life, the central value that integrates and determines the hierarchy of all his other values" (*VOS* 27).[28]

> A central purpose serves to integrate all the other concerns of a man's life. It establishes the hierarchy, the relative importance, of his values, it saves him from pointless inner conflicts, it permits him to enjoy life on a wide scale and to carry that enjoyment into any area open to his mind; whereas a man without a purpose is lost in chaos. He does not know what his values are. He does not know how to judge. He cannot tell what is or is not important to him, and, therefore, he drifts helplessly at the mercy of any chance stimulus or any whim of the moment. He can enjoy nothing. He spends his life searching for some value which he will never find. (*Playboy Interview* 36)

Because the need for a productive career to serve as one's central purpose is spiritual as well as material, Rand thinks that a career is necessary even for an independently wealthy individual.[29]

A productive career can exist "in any line of rational endeavor, great or modest, on any level of ability. It is not the degree of a man's ability nor the scale of his work that is ethically relevant here, but the fullest and most purposeful use of his mind" (*VOS* 29, cf. *Atlas* 1020).[30] Rand's appreciation of a productive career even at modest levels of ability can be seen in one of Eddie Willers's casual observations in the first scene of *Atlas Shrugged*: "He saw a bus turning a corner, expertly steered" (*Atlas* 4). One imagines the driver's focus on his driving, and his long-term commitment to (and his pride in) skillful driving, with care.

Similar examples scattered throughout *Atlas Shrugged* indicate the range of activities that Rand considers potential careers. One such example is a mother who regards raising her children as a career (*Atlas* 784–785). In an interview Rand noted, however, that parenting could only be a full-time occupation while the children are young (*Playboy Interview*, cf. *OPAR* 302).[31] As this illustrates, a career need not take the form of a lifetime commitment to a single profession; one can change careers, applying what one has learned in one field to another.

To hold purpose as a cardinal value is to be committed to *purposefulness* not only in one's career but throughout one's life. As Leonard Peikoff writes:

> The principle of purpose means conscious goal-directedness in every aspect of one's existence where choice applies. The man of purpose defines explicitly his abstract values and then, in every area, the specific objects he seeks to gain and the means by which to gain them. Whether in regard to work or friends, love or art, entertainment or vacations, he knows what he likes and why, then goes after it. ... He is the person with a passionate ambition for *values* who wants every moment and step of his life to count in their service. Such a person does not resent the effort which purpose imposes. He enjoys the fact that the objects he desires are not given to him, but must be achieved. In his eyes, purpose is not drudgery or duty, but something good. The process of pursuing values is itself a value. (*OPAR* 298)

Self-Esteem and Pride

The third cardinal value Rand identifies is "self-esteem," which she defines as "[the] inviolate certainty that [one's] mind is competent to think and [one's] person is worthy of happiness, which means: is worthy of living" (*Atlas* 1018). Self-esteem thus amounts to *self-confidence* and *self-worth*. A human being needs confidence in the efficacy of his mind in order to stand by his judgments and maintain his purposes, especially when his judgment differs from that of others with whom he must deal.[32] He needs self-worth in order to maintain his motivation to pursue his purposes especially in the face of adversity.

How are these two aspects of self-esteem related? What a person of self-esteem is confident about is not his degree of intelligence or any specific skill he may have, it is his general efficacy as a thinker and producer and value-achiever – his fitness for existence. Since life is the standard of moral value, to be characteristically inadequate for the tasks of life, when that inadequacy is due to one's chosen way of life, is to be *evil*: "to be wrong in person, to be *evil*, means to be unfit for existence" (*Atlas* 1057). Thus a judgment of one's fundamental efficacy is also a judgment of one's value as a human being – it is a judgment of one's worth.

In describing self-esteem as a value, Rand is saying that it is something one must act to achieve. Specifically, one must act to become the sort of person one judges competent and worthy.

> Just as [man] has to produce the material values he needs to sustain his life, so he has to acquire the values of character that enable him to sustain it and that make his life worth living. He is born without the knowledge of either. He has to discover both – and translate them into reality – and survive by shaping the world and himself in the image of his values. ("The Goal of My Writing" *RM* 162)

We have seen that Rand thinks of productiveness as the virtue by which one shapes the world into the image of one's values. The virtue by which one shapes oneself into the image of one's values is *pride*, which she describes as "moral ambitiousness." Galt explains the relationship between pride and self-esteem as follows:

> Pride is the recognition of the fact that you are your own highest value and, like all of man's values, it has to be earned – that of any achievements open to you, the one that makes all others possible is the creation of your own character – that your character, your actions, your desires, your emotions are the products of the premises held by your mind – that as man must produce the physical values he needs to sustain his life, so he must acquire the values of character that make his life worth sustaining – that as man is a being of self-made wealth, so he is a being of self-made soul – that to live requires a sense of self-value, but man, who has no automatic values, has no automatic sense of self-esteem and must earn it by shaping his soul in the image of his moral ideal, in the image of Man, the rational being he is born able to create, but must create by choice – that the first precondition of self-esteem is that radiant selfishness of soul which desires the best in all things, in values of matter and spirit, a soul that seeks above all else to achieve its own moral perfection, valuing nothing higher than itself ... (*Atlas* 1020 –1021)

Rand thinks that this commitment to moral *perfection* is necessary because the self-esteem one needs to achieve is an "*inviolate* certainty" of one's competence and worth. Any sort of compromise or inconsistency undermines self-esteem. The view that such compromises lead to psychological deterioration dates back to Plato and Aristotle, and Rand's acceptance of it both follows from and reinforces her reasons (discussed earlier) for thinking that one's commitment to rationality must be absolute.

Self-esteem and pride are central to the plot of *Atlas Shrugged*. Galt's pride in particular is stressed. When Dagny first meets him she notices that "[t]he shape of his mouth was pride, and more: it was as if he took pride in being proud" (*Atlas* 701), and in his speech he describes himself as "the man who has earned the thing you did not fight for, the thing you have renounced, betrayed, corrupted, yet were unable fully to destroy and are now hiding as your guilty secret" – namely the value of his own person (*Atlas* 1021). It is because of his self-esteem that Galt is unwilling to be victimized by society.

This brings us to another aspect of the virtue of pride. The virtue includes the recognition that "the proof of an achieved self-esteem is your soul's shudder of contempt and rebellion against the role of a sacrificial animal" (*Atlas* 1021). In his radio speech, Galt argues that accepting the morality of self-sacrifice undercuts one's self-esteem and makes one consent to being exploited (*Atlas* 1030, 1031, 1032–1033, 1044–1045, 1056–1057). There are many examples of this in the novel. The most prominent is the manipulation of Rearden by his wife Lillian, who has induced him to feel guilt for selfishly holding the values and practicing the virtues we have been discussing.[33] Since the morality of self-sacrifice is antithetical to self-esteem, the virtue of pride requires the repudiation of this morality, and this is the essence of Galt's strike.[34]

The Range of Life-Sustaining Values

The values that Rand thinks are required for Man's life are not limited to the obvious necessities for survival and the three cardinal values that we have already discussed. In an article endorsed by Rand, Nathaniel Branden listed "five (interconnected) areas that allow man to experience the enjoyment of life: productive work, human relationships, recreation, art, sex" ("The Psychology of Pleasure" *VOS* 72).[35] To these five areas, we might add the pleasure we have seen Rand thinks a person can take in the creation of his own character.[36] The enjoyment we find in these areas is not "causeless, irreducible and unrelated to … the needs of [our] survival." Rather, as Rand says in the case of art, each is "tied to man's survival – not to his physical survival, but to that on which his physical survival depends: to the preservation and survival of his consciousness" ("The Psycho-Epistemology of Art" *RM* 5). Reflecting on these six spheres of value, therefore, serves to broaden our understanding of Rand's view of man's life.

We have already discussed the values of productive work and of character development. Rand held that art is a crucial human value because it enables us to experience in a directly perceptual form the abstract ideas that we need to guide and motivate our actions. Since this theory is discussed at length in Chapters 16 and 17 of this volume, I will pass directly to the remaining spheres of value.

Of the six spheres, Rand and her associates commented least on recreation. Peikoff writes that recreation or leisure activities are valuable "as relaxation and reward after the performance of work" (*OPAR* 301, cf. Branden *VOS* 75). Thus, he notes, they are valuable only in the context of a life organized around a productive career. We can see this point in Rand's fiction. It is a recurrent theme in *Atlas Shrugged* that various forms of entertainment, leisure, and luxury are only truly enjoyed by the productive characters for whom they have meaning. Other characters, who have nothing to celebrate, are shown joylessly going through the motions of such activities, nervously faking to themselves and others the enjoyment that is only possible to those who have something to celebrate.[37]

The need for recreation can be fulfilled by a wide variety of activities, and indeed we see Rand's heroes resting and celebrating their achievements with a variety of leisure activities: swimming, boating, tennis, parties, and the appreciation of food and drink, of luxury items, and of natural and man-made beauty. It cannot however be fulfilled by self-destructive activities, such as drug abuse or reckless thrill-seeking.[38] Moreover, many of the forms of recreation in which Rand's heroes engage have another feature she regarded as important. As Branden puts it, they are "demanding": they require "exercising discrimination, judgment, awareness" (*VOS* 75–76). As practiced by the heroes at least, these activities involve the purposeful use of one's intellectual (and often physical) faculties with respect to a subject matter refreshingly different from one's work. Rand highlighted this feature of recreation in a brief essay, "Why I Like Stamp Collecting" (*Column*), in which she discusses one of her own hobbies, stressing the significance of both the ways in which it was like and unlike her work, and indicating the way in which it related to some of her other values.

I turn now from recreation to the value of personal relationships. The intensity with which Rand's heroes value their friends and lovers is one of their most striking features. The basis of these relationships are shared values. Even outside of the context of established relationships, we can see this focus on shared values in the joy that Rand's protagonists take in the achievements of others (large and small), in the way they sometimes feel starved for the sight of such achievements, in the great concern they show for good people who are suffering undeservedly, and in the pleasure they take in opportunities to share even minor values with others who will appreciate them.[39]

Because Rand holds that an individual's rational self-interest consists in living a productive life in which he creates life-sustaining values, rather than in living as a parasite, she thinks that there is a fundamental harmony of interest among rational people, with each person creating values that can enrich the lives of everyone else.[40] Thus Rand sees good will toward others as a concomitant of rational egoism rather than of altruism. (See "The Ethics of Emergencies" *VOS* 53–54, *Letters* 91, 345–346, and Branden, "Benevolence vs. Altruism" *TON* 1(7).)

According to Rand, a rational egoist values other people not only or primarily for the material values they produce. Rather, he values the spiritual qualities that they have or have the potential to develop. Valuing other people in this way is an extension of his own self-esteem: he recognizes that they share (or can come to share) the characteristics that he values in himself. (See *Speaking* 160–161.) In essays endorsed by Rand, Branden discusses the psychological roots of the affection that a person can feel for another – or even for an animal or a plant. Central to Rand's theory of art is that human beings have a spiritual need to experience their abstract values and convictions in perceptible form.[41] Branden argues that seeing other organisms flourish serves this need by concretizing the conviction that success is possible in life. Similarly, interacting with others who share the traits one values in oneself enables one to experience these values concretely, by perceiving the other person's actions that express the valued traits and his reactions to manifestations of the traits in oneself.[42]

The intensity of this valuable experience depends on the nature and extent of the shared values.[43] The most intense form of valuing another person is romantic love, which Rand considered to be one of "the two great values in life" (the other, being one's work) (*Speaking* 231). What one responds to in the person one loves is what Rand called the person's "*sense of life*":

> It is with a person's sense of life that one falls in love – with that essential sum, that fundamental stand or way of facing existence, which is the essence of a personality. One falls in love with the embodiment of the values that formed a person's character, which are reflected in his widest goals or smallest gestures, which create the *style* of his soul – the individual style of a unique, unrepeatable, irreplaceable consciousness. ("Philosophy and Sense of Life" *RM* 22)[44]

The topic of love brings us to our final sphere of value: "sex," Rand wrote, "is a physical capacity, but its exercise is determined by man's mind." As the most intense form of physical pleasure, "[t]o a rational man, sex is an expression of self-esteem – *a celebration of himself and of existence*" ("Of Living Death" *VOR* 54). It is an intimate pleasure that one would want to share only with someone "who reflects his deepest vision of himself" (*Atlas* 490).[45]

> Romantic love, in the full sense of the term, is an emotion possible only to the man (or woman) of unbreached self-esteem: it is his response to his own highest values in the person of another – an integrated response of mind and body, of love and sexual desire. (*VOR* 54)

This view of the nature and value of sex is an important theme in *Atlas Shrugged*. It is discussed in Francisco's speech on "The Meaning of Sex" (489–492) and dramatized in the novel's romantic relationships. Through Dagny's relationships, Rand shows how important romantic love is to people of self-esteem, and how both the joy they take in sex and the sometimes painful intensity with which they desire it stems from the deep spiritual values that they share with their lovers.[46] Through the character of Rearden, Rand shows the tremendous suffering caused to such people by a mistaken view of sex.[47] And, through the affairs of Dagny's brother Jim, Rand illustrates the distorted, joyless character of sex without self-esteem.

Love and the less intense forms of affection are *selfish*, according to Rand, in that the person one loves is valuable to one because he fulfills (a survival-based) psychological need and produces a great deal of pleasure. It should be clear that this explanation does not imply that what one really values is one's own pleasure or the satisfaction of one's psychological needs, rather than the person one loves. What Rand's theory is meant to explain is the specific need a person has for certain other people and the reason why he takes such pleasure in their company. These factors make those specific people valuable to him, and thereby make their welfare a *part* of his self-interest.[48]

> The practical implementation of friendship, affection and love consists of incorporating the welfare (the *rational* welfare) of the person involved into one's own hierarchy of values, then acting accordingly. ("The Ethics of Emergencies" *VOS* 53)

Like each of the other values we have discussed, the value to an individual of other people and of his relationships with them depends on his life and on the whole hierarchy of values that it requires, and this has implications for the sorts of people that can be of genuine value and the role that relationships can properly play in one's life. First, it is only *good* people (and what is good *in* particular people) that can be of genuine value; for evil people and traits are essentially destructive. Second, though relationships – especially relationships of romantic love – are properly among a person's highest values, they cannot be one's central purpose in life. This is because, as Roark puts it: "To say 'I love you' one must know first how to say the 'I'" (*Fountainhead* 388, cf. *Letters* 396–397). As we have seen, the value of a personal relationship depends on each person's already having a *self* – an independent purpose and an authentic self-esteem. "Your work is the purpose of your life," Galt explains, and the people you love "can be only travelers you choose to share your journey and must be travelers going on their own power in the same direction" (*Atlas* 1020).

My aim in this section has been to indicate the range of values in a life lived according to Rand's ethics. I'd like to close by stressing something that is perhaps most obvious in the case of love, but which applies to values in all the spheres we discussed, and any other spheres there may be.[49] The values that sustain a particular person's life are *concretes* such as that person's particular career, romantic partner, friends, leisure activities, favorite artworks, and so on. Because these particular, concrete values are not required for man's life as such, they are sometimes referred to as "optional values."[50] This phrase should not be understood to mean that a particular person's optional values are all things that he could live without. A person's career or romantic partner, in particular, might be essential to his life. Though he would not die immediately if the value were removed, losing it would significantly and permanently impair his ability, and will, to live. In such cases, the person ought to go to great lengths to protect the value, and it may even be rational for him to choose not to go on living without it. We will return to this issue below, in connection with the virtue of integrity.

There is an element of optionality also concerning the precise place in one's value hierarchy taken by each of the values that are required by man's life as such. For example, in discussing the cardinal values earlier, we noted the special intensity with which Dagny values purpose, whereas Galt's focus is more on self-esteem. Such subtle differences in the emphases Rand's heroes place on different aspects of morality are part of what makes each character distinct.[51] The same is true with respect to other values that are essential to life. For example art and technology are both needed for human survival, and so both will be valued by anyone who values his life, but the relative intensity with which these two values are held (properly) varies from person to person, and this explains in part why some people (reasonably) choose to become artists, while others choose to be engineers, and so on, with each productive person specializing in producing some one of the many values that human life requires. It would be immoral, on Rand's view, for someone to give up a career in a field he is passionate about in order to pursue another career that is allegedly (or even actually) more important, as judged by some standard other than his own *personal* values.[52]

The values that constitute man's life are not something above your personal values to which you must sacrifice. Rather, these values are abstractions identifying the categories of value that you, as a human being, require to survive and to enjoy your life. The purpose of these abstractions is to guide you in choosing the particular values in which your life will consist. Rather than restricting you, morality enables you to grasp what your life requires and to choose among the countless ways in which these requirements can be fulfilled. The requirements themselves are neither optional nor imposed on you from without. It is simply a fact that certain needs must be met if you are to survive, and that without these needs there would be no such phenomenon as valuing (or happiness) at all. Rand elaborates in a 1945 note:

> You set the goal and the meaning; the field of choice and possibilities is immense; the only necessity involved is that you use the material as it is and your tool (reason) as it is – that you understand them for what they are before you choose or achieve a purpose. (Do not call it a "limit." The basic fact of reality is a "limit" – the fact of existence, which presupposes an entity, which means a thing differentiated by certain intrinsic, essential attributes from that which it is not. "To be" implies a "limit" – a distinction from that which is not. If you demanded "freedom" from the natural world – you would demand, in effect, an undifferentiated chaos, the non-existence of entities, actually more than death – the annihilation of the conception of the possibility of living.) (*Papers* 032_11B_002_060–061/*Journals* 294)

The Selfishness of Virtue

The passage from Galt's speech that serves as our epigraph concludes by listing seven virtues that he goes on to describe in greater detail. We have already discussed three of them; before looking at the others, it will be instructive to consider Rand's view of virtue generally.

In "The Objectivist Ethics," Rand defines a virtue as "the act by which one gains and/or keeps" a value; later in that article and in Galt's speech, she identifies each virtue as a "recognition of [a] fact" about the "relation of existence and consciousness."[53] Let us consider how these two statements about virtue relate to one another and to the view, generally accepted by philosophers since Aristotle, that a virtue is a *state of character* – a developed, settled disposition to feel and act in characteristic ways in relevant conditions, usually without the need for (much) deliberation in the moment.

In speaking of virtue as an "act" by which one *pursues a value*, Rand emphasizes that virtue has a goal beyond itself, and must be understood in terms of this goal. In other passages she emphasizes that a specific type of action is required to achieve the goal, and that there is a specific state of consciousness from which such actions issue. She characterizes each virtue as *a recognition of a fact* and elaborates on the fact in a way that indicates the range of actions implied by recognizing it. For example, it is because a rational person recognizes that things exist and have definite identities independent of his consciousness, and that reason is his only means of grasping these identities, that he seeks to expand his knowledge by the use of reason and rejects mysticism. It is because a productive person recognizes that productive work is how he can use his mind to achieve values that he prioritizes productive work and seeks a job where he can use his mind to its utmost. And it is because a proud person recognizes that self-esteem can and must be earned that he holds himself to the highest moral standard.

Each of Rand's virtues is a recognition of a fact about how one's consciousness has to relate to existence in order for one to live. For an action to be virtuous is for it to be guided by such a recognition. And for a person to be virtuous is for this recognition to be part of his characteristic psychology – specifically, part of his *moral character*. As Onkar Ghate discusses in the next chapter, Rand has a rich moral psychological theory according to which a person's character is composed largely of "premises" about the relation between existence and consciousness – premises that have become automatized due to the person's past choices and that play a central role in generating his emotions. Thus I think it is accurate to say that, for Rand, as for Aristotle and the subsequent tradition, virtues are states of character. However, unlike this tradition, Rand understands these states as automatized recognitions of facts that require a human being to act a certain way in order to maintain his life. In her discussions of the virtues, she focuses on these facts and the actions they require, rather than on the moral-psychological issues, because it is these aspects of the virtues that reveal why the virtues are necessary to man's life.

With this in mind, we can see where Rand stands on two related issues emphasized by contemporary ethicists interested in the concept of virtue. Some ethicists think that the value of the states they identify as virtues stems from principles in accordance with which they motivate agents to act or the goals that they motivate them to pursue. However, many "virtue ethicists" maintain that the distinctive way in which a virtuous person acts is too nuanced and too sensitive to details of the situation to be expressed in or explained by any abstract moral principle or goal that does not refer back to the virtue itself. Because of this, these ethicists take virtue (or having a good character) to be the fundamental moral concept. On this view, being virtuous or acting virtuously is good in itself, and the goodness of other things is explained in terms of it. Some proponents of this view, taking their cue from Aristotle, identify flourishing (*eudaimonia*) as the ultimate end, but they define this end in terms of virtue.[54]

It should be clear that Rand does not side with such virtue ethicists on these issues. The facts of which her virtues are recognitions and the actions demanded by these facts can all be stated without making any reference to the nature of the virtues as psychological states. Moreover, the virtues are not at the foundation of Rand's moral theory; rather, they derive from the need to act in certain ways (based on certain facts) in order to achieve (first) the cardinal values and (through them) the ultimate value of one's own life. We can see the importance of this point to Rand in Galt's insistence that "virtue is not an end in itself" or "its own reward," rather "*Life* is the reward of virtue – and happiness is the goal and the reward of life" (*Atlas* 1021).[55]

This does not mean that the virtues are mere instrumental means to an end that is wholly separate from themselves. As an essential means to one's life, each virtue is a crucial constituent of the end to which it is a means. Indeed, the virtues are more central to the life which is a person's ultimate end than are such concrete values as a particular job, friend, or possession. And the virtues form part of the standard by which a person can judge whether such concretes are genuine values – that is, whether they serve his life. Nevertheless, the status of the virtues as constituents of life derives from their status as means to the cardinal values of reason, purpose, and self-esteem, and to the wider range of values that we have seen man's life requires. Thus Rand's moral philosophy is properly understood not as a virtue ethics, but as a *value ethics*.[56]

To treat virtue as one's fundamental moral concept, would be to say that a certain way of acting (and/or the psychological states that give rise to it) is good apart from its relation to the individual's life, and that he could (in principle) be called to sacrifice his life to the demands of virtue. On Rand's view, by contrast, virtue is a *selfish* necessity, because one's life depends on it.

Independence, Integrity, Honesty, and Justice as Aspects of Rationality

We have already discussed Rand's argument that life requires rationality, productiveness, and pride. Let us now discuss the four remaining virtues. In "The Objectivist Ethics," she introduces them as aspects of rationality:

> [Rationality] means one's acceptance of the responsibility of forming one's own judgments and of living by the work of one's own mind (which is the virtue of Independence). It means that one must never sacrifice one's convictions to the opinions or wishes of others (which is the virtue of Integrity) – that one must never attempt to fake reality in any manner (which is the virtue of Honesty) – that one must never seek or grant the unearned and undeserved, neither in matter nor in spirit (which is the virtue of Justice). (*VOS* 28)

Independence is the virtue of thinking for *oneself.* This policy is "the recognition of the fact that yours is the responsibility of judgment and nothing can help you escape it" (*Atlas* 1019). Of course, we can learn a tremendous amount from others, and Rand acknowledges this; however, she stresses that one must judge for oneself what one is taught rather than passively absorbing it; similarly, there are many contexts in which one needs to rely on the judgments of experts, but one must judge for oneself who is an expert and whether his opinion is consistent with the sum of one's knowledge. To do otherwise would be "the vilest form of self-abasement and self-destruction" (*Atlas* 1019). Since other people are no less capable of error and irrationality than you, to follow their opinions or wishes uncritically is essentially to act at random.

Since it is by thinking (and thought-guided action) that human beings survive, the responsibility to do one's own thinking includes the responsibility of supporting oneself via a productive career (as discussed above), rather than expecting others to produce (uncompensated) the products on which one's life depends.

Of course, forming your own judgments and values does not benefit your life, unless you translate that thought into action. This brings us to the virtue of *integrity*, which Rand defines as "loyalty to one's convictions and values; it is the policy of acting in accordance with one's values, of expressing, upholding and translating them into practical reality" ("The Ethics of Emergencies" *VOS* 52–53). Integrity means being loyal in action to the judgment of one's mind, rather than compromising one's conclusions and values to please others or out of fear of any sort.

Galt's discussion of this virtue begins by identifying it as "the recognition of the fact that you cannot fake your consciousness" (*Atlas* 1019). This formulation reflects Rand's view that a professed value or conviction on which one is unwilling to act is a mere pretense (whether it is put on for one's own benefit or for that of others). Rand thought that the values and convictions that many people claim to live by are just such pretenses, and that such people in fact lack values and convictions altogether. In her early works, where this theme is especially prevalent, she says that such people are not "living," and she describes the spiritual bleakness of their existence.[57] The life of Robert Stadler in *Atlas Shrugged* illustrates how betraying values that one once rationally held and lived by leads to similar spiritual consequences, and how this leads ultimately to the character's death (along with the destruction of countless others).

Galt goes on to describe integrity as the recognition of the fact "that man is an indivisible entity, an integrated unit of two attributes: of matter and consciousness, and that he may permit no breach between body and mind, between action and thought, between his life and his convictions" (*Atlas* 1019). To recognize this fact is to bring a wholeness to one's thoughts and actions – to *integrate* oneself. Because integrity requires acting on one's values even when it is difficult, Rand thinks of it as the virtue involved in many morally good actions that are often misidentified as sacrifices – for example, incurring costs or facing dangers to help loved ones ("The Ethics of Emergencies" *VOS* 51–52). To be indifferent in action to the interests of one's loved ones would be not to value these people, and we have already discussed why loved ones are crucial values. The same applies, though on a different scale, with actions taken to aid strangers, based on the general value one places on human life. (See Darryl Wright's discussion in Chapter 7, 163.)

In his discussion of integrity, Galt says "that courage is the practical form of being true to existence ... and confidence is the practical form of being true to one's own consciousness" (*Atlas* 1019). As integrity is an aspect of rationality, so courage and confidence are aspects of integrity. We might think of courage as integrity under fire. In addressing a military audience, Rand explained "the defense of one's country means that a man is personally unwilling to live as the conquered slave of any enemy, foreign or domestic" ("Philosophy: Who Needs It" *PWNI* 14).

It may seem like a contradiction that an egoist, who holds his life as his highest value, could risk or even lay down that very life, but remember that life is not the absence of death; it is a specific *process* of self-sustaining action. Because of this, the fundamental values that are necessary to sustain a life are thereby part of that life. This applies not only to the abstract values that are listed in a moral code, but also to the concrete values that make up an individual's life. Once a person forms such values, his refusal to go on without them is not a renunciation of his life, but a recognition that that life is no longer possible. Perhaps the clearest example of this is a person slowly dying of cancer, who chooses to end his life rather than suffer excruciating pain, or go on in a half-comatose drugged state. He is doing so out of *love of life*. What he values – life, liv*ing* – is not possible any longer, and what remains is only death, however slow. Similarly, a person who understands and values freedom will recognize that *living* is not possible if one is a slave or a subject in a dictatorship, and so he will prefer death to such a fate. Thus Galt, when threatened by a dictator, who asks if he wants to live, responds: "Passionately ... And because I want it so much, I will accept no substitute" (*Atlas* 1104). Speaking of young protestors who were willing to face a firing squad for defying the Soviet Union, Rand wrote: "they are moved by the noblest form of *metaphysical* self-preservation: the refusal to commit spiritual suicide by abnegating one's own mind and to survive as a lobotomized automaton" ("The Inexplicable Personal Alchemy" *ROTP* 124).[58]

More generally, a person of integrity will be unwilling to stand idly by while one of his highest values is destroyed. Thus he might give his life to protect someone he loves – as Galt says he would in a powerful scene from *Atlas Shrugged* (1091). Likewise, an airline pilot or ship captain, who has chosen a profession in which he is responsible for the lives of others, might choose to give his life to save a passenger. Psychologically, we are talking about situations in which an individual is not willing to go on living having abandoned the person he loved, the cause to which he dedicated his life, or the commitments inherent in his chosen profession.[59] Philosophically, in such situations, the ultimate value of one's life as a rational being is no longer possible; just as in the cancer case, *there is no longer any goal for the sake of which to act.*

However, it is only in circumstances where successful living is impossible (or may become so) that Rand thinks it is necessary or appropriate to lay down one's life, and such circumstances are rare, even in military life. The world and human nature are such that success and happiness are to be expected, if one practices the virtues human life requires. Accordingly, Rand sees integrity (including courage) not as something that may require one to forfeit one's life, but as the fortitude required to live and enjoy it.

We can think of independence and integrity as the "backbone" of Rand's morality – they are what enable a person to remain firm, rather than bending to pressure from other people or from emotionally difficult circumstances. The virtue of honesty serves a different function: it is morality's *monitor*. Galt describes the virtue as the "the recognition of the fact that you cannot fake existence" and that "the unreal is unreal and can have no value" (*Atlas* 1019).

In essentials, honesty is about remaining in full cognitive contact with reality, rather than engaging in pretense (whether to oneself or to others). Since pretense doesn't alter the facts about which one is pretending, it only undermines one's ability to deal with them. It is easiest to grasp this point in cases of deceiving oneself, but Rand holds that it applies also to attempts to attain values by deceiving others. We can see her reasons for thinking this in Peikoff's summary of a conversation she had with him on the subject.

> "The essence of a con-man's lie," she began, "of any such lie, no matter what the details, is the attempt to gain a value by faking certain facts of reality."
> She went on: "Now can't you grasp the logical consequences of that kind of policy? Since all facts of reality are interrelated, faking one of them leads the person to fake others; ultimately, he is committed to an all-out war against reality as such. But this is the kind of war no one can win. If life in reality is a man's purpose, how can he expect to achieve it while struggling at the same time to escape and defeat reality?"
> And she concluded: "The con-man's lies are wrong on *principle*. To state the principle positively: honesty is a long-range requirement of human self-preservation and is, therefore, a moral obligation." ("My Thirty Years with Ayn Rand" *VOR* 340; cf., *OPAR* 270–271 and Peikoff 2012a, 99–100)

In violating this principle, a liar places himself at the mercy of his victims' failure to notice these facts. He is "a dependent on the stupidity of others" (*Atlas* 1019). Thus Galt concludes that "honesty is not a social duty, not a sacrifice for the sake of others, but the most profoundly selfish virtue man can practice: his refusal to sacrifice the reality of his own existence to the deluded consciousness of others" (*Atlas* 1019).

Because dishonesty is self-destructive, and because a rational person never evaluates anything in isolation from its causes and effects, Rand denied that dishonestly attained goals are genuine values: "neither love nor fame nor cash is a value if obtained by fraud" (*Atlas* 1019). Though Rand speaks specifically about fraud in this case, the point is meant to apply to all forms of dishonesty. One striking feature of Rand's heroes is their recognition that things that would otherwise be great values would be entirely undermined if they were attained by faking reality. Galt, for example, insists that Dagny fully acknowledge all of the painful consequences of a decision he desperately wants her to make: "Nobody stays in this valley except by a full, conscious choice based on a full, conscious knowledge of every fact involved in his decision. Nobody stays here by faking reality in any manner whatever" (*Atlas* 794; cf. *Fountainhead*, 387–388).

The honesty Galt demands goes beyond merely abstaining from overt lies (to oneself or others). It involves actively seeking out and attending to any uncomfortable facts that are relevant to one's values and decisions. There is a striking example of this policy earlier in the novel: Rearden, after deciding on a course of action that he (mistakenly) believes is immoral, names the nature of his supposed sin, saying "I want no self-deception about it" (*Atlas* 254; cf., *Anthem* 17–18). This honesty enables him to eventually recognize the error in his moral views.[60]

Galt treats injustice as a special case of faking reality – of pretending that a person's character is other than it is. It is "moral counterfeiting," he says "to withhold your contempt from men's vices" and "moral embezzlement" to "withhold your admiration from their virtues." The virtue of justice "is the recognition of the fact that you cannot fake the character of men as you cannot fake the character of nature, that you must judge all men as conscientiously as you judge inanimate objects." It demands "that every man must be judged for what he *is* and treated accordingly" (*Atlas* 1019–1020).[61]

Justice is selfish because vicious people are destructive and the rationally selfish actions of other virtuous people produce tremendous values that can further one's own life in all the ways we discussed earlier. When we judge people by rational moral standards and reward the good and penalize the evil, as appropriate, we benefit ourselves by helping good people to flourish and leaving evil people to destroy themselves.

Since evil is irrationality, it is fundamentally impotent. Left to his own devices, an evil person will perish. He can survive only as a parasite on other, moral people, by consuming the values they produce and deflecting the destructive consequences of his actions on to them. No one can get away with existing in this manner for long, unless (otherwise) moral people unjustly allow him to, granting him what Rand calls "the sanction of the victim."[62]

Rand's conception of justice and the facts it recognizes is powerfully illustrated in *Atlas Shrugged*. The novel depicts an unjust society which, rather than treating the heroes as they deserve, condemns their virtues as vices and demands or compels them to sacrifice the products of their virtue. The heroes suffer both materially and spiritually because of their failures to recognize fully the evil of the society and to treat it accordingly. This error leads these heroes to put their virtue at the service of others' vices, and to take upon themselves the destructive consequences of the villains' actions. Galt recognizes the evil of the society, and that it is only made possible by the sanction of the victim. The strike he calls is an act of justice, and when the last of the heroes recognizes this and joins him, the evil society collapses, the villains are left with no means of survival, and the road is cleared for a new and just society.[63]

As the examples from *Atlas* indicate, Rand had distinctive views about the implications of justice (and rationality, more broadly) for what sort of personal relationships and what sorts of societies are moral – that is, compatible with the requirements of man's life. She held that justice requires that we treat other people as "ends in themselves" rather than as means to our own ends. This means dealing with them as traders, appealing to their rationality and self-interest by offering values one has created in exchange for the values one seeks. "Moochers" and "looters" violate this "trader principle" by seeking or seizing unearned benefits from others. Such parasitism is self-destructive, because it gives the producers on whom the parasites depend every reason to turn away from them or against them, as the virtue of justice demands. Galt's strike in *Atlas Shrugged* is a grand-scale illustration of this point, and the novel includes many smaller-scale illustrations.[64] I will not explore this point here, however, because Darryl Wright discusses it at length in Chapter 7, below.

I have had to be brief in my treatment of all seven virtues. More extensive discussions of Rand's view of them can be found in *OPAR* ch. 8 and in Tara Smith (2006). It should be clear from what I have said, however, why Rand views each of the virtues as a way of acting that is required by human survival and that flows from recognizing a fact about the relation between consciousness and existence.

The facts themselves are elaborations of "the primacy of existence": the metaphysical foundation of Rand's philosophy that she expresses in the form of the axiom that "existence exists." This is why Galt says (in the lines immediately preceding our epigraph) that his morality proceeds from "a single axiom: existence exists – and in a single choice: to live." As Jason Rheins discusses in Chapter 11 of this volume, Rand argues that the truth of this metaphysics is self-evident, but its application in different domains and in specific fields and circumstances is not always obvious and is never entirely automatic. A firm and deep grasp of these facts – the sort of grasp needed to guide and motivate a person in the actions that are needed to sustain his life – takes the form of states of character that are developed and sustained by the consistent choice to focus his mind, to discover the values that his life and happiness require, and to work to achieve them.

Morality and Heroism

In "About the Author," at the back of *Atlas Shrugged*, Ayn Rand is quoted as saying: "My philosophy, in essence, is the concept of man as a heroic being, with his own happiness as the moral purpose of his life, with productive achievement as his noblest activity, and reason as his only absolute" (*Atlas* 1070–1071). In this chapter we have explored Rand's view of "man's life," including how it involves holding one's own happiness as one's moral purpose, organizing one's life around a productive purpose, and maintaining an absolute commitment to reason. I would like to close by looking at her idea that such a life is heroic.

When we think of heroes, we think first of the old myths about people who performed extraordinary, even superhuman feats of courage under immensely threatening circumstances. This comes from a time when martial courage was viewed as the primary virtue. We should now generalize to all the moral virtues. Heroic *acts* are those that a person takes to pursue or defend profound values, in the most demanding circumstances. As such these acts epitomize moral virtue. But the values in which one's life consists and the virtues needed to gain and keep these values are needed not only on rare occasions, but as a consistent way of life. Man's life, as

Rand understands it, requires *a dedication to a moral ideal* – and this dedication is central to her conception of moral heroism.

We have seen both how demanding the life Rand advocates is and why she thinks that it is *selfish* to meet these demands. People who consistently think for themselves, who take full responsibility for their own lives, who are dedicated to a productive career at their highest level of ability, who pursue with intensity rationally chosen values in all aspects of life, who hold to the highest integrity and the most demanding standards throughout their lives, are moral heroes. We usually reserve the term "heroic" for those acts that are the *most* demanding, that overcome the greatest threats or temptations in the direst circumstances. But life is not primarily about such emergency situations, and the deepest heroism is exemplified in a person's pursuit of happiness *across a life*.

Most people give up their happiness and undermine their lives in big or little ways. They give up a career or love relationship because their parents disapprove. Or they adhere meekly to conventions to avoid offending their peers or relatives. Or they sacrifice something of great personal value in order to be a good Christian or Jew, or a good altruist of some other stripe. Or they just meander passively and purposelessly through their days. To care deeply and consistently about one's happiness, one must use one's mind to identify with full honesty what life requires and what one wants out of life, and then to pursue steadily the life one has chosen, steering clear of countless easier, more passive and life-denying options. This is the heroism that Ayn Rand celebrates.

What "heroism" names is not the perspective the moral person takes on himself, but his *exemplification* of a moral ideal. The hero's aim is not to be an example: he seeks only to achieve his highest values, living up to the exacting standards that he knows this achievement requires; but, in doing this, he exemplifies an ideal to which we can aspire and from which we can draw inspiration.

The term "hero" designates the exceptional, but this need not be a statistical exception. A rational ideal is the exceptional as measured against all other possibilities taken together. But Rand thinks that, as a *rational ideal*, her vision of moral greatness is open to everyone. With this issue in mind, I would like to conclude with a passage from the end of Galt's radio speech. Galt is addressing "those heroes who might still be hidden in the world," but through Galt, Rand is speaking to the potential for heroism in each of us.

In the name of the best within you, do not sacrifice this world to those who are its worst. In the name of the values that keep you alive, do not let your vision of man be distorted by the ugly, the cowardly, the mindless in those who have never achieved his title. Do not lose your knowledge that man's proper estate is an upright posture, an intransigent mind and a step that travels unlimited roads. Do not let your fire go out, spark by irreplaceable spark, in the hopeless swamps of the approximate, the not-quite, the not-yet, the not-at-all. Do not let the hero in your soul perish, in lonely frustration for the life you deserved, but have never been able to reach. Check your road and the nature of your battle. The world you desired can be won, it exists, it is real, it is possible, it's yours.

But to win it requires your total dedication and a total break with the world of your past, with the doctrine that man is a sacrificial animal who exists for the pleasure of others. Fight for the value of your person. Fight for the virtue of your pride. Fight for the essence of that which is man: for his sovereign rational mind. Fight with the radiant certainty and the absolute rectitude of knowing that yours is the Morality of Life and that yours is the battle for any achievement, any value, any grandeur, any goodness, any joy that has ever existed on this earth. (*Atlas* 1069)

Notes

1 [Note by Gregory Salmieri: Allan Gotthelf passed away before completing this chapter. There were several unwritten portions of the outline, which (in accordance with his wishes) I filled in after his death. Wherever possible, I did this by adapting material he had written earlier for other purposes (including lectures and correspondence). But substantial revision was required to fit this material into its new context and to bring the chapter as a whole into a state that (I believe) Allan would have been happy with. In some cases, I have had to supply points or formulations of my own. I am confident from years of collaboration with Allan that he would approve of my edits and additions, but he did not have the opportunity to do so. I have retained Allan's voice throughout, because in substance the chapter remains his; and in the few cases where I know he and I disagreed on how to present a point, it is his view that I followed, rather than my own. I have taken the liberty of speaking for myself in some of the notes. Those in which I do so are enclosed (like this one) in square brackets. I'd like to thank Harry Binswanger, Jim Lennox, and Robert Mayhew for comments that helped me in my revisions of the chapter, and, on Allan's behalf, I'd like to thank Cass Love and Mary Ann Sures for the feedback they gave him on his outlines and partial drafts.]

2 In speaking of a new concept of morality, Rand does not seem to have drawn a distinction between concepts and conceptions (as, for example, Rawls does in *A Theory of Justice*, 5–6). People who do draw such a distinction might think of what Rand is presenting as a new *conception* of morality – a new way of understanding a single concept that she shares with earlier theorists. I doubt that she would agree with this. Though (as we will see) she identifies commonalities between the different "concepts of morality" that makes them in an important sense share a subject matter, it is not clear that she would have regarded these commonalities as sufficient to warrant a common concept. These same points apply also to Rand's description (in the subtitle of *VOS*) of her moral theory as "a new concept of egoism."

3 [Because Galt is addressing a general audience, he speaks to the views of morality that are held by laypeople and that direct their actions. Elsewhere, Rand addresses the moral theories formulated by philosophers including Kant, Comte, and Mill, arguing that they are all variations on this theme of sacrifice of the individual's interest to some arbitrary and undefinable end that is allegedly higher than one's own life and happiness. On Rand's criticism of these ethicists, see, in the present volume 139–141 and 333–334; see also Wright 2011a.]

4 On Rand's view of objectivity, see Salmieri's discussions in this volume: 67–68 and 290–292.

5 The view that one's interests are objective and can only be achieved by following a demanding moral code was shared by the main tradition of Ancient Greek ethicists. On how Rand's view relates to this tradition, see 134–135, below; see also Wright 2011a, 9–11.

6 [The different formulations reflect the different contexts. In *Atlas*, Galt is distinguishing morality from the "codes" that determine the life-courses of other living things whose goals and actions are set by automatic (physiological or psychological) mechanisms, thus he stresses *choice* and takes the life-directing character of morality for granted.]

7 On "whim-worship" see "An Open Letter to Boris Spassky" (*PWNI* 77), "Selfishness Without a Self" (*PWNI* 68–69), *Journals* 689, and *OPAR* 228.

8 Rand's fullest treatment of this issue, especially as it relates to Kant's ethics, is her essay "Causality vs. Duty" (*PWNI*). For discussion of how the point applies to a range of classic ethical theories, see also Wright 2011a, 4–8.

9 Rand's statement about "today's moralists" should be read in the context of the moral philosophy of her time. This context is summed up nicely by Brian Medlin (1957, 111) in the first sentence of an article published just two months before *Atlas Shrugged*: "I believe that it is now pretty generally accepted by professional philosophers that ultimate ethical principles must be arbitrary." Such explicit subjectivism about ethical principles has receded over the past half-century (among academic philosophers writing in English, at any rate), but Rand would have regarded most of the views that have replaced it as involving less overt forms of non-objectivity, for she made similar criticisms of Aristotle, Hume, and Kant who are the primary inspirations for most of the work being done in ethics today.

10 [*Atlas* 991–994 is a touching description of a death that emphasizes some of the differences between life and inanimate matter that Galt describes in his speech.]

11 [This is true, Rand maintained, whether life is an emergent property or an irreducible primary: "We know the facts, we observe its existence and its attribute, but we do not know what constitutes life. If you took the purely materialistic position that life is only matter of a very complex organism which [at] a certain stage of complete complexity, acquires the attributes which we call a living organism, or whether it's an element of some kind which is not mystical, but which is not the same as what we understand by 'material' elements. ... In either case it still remains true, whether it's merely the ... complex organization that is destroyed, or the special element that's present in the living entities, and vanishes. In both cases, that which we call life in a material entity, that does go out of existence, qua life" (*Workshops* 289; ellipses represent material that is difficult to discern on the recording).]

12 [One might think that the same points apply to machines and to some non-living natural systems (e.g., perhaps, solar systems). I know of no case in which Rand discusses the seeming integration of such natural systems. Machines, of course, owe their integration to human beings, and Rand some-times speaks of them as being alive in an extended sense: "they *are* alive [Dagny] thought, because they are the physical shape of the action of a living power – of the mind that had been able to grasp the whole of this complexity, to set its purpose, to give it form. ... They *are* alive, she thought, but their soul operates them by remote control. Their soul is in every man who has the capacity to equal this achievement" (*Atlas* 246). Though not exactly literal, I think such ascriptions of life to machines here is more than mere metaphor; the machines have the attributes of life in a derivative way, because of the relationship in which the machines stand to the human beings who create, sustain, and operate them.]

13 The example is developed further by Leonard Peikoff (*OPAR* 209–211), who addresses counter-arguments that psychological factors could provide a basis for values apart from their relation to life. See also Tara Smith's (2000, 87–90) discussion of why an immortal being could not have values.

14 [This is Rand's answer to Hume's famous challenge that it is impossible to derive an "ought" from an "is" – i.e., a normative statement from a descriptive one. In two respects Rand's response to this challenge is similar to the one made by G.E.M. Anscombe (1958), in her classic paper "Modern Moral Philosophy." First, Hume's argument assumes that the only way to rationally derive an "ought" would be via a *deduction* with a normative conclusion and descriptive premises. Both Rand and Anscombe show that there are other ways in which a normative conceptualization of a fact can be rationally based on a more primitive descriptive conceptualization of it. Rand, as we've seen, writes of facts giving rise to the need for new concepts, and Anscombe writes of the "relative bruteness" of different descriptions. Second, both thinkers focus on the *needs of organisms*. (See esp. Anscombe 1958, 7–8.) Later followers of Anscombe have further developed the very Rand-like idea that each species has a distinctive *form of life*, and that morality is based in the distinctively human form. (See Foot 2003, Hursthouse 2002, and Thompson 2008.) There is no evidence that either Rand or Anscombe was familiar with the other's work; the similarities between them may be due to the common influence of Aristotle.]

15 [This formulation is often quoted as Rand's "definition" of life, but Harry Binswanger reports that she insisted to him that it was not intended as a definition.]

16 [One might object that life includes many actions aimed, not at the organism's own survival, but at reproduction or at the survival of its species (or its genes). Rand did not discuss such cases herself, but Binswanger (1990, 153–173) argues that all such actions can be understood as required for the in-dividual organism's life, since its life depends on other members of its species engaging in the actions, and (barring mutation) it cannot avoid acting in the way that is characteristic of its species. We might also take these considerations to show that, for species whose actions are selected by deterministic mechanisms, there are sometimes ambiguities about whether the individual organism or the species (or family) is the unit of life. Such ambiguities do not arise in the case of human life (on Rand's view, at least), because human action is directed by the faculty of reason, which is an attribute of the indi-vidual and functions by free will. If a human being reproduces or assists others, he does so by *choice*; and Rand holds that he should only make this choice when he has egoistic reasons for doing so. For

her view of why helping someone could be in one's interest, see below, 88–89; cf. Darryl Wright's discussion of benevolence, below, 161–163. On the value of children to a parent, see n. 43.]

17 Variants of this view can be found in Rasmussen 2002, 2006, 2007a, 2007b, and the sources cited in n. 18, below.

18 [The version of the objection presented here is a condensation of material from a talk Gotthelf delivered several times in the mid-1960s. In that talk, he speaks of "students of Objectivism" who, because they do "not fully understand the essence of the Objectivist ethics," "suddenly switch to speaking about 'the life proper to man' or 'life *qua* man'," when they are asked to explain how Rand's ethics is compatible with the fact that some vicious people live long lives. To my knowledge, this objection had not yet appeared in print, and Gotthelf may have originated it. In any case, the equivocation has since often been attributed to Rand by commentators who interpret her in the way Gotthelf warned against. For example Eric Mack (1984 and 2003) charges Rand with "shuffling" between different concepts of "life." Variants of this same objection can be found in Badhwar 1999 and 2001 and Long 2000 and 2010 and Badhwar and Long 2012.]

19 Cf. Lennox's (1995, 502) definition: Health "refers to that state of affairs in which the biological activities of a specific kind of living thing are operating within the ranges which contribute to continued, uncompromised living."

20 Branden briefly discusses a similar example in *WIAR* 26.

21 A number of scholars have described the state of successful living (of which happiness is the experience) as "flourishing." See Smith 2000, ch. 5, Hunt 1999, Miller 2005, Den Uyl and Rasmussen 1984b, 68; cf. Moen 2012, 105. The term is borrowed from Aristotelian scholarship, where it was introduced as a translation for the Greek term *eudaimonia*, which traditionally was translated "happiness" and which Aristotle equates with "living well" (*Nicomachean Ethics* 1095a19–20). (See esp. Cooper 1975, 89–90, n. 1.) Aristotle distinguishes what is required for *eudaimonia* (or "living well") from what is required for living (*Politics* 1257b41–58a1). Because of this, if one uses the term "flourishing" in connection with Rand's ethics, one must take great care not to obscure her view that the contents of a "flourishing" life can be defined only by reference to the requirements for survival.

22 As Darryl Wright (2011a, 12, n. 7) observes, in response to my earlier statement of this point about "fundamental values" in Gotthelf 2000 (83), neither I nor he (nor Rand) means to limit this point to the three cardinal values. See his discussion, with useful examples, and his reference to *Journals* 78–79.

23 On the relation between reason and emotion, see, in the present volume, 50 and 114–116; on reason's volitional character, see 63–68 and 107–112; and on the role of free will in Rand's metaphysics, see 260–264.

24 For a detailed account of what the process of thought involves, according to Rand – its basis in sense-perception, its active formation and use of concepts, the hierarchical character of these concepts, and their integration into propositions and bodies of propositional knowledge – see Gregory Salmieri's Chapter 12 below on "Objectivist Epistemology." In *VOS* Rand summarizes the heart of this process, calling it *conceptualization* ("The Objectivist Ethics" *VOS* 21–22, quoted and discussed by Salmieri, 289). On the volitional character of thought, see Salmieri's discussion (291–292), and especially Onkar Ghate's Chapter 5, "A Being of Self-Made Soul," below. On volition and causality, see Jason Rheins's discussion below, 260–262.

25 Salmieri 2009a describes this progression in detail.

26 See Wright 2011a and Salmieri 2009a, 236–247.

27 On this point, see also Branden, "The Divine Right of Stagnation" (*VOS* 141–143).

28 In the section below on "The Range of Life-Sustaining Values," we will see in greater detail how a productive purpose "integrates and determines" one's other values. However it is worth mentioning here that these other values are not all *means to* the central purpose nor do they all follow deductively from it.

29 See *OPAR* 301–302. Moreover, a wealthy person will need to productively manage his wealth, or he will soon lose it. See Branden, "Common Fallacies about Capitalism" (*CUI* 96–99, cf. Salmieri 2009a 228–229).

30 There are several characters in Rand's novels that are examples of this: I single out Eddie Willers and Rearden's secretary, Gwen Ives, in *Atlas*, and Mike Donnigan, Roark's friend the electrician, in *The Fountainhead*.

31 Of course the idea that parenting is a career presupposes that children can be a rational (selfish) value. On this point see n. 43 below.

32 See, e.g., in *Atlas*, Rearden and Dagny's certainty about the effectiveness and value of Rearden Metal and Eddie Willers's certainty in his dealings with James Taggart (e.g., *Atlas* 7–11). Indeed, as we shall see in a moment, the villains in *Atlas Shrugged* attempt to control the good characters by attacking their self-esteem (below, 86).

33 For discussion of Rearden's guilt, see Salmieri 2009b, 403–420. Another example in *Atlas* of this phenomenon is the exploitation of Cherryl Brooks first by her family and later by her husband, Jim Taggart. See *Atlas* 891.

34 On the centrality of pride and self-esteem to *Atlas*, see Ghate 2011.

35 See also Peikoff, on the range of man's proper purposefulness: "Whether in regard to *work or friends, love or art, entertainment or vacations,* he knows what he likes and why, then goes after it" (*OPAR* 297, my emphasis).

36 In the context of speaking of sex as a response to *"admiration"* – "the pleasure [one] takes in the character and achievement of another human being" – Branden observes that "of the pleasures that man can offer himself, the greatest is *pride* – the pleasure he takes in his own achievements and in the creation of his own character" (*VOS* 76). In related contexts, Rand sometimes writes of "values of character" (*Atlas* 1020, 1171, "The Goal of My Writing" *RM* 162; cf. "Philosophy and Sense of Life" *RM* 22).

37 See esp. *Atlas* 102–104, 367–378, and the discussion in Salmieri 2009a, 240–242.

38 On such "neurotic" forms of recreation, see Branden (*VOS* 75).

39 Some examples of the joy Rand's protagonists take in sights of achievement (on all scales) and their hunger for such sights can be found in *Atlas* 4, 65–67, 236–250, *Fountainhead* 527–530. For examples of their concern for victims see *Atlas* 581, 887–892. For an example of enthusiasm over shared values, see *Atlas* 61–62, 332.

40 See "The 'Conflicts' of Men's Interests" (*VOS*) and Darryl Wright's discussion of this issue, 167–172, below.

41 Rand's fullest discussion of this point is in "The Psycho-Epistemology of Art" (*RM*). See Harry Binswanger's discussion in 408–413, below.

42 Branden, "Self-Esteem and Romantic Love" (*TO* 6(12)–7(2)); see also his earlier treatment in "Benevolence versus Altruism" (*TON* 1(7), cf. Gotthelf 1998).

43 [One might wonder how Rand's theory of the value of relationships applies in the case of children, who have not yet developed their own values. Rand didn't write about this issue directly, but it is clear from her novels that she regarded children as potentially a great value. One of her heroes speaks specifically of his desire to have children (*Anthem* 99, 100, 104); her novels include several other characters whose love for their children is depicted as a sympathetic (even redeeming) feature, e.g., Guy Francon (*Fountainhead* 142–143, 703–704, 706); and Galt describes parents who do not value their children as immoral (*Atlas* 1029, cf. Wright 2011b, 102–108). Several pieces that Rand wrote or endorsed also give indications about her views on the value of children. Among these are a brief piece by Branden on the question of "the respective obligations of parents to children, and children to parents" (*TON* 1(12)), Rand's essay "The Comprachicos" (*VOR*), in which she discusses the state of modern education, Beatrice Hessen's "The Montessori Method" (*TO* 9(5–7)), Hessen's reviews of Joan Beck's *How to Raise a Brighter Child* (*TO* 7(9)), Elizabeth G. Hainstock's *Teaching Montessori in the Home* (*TO* 10(7)), and a 10-lecture course given by Reva Fox at the Nathaniel Branden Institute on the "Principles of Child Rearing," of which, to my knowledge, only the brochure (*Papers* 117_05B_013) survives. The view that emerges from these pieces is that children embody the human potential that all rational people value as an extension of valuing their own life. (See Darryl Wright's discussion of the value of the human potential, 162, below.)

Rand saw children's efforts to learn and the delight they take in doing so as epitomizing the best in human beings: "I will ask you to project the look on a child's face when he grasps the answer to some problem he has been striving to understand. It is a radiant look of joy, of liberation, almost of triumph, which is unself-conscious, yet self-assertive, and its radiance seems to spread in two directions: outward, as an illumination of the world – inward, as the first spark of what is to become the fire of an earned pride. If you have seen this look, or experienced it, you know that if there is such a concept as 'sacred' – meaning: the best, the highest possible to man – this look is the sacred, the not-to-be-betrayed, the not-to-be-sacrificed for anything or anyone" ("Requiem for Man" *CUI* 347–348).

This generic love of the human potential and its exercise and development is surely only part of the root of a parent's love for his child. If the child is his own biologically and the result of a loving relationship, the parent will soon identify in this generic potential countless small individuating features that he values in himself and his lover, and whether or not the child is biologically his, as she grows he will also observe in the child many learned characteristics he (and, if applicable, his partner) have passed on. Because of the closeness of the parent–child relationship, he will have a unique and potentially joyous perspective on the child's development of her own distinctive character, and on the specific role in this developing character of the values he cherishes in himself (and, if applicable, his partner). Thus, though the love of a parent for a child is importantly different from the love Rand discusses between adults, it is not difficult to see in outline how her theory of love can be applied in the special case of parental love.]

44 On sense of life see, in the present volume, 118–123 and 417–419.

45 Of course, there are other factors relevant to sexual attraction as well – most obviously, gender.

46 On this point, see especially Salmieri 2009a, 240–41 and Gotthelf 2009b.

47 On this and other related aspects of Rearden's development, see Salmieri 2009b, 403–420.

48 For a detailed discussion of the selfishness of friendship on Rand's view, and the objection that this view makes friends merely instrumental values, see Smith 2006, 287–304, along with Cullyer's (2011) comments and Smith's (2011a) reply.

49 An example of a value that may be an important part of someone's life without fitting straightforwardly into any of the spheres discussed above is the value certain individuals place on their way of dressing, and in general on their appearance. They might take great pride and personal pleasure in particular items of clothing and the way they match or fit them.

50 E.g., *OPAR* 323; cf. "Of Living Death" (*VOR* 55), Smith 2000, Index s.v. value(s): as optional; Smith 2006, Index s.v. values: optional values. There is also an excellent informal discussion in Peikoff 2012a, 329–341.

51 See Tore Boeckmann's discussion (436, below) of how emphases on different moral values and virtues are among the individualizing touches in Rand's characterization of her heroes.

52 For examples of this sort of immorality, see *Fountainhead* 20, 309.

53 See *Atlas* 1018–1021, where she describes each virtue as the recognition of facts, and *VOS* 28–30, where she describes rationality, productiveness, and pride as recognitions of facts.

54 Rosalind Hursthouse (2012) writes that "Virtue ethics may, initially, be identified as the [approach to normative ethics] that emphasizes the virtues, or moral character, in contrast to the approach which emphasizes duties or rules (deontology) or that which emphasizes the consequences of actions (consequentialism)." This, I may say, is a weak sense of "virtue ethics." (Notice that an ethical theory can emphasize *both* virtues and consequences.) In a stronger sense it may be defined as an approach which treats virtue as a primary concept in ethics, defining or understanding all other ethical concepts in terms of it. A good example of this stronger sense can be found in Christine Swanton's (2013, 338, n. 8) response to Robert Solomon's (2003, 140) characterization of the position she took in her (2003) book: "R. Solomon describes my view as understanding virtues as dispositions to be in various kinds of ways responsive to 'an independently justified set of values.' If that were my view, it would not be virtue ethical on this account, for it would not be even weakly virtue notion-centered."

55 On the relation between virtues as types of actions or as dispositions to act and feel in certain ways, see Smith 2006, 50–52, Hunt 2011, and Smith 2011b.

56 In correspondence, Christine Swanton has said that she does view Rand's ethics as a virtue ethics, because "I think for Rand central values are aretaic, i.e., not understood *entirely* independent of virtue" (cf. Swanton 2011a and 2011b). On this matter, however, see Tara Smith's (2011c) reply to Swanton.

57 As Salmieri explains, above, 50, this is the significance of the word "living" in the title of Rand's first novel, *We the Living*. The other early work in which this theme is most prominent is *Ideal*. For discussion, see Peikoff's introduction, *Plays* 92. On this theme in Rand's early work generally see Wright 2005, esp. 191–209.

58 It is evident from this same article (and from her own life) that Rand did not think that one is morally obligated to risk one's life to speak out in a dictatorship, and she thought it is imprudent to do so if one did not have reason to think that anything would be accomplished by it, especially if, by remaining silent, one may be able either to help overthrow the regime or to escape.

59 On the issue of risking one's life, see Branden, "The Moral Meaning of Risking One's Life" (*TON* 3(4) 15–16).

60 On Rearden's development, see Salmieri 2009b, 403–420. On the (related) development of the hero of *Anthem*, see Salmieri 2005, esp. 262–264.

61 Cf. *ITOE* 51, where Rand says that the concept of "justice" designates "the act of judging a man's character and/or actions exclusively on the basis of all the factual evidence available, and of evaluating it by means of an objective moral criterion." Also see *Atlas* 737: "justice is the act of acknowledging that which exists."

62 On the sanction of the victim, see *Atlas* 454, 470, 740; *FTNI* 47; "The Wreckage of the Consensus" (*CUI* 264); "The Principals ..." (*ARL* 2(2) 218); "The Sanction of the Victims" (*TOF* 3(1)).

63 See Salmieri 2009b, 436–450 and Smith 2009a.

64 For example, see *Atlas* 81, 916–918, 932–933, and 968–976.

References

Anscombe, G.E.M. 1958. "Modern Moral Philosophy." *Philosophy*, 33.

Badhwar, Neera K. 1999. "Is Virtue Only a Means to Happiness? An Analysis of Virtue and Happiness in Ayn Rand's Writings." *Reason Papers*, 24.

Badhwar, Neera K. 2001. *Is Virtue Only a Means to Happiness? An Analysis of Virtue and Happiness in Ayn Rand's Writings*. Poughkeepsie, NY: Objectivist Center.

Badhwar, Neera, and Roderick Long. 2012. "Ayn Rand." Stanford Encyclopedia of Philosophy. http://plato.stanford.edu/entries/ayn-rand/ (accessed June 1, 2015).

Binswanger, Harry. 1990. *The Biological Basis of Teleological Concepts*. Los Angeles, CA: Ayn Rand Institute Press.

Binswanger, Harry. 1992. "Life Based Teleology and the Foundations of Ethics." *Monist*, 75(1).

Cooper, John M. 1975. *Reason and Human Good in Aristotle*. Cambridge, MA: Harvard University Press.

Cullyer, Helen. 2011. "Rational Selves, Friends, and the Social Virtues." In Gotthelf and Lennox 2011.

Den Uyl, Douglas J., and Douglas B. Rasmussen, eds. 1984a. *The Philosophic Thought of Ayn Rand*. Champaign, IL: University of Illinois Press.

Den Uyl, Douglas J., and Douglas B. Rasmussen. 1984b. "Life, Teleology, and Eudaimonia in the Ethics of Ayn Rand." In Den Uyl and Rasmussen 1984a.

Foot, Philippa. 2003. *Natural Goodness*. Oxford: Oxford University Press.

Ghate, Onkar. 2011. "*Atlas Shrugged*: America's Second Declaration of Independence." In *Why Businessmen Need Philosophy*, edited by Debi Ghate and Richard E. Ralston. New York, NY: New American Library.

Gotthelf, Allan. 1998. "Love and Philosophy: Aristotelian vs. Platonic." Lecture. Recording available at https://estore.aynrand.org/p/376 (accessed June 1, 2015).

Gotthelf, Allan. 2000. *On Ayn Rand*. Belmont, CA: Wadsworth Publishing.

Gotthelf, Allan. 2009b. "A Note on Dagny's 'Final Choice'." In Mayhew 2009.

Gotthelf, Allan, ed., and James G. Lennox, assoc. ed. 2011. *Metaethics, Egoism and Virtue: Studies in Ayn Rand's Normative Theory*. Ayn Rand Society Philosophical Studies, vol. 1. Pittsburgh, PA: University of Pittsburgh Press.

Hunt, Lester. 1999. "Flourishing Egoism." *Social Philosophy and Policy*, 16.

Hunt, Lester. 2011. "What Is Included in Virtue?" In *Gotthelf and Lennox* 2011.

Hursthouse, Rosalind. 2002. *On Virtue Ethics*. Oxford: Oxford University Press.

Hursthouse, Rosalind. 2012. "Virtue Ethics." Stanford Encyclopedia of Philosophy. http://plato.stanford .edu/archives/sum2012/entries/ethics-virtue/ (accessed June 1, 2015).

Lennox, James G. 1995. "Health as an Objective Value." *Journal of Medicine and Philosophy*, 20(5).

Long, Roderick. 2000. *Reason and Value: Aristotle versus Rand*. Poughkeepsie, NY: Objectivist Center.

Long, Roderick. 2010. "The Winnowing of Ayn Rand." *Cato Unbound*. http://www.cato-unbound .org/2010/01/20/roderick-t-long/winnowing-ayn-rand (accessed June 1, 2015).

Mack, Eric. 1984. "The Fundamental Moral Elements of Rand's Theory of Rights." In Den Uyl and Rasmussen 1984a.

Mack, Eric. 2003. "Problematic Arguments in Randian Ethics." *Journal of Ayn Rand Studies*, 5(1).

Mayhew, Robert, ed. 2005. *Essays on Ayn Rand's* Anthem. Lanham, MD: Lexington Books.

Mayhew, Robert, ed. 2009. *Essays on Ayn Rand's* Atlas Shrugged. Lanham, MD: Lexington Books.

Medlin, Brian. 1957. "Ultimate Principles and Ethical Egoism." *Australasian Journal of Philosophy*, 35.

Miller, Fred. 2005. "Ayn Rand as Aristotelian: Values and Happiness." Paper presented to the Ayn Rand Society at the December 2005 Eastern Division Meeting of the American Philosophical Association.

Moen, Ole Martin. 2012. "Is Life the Ultimate Value? A Reassessment of Ayn Rand's Ethics." *Reason Papers*, 34.

Peikoff, Leonard. 2012a. *Understanding Objectivism: A Guide to Learning Ayn Rand's Philosophy*. Edited by Michael S. Berliner. New York, NY: New American Library.

Rasmussen, Douglas B. 2002. "Rand on Obligation and Value." *Journal of Ayn Rand Studies*, 4(1).

Rasmussen, Douglas B. 2006. "Regarding Choice and the Foundations of Morality: Reflection on Rand's Ethics." *Journal of Ayn Rand Studies*, 7(2).

Rasmussen, Douglas B. 2007a. "The Aristotelian Significance of the Section Titles of *Atlas Shrugged*: A Brief Consideration of Rand's View of Logic and Reality." In *Ayn Rand's Atlas Shrugged: A Philosophical and Literary Companion*, edited by Edward W. Younkins. Aldershot, UK: Ashgate.

Rasmussen, Douglas B. 2007b. "Rand's Metaethics: Rejoinder to Hartford." *Journal of Ayn Rand Studies*, 8(2).

Salmieri, Gregory. 2005. "Prometheus' Discovery: Individualism and the Meaning of the Concept 'I' in *Anthem*." In Mayhew 2005.

Salmieri, Gregory. 2009a. "*Atlas Shrugged* on the Role of the Mind in Man's Existence." In Mayhew 2009.

Salmieri, Gregory. 2009b. "Discovering Atlantis: *Atlas Shrugged*'s Demonstration of a New Moral Philosophy." In Mayhew 2009.

Smith, Tara. 2000. *Viable Values: A Study of Life as the Root and Reward of Morality*. Lanham, MD: Rowman & Littlefield.

Smith, Tara. 2006. *Ayn Rand's Normative Ethics: The Virtuous Egoist*. Cambridge: Cambridge University Press.

Smith, Tara. 2009a. "No Tributes to Caesar: Good or Evil in *Atlas Shrugged*." In Mayhew 2009.

Smith, Tara. 2011a. "Egoistic Relations with Others: Response to Cullyer." In Gotthelf and Lennox 2011.

Smith, Tara. 2011b. "The Primacy of Action in Virtue: Response to Hunt." In Gotthelf and Lennox 2011.

Smith, Tara. 2011c. "On Altruism, and on the Role of Virtues in Rand's Egoism." In Gotthelf and Lennox 2011.

Solomon, Robert C. 2003. *Living with Nietzsche: What the Great "Immoralist" Has to Teach Us*. Oxford: Oxford University Press.

Swanton, Christine. 2003. *Virtue Ethics: A Pluralistic Approach*. Oxford: Oxford University Press.

Swanton, Christine. 2011a. "Nietzsche and Rand as Virtuous Egoists." In Gotthelf and Lennox 2011.

Swanton, Christine. 2011b. "Virtuous Egoism and Virtuous Altruism." In Gotthelf and Lennox 2011.

Swanton, Christine. 2013. "The Definition of Virtue Ethics." In *The Cambridge Companion to Virtue Ethics*, edited by D. Russell. Cambridge: Cambridge University Press.

Thompson, Michael. 2008. *Life and Action*. Cambridge, MA: Harvard University Press.

Wright, Darryl. 2005. "Needs of the Psyche in Ayn Rand's Early Ethical Thought." In Mayhew 2005.

Wright, Darryl. 2011a. "Reasoning about Ends: Life as a Value in Ayn Rand's Ethics." In Gotthelf and Lennox 2011.

Wright, Darryl. 2011b. "Virtue and Sacrifice: Response to Swanton." In Gotthelf and Lennox 2011.

5

A Being of Self-Made Soul

ONKAR GHATE

As a novelist who self-consciously identified with the Romantic school of literature, Ayn Rand was intensely concerned with an individual's choices. She sought to understand the fundamental ideas, goals, and motives people hold and how these shape their actions, character, and happiness. As a philosopher who self-consciously originated a new system of thought, Rand was intensely interested in defining a new ideal for man to achieve. Concern for the ideal is what unites Rand's fiction and non-fiction. In both endeavors, Rand sought to understand what man is and what he can and ought to be.

In literature, Rand identified not only with the Romantic school in general, but with those she regarded as its highest exponents, particularly Victor Hugo.[1] These writers, she holds, are intensely concerned with choice both "in regard to consciousness and to existence, in regard to man's character and to his actions in the physical world." They are "*moralists* in the most profound sense of the word; their concern is not merely with values, but specifically with *moral* values and with the power of moral values in shaping human character" ("What Is Romanticism?" *RM* 99).[2]

Working within the basic principles of this literary school, Rand's particular purpose is "*the projection of an ideal man*," which means "the portrayal of a moral ideal … as an end in itself" ("The Goal of My Writing" *RM* 155). But since she disagreed with the conceptions of the moral ideal so far offered to man, she originated her own. Thus from the outset of her literary career Rand was simultaneously interested in philosophy.

> Since my purpose is the presentation of an ideal man, I had to define and present the conditions which make him possible and which his existence requires. *Since man's character is the product of his premises*, I had to define and present the kind of premises and values that create the character of an ideal man and motivate his actions. (*RM* 156–157, emphasis added)[3]

Rand argues that all individuals, as they mature into adulthood, form a set of implicit premises that represent a stand on the basic questions of philosophy. By an "implicit premise," Rand means a habitual way of facing and dealing with the world, which, if expressed in words, would be a philosophical premise.

A Companion to Ayn Rand, First Edition. Edited by Allan Gotthelf and Gregory Salmieri.
© 2016 John Wiley & Sons, Ltd. Published 2016 by John Wiley & Sons, Ltd.

> In the flux of a child's countless impressions and momentary conclusions, the crucial ones are those that pertain to the nature of the world around him, and to the efficacy of his mental efforts. The words that would name the essence of the long, wordless process taking place in a child's mind are two questions: Where am I? – and: Is it worth it?
>
> The child's answers are not set in words: they are set in the form of certain reactions which become habitual, i.e., automatized. He does not [for instance] conclude that the universe is "benevolent" and that thinking is important – he develops an eager curiosity about every new experience, and a desire to understand it. Subconsciously, in terms of automatized mental processes, he develops the implicit equivalent of two fundamental premises, which are the cornerstones of his future sense of life, i.e., of his *metaphysics* and *epistemology*, long before he is able to grasp such concepts consciously. ("The Comprachicos" *ROTP* 57)[4]

An individual's characteristic way(s) of dealing with the world, Rand holds (as we will see), is a product of his basic choices. The mind is an integrating mechanism, which sums up an individual's choices and conclusions into a way of facing existence. Part of the task of philosophy, on her view, is to help an individual take self-conscious control of the basic premises he is acquiring, to become a conscious self-programmer at this fundamental level.

> A philosophic system is an integrated view of existence. ... Your only choice is whether you define your philosophy by a conscious, rational, disciplined process of thought and scrupulously logical deliberation – or let your subconscious accumulate a junk heap of unwarranted conclusions, false generalizations, undefined contradictions, undigested slogans, unidentified wishes, doubts and fears, thrown together by chance, but integrated by your subconscious into a kind of mongrel philosophy ...
>
> You might say ... that it is not easy always to act on abstract principles. No, it is not easy. But how much harder is it, to have to act on them without knowing what they are? ("Philosophy: Who Needs It" *PWNI* 7)

Since "soul," in Rand's use of the term, refers to an individual's consciousness and its basic premises (including its basic value-judgments), we can state her point in different terms, terms Rand often used to capture a crucial principle of her philosophy: man is a being of self-made soul.

Consider the principle's significance to her ethics. The essence of morality, according to Rand, is *self*-preservation. The virtue of pride, therefore, takes on special importance for Rand. It is the virtue of building (or rebuilding) one's self in the image of an ideal.[5]

> Pride is the recognition of the fact that you are your own highest value and, like all of man's values, it has to be earned – that of any achievements open to you, the one that makes all others possible is the creation of your own character – that your character, your actions, your desires, your emotions are the products of the premises held by your mind – that as man must produce the physical values he needs to sustain his life, so he must acquire the values of character that make his life worth sustaining – that as man is a being of self-made wealth, so he is a being of self-made soul – that to live requires a sense of self-value, but man, who has no automatic values, has no automatic sense of self-esteem and must earn it by shaping his soul in the image of his moral ideal, in the image of Man, the rational being he is born able to create, but must create by choice. (*Atlas* 1020–1021)[6]

Thus for Rand man is a being of self-made soul in two senses. By his specific choices, man necessarily creates the kind of person he becomes: the basic premises and values that move him. And man's faculty of volition gives him the power to (re)shape his soul in the image of his moral ideal – a process which any individual concerned with his own self-preservation and happiness should strive to undertake.

Rand's writings on man's soul span the whole of her output, from *We the Living* in the 1930s to her non-fiction essays in the 1970s. But she developed her mature theories on this issue after finishing *The Fountainhead*. These theories are my focus. In particular, to understand Rand's view of man's soul, it is her theory of free will that we must understand. Once that is done (including considering some of the theory's direct implications for the nature and formation of a man's soul), we need to examine why, given the nature of man's free will, Rand holds that an individual by his choices develops an implicit philosophy. To do this, we need to consider three crucial issues in Rand's thought: her accounts of self-esteem (an individual's implicit evaluation of his self), of sense of life (an individual's implicit metaphysics), and of psycho-epistemology (an individual's implicit epistemology).[7]

Many of Rand's mature views on these issues were first presented in print by her student and junior colleague Nathaniel Branden and published under her editorship in *The Objectivist Newsletter* and *The Objectivist*; this is particularly true for Rand's theories of free will and self-esteem, topics which border on Branden's profession of psychology. I will refer to these essays extensively, treating them as quasi-primary.[8]

Free Will[9]

Like Aristotle and many subsequent philosophers, Rand holds that man's consciousness is born tabula rasa. An individual's consciousness begins, she writes, as a "superlative machine" ("The Objectivist Ethics" *VOS* 23) without any content, analogous to "a camera with an extremely sensitive, unexposed film (his conscious mind), and an extremely complex computer waiting to be programmed (his subconscious)" ("The Comprachicos" *ROTP* 54). Like any organism's consciousness, man's consciousness – his mind, his rational faculty – is his basic means of survival.[10]

But man possesses a control over his faculty of awareness that other organisms do not. "Nothing is given to man on earth except a potential and the material on which to actualize it," Rand writes. "The potential is a superlative machine: his consciousness; but it is a machine without a spark plug, a machine of which his own will has to be the spark plug, the self-starter and the driver; *he* has to discover how to use it and *he* has to keep it in constant action" (*VOS* 23). This, Rand holds, is the key to understanding man's nature: man must *will* his means of survival into action, that is, an individual must *choose* to activate the distinctively human level of awareness, the *conceptual* level.[11]

"The key to what you ... call 'human nature,'" Rand writes, "is the fact that *man is a being of volitional consciousness*. Reason does not work automatically; thinking is not a mechanical process; the connections of logic are not made by instinct. The function of your stomach, lungs or heart is automatic; the function of your mind is not" (*Atlas* 1012).[12]

As an advocate of free will, Rand of course holds that man has the power of *choice*: the power to *select* among alternatives, with no particular selection necessitated by antecedent factors.[13] Rand's theory of free will, therefore, is a version of self-determinism. Like any version of self-determinism, her theory raises significant metaphysical issues, including the relation of volition to the nature of consciousness and of causality, issues which I leave aside.[14] My concern is with Rand's account of the nature of man's choices, especially her view of the locus and extent of man's power of volition and how exercise of this power shapes an individual's soul.

Rand rejects any theory of volition that roots free will in a choice between particular items of mental *content*: whether to walk or ride the bus to work (selection between envisioned physical actions); whether to order the vanilla cheesecake because one is hungry or the bowl of mixed berries because one is on a diet (selection between desires or motives that will govern one's physical actions); whether to admire Mother Teresa or Bill Gates (selection of values); whether to accept the psychological theories of Freud or of cognitive psychologists (selection of ideas).[15] For Rand, all such matters are secondary and derivative: at root, free will is the power to activate one's conceptual faculty and direct its processing, or not. "All life entails and exhibits self-regulated action," writes Branden in presenting Rand's theory,

> but in man the principle of self-regulation reaches its highest expression: *man has the power to regulate the action of his own consciousness.* Man has the power to exercise his rational faculty – or to suspend it. It is *this* choice that is a causal primary. ("The Objectivist Concept of Free Will Versus the Traditional Concepts" *TON* 3(1) 3)

A crucial difference, on Rand's theory, between perceptual and conceptual awareness – between sense-perception and reason – between seeing, hearing, smelling, feeling, and tasting, on the one hand, and using concepts, developing arguments, forming principles, on the other hand – is that the latter has to be willed. Conceptual awareness requires *conscious effort* and is experienced as such. One's primary choice is to exert the full mental effort required to initiate and sustain one's conceptual awareness of the world or to refrain (partially or fully) from doing so. At the conceptual level, the human mind has the power and responsibility to activate and then regulate its processing – you must seize the mental reins, so to speak, and then direct your mind toward the goal of awareness.[16]

An individual becomes both capable and aware of his power of conscious self-regulation as his mind develops. "It must be stressed," Branden writes,

> that volition pertains, specifically, to the *conceptual* level of awareness. A child encounters the need of cognitive self-regulation when and as he begins to *think*, when and as he learns to abstract, to classify, to grasp principles, to reason explicitly. So long as he functions on the sensory-perceptual level, he experiences cognition as an effortless process. But when he begins to conceptualize, he is confronted by the fact that this new form of awareness entails mental *work*, that it requires an effort, that he must choose to generate this effort. He discovers that, on this new level of awareness, he is not infallible: error is possible; cognitive success is not automatically guaranteed to him. (Whereas to look is to see, to ask a question is not automatically to know the answer; and to know what question to ask is not automatic, either.) He discovers the need continually to monitor and regulate his mind's activity. A child does not, of course, identify this knowledge verbally or explicitly. But it is implicit in his consciousness, by direct introspective awareness. ("The Objectivist Theory of Volition" *TO* 5(1) 23)[17]

"Psychologically," Rand writes, "the choice 'to think or not' is the choice 'to focus or not'" (*VOS* 22). Rand uses the term "focus" deliberately, to draw a parallel between visual awareness and conceptual awareness. If you have ever been extremely tired or suffered a (moderate) blow to the head, you've likely had the experience of your vision being blurry and out of focus. You could not discriminate what you normally could in the world around you; you still could see some things, but the data you took in was much less than what you normally would have. Much of the world was passing you by, undiscriminated. When your mind and brain returned to normal functioning, the world came back into visual focus. Similar alternatives exist at the conceptual level of awareness, Rand maintains, except that here the degree of a mind's focus – whether it is out of focus, in partial focus, or in full focus – is set and maintained volitionally.

> Thinking requires a state of full, focused awareness. The act of focusing one's consciousness is volitional. Man can focus his mind to a full, active, purposefully directed awareness of reality – or he can unfocus it and let himself drift in a semiconscious daze, merely reacting to any chance stimulus of the immediate moment, at the mercy of his undirected sensory-perceptual mechanism and of any random, associational connections it might happen to make.
> When man unfocuses his mind, he may be said to be conscious in a subhuman sense of the word, since he experiences sensations and perceptions. But in the sense of the word applicable to man – in the sense of a consciousness which is aware of reality and able to deal with it, a consciousness able to direct the actions and provide for the survival of a human being – an unfocused mind is *not* conscious. (*VOS* 22)

A mind in full focus is a mind committed to the fundamental effort to grasp and deal with reality. To the extent of its knowledge and abilities, it works to observe and to keep its contents sharp, clear, and conceptually discriminated; it works to interconnect its data; and it works to bring to bear all its relevant data to its current situation.[18]

Since these dimensions exhibit degrees, on Rand's theory there exist not just two basic mental states at the conceptual level – a mind fully in focus or completely out of focus – but also a continuum of states of partial focus.

In describing it as the choice to think or not, Rand is obviously using "thinking" in a wide sense, to designate a mind that has taken control of its operations and is exerting the required effort, not (necessarily) a mind that is trying to solve a particular problem. Branden explains:

> To be in [full] focus does not mean that one must be engaged in the task of problem-solving every moment of one's waking existence. *It means that one must know what one is doing.* It means that one must not engage in activities which one can permit oneself only if one first suspends one's conscious mind and judgment. (*TO* 5(2) 24)

To focus, on Rand's theory, is to set awareness of reality as a goal of one's mind; a state of full focus designates a mind which has chosen to make awareness of reality its *ruling* goal. The goal of awareness entails the mental effort required to know. A mind unwilling to exert all the requisite effort does not have awareness as its ruling goal. Such a mind may have awareness as *a* goal, but not as its ruling goal; the commitment is absent; the level of goal-directedness or purposefulness is different. Such a mind, though perhaps partially activated, remains at least partially unactivated. Such a mind is not putting forth all the effort necessary to integrate its content. To such a mind, at least part of the world and part of its life is passing by, unprocessed and ungrasped. The mental state of full focus, as Leonard Peikoff characterizes it, "is the state of a goal-directed mind committed to attaining full awareness of reality" (*OPAR* 56).

A mind that is completely out of focus, therefore, is a mind that is goal-less, purposeless. Such a mind, on Rand's view, does not will the fundamental effort to understand. It has not been activated; it has not seized its reins; it is *drifting.* This does not mean that no mental processes are going on within it: it means the person is not directing or regulating them, deciding on their appropriateness to reality and to his circumstances in it. Instead, the person has relinquished control to his subconscious (to his emotional and associational mechanisms and the like).

Though one can choose not to activate one's mind, Rand maintains that the value of seizing the reins and seeking awareness is known to any mind once it reaches the conceptual level. Branden explains:

Just as man cannot escape the implicit knowledge that the function of his mind is volitional, so he cannot escape the implicit knowledge that he *should* think, that to be conscious is desirable, that his efficacy as a living entity depends on it. But he is free to act on that knowledge or to evade it. (*TO* 5(2) 23)

To place some goal above knowledge of reality means, in Rand's vivid language, to place an "I wish" above an "It is." The result is a *censored* view of reality. For instance, a person can set as his goal to grasp only things that come easily to him – or only things that he finds congenial – or only things that fit with his existing theories, social circle, or basic view of himself.

The actual process of self-censorship – the ejecting from conscious awareness of any question or datum that is uncongenial, too demanding, threatening, etc. – Rand calls *evasion*. It is

the act of blanking out, the willful suspension of one's consciousness, the refusal to think – not blindness, but the refusal to see; not ignorance, but the refusal to know. It is the act of unfocusing your mind and inducing an inner fog to escape the responsibility of judgment – on the unstated premise that a thing will not exist if only you refuse to identify it, that A will not be A so long as you do not pronounce the verdict "It *is*." Non-thinking is an act of annihilation, a wish to negate existence, an attempt to wipe out reality. But existence exists; reality is not to be wiped out, it will merely wipe out the wiper. By refusing to say "It is," you are refusing to say "I am." By suspending your judgment, you are negating your person. When a man declares: "Who am I to know?" – he is declaring: "Who am I to live?" (*Atlas* 1017–1018)

Evasion, according to Rand, is the root of evil. It is a directly willed mental state, a state of irrationality, a conscious rebellion against reality. In this sense, Rand maintains that a person *knowingly* commits evil. But there nevertheless is a point to the popular idea that no one consciously does evil. The essence of evil, on Rand's account, is to hold ideas and pursue goals that your mind would not permit you to hold and pursue were it in full focus. Evil is "not ignorance but the refusal to know"; it is a state of being out of control by choice, a state in which a motive one refuses fully to analyze or question drives one's actions. This dual nature of evil – that it is a deliberately chosen state to be out of control and driven by whims – pervades Rand's depictions and analyses of evil, both in her fiction and her non-fiction.[19] It is crucial to her view that evil is, in the end, small, petty, impotent. One important aspect of this view, which I will briefly touch on below, is that she argues that evasion has profoundly and progressively detrimental consequences for an individual's self-esteem, sense of life, and psycho-epistemology.

More widely, the commitment to one's own life is, in Rand's ethics, the root of morality, of good and evil. The choice to think or not, psychologically and existentially, is the choice to be or not to be.[20] Fully to have a self is, as a matter of policy, fully to activate one's mind. It is to assume the responsibility of (independent) judgment. And only through assuming such responsibility, Rand holds, can an individual control his fate existentially. Although *The Fountainhead* precedes Rand's full theory of volition, this primary choice is, in effect, the root of the distinction between selfishness and selflessness in the novel. First-handers assume the effort of consciousness while second-handers shirk it. Consider Peter Keating's mental processes when he is confronted with a momentous decision (to marry Dominique Francon or not): "He wanted to think that he was paralyzed. He knew that he was violently alive, that he was forcing the stupor into his muscles and into his mind, because he wished to escape the responsibility of consciousness" (*Fountainhead* 381). One's soul or self – "the real anyone" – is the "thing that thinks and values and makes decisions"; it is the "self-sufficient ego" (*Fountainhead* 441, 636). This is what Howard Roark achieves, Peter sacrifices, and Dominique deliberately tries to kill within her when she marries Peter.

The choice to "think or not" is not man's only choice, according to Rand: it is his primary choice. This choice sets a mind's regulating goal. Sub-choices then arise to the extent that there is such a goal, and are the means of implementing it.[21]

Suppose, for instance, that an individual has chosen a state of full focus. He has committed himself to grasping and dealing with reality. But what aspect of reality? He must choose. Suppose he is at work and decides that the report due on last quarter's sales results cannot wait. How will he attack this project? Will he begin by tabulating the results sent to him from his employees from the various sales divisions? Or will he first consult the previous quarter's sales report, to remind himself of all the data he will need to gather? He must choose. As Branden puts this point:

> The primary choice to focus, to set one's mind to the purpose of cognitive integration … is the highest regulator in the mental system; it is subject to man's direct, volitional control. In relation to it, all other choices and decisions are *sub*-regulators. (*TO* 5(2) 23)

The nature of these sub-choices – the alternatives which an individual is selecting among as well as what he selects – is causally shaped by at least three factors: the regulating goal he has set for himself (e.g., full focus), the ideas and values that rise to mind in his present circumstances as a result of this mental set, and the specific sub-choices he makes as he is directing his mental and physical actions.

To the extent that a mind is in partial focus, Rand holds, it exerts some control over its processing. But the sub-choices it faces are particular to its lower degree of focus. In comparison to a mind in full focus, many questions and issues on which to make a decision will not even arise for a mind in partial focus. They have, in effect, been censored as too effortful. Furthermore, some questions and issues that do arise will have to be actively ejected from consciousness.

Even an evading mind often functions by sub-choices. If some fact is to be pushed out of mind, how precisely? Will the individual do the conceptual equivalent of screaming "I'm not listening!"? Will he deliberately mischaracterize the fact and thereby attempt to rewrite it? Will he change the subject?

But whatever the regulating goal a mind has set for itself, Rand holds that this goal must be constantly renewed (or changed). Branden elaborates:

> The decision to focus and to think, once made, does not continue to direct a man's mind unceasingly thereafter, with no further effort required. Just as the state of full consciousness must be initiated volitionally, so it must be maintained volitionally. The choice to think must be reaffirmed in the face of every new issue and problem. (*TO* 5(1) 11)

But so long as an individual has set a particular regulating goal, the sub-choices he faces and makes will be his means of implementing that goal.

Despite the connection between sub-choices and the primary choice, it is important to understand the crucial way in which the two differ, according to Rand. Sub-choices are choices

111

between specific things in reality, between something and something else, between alternative ways of seeking to achieve the regulating goal a mind has set for itself (e.g., the choices of how to begin work on a sales report). The primary choice to think or not, on the other hand, is the choice between something or nothing: it is the choice to activate one's conceptual mind or to leave it unactivated (or to plunge it into darkness), the choice to orient one's mind to reality or not to do so (there exists no other reality to orient it to).

Looking at this same point from a different perspective, sub-choices have causal antecedents, which include a mind's chosen level of focus, its existing ideas and values, and the other sub-choices it has made and which have directed its current functioning. The primary choice, by contrast, has no such causal antecedents (though it does have causal prerequisites, such as a normal, wakeful brain state). "Man's freedom ... to think or not to think," Branden writes, "is a unique kind of choice that must be distinguished from any other category of choice."

> It must be distinguished from the decision to think about a particular subject: *what* a man thinks about ... depends on his values, interests, knowledge and context. It must be distinguished from the decision to think about a particular physical action, which again depends on a man's values, interests, knowledge and context. These decisions involve causal antecedents of a kind which the choice to focus does not.
>
> The primary choice to focus, to set one's mind to the purpose of cognitive integration, is a *first cause* in a man's consciousness. On the psychological level, the choice is causally irreducible ... (*TO* 5(2) 22–23)

If one were to ask the sales manager why he decided to begin working on his quarterly sales report by consulting the past quarter's report, he can cite a reason for his choice and thereby provide an explanation of his choice (e.g., he thought this course of action would prove most time-efficient). From this aspect, the choice has causal antecedents: he chooses to consult the past quarter's report because he has concluded that it will save time. But if one were to ask him why he set his mind to a state of full focus in the first place, there is no reason other than the fact that that is what he chose: he chose to focus in order to be in focus. (The same holds for drift and evasion: the individual chose not to focus in order not to be in focus, or he chose to unfocus his mind in order for his mind to be unfocused.)

As Branden states the point:

> To ask: "What *made* one man choose to focus and another to evade?" is to have failed to understand the meaning of choice in this primary sense. Neither motives nor desires nor context are causal imperatives with regard to this choice. They are not irrelevant to a man's thinking or evasion, but neither are they causally *decisive*. By themselves, they do not and cannot constitute a causal explanation.
>
> The choice to focus one's mind is a primary, just as the value sought, *awareness*, is a primary. It is awareness that makes any other values possible, not any other values that antecede and make awareness possible. ("Volition and the Law of Causality" *TO* 5(3) 44)[22]

The Primary Choice and an Individual's Social Environment

Although a version of self-determinism, Rand's theory does not maintain that an individual's environment is irrelevant to the person he becomes. In many articles, Rand discusses the fact that the rationality or irrationality of an individual's social environment can encourage thought or encourage mental passivity and evasion; and it can foster or hamper the development of his cognitive and evaluative abilities.[23]

But, leaving aside for the moment the issues of physical compulsion or incredible irrationality, Rand also insists that whatever the nature of an individual's social environment, he retains sovereign control over his mind. The reality or non-reality orientation of his mind – the fundamental morality of his actions – is his and his alone to set. Whether he chooses to think in an irrational environment (and suffer condemnation and penalties from others) or whether he chooses to surrender to that irrationality (and gain praise and rewards from others), is up to him. In Rand's novels, for instance, both Peter Keating and Howard Roark in *The Fountainhead*, and James Taggart and Francisco d'Anconia in *Atlas Shrugged*, grow up in similar social and cultural environments. The radical difference in their characters, each novel makes clear, results from the extent to which they exert independent judgment, the extent to which they use or misuse their minds. Branden puts the point as follows:

> The environment consists only of facts, the meaning of those facts ... can be identified only by a man's mind. A man's character, the degree of his rationality, independence, honesty, is determined, not by the things he perceives, but by the thinking he does or fails to do about them. ("The Objectivist Theory of Volition" *TO* 5(2) 26)

Of course a reality-oriented mind, especially in the presence of the irrationalities of others, can make errors which can hamper it, sometimes severely, both psychologically and existentially. At the conceptual level, to seek awareness is no guarantee that one will attain it.[24] But such a mind nevertheless retains the essence of a healthy character, of a moral character: sovereignty over its own functioning. This fact, in principle, makes it possible for the individual to discover and correct his errors. In his article presenting Rand's theory of volition, Branden discusses at some length the example of a boy who grows up in a bad neighborhood and becomes a criminal. Even if such a boy begins by reaching wrong conclusions which represent errors of knowledge, if he remains committed to grasping reality, he will have opportunities to correct his errors and revise his conclusions. And that commitment is his alone to set.

> If, at every turning-point, he had thought carefully and conscientiously, and had simply reached the wrong conclusions, he would be more justified in crying that he could not help it. But it is not helplessly bewildered, conscientious thinkers who fill reform schools and who murder one another on street corners – through an error in logic. (Branden *TO* 5(2) 29)

Rand's fiction contains many characters who form erroneous conclusions in the face of other people's irrationality. Consider for instance Hank Rearden and Robert Stadler in *Atlas Shrugged*. Rearden is surrounded by people who morally denounce business and treat sexual desire as degrading. He forms wrong conclusions about both issues, which become embedded in his soul. But Rearden chooses to preserve a fundamental commitment to thought. Because of this, he seeks and is open to evidence of his errors and to the effort of forming new conclusions and acting on them. Although it is a struggle, he is able to resolve his problems. Stadler, by contrast, in the face of a great deal of human irrationality, forms an erroneous conclusion about other people. But unlike Rearden, he does not struggle with his error, and constantly evades facts that would help him uncover and correct it. As a result, both his soul and his fate are radically different from Rearden's.

113

Rand does allow that a child can find himself in a social environment so irrational as to never have the chance properly to develop his mind in the first place.[25] And even apart from this kind of extreme, she often cautioned that the entrenchment of government-*enforced* irrationality and injustice in contemporary culture was reaching a stage where only individuals of exceptional moral devotion and intelligence could endure the pains and penalties and not betray their souls. Lesser men would give in or, at best, give up in bewilderment.[26]

But if we leave aside social contexts of incredible irrationality or extensive coercion, Rand's view is that what an individual becomes is a result of the mental sovereignty he retains and the resulting choices he makes in his particular environment. Much more important than the social incentives for thought or evasion to understanding an individual's development and character, on her view, is the individual's *past* primary choices. The more often an individual has exerted control over his mind's functioning, the greater his resulting knowledge, his self-confidence in his mind's power, and his conviction that the world can be dealt with. These "serve to put every emotional incentive on the side of his continuing to think," writes Branden.

> Further, they reduce the possibility of an incentive that could even tempt him to evade. It is too clear to him that reality is not and can never be his enemy – that he has nothing to gain from self-inflicted blindness, and everything to lose. (*TO* 5(2) 24)

Nevertheless, this individual remains sovereign: he must choose to continue to pursue the value of awareness by setting it as his mind's ruling goal.

By contrast, the individual who rarely seizes the mental reins meets an opposite fate. His knowledge is scant and stagnant, he has little grounds to be confident in his mind's power, and the world comes to seem an alien place that cannot be dealt with. "These feelings undercut his confidence in his ability to think, in the usefulness of thinking – and he tends to feel overwhelmed by the enormity of the mental chaos in himself which he has to untangle," Branden writes. But this individual too remains sovereign: he can choose to pursue awareness by setting it as his mind's ruling goal. And the value of awareness remains and remains known: to a sense of being out of control there is no solution but to start to exert control, even if "the mental effort he refused to exert formerly, must now be exerted tenfold" (*TO* 5(2) 25).

The point here can be broadened: on Rand's theory, the choice to think or not shapes an individual's entire emotional life, that is, whether he experiences an inner harmony or a conflict between his reason and his emotions. To understand this claim, we need to consider briefly Rand's account of emotions.

Reason and Emotion

A major aspect of the identity of man's consciousness, according to Rand, is that it integrates and then automatizes its content.

> All learning involves a process of automatizing, i.e., of first acquiring knowledge by fully conscious, focused attention and observation, then of establishing mental connections which make that knowledge automatic (instantly available as a context), thus freeing man's mind to pursue further, more complex knowledge. (*ITOE* 65)

Emotions, on her view, are an instance of this kind of automatization.

> Emotions are the automatic results of man's value judgments integrated by his subconscious; emotions are estimates of that which furthers man's values or threatens them, that which is *for* him or *against* him – lightning calculators giving him the sum of his profit or loss. ... Man's emotional mechanism is like an electronic computer, which his mind has to program – and the programming consists of the values his mind chooses. (*VOS* 30)

Each individual therefore volitionally programs his own emotional mechanism. But:

> If he chooses irrational values, he switches his emotional mechanism from the role of his guardian to the role of his destroyer. The irrational is the impossible; it is that which contradicts the facts of reality; facts cannot be altered by a wish, but they *can* destroy the wisher. If a man desires and pursues contradictions – if he wants to have his cake and eat it, too – he disintegrates his consciousness; he turns his inner life into a civil war of blind forces engaged in dark, incoherent, pointless, meaningless conflicts ... (*VOS* 31)

In contrast to an irrational person, the individual who characteristically chooses to think acquires a growing body of knowledge and rational values in his mind: he forms ideas and value-judgments that are derived from and conform to the facts of reality. To the extent that he seizes the reins and directs his cognitive and evaluative activity, he knows what ideas have been automatized by his subconscious. Such an individual is not a mystery to himself. As a rule, his emotional reactions do not surprise or puzzle him. And when they do, his policy is to engage in further thought: to recheck his conscious judgment and to try to uncover the source of his differing emotions. By this means he establishes a fundamental harmony between his reason and his emotions. Aligned as a rule with his conscious convictions and value-judgments, his emotions serve as a form of experiencing the enjoyment of himself and his values.[27]

Perhaps the best way to understand Rand's account of the relation of reason and emotion in the life of an individual is through her fiction. Examine for instance the characters of Peter Keating and Howard Roark in *The Fountainhead*; Keating experiences inner conflict as a norm, whereas Roark's soul is in fundamental harmony. The source of the difference is that Keating sacrifices his mind to the opinions of others, while Roark retains sovereignty of his. Or examine the characters of James Taggart and Dagny Taggart in *Atlas Shrugged*. Jim is the evader, and his is a life of inner conflict, haunted by the question of what is his self (*Atlas* 873). Dagny, by contrast, is a soul in basic harmony; and when she experiences conflict, hers is a ruthless policy of examining her mind, premises, and emotions, never obeying feelings she does not understand.

Thus on Rand's theory of volition, emotions are not under direct volitional control, but they are nevertheless volitional products. "As to a man's desires and emotions," Branden writes, "a man cannot will them in or out of existence directly ... Man can alter his desires and emotions only by revising the thinking or non-thinking that produced his values and premises" (*TO* 5(2) 26).

"The use or misuse of his cognitive faculty," as Rand summarizes her overall view, "determines a man's choice of values, which determine his emotions and his character. It is in this sense that man is a being of self-made soul" ("The Metaphysical Versus the Man-Made" *PWNI* 36).[28]

To understand fully why the above-quoted passage is a summary of Rand's view of man's soul we need to explore why she thinks that the exercise of man's power of volition – the choice to think or not – leads to the formation of basic premises and values (however implicit). In particular, we need to explore briefly three issues central to her account of how the choice to think shapes an individual's soul: self-esteem; sense of life; and psycho-epistemology. For Rand, these are cornerstones of a soul – and they give flesh to her idea that man is a philosophical being.[29]

Self-Esteem[30]

Rand considers consciousness a natural, biological faculty, whose vital function is to gain awareness of the organism's environment and direct its life-sustaining actions within that environment. A healthy consciousness is one that is able to do this; it is efficacious. An unhealthy or diseased consciousness is one in which this ability has been undermined or incapacitated; it is inefficacious.[31]

An individual creates an efficacious mind, according to Rand, by regularly exercising his conceptual faculty, by setting it to the task of active cognitive integration. The result, normally, is a growing body of knowledge and a mind's sense of its own power to grasp and deal with the issues that face it.

In contrast, a mind that evades, that places an "I wish" above an "It is," deliberately disintegrates its contents and sabotages its cognitive functioning.

> Whenever you committed the evil of refusing to think and to see, of exempting from the absolute of reality some one small wish of yours, whenever you chose to say: Let me withdraw from the judgment of reason the cookies I stole, or the existence of God, let me have my one irrational whim and I will be a man of reason about all else – *that* was the act of subverting your consciousness, the act of corrupting your mind. Your mind then became a fixed jury who takes orders from a secret underworld, whose verdict distorts the evidence to fit an absolute it dares not touch – and a censored reality is the result ... (*Atlas* 1037)

The consequence is a mind's growing sense of its own inefficacy.

"Self-esteem," writes Branden, "is the reputation a man acquires with himself" ("Self-Esteem" *TO* 6(5) 264). An individual must acquire some reputation with himself because free will gives him a unique perspective on his life. When an individual thinks and acts, be it to decide how to solve a problem he is having at work or to decide whether to ask out a person in whom he is interested, he knows that it is *he* who will be doing the thinking and acting. A "man's self is his mind – the faculty that perceives reality, forms judgments, chooses values" – and the self is omnipresent in thought and action ("Selfishness Without a Self" *PWNI* 68). The prospects for cognitive and existential success, and so the motivation to embark on the process of thought and action in the first place, will depend *causally* on the nature of an individual's self. Moreover, the nature of this self has been and is continually being created by numerous choices – and an individual senses this fact, precisely because he is the one making the choices.

Am I the kind of person who reaches correct decisions and makes good choices and so is deserving of success, or am I not? This is the basic issue of self-esteem. By virtue of the volitional control an individual has over his cognitive faculty and life, this issue, Rand holds, is inescapable.

> By a feeling he has not learned to identify, but has derived from his first awareness of existence, from his discovery that he has to make choices, man knows that his desperate need of self-esteem is a matter of life or death. As a being of volitional consciousness, he knows that he must know his

own value in order to maintain his own life. He knows that he has to be *right*; to be wrong in action means danger to his life; to be wrong in person, to be *evil*, means to be unfit for existence. (*Atlas* 1056–1057)

To live, Rand holds, man needs a generalized, positive estimate of his self and his ability to achieve his values. To possess self-esteem is for an individual to possess the "inviolate certainty that his mind is competent to think and his person is worthy of happiness, which means: is worthy of living" (*Atlas* 1018). A healthy human consciousness is a mind that is genuinely convinced of its efficacy in achieving awareness of the world and guiding action in it, whatever its particular circumstances. Only such a self is worthy of the painstaking attention and effort a course of genuine *self*-preservation demands.

Self-esteem is therefore both a metaphysical and a moral estimate of one's self: of one's ability to live (the metaphysical component) and one's worthiness to live (the moral component).[32]

Broadly speaking, Rand envisions three basic possibilities for the creation of self-esteem, which admit of much variation within them.

First, an individual can devote himself to the rationality of his mind's processing and the full reality of his own existence, achieve a fundamental sense of efficacy, and then judge himself by the correct standard. The proper standard by which to gauge one's self, metaphysically *and* morally, Rand argues, is an "*unbreached rationality* – not the degree of your intelligence, but the full and relentless use of your mind, not the extent of your knowledge, but the acceptance of reason as an absolute" (*Atlas* 1059). Such an individual does everything within his volitional control to create a self able to live and worthy of living, and judges himself accordingly.

Second, an individual can devote himself to the rationality of his mind's processing but judge himself by improper metaphysical or moral standards. For instance, if an individual demands the metaphysically impossible of himself – if he judges himself negatively because he does not possess the raw intelligence someone else's mind possesses or because he demands omniscience and castigates himself for not knowing yesterday what he knows today – although such a person may be rational and essentially efficacious, he will not reach full self-esteem.[33] Likewise, if an individual judges in some way that a life of rational thought and self-sustaining action is morally wrong, although such a mind may possess a conviction of basic efficacy, it will not achieve full self-esteem. Given the prevalence of anti-self and anti-self-interest moral codes, Rand holds this last to be a frequent case. Man, she writes,

has no choice about his need of self-esteem, his only choice is the standard by which to gauge it. And he makes his fatal error when he switches this gauge protecting his life into the service of his own destruction, when he chooses a standard contradicting existence and sets his self-esteem against reality. (*Atlas* 1057)[34]

Third, an individual can consistently fail to devote himself to the rationality of his mind's processing, and thereby sabotage himself. The consequent experiences of metaphysical self-doubt and moral guilt are intolerable. Rand argues, therefore, that individuals who fail to earn genuine self-esteem fake its possession. They erect some form of pseudo-self-esteem.

No man can survive the moment of pronouncing himself irredeemably evil; should he do it, his next moment is insanity or suicide. To escape it ... he will fake, evade, blank out; he will cheat himself of reality, of existence, of happiness, of mind; and he will ultimately cheat himself of self-esteem by struggling to preserve its illusion rather than to risk discovering its lack. (*Atlas* 1057)[35]

Because self-esteem is the most basic need of man's consciousness, Rand argues that the exact nature and extent of a man's self-esteem will shape his particular values, their structure and motivational force in his mind, and the essence of what he seeks to obtain in life. An individual's sense of his mind's efficacy, and the metaphysical and moral standards by which he judges his self, shape the structure of his soul.

Unsurprisingly, therefore, the issue of self-esteem pervades her fiction and non-fiction. In *The Fountainhead*, for instance, Howard Roark is the man of serene self-esteem, quietly but supremely confident in his capacity to think and judge and build, and unquestioning of his worthiness to exist. Gail Wynand, in contrast, experiences a deep and foreboding sense of unworthiness; though in a sense tremendously efficacious, he has capitulated to his society's view of life and allowed his effort to be warped from the genuine, reality-based goal of building his kind of world to that of holding power over other people. At root, his is a defensive motivation and a form of pseudo-self-esteem; he is the tragic figure of *The Fountainhead*. Dominique Francon is on a quest to strangle her self-esteem – a quest born in part from the conviction that the world will torture and kill anyone who achieves self-esteem. Peter Keating, though at first seemingly the man of outstanding success, is plagued by feelings of inefficacy and unworthiness; he is a non-thinker and parasite on other people's consciousnesses, deriving his pseudo-self-esteem from their favorable reactions to him. Ellsworth Toohey rebels against the very need to achieve self-esteem, as we see from depiction of various despicable but formative events in his childhood; his life becomes a quest to destroy the self-esteem of others.[36]

Turning to Rand's non-fiction, many of her positive philosophical essays, like "The Metaphysical Versus the Man-made" and "The Objectivist Ethics," address the proper metaphysical-moral standard by which to gauge self-esteem, and seek to teach an individual that an unbreached rationality is within his grasp – because he is the only one who can breach it (*Atlas* 1059). In "For the New Intellectual" Rand calls for a new kind of intellectual, one who will uphold and defend man's self-esteem and "the country based on the premise of man's self-reliance and self-esteem," America, the land of the producer ("For the New Intellectual" *FTNI* 50).

The issue of self-esteem also figures prominently in her more critical essays. Rand regards the philosophical theories diametrically opposed to hers as both flowing from a lack of self-esteem and leading to profound attacks on self-esteem.[37] In the Introduction to *The Virtue of Selfishness* she writes that the "attack on 'selfishness' is an attack on man's self-esteem." In "Altruism as Appeasement," she argues that intellectuals' widespread embrace of the morality of self-sacrifice is caused by a breach of self-esteem. In the "Age of Envy" she maintains that the present era is wrecked by haters of the good for being the good and analyzes various expressions of this mentality, a mentality generated by a profound default on the quest for self-esteem. In "Of Living Death" she discusses how Pope Paul VI's encyclical on sex, *Humanae Vitae*, is an attack on man's self-esteem. And in "Causality versus Duty" she argues that the (Kantian) anti-concept of "duty" is a destroyer of morality and self-esteem.[38]

Sense of Life[39]

A man's self-esteem, on Rand's view, is his fundamental estimate of his efficacy and worth. Flowing out of this estimate, she argues, is what she calls an individual's *sense of life*. A "sense of life" Rand characterizes as "a pre-conceptual equivalent of metaphysics, an emotional, subconsciously integrated appraisal of man and of existence" ("Philosophy and Sense of

Life" *RM* 24–25). It is a complex product, an implicit view of life, that, in effect, represents a metaphysical view of man: a view of his basic nature and his place in the universe – of what type of actions he is capable of and what kind of goals he can genuinely expect to reach. It represents (in part) a stand on such issues as:

> Is the universe intelligible to man, or unintelligible and unknowable? Can man find happiness on earth, or is he doomed to frustration and despair? Does man have the power of *choice*, the power to choose his goals and to achieve them, the power to direct the course of his life – or is he the helpless plaything of forces beyond his control, which determine his fate? Is man, by nature, to be valued as good, or to be despised as evil? These are *metaphysical* questions, but the answers to them determine the kind of *ethics* men will accept and practice; the answers are the link between metaphysics and ethics. ("The Psycho-Epistemology of Art" *RM* 7, cf. "Philosophy and Sense of Life" *RM* 17–18)[40]

Rand calls an individual's (usually implicit) answers to these questions his "metaphysical value-judgments" because they are metaphysical conclusions crucial to grounding his basic values. As Peikoff explains:

> The issue raised is not: "By what rules should a man live?" but, in effect, "Can man live?" – which is logically prior and which affects all of a man's specific choices and rules. If man is an efficacious being in a benevolent universe, then certain choices and actions (expressing self-assertion, ambition, idealism) are appropriate to him; if not, not. In either view (and in all the mixtures in between), metaphysics acts as man's *value conditioner*. (*OPAR* 415)

The metaphysical questions mentioned above are difficult to formulate explicitly, let alone answer correctly. But, Rand maintains, an individual nevertheless forms *implicit* answers to these questions as he grows into adulthood. In the face of numerous concrete issues and problems of his daily life, a maturing child must draw some specific conclusions, form some value-judgments, and make some choices. The rationality and accuracy of these will sum up in his mind to not just a sense of the efficacy and worthiness of his own self, but also a sense of the kind of world in which he lives. "Every choice and value-judgment implies some estimate of himself and of the world around him – most particularly, of his capacity to deal with the world," writes Rand. An individual's "subconscious mechanism sums up his psychological activities, integrating his conclusions, reactions or evasions into an emotional sum that establishes a habitual pattern and becomes his automatic response to the world around him." And so what begins

> as a series of single, discrete conclusions (or evasions) about his own particular problems, becomes a generalized feeling about existence, an implicit *metaphysics* with the compelling motivational power of a constant, basic emotion – an emotion which is part of all his other emotions and underlies all his experiences. *This* is a sense of life. ("Philosophy and Sense of Life" *RM* 15).

By a "generalized feeling about existence" Rand means a perspective on the facts of reality – on the many things and events one faces throughout one's daily life – that categorizes them into those which really count and those which don't, those which are essential and so must be taken into account in all one's thoughts and actions and those which are accidental and so should be left to one side.

For instance, in regard to artistic creation (which is a sense-of-life phenomenon according to Rand), Rand contrasts the differing generalized feelings about existence that were given form by sculptors in Ancient Greece and by sculptors in the Middle Ages.

119

An artist (as, for instance, the sculptors of Ancient Greece) who presents man as a god-like figure is aware of the fact that men may be crippled or diseased or helpless; but he regards these conditions as accidental, as irrelevant to the essential nature of man – and he presents a figure embodying strength, beauty, intelligence, self-confidence, as man's proper, natural state.

An artist (as, for instance, the sculptors of the Middle Ages) who presents man as a deformed monstrosity is aware of the fact that there are men who are healthy, happy or confident; but he regards *these* conditions as accidental or illusory, as irrelevant to man's essential nature – and he presents a tortured figure embodying pain, ugliness, terror, as man's proper, natural state. ("Art and Sense of Life" *RM* 27)

As a consequence, the work of the first artist says to the viewer, in effect: when charting your own course in life, remember that man is a being of intelligence and strength who should expect to reach not disease and pain but pleasure and success. The work of the second artist says to the viewer, in effect: when charting your own course in life, remember that man is a sordid being who should expect a life of pain and suffering. On Rand's view, this is an example of the life-shaping power of metaphysical value-judgments – and of their subconscious equivalent, an individual's sense of life.[41]

An individual's sense of life is, Rand argues, a volitional creation. In essence, it is a product of the use or misuse an individual makes of his free will. "To the extent to which a man is mentally active, i.e., motivated by the desire to know, to *understand*," Rand writes, "his mind works as the programmer of his emotional computer – and his sense of life develops into a bright counterpart of a rational philosophy." By contrast, if "evasion or lethargy is a man's predominant method of mental functioning, the result is a sense of life dominated by fear" ("Philosophy and Sense of Life" *RM* 15).

The formation of a sense of life, on Rand's theory, can be seen as a corollary process to the formation of an individual's self-esteem and, therefore, as equally necessary. Someone who is developing genuine self-esteem is acquiring, from his particular successes and assessments of them, the conviction that as a human being who exercises his rational faculty, he is capable of reaching his goals and achieving success. He has a sense of his efficacy in dealing with reality and of his worthiness to remain in it. Self-esteem is an appraisal of self – in relation to reality; sense of life is an appraisal of reality – in relation to self. Out of the sense that he is able to deal with the facts of the world grows an (implicit) sense that reality is a *realm* in which he – and any other functioning human being – can succeed. This is a feeling of living in a benevolent universe (the specifics of this feeling can vary widely) – a universe in which the attitudes of eager curiosity, confidence, earnestness, joy, and perseverance are appropriate.

Similarly, out of the sense that he is unable to deal with the facts of reality grows an (implicit) sense that reality is a *realm* in which he – and other human beings – cannot succeed. This is a feeling of living in a malevolent universe (again, the specifics can vary) – a universe in which the attitudes of passivity, doubt, and fear are appropriate.[42]

Rand describes the specific process by which a sense of life is formed as one of "emotional" generalization or abstraction:

it consists of classifying things *according to the emotions they invoke* – i.e., of tying together, by association or connotation, all those things which have the power to make an individual experience the same (or a similar) emotion. For instance ... a heroic man, the skyline of New York, a sunlit landscape, pure colors, ecstatic music – or: a humble man, an old village, a foggy landscape, muddy colors, folk music. (*RM* 16)

In *We the Living* (though the novel predates the development of Rand's theory of sense of life) there is a description of such a process. Rand writes that the heroine, Kira Argounova,

> had the same feeling for eating soup without salt, and for discovering a snail slithering up her bare leg, and for young men who pleaded, broken-hearted, their eyes humid, their lips soft. She had the same feeling for white statues of ancient gods against black velvet in museums, and for steel shavings and rusty dust and hissing torches and muscles tense as electric wires in the iron roar of a building under construction. She seldom visited museums; but when they went out with Kira, her family avoided passing by any construction works: houses, and particularly roads, and most particularly bridges. She was certain to stop and stand watching, for hours, red bricks and oaken beams and steel panels growing under the will of man. But she could never be made to enter a public park on Sunday, and she stuck her fingers into her ears when she heard a chorus singing folk songs. (*WTL* 32)[43]

Rand stresses that the process of emotional abstraction by which a sense of life is formed is rooted in the self.

> Which particular emotions will be invoked by the things in these examples, as their respective common denominators, depends on which set of things fits an individual's *view of himself.* ... The subverbal, subconscious criterion of selection that forms his emotional abstractions is: "That which is important to *me*" or: "The kind of universe which is right for *me*, in which *I* would feel at home." (*RM* 16–17)

The key concept generating the categorization inherent in a sense of life is the concept *important.*

> It is a concept that belongs to the realm of values, since it implies an answer to the question: Important – to whom? Yet its meaning is different from that of moral values. "Important" does not necessarily mean "good." It means "a quality, character or standing such as to entitle to attention or consideration" (The American College Dictionary). What, in a fundamental sense, is entitled to one's attention or consideration? Reality.
> "Important" – in its essential meaning, as distinguished from its more limited and superficial uses – is a *metaphysical* term. (*RM* 17)

An individual acquires the sense that certain things are entitled to attention (and others not) through those chosen values of his that he comes to regard as important, that is, through those values of his that reflect his sense of self and its relation to existence.

Consider two of Rand's examples: an individual who comes to believe that it "is important to understand things" and an individual who comes to believe that it "is important to obey my parents" (*RM* 18). For a person who characteristically activates his mind and seeks knowledge, a sense of efficacy will result. Such a person values understanding. And this value in turn will come to be experienced as important because it fits with his sense of self. When he gains knowledge, he has the feeling that this result is *real* and the *to-be-expected* from life. When he reaches an error, he feels that this is an *accident*, correctable if he rededicates himself to his quest. By contrast, a person dominated by passivity and lethargy will not achieve a sense of efficacy. Even if he values understanding to some extent, this value will not be experienced as important. Given what he has made of his self, he feels that his reaching knowledge is *accidental*, not the *to-be-expected*. When he fails to reach knowledge, this is experienced as *real* and the *to-be-expected* from life. Moreover, his policy of mental passivity will give rise to the need for some outside authority figure, to substitute for the mind that he has abandoned; perhaps he will regularly look to his parents, and following their judgment will become a value to him. "It is important to obey my parents" may then become an implicit conclusion of his, because the value involved reflects his deepest sense of self.

Again, to call these "implicit conclusions" or "implicit premises" is to say that they are habitual patterns of cognition and action, which, if expressed in words, would be premises. It is, Rand holds, through a series of such emotional abstractions, integrated into a sum, that an individual derives an implicit *metaphysics* – such as the sense that man is an independent being capable of surviving on his own (e.g., an aspect of Howard Roark's attitude toward life), derived in part from the conviction that it is important to understand things – or the sense that man is a collective being, doomed if separated from the group (e.g., an aspect of Peter Keating's attitude toward life), derived in part from the conviction that it is important to obey one's parents.

> "It is important to understand things" – "It is important to obey my parents" – "It is important to act on my own" – "It is important to please other people" – "It is important to fight for what I want" – "It is important not to make enemies" – "My life is important" – "Who am I to stick my neck out?" Man is a being of self-made soul – and it is of such conclusions that the stuff of his soul is made. ...
> The integrated sum of a man's basic values is his sense of life. (*RM* 18)

Thus on Rand's view an individual forms his sense of life by "deriving, subconsciously, an implicit metaphysics from his value-judgments" (*RM* 19).

The proper procedure (albeit a difficult and rare one, in today's anti-rational and anti-philosophical culture), Rand holds, is for an individual to then translate and, where required, correct his sense of life in conceptual, philosophical terms. In such a case,

> philosophy does not replace a man's sense of life, which continues to function as the automatically integrated sum of his values. But philosophy [now] sets the criteria of his emotional integrations according to a fully defined and consistent view of reality (if and to the extent that a philosophy is rational). (*RM* 19)

But whether or not an individual undertakes and successfully completes this process, "at any stage and state of its specific content, a sense of life always retains a profoundly personal quality; it reflects a man's deepest values; it is experienced by him as a sense of his own identity" (*RM* 20–21). Like an individual's self-esteem, from which it is derived, an individual's sense of life is at once highly individual and concrete, Rand maintains, and also highly generalized and abstract. Although an individual's self-esteem amounts to an abstract evaluation of himself, it is formed as a result of his specific choices and actions in specific situations over the course of his life. If an individual has a healthy self-esteem, for instance, this is a generalized confidence of being able to deal with whatever issues he will face, but it derives only from the person's specific thoughts and accomplishments. Similarly, if a person experiences a lack of self-esteem from having given in to domineering parents, this is a generalized feeling of inefficacy that nevertheless is tied to the specific incidents and conclusions of his life when dealing with his particular parents. The same holds for an individual's sense of life.

Viewed from the perspective of the *integrated* sum of an individual's basic values, a sense of life is a generalized feeling about existence. But what is being integrated into a sum, namely a vast number of emotional abstractions stemming from an individual's basic values, is highly specific to an individual (think here of Rand's description of Kira, which captures but one set of emotional abstractions). Moreover, the concrete things and events that stand united in an individual's mind by the same (or similar) emotion they invoke, will also be highly specific to an individual – dependent as this whole process is on the individual's particular experiences and his thinking and conclusions (or lack thereof) about those experiences. As we have seen, Rand describes a man's *sense* of life as a "constant, basic emotion ... which is part of all his other emotions and underlies all his experiences" (*RM* 15). The specifics of what evoke such an emotion about life, as well as how this shapes an individual's subsequent value-judgments and emotional experiences, are highly individuated. A sense of life, in effect, is an *embodied* abstraction.

That sense of life is at once highly individuated and highly abstract (and metaphysical) is vital to understanding Rand's account of two crucial aspects of human life – aspects of man's soul that she holds have been shrouded in mysticism precisely because they are at once highly personal and highly abstract: romantic love and art (both artistic creation and viewers' responses).[44]

More broadly, because sense of life is an implicit metaphysics, Rand argues that to understand an individual and his course of action it is necessary to understand not only his conscious convictions but also his sense of life (the two often clash). Moreover, she argues that some human institutions have the equivalent of a sense of life. In "Of Living Death" and "Requiem for Man," for instance, Rand explains how two recent, seemingly inconsistent papal encyclicals are understandable when seen as capturing the (evil) sense of life of the Catholic Church as an institution. And in "Don't Let It Go" Rand contrasts the American sense of life to the European and discusses the gulf between the American people's sense of life and the philosophical ideas of the nation's intellectuals.[45]

Psycho-Epistemology[46]

Just as an individual, through the volitional use or misuse of his conceptual faculty, forms his self-esteem, that is, his basic reputation with himself, and forms the equivalent of a metaphysics, that is, a view of the universe in relation to the self he has formed – so he forms, Rand argues, as a corollary component shaping both his self-esteem and his sense of life, a *psycho-epistemology*.

By an individual's "psycho-epistemology" Rand means his characteristic method of cognitive functioning, his habitual way of mentally proceeding when confronted with the need to understand and deal with the world. It is, in effect, an individual's implicit epistemology.

On Rand's view, a process of thought involves a complex interaction between the mental actions one has direct, conscious control over and the content automatized by one's subconscious mind. In an article explaining Rand's concept of psycho-epistemology, Branden writes:

> The efficacy of a man's thinking is determined not merely by the rationality of his volitional mental functions in any given moment, but by his *past* psycho-epistemological policies. The clarity or vagueness of his past identifications, the honesty or evasiveness that he has previously practiced, the order or chaos of his past knowledge – all are part of the implicit context of any new act of thinking, all affect the automatic mental functions which are involved in any thinking process. ("Psycho-Epistemology" *TON* 3(10) 44)

The root of an individual's psycho-epistemology, Rand holds, is his policy in regard to the primary choice. "Entailed by man's basic choice, to think or not to think," writes Branden, are

123

"three broad and fundamental ... alternatives in his method of cognitive functioning." These are the degree to which an individual characteristically activates and sustains "a sharp intellectual focus"; the degree to which he retains intellectual control or surrenders to his emotions, "whose validity he does not judge and/or does not care about"; and the degree to which he maintains intellectual independence or substitutes other people's "judgment for his own." "The choices a man makes with regard to these alternatives are the crucial determinants of his individual psycho-epistemology" (*TON* 3(10) 41, 43).

Because self-esteem "is reliance on one's power to think" (*Atlas* 1057), Rand maintains that self-esteem is essentially psycho-epistemological. The basic reputation one acquires with oneself pertains to one's competence as a thinker and knower. Does one characteristically exert the effort required to know, or does one give up at the first encountered difficulty? Does one characteristically face facts, even when unpleasant, or does one allow one's emotions to hold sway? Do one's emotions characteristically tempt one to evade, in effect declaring numerous conclusions and subjects as unwelcome, or do they encourage one to scrupulously consider the matter? Does one characteristically seek clarity? Does one typically renounce one's conclusions at the first sign of disagreement with others, or does one continue down the cognitive path one has glimpsed? The choices one has made in the past on such issues will affect not only the power of one's current thought processes, but also one's *estimate* of this power. The person who trusts his thinking will trust himself to judge and act; the person who does not, will not.

Because an individual's psycho-epistemology is part of the foundation of his self-esteem, Rand also maintains that it plays a pivotal role in the formation of his sense of life. The sort of world in which one would feel fully at home is the sort of world that would be suitable to the manner of one's habitual cognitive functioning ("Art and Sense of Life" *RM*). Unsurprisingly, therefore, psycho-epistemological issues feature heavily in Rand's characterization of her fictional heroes and villains.

For instance, the contrast between Roark and Peter Keating in *The Fountainhead* is psycho-epistemological (though Rand would only later identify it in these terms).[47] Roark is first-handed, the man of independence and integrity who is committed to grasping the world though his own eyes, undisturbed by the errors or objections of other people, intent on conceptualizing and summing up his experiences into principles that will govern his course through life. Keating by contrast is second-handed, a man of borrowed opinions and goals, intent on ingratiating himself with the prominent members of society, content with a splintered consciousness filled with undigested, often clashing conclusions. The nature of their thought processes, as they confront particular issues, is radically different. In seeking answers, Roark's attention habitually turns to his judgment of the facts as they exist independent from anyone's opinions; Keating's attention turns to the opinions of others.

Atlas Shrugged focuses on psycho-epistemology in more profound ways. The crucial difference between the heroes and villains is the method by which they use their minds. Dagny Taggart and Hank Rearden, for instance, are committed to integration; they seek an integrated view of life and constantly bring to the surface and try to resolve the apparent contradictions and paradoxes they face, be it the inexplicable disappearance of men of intelligence or the paradoxical power of incompetent men like James Taggart and Wesley Mouch.[48] A large part of Hank Rearden's heroism is conveyed by Rand's depiction of the unsparing, reality-oriented nature of his thought. The villains, by contrast, evade the cognitive responsibility of integration. They seek to escape the meaning and summation of their actions and ideas. This issue runs through the characterizations of James Taggart and Robert Stadler. And Galt's analysis in his radio broadcast of the functioning and motivation of such mystics is a psycho-epistemological analysis.

On Rand's view, the core of an individual's psycho-epistemology results from his choices to think or not. But his overall method of cognitive functioning is also shaped by his educational training and models of proper thinking. Rand discusses this point extensively in her essay "The Comprachicos," in which she analyzes the psycho-epistemological havoc caused by Progressive Education and by (too many) modern educators, from the nursery school to the college class-room ("The Comprachicos" *ROTP*). There she admits the possibility that this kind of education can cause irreparable damage to an individual's mind, though also saying that volition gives him "the power to correct many faults in his mental functioning, and many injuries, whether they are self-inflicted or imposed on him from the outside. The latter are easier to correct than the former" ("The Comprachicos" *ROTP* 65).

More widely, across her writings Rand argues that psycho-epistemological issues are crucial to understanding character types, human achievements, and human history. In "The Missing Link," for instance, Rand argues that there exists in today's culture a widespread mentality which she calls the "anti-conceptual mentality," characterized in psycho-epistemological terms. In "The Psycho-Epistemology of Art" she discusses why art, in bringing man's metaphysical value-judgments to the perceptual level of cognition, performs a vital psycho-epistemological function. And in the lead essay of *For the New Intellectual*, Rand argues that Western history must be understood as a battle between "those who, for good or evil, are committed to and motivated by their chosen psycho-epistemology and its corollary view of existence."[49]

Conclusion

In Rand's philosophy, man is, for good or evil, the author of his own soul. Through the primary, self-determined effort to orient his mind to the goal of grasping and dealing with reality, an individual forms his self-esteem, sense of life, and psycho-epistemology. The continual choice to expend (or not to expend) this mental effort is what separates the soul of a moral hero from that of a villain.

At the extreme of villainy is the individual who chooses to initiate a war against his own nature. Such a creature (Rand's term) rejects and seeks to negate the conceptual level of his consciousness – and yet still expects somehow to remain in existence, psychologically and existen-tially. "He is," Rand writes, "a case of arrested psycho-epistemological development" ("The Age of Envy" *ROTP* 150). Volitionally, his is a profound default. "Mental action, i.e., mental *effort* – any sort of processing, identifying, organizing, integrating, critical evaluation or control of his mental content – is an alien realm which he spends his twisted lifetime struggling to escape" (*ROTP* 151).

The ultimate consequence, Rand argues, is an individual driven by whims ("superficial and incredibly banal" emotions "to which he sacrifices his intellect" (*ROTP* 151)) and a deep lack of self-esteem. One metaphysical feeling pervades his emotional life: fear. He senses his impo-tence in the face of reality, which, given his chosen psycho-epistemology, is an unknowable and enemy realm. His sense of life becomes dominated by hatred. Fundamentally, what he comes to hate is reality – which, because of his default, threatens to consign him to the void of non-existence – but the more immediate target of his hatred is "reality's agent in human affairs, man's reason" (*ROTP* 153). Rand calls this feeling "hatred of the good for being the good"; it is a hatred of all the reality-based values that man's reason creates and which make possible a human existence. It is the hater's sense of life, Rand holds, that dominates twentieth-century culture (*ROTP* 130).[50]

At the other extreme is the soul of a moral hero. He is the individual who embraces the fact of his existence and his metaphysically given nature as a rational being. If for Rand the root of evil is an arrested psycho-epistemological development, the root of moral greatness is also psycho-epistemological.[51] It consists in expending the effort necessary to activate and consistently maintain a conceptual level of awareness of reality.

The ultimate consequence of such a policy, Rand argues, is a soul with a deeply rooted self-esteem and an accompanying sense of life that views the universe as a radiant place, a place which rewards an earnest curiosity and a rational, purposeful mind.

Toward the end of his radio broadcast, Galt tells the people struggling to understand the fate of their collapsing world that in their own minds they retain a sense of such a soul, when they experience nostalgia for a childhood before they "had learned to submit, to absorb the terror of unreason," and had instead known a moment of "a radiant state of existence ... the independence of a rational consciousness facing an open universe" (*Atlas* 1058). This is the state of soul, Galt tells them, that they have volitionally renounced but which he refused to. "I am only the man who knew that that state is not to be betrayed. I am the man who knew what made it possible and who chose consistently to practice and to be what you had practiced and been in that one moment" (*Atlas* 1058).

It is the purpose of a rational philosophy to teach man how to consistently practice this – which is why Galt the scientific inventor is also a philosopher, who studies the subject and originates his own philosophical system. In fact, in some form all of Rand's fictional heroes – Kira, Prometheus in *Anthem*, Dominique, Roark, Hank, Francisco, Dagny, Galt – do this. They seek full conscious, conceptual control over their basic premises and values, formulating their growing knowledge of the world into conscious philosophical convictions and correcting any errors they may hold.

Rand maintains that any rational person can do this to some extent, and she will often introduce the essence of her philosophy in common-sense language.[52] But such common sense needs to be translated into an explicit, systematic, consistent, and integrated set of principles. To do this is "the most difficult of human endeavors," and the tragedy of mankind's history is that "(with a few exceptions, to whom mankind owes its lives) rats rushed in where lions feared to tread" (*ROTP* 156). It is a tragedy, Rand holds, because the reward of this endeavor is full life and happiness, a soul that has earned a right to these – and consciously knows it.

In a moving scene in *The Fountainhead*, Gail Wynand, haunted by his own errors and defaults, asks Roark: "Have you always liked being Howard Roark?" In response, Roark smiles. "The smile was amused, astonished, involuntarily contemptuous. 'You've answered,' said Wynand" (*Fountainhead* 545). This, on Rand's view, is the soul of a moral hero – the radiance of an intense, quiet, *earned* pride, derived from knowing that its basic way of functioning, its basic premises, and its basic values are right for reality.

This is the type of soul man can create, Rand maintains, through a volitional commitment to love for reality, for one's self, and for "man at his highest potential" (*ROTP* 158).

Acknowledgment

I would like to thank the editors of this volume for very helpful comments on an earlier version of this chapter.

Notes

1 For Rand's analysis of Romanticism see "What Is Romanticism?" (*RM*). See also Chapter 17 of the present volume.

2 On Rand's distinction between values and moral values, see Chapters 3 and 4 of the present volume.

3 In 1934, at the age of 29, Rand began a philosophical journal; her first entries deal with the issues of ideals, reason versus faith, free will, and the possibility of an ethics based on the individual. See *Journals* 66–74.

4 One can observe Rand developing her account of implicit premises in her 1955 journals (*Journals* 667–677). I discuss Rand's concept of "sense of life" below.

5 Rand argues that crucial to this process are artistic projections of an ideal. See *RM*, especially "The Psycho-Epistemology of Art" and "Art and Moral Treason."

6 For more on Rand's account of the virtue of pride, see Chapter 4 of the present volume.

7 There are significant anticipations of her mature theories in *The Fountainhead* and other writings. For instance, Rand's first mention in print of the term "psycho-epistemology" is in the lead essay of *For the New Intellectual*, but the term "psychological epistemology" figures prominently in notes she made on psychology in 1955, in which her mature view is clearly recognizable (see *Journals* 667–674 for a portion of these notes). I will occasionally reference these earlier writings, but they are not my focus.

8 For Rand's endorsement of these essays as "authentic sources of information on Objectivism" see "A Statement of Policy" (*TO* 7(6) 471). For more on the professional relationship between Rand and Branden, see, in the present volume, 13 and 32.

9 The main sources for Rand's theory of free will are *Atlas Shrugged*, especially John Galt's radio broadcast (*Atlas* 1012–1013, 1017–1018, 1025, 1040–1041), "The Objectivist Ethics" (*VOS* 20–24), and Branden's "The Contradiction of Determinism" (*TON* 2(5)), "What is the Difference Between the Objectivist Concept of Free Will and the Traditional Concepts?" (*TON* 3(1)), "The Objectivist Theory of Volition" (*TO* 5(1–2), and "Volition and the Law of Causality" (*TO* 5(3)). See also Peikoff's treatment in *OPAR*, esp. 55–72, and Binswanger 1991. Rand uses the terms "free will" and "volition" interchangeably, and I will follow suit.

10 This point is part of the theme of *Atlas*. Rand also stresses this issue in "The Objectivist Ethics" (*VOS*).

11 On the distinction between the perceptual and conceptual levels of consciousness, see Chapter 12 of the present volume.

12 Rand accordingly rejects every version of determinism. See, e.g., "The Metaphysical Versus the Man-Made" and "The Stimulus and the Response" (both in *PWNI*); "Racism" (*VOS*); and Branden "The Contradiction of Determinism" (*TON* 2(5)). See also *OPAR* chs. 2 and 6, and Chapter 11 of the present volume.

13 See Branden "The Objectivist Concept of Free Will Versus the Traditional Concepts" (*TON* 3(1) 3).

14 But see Branden "The Contradiction of Determinism," "The Objectivist Theory of Volition," and "Volition and the Law of Causality" (above, n. 9); *OPAR* chs. 1 and 2; and Chapter 11 of the present volume.

15 See Branden "The Objectivist Concept of Free Will Versus the Traditional Concepts" (*TON* 3(1)).

16 The metaphor of mental reins is used in *OPAR* 60.

17 In a workshop, Rand was asked about the beginnings of volition and speculated that there is a period of time in which a child can will to understand, without yet knowing in any form that the process his mind engages in is that of abstraction. See *ITOE* 150–151. See also Chapter 12 of the present volume.

18 See Branden "The Objectivist Theory of Volition" (*TO* 5(1) 11).

19 For a discussion of her treatment of evil in *We the Living* and *Atlas Shrugged*, see Ghate 2012.

20 See *Atlas* 1012.

21 See also *OPAR* 62–69 and Binswanger 1991.

22 See also *OPAR* 62–69, and Chapter 11 of the present volume.

23 See, e.g., "The Comprachicos" (*ROTP*); "Our Cultural Value-Deprivation" (*VOR*); "Art and Moral Treason" (*RM*); "The Establishing of an Establishment" (*PWNI*); and Branden "The Objectivist Theory of Volition" (*TO* 5(1–2)).

24 See, e.g., Branden "Emotions and Repression" (*TO* 5(8–9)). Rand therefore maintains that in evaluating oneself and others, one must carefully distinguish between, as she puts it, errors of knowledge and breaches of morality. See *Atlas* 1059.

25 See Branden "The Objectivist Theory of Volition" (*TO* 5(2) 27).

26 See, e.g., "The Establishing of the Establishment" (*PWNI* 233), where she speaks of a "pyramid of moral endurance."

27 See "Philosophy: Who Needs It" and "Philosophical Detection" (both in *PWNI*); "Philosophy and Sense of Life" (*RM*); and also Branden "Alienation" (*CUI*). Rand of course is not denying that there are other sources of emotional problems, e.g., repression or acceptance of false philosophical ideas like the soul–body dichotomy (a major issue in *Atlas*), or that a rational person can experience individual, out-of-context or otherwise inappropriate emotions. Her point is that a characteristically rational person normally experiences a basic harmony of reason and emotion.

28 For further illustrations of Rand's view of volition, see *OPAR* ch. 2, Binswanger 1991, and Gotthelf (2000, 70–78).

29 The metaphor of cornerstones is mine, but I think it reflects Rand's discussion of man's soul in *RM*; see esp. the book's first four chapters.

30 The main sources for Rand's theory of self-esteem are *The Fountainhead*; *Atlas Shrugged*; "The Objectivist Ethics" (*VOS*); "For the New Intellectual" (*FTNI*); "The Metaphysical Versus the Man-Made" and "Selfishness Without a Self" (both in *PWNI*); "The Age of Envy" (*ROTP*); and Branden's "Mental Health versus Mysticism and Self-Sacrifice" (*VOS*), "Pseudo-Self-Esteem" (*TON* 3(5)), and "Self-Esteem" (*TO* 6(3–6 and 9)). See also *OPAR* 303–310.

31 See Branden "Mental Health versus Mysticism and Self-Sacrifice" (*VOS* 40).

32 To maintain that self-esteem is a metaphysical perspective is not to imply that it is derived from some source other than an individual's specific thoughts, actions, conclusions, successes, and failures. It is only to maintain that self-esteem is a generalized summation of the many choices an individual makes. The issue of self-esteem, therefore, is never closed. It is through the continued choices an individual makes in life, the rationality with which he deals with events, his resulting successes and failures, and the implicit or explicit conclusions he draws from these, that his continued sense of efficacy and worth depends. See Branden "Self-Esteem" (*TO* 6(5) 264–265).

33 For these and more examples see "The Metaphysical Versus the Man-Made" (*PWNI* 39–40).

34 Much of the last third of Galt's radio broadcast focuses on how irrational moral and metaphysical standards have corrupted individuals' self-esteem.

35 In *The Fountainhead* (635) Roark comments on the nature of second-handers like Peter Keating: "no man can achieve the kind of absolute humility that would need no self-esteem in any form. He wouldn't survive. So after centuries of being pounded with the doctrine that altruism is the ultimate ideal, men have accepted it in the only way it could be accepted. By seeking self-esteem through others. By living second-hand. And it has opened the way for every kind of horror." Both *The Fountainhead* and *Atlas* depict various forms of pseudo-self-esteem. See also Branden "Pseudo-Self-Esteem" (*TON* 3(5)).

36 For further discussion of motivation in *The Fountainhead*, see Ghate 2007, 243–284.

37 See esp. "For the New Intellectual" (*FTNI*) and "Philosophical Detection" (*PWNI*).

38 See the Introduction to *The Virtue of Selfishness* (quote is from xi); "Altruism as Appeasement" (*VOR*); "The Age of Envy" (*ROTP*); "Of Living Death" (*VOR*); and "Causality Versus Duty" (*PWNI*).

39 The main sources for Rand's account of sense of life are "Philosophy and Sense of Life" and "Art and Sense of Life," both in *RM* (but most of the book's essays touch on the issue); her Introductions to *The Fountainhead* and *Night of January 16th*; "Don't Let It Go" (*PWNI*); "Through Your Most Grievous Fault" (*VOR*); and "The American Spirit" (*ARL* 2(4)).

40 For further discussion of Rand's conception of metaphysics, see Chapter 11 of the present volume.

41 See also Chapter 18 of the present volume.

42 For more on the benevolent and malevolent universe premises, see *RM* and "The Metaphysical Versus the Man-Made" (*PWNI*), as well as *OPAR* 342–343 and Gotthelf 2000, 94–97.

43 One can see a somewhat similar characterization of Dagny's attitude toward life in *Atlas* 54.

44 For Rand's account of art from this perspective, see "The Psycho-Epistemology of Art," "Philosophy and Sense of Life," "Art and Sense of Life," and "Art and Cognition" (all in *RM*); for her account of romantic love from this perspective, see *Atlas* 488–493 and also Branden "Self-Esteem and Romantic Love" (*TO* 6(12)–7(2)). See also, in the present volume, 88–89, 408, and 417–419; cf., 386–387.

45 See "Of Living Death" (*VOR*), "Requiem for Man" (*CUI*), and "Don't Let It Go" (*PWNI*).

46 The main sources for Rand's account of psycho-epistemology are *Atlas*; "For the New Intellectual" (*FTNI*); "What Is Capitalism?" (*CUI*); "The Psycho-Epistemology of Art," "Art and Sense of Life," "Art and Cognition," and "Basic Principles of Literature" (all in *RM*); *ITOE*; "The Comprachicos" and "The Age of Envy" (both in *ROTP*); "The Psychology of Psychologizing" (*VOR*); *Journals*; and the first ten essays anthologized in *PWNI*; as well as Branden's "Psycho-Epistemology" (*TON* 3(10–11)).

47 This is a point that Branden also makes. See his "Psycho-Epistemology" (*TON* 3(10)).

48 For further discussion of Dagny and Rearden's thought processes, see Salmieri 2009b.

49 See "The Missing Link" (*PWNI*); "The Psycho-Epistemology of Art" (*RM*); and "For the New Intellectual" (quote is from *FTNI* 16).

50 See also *Parallels*. "Hatred of the good for being the good" captures the fundamental nature of the villains in *Atlas*; see, e.g., *Atlas* 1145–1146. For discussion, see Ghate 2012.

51 This is a point Branden also makes; see Branden "Psycho-Epistemology" (*TON* 3(10)).

52 See, e.g., her first *Los Angeles Times* column, "Introducing Objectivism" (reprinted in *VOR*).

References

Binswanger, Harry. 1991. "Volition as Cognitive Self-Regulation." *Organizational Behavior and Human Decision Processes*, 50.

Ghate, Onkar. 2007. "The Basic Motivation of the Creators and the Masses in *The Fountainhead*." In *Essays on Ayn Rand's* The Fountainhead, edited by Robert Mayhew. Lanham, MD: Lexington Books.

Ghate, Onkar. 2012. "The Death Premise in *We the Living* and *Atlas Shrugged*." In *Essays on Ayn Rand's* We the Living, 2nd edition, edited by Robert Mayhew. Lanham, MD: Lexington Books.

Gotthelf, Allan. 2000. *On Ayn Rand*. Belmont, CA: Wadsworth.

Salmieri, Gregory. 2009b. "Discovering Atlantis: *Atlas Shrugged*'s Demonstration of a New Moral Philosophy." In *Essays on Ayn Rand's* Atlas Shrugged, edited by Robert Mayhew. Lanham, MD: Lexington Books.

6

Egoism and Altruism

Selfishness and Sacrifice

GREGORY SALMIERI

When Ayn Rand is studied in philosophy classes, it is most often in connection with her defense of ethical egoism and rejection of altruism.[1] Though this is a striking aspect of her moral theory, and it is the one that she most often highlighted, she did not think that the question to which egoism and altruism are contrary answers was the central or fundamental issue in moral philosophy:

> The choice of the beneficiary of moral values is merely a preliminary or introductory issue in the field of morality. It is not a substitute for morality, nor a criterion of moral value as altruism has made it. Neither is it a moral *primary*: it has to be derived from and validated by the fundamental premises of a moral system. (*VOS* x)

For Rand, the purpose of ethics is to define "a code of values to guide [...] the choices and actions that determine the course of [man's] life" ("Philosophy: Who Needs It?" *PWNI* 4). The central question of ethics is what values are worth pursuing. In Chapter 4, above, Allan Gotthelf discusses how Rand answers this question, including her view that a philosopher's answer to this question depends on his fundamental premises about the nature of values and of human beings' need for them. Rand's position on these issues is discussed by Gotthelf in Chapter 4 (76–78) and by me in Chapter 3 (63). Both of those chapters discuss the egoistic character of Rand's ethics, but it is not their focus. In the present chapter, I discuss what it means for Rand's ethics to be egoistic.

I begin by looking at different doctrines that have been called "egoism" and situating Rand's position relative to them. Then I turn to her characterization of altruism, and identify instances of this view both in popular moral discourse and in the history of philosophy, and I survey Rand's criticisms of the view. I close with a discussion of Rand's insistence on describing the moral life as "selfish" even though, in common usage, "selfish" is a term of opprobrium and connotes a type of behavior that is incompatible with her morality.

A Companion to Ayn Rand, First Edition. Edited by Allan Gotthelf and Gregory Salmieri.
© 2016 John Wiley & Sons Ltd. Published 2016 by John Wiley & Sons, Ltd.

Situating Rand's Egoism

The term "egoism" has been used to refer to a variety of different theories about distinct but related subjects. What connects them all is the idea of *egoistic* (or selfish) action – that is, action taken with the ultimate goal of benefiting oneself. We could also describe this ultimate goal as advancing one's interest or self-interest or welfare or attaining one's good or what is good for one; I will use all of these expressions interchangeably.

Egoistic actions can be contrasted with actions that have other ultimate motivations. Such motives might include: benefiting other people, obeying some authority, or adhering to some principle (other than the principle of pursuing self-interest). What is at issue here is one's *ultimate* motivation for an action. Adhering to principles or benefiting others is egoistic, if someone does these things as a means to (or part of) advancing his self-interest. Conversely, actions taken with the proximate goal of benefiting oneself are not egoistic if one performs them only in order to benefit others or out of fealty to some authority figure or (non-egoistic) principle.

What is in an individual's interest is not always obvious – neither to the individual himself nor to a third party. It can be difficult to determine, for example, whether attending a certain school will benefit one – likewise for taking a certain job, or following a certain diet, marrying a certain person, and so on. Part of the difficulty lies in predicting the effects of each course of action; but even when all the relevant effects of each course are known, it can still be unclear which course is best for the individual. Consider for example the choice faced by Achilles in Book 9 of the *Iliad*:

> For my mother Thetis the goddess of the silver feet tells me I carry two sorts of destiny towards the day of my death. Either, if I stay here and fight beside the city of the Trojans, my return home is gone, but my glory shall be everlasting; but if I return home to the beloved land of my fathers, the excellence of my glory is gone, but there will be a long life left for me, and my end in death will not come to me quickly. (*Iliad* 9.410–416, tr. Lattimore 1951)

There are two futures open to Achilles; and, because he has divine foreknowledge, he knows just how his life would go in either case; but he still has difficulty choosing. The source of the difficulty is that the two lives open to him represent different values – glory and longevity – and he does not know which of these is *better for him*. People often face similar choices between competing values – for example, the choice between a job that is more lucrative and one that one enjoys more, or between a home that is more spacious and one that is more stylish, or between romantic relationships that engage and foster different aspects of one's character.

One reason why such choices are difficult is that it is not obvious what it is for something to be in someone's interest. Or to put this point slightly differently: *it is a substantive philosophical question what it means for something to be good for a person.* Evidently, it cannot simply be the satisfaction of the person's present desires, since people often desire things that are *bad for them* (both as judged by the people themselves and by third parties). Some theorists identify a person's good with the satisfaction of her second-order desires (i.e., with what she wants to want) or with what some idealized version of herself would want (either for her idealized self or for her actual self); other theorists identify an individual's good with certain psychological states (such as pleasure or tranquility); still other theorists identify it with the attainment of one or more ends that they take to be intrinsically valuable (such as knowledge, virtue, friendship, the development of one's talents, or the contemplation of genuine beauty).[2]

Rand held that an individual's good is "to achieve, maintain, fulfill and enjoy that ultimate value, that end in itself, which is his own life" ("The Objectivist Ethics" *VOS* 27). Because life is "a process of self-sustaining and self-generated action" (*VOS* 16, *Atlas* 1013), the life which is one's ultimate value is not a self-contained end that can be separated from the actions by which one sustains oneself; rather the end is "the support of his own life by his own effort and the achievement of his own happiness" (*Letters* 556). That it is one's own effort sustaining one's life and happiness is part of the goal. This is reflected in her choice of the word "achievement"; for happiness would not be an achievement, if it were attained in some way other than as an effect of one's own effort. In fact, Rand does not think that happiness can be attained in any other way, because she identifies happiness as the emotional form in which one experiences the achievement and value of one's life; thus life and happiness, as Rand understood them, are two aspects of a single achievement.

The function of morality, as Rand sees it, is to identify, in abstract terms, the sort of life by which a human being can sustain himself across a human lifespan. It is a life led in accordance with the virtues of rationality, independence, integrity, honesty, justice, productiveness, and pride. Such a life will be guided in all spheres by reason, will be organized around a productive career, and will include the full range of values discussed by Gotthelf in Chapter 4, above.

This abstract specification of the human form of life serves as a standard of value under the guidance of which an individual can choose the particular values and activities that make up his particular life. It is living this particular life, rather than mere conformity to an abstract standard, that constitutes the individual's interest. The goodness of this life for him is *objective* in the sense of this term in which Rand opposes it both to the *intrinsic* and to the *subjective* (see 67–68 and 290–292 in the present volume). An intrinsic good would be something that is good in virtue solely of facts independent of human consciousness, and a subjective good would be one that is good solely in virtue of consciousness, independent of facts. An objective good is something that an individual has chosen as a value for himself in accordance with a rational, fact-based standard.

Only insofar as an individual chooses values in this way does he have a self-interest at all. Values chosen subjectively, without regard for the requirements of human survival, will not form into a self-sustaining whole; so rather than a coherent self-interest that he can act to advance, the individual will have a motley assortment of conflicting desires. But neither can self-interest be intrinsic: there is an inexhaustible variety of possible combinations of values and activities that could cohere into a self-sustaining human life, and there is nothing other than an individual's choosing and pursuing one of these possibilities for himself that can make this particular life constitute *his* self-interest and ultimate goal.

In addition to disagreeing about what constitutes an individual's interest, different theories called "egoism" make different claims about the role of egoistic action in life. It is crucial to distinguish between *ethical egoism* and *psychological egoism*.[3]

Rand is an ethical egoist, and ethical egoism is a moral theory – a theory about how people *ought to act*.[4] It maintains that a person's own interest should be the ultimate goal of all of his actions. This theory can be contrasted with other moral theories – for example, utilitarianism, which holds that a person ought to act to advance the general welfare (even when this means sacrificing his own happiness), or deontologism, which holds that people ought to perform certain duties (even when doing so requires sacrificing their own welfare).

Unlike all of these theories, psychological egoism makes no claims about how people should behave; instead it purports to describe how they do in fact behave. It is the view that people always and inevitably act egoistically – that there are no actions that are ultimately motivated by anything other than self-interest.[5] Thus, psychological egoism is to be contrasted with theories that ascribe other motives to (all or some) human actions.

Not only are psychological and ethical egoism distinct theories, it is not obvious whether they are compatible. What would it mean to maintain that one *should* act in a certain manner, if one thinks that everyone inevitably will do so? The theories can be combined only if there is some difference in the respect in which we all necessarily pursue self-interest and the respect in which we ought to pursue it. For example, one could hold that people are always motivated by what *seems* to be in their self-interest, but that they should act for what is *actually* in their self-interest. On this view, immorality is caused only by the failure to recognize one's true interest, and the function of ethics as a discipline is to remedy this situation by providing the principles by which our true interest can be ascertained. This view can be plausibly ascribed to Socrates, Epicurus, and Thomas Hobbes.

Psychological egoists need not be ethical egoists. Some, like Friedrich Nietzsche, Max Stirner, and Sigmund Freud, reject morality altogether, writing about it only descriptively, without endorsing any moral theory. Other psychological egoists hold moral views according to which self-interest and morality are distinct but sometimes coincide. For example, Jeremy Bentham held that what makes an action moral is that it maximizes the general happiness, but that what makes an action good for an individual is that it maximizes her own happiness. If so, then the individual will take the moral action only when (in her own estimation) it will also maximize her own happiness. Thus Bentham focused on the issue of which social institutions would produce circumstances in which morality and self-interest coincide as often as possible.[6] Elements of this view can also be seen in Nikolai Chernyshevsky (though in other respects his view is more like that of Hobbes).

Few contemporary ethicists are psychological egoists, and Rand certainly was not. Psychological egoism is a form of determinism, a doctrine that Rand rejected.[7] Moreover, it is a theme of both *The Fountainhead* and *Atlas Shrugged* that people do not always pursue their self-interest, and *The Virtue of Selfishness* contains a brief essay by Nathaniel Branden refuting the thesis that all human action is self-interested ("Isn't Everybody Selfish?" *VOS*).[8]

Far from thinking that people automatically and inevitably pursue their self-interest, Rand did not even think that people automatically have a self-interest to pursue. As we discussed above, in order to have a self-interest, one must have rationally chosen values that cohere into a self-sustaining life, and this is not something that people automatically do; it is an achievement – a product of virtue. Once a person has achieved this, it takes continued effort on each occasion to determine whether a given course of action benefits or harms his life. People who act in a thoughtless range-of-the moment manner are not pursuing what they believe to be in their self-interest, since they are not thinking about what larger purpose (if any) is served by the immediate goals they are pursuing.

Such thoughtlessness is not the only form in which Rand thinks one can fail to pursue one's own interest; she holds that it is also possible to deliberately sacrifice what one believes to be best for one in order to fulfill what one believes is one's moral duty. Someone who makes such a sacrifice can in some sense be said to value that for the sake of which he sacrifices, but this does not make it objectively in his interest, nor does it make his mental state regarding it one of *valuing*, in the sense in which Rand used that term.

Having distinguished ethical from psychological egoism and having indicated the range of possible views of self-interest, it is instructive to compare Rand's version of ethical egoism to the

133

views of three groups of thinkers, whom I'll call egoistic consequentialists, eudaimonists, and radical individualists.

Under the heading of "egoistic consequentialists," I include Epicurus, Hobbes, and Chernyshevsky. Hobbes identified an individual's interest with the satisfaction of her desires; the other two identified it with her pleasure. On either view, the individual's interest is a psychological state that is valuable in itself, apart from any actions that may lead to it. These thinkers are *consequentialists* in that they maintain that the rightness of an action is determined wholly by consequences that are distinct from the action itself – specifically by the consequence of maximizing a psychological state that they regard as intrinsically good. Their consequentialism is *egoistic* in that it holds that one should maximize this intrinsically good state in (and for) oneself, rather than in all people impartially. Each of the three argued that certain generally recognized moral principles or virtues are indispensable means to the maximization of this state in oneself: Epicurus argued that prudence and temperance secure pleasure by silencing baseless desires that cause pain when they cannot be satisfied; Hobbes argued that it is foolish to suppose that one could get away with injustice; and Chernyshevsky argued that people's interests are so related that is impossible to benefit oneself by any course of action that is inconsistent with the general happiness.[9]

Rand was not a consequentialist. On her view, an individual's welfare is not something that can be separated from his actions and evaluated apart from them. It consists, rather, in his own rational achievement of a self-sustaining life. However, like the egoistic consequentialists, she argued that traits such as honesty, justice, and integrity are virtues precisely because they are indispensable means to further values. (See Gotthelf's discussion, above, 92–96.) Moreover, there are similarities between some of her arguments and some of theirs: *The Fountainhead*'s treatment of "secondhand" values (*Fountainhead* 633–634; cf. *Journals* 82) is reminiscent of the Epicurean doctrine of baseless desires; and Rand's arguments that parasitism is self-destructive (see 166–167, below) and that there are no conflicts of interest among rational men (see 167–172) have commonalities with the arguments from Hobbes and Chernyshevsky mentioned above (though Rand's arguments go deeper by addressing the goals of injustice as well as the means).

Eudaimonism, the dominant theory in Ancient Greek ethics, was developed in different forms by Plato, Aristotle and the Stoics. It maintains that an individual's good consists of "*eudaimonia*," a Greek word, often translated "happiness," which denotes the quality (or set of qualities) whereby a human life is flourishing or successful. Eudaimonists disagree about precisely what this quality is, but all think that it centrally involves virtue. Rather than seeing virtue as a means to maximizing some end distinct from itself, they regard virtue as an integral component of a flourishing life, and they hold up such a life as an ideal that the individual can aspire to realize (or at least approximate) in her life as a whole.[10]

Eudaimonism holds that what a person should do always coincides with her self-interest, but is ambiguous whether eudaimonism is a form of egoism, because it is not clear that, according to eudaimonism, this is the reason why the person should take the action. Ethical egoism is the thesis that what makes an action moral (or virtuous) is that it benefits the agent; whereas, according to eudaimonism, it is the virtuousness of an action that makes it part of *eudaimonia* and thus good for the agent. What then makes it virtuous? If an answer is given in terms of the agent's welfare, then eudaimonism would be a form of egoism; but eudaimonists generally define the virtues by appealing to standards of rightness or nobility that are not (at least, not obviously) based on the agent's welfare.[11]

Rand identifies the standard of value as "man's life" and has a demanding and exalted conception of the life "proper to man" ("The Objectivist Ethics" *VOS* 25–27). This has led some commentators to interpret her as a eudaimonist.[12] This is not an implausible interpretation of Rand's thought in the 1930s and 1940s, but it is not accurate for Rand's mature view. As Gotthelf and I each discuss in earlier chapters (see 60–61, 66–68, and 91–92), *Atlas Shrugged* and Rand's subsequent essays present virtue neither as intrinsically good nor as an instrument by which one maximizes some such good as pleasure, desire-satisfaction, or longevity. Rand recognized a third alternative: the moral values and virtues are essential constituents of the ultimate end that is a person's life, and they owe their status as constituents to the *causal contribution* they make to the sustenance of this life.[13] On her view, there are no values apart from an individual's ultimate value of his own life, and a person's life is made up of the values and activities by which he sustains himself.

Rand's morality is intended as an abstract specification of the human form of life – the process required of a human being if he is to sustain himself in existence, as opposed both to dying and to subsisting tenuously as a parasite. This specification serves as a standard with reference to which an individual can both select the particular values that will constitute his own life and discover the means by which these values can be achieved. Thus, for Rand, as for the eudaimonists, the content of morality is prior to any determinate ends that an individual may pursue, and it provides a standard by which such ends can be evaluated. Whether a person should pursue a particular career or relationship or material possession is not to be determined by calculating its consequences for some bottom line (whether this bottom line is conceived in terms of pleasure, desire-satisfaction, longevity, or any other maximizable good); it is, rather, to be determined by whether it is a constituent of (or a means to) leading a life of the sort proper to a human being. Unlike the eudaimonists', however, Rand's account of the sort of life that is proper to a human being is unambiguously egoistic, because she argues that what makes this form of life proper to a human being is that it is the manner in which a human being sustains *himself*.

For Rand, virtue is good neither intrinsically (as an end in itself) nor instrumentally (as a means to an end wholly distinct from itself), but as an essential contributing part of a person's ultimate end.[14] Virtue is not the only thing that she thinks is good in this way. She writes that the contemplation of art is experienced as "a self-sufficient, self-justifying primary" that "serves no practical, material end"; but she argues that art's value "*is* inextricably tied to man's survival," because it plays a psychological role that is vital to the functioning of human consciousness ("The Psycho-Epistemology of Art" *RM* 4, 5).[15] The experience of contemplating an artwork is valuable, not as a self-contained intrinsic value, nor as a mere means to some end separate from itself, but as a contributing component of the life that is one's ultimate value. Thus its value is egoistic without being instrumental.

Rand took the same view of the value of friends and loved ones: "One gains a profoundly personal, selfish joy from the mere existence of the person one loves" ("The Ethics of Emergencies" *VOS* 51). This joy is not a response to any service rendered; but it is self-interested, in that it depends on and is conditioned by the loved one's place in the self-supporting constellation of values that is one's life. Moreover, because what one values (and takes joy in) is the loved one's "mere existence," actions taken to promote his welfare needn't have any ulterior motive to qualify as egoistic.[16] Indeed, Rand speaks of "incorporating" a loved one's "welfare" into "one's own hierarchy of values" (*VOS* 53; cf. *Letters* 547). (See Gotthelf's discussion – 89, above – of the place Rand thinks that friends and loved ones occupy in a rational hierarchy of values; and see Darryl Wright's discussion – 161–163, below – of the extent to which a rational egoist values even strangers.) Each item in this hierarchy is valued neither in itself nor as a mere means, but as a contributing member of the whole that is one's life; and it is to be valued in proportion to its contribution to this whole.

I use the phrase "radical individualists" to refer to nineteenth-century thinkers like Max Stirner and Friedrich Nietzsche, who celebrated exceptional individuals and thought that part of what made them exceptional was their holding distinctive values of their own, which set them apart from others. Stirner and Nietzsche spoke favorably of selfishness (*"Eigennützigkeit"* and *"Selbstsucht"*), and they condemned morality as ignoble and as a threat to individuality and to the exceptional individuals they celebrated.[17] Neither Stirner nor Nietzsche offered a *morality* of egoism; for both saw morality as such as a constraint on individuality.[18] Largely because of this, they conceived of self-interest as subjective, they took it for granted that human beings would be in perpetual conflict, and Nietzsche celebrated attempts by (what he regarded as) superior people to dominate their inferiors.

Like Stirner and Nietzsche, Rand focused on individuals' distinctive values, she celebrated exceptional people, and she condemned altruism; but, unlike them, she was a moralist. Whereas they regarded personal values as subjective, she held that values can and should be objective and based on a principled grasp of the requirements of human survival. Far from constraining the individual's pursuit of his distinctive values, she held that moral principles are what make value-pursuit possible. (See Allan Gotthelf's discussion of Rand's view of morality in Chapter 4, above, especially 90.) Moreover, as Darryl Wright discusses in the next chapter (167–172, below), Rand held that there are no conflicts of interest among people who form their values objectively, and that there is nothing to be gained from dominating others. Thus, in place of a society in which superior people dominate inferiors, Rand advocated a society where people trade on equal terms to mutual advantage; and she held that, in such a society, people with extraordinary virtue and ability confer extraordinary benefits on others. (Lester Hunt discusses this key difference between Rand and Nietzsche in Chapter 14, below, 347.)

Like the egoistic consequentialists, Rand held that the goodness of virtues depends on their role in enabling us to secure other goods; but, like the eudaimonists, she considered virtue to be an essential constituent of the life which is a person's ultimate end, rather than a mere means to a distinct end. Like the radical individualists, she rejected altruism, but, unlike them, she thought individuals need moral principles to define and achieve their values. As we've seen, this unusual combination of views was made possible by her distinctive positions on foundational issues in ethics, including: the nature of values, the nature of life as an ultimate value, and what it is for a value to be objective.

Altruism: The Morality of Self-Sacrifice

"To say that I 'don't like' Altruism is too weak," Rand said in a 1959 interview; "I consider it evil" (*Speaking* 170). The word "altruism" is sometimes used to describe all forms of kindness or concern for other people. Of course, this was not what Rand considered evil, but neither did she use the word in some special sense distinct from its ordinary meaning; for the description of benevolent acts as "altruistic" implies a certain understanding of the nature and motive of these actions. This is reflected in the *Oxford English Dictionary*'s (2013) definition of altruism as "Disinterested or selfless concern for the well-being of others, esp. as a principle of action.

Opposed to *selfishness, egoism,* or (in early use) *egotism.*" For an action to be altruistic is for it to be aimed at others' well-being disinterestedly, meaning that this is its *ultimate* motivation rather than something that is seen as a means to or component of self-interest. When someone describes benevolent actions as altruistic, he is assuming that this is the nature of such actions. Rand emphatically rejected both this assumption about benevolent actions and the view that such disinterested action is ever moral.

Almost all moral theories maintain that people are obligated to take at least some altruistic actions. We can call all such theories "altruistic," but when "altruism" is used as the name of a moral theory (as Rand often used it), it denotes the view that being disinterested and aiming ultimately at the well-being of others is what makes an action – or a life – moral. Howard Roark defines this view as follows: "Altruism is the doctrine which demands that man live for others and place others above self" (*Fountainhead* 712; cf. *Journals* 249). Speaking in her own voice, Rand elaborated its content as follows:

> What is the moral code of altruism? The basic principle of altruism is that man has no right to exist for his own sake, that service to others is the only justification of his own existence, and that self-sacrifice is his highest moral duty, virtue and value.
>
> Do not confuse altruism with kindness, good will or respect for the rights of others. These are not primaries, but consequences, which, in fact, altruism makes impossible. The irreducible primary of altruism, the basic absolute, is *self-sacrifice* – which means: self-immolation, self-abnegation, self-denial, self-destruction – which means: the *self* as a standard of evil, the *selfless* as the standard of the good.
>
> Do not hide behind such superficialities as whether you should or should not give a dime to a beggar. That is not the issue. The issue is whether you *do* or do *not* have the right to exist *without* giving them that dime. The issue is whether you must keep buying your life, dime by dime, from any beggar that might choose to approach you. The issue is whether or not the need of others is the first mortgage on your life and the moral purpose of your existence. The issue is whether man is to be regarded as a sacrificial animal. Any man of self-esteem will answer: "*No.*" Altruism says: "*Yes.*" ("Faith and Force: The Destroyers of the Modern World" *PWNI* 83–84; cf. "Theory and Practice" *CUI* 135, "Apollo 11" *VOR* 17; Branden "Benevolence vs. Altruism" *TON* 1(7).)

It is altruism so understood that Rand thought was the generally accepted view of morality. We can see in this passage that Rand held that its essence is the *demand for self-sacrifice*, rather than any genuine concern for others. Perhaps to capture this fact, *Atlas Shrugged*, which contains Rand's most sustained discussion of this morality, rarely uses the word "altruism." In the novel's climactic speech, John Galt refers to the view as "the morality of sacrifice" (or sometimes "the morality of death").[19] However, in Rand's subsequent non-fiction (including the 1960 speech quoted above), the word "altruism" appears frequently (as it does in *The Fountainhead*), always naming the view that one is obligated to sacrifice one's values, rather than the view that one should value other people.

By "sacrifice," Rand means "the surrender of that which you value in favor of that which you don't" (*Atlas* 1028; cf. "Ethics of Emergencies" *VOS* 50). Of course there is a sense in which someone making a sacrifice can be said to regard that for the sake of which he is sacrificing as a value; often he will regard it as something "higher" or "better" than what he gives up (or than himself). But if we are to understand the action as a sacrifice, rather than as a self-interested trade or investment, we must understand the person to be giving up something that he regards as more valuable to him personally for the sake something that he sees as less a part of his personal good – even if he regards this latter thing as better in some abstract sense. For an action to be a sacrifice (as Rand understand the term, at least), it must involve placing something or someone above (what one understands to be) one's own interest.

Rand's characterization of altruism has sometimes been attacked as a straw man. Here are three examples of this criticism from ethics textbooks:

> As Ayn Rand describes it, "altruism" implies that one's own interests have *no* value, and that *any* demand by others calls for sacrificing them. Thus the "ethics of altruism" would appeal to no one, with the possible exception of certain monks. (Rachels 1999, 88)

> Similarly, Rand caricatures altruism when she argues that it sets up the self as the standard of evil. No significant version of altruism proposes to do this. (Wilkens 2011, 56)

> Nothing in the definition of altruism, nor in any well-known version of altruistic theory (e.g. Christianity or Kantianism) implies that any action taken for the benefit of others is good. Many dictators and lunatics believe that they are acting for the benefit of others ..., yet their acts are condemned by almost all moral systems. Similarly, neither the definition of altruism nor any well-known theory of altruism claims that all actions taken for one's own benefit are evil. The result of Rand's stilted definitions is that she produced a caricature of altruism that is all too easy to attack. (Palmer 2006, 107–108)

Contrary to the claims of these critics, it is easy to find examples of people endorsing altruism as Rand understood it. Let's consider some examples from popular discourse, before turning to examples from the history of philosophy.

In 2004, polls indicated that American voters regarded "moral values" as one of the most important issues in choosing a president, and these same polls made it clear that voters who prioritized values strongly preferred the Republican incumbent George W. Bush to his challenger John Kerry. Thus, in his speech accepting the Democratic Party nomination, Kerry took great pains to appeal to voters concerned about morality. Here is what he said:

> And whatever our faith, one belief should bind us all: The measure of our character is our willingness to give of ourselves for others and for our country. These aren't Democratic values. These aren't Republican values. They're American values. (Kerry 2004)

Notice that what Kerry treats as a platitude is not just that it's often good to give of oneself for others (including the others that constitute one's country), but that one's willingness to do so is *the sole measure of character*. Notice too that no reference is made to whether anyone else is actually benefited by these sacrifices. The view that Kerry said should "bind us all" is exactly altruism as Rand understood it.

John McCain, the Republican candidate in the following presidential election, is also an explicit altruist in Rand's sense. In various speeches in the years leading up to the election he said "To sacrifice for a cause greater than yourself, and to sacrifice your life to the eminence of that cause, is the noblest activity of all," and he continually challenged Americans to "serve a cause greater than self-interest" (Landon 2006, McCain 2008). Notice that what is being praised here, as in Kerry's speech, is specifically sacrifice and service, rather than anything that is supposed to be achieved by this service. True, we are told that the cause must be *higher than ourselves*, but we are not told what causes are higher than ourselves or by what standard they should be regarded as higher. McCain was not calling us to work on behalf of any specific goal, for any specific reason; he was merely extolling self-sacrifice.

Similarly, consider the following sentence, which Michelle Obama quoted approvingly in a commencement address: "Service is the rent we pay for living ... it is the true measure, the only measure of our success" (Obama 2009).[20] What difference is there between this statement and Rand's characterization of altruism (quoted above) as the view "the need of others is the first mortgage on your life and the moral purpose of your existence"?

Contrary to the charge that the altruism Rand speaks of "would appeal to no one, with the possible exception of certain monks," Kerry's, McCain's, and Obama's statements were all applauded by their immediate audiences, and there were few if any objections from the speakers' political rivals. I submit that this is because *these statements are uncontroversial expressions of the popular conception of morality.* I do not mean, of course, that everyone holds this view of morality reflectively and consistently – people do not ordinarily hold any moral views in that way – but it is no accident that such expressions occur in political discourse.

We find more frequent and more dramatic appeals to self-sacrifice as a moral ideal in the political discourse of less-free nations. Hitler, for example, claimed that the "state of mind" that "subordinates the interests of the ego to the conservation of the community, is really the first premise for every human culture." "[T]o distinguish it from egoism and selfishness," he calls this attitude "idealism" and equates it with "the individual's capacity to make sacrifices for the community, for his fellow men."[21] As Rand observed, dictators typically justify their regimes on altruistic grounds, and they could not rise to power unless they were regarded by their supporters as moral.[22] One of Rand's critics (quoted above) claimed that dictators are "condemned by almost all moral systems," and it is true that one can find examples of people appealing to various altruistic systems in the course of condemning dictators; but it is also true that every prominent dictator (including Lenin, Hitler, Stalin, Castro, Mao Tse Tung, Pol Pot, and Ruhollah Khomeini) enjoyed strident support from intellectuals who denied, minimized, or defended his atrocities on explicitly altruistic grounds.[23]

Turning now to the role of altruism in the history of philosophy, it is natural to begin with Auguste Comte, who coined the term. "*L'altruisme*" first appeared in 1851 in his *Système de politique positive* (vol. 1, p. 614), and the word entered English as "altruism" two years later in George Henry Lewes's *Comte's Philosophy of the Sciences*:

> This emotional life (*vie affective*) is divisible into Personality and Sociality. The lower animals only manifest the first; the second commences with a separation of the sexes, and grows more and more energetic in proportion to the rank of the animal in the hierarchical scale; so that all the higher animals exhibit both Personality and Sociality. These may be denominated *Egoism* and *Altruism*. (Lewes 1853, 217)

For Comte, "egoism" and "altruism" were primarily psychological terms denoting opposite impulses found across the animal kingdom, the former motivating an animal to benefit itself and the latter motivating it to benefit others.[24] Lewes explains that this distinction lies at the basis of moral thought: "Dispositions influenced by the purely egoistic impulses, we call popularly 'bad,' and apply the term 'good' to those in which altruism predominates" (Lewes 1853, 224). Thus Comte (1875, 122) wrote that the "chief problem of human life" is how to effect "the subordination of Egoism to Altruism."[25] His solution to this problem was that "all human education" should teach "every man" the following maxim: "Live for Others" (Comte 1875, 132, 143, 301, 322; 1876, 158; 1877, 33, 7, 228, 273).

The only alternative Comte envisioned to living for others was serving transient whims. Lewes explains:

> A character governed by the inferior [egoistic] instincts alone, can have neither stability nor fixed purposes; these qualities are alone attained under the empire of the impulses which prompt man

to live for others. Every individual, man or animal, accustomed to life for self alone, is condemned to a miserable alternation of ignoble torpor or feverish activity. Even personal happiness and merit therefore depend on the predominance of the sympathetic instincts. Progress towards such a moral condition should be the object of every living being. To live for others is thus the natural conclusion of all Positive Morality. (Lewes 1853, 221–222)

When Comte and Lewes speak of "the predominance of the sympathetic instincts" they do not simply mean that one should be empathetic and often act to benefit others. They mean that altruism should totally order and direct one's life so that one lives as a servant of humanity as a whole.

No being can nobly labor for itself save Humanity, her servants for the time being do but employ in the interest of her servants yet unborn the products which they get from the materials collected by her servants in the past. (Comte 1877, 285–286)

As a sign of how completely this view subordinates the self to the interests of others, consider the scope that Comte does allow to egoistic impulses. He writes that his system

alone holds at once both a noble and true language when it urges us to *live for others*. This, the definitive formula of human morality, gives a direct sanction exclusively to our instincts of benevolence, the common source of happiness and of duty. Implicitly and indirectly it sanctions our personal instincts, as the necessary conditions of our existence, with the proviso that they must be subordinate to those of altruism. With this limitation, we are even ordered to gratify our personal instincts, with the view of fitting ourselves to be better servants of Humanity, whose we are entirely. (Comte 1858, 217)[26]

In short: on Comte's view, the only justification for ever pursuing one's self-interest at all is that a total failure to do so would render one unable to serve others.

Comte is no longer much studied as a moral theorist, but his altruism was accepted wholeheartedly by his friend John Stuart Mill, who remains one of the most respected moral philosophers. Commenting on Comte, Mill writes:

All education and all moral discipline [according to Comte] should have but one object, to make altruism (a word of his own coining) predominate over egoism. If by this were meant that egoism is bound, and should be taught always to give way to the well-understood interests of enlarged altruism, no one who acknowledged any morality at all would object to the proposition. (Mill 1865, 4)[27]

We can see here that Mill accepts entirely Comte's notion of morality, and indeed Mill thinks that *everyone would*. He objects only that Comte is "a morality-intoxicated man. Every question with him is one of morality, and no motive but that of morality is permitted" (1856, 5).[28] The difference Mill sees between himself and Comte, then, is that Comte holds that self-sacrifice is good in itself, whereas Mill thinks that it is only good when it benefits others:

All honor to those who can abnegate for themselves the personal enjoyment of life, when by such renunciation they contribute worthily to increase the amount of happiness in the world; but he who does it, or professes to do it, for any other purpose, is no more deserving of admiration than the ascetic mounted on his pillar. He may be an inspiriting proof of what men can do, but assuredly not an example of what they should. (Mill 1879, 38)

The position that Mill attributed to Comte and rejected himself is the one that Rand saw as the true essence of altruism – the injunction to sacrifice as such. Though Mill thought that sacrifice is only called for in certain circumstances and that morality often permits a person to act from self-interest, notice that he did not think that, in these cases, the person is acting on "a moral motive." So for Mill, no less than for Comte, morality consists in sacrificing for others. The difference is just (as we saw) that Mill thought that morality permits us to sometimes act on non-moral motives.

In fact, whatever Mill himself may have thought, it is doubtful that utilitarianism, the ethical theory he endorsed, leaves much scope for an individual to pursue his own interests. In the past 50 years, a number of prominent ethicists have attacked utilitarianism precisely on the grounds that it requires an agent to be prepared to sacrifice lightly even values that are central to his personal identity.[29]

Though Comte coined the term "altruism," he did not claim any great originality for the idea. He regarded the opposition between egoism and altruism as identical to the opposition St. Paul spoke of "between Nature and Grace" (Comte 1875, 100; 1876, 346, 363, 416). Rand too thought that the "morality of sacrifice" had been a fixture of religious morality for millennia. In *The Fountainhead* and several later essays, she comments on the altruistic character of the codes by which primitive tribes live, and in *Atlas Shrugged* she singles out the doctrine of original sin in the Judeo-Christian tradition as a source of the conception of the self as evil (*Atlas* 1025).[30] However it is Immanuel Kant whom Rand saw as most responsible for the equation of self-interest with evil: "*His* version of morality makes the Christian one sound like a healthy, cheerful, benevolent code of selfishness" ("Faith and Force" *PWNI* 88–89).

Kant's conception of morality amounts to little more than *that on account of which one is obligated to sacrifice*. He assumes, as part of commonsense morality, that a human being's "needs and inclinations, the entire satisfaction of which he sums up under the name happiness" form a "powerful counterweight to all the commands of duty" (*Groundwork of the Metaphysics of Morals*, Ak. IV, 405, Gregor 1996). He further assumes that the morality of an action derives from its having a "purpose" based, not on "the dear self," but on "the strict command of duty, which would often require self-denial" (Ak. IV, 407). Kant derives the content of duty from these assumptions by asking himself what this content would have to be in order for duty to be capable of standing in this opponent relation to inclination.[31] Kant's approach to moral philosophy amounts to taking self-interest as the standard of the non-moral, and then understanding morality by contrast to it.[32] In this view, the distinguishing feature of moral motivation is that it includes a willingness to sacrifice one's happiness.

In essence, Rand's view of the conventional conception of morality is identical to Kant's, but whereas Kant saw this received morality as an *a priori* principle which he sought to articulate in its pure form so as to fortify us against the seductions of happiness, Rand regarded it as a vicious remnant of primordial mysticism that had to be uprooted and replaced in order to enable human beings to achieve an uncompromised happiness.[33]

Rand's Objections to Altruism

Rand's fundamental reasons for rejecting sacrifice are not distinct from her reasons for embracing her positive moral code, and these reasons have been discussed in Chapter 4 (see, especially 76–81). Here I'd like to summarize some specific objections Rand made to altruism, understood as the view that morality consists of living for others. Some, but not all, of these objections apply more generally to any moral code that demands any altruistic actions.

A first objection is that altruism does not identify any positive values to pursue, but merely instructs a person to serve others, which means to pursue for them whatever they value. Someone following this code would be a "parasite in motive" in that he would rely on those he is serving to set his goals (*Fountainhead* 712, cf. 631–632, 667–668, *VOS* viii). This objection applies only to altruism when put forward as a self-contained moral code, with no independent specification of what constitutes the welfare of others.

A related objection, which applies to all codes that demand any sacrifices of one's self-interest, is that all such sacrifices amount to sacrifices of one's *mind*. We saw earlier that Rand thought it is possible to incorporate another person's interest into one's own hierarchy of values. Since these are the values that constitute one's own interest, pursuing the other person's welfare in accordance with its place in this hierarchy is no sacrifice. It is only a sacrifice if one gives up a value that is higher in this hierarchy; and, in that case, what is sacrificed is more than the specific value involved. What the sacrificer gives up is the policy of directing his life by his own reasoning, for this policy consists in forming a rational hierarchy of values and acting in accordance with it.[34]

Several of Rand's objections to altruism relate to its effects on a person's ability to have proper relationships with and attitudes toward others.

To love someone is to intensely value that person in particular on the basis of one's own personal values and to incorporate that person's specific welfare into one's own hierarchy of values. It follows that actions taken to benefit loved ones are egoistic. Rand considers the example of: "a man who is passionately in love with his wife [and] spends a fortune to cure her of a dangerous illness." She points out that altruism would, in some circumstances at least, require the husband to "let her die in order to spend his money on saving the lives of ten other women, none of whom meant anything to him," because the husband's only reason for saving his wife rather than the ten others is that "*his* happiness requires her survival" (*VOS* 51–52). This argument applies to many (if not all) altruistic moral theories, and similar objections are now common against utilitarianism.[35]

She held that altruism is also incompatible with benevolence:

> By elevating the issue of helping others into the central and primary issue of ethics, altruism has destroyed the concept of any authentic benevolence or good will among men. It has indoctrinated men with the idea that to value another human being is an act of selflessness, thus implying that a man can have no personal interest in others – that to value another means to sacrifice oneself – that any love, respect or admiration a man may feel for others is not and cannot be a source of his own enjoyment, but is a threat to his existence, a sacrificial blank check signed over to his loved ones. ("Ethics of Emergencies" *VOS* 43).

Relatedly, altruism implies that people *owe* one another the things that might be objects of generosity, but repaying a debt is not an act of generosity, and one can neither feel benevolent about giving what one owes, nor grateful for receiving it. Thus to whatever extent a person accepts altruism, he cannot be genuinely generous, benevolent, or grateful (*Atlas* 1033, *Letters* 548).

Another line of objection is that, by pitting morality against one's self-interest, altruism leads to amorality and a lack of self-esteem.

> Swinging like a helpless branch in the wind of an uncharted moral wilderness, you dare not fully to be evil or fully to live. When you are honest, you feel the resentment of a sucker; when you cheat,

you feel terror and shame, your pain is augmented by the feeling that pain is your natural state. You pity the men you admire, you believe they are doomed to fail; you envy the men you hate, you believe they are the masters of existence. You feel disarmed when you come up against a scoundrel: you believe that evil is bound to win, since the moral is the impotent, the *impractical.*

Morality, to you, is a phantom scarecrow made of duty, of boredom, of punishment, of pain, a cross-breed between the first schoolteacher of your past and the tax collector of your present, a scarecrow standing in a barren field, waving a stick to chase away your pleasures – and *pleasure,* to you, is a liquor-soggy brain, a mindless slut, the stupor of a moron who stakes his cash on some animal's race, since pleasure cannot be moral.

If you identify your actual belief, you will find a triple damnation – of yourself, of life, of virtue – in the grotesque conclusion you have reached: you believe that morality is a necessary evil. (*Atlas* 1053; cf., 1028, 1032–1033, 1052–1054, *VOS* vii, "Causality versus Duty" *PWNI, Letters* 539)

Another of Rand's objections to altruism is that it makes suffering the focus of life. Suffering is the experiential correlate of unfulfilled needs. For Rand, one's self-interest does not consist merely in having one's needs fulfilled. Rather it consists in a specific self-sustaining life that includes fulfilling one's needs by one's own effort. Such a life is not the sort of thing that one person could attain for another, and it is not what advocates of altruism typically demand. Instead, they enjoin us to alleviate suffering. Roark comments:

> Men have been taught that their first concern is to relieve the suffering of others. But suffering is a disease. Should one come upon it, one tries to give relief and assistance. To make that the highest test of virtue is to make suffering the most important part of life. Then man must wish to see others suffer – in order that he may be virtuous. (*Fountainhead* 713; cf., *Atlas* 1031, "The Ethics of Emergencies" *VOS*, "Moral Inflation" *ARL* 3(13) 306–308)

A related objection centers on the idea that "all values have to be gained and/or kept by men's actions," and altruism creates an unjust and unjustifiable "breach between actor and beneficiary" (*Letters* 557).[36] The result is the exploitation of each person to the extent that he is a producer of values.

> Your code divides mankind into two castes and commands them to live by opposite rules: those who may desire anything and those who may desire nothing, the chosen and the damned, the riders and the carriers, the eaters and the eaten. What standard determines your caste? What passkey admits you to the moral elite? The passkey is *lack of value.*
>
> Whatever the value involved, it is your lack of it that gives you a claim upon those who don't lack it. It is your *need* that gives you a claim to rewards. If you are able to satisfy your need, your ability annuls your right to satisfy it. But a need you are *unable* to satisfy gives you first right to the lives of mankind.
>
> If you succeed, any man who fails is your master; if you fail, any man who succeeds is your serf. Whether your failure is just or not, whether your wishes are rational or not, whether your misfortune is undeserved or the result of your vices, it is *misfortune* that gives you a right to rewards. It is *pain* regardless of its nature or cause, pain as a primary absolute, that gives you a mortgage on all of existence. (*Atlas* 1032)

For Rand, values and abilities are always the results of virtue. Of course, both depend to some extent on innate endowments and on circumstances, so an individual may lack an ability or value through no fault of his own, but she holds that any value that an individual produces or ability that he develops is achievement, because whatever advantages he may have had would have gone to waste, if he had not identified and taken advantage of them by his own thought and effort. Altruism, with its focus on alleviating suffering, implies that a person's failure to achieve (whether culpable or not) entitles him to the achievements of others. And this means that a person's virtue, which is the source of his achievements, makes him an object of exploitation.

Altruism, as Rand understood it, gives a producer no moral credit for the actions he takes to satisfy his own immediate, basic needs; and, so long as others exist who are suffering, it condemns him for any further action he takes to pursue the happiness that is possible to him and that is his ultimate goal. It demands that he forgo the achievement of the positive values in which his own well-being consists, not in order to make others happy (which is impossible), but to briefly allay the suffering caused by the countless unmet immediate needs of a never-ending succession of other people.

Atlas Shrugged illustrates this effect of altruism by showing how the lives of Dagny Taggart and especially Hank Rearden are increasingly consumed by such sacrifices until they join Galt's strike. Rand's horror at this is beautifully conveyed by Rearden's thoughts during an encounter with his brother Philip, in whose "pale, half-liquid eyes" Rearden sees "the uttermost of human degradation: an uncontested pain."

> You've never suffered, the eyes were saying with self-righteous scorn – while he remembered the sensation of proud chastity with which he had fought through those moments, refusing to surrender to pain, a sensation made of his love, of his loyalty, of his knowledge that joy is the goal of existence, and joy is not to be stumbled upon, but to be achieved, and the act of treason is to let its vision drown in the swamp of the moment's torture. You've never suffered, the dead stare of the eyes was saying, you've never felt anything, because only to suffer is to feel – there's no such thing as joy, there's only pain and the absence of pain, only pain and the zero, when one feels nothing – I suffer, I'm twisted by suffering, I'm made of undiluted suffering, that's my purity, that's my virtue – and yours, you the untwisted one, you the uncomplaining, yours is to relieve me of my pain – cut your unsuffering body to patch up mine, cut your unfeeling soul to stop mine from feeling – and we'll achieve the ultimate ideal, the triumph over life, the zero! (931–932)

Altruism is evil, Rand held, because, given her understanding of an individual's interest (and, more deeply, her understanding of the nature of values), this is what any call to sacrifice for others amounts to: the demand that the life and happiness achieved by some be sacrificed in order to briefly mute the pain of others – that values be destroyed or abandoned in an attempt to escape pain.

Rand's Reclamation of "Selfishness"

Other than Rand, the few recent advocates of ethical egoism have taken pains to distinguish what they advocate from "selfishness," which is normally a term of reproach. Rand, by contrast, embraced the term.[37] When asked "Why do you use the word 'selfishness' to denote virtuous qualities of character, when that word antagonizes so many people to whom it does not mean the things you mean?" she responded "For the reason that makes you afraid of it" (*VOS* vii).[38] Rand's crusading usage of "selfish" was a means of challenging the assumptions and attitudes that underlie the conventional usage. Far from being "a mere semantic attitude or a matter of arbitrary choice," she thought that the conventional usage was "wrong" and represented an error, "which is responsible, more than any other single factor, for the arrested moral development of mankind" (*VOS* vii).

Structurally, Rand's stance here is like that of other thinkers who seek to reform language that they think reflects and reinforces widespread prejudices. In recent decades, there have been several movements, particularly by feminists and gay rights activists, to reclaim terms of denunciation or censure, such as "slut," "queer," and "bossy."[39] In each case, the reclamation involves retaining some core meaning of the term and severing it from additional connotations (both evaluative and descriptive) that the reclaimers think are improperly associated with this core meaning, because of widely held prejudices.

For example, although "slut" is conventionally "used to describe a woman whose sexuality is voracious, indiscriminate and shameful," Easton and Hardy (2009, 4) use it as "a term of approval" for "a person of any gender who celebrates sexuality according to the radical proposition that sex is nice and pleasure is good for you." In particular, they use the word for people who are "openly loving, intimate, and sexual with many people" (3). This usage retains the core meaning of "slut" as someone who is enthusiastic about sex, even outside of the context of a monogamous relationship. The additional elements in the conventional meaning of slut are informed by several widely and deeply held premises about this sort of sexuality: that it involves indiscriminateness, that it is essentially different for a woman than for a man, and that it is shameful for a woman. By using the word "slut" in a way that conspicuously contradicts the aspects of its conventional usage that follow from these premises, but that is consistent with the word's core meaning, the reclaimers simultaneously reject the premises, call attention to the role they play in our thinking, and model for us an alternative way to think about the subject of sexuality.[40]

This is what Rand does with the word "selfish" and the subjects of self-interest and morality. She observed that, "In popular usage, the word 'selfishness' is a synonym of evil; the image it conjures is of a murderous brute who tramples over piles of corpses to achieve his own ends, who cares for no living being and pursues nothing but the gratification of the mindless whims of any immediate moment" (*VOS* vii). The heroes in Rand's novels, whom she describes as "selfish," could not be further from this image. They are respectful of the rights of others, have deep friendships and romantic relationships, and are committed to long-range values and abstract principles.

Rand stresses the role of adherence to principle in particular as an attribute of selfishness. For example, in *The Fountainhead*, when Roark refuses a commission that would require compromising on his architectural principles, though he desperately needs the money, he is "incredulous" when someone describes his action as "fanatical and selfless." "That was the most selfish thing you've ever seen a man do," Roark responds (*Fountainhead* 196). By contrast, Peter Keating personifies the conventional meaning of "selfishness": he advances in his career by expropriating Roark's work, undermining others so as to take their jobs, and even precipitating a stroke in someone who stands in his way; he uses all the people around him and has no genuine friends; and he is entirely unprincipled. Yet Roark cites Keating as an example of "selflessness" (633). True selfishness, Roark thinks, entails living both *for* and *from* oneself.

> The [egoist] in the absolute sense is not the man who sacrifices others. He is the man who stands above the need of using others in any manner. He does not function through them. He is not concerned with them in any primary matter. Not in his aim, not in his motive, not in his thinking, not in his desires, not in the source of his energy. He does not exist for any other man – and he asks no other man to exist for him. This is the only form of brotherhood and mutual respect possible between men. (713–714)[41]

Speaking in her own voice, Rand writes that the "exact meaning and dictionary definition of the word 'selfishness' is *concern with one's own interests*," adding that "the concept does not include a moral evaluation" (*VOS* vii). Presumably when Rand speaks of the "dictionary definition," she means how dictionaries *ought* to define the term. Some dictionaries do define the word in (more or less) the way Rand describes, but others include evaluative content or other related elements of the popular usage to which Rand would object.[42] In particular, some dictionaries include words like "excessive" in the description of the selfish person's concern for his own interests, thereby presupposing (contra Rand) that there is some maximum appropriate amount of concern with one's own interest. Definitions that say that the selfish person is prepared to sacrifice the interests of others to his own presuppose that there are conflicts of interest between people, so that one person can attain his interests by sacrificing others. Rand rejected this presupposition, because (as discussed in Chapter 4, above) she held that a person's objective self-interest can only be attained by independent, rational action, rather than by begging from or preying on others, and because (as discussed in Chapter 7, below) she held that people's rational interests do not conflict. Both of these points rest on Rand's view (discussed in Chapter 3, above) that an individual's formation and pursuit of values is a rational, conceptual process.

Implicit in the conventional description of noble action as "selfless" and of unscrupulous behavior as "selfish" is a very different view of what it is to form and pursue values. When we call Keating's machinations "selfish," we are implying that they are motivated by a concern for himself and that he can reasonably expect to benefit by them. Moreover, we are implying that, when Roark acts in a principled manner, he forgoes such benefits and makes himself worse off. This is why the bank manager thinks of Roark's action as selfless. Behind this view lies a way of thinking that Rand, in her later works, calls a perceptual (or anti-conceptual) mentality.[43]

> A perceptual consciousness is unable to believe that ideas can be of *personal* importance to anyone; it regards ideas as a matter of arbitrary choice, as means to some immediate ends. On this view, a man does not seek to be elected to a public office in order to carry out certain policies – he advocates certain policies in order to be elected. If so, then why on earth should he want to be elected? Perceptual mentalities never ask such a question: the concept of a long-range goal is outside their limits.
>
> If a man subordinates ideas and principles to his "personal interests," what are his personal interests and by what means does he determine them? Consider the senseless, selfless drudgery to which a politician condemns himself if the goal of his work – the proper administration of the country – is of no personal interest to him (or a lawyer, if justice is of no personal interest to him; or a writer, if the objective value of his books is of no personal interest to him …). But a perceptual mentality is incapable of generating values or goals, and has to pick them secondhand, as the given, then go through the expected motions. ("Selfishness Without a Self" *PWNI* 67)

Rand challenges these assumptions of the perceptual mentality. In *The Fountainhead*, she shows that Roark benefits from his adherence to principle and that Keating suffers from his unscrupulousness. More deeply, she shows that, far from being motivated by self-interest, a "perceptual mentality" like Keating hasn't even formed any conception of his self-interest. Such a person lacks a self. "Selfishness" on Rand's view, "is a profoundly philosophical, *conceptual* achievement" (*PWNI* 68).

Notice how far Rand's view here is from Comte's. He thought that a life in pursuit of one's self-interest would necessarily be one of (as Lewes put it) "miserable alternation of ignoble torpor or feverish activity," because the only values he identified as egoistic were short-range animalistic appetites. One can acquire a stable purpose in life, Comte thought, only by subordinating these

146

appetites to altruistic impulses which are longer-range in character. This is because Comte lacks or rejects the idea that an individual's mind is capable of "generating values or goals." As Lewes (1853, 217–218) explains, Comte's system gives "predominance ... to the emotive over the merely intellectual – in opposition to the old psychology which always subordinated emotions to the intellect." Comte's distinction between the egoistic and altruistic impulses is a distinction between two different sorts of emotions. The egoistic impulses are those that have some crudely perceptible relation to one's person, the latter are all those which do not obviously relate to one's person, and which are therefore assumed to be oriented toward society.

The values Comte takes to be egoistic are values of the sort that Aristotle described as "obvious and evident – like pleasure, wealth, or honor" (*Nicomachean Ethics* 1095a22). These are the things that Aristotle says "the many" identify as "the good," and Rand's challenge to the perceptual mentality recalls a central thread in Aristotle's thinking, and in the eudaimonist tradition generally. Moral philosophy began with Socrates' reproach to his fellow Athenians: "Aren't you ashamed of your eagerness to possess as much wealth, reputation and honors as you can, while you do not care for or give thought to wisdom and truth or to the best possible state of your soul?" (Plato, *Apology* 29e.) Plato, developing a Socratic theme, argued that wisdom and virtue not only benefit their possessors, but are a precondition for anything else being of value to them, and he attributed the many's contrary view to their failure to identify themselves with their *minds*.[44] Though Aristotle differs from Plato on many central points, he accepts this pivotal idea, and like Rand, he uses it to argue against the popular usage of the word "selfish" or "self-loving" (*philautos*).

> Those who treat it as a reproach call self-lovers those who apportion the most to themselves in wealth and honors and bodily pleasures; for the many desire and are eager for these things, as if they were the best things ... Those who are greedy for these things gratify their appetites and in general their feelings and the irrational [part] of their souls. The many are this way, and that's why the epithet has come about from the ordinary type, which is base. It is just, then, to reproach those who are self-lovers in this way. It's not unclear that it is those who apportion these things to themselves that the many are wont to call self-lovers; for if someone was always eager that he himself most of all should act justly or temperately or in accordance with any of the other virtues, and in general that he secure for himself what's noble, no one will call him a self-lover or blame him for it. That sort of person, however, more than the other sort, seems to be a self-lover. At any rate, he apportions to himself what is noblest and best of all, and he gratifies the most authoritative part of himself [viz., his intellect], obeying it in all things ... this, or this most of all, is what each [of us] is, and this is what the decent man prizes most of all. That's why he most of all will be a self-lover, in accordance with another form than [the one that is] reproached; and he's as different [from the reproached form] as a life in accordance with reason is from one in accordance with feeling, and as desiring what's noble is from desiring what seems advantageous. (*Nicomachean Ethics* 1168b17–1169a)[45]

By Aristotle's lights, the popular usage of the "*philautia*" as a term of reproach is misleading because it reflects and reinforces the deeply mistaken view that virtue (or "what is noble") is one of a number of competing goods, such that a person forgoes something of genuine value to himself when he acts virtuously.[46] We can see that Rand shared this concern from her early notes for *The Fountainhead*, where she discusses why "a selfless man cannot be ethical."

> To explain what may sound like a paradox: if by ethics we understand all sets of values, all standards of conduct and thought (without specifying at present just what standards are to be considered ethical; in other words, taking merely the quality of valuing, without defining how one

147

should value), then a man who does not consider his values as *his*, but merely as prescribed to him, or – accomplishes an act which he considers virtuous – because he *has to*, not because he *wants* to – that man can hardly be considered virtuous or ethical. The man to whom virtue, or that which he considers virtue, is a necessity, not a painful duty, that man is truly ethical. As example: if a man dies for his cause, because he hates to do it, but feels that some higher power – god or state – compels him to – he is a poor hero; if a man dies because it is *his* cause and he wishes no choice but to defend it at any cost – he *is* a hero. (*Papers* 167-01B_001_004–005/*Journals* 78–79)

Most of the examples of higher values on which Rand focuses in these notes, and indeed in *The Fountainhead* itself, are moral or esthetic; and the people she denounces as selfless either fail to form such values, or else they betray their values to attain obvious things like money, power, or adulation. Rand and Aristotle – contra Comte (and before him Hobbes, Hume, Kant, and many others) – regarded an individual's good as *conceptual* rather than perceptual, and it is because of this that they thought that an individual's good can include realizing ideals.

This is the respect, discussed earlier, in which Rand's ethics is like that of the eudaimonists. But whereas they (in some cases at least) regarded virtue as an intrinsic good, Rand thought that it is good because of its role in creating the other values that life requires, and the sort of life she regarded as virtuous was significantly different from the lives celebrated by Aristotle and the other eudaimonists. One sign of this is that Aristotle thought that no one would call a virtuous man a self-lover or blame him for it. By contrast, Rand thought that admirable men were often denounced as "selfish" on account of the very traits that she regarded as their virtues. Consider the following exchange between James Taggart and Francisco d'Anconia:

> "Don't you ever think of anything but d'Anconia Copper?" Jim asked him once.
> "No." ...
> "Isn't that a very selfish attitude?"
> "It is."
> "What are you after?"
> "Money."
> "Don't you have enough?"
> "In his lifetime, every one of my ancestors raised the production of d'Anconia Copper by about ten per cent. I intend to raise it by one hundred."
> "*What for?*" Jim asked, in sarcastic imitation of Francisco's voice.
> "When I die, I hope to go to heaven – whatever the hell that is – and I want to be able to afford the price of admission."
> "Virtue is the price of admission," Jim said haughtily.
> "That's what I mean, James. So I want to be prepared to claim the greatest virtue of all – that I was a man who made money."
> "Any grafter can make money."
> "James, you ought to discover some day that words have an exact meaning." (*Atlas* 95–96)[47]

Unlike the Aristotelian self-lover, Rand's heroes pursue wealth. As a result, they are more liable to be tarred with the same brush as the Aristotelian "many," who act on irrational short-range appetites. However, Rand's heroes are fundamentally different from such people. Rather than being guided by feelings, her heroes act out of an understanding of what is good for them as human beings; and, rather than merely *allotting* to themselves the greatest share of material goods from some static pot (as "any grafter" might), they *make money* – that is, they *produce* wealth that would not have existed without them.[48] Rand, unlike Aristotle, sees *producing* values as virtuous and as an essential component of one's interest.

This is one reason why reclaiming the concept "selfish" is a crusade for Rand, whereas Aristotle's heterodox usage of *"philautos"* is not for him. By defying conventional usage, both philosophers expose confusions about what is best for a person and about the motivation for noble acts, but only Rand thought that correcting the usage also addresses a deep *injustice* that is being perpetrated against many of the people called "selfish." This is because Rand thought that the popular usage of "selfishness" serves to condemn productive men by obscuring the essential difference between them and "grafters."[49]

Rand saw the conventional usage of "selfishness" as a "package-deal" – a term that "equate[s] opposites by substituting non-essentials for their essential characteristics, obliterating differences."[50] Rand discusses many such package-deals, and in most cases she suggests abandoning the relevant words altogether. However, she was insistent on rehabilitating the word "selfish," because of the special relation in which she thought this package-deal stands to the conventional view of morality.

> Altruism declares that any action taken for the benefit of others is good, and any action taken for one's own benefit is evil. Thus the *beneficiary* of an action is the only criterion of its moral value ... (*VOS* viii)

Insofar as one accepts altruism and thinks of one's own ideals in terms of it, one will come to regard these ideals as opposed to one's own interests, thus removing all but the most perceptually accessible values from one's conception of one's self-interest. Thus, Rand thought, "Altruism *permits no concept* of a self-respecting, self-supporting man – a man who supports his life by his own effort and neither sacrifices himself to others nor others to himself" (*VOS* ix).

This last point is significant. Linguists sometime talk of a "euphemism treadmill": "People invent new 'polite' terms to refer to emotionally laden or distasteful things, but the euphemism becomes tainted by association, and the new one that must be found acquires its own negative connotations" (Pinker 1999). Because of this phenomenon, neutral or positive terms that are introduced as alternatives to negatively connoting names for persecuted groups tend to quickly take on the negative connotations of the words they were intended to replace. "Gay," for example, was introduced as a positive alternative to slurs like "faggot" or "queer" and medicalized terms like "homosexual"; but 20 years ago, when I was a teen, everyone I knew interpreted the word as an insult, and replacing it with another term would have done no good, because any word for gays would quickly become an insult in the mouths and minds of people who assumed that there was something wrong with being gay.

The same is true of any word for "selfishness" in the minds of people who assume altruism. So long as it is generally believed that people are obligated to sacrifice, any term that we might adopt to refer to the intransigent pursuit of one's self-interest would acquire the connotations that "selfishness" now has.[51] Because we need some such term, Rand concluded that "[t]o redeem both man and morality, it is the concept of '*selfishness*' that one has to redeem" (*VOS* x).[52] Thus, in describing selfishness as a virtue, Rand was urging us to rethink the concept. Part of this rethinking will involve identifying as selfish many actions that we recognize as noble, such as Roark's intransigent commitment to his architectural principles.

But Rand does not only ask us to recognize the selfishness of actions we already admire, she pushes us to reconsider our views of what is admirable. Central to the plots of her two major novels are actions taken by the heroes that, by conventional standards, are not merely selfish, but monstrously so. Roark demolishes a housing project – "the home of the destitute" – rather

149

than let it stand as a deformed version of one of his designs (*Fountainhead* 716). And Galt abandons a whole continent to chaos and mass starvation. The plot of each novel is carefully constructed to create a situation in which she thinks an action so dramatically contrary to conventional morality is right and in which she can convey its rightness to readers. In this way the novels function as complex counterexamples to the conventional altruistic morality.

More importantly, the novels hold up the ideal of the "self-respecting, self-supporting man" who neither makes nor accepts sacrifices – the sort of person who is impossible according to the premises implicit in the conventional usage of "selfishness." In the novels' philosophical discussions and in her non-fiction essays, Rand argues that this ideal is moral and achievable. Her arguments have been discussed in earlier chapters. I hope that this chapter has made clear in what sense Rand's ideal is egoist and how it relates both to altruism and to the various other views that have been called "egoism."

Acknowledgment

Notes

1 Indeed one regularly sees her as the representative of egoism in introductory textbooks or readers on ethics (or in the ethics sections of general introductions to philosophy). For example: Harris 1997, 81; Rachels 1999, 86–87; Presbey, Struhl, and Olsen 2000, 448–452; Pojman 2004, 373–380; Lawhead 2005, 449–452; Palmer 2006, 100–126; Bowie, Michaels, and Solomon 2007, 472–474; Soloman 2008, 475–478; and Wilkens 2011, 45–62.
2 The three broad alternatives presented in this sentence correspond to Parfit's (1984, 493–502) classification of theories of self-interest into Desire-Fulfillment Theories, Hedonistic Theories, and Objective List Theories. Rand's view of self-interest as objective in the sense that I go on to discuss does not fall into any of these three categories. The "Objective-List" theories are examples of what she called intrinsicism, and theories of the other two sorts are examples of subjectivism.
3 Some contemporary philosophers (e.g., Baier 1993, Hills 2010, 14, Shaver 2014,) distinguish both of these positions from "rational egoism" (in a different sense of this term than the one Rand used). Like ethical egoism and unlike psychological egoism, "rational egoism" is supposed to be a normative theory. It holds that being egoistic is what makes an action "rational," where "rationality" is understood to be a normative notion distinct from morality. Making such a distinction enables one, for example, to combine utilitarianism about moral norms with egoism about norms of rationality, and then to ponder whether it is rational to be moral – i.e., whether one's self-interest lies in maximizing the general happiness.
4 More strictly, it denotes a category of moral theories that differ from one another in their views of (among other things) what a person's interest consists of and how it can be achieved.
5 I am not sure when the term "psychological egoism" originated, but it was evidently in use and associated with both Hobbes and Bentham by the late nineteenth century. See Sorley 1885, 67, Browne 1892, 94 and Sidgwick, 1892 xxiv.
6 See Bentham's *Introduction to the Principles of Morals and Legislation*, especially I.1, the introduction to his *Constitutional Code*, and James Mill's *Essay on Government* (1824), §§IV–V.

7   On her rejection of determinism, see, in this volume 260–262; cf., 63–66, 107–112.

8   None of these pieces refer to the doctrine of psychological egoism by that name, but Rand does use that name in a 1963 letter to the philosopher W.T. Stace, in which she contemptuously rejects the doctrine (*Letters* 604). She was responding to a letter by Stace about her article "The Ethics of Emergencies" (*VOS*). The letter begins with what Stace seems to think is a concession to Rand: "Of course it is true that all actions are motivated by the pursuit of the actor's own happiness" (*Papers* 097_01x_008_001). Rand describes this sentence as an expression of "psychological egoism," and she responds: "of course it is *not* true, and nothing in my article could have conveyed the impression that I advocate such an idea" (*Letters* 604). Stace would not have seen the sentence as an expression of psychological egoism, because he held that a person's happiness, but not her self-interest, can include non-instrumental concern for other people. (See Stace 1939, 209–215.)

9   See Epicurus' "Letter to Menoeceus," Hobbes's *Leviathan* XV.4–8, and Chernyshevsky 1953, 124–128.

10 To some extent this is true of Epicurus as well. He is ambiguous between the two groups, but I class him with the egoistic consequentialists because, for him, virtue is wholly instrumental.

11 On this issue, see Sidgwick 1907, 374–375, McDowell 1980, 386, Williams 1985, 32, Annas 1993, 127, 223 and Annas 2008, Whiting 2006, 302, and Salmieri 2011.

12 Among them are Den Uyl and Rasmussen 1984b, Mack 1984, Long 2000, Badhwar 2001, Rasmussen 2002, and Swanton 2011a.

13 On the distinction between "intrinsic" vs. "instrumental" goods, see n. 14, below.

14 Rand was skeptical of the distinction between "instrumental" and "intrinsic" goods. In a letter to John Hospers, reacting to his presentation of the distinction (Hospers 1961, 104–138), she wrote: "You ask whether I would agree with the distinction you make between 'intrinsic good' and 'instrumental good.' I do not object to the concepts *as you define them*, but I would not use them, for the following reasons: A. The term 'intrinsic' is extremely dangerous to use in ethics. It can be taken to mean 'good of and by itself,' regardless of context, standard, source, recipient and recipient's knowledge. For instance, if one decided that 'security' is an '*intrinsic*' good, one would be justified in attempting to establish it by any and all means, on the ground that it would necessarily be good for all men – which is precisely the reasoning by which collectivists justify their policies. B. Values which are ends to be achieved by a certain process of action and which, therefore, could be called 'intrinsic' in that context – become means to further and wider ends and thus become 'instrumental' in a wider context. For instance, the process of writing is an 'instrumental' good in relation to creating a book, which is an 'intrinsic' good in this context; but creating a book is an 'instrumental' good in relation to achieving a literary career, which is an 'intrinsic good' in this context; and achieving a literary career is an 'instrumental' good in relation to achieving one's happiness and supporting one's life. Since I regard all values as *contextual* and *hierarchical*, I would ultimately regard only *one* good as 'intrinsic,' in your sense of the term, namely: *life* (with happiness as its corollary – as defined in my paper on 'The Objectivist Ethics,' *particularly* in [the second paragraph on *VOS* 32]).

    "Frankly, I suspect that the distinction between 'intrinsic' good and 'instrumental' good belongs to a traditional view of (or approach to) ethics which is totally different from mine. But since I do not know the full context, place and *purpose* of this distinction in *your* approach to ethics, I am open to further discussion and clarification" (*Letters* 561).

15 See Harry Binswanger's discussion below 408–413.

16 There are several examples in Rand's fiction of a hero (or heroine) valuing the mere existence of someone whom he loves even when he does not think that any relationship with the loved one is possible. See *Fountainhead* 387 and *Atlas* 765–768, and 861.

17 See Stirner 1882, 330–373 (Leopold 1995, 282–320) and Nietzsche 1908, II.9–10 (Kauffman 1989, 253–258) and 1883–1885, I.1, III.2 (Del Caro and Pippin 2006, 56, 150–153).

18 Whether Nietzsche thought this about all morality or only most forms of it is a matter of some debate, and the answer turns on how we understand the term "morality" (and how Nietzsche understood it). Leiter (2010) summarizes the issues nicely and argues that Nietzsche opposes only (what Leiter calls) "Morality in the Pejorative Sense," which presupposes that human beings have free will, can know

their own motives, and are sufficiently similar for a single moral code to apply to all. Nietzsche rejected all three of these presuppositions. Rand accepted all three, and she especially stressed the first and the third, both as presuppositions of morality and as important differences between her and Nietzsche. (See Lester Hunt's discussion in Chapter 14 of the present volume, especially 345 and 348–349.)

19 Rand uses the word "altruism" and its variants only 5 times in *Atlas* and 33 times in *The Fountainhead*, though *Atlas* is more than 50 percent longer. I don't think that, when writing *The Fountainhead*, Rand was clear that sacrifice is the essence of altruism. There are passages (e.g., 665–667) where we see this view expressed, but in that novel she still views the fundamental moral alternative as between independence and dependence, and (as we'll discuss later), she sees altruism as a form of dependence, so in that work she is more focused than she will be later on the evil of making other people's good one's central concern.

20 Ellipses in the original. Obama attributes the sentence to Marian Wright Edelman, and it is often attributed to her in earlier sources as well, though I have not found the origin of the quote.

21 This material is quoted in Peikoff *Parallels* 13.

22 For examples, see *Fountainhead* 666–667 and "Collectivized Rights" *VOS*.

23 For one example of such a defense, see Dewey 1929.

24 "Egoism," as a term denoting "the theory which regards self-interest and the foundation of morality" was in use for at least 50 years by this time. The *Oxford English Dictionary* has citations of the word in this sense going back to 1800. (There are a few earlier uses in a metaphysical sense equivalent to our "solipsism.")

25 Cf. Comte 1875 146, 155, 172, 307; 1877 283; Lewes 1853 217.

26 A similar remark of Comte's from the same work was part of a "Horror File" compiled by Leonard Peikoff and published under Rand's auspices (*TO* 10(8) 1086–1087.) This "File" is a good source for other quotes expressing altruism: "Summing up its conception of sound morality in the expression 'Live for Others,' Positivism sanctions a reasonable measure of satisfaction to the self-regarding instincts on the ground that they are indispensable to our material existence, the basis on which all our higher attributes are founded. Consequently, it censures all practices, however respective the motives inspiring them, which by excessive austerity diminish our energies and render us less fit for the service of others. By giving a social purpose to self-regarding measures it at once ennobles and controls them, steering clear of undue attention to them on the one hand, and of dangerous neglect on the other."

27 Peikoff (in his "Horror File" *TO* 10(8) 1087) reproduces a similar quote: "It is as much a part of our scheme as of M. Comte's, that the direct cultivation of altruism, and the subordination of egoism to it, far beyond the point of absolute moral duty, should be one of the chief aims of education, both individual and collective .... Every person who lives by any useful work, should be habituated to regard himself not as an individual working for his private benefit, but as a public functionary; and his wages, of whatever sort, not as the remuneration or purchase-money of his labour, which should be given freely, but as the provision made by society to enable him to carry it on ..." (Mill 1961, 146–148.)

28 Mill also objected quite strenuously to many of the social and political implications Comte draws from his ethics, describing the social system Comte advocates in his *System of Positive Polity* as "the completest system of spiritual and temporal despotism which ever yet emanated from a human brain, unless possibly that of Ignatius Loyola: a system by which the yoke of general opinion, wielded by an organized body of spiritual teachers and rulers, would be made supreme over every action, and as far as is in human possibility, every thought of every member of the community, as well, in the things which regard only himself, as in the things which concern the interests of others" (*Autobiography* [New York: 1924] 149).

29 See especially Williams 1973 and Stocker 1976.

30 For her discussion of altruism's relationship to tribalism, see "Selfishness Without a Self" *PWNI* 69–70.

31 See, in addition to the above cited passages, *Critique of Practical Reason*, Ak. V, 73.

32 For a particularly clear recent example of this same strategy, see Hills 2010.

33 Kantianism and Christianity are altruistic, but they are not forms of altruism because (as they are most often interpreted) they hold that a person is morally obligated not only to take actions aimed at others' welfare, but also to take certain actions to advance his own welfare and certain actions that aren't aimed at benefiting anyone. Rand did not regard this difference as significant, however, because (as she understood them) these moral systems are no less committed to self-sacrifice as a moral ideal than is the view that one should live for others.

34 On the way in which altruism requires the sacrifice of judgment and self-direction, see *Fountainhead* 370–376, *Atlas* 1030, "Causality versus Duty" *PWNI, Letters* 557. See also Salmieri 2005, 269–70.

35 See the sources cited in note 29, above.

36 Rand's argument here is the inverse of an argument against egoism offered by James Rachels (1999, 94–95). He claims that egoism is "unacceptably arbitrary" because it advises an individual to treat herself preferentially even though there is no difference between herself and others that could justify this differential treatment. Notice that the only preferential treatment involved is the individual's treating herself as the beneficiary of her own actions and that the individual is different from all other people with respect to those actions insofar as *she is the one performing the actions*. Rachels's argument amounts to the claim that the issue of who is performing an action is *wholly irrelevant* to whose interests the action should serve. This is disguised by Rachels's use of the passive voice: he speaks of whose "needs should be met," ignoring the issue of by whose *agency* these needs will be met.

37 For example, Robert Olsen (1965, 38) writes, "There is no reason to suppose that the man who consistently pursues his self-interest is selfish. A selfish man is simply one who fails to take an immediate, personal satisfaction in the well-being of others." John Hospers suggested a similar distinction to Rand, on the grounds that "in ordinary life" we only "dismiss" self-interested actions as "selfish" when they are indulged in "at the expense of other people by hurting other people or by cheating other people of something"; he reports that she continued her "unnecessary insistence" on "making [selfishness] term of praise" and that she "didn't care whether it was reflected in ordinary use" (Scott 2006).

38 Rand has sometimes been criticized for her combative posture here, and for saying that the question implies "moral cowardice" (Branden 1989, 335–336 [1999, 297]; Palmer 2006, 105). Notice, however that what she is responding to specifically is the suggestion that she abandon the word "selfishness" *to avoid antagonizing people*. Since she rightly regarded the substance of her position as antagonistic to millennia of entrenched moral attitudes, she reasonably regarded the suggestion that she avoid provocative language as encouragement to disguise her position so as to make it more socially acceptable.

39 Regarding "slut", see: Easton and Hardy 2009; regarding "queer," Belge and Bieschke 2011 20; regarding "bossy," Moore 2014.

40 My comparison of Rand's reclamation to Easton and Hardy's should not be taken to imply that she would agree with their reclamation of "slut," or with their sexual ethics more generally. Rand discusses sexual ethics in *Atlas* 489–492 and *Playboy Interview* 38. She argues that sex is an important value that should only be shared in the context of a serious love relationship.

41 In *The Fountainhead*, Roark says "egotist" where I have supplied "egoist." Rand later explained that "the word should have been 'egoist'," but that she had relied on an inaccurate dictionary (*Fountainhead* x). She let the text of *The Fountainhead* stand, but replaced the word when reprinting the material in *FTNI*.

42 For example the *American Heritage Dictionary of the English Language* (2001) defines "selfish" as "Concerned chiefly or only with oneself," the *Random House Dictionary* (2005) defines it as "devoted to or caring for oneself, concerned primarily with one's own interests, benefits, welfare, etc., regardless of others," and the *Oxford English Dictionary* (1983) defines it as "devoted to or concerned with one's own welfare to the exclusion of regard for others." The last two definitions go beyond Rand's if we take the remarks concerning "others" to mean that the selfish man has no regard for others at all, but not if we take it to mean that any regard he has for them is subordinate to his self-regard. *Merriam-Webster's Collegiate Dictionary* (1997) includes "excessively" in its definition of "selfish," and *Webster's Revised Unabridged Dictionary* (1996) includes "unduly." *New Lexicon Webster's Encyclopedic Dictionary*

of the English Language (1991) defines "selfish" as "concerned only to satisfy one's own desires and prepared to sacrifice the feelings, needs, etc. of others in order to do so." Similarly, the *Concise Oxford English Dictionary* (2013) defines it as "concerned chiefly with one's own profit or pleasure at the expense of consideration for others."

43 On the sort of thinking that Rand thinks is involved in having rational values, see my Chapter 3, above, and also, in this volume, 82–84, 115, and 224–225.

44 See Plato's *Euthydemus, Phaedo,* and *Republic.*

45 My translation. On *philautos* and Aristotle's reclamation of it see Salmieri 2014 and the literature cited therein.

46 This is an entrenched view in Greek culture, reflected in an inscription on a monument at Delos to the effect that "most noble is what is most just, but health is best, and pleasantest is the attaining of one's heart's desires." Aristotle begins his *Eudemian Ethics* by criticizing this inscription (1214a1–8, cf. *Nicomachean Ethics* 1099a24–30).

47 Cf. *Atlas* 410–11, 414 for the idea that money must be *made.*

48 Probably "the many" of whom Aristotle is so dismissive include people whom Rand would have regarded as virtuous, but, if so, she would argue that Aristotle misunderstands both the nature of and the motivation for their pursuit of wealth. Many of the differences in the content of their ethics flow from their differing views on how reason and virtue relate to survival and wealth. I discuss this issue in greater depth in my 2009, esp. 225–232, and in the fourth lecture of my 2003.

49 On productiveness, see, in this volume 58–63 and 84–85.

50 "How to Read (and Not to Write)" *ARL* 1(26) 3. Rand identifies the popular usage of "selfishness" as a package-deal in the introduction to *VOS* vii (cf. *Letters* 540, 554, 557). I discuss package-deals below in Chapter 12, 297–298.

51 To say that the moral theory of altruism leads to and reinforces this view of self-interest is not to say that this view can *only* arise from the idea that other people's good is the only moral standard, for we've seen that this view was prevalent in Ancient Athens and yet Aristotle tells us that "Justice is the only virtue that seems to be someone else's good"; he thereby makes it clear that it is not someone else's good that makes the other virtues virtues (*Nicomachean Ethics* 1130a4–5).

52 Cf. *AON* 119, where the case of "selfishness" is discussed as an example of the issue "when to continue using a word despite its being corrupted, and when to drop such a word."

References

Annas, J. 1993. *The Morality of Happiness.* Oxford: Oxford University Press.

Annas, J. 2008. "Virtue Ethics and the Charge of Egoism." In *Morality and Self-Interest,* edited by Paul Bloomfield. Oxford: Oxford University Press.

Badhwar, Neera. 2001. *Is Virtue Only a Means to Happiness? An Analysis of Virtue and Happiness in Ayn Rand's Writings,* with Commentaries by Jay Friedenberg, Lester H. Hunt, and David Kelley, and a Reply by Badhwar. Poughkeepsie, NY: Objectivist Center.

Baier, Kurt. 1993. "Egoism." In *A Companion to Ethics,* edited by Peter Singer. Oxford: Wiley-Blackwell.

Belge, Kathy and Marke Bieschke. 2011. "Reclaiming Our Words." In *Queer: The Ultimate LGBT Guide for Teens,* San Francisco, CA: Zest Books.

Bowie, G. Lee, Meredith W Michaels, and Robert C. Solomon. 2007. *Twenty Questions: An Introduction to Philosophy,* 6th edition. Belmont, CA: Thompson Wadsworth.

Branden, Nathaniel. 1989. *Judgment Day: My Years with Ayn Rand.* Boston, MA: Houghton-Mifflin.

Branden, Nathaniel. 1999. *My Years With Ayn Rand.* San Francisco, CA: Jossey-Bass.

Browne, Borden P. 1982. *The Principles of Ethics.* New York, NY: Harper & Brothers.

Chernyshevsky, N.G. 1953. "The Anthropological Principle in Philosophy." In *Selected Philosophical Essays.* Moscow: Foreign Languages Publishing House.

Comte, Auguste. 1851. *Système de Politique Positive, ou Traité De Sociologie, Instituant la Religion de l'Humanité*, Vol. 1. Paris: Librairie Scientifique-Industrielle De L. Mathias.

Comte, Auguste. 1858. *The Catechism of Positive Religion*, translated by Richard Congreve. London: John Chapman.

Comte, Auguste. 1875. *System of Positive Polity*, Vol. 2, translated by Frederic Harrison. London: Longmans, Green, and Co.

Comte, Auguste. 1876. *System of Positive Polity*, vol. 3, translated by Edward Spencer Beesly, Samuel Lobb, Fanny Hertz, John Henry Bridges, Vernon Lushington, and Godfrey Lushington. New York, NY: Burt Franklin.

Comte, Auguste. 1877. *System of Positive Polity*, vol 4, translated by Richard Congreve. London: Longmans, Green, and Co.

Del Caro, Adrian and Robert Pippin. 2006. *Nietzsche:* Thus Spoke Zarathustra. Cambridge: Cambridge University Press.

Den Uyl, Douglas and Douglas Rasmussen, eds. 1984a. *The Philosophic Thought of Ayn Rand*, Urbana, IL: University of Illinois Press.

Den Uyl, Douglas and Douglas Rasmussen, eds. 1984b. "Life, Teleology, and Eudaimonia in the Ethics of Ayn Rand." In Den Uyl and Rasmussen 1984a.

Dewey, John. 1929. *Impression of Soviet Russia: and the Revolutionary world: Mexico – China – Turkey*. New York, NY: New Republic.

Easton, Dossie and Janet Hardy. 2009. *The Ethical Slut*, 2nd edition. Berkeley, CA: Greenery Press.

Gregor, Mary J., ed. and trans. 1996. *The Cambridge Edition of the Works of Immanuel Kant: Practical Philosophy*. Cambridge: Cambridge University Press.

Harris, C.E. 1997. *Applying Moral Theories*, 3rd edition. Boston, MA: Wadsworth Publishing Company.

Hills, Alison. 2010. *The Beloved Self: Morality and the Challenge from Egoism*. Oxford: Oxford University Press.

Hospers, John. 1961. *Human Conduct: An Introduction to the Problems of Ethics*. New York, NY: Harcourt, Brace & World.

Kaufmann, W., trans. 1989. *On the Genealogy of Morals and Ecce Homo*. New York, NY: Random House.

Kerry, John. 2004. "Acceptance Speech and the Democratic National Convention." *The Washington Post*. Available at: http://www.washingtonpost.com/wp-dyn/articles/A25678-2004Jul29.html (accessed June 30, 2015).

Landon, Pilar. 2006. "Sen. McCain talks service, politics." *The Heights*, September 21, A1, A4.

Lattimore, Richard, trans. 1951. *The Iliad of Homer*. Chicago, IL: The University of Chicago Press.

Lawhead, William. 2005. *The Philosophical Journey*, 3rd edition. New York, NY: McGraw-Hill

Leiter, Brian. 2010. "Nietzsche's Moral and Political Philosophy." In the *Stanford Encyclopedia of Philosophy*: http://plato.stanford.edu/entries/nietzsche-moral-political (accessed June 30, 2015).

Leopold, D., trans. 1995. *Stirner: The Ego and Its Own*. Cambridge: Cambridge University Press.

Lewes, George Henry. 1853. *Philosophy of the Sciences: Being an Exposition of the Principles of the "Cours de Philosophie Positive" of Auguste Comte*. London: Henry G. Bohn.

Long, R., 2000. *Reason and Value: Aristotle versus Rand*, with commentaries by Fred D. Miller, Jr. and Eyal Moses, and a reply by Long. Poughkeepsie, NY: Objectivist Center.

Mack, E. 1984. "The Fundamental Moral Elements of Rand's Theory of Rights," in Den Uyl and Rasmussen 1984a.

McCain, John. 2008. "John McCain's New Hampshire Primary Speech." *The New York Times*. Available at: http://www.nytimes.com/2008/01/08/us/politics/08text-mccain.html?pagewanted=print&_r=1& (accessed June 30, 2015).

McDowell, J. 1980. "The Role of Eudaimonia in Aristotle's Ethics'." In *Essays on Aristotle's Ethics*, edited by A.O. Rorty, 359–376. Berkeley, CA: University of California Press.

Mill, John Stuart. 1865. "Later Speculations of Auguste Comte." *The Westerner Review*, July 1.

Mill, John Stuart. 1879. *Utilitarianism in Socialism*. Chicago, IL: Belfords, Clarke & Co.

Mill, John Stuart. 1961. *Auguste Comte and Positivism*. Ann Arbor, MI: University of Michigan Press.

Moore, Tracy. 2014. "You Don't Need to Ban 'Bossy' – You Need to Take Away Its Power." Online at: http://jezebel.com/you-dont-need-to-ban-bossy-you-need-to-take-away-1542383373 (accessed June 30, 2015).

155

Nietzsche, Freidrich. 1883–1885. *Also sprach Zarathustra*. Chemnitz: Verlog von Ermst Scmeitzner.

Nietzsche, Freidrich. 1908. *Ecce Homo*. Leipzig: Insel-Verlag.

Obama, Michelle. 2009. "Michelle Obama's Commencement Address." *The New York Times*, May 16. Available at: http://www.nytimes.com/2009/05/16/us/politics/16text-michelle.html?pagewanted=all&_r=1& (accessed June 30, 2015).

Olsen, Robert G. 1965. *The Morality of Self-Interest*. New York, NY: Harcourt, Brace & World.

Palmer, Donald. 2006. *Why It's Hard to Be Good*. New York, NY: McGraw-Hill.

Parfit, Derek. 1984. *Reasons and Persons*. Oxford: Clarendon Press.

Pinker, Steven. 1994. "The Game of the Name." *New York Times*, April 5.

Pojman, Louis. 2004. *The Moral Life: An Introductory Reader in Ethics and Literature*, 2nd edition. New York, NY: Oxford University Press.

Presbey, Gail M., Karsten J. Struhl, and Richard E. Olsen. 2000. *The Philosophical Quest: A Cross-Cultural Reader*, 2nd edition. New York, NY: McGraw-Hill.

Rachels, James. 1999. *The Elements of Moral Philosophy*, 3rd edition. New York, NY: McGraw-Hill.

Rasmussen, Douglas. 2002. "Rand on Obligation and Value." *The Journal of Ayn Rand Studies*, 4(1).

Salmieri, Gregory. 2003. *Aristotle as Ethicist*. Lecture series, available at: https://estore.aynrand.org/p/436/ (accessed June 30, 2015).

Salmieri, Gregory. 2005. "'Prometheus' Discovery: Individualism and the Meaning of the Concept 'I' in Anthem." In *Essays on Ayn Rand's* Anthem, edited by Robert Mayhew. Lanham, MD: Lexington Books.

Salmieri, Gregory. 2009. "*Atlas Shrugged* on the Role of the Mind in Man's Existence." In *Essays on Ayn Rand's* Atlas Shrugged, edited by Robert Mayhew. Lanham, MD: Lexington Books.

Salmieri, Gregory. 2011. *Egoism and Altruism*. Lecture series, available at: https://estore.aynrand.org/p/550 (accessed June 30, 2015).

Salmieri, Gregory. 2014. "Aristotle on Selfishness? Understanding the Iconoclasm of *Nicomachean Ethics* ix 8." *Ancient Philosophy* 34.

Scott, Duncan (director). 2006. *The Birth of Objectivism*, vol. 2: *A Movement is Launched*. DVD. Santa Monica, CA: The Objectivist History Project.

Shaver, Robert. 2014. "Egoism." In the *Stanford Encyclopedia of Philosophy*: http://plato.stanford.edu/entries/egoism/ (accessed June 30, 2015).

Sidgwick, Henry. 1892. *History of Ethics for English Readers*. London: Macmillan.

Sidgwick, Henry. 1907. *The Methods of Ethics*, 7th edition. London: Macmillan.

Solomon, Robert C. 2008. *Introducing Philosophy: A Text with Integrated Readings*, 9th edition. New York, NY: Oxford University Press.

Sorley, William Ritchie 1885. *On the Ethics of Naturalism*. Edinburgh, UK: William Blackwood and Sons.

Stace, W.T. 1939. *The Concept of Morals*. London: Macmillan.

Stirner, M. 1882. *Der Einzige und sein Eigentum*, 2nd edition. Leipzig: Verlag von Otto Wigand.

Stocker, Michael. 1976. "The Schizophrenia of Modern Moral Theories." *Journal of Philosophy*, 73. Reprinted 1987 in *The Virtues: Contemporary Essays on Moral Character*, edited by Robert Kruschwitz and Robert Roberts. Belmont, CA: Wadsworth Publishing.

Swanton, Christine. 2011a. "Nietzsche and Rand as Virtuous Egoists." In *Metaethics, Egoism and Virtue: Studies in Ayn Rand's Normative Theory*, edited by Allan Gotthelf and James G. Lennox. Ayn Rand Society Philosophical Studies, vol. 1. Pittsburgh, PA: University of Pittsburgh Press.

Whiting, J. 2006. "The Nicomachean Account of *Philia* 281–287." In *The Blackwell Companion to Aristotle's Ethics*, edited by Richard Kraut. Malden MA: Blackwell.

Wilkens, Steve. 2011. *Beyond Bumper Sticker Ethics: An Introduction to Theories of Right and Wrong*. Downers Grove, IL: Intervarsity Press.

Williams, Bernard. 1973. "Integrity." In *Utilitarianism: For and Against*, edited by J.C.C. Smart and Bernard Williams. Cambridge: Cambridge University Press. Reprinted 1988 as "Consequentialism and Integrity," in *Consequentialism and Its Critics*, edited by Samuel Scheffler. Oxford: Oxford University Press.

Williams, Bernard. 1985. *Ethics and the Limits of Philosophy*. Cambridge MA: Harvard University Press.

Part III

Society

7

"A *Human* Society"

Rand's Social Philosophy

DARRYL WRIGHT

Ayn Rand is an unabashed egoist. But the heroes of her novels often don't sound like most people's idea of an egoist:

> Our sole relief were the rare occasions when we could see one another. We found that we liked to meet – in order to be reminded that human beings still existed. So we came to set aside one month a year to spend in this valley – to rest, to live in a rational world, to bring our real work out of hiding, to trade our achievements – here, where achievements meant payment, not expropriation. Each of us built his own house here, at his own expense – for one month of life out of twelve. It made the eleven easier to bear. (*Atlas* 747)

This is John Galt's explanation of why the heroes of *Atlas Shrugged* spend a month each summer in Galt's Gulch. It brings out several key facets of Rand's particular form of egoism. The heroes' lives are focused on *achievement* – they are thinkers, producers, creators. They dedicate themselves to "remaking the earth in the image of [their] values" (*Atlas* 1020). Their fundamental means of dealing with one another is through *trade*: "payment, not expropriation." And though they are independent, they value each other profoundly. The trade they seek with one another is neither exclusively nor most importantly material, but *spiritual*: the experience of living together "in a rational world," "bring[ing] our real work out of hiding," and "trad[ing] ... achievements." What they seek is not just the opportunity to sell products and services in an unhampered free market (though that is crucially important) but to trade achievements *qua* achievements: to trade the sight of such a thing as achievement and of the kind of moral character responsible for it – a sight increasingly absent in the outer world depicted in the novel.[1] They *are* egoists: in the oath they take on entering Galt's Gulch, each pledges "that I will never live for the sake of another man, nor ask another man to live for mine" (*Atlas* 1069). But they are also profoundly social; they are anything but the predatory lone wolves of standard conceptions of egoism.[2]

A Companion to Ayn Rand, First Edition. Edited by Allan Gotthelf and Gregory Salmieri.
© 2016 John Wiley & Sons, Ltd. Published 2016 by John Wiley & Sons, Ltd.

Rand denies that man is a "social being" in the sense frequently given to this term: she denies that man's ideas and values are formed fundamentally by society rather than by his own individual choices, and she denies that human achievements are irreducibly collective.[3] But she considers *certain kinds* of social relationships and societies – ones not based on the foregoing premises but on a correct conception of man's nature, including a recognition of human volition – to be a deep human need: "A social environment is most conducive to [man's] successful survival – *but only on certain conditions*" ("The Nature of Government" *VOS* 125/*CUI* 378). Similarly: "Man gains enormous values from dealing with other men; living in a human society is his proper way of life – but only on certain conditions" ("A Nation's Unity" *ARL* 2(2) 127).[4] The "certain conditions" will be explored below. But the needs invoked in these passages are what the philosopher Hugh Akston has in mind when, immediately after the above paragraph from Galt, he comments that "man *is* a social being, but not in the way the looters preach" (*Atlas* 747).[5] Man needs society, and benefits from it, "if it is a *human* society" ("The Objectivist Ethics" *VOS* 35).

This chapter discusses Rand's view of the moral principles by which individuals should interact with one another and societies should be organized. It concentrates on four issues: the role of trade and the benevolent attitudes that trade relationships engender; Rand's principle that man is an end in himself; the question of whether there are conflicts among human interests; and Rand's account of individual rights.

The Trader Principle and Benevolence

The central moral principle applicable to human interaction, according to Rand, is what she calls the *trader principle*:[6]

> The principle of trade is the only rational ethical principle for all human relationships, personal and social, private and public, spiritual and material. It is the principle of justice.
> A trader is a man who earns what he gets and does not give or take the undeserved. He does not treat men as masters or slaves, but as independent equals. He deals with men by means of free, voluntary, unforced, uncoerced exchange – an exchange which benefits both parties by their own independent judgment. ("The Objectivist Ethics" *VOS* 34–35)

The first two sentences make explicit what was implied in the quote from Galt – that Rand's conception of trade applies to both material and spiritual issues. Friendship and love, as she views them, are exchanges of spiritual values, those involved in experiencing the other person's character, personality, and sense of life.[7] The passage also indicates that Rand views the trader principle as an aspect of the virtue of justice.[8] Rand considers justice an aspect of the wider virtue of rationality, and thus, as the passage indicates, considers the trader principle to be a requirement of rationality in addition to justice. I discuss the principle's relation to rationality below.

The main requirements of the trader principle are made clear in the second paragraph quoted above. One must gain values from others only by offering values in return that the other party freely accepts in exchange. One should consent to an exchange only if, by one's own independent judgment, one derives a net benefit from it, and one should expect others to adopt the same policy. Further, one should not accept values from others that one regards as undeserved.

The principle, and especially this last aspect of it, raises interesting questions of application that cannot be considered here.[9] In general, however, the principle requires that the terms of exchange in economic transactions be reached by the uncoerced agreement of those concerned, and that personal relationships and other spiritual forms of trade be based on shared values and be mutually beneficial. Personal relationships thus should not be based on duty or necessitate self-sacrifice. (In one sense, the idea of spiritual trade is clearly metaphorical, since explicit bargaining over terms is not normally a part of personal relationships. But these relationships are trades, for Rand, in the sense that each party properly expects to benefit.)[10]

Rand holds that trade, in both its material and spiritual aspects, is central to a proper conception of self-interest. The fundamental requirements of self-interest are "thinking and productive work."[11] These are indispensable for self-esteem and a sense of purpose, which Rand regards as necessary for psychological survival. They also enable one to provide for one's various needs by participating in economic trade; and they form a foundation for healthy, non-exploitative friendships and other personal relations, as indicated in the earlier passage from Galt.

More broadly, a shared commitment to the trader principle leads to, and is indispensable for, a social atmosphere of benevolence. Those who share this commitment wish each other well. They have nothing to fear from one another, and they can expect to be rewarded, not exploited, for their achievements – rewarded not just materially but also spiritually in the form of admiration, respect, good will.[13] Rand's description of the atmosphere of European society before World War I reflects the kind of spiritual climate that her ethics aims to create: "The existential atmosphere (which was then being destroyed by Europe's philosophical trends and political systems) still held a benevolence that would be incredible to the men of today, i.e., a smiling, confident good will of man to man, and of man to life" (RM vi–vii).

Rand is neither a Hobbesian nor a Humean about benevolence. That is, she holds neither that human interests are naturally antagonistic nor that human beings naturally wish each other well.[14] Benevolence, both as an individual characteristic and as an attribute of a society, depends on the moral choices of individuals. As an individual characteristic, benevolence proceeds from self-esteem, which in turn derives from moral virtue, essentially the commitment to use one's mind fully and support one's life by one's own, independent work; hostility toward others proceeds from a sense of one's own moral failings:

> One of the highest values to a man of reason and self-esteem is other human beings. Of any category in the universe, human beings are of greatest importance to him. It is only a man with an inferiority complex who despises mankind. Someone of self-esteem certainly values man, since he values himself. I don't mean that he loves his neighbor as himself, but that he attaches enormous value to man as a phenomenon. (Speaking 160; see also Nathaniel Branden, "Benevolence and Altruism" TON 2(7) 27–28, esp. 27)

Socially, for Rand, an atmosphere of benevolence depends on the moral-political principles that govern human relationships, and these, in turn, depend in complex ways on human choices. By recognizing each person's moral right to live for his own sake, the trader principle encourages such a cultural atmosphere, whereas the principle that one must make sacrifices for others undermines it. In Atlas Shrugged, Rand explores this latter idea through the story of the collectivization of the Twentieth Century Motor Company, which depicts the process by which a system of reward according to need eventually creates an environment of deep hostility and disrespect (Atlas 660–672).

She expands on the ideas of the preceding passage in her essay "The Ethics of Emergencies" (see *VOS* Chapter 3):

> A rational man does not forget that life is the source of values and, as such, a common bond among living beings (as against inanimate matter), that other men are potentially able to achieve the same virtues as himself and thus be of enormous value to him. This does not mean that he regards human lives as interchangeable with his own. He recognizes the fact that his own life is the *source*, not only of all his values, but of *his capacity to value*. Therefore, the value he grants to others is only a consequence, an extension, a secondary projection of the primary value which is himself.

Rand says that one should value others for their moral potential. That potential might be understood both metaphysically and epistemically – as the potential that a human being has by nature, and as a potential that, for all one knows, may well have been actualized in a given case. Because other people have moral potential in both senses, a given person might well deserve one's admiration and esteem.[15] Rand argues here that (absent specific contrary evidence) one should value other human beings as such on the basis of that potentiality; one should regard them as worthy of esteem unless they demonstrate otherwise. I take it that the primary way in which she holds that others might be of "enormous value" to us is simply that we benefit generally from being among and dealing with men of moral stature. The benefits can be both material and spiritual, with the latter including the benefits of being surrounded by people whom one can admire.[16] In the background of this line of reasoning is a claim that we will explore below: that there is no conflict in human interests, rightly conceived, and therefore that the virtues of one person not only uniformly benefit their possessor, but that they are never inimical to the good of others.

The above passage suggests a comparison and a contrast between self-value and other-value. The comparison is implicit but important to bring out. Both self-value and other-value require a basis; neither comes free, as it were. Rand holds that in order to live, man must value himself, but that in order to value himself he must earn self-esteem through virtue; fundamentally, through his exercise of rationality. The kinds of grounds on which one values oneself (if one does) can potentially transfer over to any given human being. In view of that possibility, Rand thinks, one's default position in regard to others should be to regard them as potential instances of "man at his best," a fully moral human being.[17] Regarded as such, each person is a potential value and a potential ally, on the same grounds that a moral person is a value and an asset to himself. Each possesses (or may possess) moral qualities that can contribute to one's life and that merit esteem on that basis. One important implication of this line of reasoning is that, although the value one ascribes to others depends on their relation to one's own life – it is not intrinsic or unconditional – *so does the value one ascribes to oneself*. This parallelism helps us see how Rand might reply to the objection that her view of other-value is unduly instrumental. It *is* instrumental in a way that is ineliminable for any egoistic theory and need not be objectionable: the value one ascribes to others is grounded in the needs of one's own life. But *what* one values in others, and the *reasons* for doing so, are parallel to what one values in oneself and the reasons for doing so. In that sense, there is no implied difference in status, as there would be if one valued others solely for their usefulness in the pursuit of narrow, practical ends.[18] Rather, others can matter to us in a way that is analogous to the way in which one matters to oneself.

At the same time, Rand makes it clear that other-value must be secondary to self-value, in two ways. First, the value one places on one's own life is the basis for all one's other values.

Second, it would be wrong to value others as highly as one values one's own life, or to treat their lives and one's own as interchangeable. These two points are related: the value ascribed to others' lives must be *subordinate* to one's self-value because it is *based on* one's self-value. It is only because of and for the sake of the value represented by one's own life that one needs or can have any other values.[19]

According to Rand, one owes strangers "[an] initial good will in the name of their human potential" ("The Ethics of Emergencies" *VOS* 54). She adds that "it is on the ground of that generalized good will and respect for the value of human life that one [properly] helps strangers" (*VOS* 54) in an emergency or in other cases of distress.[20] The help given should never come at the cost of values that are more important within one's own life (e.g., the needs of one's own family, one's career, one's financial goals, and so forth). Although Rand notes that a stranger "is potentially able to achieve the same virtues as [one's] own and thus be of enormous value" to one (*VOS* 53), the likelihood that a given stranger will have enormous or even significant personal value is small. Do such acts of benevolence, then, constitute trades that the trader principle would endorse? In a strict sense, perhaps not. But they seem to resemble trades in that one's actions are based on considerations of (egoistic) value, and they might be regarded as trades in a larger sense.

To see this, suppose that one helps a stranger whom one (somehow) knows to be morally good. The reason for doing so, on Rand's view, would be the general spiritual and practical value of living among good people – and a resulting desire to see them flourish – but not usually any specific benefit that one expects to receive from the person helped. Even so, in a general way, one would be responding to and nurturing that which is of egoistic value to oneself, namely, human moral goodness. In a similar way, in helping people on the basis of their moral potential, one acts, in effect, on the presumption of such value and responds to it accordingly.[21]

Man as an End in Himself

The moral foundation of the trader principle in Rand's ethics is the principle that *man is an end in himself*:

> The basic *social* principle of the Objectivist ethics is that just as life is an end in itself, so every living human being is an end in himself, not the means to the ends or the welfare of others – and, therefore, that man must live for his own sake, neither sacrificing himself to others nor sacrificing others to himself. To live for his own sake means that *the achievement of his own happiness is man's highest moral purpose*. ("The Objectivist Ethics" *VOS* 30)

This principle gives both positive and negative guidance. Positively, it says that a person should live "for his own sake" and that this entails making his own happiness the moral purpose of his life. To set happiness as your moral purpose is to make it *the basic goal by reference to which you deliberate* in morally optional issues.[22] In Rand's ethics, a person's own life is his proper ultimate value, and morality delineates the broad values and virtues required for sustaining and fulfilling one's life. Happiness is the overall spiritual state (i.e., state of consciousness) that results from the achievement of one's life and the subsidiary values that one's life comprises.[23] But the concept of "happiness" has a deliberative role in the choice of specific values and goals within the broad guidelines provided by morality. In effect, morality, as Rand views it, delineates

DARRYL WRIGHT

a range of possible lives, but the proper reference point for choosing among them, in her view, is the question, "What would make me happy?" One answers this question by exploring what one values and why; for instance, by exploring why one is or isn't drawn to certain careers, people, activities, and so forth. When happiness plays this role in one's deliberations, it functions as one's moral purpose.

Negatively, the principle requires "neither sacrificing [oneself] to others nor sacrificing others to [oneself]." By a *sacrifice*, Rand means the uncompensated surrender of something one values, either in material or spiritual matters. It is thus not a sacrifice, properly so called, to help a friend whose well-being is important to one's own life and happiness.[24] According to the principle, one must not make sacrifices for others, nor impose sacrifices on others. The principle thus rules out those forms of egoism which claim that a person's interests are served by exploiting others, such as the egoism of Thrasymachus in Book I of Plato's *Republic* or Callicles in the *Gorgias*.

Rand's principle differs importantly from the well-known principle that Kant formulates similarly: "Act in such a way that you treat humanity, whether in your own person or in the person of another, always at the same time as an end and never simply as a means" (Kant 1993, 36; Prussian Academy edition (Ak.) IV, 429). Kant considers the principle of personal happiness to be the most objectionable of all moral principles (Kant 1993, 46; Ak. IV, 442). Further, he argues that treating someone as an end requires making that person's ends one's own, and thus to some extent putting the ends of others ahead of one's own ends (Kant 1993, 37; Ak. IV, 430).[25] For Rand, however, that would be to treat oneself as a mere means.[26]

These differences flow from differences in value theory between the two philosophers. For Kant, an end in itself is something of intrinsic value.[27] The intrinsic value of persons generates a categorical imperative to promote their interests; this is why Kant holds that in simply refraining from coercing someone, one does not actively treat him as an end. In contrast, Rand holds that value is relational and extrinsic; what is good is so *for* a given living organism *in virtue of* its needs and goals.[28] The organism itself – its life – is the ultimate end for the sake of which anything good for it is good. What makes life an (ultimate) end, in her view, is not that it has intrinsic value but that it is *conditional* – it requires continuous action by the organism, directed at specific goals, in order to be sustained.[29] The organism's life must be the standard by which such goals are selected. Further, the conditional nature of its life is the only fundamental ground of a given organism's need to act and thus the only thing that can qualify as the ultimate end for that organism (though in regard to humans, she holds, embracing this end is not automatic but due to choice). Thus, for Rand, when we recognize that another person is an end in himself, what we recognize is not his intrinsic value (and a consequent obligation to act for his sake) but rather that he himself – his own life – is properly *his* ultimate end. We treat him as an end by leaving him free to treat himself as such.[30]

Let us examine the grounds of Rand's principle further. She presents it as a corollary of the principle that life is an end in itself, and the grounds that she adduces for these principles are related. Concerning the latter, she writes in *The Virtue of Selfishness*, "Metaphysically, *life* is the only phenomenon that is an end in itself: a value gained and kept by a constant process of action."[31] In regard to the former, she writes in *Atlas Shrugged*:

> Since life requires a specific course of action, any other course will destroy it. A being who does not hold his own life as the motive and goal of his actions, is acting on the motive and standard of death. Such a being is a metaphysical monstrosity, struggling to oppose, negate and contradict the fact of his own existence, running blindly amuck on a trail of destruction, capable of nothing but pain.

... A [moral] doctrine that gives you, as an ideal, the role of a sacrificial animal seeking slaughter on the altars of others, is giving you death as your standard. By the grace of reality and the nature of life, man – every man – is an end in himself, he exists for his own sake, and the achievement of his own happiness is his highest moral purpose. (*Atlas* 1014)

Both passages claim that life requires a constant, all-embracing course of action. The first (from *The Virtue of Selfishness*) cites life's singularity, in this regard, to support the thesis that an organism's life is its proper ultimate value.[32] The second implies that the course of action required to sustain one's life is all-embracing and therefore that any action taken apart from "the [ultimate] motive and goal" of one's own life proceeds from "the motive and standard of *death*." The passage claims, further, that one who acts in this way, by acting against metaphysically given requirements of human nature, achieves only destruction and pain. From these points, the passage concludes that "by the grace of reality and the nature of life, man ... is an end in himself ..."

On their face, these claims may appear exceedingly stark: they imply that one must choose between complete self-interest and complete self-sacrifice. But this is precisely Rand's view. Her argument is grounded in her general view of the nature and function of principles in human life, which I will briefly sketch. First, in claiming that man's life requires a constant process of action, Rand does not mean that all one's actions must be manifestly or exclusively aimed at satisfying one's own needs; she is claiming that the furtherance of one's life should be the fundamental principle by which one acts. The concrete act of buying someone a gift could proceed from this principle or from the principle of self-sacrifice. What matters, for sustaining one's life, is not primarily the concrete act but the principle behind it. It is setting aside (or subordinating) the principle of self-preservation that Rand is claiming endangers us.

Second, Rand argues that because man has no pre-programmed means of evaluating particular choices and situations, he needs the guidance of moral principles to protect his long-range survival. Discovering and applying such principles (a process that for Rand requires inductive knowledge grounded substantially in a knowledge of history) is the only means of gauging the currently unobservable long-range consequences of one's actions. To act without the guidance of moral principles, she holds, is *per se* to act self-destructively. It is to act without a clear knowledge of where one is going.[33]

Third, in Rand's view there is no principled mixture that can be formulated of self-interested and self-sacrificing elements. The best known attempt at a mixed principle is utilitarianism, on which one's own good and the good of every other person (or sentient being) is given equal weight in moral evaluation. In order to function as a principle, utilitarianism requires some way of integrating disparate assessments of the good of separate individuals into overall assessments of the goodness of outcomes. Whether or not there is a principled way of effecting such an integration has been a subject of longstanding and persistent philosophical controversy.[34] Rand's view is that such an integration is impossible, and that judgments about the general happiness or the "common good" thus remain unavoidably *ad hoc* and subjective. In her view, the only principled conception of human good that can be formulated is that of the good of an individual human being as such.[35] Though the issue cannot be discussed here, I suspect that she would have a similar response to other moral theories that are neither purely egoistic nor purely altruistic, including many of the theories in contemporary virtue ethics.[36] If her objections to these views are correct, then the attempt to act on any of the mixed principles would be equivalent in its long-term effects on a person's life to an explicit rejection of moral principles.

165

Rand holds, therefore, that there is a stark choice of principles to be made between her end-in-himself principle and the principle that man is a "sacrificial animal" whose life belongs to others. The *Atlas* passage validates the end-in-himself principle by reducing it to the fundamental choice between life and death.[37] To survive in a social context, Rand claims, man needs the moral status of an end.

In making this argument, the *Atlas* passage counterposes the claim that man's moral purpose is happiness to the claim that man should live for others. But its context makes clear what the *Virtue of Selfishness* passage states directly: that just as one must not sacrifice himself to others, one must not sacrifice others to himself. This part of Rand's principle, however, raises a question about its validation. Rand reduces the choice between the *entire* end-in-himself principle and its antithesis to the choice between life and death. But in what way is it a requirement of one's life to treat *others* as ends? Further, is the obligation to treat others as ends strictly an obligation to oneself or one that is also owed *to others*?

An analogous question will arise in regard to individual rights in Rand's politics. She is more explicit about her answer in that context, although I think she would have the same essential answer here. In part, the requirement to treat others as ends simply follows from one's self-interest. But one acquires an obligation *to others* to treat them as ends in consequence of making a parallel moral claim to be treated by them as an end, and this parallel claim is also required by one's self-interest. I will discuss this second point and then return to the first.

In Rand's view, a person's own good requires the moral protection of the full end-in-himself principle; it requires a social environment that recognizes and morally protects man's need to live for his own sake. Each person thus has grounds – in metaphysically given facts about human nature – for taking the position taken by Howard Roark in *The Fountainhead*: "I came here to say that I do not recognize anyone's right to one minute of my life. Nor to any part of my energy. Nor to any achievement of mine" (*Fountainhead* 717). According to Rand, a society's moral conditions are the fundamental determinant of whether living in that society will be inimical or beneficial to human well-being. The social recognition of one's status as an end is necessary for one's long-range survival.

This claim has its notorious doubters in the history of ethics, Thrasymachus and Callicles being prime examples. They see a strong person's advantage as lying in force and cunning and see no reason for such a person to endorse general moral restrictions on how people treat one another. How would Rand reply to them? I think her reply would begin from one given by Ragnar Danneskjöld in *Atlas Shrugged*, in speaking of those who practice what these two preach:

> If my fellow men believe that the force of the combined tonnage of their muscles is a practical means to rule me – let them learn the outcome of a contest in which there's nothing but brute force on one side, and force ruled by a mind, on the other. (*Atlas* 757)

Those who expropriate the values of others cannot succeed by force alone and, historically, have not succeeded in that way. To succeed, according to Rand, they require the "sanction of the victim" – their victims' acceptance of a moral code that sanctions the sacrifice of the individual's well-being for the sake of an allegedly superior good.[38] Even then, Rand holds, their success is at best temporary; it lasts until the victims have been drained and destroyed (the point, for instance, that prompted Glasnost and Perestroika in the USSR in the 1980s and that Venezuela and some countries in Europe may be nearing at present). But deprived of the victims' sanction, Rand holds, force cannot succeed. *Atlas Shrugged* depicts the effects on society when that sanction is systematically withdrawn. As the most creative and productive individuals go on strike against the society's moral code, its economy and culture collapse.

This is the perspective from which Rand claims that each person needs the protection of moral principles. The only possible path to human good in a social context is through independent thought, productive achievement, and trade. To pursue that path, a person must recognize his own life as an end in itself and have it recognized as such by the culture and institutions of his society; this status is necessitated by human nature and the conditions of human existence. But to justifiably assert one's moral status as an end entails a recognition of the similar status of others, Rand holds, and in that way gives rise to an obligation to treat them accordingly.[39]

Since Rand is an egoist, that obligation couldn't stand if it required sacrificing one's own good. But in her view, the same reasons that make it necessary for a person to live for his own sake, if he is to live at all, also make it to each person's advantage to treat others as ends. She holds that it is only by trading with others to mutual advantage that one benefits from their achievements over the long-term. Further, it should be noted that Rand's egoist *wants* to treat others as ends. His self-esteem and sense of purpose derive from the creative use of his mind on whatever level of ability he can reach, and from his ability to support his needs through his own productive efforts.[40] He therefore has no reason to want to exploit others. In Rand's view, the desire to seize what others produce, or to enslave the producers, has a spiritual motive and aim, rather than being aimed at material aggrandizement. It represents an attack on the person – the moral stature – of the producers, and it flows from a sense of inadequacy and self-hatred on the part of the non-producers. These are motives that her egoist entirely lacks. Rand's egoist sees a community of interests between himself and other productive individuals, and he sees a commitment to the trader principle as advancing his interests.[41] We can develop these points further by considering Rand's views about the possibility of conflicts in people's interests.

The Question of Conflicts of Interest

Most contemporary discussions of ethical egoism assume that there are unavoidable conflicts in human interests and thus that a consistent egoist would deceive, coerce, or otherwise harm others. It is also assumed that a clever egoist would conceal his moral views, advocating altruism in order to benefit from others' sacrifices.[42] The assumption of basic conflicts of interest is also a feature of game-theoretic arguments that ground morality in self-interest. Rand's ethics lies quite outside of this contemporary vein and, in this regard, belongs to an earlier tradition in the history of ethics, for which the true good of each individual is in harmony with that of every other. Rand defends this thesis in the following form: "the *rational* interests of men do not clash ... there is no conflict of interests among men who do not desire the unearned, who do not make sacrifices or accept them, who deal with one another as *traders*, giving value for value" ("The Objectivist Ethics" *VOS* 34).[43]

It is clear from this passage that Rand's harmony of interests thesis is not unrestricted; interests are subject to normative assessment as rational or irrational, and the thesis of harmony applies only to *rational* interests. Those whose interests are not rational will have conflicts of interest with others and irreconcilable internal conflicts in their own desires. In general, according to Rand, "[a] man's 'interests' depend on the kind of goals he chooses to pursue, his choice of goals depends on his desires, his desires depend on his values ..." ("The 'Conflicts' of Men's Interests" *VOS* 57). What advances one's interests is, roughly, what advances one's goals.[44] Interests inherit their normative status as rational or irrational from the goals, desires, and values underlying them, and so Rand's claim is that there will be no conflicts of interest among those whose goals, desires, and values are rational. Further, the above passage makes it clear that Rand views commitments to the end-in-himself principle and the trader principle as conditions on the rationality of a person's goals, desire, and values. This section explores the details and basis of Rand's position.

I will begin by examining a scene from *Atlas Shrugged*. Hank Rearden, on trial for the illegal sale of Rearden metal, says the following in response to the assertion that he is guilty of violating the doctrine of the supremacy of the "public good":

> Who is the public? What does it hold as its good? There was a time when men believed that "the good" was a concept to be defined by a code of moral values and that no man had the right to seek his good through the violation of the rights of another. It is now believed that my fellow men may sacrifice me in any manner they please for the sake of whatever they deem to be their own good. (*Atlas* 477)

The passage tells us that those who accept this doctrine make claims about their good purely subjectively, apart from any systematic moral theory. It also implies a distinction between moral values or principles, applicable to every human being, and a given individual's conception of his own good or interests, as a certain person. Moral principles are needed to define the good, but what they define is the good of any human being *qua* human. Rand sometimes refers to this as human good, and I will follow that usage, but it must be stressed that what is in question is the good of any *individual* human being, abstracting from personal differences. Applying these principles involves developing a specific conception of one's *personal good* – one's good as a certain person – a conception that gives concrete form to the abstractions involved in the delineation of *human good*.[45] We can express the same distinction by contrasting one's *general human interests* (the interests of a human being as such) and one's *personal interests*. The passage implies that, to be valid, a conception of one's personal good or personal interests must be formed by reference to, and must not contradict, a correct conception of human good or one's human interests.

The doctrine of the supremacy of the public good may not be based on a code of moral values, but it *is* a (freestanding) moral claim or premise. It is held as an undefined moral primary and, as Rearden says above, used to justify the sacrifices being imposed on him. And Rearden tells the judges that it is this premise which he has come to challenge:

> I could say to you that ... nobody's good can be achieved at the price of human sacrifices – that when you violate the rights of one man, you have violated the rights of all, and a public of rightless creatures is doomed to destruction. I could say to you that you will and can achieve nothing but universal devastation. ... I could say it, but I won't. It is not your particular policy that I challenge, but your moral premise. (*Atlas* 481)

What Rearden challenges is the doctrine of the supremacy of the "public good" – the doctrine that men of ability must make sacrifices for the sake of those who claim to need what they have produced. It is because Rearden challenges this moral premise that, when asked whether he puts his own interests ahead of those of the public, he answers, "I hold that such a question can never arise except in a society of cannibals" and "I hold that there is no clash of interests among men who do not demand the unearned and do not practice human sacrifices" (*Atlas*

478). The claim that there are conflicts of interest, in other words, is not theoretically innocent; it reflects either amoralism or the doctrine that the needs of some constitute a claim on the lives and efforts of others.

Even though it is this moral premise that Rearden has come to challenge, he *does* also tell the judges that the sacrifice of some to others can, in fact, achieve nobody's good, and this is also an important point in Rand's ethics. What is the relation between this point and Rearden's rejection of the supremacy of the public good? By emphasizing the latter, Rearden implies that it is more fundamental, which, crucially, it is, in Rand's view. A person's right to exist for his own sake is *not* to be derived from the inefficacy of trying to benefit some through the sacrifices of others. Nor is it to be derived from the good that men such as Rearden achieve for society (a point that Rearden also makes in this scene).

In Rand's ethics, the right to exist for one's own sake is derived from the metaphysical nature of life and the requirements of man's survival.[46] For her, the concept of "the good" pertains only to an individual human being (or other living organism); there is no valid concept of the "public good" or the "general good" in the usual senses of these terms, which entail the possibility of conflicts with the good of individuals. For an individual human being to survive and achieve his good, he must live by his own independent judgment and pursue his own independently chosen goals. But, in Rand's view, it is these same basic aspects of human nature that explain why no good can be achieved through a policy of sacrifice. Both principles are elements of an overall theory of human good, a theory of moral values.[47]

Let us consider further this latter thesis and Rand's defense of it. Rearden considers hypothetically what would follow if the thesis were false:

> If it were true that men could achieve their good by means of turning some men into sacrificial animals, and I were asked to immolate myself for the sake of creatures who wanted to survive at the price of my blood, if I were asked to serve the interests of society apart from, above and against my own – I would refuse, I would reject it as the most contemptible evil ... (*Atlas* 481)

Rearden uses this thought experiment to underline his rejection of his accusers' moral premise. But, in addition, it is significant that he does not consider the reverse scenario to the one that he projects – a scenario in which he is the beneficiary of someone else's sacrifices. He assumes that, "[i]f ... men could achieve their good by means of turning some men into sacrificial animals," there would be nothing for *him* to gain by that means, although others could gain from him. Why does he make this assumption?

The answer, I think, is that he knows who he is; he knows his abilities and the moral character through which he has developed and utilized those abilities. The broader philosophic point, however, is that according to Rand, if it is possible for someone of Rearden's moral stature to exist – and if the actualization of that possibility in a given human being depends on his own choices – then a complete conflict of human interests is impossible. The Reardens of the world, those who contribute most to producing the values required for human survival, will have nothing to gain from the sacrifices of others. They will pursue their good in the way that Rearden describes:

> I work for nothing but my own profit – which I make by selling a product they need to men who are willing and able to buy it. I do not produce it for their benefit at the expense of mine, and they do not buy it for my benefit at the expense of theirs; I do not sacrifice my interests to them nor do they sacrifice theirs to me; we deal as equals by mutual consent to mutual advantage. (*Atlas* 480)

169

If the good could be achieved through sacrifice, it would not be Rearden benefiting from the sacrifices of his brother Philip but the other way around. It should be noted that Rand considers this conclusion to be applicable at every level of human ability: in her view, Eddie Willers, though his potential for achievement is far more modest than Rearden's, is nevertheless fully equipped to achieve his own good and has nothing to gain from sacrificing those less able than himself or those who are unwilling to pull their own weight.

In this sense, the only live issue, from Rand's perspective, is whether it is possible to gain from the sacrifices of those whose productive achievements are greater than one's own, which is the issue that Rearden mentions. In effect, Rand's answer to this question is the whole of *Atlas Shrugged*. I will summarize some key points in her thinking here. As discussed in the last section, one of the themes of *Atlas* is that in order to be even semi-successful, the looters – those who expropriate the values of others – require the sanction of the victim. Rearden wins at his trial by depriving his accusers of that sanction (by refusing to defend himself against their charges); more broadly, Rand holds that without the sanction of the victim the looters will perish, and with it they will progressively destroy both their victims and, ultimately, themselves. This type of process can be observed historically in societies that expropriate and control their most creative and productive members (the collapse of communism in Eastern Europe during the 1980s is undoubtedly the most dramatic recent example of the process).

The beneficiary of the doctrine of the supremacy of the public good is, of course, supposed to be the public at large. The looters in *Atlas Shrugged* appeal to public interest and public need to justify their actions. But Rand argues that nobody's good is achieved by this doctrine. The public consists of specific individuals. The "public good" doctrine actually imposes sacrifices on some members of the public for the putative benefit of other members. But the method by which this is to be accomplished consists in stopping the victims from acting on their own independent judgment and expropriating what they produce, as Rearden is stopped from selling his metal to customers of his choice and forced to provide it to those designated to be in need. In Rand's view, such policies undermine the creation of the values they are aimed at acquiring control over. Independent thought, she holds, presupposes (at least an implicit recognition of) the moral principle that man is an end in himself. To think for yourself is to live for yourself – to form your own convictions and select your own values and goals. The principle that man must live for others requires that independent thinking be stopped. This is why every society that institutes this principle starves itself of scientific progress, innovation, technological advancement, and artistic creativity, and actively suppresses dissenters.

It is thus a central feature of Rand's account of human good that "*human* good does not require human sacrifices and cannot be achieved by the sacrifice of anyone to anyone" (*VOS* 34). The principle that each person has a right to exist for his own sake – that man is an end in himself – is also central to that account, as is the main applied principle falling under this one, the trader principle. According to Rand, it is in the context of this account of human good (and its further details in the whole of her moral theory) that one must judge one's personal good or interests.

The possession of a correct philosophical theory of human good (of moral values) is, for Rand, a necessary condition of a having fully objective and wholly correct conception of one's personal interests (other theoretical and factual knowledge is also needed). But a person can have a *rational* conception of his interests, in Rand's view, without a full grasp of the correct moral theory.[48]

In Rand's ethics, rationality is the primary moral virtue, but it is possible to possess this virtue without having full theoretical knowledge of morality. Within limits, therefore, rationality is compatible with what might be called *pure moral error*; that is, a rational person can act wrongly due to a deficiency of *moral* knowledge.[49] (*Impure moral errors* are also possible: wrong actions due to deficiencies in factual knowledge.) A rational person can also make errors in gauging his personal interests, or be unable to validate them fully, and some of his errors might be due to incomplete knowledge of moral values. But such a person has a moral stature that someone who views his interests irrationally lacks: "There is a fundamental moral difference between [for example] a man who sees his self-interest in production and a man who sees it in robbery" (*VOS* ix).

Rationality is the basic moral virtue, for Rand, because of the centrality of reason to human survival.[50] It requires:

> a commitment to the fullest perception of reality within one's power and to the constant, active expansion of one's ... knowledge. ... It means a commitment to the principle that all of one's convictions, values, goals, desires and actions must be based on, derived from, chosen and validated by a process of thought – as precise and scrupulous a process of thought, directed by as ruthlessly strict an application of logic, as one's fullest capacity permits. ("The Objectivist Ethics" *VOS* 28)

Whatever the specific circumstances, according to Rand, when a person embraces "values, goals, desires and actions" in a way that violates these commitments, he acts blindly, depriving himself of the broad context and long-range perspective he requires in order to assess the impact of his choices on his life as a whole. In so doing, he endangers himself in a fundamental way.

Rand's conception of rational self-interest applies her account of the virtue of rationality to the specific issue of judging one's personal interests. She presents this application in her article "The 'Conflicts' of Men's Interests" (*VOS*). Rational self-interest is distinguished (from irrational) by three main characteristics. The first pertains to the way in which a rational person conceives of his interests. He "sees his interests in terms of a lifetime and selects his goals accordingly" and thus

> does not regard any moment as cut off from the context of the rest of his life, and ... he allows no conflicts or contradictions between his short-range and long-range interests. He does not become his own destroyer by pursuing a desire today which wipes out all his values tomorrow. ("The 'Conflicts' of Men's Interests" *VOS* 59)[51]

The second characteristic pertains to the context of knowledge that informs a rational person's deliberations about his interests. Rational deliberation must be informed by a recognition of certain metaphysically given facts about human nature and human existence. Recognizing these facts includes both grasping them, at least implicitly, and actively relying on that grasp in making judgments about one's interests. Reliance, in this connection, refers not simply to a causal relationship, but to making epistemically appropriate use of the metaphysical context; it refers to whether one's judgments can be *justified* in light of that context.[52] Rand includes in that required context the following tenets:

(1) The recognition that reality is independent of consciousness and thus that "[t]he mere fact that a man desires something does not constitute a proof that the object of his desire is *good*, nor that its achievement is actually to his interest" (*VOS* 57).

(2) The recognition that "nature does not provide man with the automatic satisfaction of his desires" (*VOS* 57) and thus that his own action is required.

(3) The recognition that other people are not mere inanimate resources that can be exploited at will but must sustain themselves before they can be of value to oneself (*VOS* 61–62).

(4) The recognition that "neither wealth nor jobs nor any human values exist in a given, limited, static quantity, waiting to be divided" but that they "have to be produced" by human effort, and thus "that the gain of one man does not represent the loss of another, that a man's achievement is not earned at the expense of those who have not achieved it" (*VOS* 62–63).

The above points do not exhaust Rand's conception of rational self-interest, which carries the full content of the virtue of rationality into deliberation about personal interests.[53] But they are points that Rand considers especially salient in differentiating rational and irrational views of personal interests. They also underlie the third main feature of Rand's account of rational self-interest: that a rational person, deliberating from a long-range perspective and recognizing the facts listed above, will hold a view of human good that includes a commitment to the end-in-himself principle and the trader principle. Such a person sees others not as resources to be exploited, or even primarily as competitors to be outdone, but as producers to be motivated by offering one's own best efforts in exchange for theirs.[54]

Rand does not deny the potential for setbacks and disappointments inherent in the process of achieving goals by means of trade, both in the economic and personal spheres (a seller might lose market share to others; a job seeker, be passed over for another applicant; or romantic love, not be reciprocated). But someone who deliberates about his interests rationally, in Rand's sense, does not see these as conflicts of interest, because they are (as potentialities) inherent in trade, and he sees himself and others as sharing an interest in trade relationships.[55]

Individual Rights

The values of social life require not just human interactions but organized, permanent settlements – societies. We could hardly imagine any large-scale development of trade, division of labor, systematic acquisition and transmission of knowledge, and sustained human relationships beyond the family without some form of social organization and, specifically, without the existence of *political societies* under governments.[56] In Rand's view, just as individuals need moral values to guide their choices if they are to survive, so societies need to be founded on moral values if they are to be conducive to human survival. The central moral concept to guide the organization of a society, according to Rand, is that of *individual rights*.

Rand's formal definition of a "right" is as follows: "A 'right' is a moral principle defining and sanctioning a man's freedom of action in a social context" ("Man's Rights" *VOS* 110/*CUI* 369). As she views them, rights carve out a sphere of morally protected independent action within which individuals cannot properly be coercively interfered with; rights are necessary, according to Rand, in any organized society to give structure to its institutions and provide the rules of peaceful coexistence. Such rights can be seen as having two broad roles. They guide interactions among private individuals, in the sense that one person's rights impose obligations on others to respect those rights, and they guide and constrain the actions of government.[57]

But granted that some rules of social existence are necessary, why should these have the form of principles of rights, in Rand's sense? Rand's answer to any question of this form always appeals to some human need; for her, the question, "Why should we have X?" always reduces to the question, "Why do we need X?"[58] Further, the need identified is always, at root, one related to the requirements of human survival, since for Rand it is those requirements that underlie all human needs. She characterizes individual rights as *"the means of subordinating society to moral law,"*[59] and this perspective on rights helps to indicate why she considers them necessary. Society must be subordinated to moral law because, depending on its form, a society can be either beneficial or harmful to human survival. In Rand's view, the fundamental determinant of whether a given society is one or the other is *whether it respects or impairs the moral functioning of the individuals within it.*

The concept of "rights," she holds, is "the concept that preserves and protects individual morality in a social context" (*VOS* 108/*CUI* 367). Rights are often seen as protecting human interests or protecting choice, and on Rand's account they do serve both of these purposes. But in Rand's view moral principles are necessary for the successful delineation and pursuit of one's interests, and for guiding the faculty of choice. Morality, on her account, defines the "terms, methods, conditions and goals required for the survival of a rational being through the whole of his lifespan – in all those aspects of existence which are open to his choice" ("The Objectivist Ethics" *VOS* 26). What rights fundamentally protect is the individual's ability to function as a moral agent. Socially, that ability depends on *freedom from coercive interference.* It is the need for this particular form of protection that underlies Rand's claim that the principles of organized social existence must have the form of principles of rights.

Although a form of social organization cannot force a person to live morally, society can be organized either to protect or to undermine the freedom an individual needs to live a moral existence. When it does the latter – when it "compel[s] him to act against his own judgment, or ... expropriate[s] his values" ("Man's Rights" *VOS* 111/*CUI* 370) – society does not make a person immoral, but it does constrain the sphere within which a person can function as a moral agent and, in so doing, endangers his survival. The solution to this danger, according to Rand, is to place society itself (and every individual within it) under moral constraints designed to enable individual morality to flourish, and this is what the concept of "rights" accomplishes.

The specification of a set of individual rights thus depends, for Rand, on specifying the dimensions in which man's life in society requires freedom of action. "The source of man's rights," she argues, "is not divine law or congressional law, but the law of identity. A is A – and Man is Man. *Rights* are conditions of existence required by man's nature for his proper survival" (*VOS* 111/*CUI* 370). She fleshes out these claims in a manner that has provoked criticism:

> If man is to live on earth, it is *right* for him to use his mind, it is *right* to act on his own free judg-
> ment, it is *right* to work for his values and keep the product of his work. If life on earth is his pur-
> pose, he has a *right* to live as a rational being: nature forbids him the irrational. (*Atlas* 1061, *VOS*
> 111/*CUI* 370)

Rand has sometimes been accused of making an unsupported transition from claims of the form *it is right for man to x* to claims of the form *man has a right to x* (e.g., from *it is right for man to live by his own judgment* to *man has a right to live by his own judgment*).[60] Read as a self-standing deductive argument, the above passage is clearly a non sequitur. But there is no need to read it in this way and, from the standpoint of Rand's epistemology, no basis for doing so. Rand is appealing to the requirements of morality, as she has set them forth, together with the thesis that the benefits of an organized society depend on whether it protects or restricts its members' freedom to live a moral existence, in order to justify the formation of a certain conception of "rights" and a certain standard for determining the content of rights. Both the latter thesis and the principles of morality are, in her view, inductive conclusions for which history, psychology, and the events of daily life supply an evidentiary basis.[61] Given these conclusions, Rand holds that certain forms of morally protected freedom of action are a basic social need for us, and that we need to delineate and retain what these are, in order to discover and establish forms of social organization capable of securing and protecting them. To delineate and retain them, we need to form the concept of a morally protected sphere of freedom of action. The requirements of cognition and successful action thus call for the specific definition of rights that she offers, and the (independently argued for) moral standard of man's life now serves as a standard for determining the content of rights. A full defense of this line of argument would need to say much more, but it should at least be clear that the argument is complex and does not merely trade on an equivocation between "it is right for man to x" and "man has a right to x."

Rand's defense of rights is neither consequentialist nor deontological. Consequentialism allows for the recognition of rights as a strategy for maximizing the overall impersonal goodness of states of affairs, but it permits rights to be overridden when doing so would produce a better outcome.[62] Rand's argument is similar, in that it has a teleological aspect: rights are validated by reference to the good. But the relevant (and, in her view, the only objectively definable) good is the individual's good – the principles of action and the form of existence required for an individual human being's long-range survival.[63] Because the standpoint for justifying rights is individual good, and because the goods of different individuals are viewed as non-conflicting, infringements of rights are always impermissible, and individual rights are, in this sense, absolute.[64] Unlike standard consequentialism, Rand's teleological defense of rights is not concerned with maximization of the good but with securing the social conditions necessary for one's unhampered pursuit of individual good.

Her view of the stringency of individual rights brings Rand's account into contact with deontological accounts, although here again there are important differences. She does not, for instance, treat rights as correlatives of duties or as the outcome of a fair agreement over the terms of social existence (to mention two prominent deontological approaches).[65] Unlike most deontological theories, her account also denies the possibility of conflicts between rational self-interest and the rights of others, since on her view a person's interest lies fundamentally in production, trade, and the creative use of his own mind, and therefore in a way of acting that is possible only when rights are respected. Threats to rights, in her view, arise not from calculations of self-interest, but from the absence of a correct understanding of self-interest. In material issues, it is the irrational, short-range perspective of the non-thinker and non-producer that generates the motive to violate rights (to rob, expropriate, enslave those who are productive). In regard to intellectual issues, it is the religious and other advocates of doctrines that deny the efficacy of human reason whose success requires the suppression of independent thought and expression. But in Rand's view the long-term course of each group is self-destructive.[66]

Rand's justification of rights has been criticized for failing to explain their obligatory character.[67] For instance, Eric Mack writes: "If 'man's life' or people's lives generally require that (some or all) individuals be free, then ... we may value freedom for those individuals. But this hardly shows ... that persons have *obligations* to them to respect their freedom in the sense that is involved in their having a *right* to be free" (1984, 155). He thus contends that rights must be seen as "deontological claims, i.e., moral claims about how persons must ... be treated that are not determined by the consequences of persons being so treated" (156). Rand is clear, however, that there is an obligation to others to respect their rights, and that its basis is similar to that suggested above for the end-in-himself principle. She makes this kind of point in different places in her writings and speeches; for example, "The only grounds on which you can claim the right to your own life are the same grounds that support the right to life of every human" (*Answers* 115). This is a point about what other people are *entitled* to, in virtue of a (self-interested) claim one makes of them. Self-interest justifies the claim and, in Rand's view, supports respecting the entitlement. Further, the entitlement could not go through if it conflicted with self-interest. But the entitlement is also grounded in the claim to have one's own rights respected. Though there is certainly work to be done in articulating the nature of the relation between this claim and one's obligation to respect rights, that is the form that Rand's argument takes. If she is correct that one's survival requires the conditions of existence that rights protect, then arguably there is a basis in self-interest for accepting the principle of rights, including the obligation to respect the rights of others.[68]

I turn now to the substance of Rand's view of individual rights. The fundamental right, on her account, is the right to life, understood as "the right to engage in self-sustaining and self-generated action – which means: the freedom to take all the actions required by the nature of a rational being for the support, the furtherance, the fulfillment and the enjoyment of his own life" ("Man's Rights" *VOS* 110/*CUI* 369). This passage has been criticized as implying a constricted view of human freedom, on which a person should be free to do only whatever is objectively right and nothing else.[69] But that is a misreading. Rand's formulation refers to the self-sustaining actions "required by the nature of a rational being." The primary requirement, on her account, is thought and independent judgment, which she views as preconditions of successful existential action and self-esteem.[70]

Further, in a social context, the efficacy of objective judgment depends on the protection of the right to dissent.[71] In a free society, an individual has the opportunity to learn from others, while being prevented from interfering with them if he is unwilling (or unable) to learn. By contrast, to be forcibly "protected" from moral error, by protectors who were themselves insulated from objective correction, would – from Rand's perspective – amount to being deprived of one's means of survival by rulers who had surrendered theirs. Thus, among the examples of survival requirements that she gives, Rand includes "to act on his own free judgment" ("Man's Rights" *VOS* 111/*CUI* 370). Further, I take it that what she is referring to is the freedom *to be the judge of how one acts*, which would include the freedom to act against or without formulating one's *considered* judgment of how to act. On her account, what rights target for protection is the *way of functioning* that is required for man's survival. But because the rights-bearer's own choice is essential to that way of functioning, rights must protect freedom of choice, to the fullest extent compatible with extending the same protection to all,[72] even when a person's choice is irrational or mistaken.

Following Locke and the Founding Fathers, Rand holds that the right to life subsumes three others: liberty, property, and the pursuit of happiness, each of which specifies central aspects of the overall right to life. The right to liberty has already been touched on; it encompasses the freedom to act by one's own judgment. Within that sphere, the right to liberty is very broad, and we might mention several narrower rights that she would presumably view as aspects of it, such as the rights to freedom of association, freedom of speech, freedom of migration, freedom of religion, freedom of the press, freedom of contract.[73]

The right to property, Rand holds, "is the right to gain, to keep, to use and to dispose of material values" (*VOS* 111/*CUI* 370).[74] She writes: "Since man has to sustain his life by his own effort, the man who has no right to the product of his effort has no means to sustain his

175

life" (*VOS* 110/*CUI* 369). The right to *gain* property is not a right to be *provided* with property, but a right to engage in production and trade. Protection of the right to property requires a legal framework recognizing and protecting private property, for instance, by defining rules for the acquisition of property rights in unowned resources (such as land, or, once broadcasting technologies exist, airwaves),[75] rules of contract, rules concerning intellectual property, and so forth.[76] The right to property thus imposes on the government a positive obligation to establish and maintain such a framework.

Happiness, for Rand, is the central purpose of a person's life – the incentive and reward for living, and the consequence of living in accordance with the requirements of man's long-range survival. Identifying the right to the pursuit of happiness as an aspect of the right to life brings out that the latter, in her view, encompasses not just the right to exist but the right to live in the fullest sense – the right to sustain oneself both physically and psychologically.[77] The significance of the right to pursue happiness, in Rand's thought, is well indicated by her views on the ethics of abortion. She rejects abortion opponents' claim that a fetus is a person and has rights; thus she holds that abortion is within a woman's rights.[78] It is, in part, an issue of "a woman's right to her own body," which might be seen as a further aspect of the right to life (or perhaps as an aspect of the right to liberty) ("Censorship: Local and Express" *PWNI* 173). But there is also an issue of happiness involved. She comments:

> [T]he anti-abortionists obliterate the rights of the living: the right of young people to set the course of their own lives. ... Procreation is not a duty: human beings are not stock-farm animals. For conscientious persons, an unwanted pregnancy is a disaster; to oppose its termination is to advocate sacrifice, not for the sake of anyone's benefit, but for the sake of misery qua misery, for the sake of forbidding happiness and fulfillment to living human beings. ("A Last Survey" *ARL* 4(2) 383)

Thus the right to abortion is not simply an implication of the right to control one's body but, more important, of the right to pursue happiness. As examples of further aspects of the right to pursue happiness, as Rand views it, we might point to the freedom to choose one's career or the person one marries (which, as with others, may simultaneously be aspects of the right to liberty).[79]

The right to life, for Rand, is the right to act in support of one's life; it is not a right to the economic values (the goods and services) one needs in order to live. Since economic values have to be produced by human effort, a right to them would amount to a right to the lives (the life-sustaining actions) of others, Rand holds; thus, just as a person's right to liberty must be bounded by the similar right of others, so a person's right to life must be bounded by the similar right of others and cannot include a right to any portion of their time or effort. An analogous point holds concerning the rights to property and the pursuit of happiness; they are rights to act and to benefit from one's actions but not to be supported in one's efforts at others' expense.[80] Rand thus rejects the concept of welfare rights. Rights can be violated only by depriving someone of freedom, and specifically of freedom of action (and the freedom to benefit from one's actions). It is this sort of political-economic freedom that Rand considers morally valuable, on the grounds that it is this kind that we need in order to live. Arguments for welfare rights sometimes rely on a different conception of freedom – roughly, the freedom to act within the wider scope of possibilities that open up above some threshold level of economic well-being. In Rand's view, this notion of freedom is an illusory one; to attempt to protect it, she argues, would destroy the freedom of action and thus eventually the productive capacities of those who are most able to produce economic values, as well as impoverish the less able by depriving them of the crucial (for them) benefits of the "pyramid of ability." Its effect is thus to shrink rather than to expand the range of possible human action.[81]

If rights protect the freedom to act and to benefit from one's actions, then they can only be violated by actions that restrict these freedoms. According to Rand, only actions that involve the initiation (or threat) of physical force (or the indirect use of force through fraud) can have this effect. Although the initiation of force is not the only kind of moral wrong that Rand recognizes, it is, in her view, the only kind of moral wrong that diminishes its victim's effective capacity to function as a moral agent and thus to support his life. In other cases, one can disengage from a person with whom one chooses not to associate; for example, one can refuse to see a friend who has become unkind or deceptive, or fire an irresponsible employee. But it is in the nature of physical force that it does not permit its victims this option; it allows no peaceable way of protecting oneself from a value-loss. This, in Rand's view, is what makes the initiation of force a violation of rights, and one of the reasons why she holds that the institution of government is needed to respond to rights violations (an issue that is discussed in this volume, 188–190).[82] It is also why Rand holds that the retaliatory use of force against those who initiate it is morally justified: because force excludes the option of voluntary disengagement, only a coercive response can protect one against it.[83]

A "Society of Traders"

In explicating his ethics, Kant appealed to the idea of a "kingdom of ends," which he described as "a systematic union of different rational beings through common [moral] laws" in which each is treated as an end in himself (Kant 1993, 39; Ak. IV, 433). Galt's Gulch might be seen as Rand's radically different interpretation of the idea of such a union: a community of traders, who deal with one another neither as altruists nor as exploiters but as autonomous equals, each entitled to pursue his own happiness. A full-scale *society* of traders, under political laws and government, would in her view be one geared toward implementing and protecting individual rights. Politically, she holds, it would be a society of limited government; economically, a society based on private property and free markets. That is, it would be a society of full and unregulated capitalism.[84]

Galt's Gulch is not a full-fledged society,[85] but Rand's depiction of it captures the essence of her view of what a human social environment should be. "Here," explains Ellis Wyatt "we trade achievements, not failures – values, not needs. We're free of one another, yet we all grow together. ... What greater wealth is there than to own your life and to spend it on growing?" (*Atlas* 722)

Notes

1 See, in this connection, Rand's discussion of the Apollo 11 moon landing in "Apollo and Dionysus" (*ROTP* 99–118). She interprets the outpouring of public enthusiasm for the event as "the response of people starved for the sight of an achievement, for a vision of man the hero" (101). The need for people worthy of admiration is a central theme of Rand's early play *Ideal*. The screen star Kay Gonda tells a fan, Johnnie Dawes: "If all of you who look at me on the screen hear the things I say and worship me for them – where do I hear them? Where can I hear them, so that I might go on? ... A spirit,

too, needs fuel. It can run dry" ("Ideal" *Plays* 177). In *Atlas*, seeing the enormous crowds gathered for the opening of the John Galt Line, Dagny Taggart feels "a sense of fitness that they should be here, that they should want to see it, because the sight of achievement was the greatest gift a human being could offer to others" (*Atlas* 237).

2 See, e.g., Rachels 1971, 423–434.

3 For a standard formulation of the conception of man's social nature that Rand opposes, see Marx 1988. For examples in *Atlas*, see the comments of the professor of economics (27), Claude Slagenhop (135), Floyd Ferris (540), the sociology professor (607), and the newspapers (1000–1001). In Rand's view, people *can* be molded by society if, through intellectual passivity, they allow themselves to absorb social influences uncritically.

4 Rand holds that "[t]he two great values to be gained from social existence are: knowledge and trade" ("The Objectivist Ethics" *VOS* 35). In her view, a correct conception of human nature must recognize that man's consciousness – and therefore both his thinking and actions – is volitional. Cooperative achievements, she holds, can always be factored into the individual contributions of those participating in any joint undertaking.

5 The "looters" are those who expropriate the values of others. In "A Nation's Unity" (*ARL* 2(2) 127), she says that man is not a social animal (in the conventional sense) but "a *contractual* animal."

6 Rand uses this term in her notes for *Atlas Shrugged* and in a 1957 letter to a fan. See *Journals* 583–584 and 650; and *Letters* 497–498.

7 For discussion of Rand's view of friendship and love, see 88–89 and 135–136 in. this volume. For the concept of "sense of life," see *RM* 14–17, also 21–23; cf., 118–123, above.

8 See Alan Gotthelf's discussion, 96, above.

9 Should you, e.g., accept a pay raise that you don't believe you deserved? Perhaps it is sufficient if the raise is based on a factually accurate appraisal of one's work, though the standards by which that work is appraised by reasonable people (e.g., you and your boss) might vary.

10 Ordinary discourse sometimes reflects this idea, as when a relationship is described as "one-sided" or one party feels used by the other.

11 She calls these "the two essentials of the method of survival proper to a rational being" ("The Objectivist Ethics" *VOS* 25).

12 Psychological survival is in turn both the goal and a precondition of physical survival. I discuss this distinction and its significance for Rand's ethics in Wright 2008, 149–181. See also *RM* 4–5 and 162. For related discussion, see Wright 2005, 190–224.

13 See "A Nation's Unity" (*ARL* 2(2) 127).

14 For Hobbes on conflicts of interest, see *Leviathan* 6.7; and 6 and 13, *passim*. For Hume on benevolence, see *Treatise* 2.3.3.8 and 3.3.1. Hume does not claim that everyone is equally benevolent, but he sees benevolence as a psychologically basic passion, and he also holds that there is a natural principle of sympathy that well disposes us toward the good of others and thus leads us to morally approve of benevolence.

15 It seems possible to make sense of such a thought even in regard to someone who is profoundly mentally disabled from birth, insofar as we see the disability precisely as such, that is, as impeding the human potential that would normally be there. In this case, the thought would be that, had the relevant capacities not been impaired, the person might well have deserved one's moral esteem (and should be valued accordingly). This perspective emerges from viewing the person as disabled; it does not presuppose that *this* person could have existed without the disability, which, depending on the details of the case, might not be true.

16 On the ways in which we benefit from the moral stature of others, see *Speaking* 160–161.

17 Rand uses this phrase in a somewhat different manner and context in "What Is Capitalism?" (*CUI*). But it seems relevant here, also, in the sense indicated.

18 As a psychological matter, I doubt it would be possible to value *oneself* in the proper way, either, if one held this view of the value of other people. But, in any event, the important point is that this is not what Rand advocates.

19 For discussion of this thesis, see "The Objectivist Ethics" (*VOS* 16–27); *OPAR* 207–213; Wright 2011a, 8–25; and Allan Gotthelf's discussion, 89, above. In answering a question about her standard

of value, Rand offers a line of reasoning similar to that discussed in the text, but with some differences: "Only one's own life is a primary moral obligation ... because it's the only one over which you have control, the only life you can live, the only life for which ethics gives you guidance. For the same reason that you should value your own life, you should value human life as such. I'd even say that animal life has a certain value that man should respect. But that does not mean that you should indiscriminately value the life of every other human, or that you have a duty to sacrifice your own life to others, though you should, rationally, value the life of any human who corresponds to your values" (*Answers* 113).

The differences pertain to the inclusion of animals and the reasons given for holding one's own life as one's highest value. Regarding the latter, although I cannot argue the point here, I think the considerations offered in this passage turn out to be equivalent to those given in the passage discussed in the text. Regarding the former, the issue is quite complex, but it seems to me that, for Rand, the basis for valuing animals (in general) would have to do with the analogue, in them, of moral conscientiousness in a human being; namely, that an animal, by nature, strives to maintain its life.

20 At two points in "The Ethics of Emergencies" (*VOS* ch. 3), Rand says that one should only help strangers in an emergency (see 54–55). But she also says that it can be proper to help someone who is "ill and penniless," although illness is a normal occurrence rather than what she calls a "metaphysical emergency," such as a flood. Thus, her position on the scope of proper aid to strangers is somewhat unclear here. She writes, "It is only in emergency situations that one should volunteer to help strangers" (54–55). This could be read either as saying that in non-emergencies one should not help, though in emergencies one may; or, alternatively, as saying that in emergencies, but only then, one *should* help. If it has the latter sense, then Rand's view might be that in non-emergency cases of distress, such as that of illness, one *may* properly help, although it is not the case that one *should* do so (as in an emergency). Or perhaps she is distinguishing between different categories of emergency. Regardless of how one reads this part of her view, I take it that she is only concerned here to delineate the occasions on which one properly gives significant help to strangers, and not to argue that in the normal course of life one should not give strangers directions or the time, or hold a door open for them, and so forth. All of these sorts of routine kindnesses would seem clearly warranted by Rand's views about the ways in which other people as such are to be valued. One should do more, of course, for those with whom has personal relationships; on this, see above, 93.

21 My account of the place of benevolence in Rand's ethics differs from that offered by David Kelley (1996). Kelley argues that Rand's omission of benevolence from her list of major virtues constitutes a "conceptual gap in the theoretical structure" of her ethics (32). On the account given in the text, benevolence is an attitude toward others, and a way of engaging with them, that proceeds from virtue, rather than a virtue in itself.

According to Kelley, the failure to include benevolence as a major virtue "contributes to the perception of Objectivism as a cold and even cruel doctrine," and causes some adherents of Rand's views to be alienated from, and disproportionately critical of, other people (3). Kelley points to an analogy between benevolence and productiveness: Without productiveness, rationality becomes detached and contemplative, ceasing to serve one's life. Similarly, without benevolence, justice becomes cold and unfeeling.

Kelley recognizes, however, that on a correct understanding of Rand's virtue of rationality, contemplative withdrawal from the world would be wholly unwarranted; and he acknowledges that "everything I have attributed to benevolence is already entailed by the principle of justice" (33). Thus, the putative problems mentioned above, to the extent that they are not just the result of a misrepresentation of Rand's ethics, would seem to flow from a misunderstanding of the theory, in particular, from a distorted and impoverished conception of the virtue of justice. But if these problems derive from misunderstanding of Rand's ethics, and to some extent from misrepresentation (as Kelley acknowledges; see 3), then the grounds for attributing them to a "conceptual gap in the theoretical structure" of the theory disappear. Further, although Kelley goes on to say that discussion of benevolence is needed to lend specificity to the broad Objectivist principle that one should live by reason (33), it would seem more helpful and correct, and more consistent with his own analysis, to regard this discussion as unpacking the virtue of justice rather than as revealing a new, coordinate virtue that closes a gap in the theory.

There is a further problem with Kelley's comparison of benevolence to productiveness. Kelley argues that benevolence is related to justice as productiveness is related to rationality. Whereas rationality demands the recognition of what is, productiveness involves envisioning what might be; similarly, whereas justice demands the recognition of people's moral attributes and track records as they stand, benevolence involves the imaginative pursuit of the values of human interaction (see 32–33). But productiveness, for Rand, is the virtue that achieves the moral value of purpose, and the latter is one's "choice of the happiness which [one's mind] must proceed to achieve" (*Atlas* 1018). Purpose thus includes the active exploration and pursuit of the full range of values required in human life, including those pertaining to human relationships; it is not limited to the realm of material production. The associated virtue is productiveness because of the central role of productive work in maintaining an independent identity and a fully purposive existence, without which no other categories of values can be of benefit to a person. But in giving one's work this role, one is also providing for – providing, as it were, the moral-psychological soil for – the purposive pursuit of those other categories of value. The "entrepreneurial" aspects of Kelley's virtue of benevolence, therefore, are already present in a correct understanding of the value of purpose and of the relation of productiveness to this value.

Finally, Kelley's position clashes in an important respect with Rand's theory of virtue. He takes virtues to be commitments required for achieving major human values. But, for Rand, this is only a necessary condition of virtue-status (which would be shared by useful strategies or policies that are not matters of morality). The virtues also pertain to "the relation of existence and consciousness" (*Atlas* 1018). Each of the virtues involves the actively sustained recognition, in thought and action, of certain facts *pertaining to the role of man's mind in sustaining his life.* Thus justice involves "the recognition that you cannot fake the character of men," and productiveness involves the recognition "that productive work is the process by which man's consciousness controls his existence" (*Atlas* 1020). To show that benevolence was a virtue, within the terms of this overall account of the nature of virtue (with which Kelley's analysis is meant to be consistent) would require showing that benevolence consists in the actively sustained recognition of some adjacent region of *this* category of facts. Kelley's argument for a virtue of benevolence does not address this issue. To the extent that someone's lack of benevolent engagement with others did reflect a moral deficiency, it seems more likely that it would reflect a failure either of justice or purpose, or both, rather than some separate kind of moral defect. Though benevolence is clearly important to Rand, it does not itself have the status of a moral virtue.

22 Rand holds that in deliberating about what is morally right, one should refer to moral values and virtues, and that in defining the content of these one should appeal to the moral standard of "man's life." See *VOS* 25–27.

23 See *VOS* 30–32. Also see above, 80–81 and 132.

24 See "The Ethics of Emergencies" (*VOS*), and Gotthelf's discussion, above, 94.

25 Rand does not regard it as a sacrifice to act for someone else's benefit, as long as one's action is consistent with the pursuit of one's own happiness. Kant's principle excludes this constraint, which he would view as inimical to morality.

26 Another contrast is that Kant explicitly applies his principle to all rational beings (and *a fortiori* to humanity) *qua* rational, whereas for Rand it is crucial that humans are both rational beings and living organisms, for the reason explained in the next paragraph.

27 Kant defends this view of humanity not as a theoretical position but as a presupposition of practical reasoning. Accordingly, the sort of value Kant ascribes to humanity is not intrinsic in any sense that involves a metaphysical account of the nature of this value, and a better term for it might be "impersonal" or (as Kant sometimes says) "unconditional" (see Kant 1993, 7; Ak. IV, 393–394). What is crucial, in his view, is that each person has a kind of value that generates an obligation for others to promote that person's interests.

28 "The Objectivist Ethics" (*VOS* 16) and "What Is Capitalism?" (*CUI* 20–23). Also see above 63, 76–78, and 132.

29 *VOS* 16 and 67 and 76–77, above.

30 In a more extended sense, we treat him as an end by helping to create and preserve political institutions that permit every member of society to freely pursue his own happiness.

31 Rand's argument for the thesis that life is the ultimate value or end has three main parts: she argues that there are no values apart from the needs and actions of living organisms, and consequently that the concept of "value" depends on the concept of "life"; that a system of values requires an ultimate value; and that only life has the characteristics requisite for an ultimate value. The quoted statement pertains to the third part of the argument. See VOS 18.

32 For a non-human animal, the ultimate value is (roughly) the life typical for a member of its kind. What a human properly chooses as his ultimate value is his particular life as self-defined human individual. For either, the valued life may include acting to benefit others.

33 See PWNI ch. 1; OPAR ch. 6; and Peikoff "Why Should One Act on Principle?" (TIA 4(20)).

34 See, e.g., Harsanyi 1982, 39–62; Smith 2003, 576–598; and Moehler 2013, 24–47.

35 See, on this, her discussion of the "intrinsic," "subjective," and "objective" theories of the good in "What Is Capitalism?" (CUI 13–16).

36 See, e.g., Hursthouse 2002; Slote 1992; and Swanton 2005.

37 For discussion of this latter, see above, 65–67 and 78.

38 Thrasymachus' contention in The Republic that justice is "the advantage of the stronger" is an implicit recognition of the exploitative ruler's need to obtain the moral sanction of his subjects.

39 For arguments along these lines, though not specifically formulated with reference to the end-in-himself principle, see Answers 110 and 115. See also Speaking 164–165, and the section on individual rights, below. Since Rand grounds the claim made of others in human nature, her view is distinct from those (such as contractarianism) on which interpersonal moral principles are seen as a pragmatic device for coordinating behavior.

40 See Answers 115.

41 The position sketched in this and the preceding three paragraphs enables us to see how Rand would reply to the line of criticism presented by Michael Huemer (2002) in an article on Rand's egoism. Huemer disputes the claim that it is always in one's interest to respect the rights of others. He reconstructs this claim in several ways, and though his criticisms of the views stated are often apt, I think they miss the core of Rand's view. In particular, he does not consider the role of the "sanction of the victim" in sustaining those who violate rights on a wide scale, and he does not discuss Rand's moral psychology (e.g., the way in which self-esteem depends on productiveness), which is central to her conception of self-interest. It is particularly important to note, in this connection, that on Rand's view the sanction of the victim operates both materially and spiritually, providing the "looters" with both unearned wealth and unearned esteem and respect.

The view sketched in the text also makes it clear how Rand would respond to James Rachels's contention that an egoist would not consider "Because ... people may be burned to death" a "complete, sufficient reason" for not setting fire to a department store (see Rachels 1971, 423–434, esp. 432). Rachels does not explain why he thinks setting fire to a department store is something an egoist might find appealing, but it is not something that would appeal to Rand's egoist or that (in any realistic scenario) he would have reason to consider. Nevertheless, Rand's egoist would certainly find the reason that Rachels gives complete and sufficient (and the sheer pointlessness and irrationality of the act would count for him as another complete and sufficient reason). For the reasons explained in the text, he would also recognize an obligation to others to respect their lives and property.

42 For both assumptions, see, e.g., Rachels 1971, 429–430. For the second see also Frankena 1973, 19.

43 The most fully developed examples of this tradition in ethics are Aristotle's Nicomachean Ethics and Aquinas's Summa Theologica.

44 A qualification here is important: Rand denies that a person's good (or what is to his interest) can be forced on him, because human survival as such requires that a person have, as an overarching goal, the aim of living a rational life and this aim, she argues, is undermined by coercion (to whatever extent a person is subjected to it). Thus, although a person might be mistaken about his interests – e.g., if he were mistaken about what would advance some particular goal of his – and someone else might be in a position to call his attention to the error, one could not advance his interests by taking the further step of forcing him to change his course of action. Though from the perspective of that one goal, the error would be contrary to his interest, from the perspective of his entire life it would be in his interest to be free to make (and correct) his own errors, free of coercion. See "What Is Capitalism?" (CUI 23).

45 As indicated in the preceding section, I believe that it is at this point that the concept of one's happiness becomes important, within Rand's ethics, as a deliberative guide.

46 Here and elsewhere in this section, the term "rights" is used in the broad, generic sense of a moral claim, rather than in the narrower political sense of a right to be enforced by the government. In this sense, to say that man has a right to exist for his own sake is equivalent to saying that man is an end in himself. Rand frequently uses the term "rights" in this broad sense (and, as we will discuss below, in its narrower, political sense.)

47 The right to exist for one's own sake is more fundamental within Rand's ethics in that it is the basic social principle and a corollary of the ultimate value to be pursued by each individual. The inefficacy thesis helps to integrate the principle with that of egoism.

48 I will discuss Rand's views of what a fully rational conception of personal interests requires. It is also possible, in her view, for a conception to be only partially rational.

49 By "wrongly," I simply mean that the person's conduct diverges from what he morally should do (though, in the cases being considered, he himself does not grasp this, due to a lack of moral knowledge). Rearden's overindulgence of his family's demands, his condemnation of his affair with Dagny, and his acquiescence in the looters' condemnation of him are key examples in *Atlas*. For Rearden's recognition of these errors, see *Atlas* 857–860.

50 Certain other virtues, such as honesty and justice, she interprets as aspects of the broad virtue of rationality. See *Atlas* 1017–1021 and "The Objectivist Ethics" (*VOS* 28–30). Rationality is not, in her view, a pre-moral practical norm fixing one's reasons for action, as it is conceived to be in much contemporary ethical theorizing.

51 For expository convenience, I summarize the main points in this article in a somewhat different order from Rand's.

52 Rand's view of practical rationality is thus partly procedural and partly substantive. A rational person recognizes rather than evades certain readily available facts about human nature and human life (thus he holds certain substantive views as a result of a methodological commitment to focusing on reality) and deliberates about his interests from a long-range perspective. The points discussed in this section do not exhaust Rand's views of practical rationality, which, for instance, also includes the requirement to always act in accordance with one's (rational) hierarchy of values. See *VOS* ch. 3.

53 Practical rationality, for Rand, also includes the requirement to always act in accordance with one's (rational) hierarchy of values. See "The Ethics of Emergencies" (*VOS*).

54 "The 'Conflicts' of Men's Interests" (*VOS* 59–60 and 63). In regard to personal relationships, he understands that the love of one person for another is not taken from him and that "love is not a static quantity to be divided, but an unlimited response to be earned" (*VOS* 63). If a prospective romantic partner chooses someone else instead, he "could not have had what the [one chosen] has earned" (*VOS* 63).

55 For Rand's analysis of cases in which the interests of rational men may appear to conflict, see "The 'Conflicts' of Men's Interests" (*VOS*).

56 There are really two points here: that there is a need for organized, permanent settlements, and that this needs to take the form of a political society. The second point is contested by anarchism, and Rand's arguments for this point are discussed by Fred Miller and Adam Mossoff, below, 193–194.

57 Following Locke and the American Founders, Rand cites the need for organized, societal protection of individual rights as the rationale for government and therefore as limiting the proper functions of government. See "Man's Rights" (*VOS/CUI*) and 190–193, below. In addition to their roles within a society, Rand also ascribes to rights the role of morally guiding interactions among societies (this is implied, e.g., in "The Roots of War" *CUI, passim*).

58 For example, she applies this pattern of analysis to morality (Why does man need a moral code at all?), to government (Why do men need governments?), and to art (What human need is art geared to fulfill?). See, respectively, "The Objectivist Ethics" and "The Nature of Government" (*VOS*); and "The Psycho-Epistemology of Art" (*RM*). Also see, in this volume, 76–78, 188–190, and 408–413.

59 "Man's Rights" (*VOS* 108/*CUI* 367); italicized in original. The distinction I have drawn here among the roles of rights is relevant to, but not identical with, the distinction between "normative" and

"metanormative" principles made by Douglas Rasmussen and Douglas Den Uyl. Normative principles, in their sense, are moral principles for guiding individual conduct; metanormative, for guiding the formation of a constitution and legal system. Rasmussen and Den Uyl contend that Rand conflates this distinction and that viewing rights as universal moral principles to guide individuals is an error, because "[t]he justification for rights becomes dependent on trying to assess whether the protection of self-directedness will in every case promote human flourishing[,]" which "becomes an impossible task" (Rasmussen and Den Uyl 1991, 113; and see, more generally, 111–114). There isn't space here for extensive analysis of these claims. But it is not clear why the justification of an individual require-ment to respect rights should require any more than what Rasmussen and Den Uyl think is needed (and available) to justify a universal metanormative principle of rights, namely, that self-directedness "is the condition necessary for the very possibility of human flourishing," a basis for rights that "is not tied to the individual human being's actual achievement of flourishing" (114) in a given instance. Rasmussen and Den Uyl might claim that there is a collective action problem in the individual case, such that it is not always rational for the individual to respect others' rights. But that would be to embrace a conception of individual flourishing and practical rationality quite different from the one that they set out to defend. Further, if rights are not, in part, principles to guide individual conduct, it is difficult to understand the claim that there is an individual obligation to respect others' rights. In accusing Rand of conflating "normative" and "metanormative" principles, Rasmussen and Den Uyl do not consider another possibility: that she simply sees rights as falling into both categories, for there is no reason to suppose that these categories must be mutually exclusive. The text of her essay "Man's Rights" supports this interpretation (see *VOS* 109–110), with the proviso that for her the applicability of rights to guiding individual conduct depends on the existence of a legal system through which the broad principles of individual rights can be translated into objective laws defining the precise scope of a person's rights and procedures for adjudicating potential rights violations.

60 For a version of this kind of criticism, see Nozick 1997, 259–260. See also Mack 1984, 152.

61 See Peikoff 1998, lecture 3. For evidence that the inductive methodology discussed by Peikoff was used by Rand, see Salmieri 2009b, 397–452 and Salmieri 2005, 255–284.

62 I focus here on simple forms of act-consequentialism. (Rule-consequentialism faces the general problem of justifying adherence to rules that may not always maximize overall good.) On more so-phisticated forms of act-consequentialism, such as that defended by Peter Railton (see Railton 1984, 134–171), there may be room to argue that a disposition to respect rights independently of conse-quentialist calculation expands the values of social interaction and thus has a consequentialist jus-tification. Rand, though, would still object to the underlying theory of good that consequentialism employs, and to the principle, essential to consequentialism, that an individual's good is subordinate to the impersonal goodness of states of affairs. For a modified consequentialist approach to rights bearing interesting structural similarities to Rand's, though still differing in regard to basic value the-ory, see Scanlon 1977, 81–95. (Railton's and Scanlon's articles are both reprinted in Scheffler 1988).

63 See *CUI* 13–16 and, above, 77, 80, and 132.

64 Judith Jarvis Thomson distinguishes between an *infringement* and a *violation* of rights as follows: you infringe a right if you deprive someone of some of what the right protects; you violate the right if the infringement is morally wrong. The standard example of a permissible infringement would be avail-ing oneself of someone's property without consent in an emergency; the property owner had a right not to have his property used without consent, but, in the event, it was justifiable to deprive him of consent and thus there was no rights violation. Although Rand does not address these kinds of cases directly, her comments on related kinds suggest that she would see Thomson-like cases of permis-sible infringement sometimes as ones in which a right was actually violated and sometimes as ones in which the context limited either the content or the applicability of the right, so that there was no infringement. In appealing to the second possibility, her view of rights resembles what is now called "specificationism." (See Shafer-Landau 1995 for one influential statement of such a view.) Rand of-ten makes specificationist-type points in explaining different rights; on this, see n. 78, below. In Joel Feinberg's famous case of the backpacker who breaks into an uninhabited cottage during a blizzard, I suspect that Rand would not see a rights violation, though that verdict might be conditional on the

actions taken by the backpacker after the emergency had passed (did he restore order, replenish supplies, and make an attempt to notify the owner?). For Thomson's distinction, see Thomson 1986. For Feinberg's case and his discussion of it, see Feinberg 1978.

65 For examples of these approaches, see respectively, Ross 1988, 48–56 and Rawls 1999, esp. chs. 1–3.

66 Rand's account of the basis of rights is closer to at least some things that Locke says about this in the *Second Treatise of Government*, where he argues that man has rights as a matter of natural law and that natural law serves to direct man to the intelligent pursuit of his own interests (and thus that it is in our interests to respect others' rights as well as to have our own rights respected). See Locke 1980, IV.22–23, VI.54, and VI.57. Rand praises Locke's political philosophy in *Answers* 149 and she praises the Founding Fathers' conception of rights in her article "Man's Rights" (*VOS/CUI*).

67 Rand writes: "As to his neighbors, [a man's] rights impose no obligations on them except of a *negative* kind: to abstain from violating his rights." See "Man's Rights" (*VOS* 110/*CUI* 369). Subsequently, she writes that one's rights "impose no obligations on other men." But it is clear in context that she means no obligations beyond the negative obligation previously mentioned, i.e., no obligations to support the lives of others. See *VOS* 115/*CUI* 374.

68 Mack (1998, 3–21) has argued that, in Rand's thought, egoism and rights are best seen (but not always consistently presented) as coordinate aspects of the end-in-himself principle. He contrasts that interpretation to one on which she holds that rights are an application of the prior doctrine of ethical egoism, arguing that this latter interpretation cannot account for the obligation to others to respect their rights. On my interpretation, the end-in-himself principle is a corollary of the (egoistic) ultimate value and, in that sense, a consequence of Rand's egoism. But it is prior to any rational conception of one's personal interests. Obligations to others derive from egoistically grounded moral claims addressed to them. Mack's interpretation is hard to square with the texts, and he makes little attempt to do so. (But his article offers two nice examples from Rand's fiction that show that she views the obligation to treat others as ends as an obligation that is owed *to them*.) The interpretation I have developed does justice, I believe, to the range of texts in which Rand expresses her views on the relevant topics. Michael Huemer (2002, 268–269) criticizes a consistency argument that has some similarity to the arguments I have attributed to Rand in her defense of the end-in-himself principle and in her theory of rights. But in his version of the argument there is no claim addressed to others grounding the obligation to respect their rights or treat them as ends. Though I agree that his version of the argument is unsound, his criticisms of it do not carry over to the form of argument discussed in the text. The passage he quotes from Rand is somewhat ambiguous; it might be taken as an expression of that form of argument, or it might be read as making a purely strategic point that one cannot well expect one's rights to be respected if one fails to respect other people's rights.

69 See Mack 1984, 153 and 155.

70 See, for related discussion, *Speaking* 160.

71 This is part of the meaning of Rand's claim that "[t]he objective view of values permeates the entire structure of a capitalist society" ("What Is Capitalism?" *CUI* 16, and see 16–20). Capitalism, on her analysis, is the only social system with a structure that incentivizes objective judgment, not only in regard to values but in all areas. See the next chapter for discussion.

72 Thus, "those who violate [the right to life] cannot claim its protection, i.e., cannot claim the right to violate a right" ("'Political' Crimes" *ROTP* 177).

73 Many of these also have a basis in property rights, in Rand's account, and property rights will constrain the contours of many of them. For her comments on freedom of speech, in this regard, see n. 80, below. For her general views on how one determines the contours of a given right, see "Political Crimes" (*ROTP* 176–178).

74 Rand's views concerning property rights are discussed further in this volume, 193–201.

75 For some of Rand's views on how these rules should be defined, see "The Property Status of Airwaves" (*CUI* 131–140). Rand does not regard property rights as "natural rights," if this means that specific norms for property acquisition are fixed independently of human choice and law. She holds that principles of rights are objectively justifiable and definable, independently of social conventions. But these principles leave open matters of detail that need to be settled by human institutions; the latter are

not just fixed by reality independent of institutions. In her terminology, individual rights are neither subjective (arbitrarily set by society) nor intrinsic (set in full detail by mind-independent reality) but objective (to be defined by a human consciousness according to rational moral criteria derived from the nature of man and reality). Philosophy can thus define the political right to property, but specific legal property rights must be defined through the legal process of a given society.

76 See "Patents and Copyrights" (*CUI* 141–145).

77 Regarding the distinction between physical and psychological survival, see n. 12, above. See also Gregory Salmieri's and Allan Gotthelf's respective discussions in this volume, 60 and 87–90, above.

78 This at least is her view regarding the first trimester of a pregnancy. She notes: "One may argue about the later stages of a pregnancy, but the essential issue concerns only the first three months." See *ARL* 4(2) 383.

79 On Rand's view of abortion, see also Lewis and Salmieri, 383–384, below.

80 Rand makes a related point concerning freedom of speech: "The right of free speech means that a man has the right to express his ideas without danger of suppression, interference or punitive action by the government. It does *not* mean that others must provide him with a lecture hall, a radio station or a printing press through which to express his ideas" (*VOS* 114/*CUI* 373).

81 This is part of the point of the story of the town of Starnesville, and of the visit by Dagny and Rearden to Rome, Wisconsin, in *Atlas* (see *Atlas* 283–298). For the concept of the "pyramid of ability," see *Atlas* 1064–1065.

82 See *CUI* 10–11.

83 But, as Miller and Mossoff discuss in this volume, 190–191, in Rand's view the retaliatory use of force must be strictly controlled to prevent its arbitrary and unjustified use. See "The Nature of Government" (*VOS* 125–134/*CUI* 378–387).

84 Rand describes capitalism as "a society of traders" in "The Roots of War" (*CUI* 30–39). Her theory of government and her analysis and defense of capitalism are the subject of Fred Miller and Adam Mossoff's chapter in this volume.

85 See *Atlas* 747.

References

Feinberg, Joel. 1978. "Voluntary Euthanasia and the Inalienable Right to Life." *Philosophy and Public Affairs*, 7(2).

Frankena, William K. 1973. *Ethics*, 2nd Edition. Englewood Cliffs, NJ: Prentice Hall.

Harsanyi, John. 1982. "Morality, and the Theory of Rational Behavior." In *Utilitarianism and Beyond*, edited by Amartya Sen and Bernard Williams. Cambridge: Cambridge University Press.

Huemer, Michael. 2002. "Is Benevolent Egoism Coherent?" *Journal of Ayn Rand Studies*, 3(2).

Hursthouse, Rosalind. 2002. *On Virtue Ethics*. Oxford: Oxford University Press.

Kant, Immanuel. 1993. *Grounding for the Metaphysics of Morals*, translated by James W. Ellington. Indianapolis, IN: Hackett.

Kelley, David. 1996. *Unrugged Individualism: The Selfish Basis of Benevolence*. Poughkeepsie, NY: Institute for Objectivist Studies.

Locke, John. 1980. *Second Treatise of Government*. Indianapolis, IN: Hackett.

Mack, Eric. 1984. "The Fundamental Moral Elements of Rand's Theory of Rights." In *The Philosophic Thought of Ayn Rand*, edited by Douglas Den Uyl and Douglas Rasmussen. Urbana, IL: University of Illinois Press.

Mack, Eric. 1998. "On the Fit Between Egoism and Rights." *Reason Papers*, 23.

Marx, Karl. 1988. *Economic and Philosophic Manuscripts of 1844*, translated by Martin Milligan. Amherst, NY: Prometheus Books.

Mayhew, Robert, ed. 2005a. *Essays on Ayn Rand's* Anthem. Lanham, MD: Lexington Books.

Moehler, Michael. 2013. "Contractarian Ethics and Harsanyi's Two Justifications of Utilitarianism." *Politics, Philosophy, and Economics*, 12.

Nozick, Robert. 1997. "On the Randian Argument." In *Socratic Puzzles*. Cambridge, MA: Harvard University Press.

Peikoff, Leonard. 1998. *Objectivism Through Induction*. Lecture series. Recording available at estore.aynrand.org/p/107/ (accessed May 25, 2015).

Rachels, James. 1971. "Egoism and Moral Skepticism." In *A New Introduction to Philosophy*, edited by Steven M. Cahn. New York, NY: Harper and Row.

Railton, Peter. 1984. "Alienation, Consequentialism, and the Demands of Morality." *Philosophy and Public Affairs*, 13(2).

Rasmussen, Douglas, and Douglas Den Uyl. 1991. *Liberty and Nature*. LaSalle, IL: Open Court.

Rawls, John. 1999. *A Theory of Justice*, Revised Edition. Cambridge, MA: Belknap Press of Harvard University Press.

Ross, W.D. 1988. *The Right and the Good*. Indianapolis, IN: Hackett.

Salmieri, Gregory. 2005. "Prometheus' Discovery: Individualism and the Meaning of the Concept 'I' in *Anthem*." In Mayhew 2005a.

Salmieri, Gregory. 2009b. "Discovering Atlantis: *Atlas Shrugged*'s Demonstration of a New Moral Philosophy." In *Essays on Ayn Rand's Atlas Shrugged*, edited by Robert Mayhew. Lanham, MD: Lexington Books.

Scanlon, T.M. 1977. "Rights, Goals, and Fairness." *Erkenntnis*, 11(1).

Schafer-Landau, Russ. 1995. "Specifying Absolute Rights." *Arizona Law Review* 37.

Scheffler, Samuel, ed. 1988. *Consequentialism and Its Critics*. Oxford: Oxford University Press.

Slote, Michael. 1992. *From Morality to Virtue*. Oxford: Oxford University Press.

Smith, Michael. 2003. "Neutral and Relative Value After Moore." *Ethics*, 113.

Swanton, Christine. 2005. *Virtue Ethics: A Pluralistic View*. Oxford: Oxford University Press.

Thomson, Judith Jarvis. 1986. "Some Ruminations on Rights." In *Rights, Restitution, and Risk*, edited by William Parent. Cambridge, MA: Harvard University Press.

Wright, Darryl. 2005. "Needs of the *Psyche* in Ayn Rand's Early Ethical Thought." In Mayhew 2005a.

Wright, Darryl. 2008. "Evaluative Concepts and Objective Values: Rand on Moral Objectivity." *Social Philosophy and Policy*, 25.

Wright, Darryl. 2011a. "Reasoning about Ends: Life as a Value in Ayn Rand's Ethics." In *Metaethics, Egoism, and Virtue: Studies in Ayn Rand's Normative Theory*, edited by Allan Gotthelf and James G. Lennox. Ayn Rand Society Philosophical Studies, vol. 1. Pittsburgh, PA: University of Pittsburgh Press.

8

Political Theory

A Radical for Capitalism

FRED D. MILLER, JR. AND ADAM MOSSOFF

Politics, for Ayn Rand, is the branch of philosophy that "defines the principles of a proper social system" ("Philosophy: Who Needs It" *PWNI* 5). "A social system" she defines as "a set of moral-political-economic principles embodied in a society's laws, institutions, and government, which determine the relationships, the terms of association, among men living in a given geographical area" ("What Is Capitalism?" *CUI* 9). In her political writings, like the thinkers of the Enlightenment, she begins with first principles, considering first whether and why men need such an institution as government, and then drawing implications for other issues in political theory from her answers to these fundamental questions.[1]

Accordingly, Rand maintains that political theory is not a philosophical primary. "A country's political system," she writes, "is based on its code of morality" (*Atlas* 1061). One should begin a philosophical analysis of politics, according to her, only after one first understands that man's life is the standard of value, that concern with his own life is man's primary moral purpose, that reason is his basic tool of survival, and that its exercise is volitional and requires the absence of coercion.[2] These are the metaphysical facts and ethical principles on which Rand grounds her conception of and justification for *individual* rights. A *right*, as discussed by Darryl Wright in the preceding chapter, is a moral principle sanctioning an individual's freedom of action in a social context. Such principles are necessary precisely because individuals must be free from the coercion of others – no one may initiate the use of force against others. For this reason, Rand maintains that, "*Individual rights are the means of subordinating society to moral law*" ("Man's Rights" *VOS* 108/*CUI* 367). Indeed, she maintains that the protection of individual rights is the *raison d'être* of government. As Leonard Peikoff puts the point, "The goal of a proper society, accordingly, is not to compel truth or virtue (which would be a contradiction in terms), but to make them *possible* – by ensuring that men are left free" (*OPAR* 367).

In explicating Rand's political theory – in explaining why she believes that government is necessary in order to ensure the voluntary cooperation of rational individuals in a free society,[3] that is, a society in which individual rights are respected – we shall follow the same methodology. We will first present Rand's analysis of the nature of government and discuss why,

A Companion to Ayn Rand, First Edition. Edited by Allan Gotthelf and Gregory Salmieri.
© 2016 John Wiley & Sons, Ltd. Published 2016 by John Wiley & Sons, Ltd.

according to her, man needs such an institution. Then we will discuss why Rand holds that the proper purpose of government is the securing of individual rights, and why it follows from that that capitalism is the only moral social system. In detailing Rand's defense of capitalism, we will discuss why she is an ardent proponent of property rights, and thus why property rights take a central place in her writings on politics. Finally, we will discuss Rand's defense of intellectual property rights, which she views as core property rights. Ultimately, Rand's political theory represents an integrated framework in which she develops the grounds for her defense of capitalism, and it is for this reason that Rand refers to herself as "a radical for capitalism" (*Letters* 602, 666, cf. "For the New Intellectual" *FTNI* 54–55).

The Nature and Need of Government

Rand's essay "The Nature of Government" begins with a definition: "A government is an institution that holds the exclusive power to *enforce* certain rules of social conduct in a given geographical area" ("The Nature of Government" *VOS* 125/*CUI* 378). Her decision to start this way reveals that, in her view, a theoretical discussion of a topic such as politics requires clear definitions of its central concepts, such as "government." All too often, political theories proceed from vague and ambiguous notions of community, society, and state.[4] Rand does not consider definitions, though, to be stipulative or conventional; rather, they identify in fundamental terms the identity of the thing one is conceptualizing in one's theory, and they are important for that reason (*ITOE* 40, 45).[5]

Three points are especially noteworthy about Rand's definition of government. First, the italicized word "*enforce*" emphasizes that government "holds a legal monopoly on the use of physical force" ("The Nature of Government" *VOS* 128/*CUI* 381). This distinguishes governments from other kinds of social institutions that "determine the relations, the terms of association, among men living in a given geographic area" ("What Is Capitalism?" *CUI* 9). For example, a religious organization that promulgates rules for its parishioners but lacks the power to enforce them coercively is not a government. Nor is a condominium association that can enforce rules among its members a government, because it ultimately depends on the power of the police and courts if its members refuse to obey its rules. The second point is that a government possesses exclusive *territorial* sovereignty, which distinguishes it from criminal gangs like the Mafia or terrorist factions like the Irish Republican Army or the Palestine Liberation Organization, which enforce rules on their members and attack enemy groups.[6] The third point is that a government enforces "certain rules of social conduct." This applies to all forms of government, whether they are proper or improper, including the constitutional republic of the United States of America, Britain's parliamentary monarchy, or the fascist dictatorship of Nazi Germany. Rand's definition of government is purely descriptive. Ultimately, she specifies the standards for a *proper* government, but only after she establishes what a government is and examines why men need such an institution.

After clearly delineating what she means when she refers to a "government," Rand develops the case for why men need a government. In sum, her argument has three interrelated premises: first, an individual can benefit from cooperation with others only if his rights are protected from the initiation of physical force; second, the protection of individual rights requires that physical force be controlled through a system of objective rules; and, third, physical force can be placed under the control of objective rules only by means of a government. These three premises will be explained in turn.

First, a peaceful, productive, and rational society is possible only if individual rights are protected from the initiation of physical force. As discussed earlier, Rand conceives of "rights" as principles sanctioning the actions required by man's nature for his survival in a social context. She explains that the concept of rights provides the logical transition from the moral principles guiding an individual's actions to the principles guiding his relationship with others.[7] The primary function of rights according to Rand is to define and sanction a man's freedom of action in a social context, with the result that he is free to identify and pursue the values necessary for him to live.[8] It is individual rights that make it possible for the virtuous man to live in organized society, in which he is free to act on the ethical principle of rational egoism. It is only when his rights are secured against others – when each man is protected against the initiation of physical force by others – that he can interact with other men peacefully and for mutual benefit.[9]

Rand's second premise is that the protection of rights in civilized society requires an *objective* code of rules that identifies these rights, the actions that violate them, and the penalties that follow. The only action that violates another man's rights is the initiation of physical force, and thus force may only be used legitimately in self-defense. It is the government's role to provide the means by which this retaliatory use of force is employed against those who initiate force against the innocent, including police enforcement and incarceration. As Rand observes, "The retaliatory use of force requires *objective* rules of evidence to establish that a crime has been committed and to *prove* who committed it, as well as *objective* rules to define punishments and enforcement procedures" ("The Nature of Government" *VOS* 127/*CUI* 380).

These objective rules are needed to answer the many knotty, fundamental questions that naturally arise regarding crime and punishment in a way that is accessible to everyone. Let's consider some of the questions that Rand might have in mind: What evidence is sufficient to prove that an individual has committed a crime? Given that there are different sorts of criminals – pickpockets, burglars, rapists, murderers – how much force is it legitimate to use to punish each? Does it make a difference whether a criminal acted in the heat of passion or according to a deliberately executed plan? In addition to the questions concerning the capture, trial, and punishment of individuals who have already committed crimes, questions arise due to the fact that the government may also use force to prevent someone from using force against another person. For instance, in arresting individuals for such crimes as attempted murder or conspiracy to commit fraud, questions again arise concerning this legitimate use of force by the government: What are the exact conditions under which such preemptive acts are proper? What conduct is sufficient to justify classifying a murderous intent as an "attempted murder"? Again, what evidence will prove "beyond a reasonable doubt" this criminal intent? There is, finally, the formidable problem of distinguishing between criminal culpability and civil liability (the former requiring prison or punitive fines and the latter requiring the payment of compensatory damages).

Rather than leaving such decisions about when and how to use force to the discretion of individual citizens, a civilized society requires a system of objective rules. By "objective" Rand means two things: First, the rules spell out clearly in advance what actions the law forbids, why it forbids these actions, and what penalties will be incurred if anyone commits such actions. Second, they are objectively justifiable, in the sense that they are determined by the facts of reality and discoverable by a rational process.[10]

Rand's third premise supporting her thesis that men need government is that this institution is necessary in order to place the use of physical force under the control of an objective code of rules. In order to place the use of physical force under objective laws, there must be an agent to restrain and control the use of force. This agent can carry out its function only if it has the exclusive power to enforce these objective laws – exercising "the exclusive power to *enforce* certain rules of social conduct in a given geographical area" (*VOS* 125/*CUI* 378).[11] "*This* is the task of a government," concludes Rand, "its only moral justification and the reason why men do need a government" (*VOS* 127–128/*CUI* 381).

Rand makes it clear that she does not assume that men need government because they are driven by irrational passions or are incurably immoral.[12] "Whether his neighbors' intentions are good or bad, whether their judgment is rational or irrational, whether they are motivated by a sense of justice or by ignorance or by prejudice or by malice – the use of force against one man cannot be left to the arbitrary decision of another" (*VOS* 127/*CUI* 380). To see Rand's point, consider the common, run-of-the-mill disputes between neighbors, in which each neighbor accuses the other of trespassing on his property. In such cases, each party may be honestly convinced that he is in the right but also aware that the other is of the same opinion; thus, it would not be reasonable to allow the other to be the judge. To settle this disagreement, there needs to be a neutral arbiter who can resolve the dispute with reference to objective rule and enforce his decision, in other words, there needs to be a government."[13] Rand's argument for government thus stands in sharp contrast to the view expressed by James Madison in *Federalist Paper* No. 51: "If all men were angels, no government would be necessary" (Hamilton, Jay, and Madison 1961, 322). Madison assumes that men are often governed by their (irrational) passions rather than their reason.[14] If they were "angels," he implies, they could coexist in a peaceful anarchy devoid of the laws that are necessary to restrain their brutish animalistic natures. Rand not only rejects this pessimistic view of human nature, but she also maintains that, even if all men "were fully rational and faultlessly moral," they would still require government (*VOS* 131/*CUI* 384). Her main point is that the recognition and protection of individual rights requires an agent that has a legal monopoly on the use of force, that is, government.

Proper Functions of Government

Having first explained what government is and why it is necessary, Rand is now able to explain its proper role: "*A government is the means of placing the retaliatory use of physical force under objective control* – i.e., under objectively defined laws" (*VOS* 128/*CUI* 381). This makes clear the basic task of government, and hence its only moral justification. It also implies its proper functions:

> The proper functions of a government fall into three broad categories, all of them involving the issues of physical force and the protection of men's rights: the police, to protect men from criminals – the armed services, to protect men from foreign invaders – the law courts, to settle disputes among men according to objective laws. (*VOS* 131/*CUI* 384)

Rand recognizes that these three categories entail many complex issues that can be resolved only through detailed legislation, and it is the philosophy of law that must derive these necessary corollaries from the fundamental principle that the sole purpose of government is the protection of individual rights.

As such, she emphasizes that a proper government must be *limited*. Its powers must be confined to the protection of rights by the retaliatory use of force, or else the government will become the vehicle for violating the individual rights the protection of which is its sole justification. Although governments are administered by people, their activities must be subject to checks and balances so that it resembles "an impersonal robot" that is programmed to enforce the laws (*VOS* 128/*CUI* 381).[15] This accounts for a fundamental asymmetry: "A private individual may do anything except that which is legally *forbidden*; a government official may do nothing except that which is legally *permitted*" (*VOS* 128/*CUI* 381).[16]

Rand's explanation of government also necessitates that individuals *delegate* the protection of their rights to this institution, which then wields a monopoly on the use of retaliatory force. She reaffirms the principle enunciated in the Declaration of Independence that "to secure these [individual] rights, governments are instituted among men, deriving their just powers from the consent of the governed," but she understands "the consent of the governed" in a very strict sense. "There is only one basic principle to which an individual must consent if he wishes to live in a free, civilized society: the principle of renouncing the use of physical force and delegating to the government his right of physical self-defense, for the purpose of an orderly, objective, legally defined enforcement" (*VOS* 129/*CUI* 382). Hence, government is an agent of its individual citizens with specific and clearly delimited powers. Rand does not, however, subscribe to a "social contract" theory, according to which individuals allegedly consent – either actually or hypothetically – to the authority of government. For Rand, the delegation of rights is a *moral* requirement for rational individuals, not an actual claim about assent to a particular institution or government.[17]

This highlights an important difference between Rand and the natural rights philosophers, such as Samuel Pufendorf and John Locke.[18] The view that individuals can escape from the "inconveniences" of a state of nature only by compromising or outright ceding their rights to government leads all too easily to arguments that once government is created individuals must comply with the dictates of the majority. Jean-Jacques Rousseau, for example, takes social contract theory to its ultimate conclusion, arguing that once individuals have left the state of nature for civil society, they might be "forced to be free" in compliance with the "general will" (which was allegedly infallible but inscrutable except to Rousseau's "Lawgiver") (Rousseau 1997, 53, 68, 124). Rand avoids the slippery slope created by the social contract theory, leading to such things as the despotism of Rousseau's Lawgiver, because she does not view the "consent of the governed" as the standard for defining the proper functions of government. She maintains that the government has no legitimate powers except those delegated to it for the specific purpose of protecting the rights to life, liberty, and property.

Since Rand does not maintain that government arises from an *act* of consent, express or tacit, she rejects the statist implications of this consent theory, such as the power of eminent domain. The natural rights philosophers believe that eminent domain is an inherent power of sovereignty, as justified by the consent provided by individuals in forming a government that would enact laws to provide for their safety and security.[19] Hugo Grotius, the preeminent natural rights philosopher, coined the term, "eminent domain" (1925, 219, 796–797, 807), which he defines as the power of the state to take property for "public advantage" when "the body politic should be considered as desiring that private advantage should yield" (807).[20] According to Grotius, when individuals assent to create a government, the sovereign acquired preeminent dominion over their property – asserting its eminent domain – in the name of the so-called common good.

Since Rand considers consent a moral requirement of a just society, because it is consent to respecting the principle of individual rights as the only basis for social association,[21] she concludes that the government that expropriates the property of its citizens has breached its moral obligation to defend its citizens' rights to life, liberty, and property. A society is composed only of individuals, according to Rand, and therefore there is no "common good" or "social welfare" that exists over and above the government's fundamental moral obligation to protect each man's rights.[22] Rand maintains that any appeal to a "common good" that is divorced from the protection of rights will ultimately lead to the violation of those rights, because it turns this concept into an open-ended rationalization for unfettered coercion in pursuit of *anything* the government deems to be the "common good" ("The Only Path to Tomorrow" *Column* 114, "The Moral Basis of Individualism" *Journals* 249). In a constitutional republic, she explains that the government would become an instrument by which people with political clout may use legal coercion to violate the rights of other people ("What Is Capitalism?" *CUI* 12–13). The modern welfare state is evidence for this proposition, as people vote for politicians who promise to redistribute property in the name of the "common good," but Rand's insight is perhaps most dramatically revealed when the government exercises its "eminent domain" power to take someone's home from them against their will.[23]

Rand believes that the function of government is to protect individual rights, and the principle of individual rights is as inviolate as man's nature. "A is A – and Man is Man" (*VOS* 111/*CUI* 370, quoting *Atlas* 1061). Thus, the necessity and function of government – to defend man's rights against criminals – is as inviolate as the facts that give rise to it. To permit a breach of individual rights, such as violating a citizen's property rights under eminent domain, is to turn a blind eye to these facts and to convert the government itself into a criminal.[24]

As a consequence of the foregoing principles, Rand maintains that many policies of modern governments are morally illegitimate. A full discussion of the whole range of governmental policies is beyond the scope of this chapter, and so we will focus only a few examples that illustrate Rand's absolutism about the moral principle of individual rights.[25] To begin with the purest forms of statism, she condemns the policies of totalitarian regimes; for example, the concentration camps found in Nazi Germany or the gulags in the Soviet Union. In these cases a government is initiating force against its subjects in order to break them – physically, morally, and psychologically – and to make them slaves of the state.[26]

On the same grounds, Rand criticizes policies in so-called "liberal democracies" that are different in concrete form, but reflect the same underlying statist principle. One prominent example is military conscription or the draft, which is surprisingly prevalent in even relatively free countries. "Of all the statist violations of individual rights in a mixed economy, the military draft is the worst" ("The Wreckage of the Consensus" *CUI* 255–256). She argues that for the state to compel a man to risk death or injury in a war for a purpose that he may not approve of or even understand is to violate his rights of life and liberty, which it is the purpose of government to protect. The draft is involuntary servitude – literally, slavery. If men may be coerced into fighting and dying against their will, the government has defaulted on its most fundamental purpose. "Since the only proper function of government is to protect man's rights, it cannot claim title to his life in exchange for this protection" (*CUI* 255–256).[27]

Given Rand's view of the moral function of a government, she also rejects the welfare state and other forms of wealth redistribution that are just as prevalent today in modern constitutional republics. One rationale for the governmental programs that redistribute wealth from one segment of the society to another might be that the government represents some group – whether a nation, race, economic class, or some other collective entity – that has the ultimate entitlement to the life and work of the individual members of society. But, as Rand remarks, "A group, as such, has no rights. A man can neither acquire new rights by joining a group nor lose the rights which he does possess" ("Collectivized Rights" *VOS* 119–120). The view that a group has rights, according to Rand, implies "the collectivist principle that man is the rightless slave of the state" ("'Extremism,' or The Art of Smearing" *CUI* 200). Another rationale might be that government has a right to tax the wealthy in order to provide for the needy or disadvantaged through its welfare programs.[28] Rand objects that those subjected to taxation have been "deprived of rights and condemned to slave labor" for the beneficiaries of these government-run welfare programs. If it is replied that the needy have the right to jobs, food, education, and so on, Rand observes that "No man can have a right to impose an unchosen obligation, an unrewarded duty or an involuntary servitude on another man. There can be no such thing as '*the right to enslave*'" ("Man's Rights" *VOS* 113/*CUI* 373).

Since Rand rejects taxation as a violation of individual rights, the question naturally arises: How *can* the costs of legitimate governmental functions be paid without taxation? It would have to be voluntary, and Rand proposes one method whereby a government might charge fees for contracts that could be adjudicated in the courts and enforced if necessary by the police.[29] Yet Rand cautions that consideration of the institutional mechanisms by which a proper, limited government is financed is "very complex" and, importantly, "more than premature today" (*VOS* 113/*CUI* 373). It is first necessary to establish what are the proper functions of government and why the government should be limited to these functions before proposals on its operative details can be objectively evaluated.

Although the government must be limited to certain specific purposes, Rand affirms that government *is* necessary. Thus she disagrees emphatically with "libertarian" anarchists, such as Murray Rothbard and David Friedman, who claim that the initiation of force is morally impermissible but also contend that a society can banish the initiation of force without a government.[30] Rand dismisses anarchism as "a naive floating abstraction" on two grounds ("The Nature of Government" *VOS* 131/*CUI* 384). First, she explains that "A society without an organized government would be at the mercy of the first criminal who came along and who would precipitate it into the chaos of gang warfare" (*VOS* 131/*CUI* 384). Since the potential victims of such a malefactor could not appeal to an impartial protector, they would have no alternative but to organize a gang of their own in self-defense. The inevitable result is not peaceful coexistence without a government, but a descent into gang warfare on a national scale, such as the world has witnessed in the twentieth century in places like Bosnia, Lebanon, and Somalia.

Second, Rand makes the more fundamental point that "even a society whose every member were fully rational and faultlessly moral, could not function in a state of anarchy" (*VOS* 131/*CUI* 384). The reason is that this society would lack "*objective* laws" and "an arbiter for honest disagreements among men" (*VOS* 131/*CUI* 384). Just as rational individuals may not agree about the facts and circumstances of their interactions, as discussed in the previous section, they cannot be expected to agree over the procedural and substantive rules that should be applied to resolve these disagreements.[31]

The variety of anarchism endorsed by Rothbard and Friedman is known as "market anarchism" or "anarcho-capitalism." On this view, because competition is preferable to monopoly in providing economic goods in a market, it would be more efficient if there were "competing governments" among which individual citizens could choose to patronize.[32] In evaluating this variant of anarchism, Rand observes that it shares the same basic premise of statism: namely, that there is "no difference between the functions of government and the functions of industry, between force and production" (*VOS* 131/*CUI* 385). Rand identifies this fundamental distinction in social relationships as the difference between the power of the *dollar* and the power

193

of the *gun* (*Atlas* 383–387, *Journals* 623).[33] When a firm produces goods, it must rely on the rational judgment of its customers to choose to purchase them. When a government uses force, however, the judgment or choices of the targeted individuals is moot; coercion nullifies the mind and demands only obedience.[34]

This distinction becomes obvious when one considers the actual facts of how so-called "competing governments" would function, as explained by Rand:

> [S]uppose Mr. Smith, a customer of Government A, suspects that his next-door neighbor, Mr. Jones, a customer of Government B, has robbed him; a squad of Police A proceeds to Mr. Jones' house and is met at the door by a squad of Police B, who declare that they do not accept the validity of Mr. Smith's complaint and do not recognize the authority of Government A. What happens then? You take it from there. (*VOS* 132/*CUI* 385)

As Rand's hypothetical scenario makes clear, all of the complex questions underlying the need for objective laws come into play, as discussed in the previous section. Since each so-called government would have its own rules, institutions, and procedures, it would face the alternative of forcefully standing by its own decisions or else surrendering to the other so-called government. [35] As with plain old anarchism, the inevitable result is irresolvable dispute and warfare.[36]

Rand's opposition to anarchism explains her emphatic disavowal of the Libertarian movement, which coalesced in the 1970s under the intellectual leadership of Rothbard and other "anarcho-capitalists," and which cited her as an influence. (Rand's view of this movement is discussed by John Lewis and Greg Salmieri, in this volume, 381–382.) The term "libertarian" is now sometimes used (and applied to Rand) in a more general sense, as a description of a broad category of positions in political theory. As with most pieces of philosophical vocabulary, the term is defined differently by different authors. In particular, some definitions include anarchism as a form of libertarianism whereas others exclude it, and some make reference to the Lockean tradition of individual rights, whereas others do not. Rand would (properly) have rejected any attempt to classify her political thought that regarded her endorsement of individual rights as non-essential or that was so broad as to subsume anarchism. However, there are robust connections, which she readily acknowledged, between her political thought and the Lockean natural rights tradition (notwithstanding the differences we note above and below). At present there is no term that unambiguously names the broad sort of view that she shares with these thinkers. In the absence of such a term, we think it is best to describe Rand as she described herself, as a "radical for capitalism." Her reasons for this description will become clear in the following section.

Capitalism and Property

After explaining in "The Nature of Government" the objective need for government and its proper functions, she argues in "What Is Capitalism?" that there is only one *moral* social system – only one system that protects man's individual rights and secures his freedom: capitalism. "Capitalism," she writes, "is a social system based on the recognition of individual rights, including property rights, in which all property is privately owned" ("What Is Capitalism?" *CUI* 10). In defining capitalism in this way, Rand once again reveals the distinctive character of her philosophic thought.

We should emphasize at the start that Rand, unlike most political theorists and economists, understands capitalism as both a political *and* economic system, in which the government recognizes and secures all individual rights.[37] Thus, for Rand, it is a contradiction in terms to refer to fascist dictatorships, as in Latin America, as "capitalist" ("Requiem for Man" *CUI* 356–357). She dramatizes this point in *Atlas Shrugged*, in which the hero, John Galt, refuses an offer to become an economic dictator by repeatedly showing how it is impossible to make economic decisions without necessarily making what Mr. Thompson, the villainous "head of state," regards as merely political decisions (*Atlas* 1099–1101). In order to see why she thinks this we'll need to consider the roots of capitalism in the facts of human nature, that is, the metaphysical foundation for the principle of individual rights, especially the right to property.

Given that Rand believes that capitalism is an integrated political and economic system, one might wonder why she emphasizes the right to property, among all the individual rights, in her definition of this social system. The reason has to do with the special status of property as an individual right within the framework of her ethical theory.[38] She summarizes this point in her essay, "Man's Rights":

> The right to life is the source of all rights – and the right to property is their only implementation. Without property rights, no other rights are possible. Since man has to sustain his life by his own effort, the man who has no right to the product of his effort has no means to sustain his life. ("Man's Rights" *VOS* 110/*CUI* 369)

This requires some unpacking in terms of the connections Rand is making between her concept of value, her theory of virtue, and her theory of individual rights, which all lead her to identify this essential connection between the right to life and the right to property.

First, as a rational animal, man must conceptually identify and then physically act to produce the values that are necessary for him to live. Unlike the berries eaten by a wild rabbit, the values that man needs, such as clothing, food, and shelter, cannot be found ready-made in his environment.[39] Man must create values through a process of thought, identifying conceptually the skills necessary to cultivate land to grow crops, to husband animals for food and labor, and to build homes. In *Atlas Shrugged*, Rand has Francisco d'Anconia explain this in his "Meaning of Money" speech:

> Have you ever looked for the root of production? Take a look at an electric generator and dare tell yourself that it was created by the muscular effort of unthinking brutes. Try to grow a seed of wheat without the knowledge left to you by men who had to discover it for the first time. Try to obtain your food by means of nothing but physical motions – and you'll learn that man's mind is the root of all the goods produced and of all the wealth that has ever existed on earth. (*Atlas* 410)

Since man is a rational animal, if he wants to live, he must engage in production, identifying and creating the values necessary for him to survive and flourish.[40]

As explained by Allan Gotthelf (84–85, above), Rand's ethical theory maintains that such value creation is fundamentally a moral act. If man is to live, he must practice the virtue of productiveness, and it is only possible for him to live and flourish if he does so with a steadfast commitment to this requirement of his nature as a rational animal. For Rand, the source of the right to property is found in her ethical theory, as she highlights in the following passage:

> If man is to live on earth, it is *right* for him to use his mind, it is *right* to act on his own free judgment, it is *right* to work for his values and to keep the product of his work. If life on earth is his purpose, he has a *right* to live as a rational being: nature forbids him the irrational. (*Atlas* 1061)

According to Rand's ethical theory, property is the result of a virtuous man creating the values he has identified as necessary for his life and happiness,[41] and, according to her political theory, the government's sole responsibility is to secure to this man the freedom necessary to practice the virtues his life requires. She concludes: "no rights can exist without the right to translate one's rights into reality – to think, to work and to keep the results – which means: the right of property" (*Atlas* 1062). To grasp the concept of the right to property is to understand how it defines and sanctions the freedom of action necessary for virtuous men to live in society.[42]

Significantly, Rand is not saying that the right to property is a moral claim to an object: as an individual right, the right to property secures only freedom of action in a social context (*VOS* 110/*CUI* 369). The right to property secures the freedom necessary for a man to practice the virtue of productiveness – creating the values necessary for him to live. Thus, as a consequence of her understanding of the connection between property and the virtuous actions that create values, she defines the right to property as "the right to gain, to keep, to use and to dispose of material values" (*VOS* 111/*CUI* 370).

If man is not free to produce and use the values necessary to support his life – if the products of his productive labors are expropriated by the government – then, on Rand's view, he is condemned to slave labor and death. As she observes, "When unlimited and unrestricted by individual rights, a government is men's deadliest enemy" (*VOS* 115/*CUI* 374). This is not hyperbole, as attested to by the deaths of tens of millions of people at the hands of Stalin, Mao, the Khmer Rouge, and other communist dictatorships in the twentieth century.[43] The millions of deaths caused by the Nazis and other fascist regimes in the twentieth century also confirm this point.[44] The misery and destruction that have occurred in social systems that deny the right to property confirm Rand's insight that "The right to life is the source of all rights – and the right to property is their only implementation. Without property rights, no other rights are possible" (*VOS* 110/*CUI* 369).

In her analysis of the right to property, Rand's observation that the *source* of property is to be found in human nature is not an original philosophical insight. The natural rights philosophers, such as Hugo Grotius, Samuel Pufendorf, and John Locke, argue that property arises from human action; specifically, they maintain that it is the occupation and use of, or the laboring upon, materials in the world that creates a moral claim to these items – a right to property.[45] Although Rand's political theory resonates with ideas that are similar to natural rights philosophy,[46] especially as it is presented in Locke's justly famous *Second Treatise*, Rand has a distinctive approach in justifying the right to property.

Among the many important philosophical differences between Rand and Locke, two are especially relevant to their political theories: one having to do with how property is created and a second having to do with the justification of property as such. First, Rand recognizes that property is rooted in production – the rationally guided actions of a man creating the values necessary to maintain his life and to flourish. In contrast to Locke's labor theory of property, Rand explains that it is values, not productive labor, that constitute property[47]. Productive labor is only the means to create these necessary values. This leads to the second point of difference, which is how Rand answers Jeremy Bentham's criticism of the natural rights theory of property that it is "nonsense on stilts" (Bentham 1998, 67). Here, Bentham is attacking Locke's and the other natural rights philosophers' grounding of the *normative* validation of the right to property in unproven assertions; specifically, it is part of God's plans or moral commands.[48] Rand, however, develops the normative case for individual rights, working logically from the concept of value up through individualism and rational egoism to the application of these moral principles to man's life in society.

Accordingly, Rand agrees with the natural rights philosophers, who recognize that the principle of individual rights, including the right to property, is grounded in human nature. She further agrees with Locke's application of the principle of individual rights to justify limited government (although he failed to apply it consistently in justifying capitalism).[49] But in basing the concept of property in her distinctive ethical theory – maintaining in her metaethics that values for men are the result of a unity of thought and action in pursuit of a goal that maintains one's life – Rand is able to provide a unique justification for the right to property that avoids mystical commands of God or appeals to alleged moral axioms.

Since Rand's concept of value is the fulcrum in her theory of property, her theory is easily misunderstood given the widespread confusion today about the nature of "value" and its necessary connection to "human knowledge and effort" ("The Property Status of Airwaves" *CUI* 131). For instance, some critics of Rand's property theory object that land has value apart from any human action.[50] Even Locke assumes that there is a small fraction of value in land and in other objects before man labors on these things to create property.[51] For Rand, these claims assume the *intrinsic* theory of value, which holds that the good inheres in things as such, regardless of their context and consequences for man, that is, regardless of any benefit or harm that they may cause to people.

Rand argues that this theory is incoherent because it divorces the concept of value from valuer and purpose ("What Is Capitalism?" *CUI* 13–14).[52] Instead, Rand maintains the *objective* theory of value: what makes something a value is a man's identification of something in the world as important to him and then his taking action to obtain it and use it. For example, according to Rand, it is incorrect to assert that fallow land *qua* land is valuable. It is just land – no more, no less. The value in the land arises solely from the actions taken to convert it into a farm and to maintain it as such, including tilling the soil, planting and harvesting the crops, and preparing the land to be farmed again next season. This is how farms are created out of land, how livestock are created out of animals, how food is created out of plants, and how all manner of things of use to men become values.[53] In short, there are no human values without rational thought and action – creating and using the values necessary to sustain man's life.

In advanced societies with extensive division of labor and complex legal systems, such as the United States of America in the twenty-first century, most people spend their time using and profiting from longstanding pieces of property that have existed for years, if not centuries. In creating and selling complex properties in a free market, it is easy for people to forget that these derivative property interests arose from an initial act of production at some point in the past. In Rand's novel, *The Fountainhead*, the hero, Howard Roark, explains that "We inherit the products of the thought of other men. We inherit the wheel. We make a cart. The cart becomes an automobile. The automobile becomes an airplane. But all through the process what we receive from others is only the end product of their thinking" (*Fountainhead* 711). The advanced property rights that men have today, such as the right to use airplanes, all began with an initial act of productiveness by an individual who sought to create a new value; in this case, a person long ago who conceived of and built a wheel. The additional property rights that have since been created out of this initial act of creation also reflect the same virtue of productiveness – each time, there was an innovator who saw a value in a new use. "The moving force is the creative faculty which takes this product as material, uses it and originates the next step" (*Fountainhead* 711). We all live and flourish today as a result of the sum total of these individual acts of value-creation.[54]

197

Rand's justification of the right to property has important implications for the connection between that right and the right to contract. Since the right to property sanctions the freedom necessary to create, use, and dispose of values, this justifies the nineteenth-century legal doctrine known as "freedom of contract," the fundamental right to enter into contracts with others in the free trade of one's property ("The Roots of War" *CUI* 35). In sum, Rand recognizes that the right of free trade is a corollary of the rights to life, liberty, and property.

Rand has a two-part moral justification for the "freedom of contract." First, since force is banned in a free society, contracts are the only means by which men exchange their property with one another. According to Rand, this "leads to one of the most important and most complex functions of the government: to the function of an arbiter who settles disputes among men according to objective laws" (*VOS* 129/*CUI* 382). A dispute over a breach of contract can be extremely complex because it involves an *indirect* use of force, since one man has obtained property from another man without his consent. Contract violations may be criminally motivated, such as the fraudulent scheme of a conman who sells a non-existent product or service, but more often than not, contract disputes arise as a result of mistakes or irresponsibility by one of the parties in a contract between honest businessmen. In such cases, both men will have some claim to justice, and it is the critically essential function of the civil courts to use objective procedural and substantive legal rules to ascertain the truth and to compensate the victim for his loss (*VOS* 129–130/*CUI* 383–384). As discussed above in "The Nature and Need of Government," even if all men were moral, they would still require a government to adjudicate objectively disputes arising from honest errors, miscommunication, or simple negligence.[55] Thus, a social system's success is more a function of how it secures rights of property and contract in the necessarily complex interactions between private citizens than of how it performs the relatively easier task of imposing legal punishments on criminals.

Rand's second contribution to the justification of "freedom of contract" is the moral foundation that she gives to the right to contract, explaining how it follows of necessity from the right to property. Nineteenth-century American courts also saw a connection between property and contract, but the connection was made through the vague and indefinite notion that labor was the source and moral justification of property.[56] In explicitly grounding property in the concept of value, as opposed to labor, Rand is able to explain how property arises from the freedom to produce material values, and thus she is able to explain why property rights require as a logical corollary the freedom to use and dispose of these values. As she writes: "The right to property is the right of use and disposal" ("The New Fascism: Rule by Consensus" *CUI* 227).

If a man has the right to create property, but the government denies him the right to use it or to dispose of it, then it is no longer a value to him; it no longer serves his interests or benefits his life. The destruction of the right to contract necessarily entails the destruction of the right to property – and vice versa. The right to use and to dispose of one's property is secured under the law of contract, and thus the right to contract is a corollary of the right to property. Just as there cannot be a right to life without a right to property, according to Rand, there cannot be a right to property without a right to contract.

In sum, Rand believes that the right to *dispose* of one's property "in free trade, using no compulsion, no help from the government" (*Atlas* 578) is a necessary characteristic of the right to property. "Property rights and the right of free trade are man's only 'economic rights' (they are, in fact, *political* rights)" ("Man's Rights" *VOS* 115/*CUI* 374). Capitalism secures to each man his right to property – protecting under the law the freedom for man to create, use, and dispose of the values necessary to sustain his life and to flourish. This explains why Rand emphasizes the government's recognition of property rights in her definition of capitalism – it is the political right that serves as the means of implementing the right to life and makes possible the freedom to exercise the other individual rights.

Intellectual Property

Rand's justification of property as arising from man's mind-body unity – the conceptual identification and physical creation of the values necessary to live and flourish – leads her to recognize that intellectual property is a property right par excellence.[57] She identifies patents, in particular, as "the heart and core of property rights" ("Patents and Copyrights" *CUI* 145). Although intellectual property has long enjoyed legal protection in the United States,[58] Rand's account of why intellectual property is property breaks new ground in explaining *why* the government should protect the rights of inventors and authors. In her succinct formulation, intellectual property is "the legal implementation of the base of all property rights: a man's right to the product of his mind" ("Patents and Copyrights" *CUI* 141).

Since man must conceive of the means to survive and then successfully act on this knowledge, all property is fundamentally *intellectual* in the sense that it is the embodiment of what was once just an idea conceived for the purpose of benefiting man's life and happiness. "The action required to sustain human life is primarily intellectual," Rand writes, "everything man needs has to be discovered by his mind and produced by his effort. Production is the application of reason to the problem of survival" ("What Is Capitalism?" *CUI* 8). Rand's emphasis on the connection between man's mind and the value-creation necessary to sustain his life is a constant refrain in her ethical and political works.[59]

Today, many people recognize the connection between man's mind and value-creation in the context of geniuses who discover new philosophical principles or scientific theories, but Rand maintains that this is a basic truth for all men – it is inherent in man being a rational animal whose "mind is his basic means of survival" ("What Is Capitalism?" *CUI* 7). In her novel, *Atlas Shrugged*, one of the heroes, Richard Halley, who is a composer, explains:

> Whether it's a symphony or a coal mine, all work is an act of creating and comes from the same source: from an inviolate capacity to see through one's own eyes – which means: the capacity to perform a rational identification – which means: the capacity to see, to connect and to make what had not been seen, connected and made before. (*Atlas* 782–783)

It is not an accident that Rand chose a composer, someone whose creative work is secured under copyright law, to serve as her spokesman in discussing this aspect of man's mind-body unity. From the invention of the first fire-making tools up through the complex chemical formulas designed by scientists in the high-tech laboratories of modern pharmaceutical companies, Rand maintains that creative thought and action is the root of *all* productivity.[60]

This principle was implicit for much of human history, but, according to Rand, the Industrial Revolution shattered any doubts about the necessary connection between man's mind and his survival. In her essay, the "Sanction of the Victims," Rand writes:

> A great many scientific – and technological – facts were known before the Industrial Revolution, and did not affect human existence. The steam engine, for instance, was known in ancient Greece. But knowledge of that sort remained an exclusive concern that lived and died with scientists – and,

for century after century, had no connection to the lives of the rest of mankind. ("The Sanction of the Victims" *VOR* 150)

From the late eighteenth century up through the nineteenth century, technological progress skyrocketed and so did the human condition.[61] With the invention of the steam engine, the steamboat, the cotton gin, the sewing machine, vulcanized rubber, steel, railroads, electric motors, electric light bulbs, and myriad other new products and technologies,[62] it soon became clear what rendered productive the physical labor that had sustained human life throughout history – the creative human mind.

But it was not any country that demonstrated this truth, Rand held, it was the United States of America – what she refers to as the "greatest of countries" because it was explicitly built on the foundation of "the inviolate supremacy of man's right to exist" (*Atlas* 1060). Thus, it is not a historical accident that intellectual property rights – patents, copyrights, trademarks, and trade secrets – rose to prominence in nineteenth-century America.[63] It was the American government that broke with a long European tradition of defining patents and other intellectual property rights as governmental grants of special privileges, and instead first secured patents, trade secrets, and other intellectual property rights as fundamental property rights.[64]

The traditional moral justification for these intellectual property rights was the labor theory of natural rights philosophy,[65] but, as discussed above in the context of property rights in land, this labor-based metaphor is fraught with ambiguity and inevitably raises the question of *why* labor should give rise to property rights. Such concerns apply with equal force in using labor theory to justify intellectual property rights. This may explain why some people, including libertarians, have concluded that intellectual property rights are state-granted monopolies that violate the rights to liberty and property.[66] Some libertarians directly criticize Rand's defense of intellectual property, but they do so from the premise that scarcity, as opposed to value, is the root of property rights.[67]

Rand's justification for intellectual property sidesteps these problems, because she holds that it is neither labor nor scarcity, but value-creation that is the source of property rights. Of course, the means of value-creation is the virtue of productiveness. "Every type of productive work," she writes, "involves a combination of mental and physical effort: of thought and of physical action to translate that thought into material form" ("Patents and Copyrights" *CUI* 141). Thus the law focuses on labor and its creation of physical objects as objective signs of whether someone has created something deserving of legal protection as a property right. "An idea as such cannot be protected until it has been given a material form" (*CUI* 141). But the means – productiveness – is not the same thing as the source – the valuing rational mind. Intellectual property is the recognition of this basic fact. Insofar as a man identifies a new means for creating values – whether a new technology, a new book, or some other innovative commercial practice – then he has as much a valid claim to the right to use and dispose of this new value as any other value created in a parcel of land or in a chattel. Rand concludes: "thus the law establishes the property right of a mind to that which it has brought into existence" (*CUI* 142).

Although Rand is an ardent defender of intellectual property rights, she acknowledges that different types of property require different treatment under the law given their different natures (*CUI* 139). For example, she maintains that patents and copyrights should not be owned in perpetuity, like land or chattels, because the nature of the value secured as intellectual property requires term limits on its legal protection (*CUI* 142–145). She acknowledges that the issue of term limits "is an enormously complex issue" (*CUI* 144), and thus a full discussion of the justification and legal implementation of this important principle in intellectual property rights is not possible here.[68] Nonetheless, Rand's analysis of this issue in her essay, "Patents and Copyrights," reveals how she has developed an *objective* theory of property rights – recognizing that the context and purpose of each type of property is essential to defining the scope of the right to its unfettered use and disposition. This principle applies equally whether it is real estate, chattels, an invention, a book, or some other valuable product of man's creative efforts.

Conclusion

Rand's political theory is based on the normative principles that man's life is the standard of value and that concern with his own life is man's primary moral purpose, and the metaphysical facts that reason is his basic tool of survival and that its exercise is volitional and requires the absence of coercion. She maintains that government, "an institution that holds the exclusive power to *enforce* certain rules of social conduct in a given geographical area" ("The Nature of Government" *VOS* 125/*CUI* 378), is necessary for rational individuals to live virtuously in society and ultimately to cooperate to everyone's mutual benefit. The precondition for such cooperation is the protection of individual rights, including property rights, from the initiation of physical force, which requires that physical force be controlled through a system of objective laws by means of a government. A government is legitimate only if its primary functions are limited to the protection of individual rights through the police, the military, and the law courts.

The specific political system which she advocates is capitalism, which she defines as "a social system based on the recognition of individual rights, including property rights, in which all property is privately owned" ("What Is Capitalism?" *CUI* 10). This reflects her view that property rights are necessary for the implementation of the right to life and all the rights which this implies: "Without property rights, no other rights are possible." Property rights include intellectual property, that is, the right to the practical application of knowledge in the form of a physical object (e.g., an invention or composition), which may not be copied without the originator's consent. In a capitalist system individuals are free to enter into voluntary agreements and contracts for the exchange of goods and services, and the proper role of government is to protect these agreements and adjudicate any disputes that may arise according to objective laws.

Rand's political theory belongs to the individualist tradition and it shares important features with the natural rights philosophy of John Locke and with the views of the American Founding Fathers, especially Thomas Jefferson and James Madison. Her political theory is distinctive, however, in its uncompromising adherence to the principle of individual rights and, more fundamentally, in its methodology, which she summarizes as follows:

> Objectivism is a philosophical movement; since politics is a branch of philosophy, Objectivism advocates certain political principles – specifically, those of laissez-faire capitalism – as the consequence and the ultimate practical application of its fundamental philosophical principles. It does not regard politics as a separate or primary goal, that is: as a goal that can be achieved without a wider ideological context.
>
> Politics is based on three other philosophical disciplines: metaphysics, epistemology and ethics – on a theory of man's nature and of man's relationship to existence. It is only on such a base that one can formulate a consistent political theory and achieve it in practice. ("Choose Your Issues" *TON* 1(1); quoted in *CUI* vii)

Rand's account of the nature and role of government has profound implications for the philosophy of law and economics. These are the subjects, respectively, of the next two chapters.

Notes

1 See "The Nature of Government" (*VOS* 125/*CUI* 378). Rand follows a similar methodology in her work on ethics and esthetics, as is discussed above by Salmieri (63) and Gotthelf (76–78), and below by Binswanger (408–413); for a discussion of its roots in her epistemology, see Salmieri's discussion, 298–299.

2 See Salmieri (63–68), Gotthelf (76–84), Ghate (107–112), and Wright (173), above.

3 Rand disagrees with Thomas Hobbes, who held that men are naturally in a state of war with each other (see Hobbes 1958, 107). Instead, she maintains that human beings are able to deal with each other peacefully in society because, if men are free, there are no conflicts between their rational interests, and hence there is no need for an individual to be sacrificed for the sake of another. Rational individuals can thus cooperate voluntarily for mutual benefit through the growth and transmission of knowledge and through trade and the division of labor. See "The 'Conflicts' of Men's Interests" (*VOS*).

4 Rand emphasizes the importance of definitions and the hazard of using words "with the feeling 'I kinda know what I mean,'" in philosophy generally and in political philosophy in particular (*ITOE* 50–51).

5 On the place of definition in the Objectivist epistemology, see the whole of *ITOE* ch. 5, and Gregory Salmieri's discussion 292–295 in the present volume.

6 See "The Missing Link" (*PWNI* 59–60).

7 As discussed in the introduction to this chapter, Rand maintains that "*Individual rights are the means of subordinating society to moral law*" ("Man's Rights" *VOS* 108/*CUI* 367).

8 Rand notes that "the basic premise of the Founding Fathers was man's right to his own ... happiness – which means: man's right to exist for his own sake, neither sacrificing himself to others nor sacrificing others to himself; and that the political implementation of this right is a society where men deal with one another as *traders*, by voluntary exchange to mutual benefit" (*FTNI* 53). However, she observed, the moral premise of ethical egoism, as opposed to altruism, was never made explicit. Similarly, Leonard Peikoff remarks that the Founding Fathers were "political revolutionaries but not *ethical* revolutionaries," in view of their only "partial (and largely implicit) acceptance of ethical egoism" (*Parallels* 115).

9 On Rand's theory of rights, see Darryl Wright's discussion, 172–177, above. On her conception of objectivity, see n. 25 below.

10 For a fuller discussion of Rand's concept of objective law, see Tara Smith's discussion in ch. 9, below. For Rand's conception of objectivity generally, see Salmieri, 67–68.

11 See also Smith, above, 212–213.

12 This is a common viewpoint among the natural rights philosophers. Samuel Pufendorf, for instance, believes that man cannot live as the "beasts," which live in "lawless liberty," primarily because of "his greater proneness to evil" (1934, 148–149). John Locke is less cynical about human nature than is Pufendorf, but he still thinks that government is essentially required "to restrain the partiality and violence of Men" that can arise from "Passion" (Locke 1988, 275–276).

13 On a related note, Rand's argument that government is necessary is also not a "market failure" argument, as suggested by some of her critics. See, e.g., Sechrest 2007, 189–196. As a preliminary point, Rand does not believe that a free market operating within a capitalistic social system could "fail" in the manner alleged by those who use this argument, i.e., firms would fail to provide products or services that people want and for which they are willing to pay, such as lighthouses. Rational men are capable of finding alternative means of securing mutual benefits in complex situations requiring coordination of many individuals. For a detailed discussion of this issue, see Simpson 2005. See also Onkar Ghate's discussion in the present volume, 226–233. More fundamentally, Rand would maintain that

the concept of "market failure," as used in modern political theory, is invalid: the existence of a government is a necessary precondition for a free market. A free market is possible only when individuals can enter into voluntary transactions, and this is possible only if their rights – most importantly, their property and contract rights – are already protected by a government.

14 Madison reiterates this pessimistic view of human nature in *Federalist Paper* No. 55: "In all very numerous assemblies, of whatever character composed, passion never fails to wrest the sceptre from reason. ... Had every Athenian citizen been a Socrates, every Athenian assembly would still have been a mob" (Hamilton et al. 1961, 342).

15 The Founding Fathers used a metaphor that was similar to Rand's "robot." They maintained that they created a "machine that would go of itself." See Kammen 2006.

16 See 217–218, below, for a detailed discussion of some of Rand's views on the philosophy of law including her understanding of the distinction between the Rule of Law and the Rule of Men.

17 Emphasizing the moral nature of consent, Rand notes that her theory can "be put another way, [a man] must accept *the separation of force and whim* (any whim, including his own)" (*VOS* 129/*CUI* 382). In "An Untitled Letter" (*PWNI* 150–152), Rand further makes clear that she rejects social contract theory in her criticism of John Rawls's version of this political concept, i.e., his hypothetical social contract reached behind a "veil of ignorance." Nonetheless, Rand's consent theory has been misinterpreted by some critics, such as Walter Block, who objects that "there is simply no evidence that any such delegation ever took place, not anywhere, and certainly not in the United States" (Block 2002, 141–160). Block also objects that Rand's theory is inconsistent, because, even if individuals did delegate their rights in a pre-political state of nature, this would not be binding since there would be, on Rand's account, no government to legitimize their actions. Although Block's criticisms are perhaps valid against conventional social contract theorists, Rand does not advance the sort of social contract argument to which his critique is directed.

18 Rand deeply respects the achievements of the natural rights philosophers, most of all John Locke. She holds that Locke's development of the principle of individual rights, which was applied by the Founders in the Declaration of Independence, was a monumental philosophical achievement. "It took centuries of intellectual, philosophical development," she writes, "to achieve political freedom. It was a long struggle, stretching from Aristotle to John Locke to the Founding Fathers" ("Theory and Practice" *CUI* 150). Both Locke and Rand appreciate that human nature is the basis for determining a proper social system, but, according to Rand, Locke has an *intrinsic* view of rights. Rand regards this as mistaken, and thus she respects Locke's political philosophy, but she develops her own *objective* theory of rights to serve as the normative foundation for her political theory. See Salmieri's discussion, 290–292 below, of the distinction between objective, intrinsic, and subjective theories.

19 Samuel Pufendorf, for instance, maintains that eminent domain is one of the "rights which, by the nature of states and as necessary to their purpose, belong to sovereigns" (1991, 166).

20 Unlike Grotius, who believes that any "public advantage" justifies the state's exercise of eminent domain, Pufendorf argues that the exercise of eminent domain should be limited to only a "national emergency," but the two are alike in denying the absolutism of the right to property (1991, 166).

21 See passage quoted at n. 17 above.

22 Another, and more fundamental, reason for Rand's rejection of appeals to the "common good" as the standard for evaluating the legitimacy of governmental actions is that her ethics is not consequentialist.

23 This is exactly what occurred when Pfizer Inc. convinced a town in Connecticut to exercise its power of eminent domain to take the property of people who would not voluntarily sell their homes to the corporation. See *Kelo v. City of New London*, 545 U.S. 469 (2005).

24 Although he does not apply it consistently, John Locke also recognizes this about the principle of individual rights: "Should a Robber break into my House, and, with a Dagger at my Throat, make me seal Deeds to convey my Estate to him, would this give him any Title? Just such a Title by his Sword has an *unjust Conqueror* who forces me into Submission. The injury and the Crime is equal, whether committed by the wearer of a Crown or some petty Villain" (Locke 1988, 385).

25 Given her commitment to objectivity with respect to moral principles, Rand's absolutism is prominent in her normative work. See Smith 2009a.

26 For a detailed analysis of the Nazi concentration camps as an embodiment of collectivism, see Parallels ch. 13.

27 There is some evidence that Rand influenced the decision to eliminate the draft in the United States. In a speech delivered in 1967, Rand argued that the draft was in fact not necessary for the defense of a free society. See "The Wreckage of the Consensus," delivered at the Ford Hall Forum, Boston, April 16, 1967 and subsequently published in *CUI*. During the 1968 presidential campaign, Martin Anderson, an associate of Ayn Rand at the time and a contributor to *The Objectivist Newsletter*, proposed an all-volunteer military to Richard Nixon. Nixon adopted it as a campaign promise and as President in 1969 established a Commission on an All-Volunteer Armed Force (chaired by Thomas S. Gates), which included Alan Greenspan, who was at that time a very close associate of Rand, a supporter of her philosophy, and a contributor to *Capitalism: The Unknown Ideal*. Walter Oi later reported that the Commission staff members were influenced by Rand's arguments. Meanwhile Martin Anderson chaired a special committee to review reactions by governmental agencies to the Gates Commission's recommendations and to provide alternative proposals to Nixon. The Commission unanimously recommended ending the draft, which finally expired in 1973 when Congress refused to extend it. Compulsory registration for the draft was eliminated in 1975 by President Gerald Ford. Although compulsory registration was reinstated in 1980 by President Jimmy Carter, there has been no actual conscription since 1973. For background see Anderson 1982 and Griffith 1997.

28 A prominent proponent of this argument is John Rawls, whose *A Theory of Justice* is criticized by Rand in "An Untitled Letter" (*PWNI*).

29 See "Government Financing in a Free Society" (*VOS*).

30 Influential anarchistic tracts include Rothbard 1973 and Friedman 1989.

31 Some critics misrepresent Rand's argument here. Nicholas Dykes, for example, claims that "Rand posits that victims of robberies would go berserk if there was no government, but that the same people would have a 'finely-tuned sense of justice' if there were" (Dykes 2005, 104). This criticism takes Rand's argument out of context, as she explicitly states that men would need government even if they were paragons of rationality and moral virtue.

32 The proposal of anarchistic protective agencies seems to have originated with Gustave de Molinari (1977).

33 See also Binswanger 2011.

34 On this principle, see Darryl Wright's discussion above, 173, and Onkar Ghate's below, 225–226.

35 Rand mentions "actual examples of their [the anarchists'] ideals in practice": "One such example is the Mafia. The Mafia (or 'family') is a 'private government,' with subjects who chose to join it voluntarily, with a rigid set of rules rigidly, efficiently and bloodily enforced, a 'government' that undertakes to protect you from 'outsiders' and to enforce your immediate interests – at the price of your selling your soul, i.e., of your total obedience to any 'favor' it may demand. Another example of a 'government' without territorial sovereignty is offered by the Palestinian guerrillas, who have no country of their own, but who engage in terroristic attacks and slaughter of 'outsiders' anywhere on earth" ("The Missing Link" *PWNI* 59–60).

36 There have been various published responses to Rand's analysis of "anarcho-capitalism," see, e.g., Childs 1969 and Walter Block (above, n. 17). These counter-arguments, however, fail to respond to Rand's fundamental insight that anarchists accept a *statist* principle in conflating the dollar and the gun. Moreover, libertarian anarchists have attempted to draw new analogies to how actual governments interact today, such as the United States and Canada, but such arguments drop the context that, according to Rand, what makes it possible for these governments to act peaceably is that they are in fact governments – i.e., each has "the exclusive power to *enforce* certain rules of social conduct in a given geographical area" ("The Nature of Government" *VOS* 125/*CUI* 378). This is inapposite to any "competing government" scenario proposed by anarchist libertarians.

37 In one place or another, Rand recognizes that there is a wide range of individual rights beyond the rights to life, liberty, and property. For her discussion of these three basic rights, see "Man's Rights" (*VOS* 110–111/*CUI* 369–370). Throughout her writing, she recognizes many derivative rights, such as the right to self-defense (*Atlas* 1063), contract ("Collectivized Rights" *VOS* 119; "The Nature of

Government" *VOS* 129/*CUI* 382), free trade ("Man's Rights" *VOS* 114/*CUI* 373–374), freedom of speech (*Journals* 384, 367; "Censorship: Local and Express" *ARL* 2(23) 230), freedom of the press ("Thought Control" *ARL* 3(2); *ARL* 2(23) 230), a fair trial ("The New Fascism: Rule by Consensus" *CUI* 230), vote ("Representation Without Authorization" *VOR* 233), privacy (*Letters* 622), abortion ("A Last Survey" *ARL* 4(2) 382), and the pursuit of happiness ("Man's Rights" *VOS* 114/*CUI* 373). According to Rand, these and many other rights are all "corollaries" of "a man's right to his own life," which she considers to be the "one fundamental right" ("Man's Rights" *VOS* 110/CUI 369). The philosophy of law, she writes, is the field that addresses the "complex problem" of how "citizens of a free nation" develop the "specific legal procedures or *methods* of implementing their rights" (*VOS* 120–121).

38 For a discussion of her ethical theory, see Chapters 3–7, above.

39 Men can also eat wild berries, but, unlike in the case of wild rabbits, this presents two problems. First, as Rand observers, "Man could not survive even as an herbivorous creature by picking fruit and berries at random. He has no instinct to tell him which plants are beneficial to him and which are deadly poison. He can learn it only by conscious experimentation or by the observation of other living creatures who do not touch poisonous plants – a procedure, which, in either case, is a process of thought" ("The Moral Basis of Individualism" *Journals* 252). Second, even when men do learn how to identify the non-poisonous berries, the point remains that a diet of berries alone will not sustain his life, nor make it possible for him to flourish.

40 Rand writes that "Every type of productive work involves a combination of mental and physical effort: of thought and of physical action to translate that thought into a material form" ("Patents and Copyrights" *CUI* 141).

41 In her work on epistemology, Rand writes: "The concept 'property' denotes the relationship of a man to an object (or an idea): his right to use it and to dispose of it – and involves a long chain of moral-legal concepts, including the procedure by which the object was acquired. The mere observation of a man in the act of using an object will not convey the concept 'property'" (*ITOE* 37).

42 In this respect, Rand challenges most virtue-based theories of civil society, which typically argue that the government must coercively inculcate virtue in its citizens. As evidenced by Rand's political theory, it is not necessary for a virtue-based political theory to be antagonistic either to individual rights generally or to the right to property specifically. See, e.g., Miller 2006, 67–89 (explaining how Aristotle's theory of virtue ethics may be compatible with political freedom); Claeys 2009, 889–947 (analyzing the virtue theory that underlies the natural right theory of property).

43 In the twentieth century, communist governments killed approximately 100 million people. See Courtois et al. 1999, 4.

44 Although twentieth-century communist regimes murdered many more people than the Nazis (see Courtois et al. 1999), the mass murder of the Holocaust is far better known today. Although some people believe that a fascist social system secures property rights, the Holocaust belies this claim, as the Nazi government expropriated the property of Jews (and gypsies, political dissidents, and many others) during the misery and death it visited on them. As such, Rand maintains that communism, socialism, and fascism are all variants of statism, in opposition to capitalism (see "'Extremism,' Or the Art of Smearing" *CUI* 199–200). In regard to the right to property, she explicitly identifies that the difference between socialism and fascism is merely one of legal implementation of statism (see "The New Fascism: Rule by Consensus" *CUI* 226–227).

45 See, e.g., Grotius 1925, 186–191 (property arises from use and acquisition); Locke 1988, 287–290 (property arises from labor); Pufendorf 1934, 569–585 (property arises from occupation).

46 See, e.g., "Man's Rights" (*VOS* 111/*CUI* 370) claiming that "the source of rights is man's nature."

47 Locke intends his famous "mixing labor" metaphor to refer to productive actions. See Mossoff 2002, 155–164. Nonetheless, this metaphor suggests that physical labor as such is the source of property, which has led contemporary philosophers to criticize Locke's argument for property as conceptually confused and non-explanatory. See, e.g., Waldron 1983, 37–44; Nozick 1974, 174–175.

48 In the *Second Treatise*, for instance, Locke writes: "The *State of Nature* has a Law of Nature to govern it, which obliges every one: And Reason, which is that Law, teaches all Mankind, who will but consult

it, that being all equal and independent, no one ought to harm another in his Life, Health, Liberty, or Possessions. For Men being all the Workmanship of one Omnipotent, and infinitely wise Maker ... Every one as he is *bound to preserve himself*, and not to quit his Station willfully ..." (1988, 271).

49 For Locke, the function of government is the protection of the rights to life, liberty, and, most importantly, property. He writes that people "joyn in Society with others ... for the mutual *Preservation* of their Lives, Liberties and Estates, which I call by the general name, *Property*" (1988, 350). However, Locke then endorses taxation: "'tis every one who enjoys his share of the Protection, should pay out of his Estate his proportion for the maintenance of it. But still it must be with his own Consent, i.e., the Consent of the Majority, giving it either by themselves, or their Representatives chosen by them" (362).

50 One philosopher has criticized Rand's property theory, for instance, on the ground that "There is plenty of wealth ... which was never produced by any human being at all. ... Within our present system it is a fact that land, minerals, timber, etc. – regardless of whether we call them wealth or something else – will be the functional equivalents of wealth" (Mavrodes 1974, 256).

51 See Locke 1988, 296.

52 It is also an example of what Rand calls "the stolen-concept fallacy," as it takes the concept "value" out of its epistemological context, divorcing it from its necessary antecedent in the conceptual hierarchy – the concept of "life." Another example of the stolen-concept fallacy in political philosophy is the nineteenth-century socialist battle cry, "Property is theft!" (Proudhon 1994, 13). This is stealing the concept "theft," because this concept can only be valid when it refers to taking someone else's property without their consent. In other words, one can only objectively form and define the concept of "theft" on the basis of first forming the concept of "property." See 298–299 for further discussion of the stolen-concept fallacy.

53 The ways in which property rights are first acquired in originally unowned land or other things is known in the law as first-possession doctrine. An analysis of the law of first possession is beyond the scope of this chapter, but for a brief survey of this legal doctrine, see Mossoff 2003, 407–413. Rand endorses this legal doctrine in her essay, "The Property Status of Airwaves," in which she identified the Homestead Act of 1862 as a "notable example of the proper method of establishing private ownership from scratch, in a previously ownerless area" (*CUI* 132).

54 Rand emphasizes this point with the insight that there is a pyramid of ability among producers, i.e., that the "man at the top of the intellectual pyramid contributes the most to all those below him, but gets nothing except his material payment, receiving no intellectual bonus from others to add to the value of his time" (*Atlas* 1065).

55 See 190, above.

56 In 1895, the Illinois Supreme Court explained the connection between property and contract as follows: "Labor is property, and the laborer has the same right to sell his labor, and to contract with reference thereto, as has any other property owner." *Ritchie v. People*, 40 N.E. 454, 455–456 (Ill. 1895).

57 Rand recognizes that there are different types of property, such as property in land ("The Property Status of Airwaves" *CUI* 139), property in airwaves (ibid.), and property in inventions and writings ("Patents and Copyrights" *CUI* 141). In each context, the law should secure to the owner the right to acquire, use, and dispose of the relevant material value.

58 In Article I, Section 8, Clause 8, the Constitution empowers Congress to enact laws to protect patents and copyrights, and Congress immediately acted on this grant of power in enacting this important legislation in 1790.

59 Her broadest statement may be found in "The Objectivist Ethics" (*VOS* 23), but this is of course a major theme of *Atlas Shrugged*. See also "What Is Capitalism?" (*CUI*) and Salmieri 2009a, 225–236.

60 In *Atlas Shrugged*, Rand refers to an industrial machine as "the frozen form of a living intelligence" (1064), and a railroad as "the frozen form of a mind's ingenuity" (954).

61 Unfortunately, anachronisms abound in most assessments of working and living conditions in the nineteenth century. For a proper historical analysis, which compares nineteenth-century conditions to those of preceding centuries, see Robert Hessen, "The Effects of the Industrial Revolution on Women and Children" (*CUI*).

62 All of these inventions or improvements thereon were patented in the United States and thus were legally secured as property rights.

63 Given the commitment of the United States to protecting the rights to life, liberty, and property, Rand cites the success of the Industrial Revolution in the United States as central evidence for the connection between reason, freedom, and human flourishing. She writes: "The country made possible by the Industrial Revolution – the United States of America – achieved the magnificence which only free men can achieve, and demonstrated that reason is the means, the base, the precondition of man's survival" ("The Anti-Industrial Revolution" *ROTP* 285).

64 See Mossoff 2007, 953–1012; Mossoff 2003, 413–424.

65 See, e.g., *Hawes v. Gage*, 11 F. Cas. 867, 867 (C.C.S.D.N.Y. 1871) (noting that a patent is "property" because it secures for an inventor the right to "enjoy the fruits of his invention"); *Clark Patent Steam & Fire Regulator Co. v. Copeland*, 5 F. Cas. 987, 988 (C.C.S.D.N.Y. 1862) ("Congress has wisely provided by law that inventors shall exclusively enjoy, for a limited season, the fruits of their inventions"); *Davoll v. Brown*, 7 F. Cas. 197, 199 (C.C.D. Mass. 1845) ("we protect intellectual property, the labors of the mind, productions and interests as much a man's own, and as much the fruit of his honest industry, as the wheat he cultivates, or the flocks he rears").

66 See, e.g., Palmer 1990, 817–865.

67 See, e.g., Kinsella 2001, 15–22. Rand would reject scarcity as the basis for property rights because this is an example of a principle in metaphysics that she calls the primacy of consciousness. That is, an appeal to scarcity assumes, not the facts of human survival, but "unlimited desires" as the source of property rights. For this assumption see Anderson and McCheney 2003, 4–5. Rand briefly discusses scarcity in the context of property rights in broadcast spectrum (see "The Property Status of Airwaves" *CUI* 131–134).

68 Rand explains that the primary concern underlying term limits for intellectual property is that it "represents a static claim on a dynamic process of production" (*CUI* 143). In other words, the values secured by intellectual property do not represent a "static" amount of previously produced wealth, which is necessarily consumed or destroyed if not maintained, but rather represent the "dynamic" creation of new wealth through its continual reproduction in the real world, as copies of the original book or invention. For patents, in particular, according to Rand, the "legal problem is to set a time limit which would secure for the inventor the fullest possible benefit of his invention without infringing the right of others to pursue independent research" (*CUI* 144).

References

Anderson, Martin. 1982. *The Military Draft*. Stanford, CA: Hoover Institution Press.

Anderson, Terry L., and Fred S. McCheney. 2003. "Introduction: The Economic Approach to Property Rights." In *Property Rights: Cooperation, Conflict, and Law*, edited by Terry L. Anderson and Fred S. McCheney. Princeton, NJ: Princeton University Press.

Bentham, Jeremy. 1998."Anarchical Fallacies." In *Benthamiana: or, Select Extracts from the Works of Jeremy Bentham*. Holmes Beach, FL: Gaunt, Inc.

Binswanger, Harry. 2011. "The Dollar and the Gun." In *Why Businessmen Need Philosophy*, revised and expanded edition, edited by Debi Ghate and Richard E. Ralston. New York, NY: New American Library.

Block, Walter. 2002. "The Libertarian Minimal State? A Critique of the Views of Nozick, Levin, and Rand." *Journal of Ayn Rand Studies*, 4(1).

Childs, Jr., Roy A. 1969. "Objectivism and the State: An Open Letter to Ayn Rand." *The Rational Individualist*, 1(10) Reprinted 1994 in *Liberty Against Power: Essays by Roy A. Childs, Jr.*, edited by Joan Kennedy Taylor. San Francisco, CA: Fox and Wilkes.

Claeys, Eric R. 2009. "Virtue and Rights in American Property Law." *Cornell Law Review*, 94.

Courtois, Stéphane, Nicolas Werth, Jean-Louis Panné, Andrzej Paczkowski, Karel Bartošek, and Jean-Louis Margolin. 1999. *The Black Book of Communism: Crimes, Terror, Repression*. Cambridge, MA: Harvard University Press.

de Molinari, Gustave. 1977. *The Production of Security*. Edited by Richard M. Ebeling translated by J. Huston McCulloch. New York, NY: Center for Libertarian Studies; originally 1849.

Dykes, Nicholas. 2005. "The Facts of Reality: Logic and History in Objectivist Debates about Government." *Journal of Ayn Rand Studies*, 7(1).

Friedman, David. 1989. *The Machinery of Freedom: Guide to a Radical Capitalism*. LaSalle, IL: Open Court; originally 1973.

Griffith, Jr., Robert K. 1997. *The US Army's Transition to the All-Volunteer Force 1968–1974*. Washington, DC: Center of Military History, US Army.

Grotius, Hugo. 1925. *The Law of War and Peace*. Indianapolis, IN: Bobbs-Merrill.

Hamilton, Alexander, John Jay, and James Madison. 1961. *The Federalist Papers*. Edited by Clinton Rossiter. New York, NY: New American Library.

Hobbes, Thomas. 1958. *Leviathan*. New York, NY: Macmillan.

Kammen, Michael. 2006. *A Machine That Would Go of Itself: The Constitution in American Culture*. Piscataway, NJ: Transaction Publishers.

Kinsella, N. Stephan. 2001. "Against Intellectual Property." *Journal of Libertarian Studies*, 15.

Locke, John. 1988. *Two Treatises of Government*. Cambridge: Cambridge University Press.

Mayhew, Robert, ed. 2009. *Essays on Ayn Rand's Atlas Shrugged*. Lanham, MD: Lexington Books.

Mavrodes, George I. 1974. "Property." *The Personalist*, 53.

Miller, Fred. 2006. "Virtue and Rights in Aristotle's Best Regime." In *Values and Virtues: Aristotelianism in Contemporary Ethics*, edited by Timothy Chappell. Oxford: Clarendon Press.

Mossoff, Adam. 2002. "Locke's Labor Lost." *University of Chicago Law School Roundtable*, 9.

Mossoff, Adam. 2003. "What Is Property? Putting the Pieces Back Together." *Arizona Law Review*, 45.

Mossoff, Adam. 2007. "Who Cares What Thomas Jefferson Thought About Patents? Reevaluating the Patent 'Privilege' in Historical Context." *Cornell Law Review*, 94.

Nozick, Robert. 1974. *Anarchy, State, and Utopia*. New York, NY: Basic Books.

Palmer, Tom G. 1990. "Are Patents and Copyrights Morally Justified? The Philosophy of Property Rights and Ideal Objects." *Harvard Journal of Law and Public Policy*, 13.

Proudhon, Pierre-Joseph. 1994. *What Is Property?* Cambridge: Cambridge University Press.

Pufendorf, Samuel. 1934. *De Jure Naturae et Gentium Libri Octo*. Oxford: Clarendon Press.

Pufendorf, Samuel. 1991. *On the Duty of Man and Citizen*. Cambridge: Cambridge University Press.

Rothbard, Murray. 1973. *For a New Liberty: The Libertarian Manifesto*. New York, NY: Macmillan.

Rousseau, Jean-Jacques. 1997. *The Social Contract and Other Later Political Writings*. Cambridge: Cambridge University Press.

Salmieri, Gregory. 2009a. "*Atlas Shrugged* on the Role of the Mind in Man's Existence." In Mayhew 2009.

Sechrest, Larry. 2007. "*Atlas*, Ayn, and Anarchy: A Is A Is A." In *Ayn Rand's* Atlas Shrugged, edited by. Edward W. Younkins. Burlington, VT: Ashgate.

Simpson, Brian P. 2005. *Markets Don't Fail!* Lanham, MD: Lexington Books.

Smith, Tara. 2009a. "No Tributes to Caesar: Good or Evil in *Atlas Shrugged*." In Mayhew 2009.

Waldron, Jeremy. 1983. "Two Worries About Mixing One's Labor." *Philosophical Quarterly*, 33.

9

Objective Law

TARA SMITH

> If physical force is to be barred from social relationships, men need an institution charged with the task of protecting their rights under an *objective* code of rules.
>
> *This* is the task of a government – of a *proper* government – its basic task, its only moral justification and the reason why men do need a government.
>
> *A government is the means of placing the retaliatory use of physical force under objective control – i.e.,* under objectively defined laws.
>
> Ayn Rand, "The Nature of Government" (*VOS* 127–128/*CUI* 381)

A longstanding, bedrock distinction in thinking about legal systems is that between the Rule of Law and the Rule of Men. Only the former, it is widely agreed, can offer the sort of stable, reliable protections that people seek from a legal system. Legal theorists are almost entirely united both in accepting the superiority of the Rule of Law and, despite some differences over details, in understanding its core conditions.[1] Basically, the Rule of Law requires that laws be clearly formulated and extensively promulgated. They may not impose mutually conflicting demands or retroactive obligations. Their application must be consistent in that laws are enforced impartially, applied equally to all relevant parties (including government officials). Laws should be settled and stable: though they may sometimes change, they must not change frequently, without reasonable notice, or in defiance of previously approved procedures. Theorists have substantial differences, however, which I will discuss later, over the exact benefits that respect for the Rule of Law provides, and over its relation to morality.[2]

Ayn Rand agrees that the Rule of Law is imperative. Indeed, a recurring theme in her discussions of political relations is the evil of some men ruling others by physical force. The only way to avoid this, she believes, is through objective law, and her understanding of that, I think, sheds light on the value of the Rule of Law. While, as we have seen in the previous chapter, Rand directly addresses the fundamental principles of political philosophy (primarily in essays concerning the nature of government, man's rights, and capitalism), she offers no extended discussion of law as such or of the Rule of Law, in particular. Her views in legal philosophy emerge from numerous essays, often on relatively narrow topical issues, as well as from her fiction. Rand's basic views about law are not difficult to discern, however.

A Companion to Ayn Rand, First Edition. Edited by Allan Gotthelf and Gregory Salmieri.

In what follows, I will present some of Rand's express condemnations of non-objective law and then indicate the underlying principles of government that explain these assessments. I will then situate the implications of her view for the traditional Natural Law-Positivism dispute over the authority of law and for the moral status of the Rule of Law. In particular, we will see why the Rule of Law – on what she regards as a proper conception of objective law – is emphatically a moral ideal.

Rand's Condemnation of Non-Objective Law

One specific target of Rand's attack is US obscenity law, which she criticizes for its distinct lack of objectivity. The famous LAPS[3] test adopted by the Supreme Court in *Miller v. California* and *Paris Adult Theater I v. Slaton* (1973) holds that the yardstick of obscenity is

> (a) whether "the average person, applying contemporary community standards" would find that the work, taken as a whole, appeals to the prurient interest ... (b) whether the work depicts or describes, in a patently offensive way, sexual conduct specifically defined by the applicable state law, and (c) whether the work, taken as a whole, lacks serious literary, artistic, political, or scientific value.[4]

Rand observes the elastic, thoroughly unknowable meaning of the phrases "community standards" and "patently offensive" (as well as of "redeeming social value," which had been used by the Court in the earlier *Roth v. United States*, 1957) ("Censorship: Local and Express" *PWNI* 237–239, cf. "Thought Control" (in three parts) *ARL* 2(26), 3(1–2)). Defining obscenity by reference to "the prurient interest" is no help, since these are near synonyms and both are evaluative concepts which fail to inform people of the circumstances under which those evaluations are warranted. (*When* is my action "offensively or grossly indecent" or "characterized by excessive or inappropriate desire or interest"?)[5] Deference to local standards, which some justices urged, simply "passes the buck," in Rand's view (*PWNI* 241). Whether we are beholden to national or state sensibilities, laws prohibiting obscenity – when obscenity is defined by the possession of "serious" value in the eyes of the "average" person or of a particular community – represent "wanton, collectivist tyranny" ("Thought Control" *ARL* 3(1) 250, cf. 247–248). Moreover, such laws punish thought rather than action. Thought *per se*, however, is incapable of violating anyone's rights.[6]

Rand regards antitrust law as another "totally nonobjective" arena in which prohibitions of "unfair methods of competition" and "anti-competitive practices" defy objective application.[7]

> Antitrust [has grown] into a haphazard accumulation of non-objective laws, so vague, complex, contradictory and inconsistent that any business practice can now be construed as illegal, and by complying with one law a businessman opens himself to prosecution under several others. No two jurists can agree on the meaning and application of these laws. No one can give an exact definition of what constitutes "restraint of trade" or "intent to monopolize" or any of the other, similar "crimes." ("Antitrust: The Rule of Unreason" *TON* 1(2) 5)[8]

Such malleable restrictions function in the exact manner of retroactive law, such that "a man cannot know until he is convicted whether the action he took in the past was legal or illegal" ("Antitrust: The Rule of Unreason" *TON* 1(2) 5).[9]

We can see from these examples Rand's concern that laws be clearly and unambiguously stated. Where words are elastic, we enter "the foggy labyrinth of the non-objective" and the limits on officials' authority dissolve ("The Pull Peddlers" *CUI* 188). Rand cites appeals to "the public interest" as a paradigm case. She observes that the Federal Communications Commission, for instance, which is charged to evaluate broadcasting licenses on the basis of "service to public interest, convenience, or necessity," "holds an undefined power to enforce an undefinable criterion" ("The Property Status of Airwaves" *CUI* 136, "Vast Quicksands" *TON* 2(7) 25). "Since there is no such thing as the 'public interest' (other than the sum of the individual interests of individual citizens), since that collectivist catch-phrase has never been and can never be defined," the commission's power amounts to "a blank check" for appointed bureaucrats ("The Property Status of Airwaves" *CUI* 136).[10]

Leonard Peikoff elaborates on the problem as follows: when crimes (such as laws against "blasphemy," "obscenity," "immorality," "restraint of trade," and "unfair profits") "are not defined in terms of specific physical acts,"

> it is not possible to know from the statement of the law what existential acts are forbidden. Men are reduced to guessing; they have to try to enter the mind of the legislator and divine his intentions, ideas, value-judgments, philosophy. ... In practice, the meaning of such laws is decided arbitrarily, on a case-by-case basis, by tyrants, bureaucrats, or judges, according to methods that no one, including the interpreters, can define or predict. (*OPAR* 364–365)

Correspondingly, when contemporary laws require respect for such things as the "compelling state interest" served by "diversity" or "appropriate fair balance" in pharmaceuticals advertising or broadcasters' guarantee of "ample play" for the "fair competition" of opposing views or when laws prohibit a "hostile or offensive" work environment or "predatory" pricing or "predatory" lending, the individual is placed in the untenable position of not knowing what he is legally obligated to do or forbear.[11] *This*, in practice, is the Rule of Men, for it necessitates that particular bureaucrats decide arbitrarily what the law *means* on each occasion of dispute. Whatever the specific subject of a non-objective law and however benign the intentions of the lawmakers, in Rand's view, such undefinable restrictions are not truly law, "but merely a license for some men to rule others" (*TON* 2(7) 28).[12] When a law employs non-objective concepts, one has no objective way to understand and apply it. (Indeed, she observes that courts are essentially forced to legislate when lawmakers, driven by the desire to avoid antagonizing voters, deliberately adopt vaguely worded laws.)[13]

The Nature and Need of Objective Law

Although the term "objective law" is not common parlance among legal philosophers today, it is clear from the discussion of non-objective law above what Rand means by it. In another context, she said: "The 'nonobjective' is that which is dependent only on the individual subject, not on any standard of outside reality" (*AOF* 10). Something is "objective," by contrast, if it is either a fact independent of anyone's consciousness, or is based in and determined by such facts of reality. As we have seen, law fails to be objective, according to Rand, when it has no definite, determinate, stable meaning that could be known in advance, but instead acquires its meaning from the arbitrary determination of those applying the law in a particular case, whether bureaucrats or judges. Law that is objective, then, would have a definite, stable meaning of its own, graspable by a rational person prior to its application by those in power, and it would be widely promulgated and part of a consistent legal code.[14] In this sense, the law would be a stable fact, independent of anyone's consciousness.

There is a second respect, however, in which Rand held that law must be objective: its status as law is based on the facts that give rise to the need for law – and thus for government – in the first place. It must be grounded, in other words, in an objective, rational political philosophy. More specifically, Rand held that law fails to be objective when it is not grounded in the rights on which a political system is properly based. Law is not an end in itself, but the means through which government fulfills its function. The objectivity of law must, accordingly, be understood in that framework. The nature of proper laws, she observes, must "be derived from the nature and purpose of a proper government" ("The Nature of Government" *VOS* 128/*CUI* 381). Objective law conforms to the valid goals of government and establishes the institutions and rules that are necessary to achieve them. All of a legal system's activities are designed and undertaken as means to advance those ends.[15]

As explained by Fred Miller and Adam Mossoff (190–194 of this volume), Rand regards the purpose of government as the protection of individual rights. After identifying the three major instruments necessary for government to provide this protection (the police, the armed services, and law courts), Rand acknowledges that the practical implementation of proper government is "enormously complex" and involves "many corollary and derivative issues" which belong "to the field of a special science: the philosophy of law. Many errors and many disagreements are possible in the field of implementation, but what is essential here is the principle to be implemented: the principle that the purpose of law and of government is the protection of individual rights" (*VOS* 131/*CUI* 384).

A right, recall, is a sanction of a man's moral title to act by his own judgment ("Man's Rights" *VOS* 110/*CUI* 369).[16] The particular evil that rights protect the individual against is others' initiation of physical force. "The concept of a 'right' pertains only ... to freedom of action. It means freedom from physical compulsion, coercion or interference by other men" (*VOS* 110/*CUI* 369).[17] The prohibition of the initiation of force is necessary because reason is man's means of survival. Force nullifies a man's mind; it thwarts his ability to use his rational faculty. Rand writes that any threat of the form "your money or your life" amounts to the ultimatum: "your mind or your life" (*Atlas* 1023). Yet the means by which human beings sustain life is through the use of the mind.[18]

Government is "the agent of restraining and combating the use of force" and so must hold a "monopoly on the legal use of physical force." Given the tremendous power that it wields, it is imperative that its actions "be rigidly defined, delimited and circumscribed. ... If a society is to be free, its government has to be controlled." The objectivity of a legal system is our means of both constraining government and enabling it to accomplish its mission:

> Since the protection of individual rights is the only proper purpose of a government, it is the only proper subject of legislation: all laws must be based on individual rights and aimed at their protection. All laws must be *objective* (and objectively justifiable): men must know clearly, and in advance of taking an action, what the law forbids them to do (and why), what constitutes a crime and what penalty they will incur if they commit it. ("The Nature of Government" *VOS* 128–129/*CUI* 381–382)[19]

Since the reason for having government is the protection of individual rights, a law may require or forbid only as much as is necessary to secure these rights. Any step beyond that constitutes aggression by the government against the individuals it was created to defend. As such, it is a violation of rights: an unjust exercise of force.[20]

This is why Rand holds that in addition to being objectively formulated, all laws must be "objectively justifiable." The other features required for legal objectivity depend on and follow from this. When the substance of a law lacks objective warrant, it is impossible to identify standards for its proper (i.e., objective) application and, correspondingly, impossible to know how such law should be written. As Rand observes in regard to law aimed at the "public good":

> Since there is no rational justification for the sacrifice of some men to others, there is no objective criterion by which such a sacrifice can be guided in practice. All "public interest" legislation (and any distribution of money taken by force from some men for the unearned benefit of others) comes down ultimately to the grant of an undefined, undefinable, non-objective, arbitrary power to some government officials. ("The Pull Peddlers" *CUI* 188)

This is why laws that are not objectively justifiable so often employ the sort of ambiguous, elastic language that we saw in the cases of obscenity and antitrust legislation.

Since a legal system is a mechanism deliberately designed to serve a specific function, objectivity is imperative throughout. While the heart of a legal system's objectivity rests in the content of its laws, objectivity also, in Rand's view, encompasses the laws' expression and methods of adoption and application. Objectivity must be respected in the procedures by which laws are made (drafted, debated, approved, etc.) and enforced (how and when charges can be filed, rules governing suspects' detention, trials, evidence, adjudication, punishment, etc.).[21]

The broad scope of Rand's conception of objective law is explained not only by her view of the function of government, but also by her understanding of objectivity itself. In the sense in which the term applies to man-made things, objectivity is normative. When we ask whether a conclusion (policy, process, decision, etc.) is objective, we are asking a "should" question: Was it decided (structured, carried out, etc.) in the way that it needs to be in order to apprehend or reflect the relevant facts? As Gregory Salmieri explains below (274, 291–292), objectivity for Rand denotes a particular method by which a person uses his mind and arrives at a conclusion: the method of deliberate, disciplined adherence to reality by the use of logic.[22]

In assessing the objectivity of a human institution such as law, accordingly, we are assessing how well that activity is being conducted; we are employing logical, reality-governed thinking to determine whether *it* is guided by logical, reality-governed thinking. In order to do that, however, we must know which aspects of reality it should be heeding, and that depends on the purpose of the enterprise. Insofar as objectivity concerns how to think and insofar as how to do something depends on what it is that one is trying to do, the objectivity of law depends on the purpose of law. To inquire into the objectivity of a legal system is to ask, in other words, whether it is as it should be *given* its larger purpose, or given the reason for having it, at all.

It is this logical dependence of objectivity on purpose that explains why Rand thinks that objective law imposes requirements throughout several facets of a legal system. It is the particular function of protecting individual rights that dictates that law's content, adoption, expression, and application all be scrupulously objective. Government, as we saw in the previous chapter, is our means of placing the retaliatory use of force under objective control. A proper government will exert its coercive authority at all times and in all ways – and in only those times and ways – that are necessary to accomplish its mission. Law that is invalid in substance, however (prohibiting action that it has no authority to prohibit or allowing action that it should prohibit), fails to do that. Similarly, law that is adopted by non-objective means (e.g., excluding the participation of knowledgeable parties or unduly limiting time for debate), or law that is applied inconsistently, or law that is written in vague language (reasonably understood to impose conflicting demands) fails to do that.

213

At this stage, we can see how Rand's precise conception of the role of government explains her condemnation of the laws of a mixed economy (*TON* 2(7) 28, cf. *Marginalia* 198). For the "mixture" of invalid purposes (such as in regulatory and preventive laws that prohibit individuals from engaging in activities that do not infringe on others' rights) alongside valid purposes necessitates the illegitimate exercise of government power.[23] Laws whose purposes are not objectively justified cannot be objectively enforced. Their lack of objective validation means that they are enforced not by right but, ultimately, by might. While the officials enforcing such laws might dutifully comply with the laws' written provisions and thus be objective in that circumscribed respect, there is a deeper respect in which they are acting non-objectively. When the restrictions imposed by law are not themselves objectively justified, then however clear their statement and however conscientious their enforcement, these laws are necessarily enforced by means that are, in their foundations, arbitrary. The "authority" of such laws stems not from individual rights but from certain people's possession of sufficient power to impose their will. When the standard by which laws are adopted is not their service to the protection of individuals' freedom, in short, those laws cannot be applied in a way that respects that standard.

A mixed economy is a "semi-socialized economy," Rand writes ("Conservatism: An Obituary" *CUI* 214–215). It is

> a mixture of freedom and controls – with no principles, rules, or theories to define either. ... A mixed economy has no principles to define its policies, its goals, its laws – no principles to limit the power of its government. The *only* principle of a mixed economy ... is that no one's interests are safe, everyone's interests are on a public auction block, and anything goes for anyone who can get away with it. Such a system – or, more precisely, anti-system – breaks up a country into an ever-growing number of enemy camps, into economic groups fighting one another for self-preservation in an indeterminate mixture of *defense* and *offense*, as the nature of such a jungle demands. ("The New Fascism: Rule by Consensus" *CUI* 231–232).[24]

The pretense of a mixed economy is "that might and right can be safely scrambled together if we all agree never to raise this issue" ("Have Gun, Will Nudge" *TON* 1(3) 9). Its practice reflects the premise that might makes right.[25] Once a government abandons objective justification for the substance of its law, it retains no valid standard to discipline the exercise of its power. It rules not by right, but by favor ("Property Status of Airwaves" *CUI* 137), which individuals must court. The result is combat between subjective interests:

> A mixed economy is rule by pressure groups. It is an amoral, institutionalized civil war of special interests and lobbies, all fighting to seize a momentary control of the legislative machinery, to extort some special privilege at one another's expense by an act of government – *i.e.*, by force. ("The New Fascism: Rule by Consensus" *CUI* 232)[26]

Non-objective law leads to this because, without objective criteria by which to make their decisions, officials have no choice but to govern on the basis of subjective criteria (which lobbyists eagerly supply). Rand explains:

> The wisest man in the world, with the purest integrity, cannot find a criterion for the just, equitable, rational application of an unjust, inequitable, irrational principle. The best that an honest official can do is to accept no material bribe for his arbitrary decision; but this does not make his decision and its consequences more just or less calamitous. ("The Pull Peddlers" *CUI* 188)

When the law becomes an instrument of sacrifice rather than protection, the shared interest in liberty that each man holds by right is replaced, in the eyes of government, by his subjective "interests" as a farmer, homeowner, working mother, auto industry laborer, etc., which means: by the political pull of the group with which he is associated. And instead of being the protector of a man's rights, government becomes a threat: "In a mixed economy, every government action is a direct threat to some men and an indirect threat to all. Every government interference in the economy consists of giving an unearned benefit, extorted by force, to some men at the expense of others. By what criterion of justice is a consensus-government to be guided? By the size of the victim's gang" ("The New Fascism: Rule by Consensus" *CUI* 230).[27]

Non-objective law thus converts private citizens into mutual adversaries. When a government "helps" some by victimizing others, taking things it has no right to seize and giving them to those who have no right to receive them – bestowing tax breaks, price supports, licensing exemptions, or subsidies on these industries but not those, on large business owners but not small, on people with this disability but not that – individuals are pitted against one another. Other people become an ever-present threat to "justify" the loss of what belongs to a man by rights.[28] The injustice involved consists not only in the rights violations, as some are sacrificed for the (alleged) benefit of others. These cases also expose the capricious nature of the reign of non-objective law. Under such a regime, the legality of a man's actions and the meaning and extent of his rights are completely unpredictable.

In *Atlas*, Rand vividly depicts the sort of material decline that she believes results from this constriction of freedom as she catalogues a vortex of mechanical failures, delivery delays, infrastructure breakdowns, and regression to primitive living conditions. The fallout of non-objective law is not confined to a nation's economic condition, however. It also engenders intellectual and cultural stagnation. Arbitrary laws require not simply subjects' obedience, Rand contends, but, corrosively, people's constant readiness "to please," to "blindly, uncritically" satisfy whatever decrees government authorities choose to impose ("Antitrust: The Rule of Unreason" *TON* 1(2) 8).[29] The resulting servility is antithetical to innovation and progress in the creation of values. She observes:

> [W]hen men are caught in the trap of non-objective law, when their work, future and livelihood are at the mercy of a bureaucrat's whim, when they have no way of knowing what unknown "influence" will crack down on them for which unspecified offense, *fear* becomes their basic motive ... and compromise, conformity, staleness, dullness, the dismal grayness of the middle-of-the-road are all that can be expected of them. Independent thinking does not submit to bureaucratic edicts, originality does not follow "public policies," integrity does not petition for a license, heroism is not fostered by fear, creative genius is not summoned forth at the point of a gun.
>
> Non-objective law is the most effective weapon of human enslavement: its victims become its enforcers and enslave themselves. ("Vast Quicksands" *TON* 2(7) 25)

Government involvement in the realm of ideas, in particular (via National Endowments for the Arts, Humanities, or a National Science Foundation, for instance), Rand holds, creates an official orthodoxy that sows timid cautiousness which cripples intellectual life. Insofar as pull, rather than truth or objective value, is the basis for government grants, originality in the pursuit of truth or value becomes an especially risky enterprise. Non-objective law encourages conformity and conventionalism.[30]

Rand *vis-à-vis* Traditional Debates

Our discussion of Rand's conception of the basic nature of legal objectivity puts us in a position to appreciate Rand's positions on two longstanding debates in legal theory. One concerns whether law is natural or posited, and the other, whether the rule of law is a moral or a morally neutral ideal. The Natural Law versus Positivism debate concerns the fundamental source of legal authority. While it is easy to see why it is prudent to obey the law – disobedience will be visited with penalties – many people also believe that a person *really should* obey the law in some further sense, for reasons quite apart from the risks of being caught and punished for a legal breach. If that is so, though, and if it is legitimate for the government to punish those who break its laws, what is the nature and source of this legal authority?

Natural Law advocates maintain that law's authority is not supplied by any external considerations, but is internal to the law itself. Law contains within it the moral authority that renders it legitimate, genuinely obligatory as *law*. In this view, among the criteria of legal legitimacy are moral criteria; legal norms must, in order to truly *be* legal norms, satisfy certain moral conditions (Murphy 2007, 35–36, cf. 2005, 15). Positivism denies any such necessary connection between law and morality (Bix 2005, 36). It insists on the strict separation of questions concerning the existence of law from questions concerning the morality of law. On the Positivist thesis, law is a social convention; its existence is a matter of social fact, wholly a product of choices that particular human beings happen to have made (Murphy 2007, 25–26; Bix 2005, 29–32). No moral standards need be met in order for a law to carry authority.[31]

From the perspective of Rand's theory, neither Positivism nor Natural Law offers a valid account of law's authority. The authority of law is not simply a product of social convention, on her view, but nor is it an intrinsic feature naturally embedded in certain social rules. Her reasons reflect her understanding of objectivity.

Recall that Rand distinguishes the objective from the intrinsic ("What Is Capitalism?" *CUI* 13–14).[32] Correspondingly, law whose authority is objectively valid is not a special subset of putative law that is distinguished by its independent possession of certain qualities that we can simply spot or recognize as the source of its claim to our obedience. Nor, however, is objective law the unconstrained, amoral invention of a particular group of men. A system of law has a job to do, namely, to protect individual rights. Its claim to authority depends on how well designed it is to do that and that, in turn, depends on the method employed in establishing its powers, structure, rules, and activities. Only a legal system guided by certain mechanisms of adoption, enforcement, and so on, can achieve the purpose for which we have a legal system in the first place.[33]

The Natural Law/Positivism divide, from this perspective, reflects the false dichotomy of intrinsicism vs. subjectivism. Law *is* a convention, but it cannot be constructed subjectively if it is to serve its purpose effectively. Since human beings do not find objective law ready-made, we must create it, as the Positivists realize, but we are not free to construct the law in any way that we please. It – and we – must answer to reality. Facts about human nature constrain our options (in particular, facts about man's fundamental need for reason and freedom), dictating that only certain kinds of legal institutions will enable the government to provide the protection needed from it.

Natural Law advocates are correct, then, to the extent that law's authority is dictated in part by metaphysical reality – specifically, by the fact that reason is man's means of survival and that physical force cripples a man's ability to use reason. These facts limit the kinds of legal framework that can successfully serve government's function and thereby warrant respect. Positivists are correct that a legal system is constructed by us. By Rand's lights, however, neither camp understands the full significance of these facts or the relationship between them. Given that government enjoys the unique prerogative to impose its will by force, its authority depends on whether it does that according to strictly objective methods.[34]

Finally, we can turn to the moral status of the Rule of Law. While many view this ideal as desirable on purely prudential grounds, Rand regards it as a moral ideal. The reasons again stem from her views of government and objectivity.

Observe that the distinction between the "Rule of Law" and the "Rule of Men" is crudely labeled. Since the rules that men in civil society respect as laws are made by human beings,[35] the alternative is actually between two types of "Rule of Men." Thus we need a more precise understanding of what distinguishes these models. The Rule of Law consists of men ruling *in what particular way?* By what guidelines?

Rand's analysis suggests that the propriety of the Rule of Law rests, at bottom, in its objectivity. The Rule of Law banishes subjectivism. The classic example of the Rule of Men occurs when government officeholders do not confine the exercise of their authority to its intended purpose, but exploit their position to advance extraneous, personal agendas. What the designation "Rule of Men" conveys is the fact that such men elevate their subjective desires above the laws. Indeed, the laws under such a regime are a sham, present in name only. For laws that are subordinate to particular men's wishes about whether and how to enforce them do not function as laws, at all.

When a society is governed by the Rule of Law, by contrast, the rules are firm and their sovereignty is constant; it is the laws that reign and men's wills are secondary. The application of those laws is not subservient to anyone's personal ends. All individuals' ends, those of government officials as well as of private citizens, are pursued strictly within the confines authorized by valid laws. When those charged to administer the legal system respect its rules as the highest arbiter, what is achieved through government power is, in fact, a *law*-governed society.

Government officials' deliberate manipulation of power to serve private agendas is only one way, of course, in which a legal system could fail to deliver the Rule of Law. Yet the subjectivism that is so glaring in this sort of case is operative in any violation of a Rule of Law condition. The motivations behind particular failings needn't be sinister in order to be subjectivist. Ambiguous language in the statement of law could be unintentional, for instance, just as the adoption of laws that impose mutually conflicting demands could be inadvertent and recognized only after the laws' application to actual cases. Nonetheless, such deviations make it impossible for citizens to know the rules to which they will be held accountable (and thus, to have a fair chance to comply). When it comes time to apply such laws to specific disputes, the beliefs and attitudes of the particular officials empowered to resolve those cases are decisive. Individuals' legal obligations become, in principle, as inscrutable as they would be under an erratic despot.[36]

Departures from Rule of Law conditions are, fundamentally, departures from objectivity. As such, they sabotage the function of government. On Rand's view, the protection of rights requires rules that are objective in content as well as in operation, functioning *as rules* via appropriate forms of enactment, expression, and application. Laws that fail to function in that way fail to perform the work of the law. Far from having one's rightful freedom safeguarded, under "laws" whose practical meaning is determined on a case-by-case basis, nothing is secure.

On Rand's analysis of objectivity, then, the difference between the Rule of Law and the Rule of Men, distilled to its essence, is the difference between a society ruled by reason and a society ruled by force.[37] This, given her conviction that rationality is the fundamental virtue and that force is the major social evil, is why she regards the Rule of Law as a moral ideal.[38] The rule of reason is reflected in the establishment of a government designed to protect individuals' freedom. On the premise that human beings survive by reason and that the exercise of reason requires freedom from force, a system of objective law is the rational means by which man can protect the conditions of his existence. The specific conditions required by the Rule of Law maintain this dedication to the propriety of reason. In a system that upholds them, the laws function as the final arbiter of disputes; government officials serve only as its handmaidens.

Under the Rule of Men, means and ends are reversed. This is obvious when rulers deliberately treat the law as a tool of convenience and their subjective desires function as final arbiter; these individuals, personally, are sovereign, subject to no rational limits. Even when the problem is not intentional abuse, however, this is what occurs. When a legal system fails any of the Rule of Law requirements (concerning laws' clarity, stability, mutual compatibility, and so on), the effect is the same: the government's use of force is unleashed beyond its objectively valid boundaries. And individual rights lose their protection.

In Rand's view, the Rule of Law is not simply a formal device for coordinating large numbers of people. The Rule of Law is a moral *ideal*, something to which man should earnestly aspire, because it is essential to the rule of rights – to protecting individuals against the *evil* of the initiation of force.[39]

Conclusion

The function of government, in Rand's view, is the protection of individual rights; a legal system is the mechanism through which government fulfills that function. The system's objectivity is essential in order for government to serve its purpose and to serve only that purpose. Because government power is coercive – the power to achieve ends by physical compulsion rather than persuasion – to the extent that any aspect of law's design or application defies the requirements of objectivity, it represents the unjustified use of force, compelling individuals to comply with restrictions that the government has no authority to impose. As such, it extinguishes individuals' freedom. And the enforcement of such laws inescapably replaces the rule of valid law with the Rule of Men.

In claiming that rights protect individual freedom against the initiation of physical force, Rand identifies the object of rights much more precisely than had previous rights theorists. This, I think, provides the basis for her comparatively exact standard for measuring the objectivity of law as well as for her viewing the stakes of legal objectivity in morally severe terms.[40] Non-objective law is deadly, in Rand's view, because the alternative between objective law and non-objective law is the alternative between societies in which men deal with one another as thinkers, using reason, or as beasts, using muscle. Human existence, she argues, depends on the former.

Acknowledgments

Thanks to Greg Salmieri and Allan Gotthelf for extremely valuable comments on earlier drafts, as well as to Onkar Ghate and Harry Binswanger for helpful discussion of some of the surrounding issues.

Notes

1 See, e.g., Fuller 1964; Tamanaha 2004; Fallon 1997; Marmor 2004; and Raz 1979. What follows is not an exhaustive list of the Rule of Law's essential elements, but those most widely agreed upon.

2 Among those contending that the Rule of Law is a morally substantive ideal are John Finnis, Richard Epstein, Randy Barnett, Frank Michelman, and Michael Moore, cited in Fallon 1997, 2, 22. Prominent figures who see it as value-neutral include Raz and Kramer (see Kramer 2007, 102, 164, 210).

3 "LAPS" is an acronym for literary, artistic, political, or scientific.

4 Quoted in Rand, "Censorship: Local and Express" (*PWNI* 236).

5 These are among the *Oxford English Dictionary*'s definitions of "obscene" and "prurient."

6 See *ARL* 3(1) 247–250. Regulations banning "indecent" speech on the airwaves face comparable problems.

7 "Totally nonobjective" is Rand's characterization (*Answers* 39). The other quoted terms are from the Federal Trade Commission Act of 1914, quoted in Hull 2005, 164.

8 Also see her review of Harold Fleming, *Ten Thousand Commandments: A Story of the Antitrust Laws* (1951), praising his account of court rulings that must grapple with "non-objective, undefinable" antitrust statutes (*TON* 1(4) 14).

9 Also see "America's Persecuted Minority: Big Business" (*CUI* 47–48) and *Answers* 6. In *Atlas Shrugged*, Rearden confronts this predicament; see, e.g., 383.

10 Also see "The Pull Peddlers" (*CUI* 188–189), and this passage from "America's Persecuted Minority: Big Business" (*CUI* 50; emphases in original; paragraphing removed): "Mr. Fleming's book [Fleming 1951, 22 (see n. 8 above)] quotes the following statement made by Emanuel Celler, Chairman of the House Judiciary Committee, at a symposium of the New York State Bar Association, in January 1950: 'I want to make it clear that I would vigorously oppose any antitrust laws that attempted to particularize violations, giving bills of particulars to replace general principles. The law must remain fluid, allowing for a dynamic society.' I want to make it clear that '*fluid law*' is a euphemism for '*arbitrary power*' – that 'fluidity' is the chief characteristic of the law under any dictatorship – and that the sort of '*dynamic society*' whose laws are so fluid that they flood and drown the country may be seen in Nazi Germany or Soviet Russia."

11 *Grutter v. Bollinger*, 539 US 306 (2003) and Coleman and Palmer 2007; Daily 2008, 106, also see 97 and 105–106 for other aspects of FDA requirements' non-objectivity. On the Fairness Doctrine (the broadcasting guarantee), which was in effect from 1949 until 1987 and whose reinstatement has recently been urged by prominent senators, see "Let the Blowhards Blow," *The Economist*, July 21, 2007, 46; John Fund, "'Fairness' Is Foul – Liberals vs. the First Amendment," *Wall Street Journal*, October 29, 2007; and Bob Cusack, "Schumer on Fox: Fairness Doctrine 'Fair and Balanced,'" *The Hill*, November 4, 2008. On harassment, see Equal Employment Opportunity website, http://www.eeoc.gov/ (accessed May 26, 2015). And on predatory pricing and lending, see the Robinson-Patman Act of 1936, the Anti-Price Discrimination Act, 15 U.S.C. Sec. 13, and the Home Ownership and Equity Protection Act of 1994. In the United Kingdom, a person is subject to legal penalties for "anti-social behavior" (Housing Act 1996, Chapter 52, Section 153).

12 Also see "America's Persecuted Minority: Big Business" (*CUI* 50).

13 WKCR interview on "The American Constitution" (*Speaking* 56–57).

14 Not all laws can be readily intelligible to a layman. Certain laws involve complex issues (e.g., toxins, property rights in genetic materials, or cyberspace), the understanding of which may require specialized knowledge. While we may sometimes need to hire specialists to decipher legal requirements in highly technical areas, objectivity demands that laws can be readily understood by those possessing the relevant expertise. Any difficulty in understanding a law should arise from the nature of its subject matter, rather than from inexact formulation.

15 This does not entail that only one set of rules can serve those ends. On certain matters, officials have legitimate options within an objectively valid range.

16 See also Darryl Wright's discussion of Rand's conception of rights in Chapter 7 (172–177).

17 Also see *Answers* 5, and Smith 1995.

TARA SMITH

18 Peikoff offers an extended explanation in *OPAR* 310–323. For further discussion of force as paralyzing the mind, see Smith 2009b and Wright 1999.
19 Emphasis hers. In an interview, Rand observes that objective law must be graspable by a rational consciousness (WKCR interview on "Objective Law" *Speaking* 59).
20 See *OPAR* 365.
21 "The Nature of Government" (*VOS* 127–129/*CUI* 380–382); *Answers* 6; and *OPAR* 364–365.
22 Peikoff provides a thorough analysis of Rand's understanding of objectivity, *OPAR* 110–151, esp. 116–121. Rand does distinguish metaphysical from epistemological objectivity, though she seems to regard the latter as its principal meaning (see "Who Is the Final Authority in Ethics?" *VOR* 18, and *ITOE* 46–47, 52–54, 82; also the discussion of this in Smith 2004 and 2008).
23 In the interview referred to earlier (n. 19), Rand says that preventive law is a "strictly statist" concept that has "no conceivable justification" and belongs only in a dictatorship (*Speaking* 63). Notice that preventive law withdraws the presumption of innocence, penalizing individuals by restricting their freedom before – indeed, in the absence of – their violation of others' rights. For further discussion of preventive law, see Harry Binswanger, "What Is Objective Law?" (*TIA* 6(1) 8–14).
24 Emphasis hers. On why controls will expand, see "The Anatomy of Compromise" (*CUI* 160) and *Marginalia* 201.
25 For more on this, see *OPAR* 373–375, "America's Persecuted Minority: Big Business" (*CUI* 45), "The Obliteration of Capitalism" (*CUI* 206), and "Conservatism: An Obituary" (*CUI* 214–215).
26 Also see "The Roots of War" (*CUI* 31–32), "The Pull Peddlers" (*CUI* 186), and *Atlas* 596 and 1065.
27 On the impossibility of rationally applying irrational principles, see "The Pull Peddlers" (*CUI* 188) and Smith 2005.
28 Rand limns the resentment she believes this breeds in the account of the Twentieth Century Motor Company in *Atlas*.
29 Even illegitimate threats that are not subsequently acted on (such as unjust laws that citizens obey) constrict freedom by intimidating men into submission to demands that the threatener would not be justified in enforcing. Under such laws, citizens must, in order to avoid legal sanction, obey rules that are justified as well as rules that are not. This violates their rightful freedom.
30 "The Establishing of an Establishment" (*PWNI* 220–33, see esp. 222, 224–225, 229–230).
31 While each of these schools includes differing species and the exact nature of the competing positions is itself a subject of some dispute, this portrait should suffice for our purposes. For details of such differences, see Murphy 2005 and Bix 2005.
32 See also Gregory Salmieri's discussion in Chapter 12 (290–292).
33 No system can guarantee that rights will never be infringed, of course.
34 Rand emphatically rejects Legal Realism, calling the claim that "law is what judges say it is" a "formula for tyranny" that represents "pure non-objectivity" and the destruction of law (*Speaking* 60).
35 Even Natural Law theorists acknowledge this.
36 Plato's Philosopher Kings do not aim at *personal* advantage, yet insofar as the rules they impose are, according to Plato, justified by those individuals' enlightened status *as men* rather than by the character of those laws, they are completely unpredictable.

Separately, note that objective law does not require that the numerous government officials who resolve different disputes all issue identical rulings. Many particulars are legitimately discretionary *within* the parameters set by the relevant principles. Violations of the Rule of Law ideal, however, violate those principles.
37 Rand portrays this contrast starkly in *Atlas*, where, by the climax, guns settle disagreements. Aristotle also conceived of the difference in this way. See *Politics*, III 1287a28–b6, and, more broadly concerning the Rule of Law, 1282b1–12. Aristotle's reasoning for the superiority of the Rule of Law to the Rule of Men is not the same as Rand's, however. He believes that because law is made through the deliberations of many men, we can expect important benefits from the Rule of Law that would not be equally available under the rule of individual men. The many are less susceptible to passion and to corruption, he argues, and more likely to arrive at wisdom. (He hardly advocated unrestrained democracy, however.) For his somewhat complicated view, see *Politics*, III 1286a1–b41 *passim* and IV

1292a30–37. For brief comment on Aristotle's view, see Tamanaha 2004, 122 and 125, and for a fuller discussion, Miller 1995, 79–84, and Miller 2007, 99–102.

38 See the discussions of the virtue of rationality and of force by Gotthelf (Chapter 4, 82–84) and Wright (Chapter 6, 177), above.

39 Also see her remarks on non-objective law as a tool of tyranny in her WKCR interview on "Objective Law" (*Speaking* 60–61).

40 In *Atlas*, Judge Narragansett, one of the virtuous strikers, condemns non-objective law as "humanity's darkest evil" (737).

References

Bix, Brian H. 2005. "Legal Positivism." In Golding and Edmundson 2005.

Coleman, Arthur L., and Scott R. Palmer. 2007. "A More Circuitous Path to Racial Diversity." *Chronicle of Higher Education*, July 13, B10.

Daily, Stella. 2008. "How the FDA Violated Rights and Hinders Health." *The Objective Standard*, Fall.

Fallon, Richard H. 1997. "The Rule of Law as a Concept in Constitutional Discourse." *Columbia Law Review, 97*.

Fleming, Harold. 1951. *Ten Thousand Commandments: A Story of the Antitrust Laws*. New York, NY: Prentice Hall.

Fuller, Lon. 1964. *The Morality of Law*. New Haven, CT: Yale University Press.

Golding, Martin P. and William A. Edmundson, eds. 2005. *Blackwell Guide to the Philosophy of Law and Legal Theory*. Oxford: Blackwell Publishing.

Hull, Gary, ed. 2005. *The Abolition of Antitrust*. New Brunswick, NJ: Transaction.

Kramer, Matthew H. 2007. *Objectivity and the Rule of Law*. New York, NY: Cambridge University Press.

Marmor, Andrei. 2004. "The Rule of Law and Its Limits." *Law and Philosophy, 23*.

Miller, Fred D. 1995. *Nature, Justice, and Rights in Aristotle's* Politics. Oxford: Oxford University Press.

Miller, Fred D. 2007. "Aristotle's Philosophy of Law." In *A History of the Philosophy of Law from the Ancient Greeks to the Scholastics*, edited by Fred D. Miller, Jr. in association with Carrie-Ann Biondi. Dordrecht, Netherlands: Springer.

Murphy, Mark C. 2005. "Natural Law Theory." In Golding and Edmundson 2005.

Murphy, Mark C. 2007. *Philosophy of Law*. Oxford: Blackwell Publishing.

Raz, Joseph. 1979. "The Rule of Law and Its Virtue." In *The Authority of Law*. Oxford: Clarendon Press.

Smith, Tara. 1995. *Moral Rights and Political Freedom*. Lanham, MD: Rowman & Littlefield.

Smith, Tara. 2004. "'Social' Objectivity and the Objectivity of Value." In *Science, Values, and Objectivity*, edited by Peter Machamer and Gereon Walters. Pittsburgh, PA: University of Pittsburg Press.

Smith, Tara. 2005. "How 'Activist' Should Judges Be? Objectivity in Judicial Decisions." Recorded lecture available at https://estore.aynrand.org/p/160 (accessed May 26, 2015).

Smith, Tara. 2008. "The Importance of the Subject in Objective Morality: Distinguishing Objective from Intrinsic Value." In *Objectivism, Subjectivism, and Relativism in Ethics*, edited by Ellen Frankel Paul, Fred D. Miller, and Jeffrey Paul. New York, NY: Cambridge University Press.

Smith, Tara. 2009b. "'Humanity's Darkest Evil': The Lethal Destructiveness of Non-Objective Law." In *Essays on Ayn Rand's* Atlas Shrugged, edited by Robert Mayhew. Lanham, MD: Lexington Books.

Tamanaha, Brian Z. 2004. *On the Rule of Law: History, Politics, Theory*. Cambridge: Cambridge University Press.

Wright, Darryl. 1999. *Reason and Freedom*. Second Renaissance Books. Audio recording.

10

"A Free Mind and a Free Market Are Corollaries"

Rand's Philosophical Perspective on Capitalism

ONKAR GHATE

Ayn Rand is perhaps most widely known as an uncompromising advocate of laissez-faire capitalism. She argues that to understand and defend this political-economic system, one must understand that it requires a definite moral-philosophical base: a base of individualism, self-interest, and reason. The first paragraph of her introduction to *Capitalism: The Unknown Ideal* reads: "This book is not a treatise on economics. It is a collection of essays on the *moral* aspects of capitalism" (*CUI* vii).[1] Rand thought such a book vital because capitalism was perishing from lack of a base. In the nineteenth and especially twentieth century, she argues, the United States (and Britain) moved away from capitalism, after having approached laissez-faire, because of a dramatic intellectual and cultural shift. Collectivism replaced individualism, altruism replaced self-interest, and various forms of mysticism replaced reason. Capitalism's alleged champions were unable or unwilling to mount an effective response: they accepted the basic philosophical tenets of the mystic-altruist-collectivist axis.[2]

Rand's distinct perspective on the free market, therefore, is not that of the economist, who studies the principles by which economic production and trade among free individuals take place. Her perspective is that of the philosopher, who studies the view of man, knowledge and values embodied in the nature and workings of the free market. In fighting for capitalism Rand is fighting, she writes, "for that philosophical base which capitalism did not have and without which it was doomed to perish" ("Choose Your Issues" *TON* 1(1) 1). To read Rand's writings as primarily about politics or economics (as too many free-market sympathizers do) – even those articles addressing political or economic topics – is to misunderstand what she is doing. Rand's perspective is more abstract and fundamental: to understand and explain why "*Intellectual* freedom cannot exist without *political* freedom; political freedom cannot exist without *economic* freedom; *a free mind and a free market are corollaries*" (*FTNI* 21). This connection between mind and market is what I will explore.

In previous chapters, Miller and Mossoff addressed Rand's account of proper government and her definition of capitalism as "a social system based on the recognition of individual rights,

---

A Companion to Ayn Rand, First Edition. Edited by Allan Gotthelf and Gregory Salmieri.
© 2016 John Wiley & Sons, Ltd. Published 2016 by John Wiley & Sons, Ltd.

including property rights, in which all property is privately owned" ("What Is Capitalism?" *CUI* 10), and Smith addressed the non-objective, ultimately dictatorial nature of regulations that interfere with the operations of the free market. My focus in this chapter is on Rand's account of some of the other crucial philosophical premises implicit in the operations of a free market.

For my discussion, it will be important to keep in mind a few of the main points from these previous chapters, especially the point that according to Rand capitalism designates a political-economic system in which the government's power is (a) explicitly limited by the principle of individual rights and (b) directed solely toward the purpose of securing and protecting the rights of each individual citizen.

This necessitates, Rand argues, a body of objective laws that specify how and under what circumstances the government can use its coercive power.[3] Laissez-faire requires that the law prohibit the government from interfering with the intellectual judgments and lives of citizens: there must be full freedom of thought and speech and full separation of church and state and of education and state. The government has no power to ban books, prohibit obscenity or blasphemy, establish churches, run schools, set curricula, offer scholarships, subsidize scientific research, award artistic grants, and so on. Laissez-faire also requires that the law prohibit the government from interfering with the economic judgments and lives of citizens: there must be full freedom to produce, contract, and trade, and so full separation of economy and state. The government has no power to set pharmaceutical testing or manufacturing processes (e.g., the FDA), legislate accounting standards (e.g., the SEC), dictate employment terms (e.g., a minimum wage), erect tariffs, run banks, ban gold, or otherwise control the money supply (e.g., the Federal Reserve), bail out failing companies, license broadcast frequencies (e.g., the FCC), and so on. In the final chapter of *Atlas Shrugged*, Judge Narragansett crosses out the contradictions in the US Constitution's statements "that had once been the cause of its destruction" and adds a new clause: "Congress shall make no law abridging the freedom of production and trade ..." (*Atlas* 1167–1168).

Economically, therefore, capitalism means a *free* market, that is, a complete "separation of state and economics, in the same way and for the same reasons as the separation of state and church" ("The Objectivist Ethics" *VOS* 37). Production and trade, like all other relationships in a capitalist system,

> are voluntary. Men are free to cooperate or not, to deal with one another or not, as their own individual judgments, convictions, and interests dictate. They can deal with one another only in terms of and by means of reason, i.e., by means of discussion, persuasion, and contractual agreement, by voluntary choice to mutual benefit. The right to agree with others is not a problem in any society; it is the right to disagree that is crucial. It is the institution of private property that protects and implements the right to disagree – and thus keeps the road open to man's most valuable attribute (valuable personally, socially, and objectively): the creative mind. (*CUI* 11)

The economic result of the free market, Rand holds, is a complex *integration* of production and trade created by individuals' voluntary decisions (including their voluntary division of labor). A full understanding and evaluation of this economic integration, on Rand's view, requires a proper philosophical perspective.

In the next section I cover briefly the basic approach to knowledge and values that Rand argues is implicitly embedded in the operations of a free market. I then move to a discussion of her view of how this approach plays out: that it is the producers of economic values (not the consumers) who govern the operations of a free market. In the last major section, I explore her idea that statist systems are not alternative forms of economic production but simply the destruction, partial or total, of producers. In the conclusion, I sketch Rand's views on the relation of philosophy to economics and discuss her evaluations of some free-market economists.

Although Rand was interested in capitalism and free markets throughout her life, her primary writings on the topic are *Atlas Shrugged*, "For the New Intellectual" (*FTNI*), *Capitalism: The Unknown Ideal* (the lead essay of this book, "What Is Capitalism?," is especially important), and a number of essays from the 1970s (originally appearing in *The Ayn Rand Letter*) in which she discusses current economic events. These will be my focus.

Preliminaries: Knowledge, Values, and Man's Life

The key, I think, to understanding Rand's philosophical account of the free market (and of its destruction) is her claim that the free market, by protecting voluntary relationships, embodies an *objective* view of knowledge and values.

"The action required to sustain human life," Rand argues, "is primarily intellectual: everything man needs has to be discovered by his mind and produced by his effort. Production is the application of reason to the problem of survival" (*CUI* 8). The proper use of man's rational faculty, according to Rand's epistemology, is volitional and complex.[4] To reach conceptual knowledge is an achievement.

It requires, she argues, a mind that chooses to follow the evidence and the principles of logic wherever they lead. It requires a mind seeking a non-contradictory identification of reality. To achieve this, a mind must survey and integrate its ideas to ensure they are rooted in fact without contradiction. A mind must be *objective*. The moment a mind allows in a consideration other than discovery of *truth*, the moment it exempts some *idea* from logic and fact and accepts it on faith (i.e., emotionally), it derails the process of integration that is the essence of *thought*.

The same holds for values. By virtue of the nature of value and of the good, Rand argues, their achievement requires an intellectual process: an act of evaluation.

> The *objective* theory [of values] holds that the good is ... *an evaluation* of the facts of reality by man's consciousness according to a rational standard of value. ... [T]hat *the good is an aspect of reality in relation to man* – and that it must be discovered, not invented, by man. Fundamental to an objective theory of values is the question: Of value to whom and for what? (*CUI* 14)

In *Atlas Shrugged* and "The Objectivist Ethics" Rand explicitly asks and presents her answers to these two questions: by the nature of what a value is, the rational standard of value is man's life and the purpose of pursuing values is to achieve one's own life.[5]

The act of evaluating – the root process of pursuing the good – is, according to Rand, a complex intellectual act of integration: of identifying the requirements of life and happiness, of discovering how to create and produce these requirements, of ascertaining how a particular goal fits with the rest of one's goals, and thereby establishing a rational hierarchy of values.[6] As a complex form of thought, this process, too, requires strict objectivity. The moment a mind allows in a consideration other than discovery of the *good*, the moment it exempts some *desire* or *goal* from logic and fact and embraces it on faith (i.e., emotionally), it derails the process of integration that is the essence of *evaluation*.

To pursue the *true* and the *good*, and thus to pursue life, Rand's philosophy maintains, is to choose to exert the effort of cognitive integration. This is the essence of reason *and* morality.[7] To subvert the integrative process is to subvert the mind: it is the essence of irrationality *and* evil. Thus Rand writes, in a formulation capturing her view of the unity of thought and evaluation:

> Whenever you committed the evil of refusing to think and to see, of exempting from the absolute of reality some one small wish of yours, whenever you chose to say: Let me withdraw from the judgment of reason the cookies I stole, or the existence of God, let me have my one irrational whim and I will be a man of reason about all else – *that* was the act of subverting your consciousness, the act of corrupting your mind. Your mind then became a fixed jury who takes orders from a secret underworld, whose verdict distorts the evidence to fit an absolute it dares not touch – and a censored reality is the result, a splintered reality where the bits you chose to see are floating among the chasms of those you didn't, held together by that embalming fluid of the mind which is an emotion exempted from thought. (*Atlas* 1037)[8]

Precisely because capitalism upholds rights and bans coercion from dictating the terms of association – under laissez-faire each individual has the right to think, earn property, and pursue his happiness – the individual, Rand argues, is able to perform the life-giving processes of integration: thought and evaluation. "It is the basic, metaphysical fact of man's nature – the connection between his survival and his use of reason – that capitalism recognizes and protects" (*CUI* 11).

To initiate force against another individual and substitute coercion for agreement – to torture him to accept some religious tenet or to point a gun and demand that he hand over his wallet – is, Rand maintains, to compel him to drop reason and act on *faith*. It is to *disintegrate* his consciousness. The result is "to negate and paralyze his means of survival" (*Atlas* 1023). It negates it, because the individual's uncoerced judgment is telling him to think or to do the opposite of what the force-initiator is commanding. Force paralyzes the mind, because so long as a mind chooses to remain true to truth, it cannot proceed cognitively in compliance with the force-initiator's dictates.[9]

Suppose an atheist is being tortured and told to repent his sin and accept God. So long as he remains true to his grasp of logic and facts, he has no alternative but to still accept and espouse atheism. If he puts objectivity aside and accepts God on faith (out of pain or fear), or if he simply spouts the words "God exists" to stop the torture, no integrative process occurs in his mind. Likewise, if a mugger tells you to hand over your wallet, and you are convinced that it is your money, that the mugger is in the wrong, that it would be unjust for him to take your money, and that you would kill the mugger if you could, this is your objective evaluation. When the mugger demands that you hand over your money regardless of your own evaluation, Rand argues that you are being placed in an impossible metaphysical situation. "Reality threatens man with death if he does not act on his rational judgment," but the forcer-initiator threatens man "with death if he does." He places man in "a world where the price of … life is the surrender of all the virtues required by life" (*Atlas* 1023). If you comply with the mugger's demand and hand over your wallet because of the gun pointed at your head, of course this action of yours is a result of your mental processes – but in a more fundamental sense, Rand maintains, cognition and evaluation about the matter have ceased. The metaphysical contradiction in your mind has *not* been resolved. Obedience is not understanding.[10]

Rand's account of the objectivity of *knowledge* and of *values* is necessary to understand her philosophical account of both the nature and workings of the free market and of its opposite. The free market, she holds, unleashes the rational, creative minds of producers. In a division-of-labor economy, the result of their work is an enormous, ever-growing integration of both production and trade. Non-capitalist systems, by allowing force to dictate the terms of association, *stop* the minds of producers. The extent to which a social system departs from the free market by permitting the initiation of force, Rand argues, is the extent to which economic production *disintegrates* (or never occurs in the first place). The full initiation of force, as in various totalitarian systems, is the full destruction of economic production.[11]

Let us explore both of these ideas, first by considering in more depth Rand's philosophical account of the basic principles ruling a free market, particularly why she thinks a free market is ruled by producers, and then by considering her account of what happens to producers in non-capitalist systems.

The Free Market: Rule by Producers

A genuine market, Rand argues, is a market of *producers*: an individual can consume or trade only that which he has produced (or that which he has been given by a producer). "Consumption," Rand writes, "is the *final*, not the *efficient*, cause of production" ("Egalitarianism and Inflation" *PWNI* 178). This means that

> consumers *qua consumers* are not part of anyone's market ... Nature does not grant anyone an innate title of "consumer"; it is a title that has to be earned – by production. Only *producers* constitute a market – only men who trade products or services for products or services. In the role of producers, they represent a market's "supply"; in the role of consumers, they represent a market's "demand." The law of supply and demand has an implicit subclause: that it involves the same people in both capacities. (*PWNI* 176)

But nature also does not grant anyone an innate title of "producer." No individual is born knowing *what* to produce or *how* to produce it. In a genuine market, each individual must *earn* his way: each must attain the knowledge and perform the actions that the production of values demands.

Insofar as he is a creator and innovator, an individual forges new thoughts and new products and thereby serves as mankind's teacher. Insofar as he isn't, he must learn his method of survival from others. Mankind's progress depends on the existence of creators and innovators. Vital to the story of *Atlas Shrugged* is that there exist Atlases – individuals of astounding intelligence and ability – who serve as the inventors and teachers of men's productive activities. There is a "pyramid of ability," with the individuals at the top the generators of *knowledge*: new ideas, new methods, and new principles.[12]

> What determines the material value of your work? Nothing but the productive effort of your mind – if you lived on a desert island. The less efficient the thinking of your brain, the less your physical labor would bring you ... But when you live in a rational society, where men are free to trade, you receive an incalculable bonus: the material value of your work is determined not only by your effort, but by the effort of the best productive minds who exist in the world around you.
>
> When you work in a modern factory, you are paid, not only for your labor, but for all the productive genius which has made that factory possible: for the work of the industrialist who built it, for the work of the investor who saved the money to risk on the untried and the new, for the work of the engineer who designed the machines of which you are pushing the levers, for the work of

the inventor who created the product which you spend your time on making, for the work of the scientist who discovered the laws that went into the making of that product, for the work of the philosopher who taught men how to think ...

[T]he man who produces an idea in any field of rational endeavor – the man who discovers new knowledge – is the permanent benefactor of humanity. Material products can't be shared, they belong to some ultimate consumer; it is only the value of an idea that can be shared with unlimited numbers of men, making all sharers richer at no one's sacrifice or loss, raising the productive capacity of whatever labor they perform. It is the value of his own time that the strong of the intellect transfers to the weak, letting them work on the jobs he discovered, while devoting his time to further discoveries. This is mutual trade to mutual advantage; the interests of the mind are one, no matter what the degree of intelligence, among men who desire to work and don't seek or expect the unearned. (*Atlas* 1064–1065)

Once an individual acquires the knowledge of how to produce, he must decide, of all the things he has learned to produce, what it is most *valuable* to produce. A complex calculation, an act of *evaluation*, is required. This is true of an individual on a self-sustaining farm – should he grow wheat or corn, raise cattle or pigs, keep chickens or ducks, or some combination of all these? And it is true of an individual in a division-of-labor economy. If the farmer starts to specialize and trade his goods with others – for bread and firewood, say – he must now evaluate what it would be most *valuable* to produce in order to *exchange it on the market*. The answer is not self-evident.

In an advanced, industrial economy the individuals who charge themselves with the task of figuring out what is most valuable to produce are the entrepreneurs and businessmen. On whatever scale they operate, from an individual running a small grocery store and employing two clerks to Bill Gates running Microsoft and employing tens of thousands of people, they organize and direct – they *integrate* – men's productive activities.

The businessman carries scientific discoveries from the laboratory of the inventor to industrial plants, and transforms them into material products that fill men's physical needs and expand the comfort of men's existence. By creating a mass market, he makes these products available to every income level of society. By using machines, he increases the productivity of human labor, thus raising labor's economic rewards. By organizing human effort into productive enterprises, he creates employment for men of countless professions. *He* is the great liberator who, in the short span of a century and a half, has released men from bondage to their physical needs ... (*FTNI* 23)

Rand's outline of the development of economic production is this. First men must discover the rudiments of what to produce and how to produce it. To progress beyond a hand-to-mouth existence, men must continue to acquire knowledge so that they are able to produce more than required for immediate consumption. They can then save some of what they have produced or use some of their newly-released time to further production. They can plant leftover seeds or use their free time to make a spear or a plow. When they learn to trade (and develop a medium of exchange), they can specialize, which makes possible further expansion of their individual knowledge and abilities. In an advanced economy, entrepreneurs and businessmen assume the risk of organizing and directing the processes of production and trade. They combine the savings of some individuals with the specialized work of others to form business enterprises, some of incredible scope and complexity.[13]

On Rand's view, the free market is a complex integration of individual knowledge and consequent productive action, which "demands the best of every man – his rationality – and rewards him accordingly" (*FTNI* 21). Accordingly, it is "men of the mind" (to use the formulation from *Atlas Shrugged*) who rise and prosper in the free market.

But there are opponents of the free market who coercively seek to override its processes and outcomes. Fundamentally, Rand argues, these opponents are motivated by what she calls the *subjective* or the *intrinsic* theories of values. The subjective theory

> holds that the good bears no relation to the facts of reality, that it is the product of a man's consciousness, created by his feelings, desires, "intuitions," or whims, and that it is merely an "arbitrary postulate" or an "emotional commitment."

The intrinsic theory

> holds that the good is inherent in certain things or actions as such, regardless of their context and consequences, regardless of any benefit or injury they may cause to the [individual] actors and subjects involved. It is a theory that divorces the concept of "good" from beneficiaries, and the concept of "value" from valuer and purpose – claiming that the good is good in, by, and of itself. (*CUI* 13–14)[14]

Both approaches to value, Rand argues, lead to the notion that the initiation of force is a means of achieving the good.

> If a man believes that the good is a matter of arbitrary, subjective choice, the issue of good or evil becomes, for him, an issue of: *my* feelings or *theirs*? ... Reason is the only means of communication among men, and an objectively perceivable reality is their only common frame of reference; when these are invalidated (*i.e.*, held to be irrelevant) in the field of morality, force becomes men's only way of dealing with one another. If the subjectivist wants to pursue some social ideal of his own, he feels morally entitled to force men "for their own good," since he *feels* that he is right and that there is nothing to oppose him but their misguided feelings.

Similarly, if

> a man believes that the good is intrinsic in certain actions, he will not hesitate to force others to perform them. If he believes that the human benefit or injury caused by such actions is of no significance, he will regard a sea of blood as of no significance. If he believes that the beneficiaries of such actions are irrelevant (or interchangeable), he will regard wholesale slaughter as his moral duty in the service of a "higher" good. It is the intrinsic theory of values that produces a Robespierre, a Lenin, a Stalin, or a Hitler. It is not an accident that Eichmann was a Kantian. (*CUI* 14–15)

One constant line of attack against capitalism, Rand is arguing in effect, is the protest that the protesters themselves do not *like* some outcome generated on the free market. For instance, they feel it is unfair that a small grocery store, which some people enjoyed shopping at and which for a time was profitable, should be put out of business by Walmart. The objection amounts to: "The free market is dictatorial – and I (we) don't like what it dictates! ... There ought to be a law." To rectify the alleged injustice, those at the top must be legally chopped down (e.g., by such measures as anti-trust laws, progressive taxation, and zoning restrictions) and those at the bottom must be legally propped up (e.g., by such measures as subsidies, corporate bailouts, unemployment "insurance," and minimum wage laws).

Another constant line of attack, Rand is arguing, is the protest that the outcomes on the free market simply do not coincide with "the good." It is obvious, this kind of complaint goes, that Einstein's work is more valuable than Elvis Presley's and that the microscope is more valuable than lipstick (to use two of Rand's examples from "What Is Capitalism?") – so why should Presley earn more than Einstein and the lipstick industry more than the microscope industry? The objection amounts to: "The free market is arbitrary and immoral – it dictates the morally wrong outcome! ... There ought to be a law." And therefore, in the name of the good, wealth must be legally "redistributed" from the morally undeserving "haves" to the morally deserving "have-nots" (e.g., by such measures as subsidies to the arts, sciences, and "essential" industries; public education; and Medicare).

These two lines of attack, Rand maintains, although they voice different theories of values, actually have their roots in the same mentality and blend in practice. The first line of attack derives from the subjectivist theory of values. These moral critics, Rand argues, *feel* that the small grocery store should remain in business, and therefore coercively seek to override the individual, voluntary decisions that generate the free market's prices and outcomes. The second line of attack derives from the intrinsic theory of values. By reference to the nature of the good, intrinsic in the very nature of reality, these moral critics contend that it is wrong for Presley to make more than Einstein or for a symphony orchestra to struggle financially while "American Idol" makes millions. Thus these critics too seek to override the individual, voluntary decisions that generate the free market's prices and outcomes. But, Rand asks rhetorically, "by what means do the moralists of the intrinsic school discover their transcendental 'good,' if not by means of special, non-rational intuitions and revelations, *i.e.*, by means of their *feelings?*" ("What Is Capitalism?" *CUI* 15, emphasis added; see also Smith 2000, 66–71.)

On Rand's view, whenever either of such moral critics of capitalism manages to enact economic controls, what is in fact happening is that the critics' *feelings* are being given the backing of physical force, so that these critics can override the thoughts, evaluations, and resulting economic decisions and transactions of other individuals – that is, so that the critics can override the very *process* by which an individual reaches knowledge and achieves values.

> A value which one is forced to accept at the price of surrendering one's mind is not a value to anyone; the forcibly mindless can neither judge nor choose nor value. An attempt to achieve the good by force is like an attempt to provide a man with a picture gallery at the price of cutting out his eyes. Values cannot exist (cannot be valued) outside the full context of a man's life, needs, goals, and knowledge. (*CUI* 15–16)

The nature of the free market, therefore, cannot be understood or defended, Rand argues, unless one grasps that the free market

> represents the *social* application of an objective theory of values. Since values are to be discovered by man's mind, men must be free to discover them – to think, to study, to translate their knowledge into physical form, to offer their products for trade, to judge them, and to choose, be it material goods or ideas, a loaf of bread or a philosophical treatise. Since values are established contextually, every man must judge for himself, in the context of his own knowledge, goals, and interests. Since values are determined by the nature of reality, it is reality that serves as men's ultimate arbiter: if a man's judgment is right, the rewards are his; if it is wrong, he is his only victim.
>
> It is in regard to a free market that the distinction between an intrinsic, subjective, and objective view of values is particularly important to understand. The market value of a product is *not* an intrinsic value, not a "value in itself" hanging in a vacuum. A free market never loses sight of the question: Of value *to whom?* (*CUI* 16)

In a free market, a trade requires the voluntary agreement of both parties. Each is free to discover and deploy knowledge, to assess the potential exchange in light of his own life, circumstances and values, and to thereby make a rational decision. Free-market prices are a product of individuals' knowledge, evaluations, and consequent decisions to trade. In this sense "the free-market value of goods and services," Rand writes, represents their "*socially objective value, i.e.*, the sum of the individual judgments of all the men involved in trade at a given time, the sum of what *they* valued, each in the context of his own life" (*CUI* 16). This new concept, Rand argues, is crucial to understanding the outcomes of the free market.

The fact that in a free market an individual is free to reach an objective evaluation and make a rational decision in matters of production and trade is no guarantee that he will. No economic system can rewrite the metaphysically given fact of free will (and none should try): man's primary choice is to think or not.[15] But a free market (i.e., a capitalist social system) also contains no coercive mechanisms that attempt to rewrite another metaphysically given fact: the fact that the achievement of values, of happiness, and of life requires rational thought. No governmental unemployment "insurance," no governmental bailouts, no governmental safety nets exist to try to insulate people from their erroneous or irrational decisions. For instance, Rand writes, if a

> stenographer spends all her money on cosmetics and has none left to pay for the use of a microscope (for a visit to the doctor) *when she needs it*, she learns a better method of budgeting her income; the free market serves as her teacher: she has no way to penalize others for her mistakes. If she budgets rationally, the microscope is always available to serve her own specific needs *and no more*, as far as she is concerned: she is not taxed to support an entire hospital, a research laboratory, or a space ship's journey to the moon. Within her own productive power, she does pay a part of the cost of scientific achievements, *when and as she needs them*. She has no "social duty," her own life is her only responsibility – and the only thing that a capitalist system requires of her is the thing that *nature* requires: rationality, *i.e.*, that she live and act to the best of her own judgment. (*CUI* 17–18)

Although the specifics can vary widely, in some form an individual who thinks and evaluates non-objectively and thus makes irrational decisions suffers the economic consequences: at the very least, he will fail to obtain in the market the value he could have obtained had he acted rationally. In this way a free market, Rand writes, "teaches every participant to look for the *objective* best within the category of his own competence, and penalizes those who act on irrational considerations" (*CUI* 18).[16]

Thus when Rand argues that the free-market value of a good or service represents its socially objective value, she is not arguing that one must adopt an amoral neutrality toward market prices, that is, regard them as exempt from any further form of evaluation.

First, a product's socially objective value may reflect non-objective evaluations and irrational decisions. Businessmen (and other free-market participants) must consider and evaluate this issue constantly. For instance, if non-motorized scooters start selling like hotcakes, a bicycle manufacturer may be tempted to retool his factories to manufacture scooters. But he must assess the source of the change in demand. If he thinks, for instance, that it is a fad that will not last – that buyers' motivations are second-handed ("everyone is buying a scooter, so I will too!") and that in a few months the scooters will sit in people's garages, unused and never to be worn out or replaced – he will not retool. He will expect the market to correct, that is, people's evaluations to become more objective and their actions more rational. By contrast, if a maker of film cameras thinks that digital cameras are a fad that won't last – he likely will go out of business.[17]

Second, and related to the first issue, one can view a good or service from the perspective of what Rand calls its *philosophically objective value*.

> By "philosophically objective," I mean a value estimated from the standpoint of the best possible to man, i.e., by the criterion of the most rational mind possessing the greatest knowledge, in a given category, in a given period, and in a defined context (nothing can be estimated in an undefined context). For instance, it can be rationally proved that the airplane is *objectively* of immeasurably greater value to man (to *man at his best*) than the bicycle – and that the works of Victor Hugo are *objectively* of immeasurably greater value than true-confession magazines. But if a given man's intellectual potential can barely manage to enjoy true confessions, there is no reason why his meager earnings, the product of *his* effort, should be spent on books he cannot read – or on subsidizing the airplane industry, if his own transportation needs do not extend beyond the range of a bicycle. (Nor is there any reason why the rest of mankind should be held down to the level of his literary taste, his engineering capacity, and his income. Values are not determined by fiat nor by majority vote.) (*CUI* 16–17)[18]

To say that the philosophically objective value of the works of Hugo is vastly greater than that of true-confession magazines is to say (in part) that in an advanced culture (and not, say, a clan of hunter-gatherers unable to read and possessing no leisure time) the inspiration offered by Hugo's works is such that they (and not true-confession magazines) can fuel the minds, courage, and lives of rational, intelligent men of achievement.[19] To say that the philosophically objective value of the airplane is greater than the bicycle's is to say (in part) that in an advancing industrial economy, the invention of the airplane makes possible a new level of action and of integration of men's productive activities that, comparatively, the invention of the bicycle never did (think for instance of the creation of Federal Express and all the companies using its services to ship goods across the planet). From an economic perspective, people rightly speak of the age of air travel; they don't speak of the (prior) age of bicycle travel.

The evaluative perspective of "philosophically objective value" is crucial to understanding the workings of the free market, Rand maintains, because it is the philosophically objective value of a product that motivates the great creators who abound under capitalism – the great scientists, inventors, investors, and businessmen – and explains one crucial way in which they are mankind's teachers.

These individuals are idealists – they have a vision of what can and ought to be, of what is possible to man at his best – and they strive to bring this vision into reality. This is what motivates the architect Howard Roark in *The Fountainhead* and the businesswoman Dagny Taggart, the industrialist Hank Rearden, the banker Midas Mulligan, and the inventor-philosopher John Galt in *Atlas Shrugged*. This is what motivates Edison with his vision of electrical light illuminating the night, Rockefeller with his vision of a world awash in oil, and Bill Gates with his vision of a computer on every desk.[20] And from these individuals' vision and productivity, other (rational) individuals in a free market learn.

> [T]he intellectual criteria of the majority do not rule a free market or a free society – and ... the exceptional men, the innovators, the intellectual giants, are not held down by the majority. In fact, it is the members of this exceptional minority who lift the whole of a free society to the level of their own achievements, while rising further and ever further. ... While the majority have barely assimilated the value of the automobile, the creative minority introduces the airplane. The majority learn by demonstration, the minority is free to demonstrate. The "philosophically objective" value of a new product serves as the teacher for those who are willing to exercise their rational faculty, each to the extent of his ability. Those who are unwilling remain unrewarded – as well as those who aspire to more than their ability produces. (*CUI* 18)[21]

231

In recent times the computer industry may be taken as a vivid example of the process Rand is describing. While many people viewed the first computers as interesting curiosities, with at best limited application, the visionaries in the field saw the ways in which computers could revolutionize business and the world, forged ahead, and triumphed. Rand observes:

> A given product may not be appreciated at once, particularly if it is too radical an innovation; but, barring irrelevant accidents, it wins in the long run. It is in this sense that the free market is not ruled by the intellectual criteria of the majority, which prevail only at and for any given moment; the free market is ruled by those who are able to see and plan long-range – and the better the mind, the longer the range. (*CUI* 19)

This is the deepest sense in which, according to Rand, *producers* not consumers rule the free market (even though consumption is the final cause of production). No individual is born with the knowledge of what to consume – of what is *objectively* valuable because it furthers life. This knowledge must be discovered – and it is the visionary thinkers and producers in a free society who discover it, who teach men *what* to value and how to produce these values.[22]

From the perspective of an objective theory of values, Rand therefore maintains, the incredible progress that occurs in a free society is non-sacrificial (*CUI* 21).[23] Each individual must earn his way and persuade, not coerce, others to deal with him. In the free market the "economic value of a man's work is determined ... by a single principle: by the voluntary consent of those who are willing to trade him their work or products in return. This is the moral meaning of the law of supply and demand" (*CUI* 19). To override the outcomes of the free market is to sacrifice the rational interests of individuals for the sake of some subjective or alleged intrinsic (i.e., non-existent) good – that is, for the sake of someone's feelings which are being treated as moral absolutes.

From the perspective of the objective theory of values, therefore, Walmart *should* be able to displace a small grocery store if consumers judge that Walmart offers superior value and choose to shop there. No firm can stay in business just because some people *wish* it would. Values are not subjective. The lipstick industry may well make more money than the microscope industry "even though it can be rationally demonstrated that microscopes are scientifically more valuable than lipstick," Rand writes. "But – valuable *to whom?* A microscope is of no value to a little stenographer struggling to make a living; a lipstick is ..." (*CUI* 17). Similarly, Presley can make more money than Einstein even though Einstein's achievements are the greater because

> men work in order to support and enjoy their own lives, and if many men find value in Elvis Presley, they are entitled to spend their money on their own pleasure. Presley's fortune is not taken from those who do not care for his work (I am one of them) nor from Einstein – nor does he stand in Einstein's way – nor does Einstein lack proper recognition and support in a free society, on an appropriate intellectual level. (*CUI* 20)

Values are not intrinsic. Values are objective – and, as Rand states her principle, the "objective view of values permeates the entire structure of a capitalist society" (*CUI* 16).

As Rand's statement of her principle implies, there are many further ways in which she holds that the objective theory of values is necessary to understand the nature of capitalism and properly to defend it. Although I do not have space to address these, let me mention one other.[24] In *Capitalism: The Unknown Ideal* Rand advocates a gold standard because crucial to the objectivity of a capitalist system and the free market, she maintains, is the objectivity of money.

This requires that money be an actual good (e.g., gold) freely chosen by men to serve as their medium of exchange. Those who attack the free market invariably seek to control the money supply. By coercively substituting for gold paper bills backed by nothing, by debasing money (and causing inflation), these economic "planners" undermine economic production. Among other problems, the market now contains consumers who were not first producers – economic parasites or "hitchhikers on virtue."[25]

Statist Economies: The Destruction of Producers

Capitalism, Rand argues, is the system of individual rights. In contrast, a "statist system – whether of a communist, fascist, Nazi, socialist or 'welfare' type – is based on the ... government's unlimited power" ("War and Peace" *Column/TON* 1(10) 44), which means governmental power is not limited by the principle of individual rights. In such a system the state "has the right to *initiate* the use of physical force against its citizens. How often force is to be used, against whom, to what extent, for what purpose and for whose benefit" are details ("America's Persecuted Minority: Big Business" *CUI* 44). Economically, in statist social systems there exists no separation of state from production and trade. To some degree, the government intervenes in the economy. Stripped of all euphemisms and semblances of legality, Rand holds, and whether one is examining a mixed economy, a welfare state, a socialist or communist or fascist dictatorship, or a theocracy, statism means gang warfare: "some men have the right to force, coerce, enslave, rob, and murder others" (*CUI* 44). Economic exploitation of producers is *institutionalized*.

> When individual rights are abrogated, there is no way to determine who is entitled to what. ... The criterion, therefore, reverts to the tribal concept of: one's wishes are limited only by the power of one's gang. ... A dictatorship is a gang devoted to looting the effort of the productive citizens of its own country. ("The Roots of War" *CUI* 32)[26]

The degree of statism in an economy, Rand holds, is the degree to which the minds and work of producers are stopped.

If, for instance, in a mixed economy the government decrees that some area of reality, say stem cells, is off limits to scientific research – if the SEC declares that certain accounting rules must be used, regardless of the company's judgment of the rules' merits – if the FCC orders that radio broadcasts must not be "obscene," the EPA orders that a real estate developer must get its approval to the effect that a proposed development does not "unduly interfere" with swamps and other wilderness – if the Justice Department orders that offering a software program for free to customers is "anti-competitive," or the FDA orders that pharmaceutical companies must use certain manufacturing processes and get its agreement that a new drug is "effective" – the government stops the minds of producers.[27] Production and trade on a free market demand of producers constant effort: to pursue new lines of research, establish new accounting principles or manufacturing processes, launch new products, invent new drugs. "I must do these things," a producer thinks to himself. "You can't," the government's gun declares. The result is to paralyze thought.

The same holds, Rand argues, if the government's interference is not to prohibit but to support specific avenues of production. Whenever the government offers grants, monopoly privileges, import restrictions, subsidies, and so on, it is offering the *unearned* – offering the rewards of thought without the need for thought. How can it do so? Only by handcuffing actual producers: by robbing them of their earnings (e.g., corporate taxes), restricting their freedom to trade (e.g., tariffs), preventing them from outcompeting economic inferiors (e.g., government-enforced monopolies and anti-trust laws). The enormous thought and action these producers would have engaged in had they been free to earn, to keep what they earned, and to use it productively, is extinguished. What replaces it is the bloat of government-subsidized and government-protected companies. The lethargy of such companies is, fundamentally, mental lethargy.[28]

In statist systems, the government's interference with the thought of individual producers and traders gains sanction from non-objective theories of values. Rand argues that, viewed in terms of fundamentals, both theories obliterate the individual. Moralists of the intrinsic school feel that some disembodied cause or group – the public, the nation, the race, the proletariat, God – transcends the individual, his evaluations, and his good. Moralists of the subjectivist school believe that values are rooted in desires and "emotional commitments," and so values are fundamentally divorced from reason and objective reality. If the essence of viewing man as an individual is the fact that man's mind is volitional and the use or misuse he chooses to make of his rational faculty determines his basic premises and values – as Rand argues it is – then such moralists obliterate the individual.[29] Instead, most view man as a *pack* animal and regard the group as possessing (metaphysical, epistemological, and moral) primacy; theirs is a "tribal view of man," to use Rand's terminology.[30]

In practice, Rand argues, both types of moralists routinely advocate sacrifice of the individual's interests to some collective. Both demand that you, in the words of America's forty-third president, "serve in a cause larger ... than yourself." Both champion the mystical "public interest" (or some equivalent, like "the common good" or "the welfare of society"). The basic justification of the SEC, FDA, EPA, FCC, Social Security, Medicare, tariffs on foreign producers, subsidies to the sciences and arts, and anti-trust legislation, for example, is moral appeal to the mystical-altruistic-collectivist notion of "the public interest."[31] At root, Rand holds, such a justification is non-objective.[32]

In short, just as the objective theory of values permeates a capitalist economy, so Rand argues that (to the degree of its statism) the intrinsic and subjectivist theories of values permeate a statist economy.

Since the moral meaning of the law of supply and demand is denied by statist theories, statism in practice treats the law itself as dispensable. In the free market, by virtue of the law, individual producers rise as each pursues his self-interest. Under statism, such men are punished and destroyed. Replacing them, Rand argues, are various sorts of parasites: unproductive consumers, bureaucrats, "pull peddlers," and dictators.[33] These men are economic *disintegrators*.

A modern, industrialized economy is a vast and complex division of thought and action, all integrated by the voluntary agreements of individual producers. In a division-of-labor economy, each individual counts on the continued rational thought and productive actions of other individuals. As government intervention brings such thought and action to a halt, replacing the producer with the parasite, this economic integration breaks down.

Atlas Shrugged of course depicts just such a scenario. As one area of thought and production is killed off, all those in the economy who were depending on that area are negatively impacted, and then those who depend on the latter are in turn negatively impacted, and so on.[34] The economic destruction extends through the system. Producers like Dagny Taggart and Hank Rearden can and do strive to reorganize and realign, given the areas that have newly been killed off, but the more areas are killed off, the harder it becomes. A straitjacket is being woven and is essentially completed with the passage of Directive 10-289, the "moratorium on brains." John Galt, who has identified the philosophical nature and causes of this disintegrative process, of course accelerates it by persuading thinkers and producers, in vital area after vital area of the economy, to strike. But it is only an acceleration.[35]

Rand patterned the economic disintegration in *Atlas Shrugged* on the actual economic disintegration of nations, and argued in many subsequent essays that the United States was in the beginning throes of such a disintegration.[36] In regard, for instance, to Nixon's wage and price controls and the temporary economic straitjacket (Nixon's word) they imposed, Rand commented in her article "The Moratorium on Brains":

> [T]he men of intelligence, the nonconformists, the originators, the innovators ... do not function on the expediency of the moment. The better the mind, the longer the range. Scientists, inventors, discoverers work and plan in terms of decades. To a pragmatist or a politician, ten years is the unknowable; to a great mind pursuing a great achievement, it is just one step. The steadfast confidence required for such work is based on certainty, not the certainty of guaranteed success, but the certainty of one's freedom to take calculated – and calculable – risks. Can you see such a mind venturing out on such a road, with the knowledge that a single sentence broadcast over the air without warning can stop him dead at any moment? Can you see him pleading with a board for permission to continue? Can you see him entering the game of pressure politics and wriggling his way through a maze of boards with built-in uncertainty in their functions? If not, then you know what this country will lose and what incalculable loss it has sustained already – in the form of a traumatic shock of helpless discouragement sustained by a young mind on hearing Mr. Nixon's freezing bombshell, a young mind that could have become a skyrocket lighting the world, but will never be heard from or seen. And we will never know how many hopes, half-formed plans, and half-grasped visions died in lesser men that night, along with the best within them. (*ARL* 1(2) 13)[37]

Rand viewed many of the economic policies of her day as at war with producers, especially persistent inflation. In "Egalitarianism and Inflation," the one essay of Rand's that extensively addresses an issue directly in economics, she discusses the basic factors (such as savings, money, and investment) that lie at the root of the incredible economic integration of a modern, industrial economy, all driven by the activities of producers. She argues that inflation undermines this integration and destroys producers, and that inflation is a crime statists have been perpetrating for centuries because "its size is its protection: the integrating capacity of the victims' minds breaks down before the magnitude – and the seeming complexity – of the crime, which permits it to be committed openly, in public" (*PWNI* 169). And in the face of America's resulting desperate "need for men of productive ability" (183), she evaluates as morally obscene those intellectuals advocating egalitarian schemes for "equal rewards for unequal performance" (163), schemes whose only consequence is to destroy the competent.

As a country moves further and further toward some variant of statism and the thinkers and innovative producers – the preeminent economic integrators in the free market – disappear (or never appear in the first place), no longer able to function, who replaces them?

The process, as Rand sketches it, begins with unproductive consumers, men of "need," to whom the nation is told to sacrifice the producers. This requires bureaucrats to administer the so-called public interest – to decide in case after case who counts and who does *not* count as "the public." Since this notion of "the public interest" is undefined and indefinable, no *objective* standards exist by which a bureaucrat can function. His arbitrary power over individuals' work and lives, Rand insists, cannot be wielded honestly:

The wisest man in the world, with the purest integrity, cannot find a criterion for the just, equitable, rational application of an unjust, inequitable, irrational principle. The best that an honest official can do is to accept no material bribe for his arbitrary decision; but this does not make his decision and its consequences more just or less calamitous. ("The Pull Peddlers" *CUI* 188, cf. "The Establishing of an Establishment" *PWNI*)

Thus the bureaucrat is worse than the unproductive consumer – he is not just a drain on but an active obstacle to production. Moreover, the prospect of arbitrary power attracts vicious men who want to wield it – thus the rise of pull peddlers in and around government (which includes many scientists, businessmen, etc., who "adjust" to the system). The free market's "pyramid of ability" is replaced by an "aristocracy of pull" (*Atlas* 404). And in a competition between all these force-initiators, "the murderer wins over the pickpocket" (*Atlas* 413). Hence eventually the rise of mindless, brutish thugs and dictators.

This is the pattern in *Atlas Shrugged*. The calls, in the name of morality, for sacrifice to the public interest lead to the installation of bureaucrats, such as Wesley Mouch, with ever wider arbitrary powers to administer sacrifices for whatever they determine to be the public's interest. Like flies to a rotting corpse, this arbitrary power attracts men like Jim Taggart, Orren Boyle, and many unnamed minor pull peddlers – men whose personal influence over the politicians enables them to collect sacrifices by assuming the "magic title" of the public (*Atlas* 504).[38] The system becomes entrenched and unquestioned, with bureaucrats embedded in industry after industry, like the Wet Nurse in Rearden Steel's operations and Clem Whetherby in Taggart Transcontinental's, and with sundry pull peddlers trading their influence over these bureaucrats. As a result, men grow rich not by the voluntary exchange of values, and the long-range productive activity it makes possible, but by looting. And the looting becomes increasingly crude and short-range, with the likes of Mouch, Taggart, and Boyle being replaced by such "undisguised gangsters" as Cuffy Meigs (*Atlas* 914).[39]

In articles like "Egalitarianism and Inflation," "The Moratorium on Brains," and "Don't Let It Go,"[40] Rand argued a similar disintegration was occurring in the United States, though the country was not yet so far gone as to descend into dictatorship. But so long as the mystical-altruistic-collectivistic advocacy of statism continued, even if only by virtue of the void of no one advocating better ideas, the ultimate destination, she argued, was inevitable.

Conclusion

Rand's philosophical view of the fundamental economic difference between capitalism and statism is encapsulated in her distinction between economic and political power. Economic power "is the power to produce and to trade what one has produced" ("America's Persecuted Minority: Big Business" *CUI* 44). It is a real power: production and trade on a market are a means of furthering one's life. This creative power "is exercised by means of a *positive*, by offering men a reward, an incentive, a payment, a value" (*CUI* 45).[41] Political power, in contrast, is the power of the government to wield force. It too is a real power, but it is the power of destruction.

In a free market, no laws exist to limit, interfere with, control, or curb the exercise of economic power. Political power, by contrast, is strictly limited: force can be used only against those who violate the rights of the individual by initiating force. *The power of destruction can be used only against the initiators of destruction.* The mind of the creator is free – and economic production abounds.

In a statist economy, economic power is curtailed. Political power, by contrast, is unrestrained by any principle. The power of destruction is unleashed against the minds and lives of creators. The consequence is the disintegration of economic production. If the coercion is severe and widespread enough, the result is economic collapse.

A free mind and a free market are corollaries – and so too are a shackled mind and a shackled market.

The science of economics, on Rand's view, has an important but delimited purpose.

> An industrial economy is enormously complex: it involves calculations of time, of motion, of credit, and long sequences of interlocking contractual exchanges. This complexity is the system's great virtue and the source of its vulnerability. The vulnerability is psycho-epistemological. No human mind and no computer – and no planner – can grasp the complexity in every detail. Even to grasp the principles that rule it, is a major feat of abstraction. (ARL 342)[42]

To grasp and define these principles, is the task of economics.

Economics studies production and trade under the division of labor. It presupposes philosophy in definite ways. Like any (specialized) science, it presupposes epistemology: it must employ man's proper method of cognition.[43] Like any social science, it rests on a metaphysical view of man. For instance: Does man have free will? Is he a rational being or a being driven by emotions and impulses? Is he automatically self-interested or must he choose to become so?[44] And like any science that studies normative phenomena, economics presupposes ethics: the concepts of value, production (the creation of material values), and trade (the exchange of values) are all at root moral concepts. The objectivity of the science of economics depends on the objectivity of the concepts at its base.[45]

But despite this connection, one must distinguish Rand's evaluation of a thinker *qua* economist and *qua* (moral-philosophical) advocate and defender of capitalism. Her periodicals, for example, contain favorable book reviews of some of Henry Hazlitt's and especially Ludwig von Mises's works in economics.[46] The Recommended Bibliography of *Capitalism: The Unknown Ideal* contains books by the economists Bastiat, Böhm-Bawerk, Hazlitt, and von Mises, while cautioning that these recommendations "should not be understood as an unqualified endorsement of their total intellectual positions" (CUI 388–391). In a question period she said "Adam Smith was a brilliant economist; I agree with many of his economic theories" (Answers 27). And in "The Fairness Doctrine for Education" she argues that von Mises should be taught in economics courses (PWNI 271).

But as advocates of capitalism, she regarded both Hazlitt and von Mises as undermined by false philosophical and moral assumptions. In two 1946 letters to Rose Wilder Lane, for example, Rand criticizes Hazlitt's *Economics in One Lesson* and von Mises's *Omnipotent Government* (books included in the Recommended Bibliography of *Capitalism: The Unknown Ideal*) on the grounds that they try to divorce economics from morality, which is impossible (Letters 307–309, 330–332). In Rand's marginal comments on her copy of von Mises's *Human Action* (also included in her Recommended Bibliography), she criticizes von Mises for denying the relevance of philosophy to economics while simultaneously feeling the need to delve into philosophical issues, which he gets wrong; she indicates that his errors undermine both philosophical and economic truths (Marginalia 104–141). And in answer to a question in 1977 about her view of the Austrian school of economics, Rand said

> I think they are a school that has a great deal of truth and proper arguments to offer about capitalism – especially von Mises – but I certainly don't agree with them in every detail, and particularly not in their alleged philosophical premises. They don't have any, actually. They attempt – von Mises particularly – to substitute economics for philosophy. That cannot be done. (Answers 43)[47]

Similarly, though she praised Adam Smith's contributions to economics, she said in answer to a question, "I am *not* an advocate of Adam Smith's philosophy. ... Altruism is what's destroying capitalism. ... I disagree with his attempt to justify capitalism on altruistic grounds" (*Answers* 27).

Part of what Rand respected about a thinker like von Mises, I suspect, was the extent to which his work embodied explicit or implicit individualistic premises. She was much harsher in her judgment of Milton Friedman and Friedrich Hayek, because she thought that collectivist philosophical premises were so central to their work as to undermine many of their economic points and prevent them from being advocates of capitalism at all, though they posed as such. Her earliest discussion of Friedman comes in a series of letters from 1946 and 1947 concerning a pamphlet he co-wrote with George Stigler called *Roofs or Ceilings?* (Friedman and Stigler 1946). The pamphlet describes the free market and governmental controls as alternative methods by which a society can "distribute" a good "among those who want it," and they argue against rent controls on the grounds that free market "price rationing" is more efficient. Rand viewed the pamphlet as "without exception, the most pernicious thing ever issued by an avowedly conservative organization," because

> it advocates collectivism in its premises and implications; because it hints that the nationalization of private homes might be the proper solution for the housing shortage; and because there is no excuse for anyone in his right mind to call the free-market, free-enterprise system a "system of rationing." (*Letters* 320, 357)

The collectivist premises that Rand identified in Friedman did prevent him from advocating the separation of state and economy and state and education that Rand held were essential to capitalism. For example, it led him in 1962 to endorse both wealth redistribution (in the form of a negative income tax) and governmental involvement in education (Friedman 2002, 85–107,190–195). Rand summed up her ultimate view of Friedman in a 1980 response to a question about his television program "Free to Choose": "He is not for capitalism; he's a miserable eclectic. He's an enemy of Objectivism, and his objection is that I bring morality into economics, which he thinks should be amoral" (*Answers* 43).[48]

This same criticism dominates her marginal comments on Hayek's *The Road to Serfdom* (*Marginalia* 145–160). She notes that he endorses free markets only as the best "method of guiding economic activity" and that he holds that there are cases in which "the holder of coercive power" will need to employ alternative methods.[49] The essentially collectivist character of Hayek's argument explains why Rand, in a 1946 letter, classified him as "real poison" and an enemy of her cause (*Letters* 308, cf. *Marginalia* 145–160).

Thus Rand rejected Hayek and Friedman (and, to a lesser extent, Smith, von Mises, and Hazlitt) as *advocates of capitalism*. But this is not to say that she dismissed them *as economists*, for she did not think that this sort of advocacy was the task of economics. Indeed, in a fundamental sense for Rand there are not different *economic* systems from which to choose and advocate (and there certainly exists no standard of "economic efficiency," separable from morality, by which to evaluate different systems). There is only production and trade under freedom, the governing principles of which economics studies and codifies. When rights are violated, and statism ensues, economics studies how production and trade are distorted and ultimately extinguished. Thus the basic task of economics is to enable man to grasp *how* production and trade on a free market occur, not why they should occur.

Rand's criticism of these thinkers, therefore, should not be taken as a denial that their work contains valuable insight into economics. Nevertheless, she would insist that (what she identified as) their philosophical errors undermine, not just their advocacy of capitalism, but their work as economists. For, as we have seen, she held that a moral-philosophical perspective on capitalism is not only fundamental to understanding the nature, justification, and basic principles of the free market, it is also necessary for defining and grounding the specialized science of economics.

Acknowledgments

I wish to thank Rob Tarr for discussion of issues in this essay and the editors of the present volume for very helpful comments on a previous draft.

Notes

1 A few paragraphs later she writes "I want to stress that our primary interest is not politics or economics as such, but *'man's nature and man's relationship to existence'* – and that we advocate capitalism because it is the only system geared to the life of a rational being. ... In this respect, there is a fundamental difference between our approach and that of capitalism's classical defenders and modern apologists."

2 See esp. "What Is Capitalism?," the introduction to CUI, and "For the New Intellectual" (*FTNI*). See also Lewis and Salmieri's discussion, 356, below.

3 See "Man's Rights" and "The Nature of Government" (both in *VOS* and *CUI*).

4 See *Atlas* 1009–1069, "The Objectivist Ethics" (*VOS*), "Who Is the Final Authority in Ethics?" (*VOR*), *ITOE*, and *OPAR* 37–186. See also, in this volume, 63–68, 78, 82–83, 107–112, and 291–300.

5 See also Chapters 3 and 4 of the present volume.

6 See "The Objectivist Ethics" and "The Ethics of Emergencies" (both in *VOS*), and *ITOE* 32–34.

7 In *Atlas* 1017, John Galt says in his radio broadcast: "You who speak of a 'moral instinct' as if it were some separate endowment opposed to reason – man's reason *is* his moral faculty. A process of reason is a process of constant choice in answer to the question: True or False? – *Right or Wrong?*"

8 See also Nathaniel Branden, "Mental Health versus Mysticism and Self-Sacrifice" (*VOS*).

9 See Darryl Wright's discussion of force, 176–177, above.

10 Moreover, force-initiators who seek to coercively control men's actions render thought purposeless – because an individual cannot make use of his conclusions to guide his pursuit of values – and so destroy the reality-oriented motivation that thought demands, further paralyzing man's mind. For more on Rand's view of force and mind, see *Atlas*, esp. 1022–1024 and 1089–1146, and *OPAR* 310–323.

11 For further discussion of Rand's views of the objectivity of knowledge, the objectivity of values, reason and volition, and the evil of the initiation of force, see, respectively, Chapters 11 and 12, 3 and 4, 5, and 7 in the present volume.

12 The metaphor of an intellectual pyramid is used in *Atlas* 1065; in "The Establishing of an Establishment" (*PWNI* 233), Rand refers to the point as the "pyramid of ability."

13 See esp. "Egalitarianism and Inflation" (*PWNI*).

14 For more on these theories of value, and why Rand regards them, and the underlying theories of subjectivism and intrinsicism in epistemology, as false dichotomies plaguing philosophy, see "For the New Intellectual" (*FTNI*), *ITOE*, "Who Is the Final Authority in Ethics?" (*VOR*), and *OPAR* 241–248. For discussion, see 67–68, 74–75, and 290–292 in the present volume.

15 See "The Objectivist Ethics" (*VOS*). On the issue of rewriting metaphysically given facts, see "The Metaphysical versus the Man-Made" (*PWNI*). See also, in the present volume, reverse order of these page numbers so 171–172 and 262–265.

16 The stenographer may continue to purchase a lot of lipstick and so repeatedly have insufficient funds to see a doctor, but the penalty she pays is precisely that she's repeatedly unable to afford to see a doctor. Because the free market does not mandate uniformity, other individuals are free to budget differently, and she is free to observe and learn from their example: to observe that their actions allow them to gain in a way that she does not.

17 Early in *Atlas*, Hank Rearden can find few buyers for Rearden Metal other than Taggart Transcontinental, but he forges ahead because he regards as irrational people's negative evaluation of Rearden Metal. Of course the fact that a product's socially objective value and so its market price may reflect non-objective evaluations and irrational decisions does not, for Rand, mean that the market price should be overridden. There is no way to force people to be rational (and no way to know what the price of a good would have been, had participants acted objectively).

18 For a penetrating discussion of Rand's distinction between socially objective value and philosophically objective value, see *OPAR* 395–400.

19 For Rand's view of the life-serving role of art and the nature of objective esthetic standards, see *RM*, *OPAR* ch. 12, and Chapters 16 and 17 of the present volume.

20 From Rand's perspective, therefore, it is an error to think of competition as the essence of a free market. "Competition is a by-product of productive work, *not* its goal. A creative man is motivated by the desire to achieve, *not* by the desire to beat others." Rand describes the latter desire as "shameful if and when it serves as a *primary* motive." And she criticizes Nixon for attempting to promote economic productivity by appeal to the "competitive spirit," saying that this amounts to erecting an "envy-ridden, 'competitive' second-hander as a national ideal" ("The Moratorium on Brains" *ARL* 1(2) 8).

21 As I understand the idea, the philosophically objective value of a product reflects directly volitional, indirectly volitional, and non-volitional factors: a fully rational mind, with the greatest attainable knowledge (in a given category, period, and context), and with the greatest intellectual and productive potential and ability. Though the philosophically objective value of a product serves as the teacher on a free market, it does so for "those willing to exercise their rational faculty, *each to the extent of his ability*. Those who are unwilling – as well as those who aspire *to more than their ability* produces" [emphases added] are penalized. This I interpret to mean that the philosophically objective and the socially objective values of a product will not (normally) coincide, even over time and if all market participants are rational. But for what I take to be a different view, see *OPAR* 399: "Market value, in essence, is the most rational assessment of a product that a free society can reach at a given time; and there is always a tendency for this assessment to approach the product's philosophically objective value, as people gain the requisite knowledge. In time, barring accidents, the two assessments coincide."

22 Galt says in his radio broadcast: "We are the *cause* of all the values that you covet, we who perform the process of *thinking* ... We taught you to know, to speak, to produce, to desire, to love. You who abandon reason – were it not for us who preserve it, you would not be able to fulfill or even to conceive your wishes. You would not be able to desire the clothes that had not been made, the automobile that had not been invented, the money that had not been devised, as exchange for goods that did not exist, the admiration that had not been experienced for men who had achieved nothing, the love that belongs and pertains only to those who preserve their capacity to think, to choose, to *value*" (*Atlas* 1038).

23 See also "The 'Conflicts' of Men's Interests" (*VOS*).

24 For discussion of more such issues, see *OPAR* 400–406.

25 See "Egalitarianism and Inflation" (*PWNI*), Greenspan, "Gold and Economic Freedom" (*CUI*), Branden, "Common Fallacies About Capitalism" (*CUI*), and *Atlas* 410–415 (the quote is from 413). When Greenspan wrote his article on gold and economic freedom, he was an advocate of laissez-faire; his later career suggests he changed his mind. On Greenspan's relationship to Rand, see 30, 32 and 33, above.

26 See also "The Pull Peddlers" (*CUI* 184–190). In "Egalitarianism and Inflation" (*PWNI*), Rand writes "In respect to its legitimate functions – which are the police, the army, the law courts – it [the government] performs a service needed by a productive economy. When a government steps beyond these functions, it becomes an economy's destroyer" (180).

27 Rand was particularly critical of the FCC and of the antitrust laws, viewing their non-objective powers as grave threats to intellectual and economic freedom. See, e.g., "Choose Your Issues," "Antitrust: The Rule of Unreason," and "'Have Gun, Will Nudge'" in *TON* 1(1–3). For discussion, see 210–211, above, and 357–359, below.

28 Rand argues that this principle applies in the intellectual realm as well, when government funds the sciences and arts. "Governmental encouragement does not order men to believe that the false is true: it merely makes them indifferent to the issue of truth or falsehood." And: "In business, the rise of the welfare state froze the status quo, perpetuating the power of the big corporations of the pre-income-tax era, placing them beyond the competition of the tax-strangled newcomers. A similar process took place in the welfare state of the intellect. The results, in both fields, are the same." See "The Establishing of an Establishment" (*PWNI*, quotes are from 222 and 231–232).

29 I discuss Rand's view of free will and character in Chapter 5, above.

30 See esp. "What Is Capitalism?" (*CUI*), and "The Missing Link" and "Selfishness Without a Self" (both in *PWNI*); the quote is from *CUI* 2.

31 For Rand's discussion of the mystic-altruist-collectivist axis, see "The Intellectual Bankruptcy of Our Age" (*VOR*) and "Is Atlas Shrugging?" (*CUI*). On the "public interest" see 210–211, above, and 358, below.

32 See "What Is Capitalism?" and "The Pull Peddlers" (both in *CUI*). See also, in the present volume, 191–192 and 212–213.

33 The term "pull peddler" is introduced in *Atlas* 913 (cf. 392–396, 404, 410–415). There it describes businessmen "whose only asset and sole investment consisted of an item known as 'friendship'" – i.e., influence over politicians. She would later use the phrase as the title for an article about lobbyists: "'Lobbying' is the activity of attempting to influence legislation by privately influencing the legislators. It is the result and creation of a mixed economy – of government by pressure groups. Its methods range from mere social courtesies and cocktail-party or luncheon 'friendships' to favors, threats, bribes, blackmail" ("The Pull Peddlers" *CUI* 186).

34 See, e.g., *Atlas* 496–498 for the cascading results of the loss of the nation's primary coal provider.

35 The economy-wide disintegration in *Atlas* is a macrocosm of the disintegration and destruction of the Twentieth Century Motor Company and Starnesville. Both disintegrations are driven by a non-objective approach to values – by the slogan "from each according to his ability, to each according to his need" and similar mystical-altruistic-collectivistic quests for the unearned.

36 See, e.g., "The Moratorium on Brains" (*ARL* 1(2); "Don't Let It Go" (*PWNI*); and "A Preview" *ARL* 1(22–24), "A Nation's Unity" *ARL* 2(1–3), and "The American Spirit" *ARL* 2(4).

37 A similar demoralization occurs in intellectual fields under statism, Rand argues, and there exists, she says, instead of a "pyramid of ability" a "pyramid of moral endurance" among those able to hold on. See "The Establishing of an Establishment" (*PWNI*). We witness these kinds of destruction in *Atlas*, as men like Dan Conway give up and men like Quentin Daniels never rise to the place they should. We see how the long-range plans of producers like Hank Rearden are dashed by legislative fiat. After Directive 10-289 is passed, Hank is reduced to a criminal's range-of-the-moment existence and creates little; for the first time in his life, he is bored to death.

38 *Atlas* describes the birth of several pull-peddling professions: the freezing of railroad bonds leads to the advent of "defreezers" (352), and Directive 10-289 lead to "many breeds" of pull peddlers: "those of 'transportation pull,' and of 'steel pull,' and 'oil pull' and 'wage-raise pull' and 'suspended sentence pull'" (912).

39 Within this basic pattern, Rand holds, there can be much variation. For instance, there are reasons why in *Atlas* it is not a flamboyant dictator but a zero like Mr. Thompson who rises to the very top of political power, while brutes like Meigs function (for a time) more on the periphery. Or, to take another example, in a later essay Rand comments: "It is the creators of wealth, the Hank Reardens,

who are destroyed under any form of statism – socialist, communist, or fascist; it is the parasites, the Orren Boyles, who are the privileged 'elite' and the profiteers of statism, particularly of fascism. (The special profiteers of socialism are the James Taggarts; of communism – the Floyd Ferrises)" ("The New Fascism: Rule by Consensus" *CUI* 245).

40 "Egalitarianism and Inflation" (*PWNI*), "The Moratorium on Brains" (*ARL* 1(2), "Don't Let It Go" (*PWNI*).

41 See also *OPAR* 402–406, and Binswanger 2011, 269–275.

42 For discussions of Rand's concept of psycho-epistemology, see 123–125, above, and 409, below.

43 See *ITOE* 104.

44 See "What Is Capitalism?" (*CUI* 1–9).

45 For more on Rand's view of the relation of philosophy to economics, see "Egalitarianism and Inflation" (*PWNI*) and *OPAR* 378–379. On the objectivity of concepts generally, see 289–292 in the present volume.

46 See *TON* 1(1), 1(2), 1(5), 1(9), 2(9), 3(9), and *TO* 10(8).

47 In 1996 George Reisman, a student of von Mises who had also been a student of Rand's (see above, 30) published *Capitalism: A Treatise on Economics* (Ottawa, IL: Jameson Books). The book is an attempt both to integrate the teachings of the Austrian and Classical schools of economics and to approach the science of economics from the base of Rand's philosophy.

48 In "Ideas v. Goods" (*ARL* 3(11)) and "Ideas v. Men" (*ARL* 3(15)), Rand comments on the errors, ignorance, and intellectual superficiality in a lecture given by an alleged free-market economist (Ronald H. Coase) who denies the relevance of morality to economics.

49 The quotes are from Hayek 1944, 35, 36; for Rand's remarks on them, see *Marginalia* 148–149.

References

Binswanger, Harry. 2011. "The Dollar and the Gun." In *Why Businessmen Need Philosophy*, revised and expanded edition, edited by Debi Ghate and Richard E. Ralston. New York, NY: New American Library.

Friedman, Milton. 2002. *Capitalism and Freedom: Fortieth Anniversary Edition*. Chicago, IL: University of Chicago Press. Reprint of *Capitalism & Freedom: A Leading Economist's View of the Proper Role of Competitive Capitalism*. Chicago, IL: University of Chicago Press. 1962.

Friedman, Milton, and George Stigler. 1946. *Roofs or Ceilings? The Current Housing Problem*. Irvington-on-Hudson, NY: The Foundation for Economic Education.

Hayek, Friedrich. 1944. *The Road to Serfdom*. Chicago, IL: University of Chicago Press.

Smith, Tara. 2000. *Viable Values: A Study of Life as the Root and Reward of Morality*. Lanham, MD: Rowman & Littlefield.

Part IV

The Foundations of Objectivism

11

Objectivist Metaphysics

The Primacy of Existence

JASON G. RHEINS

The heroes and villains of *Atlas Shrugged* are distinguished, ultimately, by their opposite metaphysical premises, and, speaking to an audience of college students, Rand argued that "the nature of your actions – and your ambition – will be different, according to which set of answers you come to accept" to the questions of metaphysics ("Philosophy: Who Needs It" *PWNI* 3). What are the questions – in a field whose name has become all but synonymous with abstruse speculation – whose answers Rand thought shape a person's character and fill a basic, practical human need? What are her answers to these questions, and how does she conceive of the alternatives? This chapter addresses these questions and aims to shed light on Rand's characteristic approach to metaphysical concepts and principles – an approach that focuses on their practical import, without being pragmatist; on their role in human existence, without being existentialist; and on their axiomatic, self-evident status, without being Cartesian.

Rand described the "province of *metaphysics*," as the "study of existence as such or, in Aristotle's words, of 'being qua being'" (*PWNI* 2). Unlike the other fields of human knowledge, which have a *specific* subject matter, metaphysics is about all that is. However, metaphysics does not endeavor to tell us everything about everything. It describes what holds true of a thing just insofar as it *exists*.

Metaphysics, then, is meant to deal with the most *fundamental* facts of reality. For a fact to be "fundamental" within a given context means that it gives rise to or causes the greatest number of other facts in that context, or that it is the fact on which the greatest number of other facts depend. Epistemologically, fundamental facts are those facts within a given context that must be known in order for the other facts to be known, and fundamental facts can explain the most other facts within that context.

For human beings, the most fundamental facts of reality include those that are absolutely fundamental in *any* context, but also ones specifically fundamental to *human* existence, including the fact that we are conscious, living animals, and certain unique but fundamental features of human consciousness. Thus, in addition to ontology, the study of existence as such, the Objectivist metaphysics also subsumes some topics of "philosophical anthropology," the basic

A Companion to Ayn Rand, First Edition. Edited by Allan Gotthelf and Gregory Salmieri.
© 2016 John Wiley & Sons, Ltd. Published 2016 by John Wiley & Sons, Ltd.

description of the essential characteristics of human nature.[1] The latter are discussed by Onkar Ghate in Chapter 5, while this chapter primarily focuses on the former.

To orient ourselves, we will begin by considering two quotations, which respectively provide a (partial) summary of what Rand regarded as the key questions of metaphysics and an outline of the central principle of her metaphysics:

> Are you [I] in a universe which is ruled by natural laws and, therefore, is stable, firm, absolute – and knowable? Or are you in an incomprehensible chaos, a realm of inexplicable miracles, an unpredictable, unknowable flux, which your mind is impotent to grasp? [II] Are the things you see around you real – or are they only an illusion? Do they exist independent of any observer – or are they created by the observer? Are they the object or the subject of man's consciousness? [III] Are they what they are – or can they be changed by a mere act of your consciousness, such as a wish? (*PWNI* 3, numerals are my addition)

Here, we begin to see the key issues of metaphysics (and their epistemological implications) that Rand is concerned with: Do things possess a determinate nature, one that is amenable to comprehension and prediction? Is what we perceive real and mind-independent or mind-dependent, being created or shaped by the perceiver? Does consciousness have the power to directly alter the facts of reality?

Where does Rand stand on these issues, and how does she characterize and understand the alternative positions? Here she writes of "the basic metaphysical issue that lies at the root of any system of philosophy: *the primacy of existence* or *the primacy of consciousness*" ("The Metaphysical Versus the Man-Made" *PWNI* 32). The "primacy of existence" is the view she endorses of existence, consciousness, and the relationship between them, while the "primacy of consciousness" names the opposite view. She summarizes the key points of the primacy of existence thus:

> The primacy of existence (of reality) is [A] the axiom that existence exists, i.e., that the universe exists independent of consciousness (of *any* consciousness), [B] that things are what they are, that they possess a specific nature, an *identity*. The epistemological corollary [C] is the axiom that consciousness is the faculty of perceiving that which exists – and that man gains knowledge of reality by looking outward. (*PWNI* 32, letters are my addition)

Thus the primacy of existence holds that there is a mind-independent reality, which can be perceived and understood by (human) consciousness, but which is not created or directly shaped by consciousness. This principle integrates the three primary axioms of Objectivist metaphysics:

The axiom of *existence*: "Existence exists" – what is, is;

The axiom of *identity*: "A is A" – each thing is what it is;

The axiom of *consciousness*: "Consciousness is conscious" – the *awareness* of reality is the awareness *of reality*.[2]

Together with the three primary axioms that it integrates, the primacy of existence forms the core of the Objectivist metaphysics.

Continuing the quote immediately above, Rand characterizes the alternative view, "the primacy of consciousness," in its purest expression as the view that:

> the universe has no independent existence, that it is the product of a consciousness (either human or divine or both). The epistemological corollary is the notion that man gains knowledge of reality

by looking inward (either at his own consciousness or at the revelations it receives from another, superior consciousness). (*PWNI* 32–33)[3]

Just as the primacy of existence stems from the joint acceptance of the three axioms above, the primacy of consciousness is based on the rejection of these axioms and "represents a reversal" of the priority between existence and consciousness.

The first section below concerns the axioms of existence and identity, their respective concepts, and then their validation and cognitive roles. The next two sections consider Rand's view of entities and causation. After that we will turn to consciousness, then to its dependence on existence (i.e., the primacy of existence). In the penultimate section we discuss Rand's view of free will (a fundamental feature of human consciousness) and the related distinction Rand draws between "metaphysically given" and "man-made" facts. We conclude with a word or two on the relationship between the primacy of existence and Rand's conception of objectivity. Throughout, reference will be made to the practical function of metaphysics: its guiding, cognitive role for all spheres of human life and thought, from the theoretical to the mundane.

The Axioms of Existence and Identity

According to Rand, the most fundamental fact and the first axiom of all metaphysics, all philosophy, indeed of all knowledge, is that "Existence exists." In this statement, "existence" is a collective noun referring to everything that exists, so the statement simply reaffirms the existence of whatever exists. Rand writes that this "repetition" is the only way to formulate as a proposition the basic fact grasped by the concept "existence," but she did not regard it as a vacuous tautology.

> Axioms are usually considered to be propositions identifying a fundamental, self-evident truth. But explicit propositions as such are not primaries: they are made of concepts. The base of man's knowledge – of all other concepts, all axioms, propositions and thought – consists of axiomatic concepts. (*ITOE* 55)

The axiom "*existence exists*" is an expression of the concept "existence," and it can only be a repetition, because "existence" is itself an *axiomatic concept* and, thus, an irreducible and unanalyzable primary.[4] However, the repetition serves a "special underscoring" function that Rand argues is "a matter of life and death for man" (*ITOE* 59). The axiom is a statement that there are things that exist, and it is a touchstone of thought, reminding us and emphasizing to us that all those things that exist *do* in fact exist. Thus, the axiom of existence names that most fundamental and basic fact that everything that is *exists*. This statement is perfectly universal in its scope: there is nothing it fails to refer to since, as Parmenides first recognized, there is nothing that "is not."[5] There is no non-existence; there is only what is, namely, *everything* that is.[6]

But why is this "a matter of life and death for man"? Firstly, the axiomatic concepts are cognitive necessities for conceptual beings who must be able to predict, plan for, and act with a view toward the future. To do so requires that we be able to generalize across cases and to relate past, present, and future.[7] This is only possible if we grasp that reality is one and continuous and that we, our conscious selves, are continuous. Rand writes:

> Axiomatic concepts are the *constants* of man's consciousness, the *cognitive integrators* that identify and thus protect its continuity ... [C]onceptual awareness is the only type of awareness capable of

247

integrating past, present and future ... It is only conceptual awareness that can grasp and hold the total of its experience – extrospectively, the continuity of existence; introspectively, the continuity of consciousness – and thus enable its possessor to project his course long-range. It is by means of axiomatic concepts that man grasps and holds this continuity, bringing it into his conscious awareness and *knowledge* ...

If the state of an animal's perceptual awareness could be translated into words, it would amount to a disconnected succession of random moments such as "Here now table – how now tree – here now man – I now see – I now feel," etc. – with ... only a few strands of memory in the form of "This now food" or "This now master." What a man's consciousness does with the same material, by means of axiomatic concepts, is: "The table exists – the tree exists – man exists – I am conscious." (*ITOE* 56–57)

Additionally, because conceptual consciousnesses are volitional and fallible, they must be able to distinguish states of mind (which may be errant) from the world.[8] Moreover, "existence" and the other axiomatic concepts help us mark off and steer clear of the "void of unreality" that we can cognitively stumble into (*ITOE* 59). A simple example is when a person catches herself spending too many cognitive resources on an unreal context – a world, say, in which she had made a slightly different decision that would have prevented her present problems – or when she senses that her course of action is increasingly quixotic. In such cases, one can remind oneself that only existence exists, and thus bring oneself back to reality and back to the kind of thinking that will make a difference in reality.[9]

A more radical example is the active evasion of the existence of unwelcome facts on the unspoken premise that what exists need not exist if one chooses not to acknowledge it (*Atlas* 1017–1018). Engaging in such evasion is the fundamental evil according to Rand's ethics, and it is dramatized in *Atlas Shrugged* by the lives of the villains – especially James Taggart:

> ... danger, to him, was a signal to shut off his sight, suspend his judgment and pursue an unaltered course, on the unstated premise that the danger would remain unreal by the sovereign power of his wish not to see it – like a fog horn within him, blowing, not to sound a warning, but to summon the fog. (*Atlas* 868)[10]

The only alternative to Taggart's manner of functioning is to remember and live by the axiom of existence, which is to accept that facts are facts and to think and act accordingly.

"Existence," like the other axiomatic concepts which we will discuss later, is an irreducible primary that cannot be defined, analyzed, or explained in any more primitive terms. Rand writes:

> An axiomatic concept is the identification of a primary fact of reality, which cannot be analyzed, i.e. reduced to other facts or broken into component parts. It is implicit in all facts and in all knowledge. It is the fundamentally given and directly perceived or experienced, which requires no proof or explanation, but on which all proofs and explanations rest. (*ITOE* 55)

One *defines* a concept by citing the features that distinguish its units from other existents – for example, one defines "human being" by citing the facts that distinguish human beings from other animals. But there is nothing from which one can similarly distinguish existence as such, for there are no non-existents.[11]

One *analyzes* an existent by breaking it down into component parts, either its literal parts or its distinguishable characteristics. For example, one analyzes water (H_2O) by reference to its constitutive ions of hydrogen (H+) and hydroxide (OH-), which in turn are understood by reference to the basic atomic elements of hydrogen and oxygen, and those elements in turn by reference to protons, electrons, neutrons, and so on. But there are no parts into which the fact of existing can be broken down, nor are there prior facts by reference to which it can be understood, since any such parts or facts would themselves have to exist. Likewise, Rand did not regard existence as an attribute of a subject such that it could be isolated in an analysis. Before any attribute could belong to the subject, the subject would have to exist.

Finally, one *explains* a fact by specifying other existents that cause or underlie it. For example, one can explain a black eye by analyzing it as a hematoma (bruise) due to burst capillaries, or, in another sense, one can explain it by its cause, the punch and the man who threw it. We have already seen that existence cannot be analyzed, and any attempt to explain it by reference to a cause would need to treat the cause as external to existence. There is nothing outside of existence to give rise to existence.[12] Thus, Rand thought that questions such as "Who created the universe?" or "Why is there something rather than nothing?" revealed "in what manner people do not believe that 'existence exists'" (*Biographical Interviews* 569).[13] One function of the axiom of existence is to make salient the mistakes behind such questions.

The axiom of *identity* holds that each thing is *itself*, or, as Rand frequently puts it: "A is A." The force of this statement is perfectly captured in Bishop Butler's famous remark, "Every thing is what it is, and not another thing."[14] "Identity" names the fact that everything that is is something in particular. A given thing's identity is the sum total of all of its characteristics. Synonyms for something's "identity" might be its "character" or its "nature," so long as it is understood that a thing's identity at any given moment refers to all of its attributes, actions, relations, and so on.

Like "existence," the concept "identity" denotes a primary – something that is not subject to definition, analysis, or explanation. One can elaborate on the concept as I have done here, or restate the idea in different (equivalent) ways, but there is nothing more primitive by reference to which we can analyze or explain a thing's being what it is. (The same goes for the axiom of identity's corollary, the law of non-contradiction, which states that a thing is not what it is not.)

The axioms of existence and identity are closely related. Both are universal in scope, applying to all existents. And in one very important respect, they do not even designate distinct facts: having an identity is not something over and above existing, as though it were possible to merely *be*, without *being something*.[15] Rand emphasized this point saying, "Existence is Identity."[16] However the two axioms are distinct in what they underscore.[17] As applied to a specific existent, the axiom of existence reminds us that it *is*, whereas the axiom of identity reminds us that it is *what it is*.

For example, if one were to pretend, as Galileo's detractors did, that the mountains and craters observable on the surface of the Moon do not exist, then the axiom of existence would chasten him. Similarly, if one were to persist in maintaining that something is *other* than it really is, for example, that the collapse of the banking system *is not* an economic crisis, then the Law of Identity would name his fundamental error. However, because existence is identity, the difference between these errors is itself a matter of emphasis or formulation: that the moon *is not* a perfect sphere and that *there are* craters and mountains on the moon are two ways of formulating the same fact.

The Epistemological Basis and Function of the Axioms

How are the axioms known? Rand maintained that the fundamental facts identified by the axioms of metaphysics are known in some form by all human beings – indeed by all conscious creatures – for the awareness of this basic fact is implicit in every act of perception. It is, she would say, perceptually self-evident.

In calling the axioms not merely "self-evident" but "*perceptually* self-evident," Rand means that the facts necessary to validate the axioms can be directly perceived and that everything that can ever be grasped by means of an axiomatic concept is present in each act of sense perception.

A single act of perception by an infant or an animal does not include in it the concepts necessary to formulate this information explicitly. It includes only the *content* that an adult human being can conceptualize in this way. However, an adult knows nothing more about what it is to exist than an infant does, even if the adult knows about the existence of many more things. But what is evident to even the child or the animal in an act of perception is that there *is* something. It is in this sense that Rand believes that to perceive anything is the fully sufficient grounds for knowing that it (thus something) *is* (= existence), and that it is *whatever* it is (= identity). Thus the axiomatic concepts of "existence" and "identity" are implicit in perception. The axiomatic concept of "consciousness" (discussed in detail below) is likewise implicit in perception, that is, in what is a *conscious* activity.

Because the axioms are implicit in all acts of awareness, and because they must be presupposed for any knowledge or any form of proof to be valid, they cannot themselves be "proven." They can only be directly perceived. The axioms of metaphysics are for Rand, like for Aristotle, indemonstrable. However, according to both Rand and Aristotle it is demonstrable that the axioms are *axioms* – that is, it can be proven that they are primary and fundamental such that all other knowledge is posterior to and dependent upon them.

The type of argument by which it is demonstrated that the axioms are themselves indemonstrable *and* that they cannot even be coherently denied (i.e., that they are presupposed in all cognition) is traditionally known as "reaffirmation through denial," although Aristotle refers to it in the *Metaphysics* as an "elenchtic" or "refuting demonstration" (Aristotle *Metaphysics* Γ.3–4).[18] In such an argument, the very attempt to deny an axiom refutes the denier, since the meaningfulness or force of his would-be denial is shown to presuppose the axiom in question. For instance, to say that one is denying "existence exists" one must grant existence to oneself or at least to one's statement of denial. Similarly, one cannot coherently deny the axiom of identity, for one's denial of it would not even be a denial unless things are what they are and not something else.

If the axioms are omnipresent and perceivable, then why formulate them *explicitly?* The distinctively human mode of conceptual cognition gives mature human beings the ability and the need to hold this knowledge in the form of explicit concepts and propositions. We need this because merely perceiving a fact does not force us to *accept* it or enable us to accept it *consistently* by adhering to its implications in all departments of knowledge and areas of life. Holding the axioms explicitly guides us at the conceptual level, helping to prevent certain sorts of errors and evasions.

The axioms of existence and identity serve the needs of a conceptual consciousness, "a consciousness capable of conceptual errors, that needs a special identification of the directly given, to embrace and delimit the entire field of its awareness – to delimit it from the void of unreality to which conceptual errors can lead" (*ITOE* 58–59). Without the axioms to serve as "epistemological guidelines," one can stray into that "void of unreality" in which one can evade even the most crucial facts for human existence – that is, the facts of human nature.

> All the disasters that have wrecked your world, came from your leaders' attempt to evade the fact that A is A. All the secret evil you dread to face within you and all the pain you have ever endured, came from your own attempt to evade the fact that A is A. The purpose of those who taught you to evade it, was to make you forget that Man is Man. (*Atlas* 1016)

Thus, while the axioms are perceptually self-evident and are implicit in every act of awareness, their consistent application at the conceptual level is not automatic. It becomes ever more possible to fail to adhere to them as one's thought becomes more abstract, which is to say more removed from sense perception. It therefore becomes essential to formulate *explicitly* these fundamental facts into principles to help us retain our ties to reality. Where one cannot immediately *see* that what is is or that A is A, it becomes possible to misclassify things, to succumb to confirmation bias and selective observation, to waste effort pursuing ill-formed questions, and so forth. Even worse, people who seek to evade the facts of reality will actively seize upon these possibilities. The axioms, formulated explicitly as principles, are also the cognitive defense of the intellectually honest from the creeds by which evaders attempt to subvert reality in order to fulfill their whims or to prolong their illusions. To better illustrate these points, we shall consider the application of the axioms of existence and identity to logic and cosmology.

The axioms of existence and (especially) identity play the same role in Rand's philosophy as is played in Aristotle's by the propositions that he identified as "common axioms," such as the Law of Non-Contradiction.[19] They are *primary* facts about reality and so give rise to the *fundamental rules of thought* – that is, to logic.[20] They *must* be grasped and adhered to by human beings because it is possible for human thought to veer off from existence, and even to suppose that there is some alternative to existence or that a thing can be other than what it is.

Rand's Aristotelian approach to metaphysical axioms should be distinguished from the "rationalist" approach (represented by such thinkers as Descartes and Spinoza) according to which metaphysics or knowledge in general consists of self-evident axioms and the theorems that are then deduced from them.[21] Like Aristotle, Rand does not attempt to derive from "existence" and the Law of Identity any specific claims about the particular kinds of things that exist or their natures.[22] At the same time, the Aristotelian approach should also be contrasted with the constructivist view (represented by Peano, Russell, and others) according to which axioms are mere truths of language, conventions, or propositions chosen pragmatically for their capacity to generate subsequent theorems. For Aristotle and Rand, the axioms are the proper principles of thought only because they identify fundamental metaphysical facts.

The traditional laws of logic are the Law of Identity, and Aristotle's first two "common axioms": The Law of Non-Contradiction, and the Law of the Excluded Middle. Rand regards the Laws of Non-Contradiction and the Excluded Middle as corollaries of Identity. The Law of Non-Contradiction takes the law of identity (that *A is A*) and extends it into a proscription against the denial of Identity, that is, against what identity renders meaningless and impossible. Consider, again Butler's formulation that "Every thing is what it is, and not another thing." The Law of Identity would be the first part "Every thing is what it is." Non-Contradiction is the negative emphasis of the second part: "and not another thing." A is A, and thus A is not non-A, that is, anything *other than* A. The Law of the Excluded Middle takes this one step further: if everything has a definite and non-contradictory identity, then for any well-defined attribute X, a given subject is either X or it is non-X (where that means being anything other than X).[23]

While they constrain our thoughts to the non-contradictory, the axioms do not and cannot specify which specific existents with what specific identities there are (or are not) to be discovered in the world. That is to say that Rand does not believe that the content of the natural or human sciences can be deduced from metaphysics. She thought that the area of science that has most frequently and disastrously been encroached upon by overweening metaphysics is cosmology. For example, she wrote that, after "Aristotle established the right metaphysics by establishing the law of identity," he "destroyed his metaphysics by his cosmology – by the whole nonsense of the 'moving spheres,' 'the immovable mover,' teleology, etc." Her paradigm example of this error was Thales' attempt "to prove by philosophical means that everything is literally and physically made of water or that water is a kind of universal 'little stuff.'" This approach amounts to "rationalizing from an arrested state of knowledge" so that "every new step in physics has to mean a new metaphysics." As a result, "philosophy has dangled on the strings of physics ever since the Renaissance" (*Papers* 033_15x_012_003–005/*Journals* 698–699).

However, there are certain positions that might be called "cosmological" that Rand thought were implicit in the axioms of existence and identity. Chief among these implications is that the universe as a whole is eternal, and that the idea that it could be "created" or "destroyed" is incoherent. Rand held to this on metaphysical grounds similar to those of Parmenides and Aristotle.

> To grasp the axiom of existence exists, means to grasp the fact that nature, i.e., the universe as a whole, cannot be created or annihilated, that it cannot come into or go out of existence. (*PWNI* 33)

> "Creation" does not (and metaphysically cannot) mean the power to bring something into existence out of nothing. "Creation" means the power to bring into existence an arrangement (or combination or integration) of natural elements that had not existed before. (*PWNI* 34)

It is existence (not non-existence) that exists, so there is no "nothing" from which existence could come to be or pass away into.

This is not a denial of any specific claims about the observable history of the cosmos, but of faulty metaphysical claims. Consider the "Big Bang," which is currently thought to have occurred 13.8 billion years ago. Rand's metaphysics is silent on the question of whether or not an ancient expansion is responsible for the present state of the universe or those parts of it that are currently observable; but it does say that if so, it was an expansion of *something* that already existed. The idea of the universe exploding into existence from nothing is incoherent, and in fact it is not something that is (or could be) supported by physical evidence; rather, it is a *metaphysical* view or interpretation that certain people (some of whom happen to be physicists) have about the significance of an event for which there is physical evidence. If there was a Big Bang, metaphysics tells us that the universe existed before it in *some* form. It cannot tell us in what specific form it existed: for example, it cannot tell us whether the Big Bang was preceded by a "Big Crunch" (as some physicists believe) or even an infinite number of such crunches and bangs. It can only tell us that, if there was such a crunch or if there is one to come, it will not be a collapse into non-existence.

Likewise, consider the statement that "elements" or "matter" can be rearranged but not created or destroyed. If we interpret this as a *metaphysical* principle, then "element" cannot be referring to any specific chemical elements (e.g., to those arranged on the Periodic Table), and "matter" cannot be referring specifically to mass or any particular form of mass-energy. These terms merely denote the ultimate constituents of the universe, whatever these constituents may be. The specific identities of the constituents and the forms they can take is something to be discovered by the physical sciences. Metaphysics says only that they neither come into existence from nothing, nor pass away into nothing. Furthermore, Rand refused to speculate about the categorical status of yet to be discovered sub-atomic existents. That is to say that she did not believe that one could mandate, *a priori*, that what would be found would even be entities conceptually distinguishable from their qualities or actions.[24]

There are other limitations that Rand thought metaphysics places on physical theories. On the grounds of the axiom of identity, she maintained that the universe contains a definite and therefore finite amount of matter (or whatever it is that things are ultimately constituted from), since positing an "infinite" amount would mean that the matter lacked a *specific* quantity, and in this respect would lack identity.[25] Her position here is much like Aristotle's, and also like Aristotle, she denied that there are voids.[26] Here "void" must be understood in a strictly metaphysical sense as a place where there is literally nothing, not just a lack of massive bodies.[27]

Entities

Once a child has an implicit grasp of "existence," but before he can grasp "identity," he must implicitly grasp the concept of "entity." A constant flux of inconstant and disparate sensations would not afford the child adequate grounds to grasp "identity" even implicitly. That is to say that on the way to seeing that things have identities, they must first grasp that the world is made up of stable "things."

> (It may be supposed that that the concept "existent" is implicit even on the level of sensations – if and to the extent that a consciousness is able to discriminate on that level ... A sensation does not tell man *what* exists, but only *that* it exists.)
> The (implicit) concept "existent" undergoes three stages of development in man's mind. The first stage is the awareness of objects, of things – which represents the (implicit) concept "*entity*." The second and closely allied stage is the awareness of specific, particular things which he can recognize and distinguish from the rest of his perceptual field – which represents the (implicit) concept "*identity*".
> (*ITOE* 6)

What is the significance of beginning with an awareness "of objects, of things"? Rand held what she referred to as an Aristotelian (as against a Platonic) view of reality. Part of what she meant by this is that everything that exists is a particular with a determinate identity. The universal "forms" or "ideas" that Plato posited do not exist: there is no beauty, or circularity, or manness, apart from particular beautiful things, circles, and men. Rand argued that universal concepts (such a "man," "circle," and "beautiful") are categorizations of particulars formed by the human mind on the basis of observed facts about the particulars. However, her own view of the process by which these categorizations are formed and its metaphysical basis is different from Aristotle's view – "moderate realism" – as it is usually understood and as Rand understood it (*ITOE* 2, 307). In particular, she denies universal essences that exist within the individual members of a kind (e.g., a universal manness that exists in all men). Nevertheless, like Aristotle and unlike nominalists (e.g., Berkeley, Hume, Wittgenstein, and Quine), she maintained that there is a metaphysical basis for the particular categorizations we form and for identifying certain features as essential.[28]

Rand's metaphysics is Aristotelian in another, related respect. Aristotle distinguished between different "categories" of existents: entities (which he called "substances"), actions, qualities, relations, and so on, and he regarded individual entities as fundamental to all other existents. Rand endorsed this position, explaining: "What [Aristotle] meant is that the primary existent is an entity. And then aspects of an entity can be identified mentally, but only in relation to the entity. There are no attributes without entities[;] there are no actions without entities" (*ITOE* 264).

Actions are always the actions of *some* entity, attributes are the attributes of an entity (or of another attribute or action which is ultimately of some entity), and for a relationship to exist is for some entitles (or their respective attributes, actions, etc.) to stand in it.

This Aristotelian view of categories can also be contrasted with those metaphysical systems that take either actions or events/states of affairs (understood as mosaics of properties) as metaphysically fundamental, and treat entities as their conglomeration, as apparent islands of stability within the kaleidoscope of sensations, formed when several different activities or qualities temporarily coincide.[29]

Speaking from the point of view of Rand's metaphysics, Nathaniel Branden responds to this view as follows:

> When neo-mystics challenge the concept of "entity" and announce that, "naive" reason not withstanding, all that exists is change and motion – ("There is no *logical* impossibility in walking occurring as an isolated phenomenon, not forming part of any such series as we call a 'person,'" writes Bertrand Russell) – they are sweeping aside the fact that only the existence of entities makes the concepts "change" and "motion" *possible*; that "change" and "motion" presuppose *entities* which change and move; and that the man who proposes to dispense with the concept of "entity" loses his logical right to the concepts of "change" and "motion": having dropped their genetic root, he no longer has any way to make them meaningful and intelligible. ("The Stolen Concept" *TON* 2(1) 2)[30]

In addition to the points about metaphysical dependence already made, Branden's argument presupposes Rand's view that integrated objects (i.e., entities) rather than isolated sense-data are the given in sense perception. In the view Russell takes in *The Analysis of Mind*, which Branden refers to above, the only true particulars are discrete sensations experienced at precise moments. Russell thought that so-called "individuals" (e.g., a cat) are in fact the amalgamation of many such particulars. He concludes from this that there is no basis for thinking that actions or attributes depend on entities. However, Rand has a different view of what is perceptually given and so sees this issue very differently. On Rand's view, the various attributes of an individual (e.g., the color of the cat's nose, the sway of its tail, etc.) can only exist as "parts" or (more precisely) *aspects* of the individual, and can only be grasped in isolation from the individual by means of abstraction.[31]

For human beings and other animals with sense perception, entities – the perceptually given – are first and foremost individual, physical objects. Thus at the starting point of our cognition and practical engagement with the world, actions, attributes, relationships, and so on are always at least initially perceived as the attributes, actions, and so on *of some entity*. Once we reach higher levels of abstraction, we can speak of the attributes, relationships, actions, and so on of things other than individual, physical entities.

On the other hand, Rand does not wish to over privilege the ontological categories of the human scale by presuming that they can be extended to all other scales. This is pursuant to her deliberate opposition to letting metaphysics do the work of cosmology. For instance, Rand refused to pontificate about the categorization of undiscovered levels of physical reality. She did not think that metaphysics could tell us whether, as science progresses deeper into the sub-atomic domain, those "things" that it will discover shall easily fit the category of entity or if other aspects of their identity will fall into the same subordinate categories familiar at the perceptual level in the same ways (e.g., attribute, action).[32] All that metaphysics guarantees is that they would "be" whatever they are and "do" whatever they do. Metaphysics cannot tell us that they must be bodies that have extension or mass, for instance.

Moreover, Rand was intentionally flexible in her usage of the term "entity." Unlike Aristotle, she does not limit entities to everyday sized objects (and god), nor claim that natural entities are more fully entities than artificially crafted ones. What counts as an entity will vary from context to context, and Rand was prepared to call any combination or conglomeration of other entities an "entity" as well, so long as there was something uniting its parts in such a way that there is something we could learn about that "entity" as a whole. The unity need not be physical: it could be glue sticking together a pile of dirt to make it a "clod," or the laws holding together the people in a given area to make them a "nation." Similarly, she would call any part of an entity an entity, so long as there were some informative basis for distinguishing it from other parts of the whole. Whether there is such a basis is not determined by a general metaphysical rule or principle of individuation. It does not depend on an *a priori* rule about spatial distinctness, for example. (Rand is prepared to call a valley an entity, or a walk-in closet an entity distinct from the room.) It is an epistemic judgment, specific to that context, of whether the factors uniting or dividing suffice to make it worthwhile to refer separately to that part or conglomeration, and thus call it an "entity."[33]

Causality

We have seen that, on a generally Aristotelian metaphysics, actions presuppose entities (broadly conceived). Moreover, specific actions presuppose entities of specific sorts: an iguana cannot perform a symphony, a battleship cannot fly, and reality cannot contain actual contradictions. What a given entity can and must do in a given circumstance is determined by the entity's identity. Thus Rand sees causality as a corollary of identity:

> The law of causality is the law of identity applied to action. All actions are caused by entities. The nature of an action is caused and determined by the nature of the entities that act; a thing cannot act in contradiction to its nature. (*Atlas* 1037)

Identity is the fact that each thing is what it is. And it is because an entity is precisely what it is that it does precisely what it does. A penny cannot behave like a wooden barrel, a man cannot (successfully) behave on instinct like a wolf or a sheep. The Law of Causality identifies the fundamental fact that each entity will do what is in its nature to do and that it can do nothing else. A shoddily constructed bridge will collapse under the weight of a train, because it cannot bear the weight that a properly built bridge can and will. An open flame will eventually burn human flesh, but a bowl of cool water will not.

Notice that, on this Aristotelian conception of causality, a cause, in the first instance, is an entity, while effects are the actions of the entity. This view of entities as causes was generally accepted among the Ancient Greek philosophers. Since the seventeenth century (and especially after David Hume in the eighteenth century) it has become common to think of causality as a relationship between two successive events (or states), and the subsequent debate has been whether the earlier event (the cause) *necessitates* the latter (the effect) or merely regularly precedes it.[34] Hume famously concluded that there is no (knowable) necessary connection between one set of simple "impressions" or "ideas" and the next. Rand rejected the modern conception of causality because she denied that there can be actions or changes or events without things that act or change. The "necessary connection," she maintained, is not between an event and another event, but between what a thing is and what it therefore does or can do.[35]

By specifying that actions do not come about without the appropriate causes, the Law of Causality identifies the fact that results cannot be obtained without the proper means. As Galt puts it in his speech, "The law of identity does not permit you to have your cake and eat it, too. The law of causality does not permit you to eat your cake *before* you have it" (*Atlas* 1037). This means that if one seeks an effect one must earn it by enacting its cause(s). This is how the heroes in *Atlas Shrugged* behave, while the villains characteristically seek the "*unearned.*" Whether it be wealth that they did not create, credit for what they did not do, or undeserved love, they seek effects divorced from their causes. Worse, they impede or destroy the causes of the effects they seek (namely, the creative and productive activity of the heroes).

One theme of the novel is that seekers of the unearned attempt not only to defy the law of causality but also to reverse it – attempting to achieve a cause by means of its effects. Galt explains:

> The corollary of the *causeless* in matter is the *unearned* in spirit.
>
> Whenever you rebel against causality, your motive is the fraudulent desire, not to escape it, but worse: to reverse it. You want unearned love, as if love, the effect, could give you personal value, the cause – you want unearned admiration, as if admiration, the effect, could give you virtue, the cause – you want unearned wealth, as if wealth, the effect, could give you ability, the cause ... (*Atlas* 1038)[36]

For instance, by appearing to be responsible for Taggart Transcontinental's successes, James Taggart hopes to gain the respect that is properly due to his sister, Dagny. To what end? In deceiving others, he hopes to deceive himself; by receiving credit, he erroneously believes that he will feel as if he deserved it, and this will afford him self-esteem (though, in fact, self-esteem is impossible to a man devoid of virtue).

Galt indicts a number of influential theories as mere rationalizations for such reversals:

> you support the doctrines of your teachers, while they run hog-wild proclaiming that [*apud* Keynes] spending, the effect, creates riches, the cause, that [*apud* Marx] machinery, the effect, creates intelligence, the cause, that [*apud* Freud] your sexual desires, the effect, create your philosophical values, the cause. (*Atlas* 1038)[37]

As this quote indicates, Rand's account of causality is not limited to entities (in the narrow, primary sense), even though it centers on them. In many contexts, existents that fall into other ontological categories can and should also be considered causes. What remains the same is that *something* with a certain identity is responsible for a certain kind of result. This will be true when we consider consciousness, as well; that the mind has a definite identity and is a cause of certain kinds of mental and physical activities is central to Rand's approach to the third and last axiom: consciousness.

Consciousness

The third (and final) axiom of Rand's metaphysics is that "consciousness is conscious." As in the case of "existence exists" the repetition is a means to underscoring and giving propositional form to an axiomatic concept. Like "existence" and "identity," the axiomatic concept of "consciousness" is a foundation of and is implicit in all other knowledge. In one sense, the concept of "consciousness" is more limited in scope than "identity" or "existence." These concepts include everything (including consciousness), while consciousness is "an attribute of certain living entities."[38] However, the axiom of consciousness is universal in the sense that it is applicable to every thought, feeling, perception, and so on that one has and to every act of perceiving, imagining, thinking, and so on. "Consciousness" here refers to any state of awareness: "the units of the concept 'consciousness,'" Rand writes, "are every state or process of awareness that one experiences, has ever experienced or will ever experience (as well as similar units, a similar faculty, which one infers in other living entities)" (*ITOE* 56).

In being aware of any fact of reality, there is a conscious being that is aware: "Existence exists – and the act of grasping that statement implies two corollary axioms: that something exists which one perceives and that one exists possessing consciousness, consciousness being the faculty of perceiving that which exists" (*Atlas* 1015). In calling consciousness "the faculty of perceiving that which exists," Rand is referring to the fact that consciousness is principally a faculty of awareness of reality. Consciousness is axiomatic and implicit in all knowledge: the mind must be aware of reality for there to be knowledge. Indeed, Rand held that the concept of "knowledge" only has meaning if existence and consciousness are distinct and the latter is of the former (*ITOE* 57). As with the other axioms, it is self-refuting to deny the axiom of consciousness, that is, to deny that one is conscious. If one denies the validity of consciousness as such, then one refutes oneself. If we know nothing, then we do not even know that.

On Rand's view, sense perception is the primary form of consciousness possessed by animals, and it is a direct grasp of reality. The modes of perception differ in form, in the aspects of reality to which they are attuned, and in the range and precision of their discriminations. But the objects of perception – whatever facts of reality a sense modality is sensitive to – are, according to Rand, a part of reality itself, and not merely "representations" or "images" of reality within consciousness. Rand takes a direct realist and infallibilist view of perception: the senses give us an awareness of reality that is direct and inerrant.[39]

Rand rejected the notion that consciousness simply could be generating its own sensory content, in the manner of a perpetual hallucination, or as in various forms of idealism. As Rand puts it, "consciousness conscious of nothing but itself is a contradiction in terms" (*Atlas* 1015; cf. *ITOE* 246 and 55).[40] For her, first and foremost, consciousness is the grasp of existence beyond itself, that is, the "external" world. Eventually humans can become self-aware by reflecting on the nature of their awareness of external things. But were there no awareness of other things to begin with, consciousness would have nothing to grasp or perceive in its self-identification. On Rand's view there is no self-consciousness without consciousness, that is, consciousness of an external world.

The impossibility of a total failure of consciousness is implicit in the axiom of consciousness. Consciousness is primarily awareness, and awareness is relational. Consciousness thus has no content of its own; there is no way it can execute its primary function without things other than itself to serve as relata. If the objects of consciousness were not existent prior to the awareness of them, then they could not be perceived. The very idea of a state of consciousness that fails to present us with reality can only be conceived of if one first has a grasp of reality and knowledge of veridical states of awareness to compare a dream or hallucination against.

The concept of "consciousness" thus serves as a defense against skepticism. This includes various forms of philosophical skepticism, but also certain kinds of everyday self-doubt. For instance, early in *Atlas Shrugged*, when James casts vague and baseless doubts on Dagny's well-reasoned conclusions about Rearden Metal, she responds by deploying the axiom: "When I see things, I see them" (*Atlas* 21). Cognition can go wrong in various ways, but it also can and does go right. The repetition of the axiom serves as a reminder that one does indeed know things, and can do so even when it is difficult; it helps one to muster courage when in uncharted territory and to maintain confidence in one's conclusions when facing opposition.

Rand also held that there was a wider meaning of "consciousness." She did not think that every aspect of consciousness is an immediate and infallible direct grasp of reality like sense perception. In the case of human conceptual error, our rational faculties *fail* to grasp reality (or we fail to even try, when we evade). Some activities of consciousness, such as a choice to move, are directive of action, rather than cognitive grasps. So, not every state of consciousness is a perception of reality, when "consciousness" is taken broadly. However, even in this sense, to say that "consciousness is conscious" is still to state the existence and identity of consciousness; it *exists*, and it is consciousness, not non-consciousness. Thus we who possess consciousness are conscious; we are not automata. Our conscious states are just that: conscious states, and not whatever objects or ends that they purport to be aware of or to be moving us toward. To deny consciousness in this sense, as eliminative materialists do, is also self-refuting. One cannot claim to *believe, think, conclude,* or *have reasons* for denying consciousness, unless one has the *conscious states* of believing, thinking, judging, and so on.

Consciousness, like existence and identity, is a primary and fundamental fact of reality, which means both that it cannot be demonstrated from something else and it cannot be decomposed into other things in order to define it.

According to Rand, one cannot prove that there is consciousness, in as much as proofs and the concept of "proof" presuppose consciousness. There would be no mind that required proof if there were there no minds. Nor would any evidence any mind adduced count toward a proof either that there is consciousness or that it is the awareness of reality, unless the faculty of awareness had some real grasp of reality.

Rand also held that consciousness is not completely reducible to non-consciousness. While consciousness depends upon the proper functioning of certain body parts of living animals, states of consciousness are not identical with those body parts or with the physical activities that they perform. The denial of one for not being the other is, according to Rand, an invalid ultimatum that one poses to reality: that all things must fit one's impoverished conceptual scheme (e.g., idealism or materialism) or else not exist. Consciousness has its own distinct identity and its properties need not be reducible to or identical with the physical properties of the (physical) objects of consciousness, including those physical objects (brains, eyes, etc.) that are the organs of consciousness. Rand, then, is a kind of dualist. She frequently emphasizes that man is "an indivisible entity of matter and consciousness," and that it is a serious failure to neglect either side of this duality.[41] But she does not mean this in a Cartesian way. Consciousness is not a substance or independent entity – consciousness is "inseparable" from its material organs. It is a kind of activity performed by certain kinds of entities. Nevertheless, it has properties and features of its own that are not reducible to strictly physical properties. For human conceptual consciousness, one such feature is volition, discussed below and in Chapter 5, above, at some length.

The Primacy of Existence

While consciousness is in an important sense irreducible, it is not primary in every sense. According to Rand, existence precedes consciousness; something must first be before there can be awareness of it.[42] As we saw, this implies that the awareness of something independent of awareness itself is a precondition of the eventual possibility of self-consciousness. That is, extrospection must always precede introspection. When a child learns to distinguish her own awareness of things from the existence of the things of which she is aware, she is recognizing, implicitly, that her own mind is not the creator or sustainer of the objects which she perceives; they do not depend on her. The content of her awareness depends on them. When formulated explicitly, as a principle of metaphysics, this is the Primacy of Existence.

The Primacy of Existence can basically be explicated in two ways that differ in their emphases but make the same claim. Emphasizing the "consciousness" side of things, the Primacy of Existence states that consciousness is receptive rather than creative – it does not create its object.[43] This is an integration of "identity" with "consciousness" – a statement of the nature (and limits) of consciousness. If one were to ask what is consciousness's identity, the answer would be: to be aware of what is, but not to make it. In Rand's words, "Consciousness is Identification" (*Atlas* 1016).

Emphasizing the "existence" side of things, the Primacy of Existence states that the world is mind-independent. Things are what they are whether or not there is consciousness of them. Relating "existence" to "consciousness," the Primacy of Existence attributes *ontological* and *justificatory* priority to existence over consciousness, which respectively mean that something must first exist before we can be conscious of it, and the contents of consciousness (in cases where they are fallible) must be shown to comply with existence.[44]

Obviously some things in the world are, in various senses of the term, "mind-dependent." Perception, concepts, thoughts, and so on depend upon a living thing possessing consciousness, of which they are parts. The mind has "states," activities, or, in the case of individual items of knowledge such as a concept, a unique category that Rand called "mental 'entities'" ("entities" typically kept in scare-quotes to remind her reader that such a thing was not to be regarded as a literal entity). By claiming that the world is mind-independent, Objectivism does not mean to deny that there are minds, nor that agents can make up their own minds, nor even that consciousness is a cause of events in the world – for when a rational agent uses her mind to decide to do something, the resultant action will alter the rest of existence.

The point is, rather, that whatever exists has the identity it does, not because some subject is conscious of it, but simply because it *exists* and has *identity*. This is the case even with regard to the existence and identity of acts of consciousness. For example, if I am fantasizing about someone whom I desire, then I really am having those thoughts, regardless of whether I am keeping track of my day-dreaming or whether I am willing to identify and admit to myself this desire. Moments from now, it will still be the case that I had those thoughts and attendant emotions, even if I deny or attempt to repress them. It is in that sense that the Primacy of Existence claims that all things in existence, including mental "entities," are "mind-independent." Likewise, whether or not I have the honesty (and introspective capacity) to identify these feelings and admit them to myself is a measure and a means of my fidelity to the facts of reality. A distinctive trait of Rand's heroes is their brutal honesty with themselves about their motives and emotions. For example, throughout *Atlas Shrugged*, Rearden insists on making his motives explicit even when he (mistakenly) thinks that they brand him as immoral. By contrast (as we have seen) villains such as James Taggart go to great lengths to conceal *from themselves* their true motives.

Onkar Ghate discusses this issue in more detail in Chapter 5. Here it is worth noting that the sort of dishonesty displayed by her villains is indicative of a reversal of the relationship between consciousness and existence. Rand considered this the antithesis of her own view and dubbed it the Primacy of Consciousness. In a metaphysics committed to the Primacy of Consciousness, the nature of reality or the existence of the universe itself is established by some consciousness. The simplest example would be a theistic conception in which an antecedently existing God or some divine mind(s) decides how the world should be or even that it should be at all. On such a view there is an absolute starting point; i.e., the theist answers the child's innocent query, "Then who made God?" not with an infinite regress of Ur-Gods, but with the assertion that God is an absolute – "No one made God. God has always been." In so saying, the theist accepts that there must be some starting point, but opts that that starting point be a consciousness rather than existence. Conversely, on the Primacy of Existence, reality is taken to be a given, making questions about its purpose in existing or its ultimate cause inherently misguided.

Rand identifies a given philosophical system as committed to the Primacy of Consciousness if and when it takes the facts of existence to be dependent on consciousness (or multiple consciousnesses) and/or takes the content of consciousness as a primary, which is not answerable to antecedent standards set by reality, and which sets conditions on existence.

Free Will

As we have seen, Rand held that consciousness, like everything else in existence, has an identity, and that its identity is not the power to create reality, but principally to grasp it. Beyond direct sensory perception, this awareness is not an immediate and infallible grasp of reality. The human, *conceptual* level of consciousness is neither an infallible nor an *automatic* grasp of reality. For Rand this meant that part of the identity of a rational consciousness is its being volitional ("The Objectivist Ethics" *VOS* 21).

The fundamental locus of the power of volition is the conceptually conscious being's "primary choice." Rand calls this primary choice, whereby a human being chooses to actively orient his mind, the choice "to focus" or "to think" (*VOS* 22).[45] For our purposes, it will suffice to point out that, according to Rand, the primary choice (and subsequent or secondary choices, e.g., of particular actions) is volitional or free, in a metaphysical sense.[46] This means that prior to a given choice being made, two (or more) futures are open, and the agent by his choice brings one into reality rather than the other(s).[47]

Rand advocates what contemporary analytic philosophers often call a "*libertarian*" view of free will.[48] Rand (1) is an incompatibilist and so regards freedom of the will and determinism as incompatible, and she (2) rejects determinism, the view that every event is determined and necessitated by antecedent events. She additionally advocates for what are called agent causes; she (3) holds that choices are causal, specifically they are self-caused.[49]

(1) According to compatibilist theories, determinism and freedom are compatible, because "freedom" is understood as a certain way in which one's actions are predetermined. According to various compatibilist theories, we are free if our actions are predetermined by internal rather than external factors, or if they or the desires that produce them are in accordance with our (predetermined) higher-order desires, or if one has the power to do what one (predeterminatedly) wants to do.[50] Against this, Rand maintains that metaphysical freedom (and moral responsibility) presuppose an agent being able to act differently than he does (even if all other factors are the same). This is referred to by contemporary philosophers as "the principle of alternative possibilities."

(2) Rand endorses incompatibilism and free will, hence she rejects determinism. Her distinctive perspective on identity and causality are essential to this. It is often thought that determinism is entailed by the concept of "causation" as such. As noted above, the modern conception of cause and effect is one of antecedent events (the causes) leading to subsequent events (the effects). If one thinks that a given state of affairs (cause) necessitates the next state of affairs (effect), then everything will happen of necessity. The future is always preceded by the past, and on this view it is always predetermined by the past as well. Hence the "state" of a person and her environment immediately prior to making her choice necessitates her next state. Hence her "choice" is determined.

"Indeterminists" attempt to resist this conclusion by maintaining that the subsequent state (effect) is not determined by the antecedent state (cause). Given their usual background views about the nature of causation, though, this means that they claim that choices *have no causes*. Choices are not determined by anything. They are purely random.

(3) Rand rejects this view as well. The fact that we act in one way rather than another is not uncaused, but rather the agent herself is the cause of her chosen action. So, in rejecting determinism, Rand does not reject the principle of causality as she understands it. Rather, she claims that, in the act of choosing, the human agent is acting in accordance with her nature, her *volitional* nature. Her nature is such that she *must* choose. However, the action that the agent takes is still a choice, for which option she selects is up to her. It is self-determined.

Roderick Chisholm (1976) and subsequently other, contemporary defenders of a libertarian conception of free will appeal to the idea that people are the causes of their actions. One key difference between Chisholm and Rand, though, is that while he analyzes agent causation in explicitly Aristotelian terms, he understands all non-agent causation in the same event-event Humean manner as his determinist and indeterminist opponents. This makes agent causation appear to be a mysterious, metaphysical oddity or simply a case of special pleading.

Rand held that our concept of causation must be wide enough to include all the forms of causation that we encounter in reality. All causation (in the primary sense) is an entity acting in accordance with its identity. One such type of causation is the human, volitional form of causation, and it need not operate identically to the mechanistic kind of physical causation that is assumed to hold for bodies, at least those that are above the scale of quantum-level phenomena.[51]

According to Rand, the fact of this agent causation (that the agent chooses for himself or herself whether, e.g., to come into focus or not) is axiomatic. Like the axiom of consciousness, it is experienced directly. We have a direct introspective awareness of effortful focus and deliberation.[52] And, as with the other axioms, the denial of free will is self-refuting. Anyone who wishes to deny volition and makes an argument to the effect that there is no free will is effectively saying to his listeners that they have the ability to choose whether or not to accept his argument and its evidence *and* that the evidence points to the fact that they have no such choice. If we are to be able to make up our minds, including about free will, then we must be able *to make* those minds up.[53]

A determinist could coherently state that he was antecedently determined to believe in determinism by factors beyond his powers of choice; that he is currently determined to be uttering an "argument" for determinism; and that his listeners are themselves determined to either give or withhold assent to his utterances. In that case, such terms as "reason," "assent," "evidence," and so on turn out to refer, at most, to a series of mechanistic reactions, erroneously regarded in folk-belief to be "voluntary." What the determinist cannot say is that one *should* endorse determinism. The determinist cannot consistently retain the normative dimensions of such terms while denying their volitional basis.[54]

Just as free will is a case of causality, so too is it a case of identity. Human beings can only make certain choices at certain times and we cannot instantaneously choose to alter our character; nor can we choose not to have choice as such. Thus Rand's endorsement of self-created character and free will is not an endorsement of the existentialist position that human "nature" or identity is contrary to or negated by choice.[55]

The Distinction Between the Metaphysically Given and the Man-Made

In order for a human being to maintain the proper relationship to reality, he must choose to keep his consciousness focused upon, and his thoughts and actions guided by, the facts of existence. A crucial conceptual means for doing so is the recognition of the distinction between what Rand calls "the *metaphysical*" or "the *metaphysically given*," on the one hand, and "the *man-made*" on the other.

According to Rand, the distinction between the metaphysically given and the man-made is the only fundamental distinction between different kinds of facts. A man-made fact is one that is the product or result of human choice.[56] Metaphysically given facts result from the natures and actions of everything in reality that lacks volition or is not open to choice. Thus, man-made facts are *contingent*. They are dependent upon the choices of volitional beings and so could have been otherwise. Metaphysically given facts are not so dependent and could not have been otherwise; they are *necessary*.[57]

Once performed, actions and events, whether volitional or automatic, cannot be undone. Past choices did not *happen necessarily*, but *they are*, necessarily, *what happened*. To think otherwise and claim that the past was not what it was will not change the facts. That, Rand might say, is because existence has primacy over consciousness, because what is, is. A is A. On the other hand, to think of *human* history as metaphysically given, a species of natural history, would be equally disastrous. We would be incapable of learning from human history or morally evaluating the past actions and ideas of human individuals and societies if we did not recognize that they *were chosen*, that is, man-made.

Rand identified the ability to draw the crucial distinction between the metaphysically given and the man-made as an important mark of a civilization leaving its pre-philosophical childhood and beginning its maturation into philosophical adulthood.[58] To a primitive culture that has not yet grasped the distinction between the metaphysical and man-made or between what is by nature (*phusis*) and what is by custom or convention (*nomos*), to use the terms by which the Greeks first grasped this distinction, the world is mysterious and terrifyingly unpredictable, full of gods and demons. A good year's harvest indicates the favor of the gods or spirits (of sun and rain, of soil and crop), while drought and famine imply that some gods or spirits are upset with us. Even "human" events, such as the outcome of a battle or a person's happiness or misfortune, are in the hands of the spirits. In such belief "systems" there is no well-marked distinction between natural and human events. "Nature" – to use a term such peoples do not have – acts just like we act; thus the method for dealing with it is to approach it just as one does people (very powerful people), offering them gifts, asking them for mercy, pleading for forgiveness, and so on.

Such people were to be pitied, living in an understandable initial state of ignorance and confusion.[59] However crudely he might describe it, a primitive person knows by introspection that *he* acts according to his desires and thoughts. The manner of causality whose nature is most immediately intelligible to us is our own intentional, voluntary action. It is to be expected that pre-philosophical humans would believe that other things in the world around them act similarly. Understood very broadly, animism is the default.

However, at the point when we begin to grasp the concept of "nature," as the Greeks did in the sixth and fifth centuries BCE, we grasp that some objects, at least the non-living ones or non-animals, do not act according to their thoughts or choices (or any state of mind or "soul"), but simply according to certain inexorable laws of their own internal motion and the motions conveyed to them from without. If that is so, then the only way to deal with them is to learn what the rules of their activities are and then harness them in accordance with those discovered rules. Bacon famously formulated this point in one of Rand's favorite aphorisms: "Nature to be commanded must be obeyed."[60] One must approach and act toward what is natural and meta-physically given in one way – a way that begins by accepting it as inalterable – and toward what is man-made or the result of a volitional consciousness in an altogether different way – one that begins by recognizing that such things could have been otherwise. Thus it becomes crucial that one be able to distinguish between and properly identify what belongs to each category and to act accordingly. Despite its theistic beginning and its implications that our character is due to god, Rand thought that the "serenity prayer" recited by Alcoholics Anonymous eloquently summed up the vital need to make and respect this distinction:

> God, grant me the serenity to accept the things I cannot change,
> The courage to change the things I can,
> And the wisdom to know the difference.

While we are unlikely to act or believe as humans did before the discovery of these concepts, Rand holds that we still all too often ignore or evade this distinction.

Consider, on the one hand, mistaking what is metaphysically given for being man-made. For example, a dictator who demands that scientists or industrialists do the impossible and then blames their inability to fulfill his whims on their unwillingness.[61] This inversion of the metaphysically given and the man-made is present in social forms of the primacy of consciousness (e.g., in the view that communism would work if only people were less selfish, or that the economy would grow, despite crippling new regulations, if only consumers had more confidence).

The same inversion is present (and even more obvious) in supernatural forms of the primacy of consciousness (e.g., in the belief that an earthquake in Haiti was retribution for a pact with the devil, just as one in Portugal was punishment for Catholicism, or perhaps Protestantism) or in the belief that you survived a car accident, not because you were cushioned by an airbag, har-nessed by a seat belt, and cradled in a reinforced steel cage, but because you were touched by an angel. None of these "primacy of consciousness" explanations is true. Worse: they distract and dissuade people from searching for the real causes; the future actions that they suggest do noth-ing to address the real causes at issue; and, at the same time, they lead to the suppression and punishment of whatever or whoever is thought to have offended the spirits. This usually turns out to be whatever or whoever offends the mystics who claim to speak for the spirits. All manner of events both public and private are presumed to have happened for "a reason" according to

"God's plan." This leads to passivity with respect to things that we can change, futile resentment and foolish reaction over things we cannot, and the incapability to tell the difference or to properly understand (or enjoy) either.[62]

It does not matter here that these events are explained as "God-made" rather than man-made. They still are seen to be the result of a consciousness that can be swayed (by changing human actions or opinions). It may be true that there are measures that we can take to prevent certain disasters in the future, just as today there are measures we can take to reduce their impact. But any such measures would require understanding the metaphysically given natures of the relevant entities (e.g., tectonic plates) and interacting with them accordingly, rather than *persuading* any divine minds not to shake our cities.

On the other hand, it is equally common to mistake what is man-made for something that is metaphysically given; we all too often regard the current modes of social behavior as simple facts of the world around us, giving little thought to how those facts and practices came to be and what alternatives might be possible and preferable. It is said one "cannot fight City Hall," but the current laws and power structures in a society are man-made, and they can and often should be fought. It is only reality that one cannot fight. One cannot repeal the law of gravity. If taken very literally and seriously, Ben Franklin's witty adage that "the only certainties are death and taxes" would be a perfect case of ignoring the difference between the metaphysically given and the man-made and thus elevating the man-made to the status of a metaphysical absolute or "certainty." While death is a metaphysical given for organisms, taxes are not. Political institutions could be changed so as to eliminate them.

It is not always easy to determine what is metaphysical and what is man-made, but this does not relieve the necessity of making such distinctions. It only makes that need more pressing. Among the most difficult cases are distinguishing metaphysically given features of human nature (or of a particular person's nature) from chosen and morally evaluable traits. It is easy to think that common affects, beliefs, or tendencies that are deeply rooted and prevalent in one's own society are part of human nature. For millennia, even the most enlightened of philosophers regarded the institution of slavery as a natural state of affairs based on (and justified by) supposedly natural differences between freemen and "natural slaves" – for instance, between Greeks and Barbarians or whites and non-whites. The same holds for the subjugation of women. Today, we rightly hold these practices in contempt and we recognize that the beliefs used to justify them were always false. But we should not assume that their falsehood was always obvious.

In many issues of human psychology, identifying and distinguishing the metaphysically given from the man-made remains challenging. Depression, for instance, is known to be "heritable," which, in the context of treatment, simply means that parents' depression is highly predictive of their children's depression. But it remains unclear to what extent a disposition toward depression is *inherited* through one's genes (and, therefore, metaphysically given), rather than *taught* by parental modeling, *perpetuated* through a painful cycle of parent–child interaction, or even *inculcated* through more subtle aspects of the home environment. If we had this knowledge, we would be better able to develop and administer interventions to prevent or treat depression.

Finally, with respect to one's own psychology, it can be difficult to determine what is in one's power and what is not. We cannot change our past, and at any given point in time, like it or not, we have those dispositions that we have acquired. We may be able to change ourselves, but it is not always obvious what we can change, how quickly, and in what manner. One cannot, after years of abusing drugs, wake up one day and decide that without any work or struggle one will have no problems whatsoever in giving them up. Likewise, one cannot simply order oneself to stop loving another or to believe otherwise than one does and expect anything like immediate self-compliance. Here again, consciousness has identity, and volition is not a violation of identity or causality. We have a nature: both human nature proper, over which we have no control, and what Aristotle called our "second nature," that is those characteristics that we developed (usually voluntarily) and now possess, and perhaps can change, but not instantaneously and by any means (or no means) whatsoever.

Objectivity as Respect for the Primacy of Existence

The Primacy of Existence is, in the first place, a fundamental claim about the relationship between the world, which is identified as mind-independent, and the mind, which is awareness of the world. By extension, the Primacy of Existence and its antithesis, the Primacy of Consciousness, name the basic orientations of any system of thought with respect to how one gains knowledge of the world. If the world is mind-independent, then one must look out at the world. If the world is mind-dependent, then one can look inward, into the structure of one's mind, or God's, or the collective's (un)consciousness to determine how things must be.

If existence exists and has its identity independent of consciousness, then a being with a volitional and fallible consciousness must act to keep its thoughts and actions in compliance with that unswervingly lawful reality, or else face the consequences of running headlong into the immovable. In other words, humans must bring the man-made into compliance with the metaphysically given. Rand called a conceptual consciousness's volitional adherence to reality "objectivity." Objectivity would be neither possible nor necessary if reality and consciousness were not distinct, or if there were no possibility of a consciousness failing to adhere to reality.

It is axiomatic concepts that identify the precondition of knowledge: the distinction between existence and consciousness, between reality and the awareness of reality, between the object and the subject of cognition. "Axiomatic concepts are the foundation of *objectivity*" (*ITOE* 57).

How does one maintain the proper relationship between consciousness and existence? Philosophy answers this question with regard to knowledge through epistemology and with regard to action through ethics. Rand's view is that successfully and consistently achieving and maintaining objectivity requires, at minimum, the ability to distinguish between reality and consciousness and between what is an immutable part of the former's identity or a volitional aspect depending on the latter. As we have seen, she regards explicit knowledge of the axioms as epistemologically and practically essential, while to actually implement the Primacy of Existence in one's voluntary cognition and behavior requires a respect for the distinction between the metaphysically given and the man-made.

In naming her philosophy "Objectivism" Rand meant to convey that it was based entirely on the primacy of existence and fidelity to it: respecting reality by bringing one's thoughts and actions into accordance with it, rather than vainly demanding that it bow to consciousness. In *Atlas Shrugged*, Ayn Rand has Galt encapsulate his ethics as an axiom and a choice: "My morality, the morality of reason, is contained in a single axiom: existence exists – and in a single choice: to live" (*Atlas* 1018). To live is to remain in existence; the only means to do this is to accept and cleave to the axiom.

Notes

1 See *Workshops* 349–351.

2 Quoted formulations from *Atlas* 1015–1016. Cf. Rand's formulations in *ITOE* ch. 6, esp. 59.

3 Rand believed that most philosophers were *primarily* committed to the primacy of consciousness, but many constituted mixed cases. For instance, Rand considered idealists such as Kant and Hegel as more consistently committed to the primacy of consciousness than figures such as Descartes. However, she still regarded a representationalist such as Descartes to be fundamentally in the primacy of consciousness camp because of his commitment to the prior certainty of consciousness and his creationary theism. See Lennox, below, 330.

4 About axiomatic concepts, see more below. For the same reason, the axioms of identity (A is A) and of consciousness (consciousness is conscious) are also repetitions, underscoring the fundamental facts apprehended in the axiomatic concepts of "identity" and "consciousness" respectively.

5 DK 28B2.5–6, 6.1–3, 7.1–2. For Parmenides and the explicit identification of "existence" see *ITOE* 262.

6 Rand accepted the valid use of "non-existence" as a relative term, i.e., at a certain time such and such *was not* while at some other time it was; or that such and such exists as a character of literary fiction, but was never an historical person. She rejects there being anything that is referred to by an absolute sense of "non-existence." "It may be said that existence can be differentiated from non-existence; but non-existence is not a fact, it is the *absence* of a fact, it is a derivative concept pertaining to a relationship, i.e., a concept which can be formed or grasped only in relation to some existent that has ceased to exist. ... Non-existence as such is a zero with no sequence of numbers to follow it, it is the nothing, the total blank" (*ITOE* 58).

7 This is what Rand means by saying that "[axiomatic concepts] identify explicitly the omission of psychological time measurements, which is implicit in all other concepts" (*ITOE* 56–57).

8 Rand goes on to say that it is only in this way that we are able to distinguish subject from object, i.e., our consciousness from the external world. For reasons of space, the technical details of her view on this point must be omitted.

9 Note the way that the idiom "It is what it is" is used in just this manner.

10 Salmieri 2009a, 224–225, 249 n. 20 observes that similar fog imagery is used to describe the look Hank Rearden sees in the eyes of his wife, Lillian: "not the look of understanding, but of a furious refusal to understand – as if she wanted to turn the violence of her emotion into a fog screen, as if she hoped not that it would blind her to reality, but that her blindness would make reality cease to exist" (*Atlas* 528). On evasion as the fundamental evil in Rand's ethics, see 64, 83, 110, and 125–126, above.

11 In holding this, Rand is opposing the view, first maintained by the Stoics, that existence is a predicate or attribute that qualifies some wider and ontologically ambiguous category that includes both "things" that exist and those that do not. See Seneca *Ep.* 58.13–15 = LS 27A, Sextus *M.* 10.218 = LS 27D. See also Alexander *In Ar. Top.* 301, 19–25 = LS 27B, where he rejects the Stoics' subsuming of beings into the broader genus of "somethings" on Aristotelian grounds.

12 Compare to Parmenides DK 28B8.5–21.

13 One might think to explain all the "natural" parts of existence by reference to a "supernatural" part of existence such as God. To do so, though, would be to assume that the existence of all of the known, observable universe requires a cause or explanation (outside of all that is known and observed to exist). This is effectively to presume that existence need not exist. Furthermore, if someone in likewise manner demanded from the supernaturalist a cause or explanation of God, the supernaturalist would either fall into an infinite regress, or he would have to concede that he will accept an irreducible primary, but only so long as, as with God, it is a form of consciousness. This is the primacy of consciousness: i.e., the view that existence is conditional and/or dependent on consciousness.

14 "Fifteen Sermons Preached at the Rolls Chapel," Preface §39 in White 2006, 44.

15 Rand held that existence is not a predicate or an attribute. The alternative view – which we first find with the Stoics and which might be attributed to Russell among other moderns – holds that existence

is a qualification given to some ontologically ambiguous notion. On such a view, the widest class is "things" (rather than beings or existents), both those that exist and those that do not, and among them some fall into the class of things that exist. Rand rejects this, in as much as there is nothing to which existence does not apply; it has no contrary. If existence is not a finishing touch adding the perfection of being to totally qualified non-beings, an ontological spark that breathes reality into the nose of a fully articulated statue made of nothing, then neither is it a bare template to which attributes and qualifications are subsequently added. This view, that there is prime-matter or an underlying substratum that simply is, but is not yet one thing rather than another, is sometimes called the "pincushion" view. Rand rejected it; on her view both the scholastic prime-matter that *is no-which-way* and the Stoic or Russellian *just-such-a-thing-that-is-or-isn't* are the products of the same deep metaphysical error – the separation of existence from identity.

16 She also states that the concept of "identity" is a corollary of the concept of "existence" (*ITOE* 55).

17 This point could be made by saying that existence and identity are distinct *epistemologically* but not *metaphysically*. This distinction is employed in several closely related ways by Rand, especially in discussing axiomatic concepts in *ITOE* ch. 6, 56–58. See also Peikoff, "The Analytic-Synthetic Dichotomy" (*ITOE* 98). See 249–251, below, on the content and function of axiomatic concepts.

18 *Metaphysics* Γ.4.1006a11–18. For Aristotle on the Law of Non-Contradiction as an axiom see Γ.3–4.1005b8–1006a11. Aristotle's own elenchtic demonstration follows at Γ.4.1006a18–b18.

19 See Lennox's discussion of the relation between Rand's axioms and Aristotle's, 336, below.

20 *ITOE* 58; "although they designate a fundamental *metaphysical* fact, axiomatic concepts are the products of an *epistemological* need." For Aristotle's view of the common axioms, see *Metaphysics* Γ.3–4.

21 For Descartes, see his second set of replies to objections to the *Meditations*, AT VII.155–170. For Spinoza see *Ethics*, esp. Books I and II.

22 "The concept 'existence' does not indicate what existents it subsumes: it merely underscores the primary fact that they *exist*. The concept 'identity' does not indicate the particular natures of the existents it subsumes: it merely underscores the primary fact that *they are what they are*. The concept 'consciousness' does not indicate what existents one is conscious of: it merely underscores the primary fact that one is *conscious*" (*ITOE* 59).

23 By "well defined" I mean that: When X and non-X are well defined they really are contradictories, such that they are mutually exclusive and jointly exhaustive.

24 On the issue of the ultimate constituents of the universe, see *ITOE* 290–295.

25 Aristotle argues that the eternity of the universe is fully compatible with his denial of the existence of any actual, simultaneous infinite quantity. At any given moment there are only finite quantities in the cosmos, and they are always succeeded by finite quantities. Rand would likely have agreed with this analysis. For details on Aristotle's position, see White 2009.

26 For Rand's positions on the nature of space and the finite size of the universe, see Lecture 2 of Leonard Peikoff's "The Philosophy of Objectivism" lecture series (*TPO*), which Rand endorsed.

27 In the nineteenth century, many physicists postulated the existence of a substance called ether that filled the spaces between massive bodies and served as a medium for the propagation of light. This view is widely thought to have been disproven by experiments performed by Michelson and Morley in the 1880s and by a series of subsequent experiments in the early twentieth century. Rand briefly discusses these experiments in *ITOE* 303, arguing that they do not establish that space is an absolute vacuum. The experiments set the context in which Einstein's theory of Special Relativity was received. Though Einstein's theory is often thought to dispense with the ether altogether, it is significant that this was not Einstein's own view. He thought that the experiments and his theory showed only that the ether did not have the mechanical properties attributed to it by earlier physicists, and he sometimes referred to the gravitational field posited by his theory of General Relativity as "ether": "we may say that according to the general theory of relativity space is endowed with physical qualities; in this sense, therefore, there exists an ether. According to the general theory of relativity space without ether is unthinkable; for in such space there not only would be no propagation of light, but also no possibility of existence for standards of space and time (measuring-rods and clocks), nor therefore any space-time intervals in the physical sense. But this ether may not be thought of as endowed with the quality characteristic of

ponderable media, as consisting of parts which may be tracked through time. The idea of motion may not be applied to it" (Einstein 1983, 23–24).

Some contemporary physicists, following Einstein's lead, have emphasized the relativistic and spectroscopic properties of space. Robert Laughlin writes that "[Space] is filled with 'stuff' that is normally transparent but can be made visible by hitting it sufficiently hard to knock out a part. The modern concept of the vacuum of space, confirmed every day by experiment, is a relativistic ether. But we do not call it this because it is taboo" (Laughlin 2005, 121). For more on these issues, see Kustro 2000. My thanks to Travis Norsen, Eric Dennis, and Matt Bateman for supplying me with many of the details concerning the theory prior to Einstein and to the revival of ether, as it were.

28 Her position on this issue, which she regarded as epistemological rather than metaphysical, is discussed in the next chapter.

29 The paradigmatic example of such a view is Hume's *Treatise on Human Nature* (T 1.2.3.4). In the twentieth century, such views were endorsed (by way of sensations) by several logical positivists and other early analytic philosophers (Russell 1912 and Broad 1925) and (by way of activities) by process-philosophers such as Whitehead.

30 Quoting Russell from *The Analysis of Mind*, lecture X.

31 See *ITOE* 264–266, 276. In order to characterize the relationship of dependence between attributes, actions, etc. and entities, we should distinguish between what are merely logical parts from what are mereological or proper parts. What is actually a physically separable part of an entity can itself be regarded as an entity: my hand is a part of my body, and if severed from my body it would be a severed hand, but still a separate entity. By contrast my height cannot be detached from my body except "logically," in thought, as a matter of selective attention and abstraction. It cannot exist on its own, apart from that which it is the height of. It is merely a logical part of me, whereas my hand is a mereological or proper part. It is an actually separable thing that is potentially its own entity. Therefore it is metaphysically illicit (a kind of *category mistake*) to posit processes or relationships without the entities undergoing said processes or standing in said relationships.

32 See *ITOE* 292–295.

33 See *ITOE* 269–273.

34 See Windelband 1958, 410 (cited by Branden in "Volition and the Law of Causality" *TO* 5(3) 43–44). See also Frede 1980 and Runggaldier 2014.

35 For thoughts in a similar vein see Machamer, Darden, and Craver 2000.

36 See Gotthelf's discussion (82, above) of the virtuous person's attitude toward causality.

37 The bracketed names are my own postulation of the theorists whose views are most likely being referenced.

38 Consciousness is an attribute of living entities, but it is not an attribute of their mental states. Just as existence is not a property of existing things, but is them, so too consciousness is "not an attribute of a given state of awareness, it *is* that state."

39 On these issues, see Salmieri's treatment, 281–282, below. See also Salmieri 2013a, 46–8, Ghate 2013a, 94–103, and Bayer 2013, 251–253.

40 See Salmieri's treatment of the validity of sense perception and Objectivist responses to traditional skeptical arguments, 279–282 and 299, below.

41 E.g., *Atlas* 1026–1027.

42 Cf. Aristotle *Metaphysics* Γ.5.1110b31ff.

43 *Receptive* is distinguished here from *creative* or *productive*; it specifies that consciousness does not create its object. *Receptive* does not imply *passive*. In characterizing theories of cognition Rand uses the distinction of epistemologically *passive* vs. epistemologically *active* consciousness to separate those theories that treat all cognition, especially conceptual consciousness, as an automatic product received from the world (passive) as against views such as her own in which conceptual consciousness requires that the subject actively form concepts by acts of volition. However, that the subject must *actively* choose to do something in order to achieve this level of cognition does not imply that the act of cognition is *creative* in the sense of making the object of awareness what it is. See Salmieri's discussion, below, 290–291.

44 This stands in opposition to the strategy of the Kantian "Copernican revolution," wherein one imputes to phenomenal experience that which would make it conform to the possibility of alleged knowledge.

45 Cf. *Atlas* 1012. Onkar Ghate discusses focus at length in Chapter 5, above.; see esp. 108–109; cf. Allan Gotthelf's discussion 82–83.

46 Based on Branden's formulations in "The Objectivist Theory of Volition" (*TO* 5(1–2)), it could be inferred that Rand only regarded the primary choice of whether or not to think (i.e., be in a state of "focus") as the only absolutely free choice, with all other choices being more or less determined by the primary choices. Most interpreters, including the author, believe that Rand's considered view is that secondary choices are (at least usually) free as well. Her point – perhaps not well expressed by Branden – is that secondary choices, say over actions, would not be free unless we had some (long-term) form of volitional control over our motives/values and beliefs/concepts. For this to be possible we must have volitional control over the primary choice – whether or not to actively think, whether or not to face reality or to ignore or even actively evade it. Secondary choices would not be free unless the primary choice were free, but that the primary choice is free certainly does not entail that secondary choices are unfree. Similarly, considered in isolation from any other concomitant choices or actions, the choice to be in focus has no antecedent motive – for it determines whether and what kind of facts/values will be considered, so as to motivate us. Secondary choices do have such motivation. However, this too does not exclude their freedom, for Rand's view of volition is not a freedom of indifference theory.

47 One cannot unchoose a past choice that one has already made, but one did not have to make the choice that one did; the point is that an agent who chooses *could have done otherwise*.

48 This is not to be confused with political libertarianism.

49 See Branden, "Volition and the Law of Causality" (*TO* 5(3) 4–44).

50 For freedom as determinism by internal factors, see the Stoics (e.g., Cicero *De Fato* 39–43 = LS 62C and Alexander *De Fato* 181,13–182,20 = LS 62G) who held that what comes about "*through us*" is "*up to us*" or "*in our power*," even though it is fated. For freedom as determination of action through (predetermined) higher-order desires, see Frankfurt 1971. For freedom as the power do what one (predeterminately) wants, see Hobbes's *Leviathan* (I.21.1–4) and Hume's *Enquiry Concerning Human Understanding* (E 8.23).

51 Our notion of deterministic action, which is not self-evident, is applied by us to physical bodies and quite successfully, judging by the progress of the physical sciences since the seventeenth century. However, in my view, at least, Rand's principles of causality and identity do not guarantee that at *every* physical level science will ever discover that one antecedent state will produce one and only one consequent state. The nature of a cause determines and delimits it to performing actions from a finite range of effects, and things cannot act contrary to their nature by doing what is beyond their range of possible actions, but their nature may be such as to give rise to a limited disjunctive set of outcomes from one and the same initial condition. I must stress that this is my own opinion as to what Objectivist metaphysics need and need not be committed to with respect to causality – i.e., it need not assume that there is a strict one-to-one determinacy of all physical actions. Rand herself may have accepted more than this, though, taking all physical causation to be deterministic. If so, it is unknown to me how strongly she held this view and for what reasons. It may not have been a conscious theoretical commitment, but simply a default assumption; she may not have taken no-tice of this point. It is also conceivable that her view was colored by the prevailing interpretations of quantum mechanics at that time, e.g., the Copenhagen interpretation, which she regarded as a rejection of non-contradiction (as did some of its formulators such as Bohr). If her understanding of the situation was that (some) physicists doubted or denied a strict one-to-one physical determinacy *because* they rejected the axiom of identity, then she probably would not have seen any strong reason to consider such a possibility. However, as we saw earlier, Rand deliberately avoided legislating the ontology of undiscovered physical things from the throne of metaphysics. Therefore, I believe that my interpretation is in the proper spirit of her fundamental views regarding identity and causality.

52 If anything, the primary choice is less easy to directly introspect, inasmuch as choosing to focus is chosen in tandem with some other more particular choice(s) of how to direct one's consciousness or body. Cf. "The Objectivist Ethics" (*VOS* 22).

53 See Branden, "The Contradiction of Determinism" (*TON 2:3*) and Peikoff, *OPAR* 71–72. Similar arguments can be found in Epicurus (VS 40), Kant (Ak. IV, 448), and Searle (2001).

54 A typical strategy at this point is for the determinist to turn to epistemic externalism and thus redefine the ideas of norms, especially justification. It is permissible for the internalist to reply that no one means by justification the externalist's revisionary notion, and that external "justification" is, practically speaking, a concept that cannot do any work for us (or at least none of the work that the traditional, "internal" concept of justification did). In so saying, the internalist would be reaffirming that our concepts of conceptual-level justification *do* in fact presuppose a volitional basis, and that the externalist's replacements would fail to do the work of guiding a volitional, conceptual consciousness (since they deny said volition). Again, this would not prove the fact of volition, which Rand regarded as self-evident through introspection, but it would show which other facts and concepts the externalist was not entitled to, because they are (or are inherently regarded by all to be) dependent on volition. Thus Rand would regard it as a case of the fallacy of the stolen concept (on which, see below, 298–299). It should be noted, however, that Rand would not accept typical internalist conditions for the justification of sense perception or of relying on perception. That is, we do not need to *know that* perception is a valid form of awareness in order for it to be valid for us to depend upon it. (On the relation of Rand's epistemology to internalist and externalist views of justification, see Salmieri 2013a, 75–84.)

55 For more on the relationship between free will, human nature, and character, see Ghate's Chapter 5, above.

56 The category is restricted to *human* choice, since human beings are (as far as anyone knows) the only beings to possess reason and free will. If other rational creatures were to be discovered – something Rand considers with a fanciful example in *ITOE* 73 – then the terminology would need to be adjusted to include them.

57 This is the only *metaphysical* distinction that Rand endorses between modalities. As should be clear from the sections on identity and causality, Rand is perfectly comfortable with speaking of the capability or *potentiality* of performing some action or being in some future state that various things either have or lack. In this sense she will sometimes speak of something being "possible" or "impossible," as one typically does in English. However, Rand was emphatic that conceivability or inconceivability, for instance, was not a criterion for determining whether or not something is necessary or contingent, and she recognized no gradations between "metaphysical," "logical," "physical," etc. necessity. See Peikoff, "The Analytic-Synthetic Dichotomy" (*ITOE* 88–121).

58 See "The Missing Link" (*PWNI* 42–43).

59 Rand had contempt for those modern people who would ignore or worse still attempt to undermine and undo this conceptual foundation of advanced civilization. Furthermore, the veneration of such primitive civilizations (or the preferment of them over more advanced societies) was repugnant to her. See "Apollo and Dionysus" (*ROTP*).

60 *Novum Organum*, Book I, Aphorism 3. Rand quotes or refers to this aphorism often. See "The Metaphysical Versus the Man-Made" (*PWNI* 34 and 43), "For the New Intellectual" (*FTNI* 9), *ITOE* 82, "Introducing Objectivism" (*Column* 3), and "Who Is the Final Authority in Ethics?" (*VOR* 18). Cf. "The Stimulus and the Response" (*PWNI* 202), where she remarks on B.F. Skinner's "unconscionable misuse" of the aphorism.

61 For examples, see *Atlas* 977–987, 1112–1115.

62 Nietzsche speaks powerfully to this point in §I.33 of *Daybreak*, subtitled "Contempt for causes, for consequences, and for reality."

References

Bayer, Benjamin. 2013. "Keeping Up Appearances: Reflections on the Debate Over Perceptual Infallibilism." In Gotthelf and Lennox 2013.

Broad, C.D. 1925. *The Mind and Its Place in Nature*. London: Routledge & Kegan Paul.

Chisholm, Roderick. 1976. "The Agent as Cause." In *Action Theory*, edited by M. Brand and D. Walton. Dordrecht, Netherlands: D. Reidel.

Einstein, Albert. 1983. "Ether and the Theory of Relativity." In *Sidelights on Relativity*, translated by G.B. Jeffery and W. Perrett. New York, NY: Dover.

Frankfurt, H. 1971. "Freedom of the Will and the Concept of a Person." *Journal of Philosophy*, 58(1).

Frede, Michael. 1980. "The Original Notion of Cause." In *Doubt and Dogmatism: Studies in Hellenistic Episte-mology*, edited by J. Barnes, M. F. Burnyeat, and M. Schofield. Oxford: Oxford University Press. Reprinted 1989 in M. Frede, *Essays in Ancient Philosophy*. Oxford: Oxford University Press.

Ghate, Onkar. 2013a. "Perceptual Awareness as Presentational." In Gotthelf and Lennox 2013.

Gotthelf, Allan, ed., and James G. Lennox, assoc. ed. 2013. *Concepts and Their Role in Knowledge: Reflections on Objectivist Epistemology*. Ayn Rand Philosophical Studies, vol. 2. Pittsburgh, PA: University of Pittsburgh Press.

Kustro, Ludwik. 2000. *Einstein and the Ether*. Montreal: Apeiron.

Laughlin, Robert B. 2005. *A Different Universe: Reinventing Physics from the Bottom Down*. New York, NY: Basic Books.

Machamer, Peter, Lindley Darden, and Carl Craver. 2000. "Thinking About Mechanisms." *Philosophy of Science*, 67, March.

Runggaldier, Edmund. 2014. "Aristotelian Agent-Causation." In *Neo-Aristotelian Perspectives in Metaphysics*, edited by Daniel D. Novotný and Lukás Novák. New York, NY: Routledge.

Russell, Bertrand. 1912. *The Problems of Philosophy*. Oxford: Oxford University Press.

Salmieri, Gregory. 2009a. "*Atlas Shrugged* on the Role of the Mind in Man's Existence." In *Essays on Ayn Rand's* Atlas Shrugged, edited by Robert Mayhew. Lanham, MD: Lexington Books.

Salmieri, Gregory. 2013a. "Conceptualization and Justification." In Gotthelf and Lennox 2013.

Searle, John. 2001. "Freewill as a Problem in Neurobiology." *Philosophy*, 76(4).

White, D., ed. 2006. *The Works of Bishop Butler*. Rochester, NY: University of Rochester Press.

White, Michael. 2009. "Aristotle on the Infinite, Space, and Time." In *Companion to Aristotle*, edited by G. Anagnostopoulos. Oxford: Wiley-Blackwell.

Windelband, Wilhelm. 1958. *A History of Philosophy*, Vol. II. New York, NY: Harper & Row.

271

12

The Objectivist Epistemology

GREGORY SALMIERI

Philosophy is primarily epistemology – the science of the means, the rules and the methods of human knowledge. It is the base of all other sciences and one necessary for man because man is a being of volitional consciousness – a being who has to discover, not only the content of his knowledge, but also the means by which he is to acquire knowledge.

Papers 033_15x_012_005–006/Journals 699 (cf. *ITOE* 78–79, "Philosophy: Who Needs It" *PWNI* 3–4)

Rand described herself as "primarily" an "advocate of reason," adding that this was the basis of her other philosophical positions, including her commitments to egoism and capitalism ("Brief Summary" *TO* 10(9) 1089; cf. "Credibility and Polarization" *ARL* 1(1) 1). Almost all philosophers claim to support their positions with rational arguments, but Rand meant more than this. Her ethics and politics derive from her view of the nature of reason and its essential role in human life: egoism, as she understood it, is consistent rationality in conceiving, choosing, and pursuing values, and capitalism is the political system that protects the freedom that a person needs to live by reason.[1] This is why, in a lecture Rand endorsed, her whole philosophy could be summarized by the sentence: "Man must live exclusively by the guidance of reason."[2] As she says in the passage above that serves as this chapter's epigraph, people do not automatically reason or even know how to do so. To avoid ignorance and error and to achieve the knowledge our survival and happiness require, we must discover and practice the proper methods of cognition. Thus we need epistemology, the "science devoted to the discovery of the proper methods of acquiring and validating knowledge" (*ITOE* 36).

Rand thought that Aristotle had discovered the outlines of the right approach, and she credited an (often implicit and unacknowledged) Aristotelian epistemology for such achievements as the Renaissance, the Enlightenment, the Scientific Revolution, and the Founding of the United States of America ("Review of Randall's *Aristotle*" *VOR* 6, *FTNI* 22).[3] The philosophers of the seventeenth and eighteenth centuries recognized that the guidance Aristotle offered was incomplete, and they sought to define a proper methodology. However, they proved unequal to the task, and by the nineteenth century, all of the prominent voices in philosophy were agreed that reason is not competent to guide the choices that determine the course of a human life. Philosophers (some more explicitly than others) encouraged

A Companion to Ayn Rand, First Edition. Edited by Allan Gotthelf and Gregory Salmieri.

people to live by the guidance of their emotions or to submit to the authority of others. An implicitly Aristotelian respect for reason persisted in the Western mind throughout the nineteenth century, and Rand saw this as the driving force behind the Industrial Revolution, the continued advances in the physical sciences, the abolition of slavery and serfdom, and the Romantic Movement in art.[4] But without a philosophical defense, this implicit pro-reason orientation could not hold out against the tide of increasingly explicit irrationalism. The result of its fading in the twentieth century was a general cultural dreariness, the rise of totalitarian governments in Europe, and the erosion of liberty even in the United States (where the Enlightenment's influence was strongest).[5] These developments could only be reversed, Rand argued, by "a *philosophical* revolution or, rather, a rebirth of philosophy," and "It is with a new approach to epistemology that the rebirth of philosophy has to begin" ("The Comprachicos" *ROTP* 93, *ITOE* 74; cf. *Journals* 699). Thus epistemology was to be the "predominant" subject of a treatise she planned to write, systematically presenting her philosophy (*ITOE* 36, *FTNI* vii).

The treatise was never completed, but Rand published a "preview" of it in the form of her longest continuous work of non-fiction, the monograph *Introduction to Objectivist Epistemology* (*ITOE*). *ITOE* is not, as its title might suggest, a survey of Rand's epistemology intended for a general audience. Rather it is "a summary of one of its cardinal elements – the Objectivist theory of concepts," and the intended audience is "philosophy students" who are well versed in Objectivism, as presented in earlier works by Rand and her associates.[6]

My aim in this chapter is to make *ITOE* more accessible both to students of epistemology without a background in Objectivism and to students of Objectivism without a background in epistemology. To this end, I will fill in some of the presupposed context, and connect the monograph's project to other aspects of Rand's thought and to more familiar issues and views in (contemporary and historical) epistemology. In doing so, I will make liberal use not only of *ITOE* and Rand's other published writings, but also of her private notes on epistemology and psychology, the transcripts of workshops she conducted on epistemology (an edited version of which is included in current editions of *ITOE*), and lectures that were given by her associates with her endorsement.

I begin with a discussion of some figures and issues in the history of philosophy that will help us to appreciate what Rand meant by the advocacy of reason and why she saw the issue of concepts as central to epistemology. I then discuss her view of consciousness and sense perception before turning to the theory of concepts presented in *ITOE* and its implications for other issues in epistemology.

The Earlier Advocates of Reason: Rand and the Enlightenment

Rand's exalted view of reason and its role in human life harkens back to the Enlightenment, an intellectual movement that began in the seventeenth century and became the dominant cultural force in eighteenth-century Europe and North America. Leonard Peikoff (writing under Rand's editorship) describes the zenith of this movement as "the first time in modern history" when "an authentic respect for reason became the mark of an entire culture" ("America's Philosophic Origin" *ARL* 3(5) 268, cf. *Parallels* 100–101). The extent of Rand's affinity to the Enlightenment can be glimpsed in historian Isaac Kramnick's apt summary of the movement's dominant ideas:

> They believed that unassisted human reason, not faith or tradition, was the principal guide to human conduct. ... Pleasure and happiness were worthy ends of life and realizable in this world. The

natural universe, governed not by the miraculous whimsy of a supernatural God, was ruled by rational scientific laws, which were accessible to human beings through the scientific method of experiment and empirical observation. Science and technology were engines of progress enabling modern men and women to force nature to serve their well-being and further their happiness. Science and the conquest of superstition and ignorance provided the prospect for endless improvement and reformation of the human condition, progress even unto a future that was perfection. The Enlightenment valorized the individual and the moral legitimacy of self-interest. It sought to free the individual from all varieties of external corporate or communal constraints, and it sought to reorganize the political, moral, intellectual, and economic worlds to serve individual interest. (Kramnick 1995, xi–xii)

The Enlightenment intellectuals were motivated by the conviction that human reason is capable of discovering profound and empowering truths, but they were keenly aware of human fallibility – indeed, they contemptuously rejected much of what had passed for knowledge in earlier ages. To avoid errors, and to reach the knowledge we need to guide our lives, these thinkers argued, we need to learn and practice the proper method of using our minds. Among the movement's most revered figures were three philosophers who sought to define such a method: Francis Bacon, René Descartes, and John Locke.[7] Each of the three identified some form of cognition as the foundation for knowledge, and each taught individuals to build upon this foundation by deliberate steps. Implicit in their emphasis on method is the view that knowledge is an *achievement* – an effect that a person brings about in himself by implementing the relevant causes. Rand formulates this point by reworking a famous aphorism by Bacon: "*nature*," she writes, "*to be apprehended, must be obeyed*" (*ITOE* 82). This is the core of her conception of "objectivity":

Objectivity is both a metaphysical and an epistemological concept. It pertains to the relationship of consciousness to existence. Metaphysically, it is the recognition of the fact that reality exists independent of any perceiver's consciousness. Epistemologically, it is the recognition of the fact that a perceiver's (man's) consciousness must acquire knowledge of reality by certain means (reason) in accordance with certain rules (logic). This means that although reality is immutable and, in any given context, only one answer is true, the truth is not automatically available to a human consciousness and can be obtained only by a certain mental process which is required of every man who seeks knowledge – that there is no substitute for this process, no escape from the responsibility for it, no shortcuts, no special revelations to privileged observers – and that there can be no such thing as a final "authority" in matters pertaining to human knowledge. Metaphysically, the only authority is reality; epistemologically – one's own mind. The first is the ultimate arbiter of the second. ("Who Is the Final Authority in Ethics?" *VOR* 18)

The commitment to (what Rand called) objectivity is what gave the Enlightenment intellectuals the confidence to reject long-established doctrines and institutions and to conceive new theories, new ways of life, and new forms of government, which they propagated, not by citing ancient authorities, but by submitting arguments to the judgment of individuals.

The knowledge that the Enlightenment sought, and upon which it sought to reform civilization, was *scientific knowledge*, in a demanding sense of that term that has its origins in classical Greek philosophy. Science (so understood) is the systematic understanding of a domain in terms of its fundamentals – the features that cause and explain the greatest number of others.[8] Aristotle contrasts scientific knowledge with mere experience. The person who is merely experienced with respect to a domain has observed patterns of phenomena within the domain, and he expects these patterns to continue, but he does not know why the phenomena occur. The possessor of scientific knowledge, by contrast, understands these phenomena (and other facts) as necessary consequences of a set of *principles*. The principles of a science comprise a set of axioms and the definitions of a battery of concepts. The axioms identify the fundamental factors operative within the science's domain, the concepts categorize the items within the domain, and the definitions articulate the *essences* of these items – that is, those fundamental features of the items in virtue of which they fall under the concepts they do.[9] Because the possessor of scientific knowledge understands the facts of the domain in terms of the relevant concepts and in light of the relevant principles, he apprehends why these facts obtain, and he can be certain that they will obtain even in new cases or circumstances.[10]

The development of ancient geometry provides the most striking example of the difference between science and mere experience. Many of the geometric facts that form the theorems in Euclid's *Elements* had been noticed centuries before the development of geometry as a science. The Egyptians and Babylonians, for example, had noticed that the sides of right triangles are so related that a square based on the longest side has an area equal to the sum of the areas of the squares based on the two smaller sides. However, the Greek geometers were the first to see this fact as necessitated by essence of right triangles and squares, and by a comparatively few fundamental facts about shapes, and they went on to integrate this and myriad other proofs about shapes into an axiomatized body of knowledge.[11]

Since the time of Plato and Aristotle, the achievement of the Greek geometers has served as the paradigm of rational understanding. Both the Greek philosophers and the thinkers of the Enlightenment sought to emulate this example in other domains – including, especially, morality and the natural world. Bacon wrote of a future in which human beings would acquire great power over nature by comprehending its principles.[12] Descartes made considerable advances in geometry – most notably the integration of the field with algebra. He also claimed to have discovered the principles governing the motion of bodies. However, his theories on this subject were quickly displaced by the Enlightenment's proudest scientific achievement, Newton's *Mathematical Principles of Natural Philosophy*, which took its place alongside Euclid's *Elements* as a paradigm of science. Even Locke, who was skeptical that our cognition of the natural world could ever rise to the level of a science, was convinced that we could develop a science of morals.[13]

Rand shared the Enlightenment's ambition for scientific knowledge – including a scientific morality. In a 1934 journal entry, she wrote of working towards "a logical system, proceeding from a few axioms in a succession of logical theorems" (*Papers* 166_04x_001_017/*Journals* 72), and she followed this structure in an aborted treatise on morality that she worked on in the 1940s (see *Journals* 287–288, 299–300).[14] None of her completed works are organized in this way, but they do make frequent reference to the hierarchical structure of ethics, and (more generally) of philosophy and of knowledge as a whole. For example, in "The Objectivist Ethics" (*VOS*), she defends a standard of value on the basis of theses about the fundamental nature of human beings and of values, and then she shows how this standard requires a certain set of cardinal values, which in turn require certain virtues.[15] In "What Is Capitalism?" she argues that the need for capitalism follows from man's essence as a rational animal (*CUI* 7–10), and in "The Psycho-Epistemology of Art" she does the same for the need for art (*RM* 5–8).[16] As John Lewis and I discuss in Chapter 15, below, an omnipresent theme in her political commentary is that concrete political issues can only be understood and evaluated by reference to political principles, which depend on a moral code, which in turn depends on metaphysics and epistemology.

When "considering a specific political event," Rand wrote, "a *rational* man"

> will call on his *conceptual* knowledge to identify the event by means of its essence: he will observe, for instance, that a given law establishes government controls and he will estimate it as evil, by means of his previously reached conviction that government controls are evil; he will not need to examine every concrete detail of the law nor ponder over all its future consequences; his conceptual grasp of the *essential* element involved will contain and cover all those concretes. (*Papers* 035_21F_003_004/*Journals* 676)

This is what Rand means when she speaks of being *guided by reason*. In her view, the only alternative to this approach is "the 'emotional' epistemology of the 'perceptual' level'" (*Papers* 035_21F003_001/*Journals* 674). Someone functioning at this level

> is helpless and lost before the complexity of the same law; his only method of *condensing* the meaning of that law is his emotion, backed by the context of his memories, which are loosely stored by resemblance, similarity, or chance association; he has no way of determining what *is* essential in that law, and thus his *emotion* becomes the *essential* – and, without examining or analyzing that law (which he cannot begin to do and would not know how), he concludes that the law is "*bad*" or "*good*" according to whatever aspect of it has the strongest emotional meaning for him, the strongest emotional associations or connotations. *This* is the reason why such men jump to conclusions rashly, on the mere hint of some isolated aspect of an issue, and miss the most important, essential, or relevant points, regardless of their intelligence and perceptiveness. (*Papers* 053_21F_003_004/Journals 676–677)[17]

Rand referred to people who function in this way as "concrete bound" or as "anti-conceptual mentalities."[18] These mentalities have "not discovered the process of conceptualization in conscious terms" and so they are only able to perform the process at the most rudimentary level (*ITOE* 76). They possess concepts for perceptual objects and their obvious attributes, and so they are able to record observations at a superficial level. But they do not understand more abstract concepts, though they may use the words corresponding to them.

> Words, as such people use them, denote unidentified feelings, unadmitted motives, subconscious urges, chance associations, memorized sounds, ritualistic formulas, second-hand cues – all of it hung, like barnacles, on some swimming suggestion of some existential referent. (76)

People functioning in this manner are not equipped to reason about the complex issues that determine the course of a human life, so they are left with no guide except their emotions – most notably the emotion of fear, which leads them to seek security in the opinions of others.

Rand's analysis is reminiscent of Enlightenment philosophy, especially Locke's. He, too, thought that much irrationality and vice was due to accidental "associations of ideas" occupying the place in a person's mind that should be filled by rational connections. This happens, he argued, because the practice of "learning Names before the Ideas they belong to" leads to using "Words without any, or without clear ideas," and he detailed the ways in which ideas could be defective ("confused," "obscure," "inadequate," "fantastical," "false") and retard thinking.[19] Locke's solution to this problem was to trace "even the most abstruse ideas" back to the data of "sensation or reflection" from which they were originally derived (*Essay* II.xii.8, cf. *Of the Conduct of the Understanding* §9, §28). Rand concurred:

> One of the cardinal points I make throughout [*ITOE*] is that, to be valid, the most abstract concept – the concept that is removed from concretes by a long conceptual, hierarchical chain – has to be broken

down, analyzed, brought back to the perceptually given. If it cannot be brought back, it is not a valid concept. Or, what is more practical, if a person using a concept cannot indicate specifically on what aspects (ultimately resting on the perceptually given) his concept rests – if he cannot bring it back down to earth – then he is using his concepts improperly and the deductions or conclusions he will make from them are improper. (*Workshops* 27)[20]

The view that all of our concepts are derived ultimately from sense perception dates back to Aristotle.[21] Plato, by contrast, had held that concepts – either all of them or those most needed for scientific knowledge – cannot be formed or defined on the basis of sense perception, but must be possessed innately.[22] In the seventeenth century, this Platonic position was taken up by Descartes, among others.[23] Bacon and Locke took up Aristotle's position, but they focused more than he had on the process by which concepts (or "ideas" or "notions") are formed, and on the methods one must follow to ensure that one's concepts are properly grounded in perception.[24]

The position shared by Aristotle, Bacon, Locke, and Rand (among others) is often referred to as "empiricism," where this term is taken to mean the view "that sense experience is the ultimate source of all our concepts and knowledge" (Markie 2013).[25] Rationalism, in turn, is defined as the (Platonic) view that "there are significant ways in which our concepts and knowledge are gained independently of sense experience" (Markie 2013). Thus it is often thought that every theory of knowledge is either empiricist or rationalist. However this way of classifying obscures fundamental differences among the "empiricist" positions and fundamental affinities that some of these positions have with rationalism.[26]

The first thinkers to identify themselves as "empiricists" were a school of Hellenistic doctors who thought that it was impossible to come to know the fundamental causes of disease and health, so doctors should restrict themselves to describing and predicting patterns of symptoms and recommending treatments on the basis of such predictions.[27] Medicine, as these empiricists practiced it, was not scientific in Aristotle's sense; it was limited to the sort of knowledge he called "experience" – *empeiria*, in Greek. At least some of the these empiricists thought that scientific knowledge was impossible in all fields, because (siding with Plato over Aristotle) they believed that in order to know the principles required for scientific knowledge, human beings would need an intellectual faculty independent of the senses, and (siding with Aristotle over Plato) they denied that human beings have any such faculty.[28]

In the eighteenth century, David Hume developed a version of this same empiricist position. He argued that all cognition is based on sensory experience, and that it is impossible to derive from sensory experience the knowledge of *necessary causal connections* that is central to the classical conception of scientific knowledge. According to Hume, our talk of causal connections is the expression of a non-rational propensity human beings have to form *associations* between phenomena that we have often observed together.[29] Thus, on Hume's view, scientific knowledge as classically conceived is impossible, and any "causal" or "scientific" knowledge we might claim to have can be nothing more than a body of observations and expectations concerning patterns of observed phenomena.[30]

Aristotle's position is as different from empiricism (as exemplified by Hume and the medical empiricists) as either is from rationalism (as exemplified by Plato and Descartes), so it is best to consider the Aristotelian view a third school of thought.[31] This seems to have been Rand's view, since she saw her epistemology as (broadly) Aristotelian and regarded the rationalism-empiricism dichotomy as a false alternative (*FTNI* 27, "Review of Randall's *Aristotle*" (*VOR* 6–7), *Parallels* ix; cf., *HOP1*). According to the Aristotelian position, human beings can form concepts, based on the evidence of our senses, which enable us to advance beyond the level of mere experience to an abstract and systematic understanding of the world in terms of fundamentals. It is this sort of cognition that Rand has in mind when she speaks of "conceptual knowledge," and this is the kind of knowledge by which she and the Enlightenment thinkers thought reason could direct the course of human life.

However, Rand thought, the Enlightenment was undermined by philosophical failings. At the same time that the Aristotelian commitment to observation-based, abstract reasoning caught on in the culture at large, "reason was pushed off the philosophical scene, by default, by implication, by evasion."

> Most philosophers did not intend to invalidate conceptual knowledge, but its defenders did more to destroy it than did its enemies. They were unable to offer a solution to the "problem of universals," that is: to define the nature and source of abstractions, to determine the relationship of concepts to perceptual data – and to prove the validity of scientific induction. (*FTNI* 26)

Peikoff makes this point about Locke, specifically: "When the men of the Enlightenment counted on Locke (and his equivalents) as their intellectual defender, they were counting on a philosophy of reason so profoundly undercut as to be in process of self-destructing" (*ARL* 3(6) 275/*Parallels* 113).

Locke doubted that a science of nature was possible, because he did not think we could discover the fundamental properties of natural objects and form adequate concepts of them. Well-defined concepts adequate for science could be formed in the domain of mathematics, he thought, only because there are no mind-independent objects to which mathematical concepts are supposed to correspond.[32] Hume, Kant, and their successors carried this view to its logical conclusion: the features that make possible the rigor and certainty that had made geometry the paradigm of scientific knowledge since antiquity also prevent geometry from telling us anything about reality as it exists independent of the human mind, and the same applies to any other body of knowledge that conforms to the classical conception of a science.[33] Peikoff summarizes the version of this view that dominated philosophy departments in the middle decades of the twentieth century:

> If [a statement] is demonstrated by logical argument, it represents a subjective convention; if it asserts a fact, logic cannot establish it. If you validate it by an appeal to the meanings of your *concepts*, then it is cut off from reality; if you validate it by an appeal to your *percepts*, then you cannot be certain of it. ("The Analytic-Synthetic Dichotomy" *ITOE* 94)[34]

Most of the philosophers who shared this consensus view thought of themselves as proponents of science and reason, but their position excludes the possibility of identifying the essence of a phenomenon, forming and defining one's concepts accordingly, and demonstrating that certain attributes are necessitated by this essence. This rejected, essentialist way of thinking is at the core of science according to the classical conception, and it is what Rand thinks distinguishes a "rational man" from an "anti-conceptual mentality." Accordingly, this sort of thinking is ubiquitous in the works of Rand and her associates.

On subjects as diverse as metaphysics and economics, these writings are filled with arguments that certain definitions, rather than common alternatives, correctly identify the essence of their definienda, and that certain truths follow from or are explained by these definitions. For example, Rand avers to the definition of man as "the rational animal" in explanations of the nature of free will and morality, and in accounts of why we need self-esteem, philosophy, art, capitalism, political freedom, property rights, and representative government.[35] And she discusses and rejects alternative definitions that identify the human essence as – being a tool-maker, having an opposable thumb, or being produced or conditioned by various chemical, social, or economic forces.[36] Again, she argues for a distinctive definition of capitalism, in terms of which she explains a range of historical events, and from which she and her associates argued that such evils as coercive monopolies are logically impossible under capitalism.[37] According to the prevailing epistemology of the time, such arguments are mere semantics. Peikoff summarizes one philosophy professor's response to this last argument: "You're merely saying that, no matter what portion of the market it controls, you won't call a business a 'coercive monopoly' if it occurs in a system you call 'capitalism.' Your view is true by arbitrary fiat, it's a matter of semantics, it's *logically* true, but not *factually* true" (*ITOE* 88).

To defend her arguments and to flesh out her conception of rationality, Rand needed to show that definitions are not arbitrary, but could be objective – that is, that certain definitions are true and their alternatives false; and that there is a certain mental process that a thinker must implement in order to reach a concept's true definition (in a given context of knowledge). More generally, she needed to show that how we conceptualize the world is not arbitrary – that, in order to grasp the facts, we must form and apply certain concepts in certain ways, based, ultimately, on perceptual evidence. This is the task at which she thought the philosophers of the Enlightenment had failed.

One cause of this failure was a costly error that Locke inherited from Descartes concerning the foundations of knowledge: the idea that our most immediate and certain knowledge is of our own mental states, rather than objects in the external world. The senses, they thought, provide us with a direct awareness of certain "ideas" that are produced in our minds when external stimuli impinge on our sense organs. These "ideas of sensation" (or "sense data" as they came to be called) lack much of the content that (we will see) Rand thought is part of sense perception and needed for the formation of concepts. Moreover, the Cartesian view creates a divide between what appears to us and what exists in its own right. This divide would lead in time to Kant's view that human knowledge is confined to the realm of appearances, and cannot extend to "things-in-themselves" that lie behind the appearances. Because there are assumptions we need to make about this unknowable reality in order to lead our lives, Kant argued, our actions may and must be based in part on certain articles of faith.[38] To understand Rand's objection to this line of thought, and her alternative to it, we will consider her view of consciousness and sense perception in the next section.

The subsequent section will discuss her view of the process by which concepts and a whole system of conceptual knowledge are built upon a perceptual foundation. We will then look more closely at Rand's conception of objectivity and how it relates to her theory of concepts. From there we will turn to her view of definitions, considering both how they are objective and the role they play in making possible the sort of knowledge prized by the Enlightenment. Finally we will consider the standards that follow from Rand's theory for the proper formation and use of concepts.

Consciousness and Sense Perception

"Consciousness," as Rand uses the term, is synonymous with "awareness" or with the widest sense of the term "perception" (embracing propositional knowledge as well as sense perception). It can refer both to active states of awareness (such as seeing a tree or solving an equation) and to the faculty of which these states are exercises.

She regarded "consciousness," along with "existence" and "identity" as axiomatic concepts – ones that denote unanalyzable facts that are "directly experienced" and are "implicit in all facts and in all knowledge" (*ITOE* 55).[39] Implicit in any state of awareness is the awareness that something exists possessing an identity, and the awareness "that one exists possessing consciousness, consciousness being the faculty of perceiving that which exists" (*Atlas* 1015).[40]

Thus for Rand, no less than for Descartes and Locke, one's awareness of one's own consciousness is fundamental and incontestable.[41] However, Rand rejected as incoherent the Cartesian notion of a consciousness that could exist with no external objects.

> If nothing exists, there can be no consciousness: a consciousness with nothing to be conscious of is a contradiction in terms. A consciousness conscious of nothing but itself is a contradiction in terms: before it could identify itself as consciousness, it had to be conscious of something. If that which you claim to perceive does not exist, what you possess is not consciousness. (*Atlas* 1015, cf. *ITOE* 250–251)[42]

Rand does not mean to deny that people sometimes misidentify what they perceive, and so come to believe that they are perceiving things that do not in fact exist, and she recognizes that people can fail to distinguish between their perceptions and other states of consciousness, such as desires, intentions, emotions, and dreams.[43] However, whatever errors and non-cognitive states the faculty of consciousness may be capable of, Rand holds that it is fundamentally a faculty of perceiving existence and that all its other states or activities have content that is "derived from one's awareness of the external world" (*ITOE* 29). It follows that, whatever doubts may be warranted about our identifications of specific items in that external world, there can be no rational doubt that there is such a world and that we are aware of it.

Rand held that "sensory perception" is the fundamental form this awareness takes: "Man's senses are his only direct cognitive contact with reality and, therefore, his only *source of* information" ("Kant vs. Sullivan" *PWNI* 121). Thus, to deny "the validity of senses," in her view, is tantamount to denying that one is conscious (*ITOE* 3). Since our other forms of awareness depend on the senses, if we were not aware of reality in sensory perception, then we would not be aware of it at all – which means that we would not be conscious.

Henceforward I will use the word "perception" (as Rand often does) to refer specifically to sensory perception, rather than in the more general sense in which I've been using it up to now. "Perception," in this narrow sense, names a specific form of awareness possessed by human beings and certain other animals; Rand distinguished it both from conceptual knowledge and from sensation.[44] By "sensation," she meant a discrete and transient form of awareness "produced by the automatic reaction of a sense organ to a stimulus from the outside world." By contrast: "A 'perception' [or 'percept'] is a group of sensations automatically retained and integrated by the brain of a living organism, which gives it the ability to be aware, not of single stimuli, but of *entities*, of things" ("The Objectivist Ethics" *VOS* 19–20, cf. *ITOE* 5).

Rand thought that there was a developmental stage during which infants, like lower animals, experience the world in the form of sensations, but she denied that an adult "is able to experience a pure isolated sensation."

> It is in the form of percepts that man grasps the evidence of his senses and apprehends reality. When we speak of "direct perception" or "direct awareness," we mean the perceptual level. Percepts, not sensations, are the given, the self-evident. The knowledge of sensations as components of percepts is not direct, it is acquired by man much later: it is a scientific, *conceptual* discovery. (*ITOE* 5, cf. 136)

What Rand means in calling perception "direct" is that our perceptual awareness of objects is not inferred from or otherwise based on sensations or any prior mental state. Philosophers of perception call this position "direct realism," and it is best explained by contrast with the dominant view of perception, which can be called "perceptual subjectivism." A perceptual subjectivist holds that "what we are immediately aware of in perceptual experience is something subjective," typically a mental image in the case of vision (or some analog in the cases of the other senses).[45] Some perceptual subjectivists, called "phenomenalists," deny that we are ever aware of mind-independent objects; often these philosophers embrace "idealism," the metaphysical doctrine that nothing exists independently of the mind. This view is most famously associated with George Berkeley, and (in a different form) Hegel. Most perceptual subjectivists, however, are "representationalists" (also known as "indirect realists"): they hold that "the immediate objects of experience represent or depict physical objects in a way that allows one to infer justifiably from such experience to the existence of the corresponding 'external' objects" (BonJour 2007). This was the view of Descartes and Locke; and, in one form or another, it has been held by most epistemologists since. By contrast to both sorts of perceptual subjectivists, "direct realists hold that perception is an immediate or direct awareness of mind-independent physical objects or events in the external world" (Le Morvan 2004, 221).

Rand held that every "state of awareness," including perception, is "not a passive gaze, but an active process" (*ITOE* 5), but unlike the processes of reasoning, which are under a person's conscious control and must be initiated and sustained volitionally, the process of perception is performed automatically by the nervous system. In this respect perceptual awareness is "the given" upon which we build conceptual knowledge. As Wright (2008, 160–164) points out, Rand does not think it is always evident to a person whether or not a given state of consciousness is part of this given. Indeed she complains that many people regard certain of their own concepts "as if they were percepts" (*ITOE* 76).[46] Distinguishing between perception and reasoning and taking responsibility for the latter is an achievement.

> The day when [a man] grasps that the reflection he sees in a mirror is not a delusion, that it is real, but it is not himself, that the mirage he sees in a desert is not a delusion, that the air and the light rays that cause it are real, but it is not a city, it is a city's reflection – the day when he grasps that he is not a passive recipient of the sensations of any given moment, that his senses do not provide him with automatic knowledge in separate snatches independent of context, but only with the material of knowledge, which his mind must learn to integrate – the day when he grasps that his senses cannot deceive him, that physical objects cannot act without causes, that his organs of perception are physical and have no volition, no power to invent or to distort, that the evidence they give him is an absolute, but his mind must learn to understand it, his mind must discover the nature, the causes, the full context of his sensory material, his mind must identify the things that he perceives – *that* is the day of his birth as a thinker and scientist. (*Atlas* 1041)

When Rand says that the senses are "valid" and cannot "deceive" us, she means that there is no such thing as *misperception*. This is significant because it makes perception an inerrant foundation on which knowledge can be built.[47] It is widely thought that, if sense perception involves an inerrant awareness of anything, it cannot be of external objects, because perceivers are mistaken about external objects when they experience illusions.[48] Indeed it is the phenomenon of illusion, taken together with the search for an inerrant foundation of knowledge that has motivated so many epistemologists to accept perceptual subjectivism. By contrast, Rand held that, even in cases of illusion, we non-erroneously perceive external objects. Any errors we make lie in our *interpretation* of what we perceive.[49] For example, when looking at a straight stick that appears bent because it is partially submerged in a bucket of water, we do not experience a mental image of a bent stick that misrepresents the straight stick (as representationalists maintain); nor do we mistakenly perceive the straight stick as bent (as most direct realists maintain). Rather, because partially submerged straight sticks resemble bent sticks, it is easy for naïve observers to mistake the former for the latter.[50]

When discussing illusions and other phenomena that seem to pose challenges to the validity of the senses, Rand and her associates sometimes distinguish the *form* of perception from the *object* of perception (or "the how" from "the what").[51] This distinction can be brought out by means of an extended example. Suppose that a leaf is perceived from roughly the same vantage point by five perceivers: a hawk, a bee, a bat, a myopic man, and a woman with normal vision. All five perceivers are aware of the leaf and specifically of its shape. This is the *object* of perception. The five perceivers differ in the *way* they perceive this object. The normally sighted woman sees the shape in greater detail than does the myopic man, and there is a qualitative difference between their visual experiences. The hawk sees the shape in greater detail than either human being, and presumably the quality of his experience differs from that of the normally sighted woman's in something like the way that hers differs from the myopic man's. The vision of these three perceivers is similar as contrasted to that of the bee, who has a compound eye and a color-perception extending into the ultra-violet range. But, though the bee sees the leaf quite differently, she too sees its shape. The bat's perception of the shape will be more different still, as he perceives it via echolocation, a faculty that the other four perceivers lack entirely. *What* the five perceive is the same, but *how* they perceive it differs.[52] They perceive the same *object*, but each perceives it in a different *form*. This same point applies to a single perceiver as the condition of her sense organs changes, or as she perceives the same object via different sense modalities – for example, a human being will see the leaf differently if she squints than if she looks at it normally, and she can perceive its shape either visually or tactilely.

The form of a perception is the *identity* of that perception, as distinguished from other (possible) perceptions of the same object. The concept of "form" enables Rand (and her associates) to defend the *directness* of perception against arguments that (e.g.) the two human beings must be perceiving different (subjective) objects when looking at the same leaf, because the leaf appears blurry to one and well-defined to the other: the blurriness or definition is not an attribute of *what* the two see, but of *how* they see it. Similarly, the distinction enables one to respond to arguments that the myopic man's senses deceive him, because the leaf is not really blurry – or that the normally sighted woman's senses deceive her since, on a microscopic level, the leaf is a blur of moving particles.

More generally, Rand held, all attempts to draw a distinction between things *as they appear to us* and things as they exist *in themselves* involve mistaking the *forms* in which someone perceives for features of the perceived *objects*. She identified this mistake as the root of Kant's conclusion that (as she put it) we cannot grasp "the world of 'real' reality, 'superior' truth and 'things in themselves' or 'things as they are' – which means: things as they are *not* perceived by man" (*FTNI* 28). Kant's argument, she wrote, amounts to the following:

> Man is *limited* to a consciousness of a specific nature, which perceives by specific means and no others, therefore, his consciousness is not valid; man is blind, because he has eyes – deaf, because he has ears – deluded, because he has a mind – and the things he perceives do not exist, *because* he perceives them. (*FTNI* 28)[53]

282

This Kantian position is the consistent development of "the unchallenged premise that any knowledge acquired by a *process* of consciousness is necessarily subjective and cannot correspond to the facts of reality, since it is '*processed* knowledge'" (*ITOE* 81). This assumption, which Rand thought ran through much of the history of epistemology, amounts to the idea that "*identity* [is] the *disqualifying* element of consciousness," "that only an ineffable consciousness can acquire a valid knowledge of reality, that 'true' knowledge has to be causeless, i.e., acquired without any means of cognition" (80).[54] Against this assumption, Rand maintained that consciousness, like everything else, has identity, and operates by specific means.

> All knowledge *is* processed knowledge – whether on the sensory, perceptual or conceptual level. An "unprocessed" knowledge would be a knowledge acquired without means of cognition. Consciousness (as I said in the first sentence of this work) is not a passive state, but an active process. And more: the satisfaction of every need of a living organism requires an act of *processing* by that organism, be it the need of air, of food or of knowledge. (*ITOE* 81)

In *Atlas Shrugged*, Galt says that consciousness is a process of "identification" (1016), and *ITOE*'s first sentence (which Rand references in the above quote) names "differentiation and integration" as the process's "two essentials" (*ITOE* 5). Even a sensation identifies something (for example, heat or light or sweetness) by differentiating it from something else (cold, dark, or bitterness). Similarly, the act of perception identifies entities by differentiating them from their surroundings, and this differentiation is achieved and maintained by an automatic, neurological process of integrating sensory material.

Rand held that reasoning, too, is a process of differentiating and integrating. She defined reason as the "faculty that identifies and integrates the material provided by man's senses" ("The Objectivist Ethics" *VOS* 22, "Philosophy: Who Needs It?" *PWNI* 3–4, "The Left: Old and New" *ROTP* 162).[55] A human being uses concepts to identify what he perceives, and a concept is formed by first differentiating a class of similar items from the rest of existence and then integrating these items into a new mental unit.

The Process of Concept-Formation

We will be better able to grasp what is distinctive about Rand's theory of concept-formation, if we first look briefly at Locke's account of how concepts (or "general ideas") are abstracted from sensory material. He explains it as follows:

> [T]he mind makes the particular ideas, received from particular objects, to become general; which is done by considering them as they are in the mind such appearances, separate from all other existences, and the circumstances of real existence, as time, place, or any other concomitant ideas. This is called ABSTRACTION, whereby ideas taken from particular beings become general representatives of all of the same kind; and their names general names, applicable to whatever exists conformable to such abstract ideas. Such precise, naked appearances in the mind, without considering how, whence, or with what others they came there, the understanding lays up (with names commonly annexed to them) as the standards to rank real existences into sorts, as they agree with these patterns, and to denominate them accordingly. Thus the same colour being observed to-day in chalk or snow, which the mind yesterday received from milk, it considers that appearance alone, makes it a representative of all of that kind; and having given it the name *whiteness*, it by that sound

signifies the same quality wheresoever to be imagined or met with; and thus universals, whether ideas or terms, are made. (*Essay* II.xi.9)

On this account, a concept is formed by noticing some identical characteristic(s) that is common to the several individuals and then mentally isolating that characteristic from the individuals' other characteristics. This purified awareness of the characteristic(s) then applies equally to all objects possessing it. Kant aptly described the resulting concept as "a partial representation" of a perceived object "which can be common to several" objects (Ak. XXIV, 573, cf. 904–905). As "white" is formed by abstracting a single color that is observed on different occasions in snow, chalk, and milk, so children form the concept "man" when they "leave out of the complex idea they had of Peter and James, Mary and Jane, that which is peculiar to each, and retain only what is common to them all" (*Essay* III.iii.7). The process can be described as one of "context omission," because it consists in isolating a perceptible characteristic(s) from the context of other characteristic(s) with which it is found.[56]

There are severe problems with this position, which have been pointed out by centuries of critics, from Berkeley and Hume to Peter Geach (1951) and Wilfrid Sellars (1963). Most notably, only in rare cases are there any perceptibly identical characteristics shared by all of the things to which a concept applies. Even the whites of snow, milk, and chalk differ, as can be seen if one places these substances side by side. And, as Rand points out in connection with an example like Locke's of Peter, James, and Mary:

> The three persons are three individuals who differ in every particular respect and may not possess a single *identical* characteristic (not even their fingerprints). If you list all their particular characteristics, you will not find one representing "manness." (*ITOE* 2)

Berkeley and Hume observed that, if one mentally removes from one's perception of a given man, triangle, or white object, every characteristic in which it differs from other objects of the same kind, one will be left not with a generalized representation of the kind, but with nothing at all (Berkeley, *Principles of Human Knowledge*, introduction, §6–24, esp. §13; Hume, *A Treatise of Human Nature* T 1.1.7).

Many have concluded from the failure of the theory of context-omission that concepts cannot be based on perception and must be either innate ideas or free creations of our own minds. Rand, by contrast, held that concepts are formed from perception by a process, not of context-omission, but of *measurement-omission*. Consider her description of how a child would form the concept "length":

> If a child considers a match, a pencil and a stick, he observes that length is the attribute they have in common, but their specific lengths differ. The *difference is one of measurement*. In order to form the concept "length," the child's mind retains the attribute and omits its particular measurements. Or, more precisely, if the process were identified in words, it would consist of the following: "Length must exist in *some* quantity, but may exist in *any* quantity. I shall identify as 'length' that attribute of any existent possessing it which can be quantitatively related to a unit of length, without specifying the quantity." (*ITOE* 11)[57]

Length is a particularly difficult case for context-omission; for, as Hume put it, "'tis evident at first sight that the precise length of a line is not different nor distinguishable from the line itself, nor the precise degree of any quality from the quality" (T 1.1.7.3). The child in Rand's example does not discover a common attribute shared by the pencil, the match, and the stick, which is distinct from the attribute in which the three differ. Rather, he grasps that the three entities are *commensurable* – that the relevant difference between them is one of degree. The child notices that, if he takes any one of the three entities as a unit, there is something about each of the others that can be measured in terms of it: the pencil and the stick are each so many match-lengths long; and, conversely, the match is a certain fraction of a pencil-length. By omitting these measurements, the child forms a concept of the *dimension* – length – along which the three lengths and indefinitely many others can be measured.

The omission involved here is quite unlike that involved in context-omission. In context-omission what is omitted is fully distinct from what is retained; it is an obstacle to be removed before a "representation" (to use Kant's phrase) can become "common" to several objects. In measurement-omission, by contrast, "that the measurements *must* exist is an essential part of the process. The principle is: the relevant measurements must exist in *some* quantity, but may exist in *any* quantity" (*ITOE* 12). Rather than ignoring the measurements and turning our attention to something else, in forming concepts we *despecify* the measurements so as to project a whole dimension along which the measurements fall. Whereas context-omission involves only *differentiating* a shared feature from a host of differing ones, the process Rand describes is primarily one of *integrating* the differing measurements into a new whole. This is reflected in her definition of a concept as: "a mental integration of two or more [items] possessing the same distinguishing characteristic(s), with their particular measurements omitted" (13).[58]

The formation of the concept "length" is an unusually simple example in two respects. First, the concept embraces an entire axis of measurement. By contrast, a typical concept embraces a range of items along an axis – items that are commensurable not only with one another but also with other items from which they are contrasted. Take, for example, the concept "blue": two shades of blue are commensurable with one another but also with a shade of red, and all the shades fall along the axis hue. The second respect in which the example of "length" is unusually simple is that there is only a single axis along which lengths are commensurable, whereas most things are measured along several axes. Colors, for example, can be measured along the axes of hue, saturation, and brightness; entities can be measured along innumerable axes.

Let us consider Rand's description of the formation of a concept of an entity – the concept "table":

> The child's mind isolates two or more tables from other objects, by focusing on their distinctive characteristic: their shape. He observes that their shapes vary, but have one characteristic in common: a flat, level surface and support(s). He forms the concept "table" by retaining that characteristic and omitting *all* particular measurements, not only the measurements of the shape, but of all the other characteristics of tables (many of which he is not aware of at the time).
>
> An adult definition of "table" would be: "A man-made object consisting of a flat, level surface and support(s), intended to support other, smaller objects." Observe what is specified and what is omitted in this definition: the distinctive characteristic of the shape is specified and retained; the particular geometrical measurements of the shape (whether the surface is square, round, oblong or triangular, etc., the number and shape of the supports, etc.) are omitted; the measurement of size or weight are omitted; the fact that it is a material object is specified, but the material out of which it is made is omitted, thus omitting the measurements that differentiate one material from another; etc. Observe however, that the utilitarian requirements of the table set certain limits on the omitted measurements, in the form of "no larger than and no smaller than" required by its purpose. This rules out a ten-foot tall or a two-inch tall table (though the latter may be sub-classified as a toy or a miniature table) and it rules out unsuitable materials, such as non-solids. (*ITOE* 11–12)

Here we can see more aspects of Rand's theory of concept-formation in action. The process begins with the isolation of a group of similar existents – in this case, some tables. Rand uses the term "unit" for "an existent regarded as a separate member of a group of two or more similar members" (6). Thus each of the tables of which the child is aware would be a unit of the relevant group. The units are seen as similar when contrasted to some foils – in this case the foils might be chairs or other household items. To see the units as similar is to see the difference between them as slight in comparison with their differences from the foils. This requires that there be some axis of measurement along which the units and the foils can be compared. Rand coined the phrase "conceptual common denominator" (or "CCD" as it is often abbreviated) for this axis.[59] She defined it as follows: "The characteristic(s) reducible to a unit of measurement, by means of which man differentiates two or more existents from other existents possessing it" (15).

The CCD that Rand thinks a child would use in forming the concept "table" is shape. Unlike length or hue, shape is not a simple characteristic that can be measured along a single axis. Nevertheless, as Rand notes, "any shape can be reduced to or expressed by a set of figures in terms of *linear measurement*," and "a vast part of higher mathematics, from geometry on up, is devoted to the task of discovering methods by which various shapes can be measured" (14). Of course, Rand did not think that this complex mathematics is needed to notice similarities in shape: "When, in the process of concept-formation, man observes that shape is a commensurable characteristic of certain objects, he does not have to measure all the shapes involved *nor even to know how to measure them*; he merely has to observe the element of *similarity*." In many cases, "similarity is grasped *perceptually*" (14). In such cases, she held that what is grasped perceptually is the very same relationship that geometry enables us to grasp with mathematical precision. Thus she differentiated her view from that of "modern philosophers, who claim that 'similarity' is a vague, undefinable or ineffable term" (*Papers* 109_30x_002_15, cf. *ITOE* 140–141).[60]

Once the tables are isolated by contrasting them with other items sharing the CCD, the concept "table" is formed by omitting measurements within what we might call the table-range of measurements along the CCD. This range of measurements constitutes the "distinguishing characteristic" of tables. However, Rand thinks, it is not only along the CCD that we omit measurements and retain ranges. If we did, the result would be not the concept "table" but a concept "table-shaped." In forming the concept "table," one omits measurements and retains ranges for *all* the characteristics of tables – for example, the material they are made of, their color, weight, and cost, who owns them, and so on. One does this for all of the characteristics one knows tables to have, and one does it also for the characteristics that one does not yet know, by instituting a *policy* of omitting measurements (and retaining ranges) of new characteristics as they are discovered.

To have the concept "table" is to regard everything within the table-range a certain way – as a table. Part of what it means to regard something this way is that when one finds it to have any characteristic, one expects there to be a corresponding characteristic in other tables that is commensurable without (necessarily) being quantitatively identical, so one ascribes the characteristic with its measurements omitted to all tables. This means that, in forming a concept, one commits oneself to a policy of *induction*. Rand regarded defining the proper rules of induction as an important outstanding philosophical question, which she intended to address in her treatise on Objectivism (*ITOE* 303–304, *Journals* 700).[61]

Though the child in Rand's example isolates the tables from other items along the CCD of shape, it is not just the shapes, but the tables *as complete entities* that he regards as similar and resolves to treat as units in his further thinking. Evidently, this is because he views the similarity in the shapes, not as an isolated phenomenon, but as one of many related similarities between the tables. Rand's "adult definition" of table indicates some of the relations between the different respects in which tables are similar to one another: in particular, she notes that "utilitarian requirements of the table set certain limits" on the sizes and shapes that tables can take. A child first forming the concept would not yet be able to formulate such a definition, but presumably Rand thinks he would be aware in a less articulate form of the relation between a table's function and its shape and size. In a discussion of this example, she noted that a table's function (or at least some of its uses) is "observable directly" (Workshops 141/*ITOE* 209–210).

The process of concept-formation makes use of a great deal of unconceptualized knowledge. As Rand stressed, it is concepts of perceptible entities (like dogs, tables, or balls) that children form first.[62] It is only later that a child conceptualizes the attributes (or actions or relations) of these entities. However, in order to form the first entity concepts, a child must already be aware of some of the entities' attributes and of some of the relations among these attributes. Just as one does not always need to know how to measure an attribute in order to grasp similarity, so too Rand thought that one does not always need to have a concept of an attribute to be aware of it in the way needed for the formation of other concepts. The awareness of attributes (and actions and relations) that children use to form their first concepts of entities is *perceptual* rather than *conceptual* in form (*ITOE* 15).

The perceptual level of consciousness, as Rand understood it, is rich. It includes an awareness of "entities, motions, attributes, and certain numbers of entities," and, importantly, the awareness of certain similarities and differences (15). However, it does not include an awareness of attributes *in abstraction from the entities that they characterize*, and it does not include the ability to regard each of several similar existents as a distinct member of a group of similar things – that is, to view them as *units*. This perspective on an existent as *one of a group of similar existents* represents the first step into the *conceptual level* of consciousness.

However, to take this "unit-perspective" on an item is not yet to have a concept.[63] The perspective requires only regarding a particular in light of the relationships of similarity and difference in which one has observed it to stand to other particulars. Someone regarding a particular in this way may be able to apply to it things he has learned about other units, but his knowledge and thought remain concerned with the units as individuals. He is able, in effect, to reason analogically, but not inductively or deductively.

A concept is formed when the group of similars is *integrated* by the act of measurement-omission into a unitary and open-ended awareness of all similar existents. The result is "a *single* new *mental* entity which is used thereafter as a single unit of thought" (10). Rand analogizes this mental entity to "a file folder in which man's mind files his knowledge of the existents it subsumes."[64]

> The content of such folders varies from individual to individual, according to the degree of his knowledge – it ranges from the primitive, generalized information in the mind of a child or an illiterate to the enormously detailed sum in the mind of a scientist – but it pertains to the same referents, to the same kind of existents, and is subsumed under the same concept. This filing system makes possible such activities as learning, education, research – the accumulation, transmission and expansion of knowledge. (66–67)

The concept is able to function as a single unit in thought because it is represented by a *perceptible* symbol – a *word*. Without the word, the unit-perspective would remain fleeting and could only be maintained with effort – by holding in mind several items at once and comparing them. The introduction of a word completes the act of integration, creating the "mental equivalent of [a] concrete" (10). Extending Rand's file-folder analogy, one might think of the word as the physical folder – the sheet of stiff paper that holds a set of documents together by being literally folded around them. The file itself – say one's file of 2013 business receipts – is not the same thing as the physical folder: since the relevant documents could have been held together by a different piece of stiff paper, and that piece of paper could have been folded around different documents. The file is, rather, the *organization* of documents that is implemented by means of the physical folder. Likewise, a concept is an organization of information that is implemented by means of a word. (The same concept could be denoted by a different word, as it is in other languages, and the same auditory symbol might stand for different concepts, as in the case of homonyms.) The word provides stability and unity to the unit-perspective: once the use of the word has been automatized, this perspective is readily available to a thinker and can be held in mind as a single unit.

The integration provided by words makes possible what Rand identifies as "the cognitive role of concepts."[65] Referencing an informal experiment that showed that crows are able to keep track of three men at a time, but not five, Rand makes the point that there is a limit to the number of separate units that any consciousness can hold in mind simultaneously (62–63).[66] Man's "incomparable cognitive power," she concludes, is due to "the ability to reduce a vast amount of information to a minimal number of units" (63). This is the ability provided by concepts.

> A concept substitutes one symbol (one word) for the enormity of the perceptual aggregate of the concretes it subsumes. In order to perform its unit-reducing function, the symbol has to become automatized in man's consciousness, i.e., the enormous sum of its reference must be instantly (implicitly) available to his conscious mind whenever he uses that concept, without the need of perceptual visualization or mental summarizing – in the same manner as the concept "5" does not require that he visualize five sticks every time he uses it. (64)

Forming a new concept (whether one is forming it for the first time or learning it from someone else) requires "fully conscious, focused attention and observation"; and, for a time, using the concept is taxing, but eventually one "establish[es] mental connections" that make the knowledge integrated by the concept "automatic (instantly available as a context) thus freeing [one's] mind to pursue further, more complex knowledge" (65).

The wealth of new knowledge that is made possible by our earliest concepts leads to the need for further concepts, which enable further knowledge, and further concepts to integrate that knowledge. Thus the process of conceptualization produces "a system of mental filing and cross-filing, so complex that the largest electronic computer is a child's toy by comparison" (69). At the base of this system are concepts of the sort we form first as children: concepts denoting perceptible entities (e.g., "dog" or "table"). As we discussed earlier, to form such concepts, our perceptual awareness of the entities must include an awareness of many of their attributes, actions, and relations. The unit-economy provided by the concepts a child forms of these entities frees his mind to then focus selectively on these characteristics, treating them as separate units of thought, which he will then integrate into further concepts (e.g., "furry," "barking," "tail").

The unit-economy provided by our first concepts also enables us to notice more remote similarities than we could at first, and this leads us to form wider concepts such as "animal," (integrating such concepts as "dog," "bird," and "fish") or "furniture" (integrating "table," "bed," etc.). Similarly, having a concept enables us to focus on subtle similarities and differences among its units that we could not otherwise attend to. This makes possible the formation of narrower concepts that subdivide its units – for example, the concepts "parrot" and "finch" are made possible by "bird." Concepts also enable us to discover or invent things that then need to be conceptualized (e.g., "atom," "gene," "field," "television," "marriage," "government," etc.).[67]

The "filing-system" that comprises all of our concepts "serves as the context, the frame-of-reference, by means of which man grasps and classifies (and studies further) every existent he encounters and every aspect of reality" (69). And Rand sees the activity by which one builds, maintains, and uses this system as a continuation of the process of concept-formation.

> The process of concept-formation does not consist merely of grasping a few simple abstractions, such as "chair," "table," "hot," "cold," and of learning to speak. It consists of a method of using one's consciousness, best designated by the term "conceptualizing." It is not a passive state of registering random impressions. It is an actively sustained process of identifying one's impressions in conceptual terms, of integrating every event and every observation into a conceptual context, of grasping relationships, differences, similarities in one's perceptual material and of abstracting them into new concepts, of drawing inferences, of making deductions, of reaching conclusions, of asking new questions and discovering new answers and expanding one's knowledge into an ever-growing sum. The faculty that directs this process, the faculty that works by means of concepts, is: *reason. The process is thinking.* ("The Objectivist Ethics" *VOS* 21–22)

The Objectivity of Conceptual Knowledge

Rand intended her theory of concepts as a solution to the "Problem of Universals." As with most longstanding philosophical disputes, this problem is understood differently by members of different traditions.[68] Rand's thinking about universals was stimulated by a conversation "with a Jesuit who philosophically was a Thomist," and her characterizations of the problem show the influence of twentieth-century neo-Thomist thought (*ITOE* 307).[69] Here is how the problem is formulated in an often-cited neo-Thomist source:

> The problem of universals is the problem of the correspondence of our intellectual concepts to things existing outside our intellect. Whereas external objects are determinate, individual, formally exclusive of all multiplicity, our concepts or mental representations offer us the realities independent of all particular determination; they are abstract and universal. The question, therefore, is to discover to what extent the concepts of the mind correspond to the things they represent; how the flower we conceive represents the flower existing in nature; in a word, whether our ideas are faithful and have an objective reality. (De Wulf 1913, 90)[70]

Rand's goal, like the neo-Thomists', was to show that concepts are "objective" and "correspond to something that is to be found in reality."[71] But she did not share their view of objectivity and of what it is for a concept to correspond to reality. According to the neo-Thomists, in order for concepts to correspond to reality, each concept would need to correspond to some object that exists independently of the mind. This condition is satisfied by two of the four traditional theories of universals that the neo-Thomists recognized (de Wulf 1913).

The first of these theories is "extreme realism" (or "exaggerated realism"), the neo-Thomists' name for Plato's view that universals exist independently of the perceptible world as eternal archetypes of which perceptible objects are imperfect and transient manifestations. The neo-Thomists saw this view as "extreme" by comparison to their own position, which they called

289

"moderate realism." According to moderate realism, a concept corresponds to a "common nature" or "essence" that is "immanent in individuals and is multiplied in all the representatives of a class" (de Wulf 1913). Because all the members of the class have "perfectly similar natures," the concept is able to correspond to something that "is really in each and every one of the individuals" (Maher 1900, 249; Coffey 1938, 7–8; cf. Coffey 1958, 270–271, 277–278). And because these individuals are perceptible, "the content of our universal concepts is really in the data of sense," so concepts can be formed by the process of context-omission that we discussed earlier in connection with Locke (Coffey 1958, 290).[72]

According to both "realist" views, a concept is an apprehension of a universal whose existence and relation to the particulars is independent of the mind. The remaining two theories of concepts (in the neo-Thomists' fourfold classification) deny this. *Conceptualism* maintains that concepts are formed by the mind rather than received from without, so conceptualists conclude that (so far as we can know) our concepts do not correspond to anything that exists independently of the mind.[73] *Nominalism* denies the existence of concepts as distinct from words and linguistic habits. According to this view, the content of thought is always particular, but people use the same name for multiple particulars when they resemble one another, and this leads us to apply what we have learned about one resembling particular to the others.[74]

Both non-realist theories stress the mind's *activity* – whether in forming concepts or in using language – but they think that this activity makes concepts (or word usages) subjective. The realists, by contrast, have an essentially *passive* view of conceptual thought. Their account of the objectivity of concepts does not make reference to anything the mind *does* or *produces*, but only to the existence of a universal to which the concept corresponds. The mind receives its universal content from without, and needs only to separate this content from any other material that may be present with it.

Behind this constellation of theories, Rand saw the premise that in order to apprehend reality accurately, a consciousness would have to passively mirror it. This premise generates a false dichotomy between the "intrinsic" and "subjective" that she thought had "played havoc" with "every issue involving the relationship of consciousness to existence."[75]

Something is *intrinsic* if it is a feature of reality "unrelated to man's consciousness" that can be "perceived by man directly," on the model of sense perception, without requiring any *volitional work*. Something is *subjective* if it is an arbitrary creation "of man's consciousness, unrelated to the facts of reality." Both forms of realism regard universals or concepts as intrinsic, and the conceptualist and nominalist schools regard them as subjective.

> None of these schools regards concepts as *objective*, i.e., as neither revealed nor invented, but as produced by man's consciousness in accordance with the facts of reality, as mental integrations of factual data computed by man – as the products of a cognitive method of classification whose processes must be performed by man, but whose content is dictated by reality. (*ITOE* 54)

Objectivity, as Rand understands it, is not a matter of the mind's passively mirroring intrinsic features or structures in reality. Rather it consists in identifying existents by implementing a specific process of volitional action that is required by the nature of man's cognitive faculties and the natures of the existents to be identified.[76] Concepts are produced by the mental act of *integration*.[77] Independent of this act and of the cognitive need that it serves, a concept's units do not contain or form a unity. Therefore, there is no intrinsic universal. But concepts are not subjective, because integration by measurement-omission is not an arbitrary process. It is possible only when the units stand in the relation of commensurability, which exists indepen-dent of the mind and its needs. Moreover, the nature of human consciousness – specifically, its need for unit economy – makes it necessary for a human being to form certain concepts (and not others), if he is to integrate and expand his knowledge.

Rand's view of objectivity colors what she means when she speaks of the *correspondence* of concepts to reality. Philosophers discuss correspondence most often in connection with the "correspondence theory of truth." Both proponents and critics of this theory often hold that for thought to correspond to reality would mean for its structure to be isomorphic with that of reality: each concept would correspond to some discrete object, and each proposition would correspond to a fact composed of such objects.[78] Conceived in this way, the relation-ship between thought and reality does not involve any activity on the mind's part. Accordingly, theorists who stress the role of mental activity in the meaning of concepts and propositions are often led to reject the idea of correspondence – to reject intrinsicism in favor of subjectivism.[79] Rand, by contrast, viewed the correspondence of cognition to reality in active terms. She defined "truth" as the "recognition of reality" (*Atlas* 1017), and she saw this as a formulation of the "correspondence theory" ("Philosophical Detection" *PWNI* 19, cf. *OPAR* 165).[80] Truth, and successful cognition generally, corresponds to reality in that it is "a mental identification or classification of what actually exists" (*TPO* 6 2:03:47/*Answers* 158).[81] A valid concept, in par-ticular, corresponds to reality because it is based on facts, which it enables a person to integrate into an ever-expanding body of knowledge.[82]

As we saw earlier, Rand held that consciousness is an active process even at the perceptual level, but the activity involved in sense perception is physiological and automatic. What sets the conceptual level apart is that the process of conceptualization must be performed volitionally. As a result, human beings do not automatically form all the knowledge that we need and are capable of, and the conclusions we do form can be in error. This is why, Rand held, we need epistemology.

> Man is neither infallible nor omniscient; if he were, a discipline such as epistemology – the theory of knowledge – would not be necessary nor possible; his knowledge would be automatic, unquestion-able and total. But such is not man's nature. Man is a being of volitional consciousness: beyond the level of percepts – a level inadequate to the cognitive requirements of his survival – man has to ac-quire knowledge by his own effort, which he may exercise or not, and by a process of reason, which he may apply correctly or not. Nature gives him no automatic guarantee of his mental efficacy; he is capable of error, of evasion, of psychological distortion. He needs a *method* of cognition, which he himself has to discover: he must discover how to use his rational faculty, how to validate his conclusions, how to distinguish truth from falsehood, how to set the criteria of *what* he may accept as knowledge. (*ITOE* 78–79, cf. *PWNI* 3–4)

Rand saw this need as the context for the concept "objectivity." The concept integrates the knowledge both that we need to correspond to reality in our thinking and that doing so requires a fact-based method.

> Objectivity begins with the realization that man (including his every attribute and faculty, includ-ing his consciousness) is an entity of a specific nature who must act accordingly; that there is no escape from the law of identity, neither in the universe with which he deals nor in the working of his own consciousness, and if he is to acquire knowledge of the first, he must discover the proper method of using the second; that there is no room for the *arbitrary* in any activity of man, least of all in his method of cognition – and just as he has learned to be guided by objective criteria in making

his physical tools, so he must be guided by objective criteria in forming his tools of cognition: his concepts.

Just as man's physical existence was liberated when he grasped the principle that "nature, to be commanded, must be obeyed," so his consciousness will be liberated when he grasps that *nature, to be apprehended, must be obeyed* – that the rules of cognition must be derived from the nature of existence and the nature, the *identity*, of his cognitive faculty. (*ITOE* 82)

Thus "to be 'objective'," as Peikoff aptly puts it, "is volitionally to adhere to reality by following certain rules of method, a method based on facts *and* appropriate to man's form of cognition" (*OPAR* 117).

Of course, Rand did not think that a child needs to have an explicit method to take his first steps into the conceptual level. The processes of forming and applying concepts that denote directly perceptible objects and their perceptible attributes can be performed unselfconsciously. It "is learned as one learns to speak, and it becomes automatic in the case of existents given in perceptual awareness, such as 'man,' 'table,' 'blue,' 'length,' etc." (*ITOE* 28). Thus we find it easy "to identify with full certainty the perceptual referents of simple concepts" (50). However, when people use the words denoting more advanced concepts, they are too often "guided by the feeling 'I kinda know what I mean'" (21). This is because "as man's concepts move farther away from direct perceptual evidence," the process becomes "progressively more difficult" and "requires a new cognitive effort" (28).

People who do not put forth this effort in the realm of higher abstractions function by memorization and imitation of formulas that they do not understand. Instead of genuine concepts, they form "floating abstractions" with only approximate meanings (76). The result is the "concrete-bound" or "anti-conceptual" mentality, which "treats the first-level abstractions, the concepts of physical existents, as if they were percepts, and is unable to rise much further, unable to integrate new knowledge or to identify its own experience" (*ITOE* 76, cf. "The Missing Link" *PWNI* 51).

In order to consistently sustain a genuine process of conceptualization after the point at which it becomes "fully volitional," one must "adopt it as an active, continuous, self-initiated policy," and this requires knowing the process "in conscious terms" (*PWNI* 51, *ITOE* 76). This requires "rules of thinking" that articulate the "epistemology" that is already "implicit in [man's] thinking, but unidentified" (*Papers* 033_15x_12_007–008/*Journals* 699). In addition to the traditional laws of logic (which are discussed by Jason Rheins, 251, above), these "rules of thinking" include standards that derive specifically from Rand's theory of concepts. These standards concern how concepts should be formed and defined. We will consider the issue of definition first, because the distinctive view of essences at the core of her theory of definition plays a significant role in her view of when it is (and is not) proper to form a new concept.

Definitions and the Objectivity of Essences

It is the epistemological obligation of every individual to know what his mental file contains in regard to any concept he uses, to keep it integrated with his other mental files, and to seek further information when he needs to check, correct or expand his knowledge. (*ITOE* 67)

Once one reaches the fully volitional level of knowledge, Rand held, definitions are the indispensable means of fulfilling this obligation.[83] A definition specifies "the nature of the units subsumed under a concept," thereby enabling us "to distinguish a concept from all other concepts and thus to keep its units differentiated from all other existents" (40). In this way it enables one to "identify and *retain*" a concept – that is, to make self-conscious the policy on which one is integrating the units and to carry this policy forward consistently.

This is the primary function Rand accords to definitions, but they also serve a second function: because the definition of each concept is formulated in terms of others, definitions also enable one "to establish the relationships, the hierarchy, the *integration* of all his concepts and thus the integration of his knowledge" (40). For example, defining "man" as a type of animal, and "animal" as a type of organism, serves to situate our knowledge of human beings within the wider context of our knowledge of living things. And specifying that man is the *rational* animal, reminds us of the difference between man and the other animals – a difference that we must always bear in mind when applying our general biological knowledge to human beings.

Rand accepted two traditional Aristotelian rules of definition. First, that definitions should be formulated in terms of a genus (that "indicates the category of existents from which [the units] were differentiated") and a differentia (which "specifies the distinguishing characteristic(s)" that set the units apart from other members of the genus) (41). Second, she accepted and emphasized what she called "the rule of *fundamentality*":

> When a given group of existents has more than one characteristic distinguishing it from other existents, man must observe the relationships among these various characteristics and discover the one on which all the others (or the greatest number of others) depend, i.e., the fundamental characteristic without which the others would not be possible. This fundamental characteristic is the *essential* distinguishing characteristic of the existents involved, and the proper *defining* characteristic of the concept. (*ITOE* 45)[84]

The "*essential* characteristic" is the one "without which the units would not be the kind of existents they are" (42). Rand reinterprets this traditional Aristotelian idea in light of her view that concepts are objective rather than intrinsic. If kinds are not intrinsic features of reality, but objective products of human cognition, then the status of an existent as a member of a kind (i.e., as a unit of a concept) is not intrinsic but objective, and so there cannot be any characteristic of the units that, wholly independent of the mind and its needs, makes them members of the kind.

Essences in Rand's view are *epistemological* rather than *metaphysical*. A person properly forms a concept that classifies existents into a kind when he has observed that they are similar to one another. This initially observed similarity will typically be complex: it will include many related respects in which the units are like one another as opposed to other things. And the concept enables the person to discover (and to retain) more of what the units have in common. Thus the possessor of a concept has a wealth of knowledge about the units *as such* – that is, about the units insofar as they are similar to one another as opposed to other things. The essential characteristic condenses this body of knowledge into a unit-economical form. By implying as many as possible of the unit's other known distinguishing characteristics, the essential characteristic enables the concept-possessor to hold in mind as a single unit his complex reason for classifying the concept's units as he does. (Usually the essence will be a single characteristic, but Rand allows that in some cases, it may be more than one; thus she writes of the "essential characteristic(s).")

The essence is whichever characteristic(s) serves this function, and this will necessarily be *relative to a given context of knowledge*. As Allan Gotthelf (2013, 33) puts Rand's point: "The essential characteristic of a concept, then, is that distinguishing characteristic of its units, *from among those known*, which is *known* to be responsible for (and thus explanatory of) the greatest number of other *known* distinguishing characteristics." Contexts of knowledge vary from individual to individual, so the same concept can have different essences for different people, and what is essential for a given person can change as he discovers more distinguishing characteristics of the units, learns more about the causal relations between the distinguishing characteristics, or discovers more existents from which the units of the concept need to be distinguished.[85]

"An objective definition valid for all men" can be "determined according to the widest context of knowledge available to man on the subjects relevant to the units of a given concept" (*ITOE* 46). But this definition, too, can change as science progresses and mankind's knowledge grows.[86] From Rand's point of view, such a change of definition is not a matter of correcting an earlier error and discovering what the essence really was all along. Rather, if one of the earlier-known distinguishing characteristics really explains (in whole or in part) most of the other then-known distinguishing characteristics, then that characteristic really is essential *relative to that earlier context of knowledge*, and this is not altered by the subsequent discovery of a deeper explanation or of new foils from which the units must also be differentiated. Such new discoveries simply create a new context in which the relevant characteristic is *no longer* the essential one and so is *supplanted* by a new essential characteristic.[87]

Essences, so understood, are *objective*, as opposed to being either intrinsic or subjective. They are not intrinsic because a characteristic's status as essential is the product of a human cognitive need and, therefore, is relative to a given context of knowledge. This does not make them subjective, however, because within any given context of knowledge, it is a factual matter (independent of anyone's wishes) which attributes of a group of existents serve this need and should be designated as essential. A definition is "false and worthless," Rand argued, "if it is not *contextually* absolute – if it does not specify the known relationships among existents (in terms of the known *essential* characteristics) or if it contradicts the known (by omission or evasion)" (*ITOE* 47). Rand and her associates criticized many such "definitions by non-essentials" in articles on a wide range of topics, and they argued for alternatives.[88]

To illustrate Rand's view of definitions and the role they play in thought, let us consider her definitions of two concepts that figure prominently in her works: "capitalism" and "Romanticism." Both concepts were first formed in the nineteenth century to designate phenomena that had only recently come into existence. It was already the "era of philosophy's post-Kantian disintegration," so there was little interest in developing the observationally grounded essentialized understanding of the world that was characteristic of the Enlightenment. Thus, Rand thought, philosophers did not provide the "epistemological criteria" that the new field of political-economy needed ("What Is Capitalism?" *CUI* 2), and they "defaulted in regard to aesthetics as they did in regard to every other crucial aspect of the nineteenth century" ("What Is Romanticism?" *RM* 97).

The concept "capitalism" was formed to denote a distinctive social system that was then emerging. Rand contemptuously quotes an encyclopedia article that characterizes it as "the economic system that has been dominant in the western world since the breakup of feudalism"; the article says a fundamental role is played in this system by "the relations between private owners of nonpersonal means of production ... and free but capitalless workers, who sell their labour services to employers" (*CUI* 4). Elsewhere Rand notes that capitalism is often defined in terms of competition in a marketplace ("How to Read (and Not to Write)" *VOR* 131–132). Rand did not think these features were fundamental, and she sought to understand the essence of the system – the feature that caused and explained such distinguishing features of capitalist countries as rapid industrialization and a rise in the standard of living. The characteristic she identified as essential was the respect for individual rights, and the consequent separation of the government from the economy. Thus she defined capitalism as: "a social system based on the recognition of individual rights, including property rights, in which all property is privately owned" (*CUI* 10). This definition (when taken in the context of other aspects of her developing philosophical system and of her understanding of world history) enabled Rand to evaluate capitalism morally, and to explain: why it arose when it did historically; why it led to such effects as the Industrial Revolution, the near century of peace Europe enjoyed between 1815 and 1914, and the end of slavery, of serfdom, and of child labor; and why it increasingly came under attack in the late nineteenth and early twentieth centuries. The definition also enabled her to see that capitalism had never been fully and consistently implemented, and to identify the steps by which specific departures from (or failures to implement) the essence of capitalism explained such nineteenth-century developments as railroad and utility monopolies. The fact that the essence of the new social system wasn't properly identified in the nineteenth century also explained why it could not be implemented consistently or defended intellectually. The definition thus condenses, organizes, and facilitates a vast body of causal knowledge. This is what justifies the definition. If Rand's explanations were mistaken, then the definition would be as well. And if, in the future, new knowledge makes possible deeper explanations of these phenomena in terms of some other characteristic, then the definition would become obsolete and would need to be replaced.[89]

Romanticism is an artistic movement that flourished in the nineteenth century. According to the most common definition (both at the time and during the period when Rand was writing), it is "an esthetic school based on *the primacy of emotions.*" Rand observed that the "emotional intensity" that Romantic art projects and evokes is only one of several consequences of the artists' "value-oriented view of life." In the context of the knowledge available to the nineteenth-century estheticians, it would have been proper to define Romanticism as the esthetic school committed to "the primacy of values." But Rand thought her own context of knowledge was wider. She had identified the focus on personal values as itself a consequence of the (at least implicit) belief in free will, so she concluded that: "following the rule of fundamentality, it is as a *volition*-oriented school that Romanticism must be defined – and it is in terms of this essential characteristic that the nature and history of Romantic literature can be traced and understood" (*RM* 96–97, 99).[90]

Rand held that "*reason* is the faculty of volition" (*RM* 97) and individual rights are the principles that define and sanction the freedom human beings need to live by their reasoning. So both capitalism and Romanticism are creatures of the rational way of life that Rand extolled. They were both products of the Enlightenment's valorization of reason, but they emerged in a post-Enlightenment world, where no serious attempt was made to identify their essence and provide the guidance needed to implement them consistently.[91] Thus, Rand thought, these Enlightenment orphans were left ill-equipped and defenseless. It was in order to defend these values and the rational life of which they are parts that Rand needed to develop the objective theory of concepts and definitions that she thought Enlightenment philosophers had failed to provide.

Standards of Conceptualization

Thus far we have been discussing valid concepts, but Rand thought that there are also "invalid concepts" – ones that hamper thinking rather than facilitate it. "An invalid concept invalidates every proposition or process of thought in which it is used as a cognitive assertion" (*ITOE* 49).

Invalid concepts include those for entities that are mistakenly believed to exist (e.g., the concepts "ghost" and "god"), and those that attempt to classify entities on the basis of attributes that they do not really possess (e.g., the early medical concept "choleric") (239). In these cases, the errors are prior to the process of concept-formation, but Rand thought that some concepts are invalid due to errors within the process of concept-formation itself. Real existents can be improperly integrated on the basis of real, but non-essential attributes.

This cannot occur with first-level concepts, which are based on the causally significant similarities that are salient in perception. But, once someone has reached the fully volitional level of conceptualization, he has a large body of concepts that enables him to observe and describe all manner of complex or subtle similarities and to group accordingly. For example, think of all the similarities by which people could be grouped (similarities in age, skin color, religion, income, moral character, etc.), or all the groups one can form of countries that are similar in some respect (those with centrally located capitals, those founded in the twentieth century, those with governments based on the principle of individual rights, etc.). There are contexts in which one might want or need to think about any of these groups, and one can always do so by means of descriptive phrases. But to form a separate concept for every such group would be stultifying.

Rand thought that the "principal" factor determining whether one should form a new concept is "the requirements of cognition (or further study)." She also names two other, lesser factors: "the descriptive complexity of a given group of existents" and "the frequency of their use." Taken together, these factors determine whether forming a new concept would serve or frustrate the need for unit-economy.

The first (and principal) factor tells us that it is unit-economical to form a new concept only when there is a lot to know about its units *as such*. Whenever this is the case, it will be possible to specify an *essential* characteristic that explains a host of others. Thus, once one reaches the fully volitional level of conceptualization, one should form concepts only when one is in a position to define them in this way. To illustrate this point, Rand writes of the "senseless duplication of cognitive effort" and the "conceptual chaos" that would result if someone formed a concept denoting "beautiful blondes with blue eyes, 5′ 5″ tall and 24 years old":

> everything of significance discovered about that group would apply to all other young women as well. There would be no cognitive justification for such a concept – unless some *essential* characteristic were discovered, distinguishing such blondes from all other women and requiring special study, in which case a special concept would become necessary. (*ITOE* 71)

Since essences are contextual, discovering an essential characteristic needn't require advanced scientific knowledge, but it does require an awareness of multiple distinguishing characteristics and of some explanatory relationships among them.

Rand held that "there is a great deal of latitude, on the periphery of man's conceptual vocabulary, a broad area where the choice is optional" (*ITOE* 70). But there are cases where forming a concept is mandatory because "the mental weight of carrying these existences in one's head by means of perceptual images or lengthy verbal descriptions is such that no human mind could handle it." And there are cases where forming a concept would be impermissible.

> The requirements of cognition determine the *objective* criteria of conceptualization. They can be summed up best in the form of an epistemological "razor": *concepts are not to be multiplied beyond necessity* – the corollary of which is: *nor are they to be integrated in disregard of necessity.* (72)

A concept denoting beautiful blue-eyed blondes would be an example of multiplying concepts beyond necessity.[92] As a second example of this error, Rand discusses why it would have been a mistake to form a new concept for black swans when they were first discovered, rather than subsuming them under the existing concept "swan": "virtually all their characteristics are similar to the characteristics of the white swans, and the difference in color is of no cognitive significance" (*ITOE* 73, cf. *Workshops* 150–151, where she makes the same point about white-skinned and black-skinned human beings). A third example can be found in Rand's correspondence with John Hospers, who scolds Rand for "condemn[ing] 'logical positivism' as if it were ONE doctrine, without separating out SPECIFICALLY the various views that may fall under this head" (*Papers* 141_HO2_019_002). Having distinguished a dozen minutely different versions of logical positivism, Hospers is unwilling to discuss the merits of logical positivism *as such*. Rand replies that what she rejects is the logical positivists' "basic premise and approach (which is implicit in their specific, individual theories)," and she points out that, if one proceeded by Hospers's methods, one could not say anything about Christianity as such, but would have to comment separately on each of its "over three hundred sects" (*Letters* 520).[93] The issue at stake in all of these examples is that, since a valid concept is based on an essential similarity, the concept's units must not be *arbitrarily* subdivided into minute sub-groups; any finer distinctions that may be properly drawn among the units must always be understood in the context of the units' essential similarity.[94]

"In the process of determining conceptual classification," Rand wrote, "neither the essential similarities nor the essential differences among existents may be ignored, evaded or omitted once they have been observed" (*ITOE* 71). Multiplying concepts beyond necessity amounts to disregarding essential similarities. Integrating concepts "in disregard of necessity" is the converse error, and it involves disregarding essential differences. Rand gives a fanciful example that parallels the case of a black swan: if a "rational spider from Mars" were discovered, should it be classified as a human being? In our actual context of knowledge, man is properly defined as "the rational animal," but if rational spiders from Mars were discovered, that definition would need to be changed and "the formation of a new concept to designate the Martians would be objectively mandatory." This is because "the differences between [the spider] and man would be so great that the study of one would scarcely apply to the other" (73). Of course the Martian would have a significant commonality with human beings, and surely Rand would acknowledge that there could be some wider concept subsuming both. But any such concept would have to be *posterior* to the concept "man" and to the new concept that would be needed to designate the Martians. Unlike the differences between white and black swans, the difference between a human being's body and a spider's is essential: nearly all of our medical knowledge, for example, would be inapplicable to Martian spiders, and even the things that would hold true of both human beings and Martian spiders in virtue of their both being rational would apply very differently in the two cases.

Rand called the error of disregarding essential differences "package-dealing," and she thought it was common. *ITOE* mentions one non-hypothetical example: "schools of biology and psychology, whose false definition of the concept 'learning' has led to attempts to equate the 'behavior' of a piece of magnetized iron with the 'behavior' of man" (72).[95] In other works, she identifies and analyzes a wide array of package-deals, including: "extremism," "isolationism," "McCarthyism," "polarization" (when used as a political term), "rationing" (when applied to prices set on a free market), "ethnicity" (which treats cultural characteristics as racial), "pollution" (when applied to things other than noxious chemicals), "Romantic" (when used to liken the Romantic movement in philosophy with Romantic art), "necessity" and "contingency" (as those concepts are often used in metaphysics), "national security" (when applied to issues not directly related to defense from foreign aggressors), "power" (when used indiscriminately for political and economic power), "meritocracy" (which equates achievement with political power), "free speech" (when applied to actions that violate property rights), "service" (when used to imply that providers of services are or should be servile), "we" (when used by the characters in *Anthem* to obscure the difference between one's own consciousness and others'), "experience" (as used by pragmatist philosophers), "conservatism" (which combines capitalism with theocracy), "libertarian" (which combines capitalism with anarchism), and the conventional usage of "selfish."[96]

Though Rand recognized that package-deals can result from honest errors, she did not think that this was the case with most of the terms in the list above. Rather, she regarded them as *anti-concepts*. "An anti-concept is an unnecessary and rationally unusable term designed to replace and obliterate some legitimate concept. The use of anti-concepts gives the listeners a sense of *approximate* understanding" ("Credibility and Polarization" *ARL* 1(1) 1; cf. "Causality vs. Duty" *PWNI* 128, *ITOE* 71, and "Extremism: The Art of Smearing" *CUI* 195).[97] By thwarting the process of identifying existents in essentials, anti-concepts enable people to avoid naming unwelcome facts and to act on unadmitted motivations. Thus they are tools of evasion and deception. In particular, Rand thought they were often used by intellectuals and politicians who did not dare name to their constituents (and, in some cases, even to themselves) the nature of the political systems they were advocating.[98]

Rand held that even properly formed concepts become invalid when they are not used in accordance with certain principles. One principle is that we must always know what we mean by the words we use, and never engage in "floating abstractions." A second principle is that we must keep in mind that each concept subsumes all the essentially similar items, including ones that may be non-obvious or unfamiliar. To violate this principle is to commit "the fallacy of the frozen abstraction," "which consists of substituting some one particular concrete for the wider abstract class to which it belongs" ("Collectivized Ethics" *VOS* 94, cf. *Journals* 295–296 and 640–641). One case of this fallacy is the failure to recognize that the concept "ethics" applies to codes other than altruism ("Collectivized Ethics" *VOS* 94).[99] A second case, discussed by Alan Greenspan (in an essay endorsed by Rand), concerns an unduly narrow conception of "competition," which led many to interpret the market influence of major nineteenth-century industrialists as a threat to competition rather than an instance of it, and so led them to mistakenly conclude that much of classical economics had been refuted ("Antitrust" *CUI* 68).

Another principle to which Rand frequently appeals derives from the ways (discussed earlier) in which many of our concepts depend on earlier concepts. Nathaniel Branden explains: "When one uses concepts, one must recognize their genetic roots, one must recognize that which they logically depend on and presuppose" ("The Stolen Concept" *TON* 2(1) 2). This attention to the "genetic roots" of concepts figures prominently in the central argument in Rand's ethics, which turns on the premise that "the concept of 'value' is genetically dependent on and derived from the antecedent concept of 'life'" ("The Objectivist Ethics" *VOS* 18, cf. *Atlas* 1012–1013, *Letters* 562).[100]

A failure to attend to the genetic roots of concepts leads to what Rand called "the fallacy of the stolen concept" (*ITOE* 3, "The Cult of Moral Grayness" *VOS* 87, *Letters* 524, cf. *Atlas* 1039). The fallacy consists in "using a higher-level concept while ignoring or denying the validity of its genetic roots" – that is, ignoring or denying "one or more of the earlier concepts on which it logically, hierarchically depends" (*TPO* 5 01:33:55–34:15, cf. *OPAR* 136). To resume our earlier example: "because the concept 'value' has no other source, base, meaning or possibility of existing" outside of the context of an organism sustaining its own life, Rand holds that "by accepting the concept 'value'," a person accepts his own life as his only possible ultimate value; therefore, "to choose any value, other than one's own life, as the ultimate purpose of one's actions is to be guilty of a contradiction and of the fallacy of the 'stolen concept'" (*Letters* 562).

Another example of this fallacy, cited by Branden (*TON* 2(1) 2) is Bertrand Russell's statement that "there is no *logical* impossibility in walking occurring as an isolated phenomenon, not forming part of any such series as we call a 'person'" (Russell 1921, 195). Russell is stealing the concept "walking"; for "*motion* presupposes the thing which moves" so that "without the concept of entity, there can be no such concept as 'motion'" (*Atlas* 1039, cf. 682, *Journals* 86, and *Letters* 524–525).[101]

We have already discussed two other views that Rand diagnosed as instances of concept stealing. When Rand rejects "as a contradiction in terms" the Cartesian notion that consciousness could exist without any external objects to be conscious of, she is accusing Descartes (and most subsequent epistemologists) of stealing the concept "consciousness." And her objection to views that deny "the validity of the senses" is that they are "merely variants of the fallacy of the 'stolen concept,'" since the senses are the source of the knowledge needed to give meaning to the terms in which such views are formulated (*ITOE* 3). Peikoff explains how the same line of argument applies to any form of global skepticism:

> "Error" signifies a departure from truth; the concept of "error" logically presupposes that one has already grasped some truth. If truth were unknowable ... the idea of a departure from it would be meaningless.
>
> The same point applies to concepts denoting specific forms of error. If we cannot ever be certain that an argument is logically valid, if validity is unknowable, then the concept of "invalid" reasoning is impossible to reach or apply. If we cannot ever know that a man is sane, then the concept of "insanity" is impossible to form or define. If we cannot recognize the state of being awake, then we cannot recognize or conceptualize a state of *not* being awake (such as dreaming). If man cannot grasp X, then "non-X" stands for nothing. (Peikoff, "Maybe You're Wrong" *TOF* 2(2) 9, cf. Branden, "The Stolen Concept" *TON* 2(1) 2, 4)[102]

Unlike the concept stealer, who treats each concept as a self-contained item, the Objectivist epistemology maintains that we must always use each concept in a way that maintains its connection with the hierarchy of prior concepts and knowledge on which it depends for its meaning. This is demanding intellectual work, but Rand thought that our cognitive responsibility extends much further than maintaining the connection between each concept and those that are its genetic roots. This brings us to a final principle of Objectivist epistemology: "No concept man forms is valid unless he integrates it without contradiction into the total sum of his knowledge" (*Atlas* 1016).

No item of knowledge, for Rand, can be self-contained and separate from the whole; for consciousness as such is relational. To be aware of something, even at the perceptual level, involves differentiating it from its surroundings. Concept-formation involves integrating a group of units that one has first differentiated from other things. And (except in the most elementary cases) we cannot retain and use a concept without a definition to "distinguish [it] from all other concepts and thus to keep its units differentiated from all other existents" (*ITOE* 40). Therefore, when one identifies a unit by means of a properly formed and defined concept, one relates the unit not only to the other units of the concept, but to the whole of the known universe. To form even a single concept is to commit to a lifelong project of discovering and organizing new knowledge about the units, and about everything they might be distinguished from, characterized by, or otherwise related to – a project that will require the formation of new concepts, the forming (and, in some cases, revising) of definitions, theories, and entire sciences.

Conceptually identifying individual entities and their characteristics enables us to grasp the (often complex) causal relations between them, and in this way too to integrate them into a larger context in terms of which they can be understood and evaluated. We can see this in the composition of *Atlas Shrugged*: the perceptive reader is led to conceptualize the characters and events of the story in increasingly complex ways that enable him to appreciate ever larger causal connections; by the end of the novel we are in position to regard everything that happens to hundreds of characters and an entire society over the course of 12 years as the intended effect of a stand taken by a single man in the name of a metaphysical axiom.[103] We see a similarly grand-scale integration across time and across fields in Rand's interpretation of the events of her time (as John Lewis and I discuss in Chapter 15, below).[104]

In all the ways we have discussed, the process of conceptualization is "an actively sustained process of identifying one's impressions in conceptual terms ... and expanding one's knowledge into an ever-growing sum" ("The Objectivist Ethics" *VOS* 22). Individual concepts and propositions arise as parts of this growing sum, and they only have meaning in the context of this whole. Thus, Rand frequently criticizes thinkers for "context-dropping."[105]

As Jason Rheins discussed in the previous chapter, this ever-growing sum of our knowledge is integrated by the axiomatic concepts of "existence," "identity," and "consciousness." The concept "existence" identifies at the most abstract level the object that we seek to know, and the concept "consciousness" identifies oneself as the knower, thereby enabling self-direction. "Identity" names the fundamental fact that to exist is to be *something*: "An atom is itself, and so is the universe; neither can contradict its own identity; nor can a part contradict the whole." To be conscious of existence – whether of a specific existent or of existence as a whole – is to *identify* it, and to do so *without contradiction*. Thus the axiom of identity provides the fundamental guidance we need to expand our consciousness of existence into an ever-growing sum. It tells us that we must develop and practice logic, "the art of *non-contradictory identification*" (*Atlas* 1016).

Rand held that these axioms are implicit in sense perception and that the volitional recognition of them in one's thought and action is constitutive of rationality – a moral virtue that includes "a commitment to the fullest perception of reality within one's power and to the constant, active expansion of one's perception, *i.e.*, of one's knowledge" ("The Objectivist Ethics" *VOS* 28). But to achieve the fullest perception of reality within a human being's power, one needs more than the self-evident guidance contained in the axioms themselves. One needs to identify explicitly the specific nature of human consciousness and, therefore, of the methods we must deliberately implement to expand and to check our knowledge. This is what is required for *objectivity* and it is what Rand thought previous philosophers had failed to provide.

> Cognitive *objectivity* has existed in the world as a kind of unofficial, unrecognized underground, in isolated instances and sporadic snatches, fed by such partial leads as could be found in Aristotle's far from perfect system. Objectivity has never had a full statement, a consistent theory or a firm epistemological foundation; and, even though it represented the *implicit* method practiced in every scientific achievement, particularly in the spectacular progress of the physical sciences, it was not identified nor acknowledged even by its practitioners – which is an eloquent illustration of the ultimate futility of practice without theory, of man's helplessness when he lacks an explicit statement of his merely implicit knowledge. (*Papers* 031_04x_005_001–002/*Journals* 692)

Rand never gave the "full statement" of what objectivity requires that she envisioned when writing these notes, but *ITOE* presents the theory that she saw as the "epistemological foundation" of the method of conceptualizing. This is why, in a 1971 review of the pieces she had written over the past 19 years, Rand identified *ITOE* as "the outstanding one, in terms of long-range importance" ("Brief Summary" *TO* 1090). We should now be in a position to appreciate both the historical significance Rand accorded to her theory of concepts and the role that the theory played in her own thought.

Acknowledgments

I would like to thank several friends for their input on this chapter, which has come in many forms over the many years I was working on it: Matt Bateman, Ben Bayer, Harry Binswanger, Allan Gotthelf, Mike Mazza, Shoshana Milgram, Travis Norsen, Karen Salmieri, Alex Silverman, and Dan Schwartz.

Notes

1 Note in this connection, her statement of *Atlas*'s theme: "the role of the mind in man's existence – and, as a corollary, the demonstration of a new moral philosophy: the morality of rational self-interest" ("For the New Intellectual" *FTNI* 97). In Salmieri 2009a, I discuss the novel's key theses about the role of the mind in individual's life, and in 2009b, I discuss the manner in which the novel argues for these theses.

2 The quoted sentence appears on *VAR* 2. On the questionable provenance of this book and the recordings on which it is based, see Bibliography #51. However, Branden's use of the early version of Rand's definition of reason (see n. 55, below) immediately before this quote indicates that this material dates from before 1965 and was part of the version of the course Rand endorsed.

3 See also Lennox's discussion of Rand's view of Aristotle, 334–337, below.

4 On the Industrial Revolution, see *FTNI* 23; on slavery and serfdom, see "Racism" (*VOS* 150–151); on Romantic art's relation to rationality, see below 295 and Tore Boeckmann's discussion in ch. 17, 446–447.

5 For Rand's account of the failings of contemporary epistemology and its consequences, see "For the New Intellectual" (*FTNI* 24–36), *ITOE* 3, 79–82, "The Cashing-In: The Student 'Rebellion'" (*CUI* 279–281/*ROTP* 15–17), "The Chickens' Homecoming" (*ROTP*), and many of the essays in *PWNI*: "Philosophy: Who Needs It" (8–9), "Philosophical Detection" (24–28), "Faith and Force: The Destroyers of the Modern World" (85–88), "From the Horse's Mouth," and "Kant vs. Sullivan." See also, Leonard Peikoff's *The Ominous Parallels* and *OPAR* 452–460.

6 The monograph's foreword makes this clear by reminding readers of a number of theses and concepts that are "taken for granted" in what follows (*ITOE* 3–4). In particular Rand mentions "the fallacy of the 'stolen concept'" (on which, see below 298–299), the "validity of the senses" (below, 281–282), and the axiom that "existence exists" (see Jason Rheins's discussion, above 247–249). All of these topics had been introduced in Galt's Speech in *Atlas Shrugged* (1039–1040, 1015–1016), and Nathaniel Branden had elaborated on "The Stolen Concept" in an article by that title (*TON* 2(1)).

7 They are three of the four "principal geniuses" whom the Encyclopedist Jean Le Rond d'Alembert named among the "great men" who "prepared from afar the light which gradually, by imperceptible degrees, would illuminate the world" (d'Alembert 1995, 85, 74). The fourth genius was Isaac Newton, whose *Mathematical Principles of Natural Philosophy* stands as the Enlightenment's greatest example of scientific knowledge. Thomas Jefferson referred to Bacon, Newton, and Locke as "my trinity of the three greatest men the world had ever produced" (Jefferson 1811).

8 The Greek word for "scientific knowledge" is *epistēmē*. It is the subject of Plato's *Theaetetus* and Aristotle's *Posterior Analytics*. The corresponding word in Descartes and Bacon's Latin is *scientia*. In Locke the equivalent is "science" or "demonstrative knowledge" (see *Essay Concerning Human Understanding* IV.ii). On the centrality of (what I am calling) the classical conception of science to Enlightenment epistemology, see Hatfield 2003, 10. On the different ways in which this idea was developed in the seventeenth and eighteenth centuries, see Cassirer 2009, 5–27.

9 Aristotle (and parts of the subsequent tradition) uses the word "hypothesis" for the principles I call "axioms," and he reserves the word "axiom" for principles that are shared by multiple sciences. Euclid's word for what I called axioms is "postulates" (*aitēmata*). Descartes and Locke do not have a distinct term for these items, but speak of them as objects of "intuition" (*intuitus*). (See *Rules for the Direction of the Mind*, Rule III, and *Essay* IV.I.) This sense of "intuition" derives from the use of the word to translate "*nous*," Aristotle's name for the knowledge of principles (*Posterior Analytics* II.19, *Nicomachean Ethics* VI.6).

10 I discuss Aristotle's conception of science in Salmieri 2014. See the literature cited therein for the range of different interpretations of Aristotle's position.

11 On the origins of Greek geometry, see Heath 1921, esp. 118–169.

12 Bacon, Preface to *The Great Renewal*.

13 Locke, *Essay Concerning Human Understanding* IV.III §26, IV.XII §10, IV.XI §16–18, IV.XII §8.

14 For Rand's view on the respects in which mathematics is and is not a model for other areas of knowledge, see *ITOE* 201–203. On Rand's aborted treatise on ethics and its role in her development, see Wright 2009.

15 See Allan Gotthelf's discussion of Rand's morality in Chapter 4, above for details.

16 None of these derivations is presented as a series of formal deductive arguments, though some can (arguably) be laid out as such. This might be thought of as a disanalogy between Rand's thought and geometry. However, the proofs of Euclid are construction proofs rather than syllogisms (and it is not obvious how or whether they can be recast as formal syllogisms, at least using the logic available at the time). Of the Enlightenment thinkers who saw geometry as a model for ethics, some like Spinoza seem to have interpreted geometrical argument as syllogistic in character. But others, like Descartes and Locke, seem not to have done so. (See Locke, *Essay* IV.XVI §4. For discussion of Descartes on this issue, see Hatfield 2014, 12 and 346–353.)

17 Cf. "Introduction to *Ninety-Three*" (*RM* 151–152), where Rand discusses the "tragic" case of a great artist, Victor Hugo, who deals with philosophical issues in this non-conceptual manner.

18 See *ITOE* 76–77 and "The Missing Link" and "Selfishness Without a Self" (both in *PWNI*).

19 See especially *Essay* II.xxxiii and III.x–xi and *Of the Conduct of the Understanding* §3, §5, §28, §30, §39. On the need to properly define concepts and the methods for doing so, see also Spinoza, *Treatise on the Emendation of the Intellect* §94–97.

20 I have very lightly edited this quote to remove some grammatical errors.

21 See *Posterior Analytics* II.19 and *Metaphysics* A.1.

22 See esp. Plato's *Phaedo* 72e–77a.

23 Descartes, *Meditations on First Philosophy*, Meditation 2, cf. Leibniz, *New Essays on Human Understanding* A VI vi 48.

24 Though both Bacon and Locke qualify as "Aristotelians" in the broad sense in which I'm using the term here, both were very critical of Aristotle. Bacon, in particular, considered Aristotle a rationalist, who paid lip service to perception, but did not in fact try to derive his principles from it (*New Organon* I.62–63).

25 Kelley (1984) defines empiricism along these lines, and so describes both Aristotle and Rand as empiricists. Hollinger (1984, 55) describes Rand as an empiricist for the same reasons.

26 On the problems with this way of classifying, as it applies to Aristotle, see Ferejohn 2009 (esp. 79–80), Helmig 2012 (esp. 340), and Salmieri 2014. For similar problems related to Bacon, see Woolhouse 1988, 15–16, Sargent 2001, Rossi 2003, 75–79, and Snyder 2006, 75–79. And in relation to Locke, see Loeb 1981, 36–55, Loeb 2010, Woolhouse 1988, 1–8, 94, and Ayers 1991, 154–161.

27 On the medical empiricists, see Edelstein 1967, Frede 1988, Allen 2001, 89–97, and Pellegrin 2006, 671–682.

28 Even prior to the self-conscious empiricist movement in medicine, there were empirical physicians who contented themselves with observing patterns of symptoms and figuring out how to treat them by trial-and-error without an understanding of the underlying causal structure. Aristotle contrasted the knowledge of such physicians with the sort of knowledge to which human beings can and should aspire (*Metaphysics* A.1 981a1–12). There were empirical physicians in the modern world as well, and both Bacon (*New Organon* I.64, 117) and Leibniz (*Monadology* §28) disparage them.

29 Locke and Hume's differing view of "association" represents a fundamental difference between the two thinkers that is too often overlooked. For Locke's view see *Essay* II.XXXIII; for Hume's, see *Treatise* 1.4, 3.2–4, 3.14.

30 For Hume's treatment of these subjects, see *Treatise* §3 and *An Enquiry Concerning Human Understanding* §3, §7.

31 The three positions can be compared and contrasted as follows: Aristotelians and rationalists agree (contra the empiricists) that scientific knowledge (as classically conceived) is possible, but they disagree on what makes it possible, with the Aristotelians maintaining that the principles are grasped based on sense perception, and the rationalists maintaining that they are known independently of sense perception. Aristotelians and empiricists agree (contra the rationalists) that all knowledge is based on sense perception, but they disagree about whether scientific knowledge is possible on this basis. And, rationalists and empiricists (contra the Aristotelians) agree that the principles of scientific knowledge cannot be derived from sense perception, but they disagree about whether such knowledge is possible, because they disagree about whether we have an independent faculty by which to apprehend the principles.

32 On the reasons why demonstration is possible in geometry, see *Essay* IV.III §18–20. The crux of the issue is that Locke thinks that demonstration is possible in the case of "modes," but impossible for "substances," because ideas of modes contain only a finite set of known attributes, whereas the ideas of substances make reference to some unknown underlying cause that is responsible for the known attributes and for many others that may be unknown. Hence ideas of modes, unlike ideas of substances, are "adequate" (II.XXXI §14). Browne (2001) and Long (2005a, 2005b) recommend what amounts to this same position to Objectivists. See nn. 85 and 92, below, for discussion.

33 In formulating the issue this way, I am eliding some significant differences between Hume's position and Kant's. Hume held that all truths were either relations of ideas (as in logic or geometry) or matters of fact (as in natural science) and that demonstrative knowledge was only possible in the former realm. Kant reformulated this distinction as one between "analytic" and "synthetic" judgments. In analytic judgments the meaning of the predicate is already contained in the meaning of the subject, so the judgment is necessarily true and can be known to be so without consulting experience, but the judgment is uninformative. The predicate of a synthetic judgment adds something new that is not contained in the subject, so these judgments are informative. But in most cases – those corresponding to Hume's "matters of fact" – synthetic judgments can only be known to be true by observation, and so they cannot be known to hold necessarily or universally. Kant argues that mathematical truths and the principles of natural science belong to a third class of judgments that are informative but can be known to hold true necessarily and universally of all the objects of our experience. Such judgments are possible because the objects of experience are constructed by mechanisms in the mind that guarantee the objects' conformity to these judgments. However, these same mechanisms preclude us from knowing reality as it exists in its own right, independent of the mind. The nineteenth and twentieth centuries saw many variations on the idea that universal and necessary knowledge is possible only of objects that are constructed in part by the mind's own activity. Kant himself held that the structures by which the mind constructs objects are fixed and shared alike by all rational beings. Subsequent thinkers (e.g., Fichte, Schelling, Hegel, Marx, Bradley) saw them as subject to change. The dominant traditions in twentieth-century philosophy (especially in the English-speaking world) saw the relevant structures as linguistic and conventional. For Rand's (brief) criticisms of some of these post-Kantian views, see *FTNI* 33–36. The interpretation of Kant that Rand assumes (and that I have sketched here), has with excellent reason remained the dominant interpretation over the centuries, but as is always the case with historical philosophers of stature, there are alternative interpretations

in the literature. For a compelling defense and detailed exposition of this traditional interpretation of Kant, see Guyer 1987 and 2014.

34 Peikoff's article is a criticism, based on Rand's theory of concepts, of the analytic-synthetic dichotomy, which he says "is accepted, in some form, by virtually every contemporary philosopher – pragmatist, logical positivist, analyst, and existentialist alike" ("The Analytic-Synthetic Dichotomy" *ITOE* 90). He focuses on the "dominant contemporary form" of the distinction – the view of the twentieth-century empiricists that all meaningful statements are either analytic, *a priori*, and necessary, or else synthetic, *a posteriori*, and contingent. It is curious that Peikoff does not mention Quine, whose (1951) critique of the dichotomy has had a great influence on analytic philosophy. However, from the standpoint of Rand's interests, Quine's position is not fundamentally different from the one he attacks: for he too holds that insofar as our beliefs are grounded in experience they are uncertain, and that what certainty or stability they have comes from our commitment to maintain them "come what may"; his innovation is the idea that our beliefs are so interrelated that it is possible to maintain or to reject any proposition (from the most trivial observation, to the laws of logic) in the face of any set of experiences, so long as one is willing to revise enough other beliefs to accommodate one's choice. The later challenges to the dichotomy based on externalist theories of meaning (e.g., Kripke 1972 and Putnam 1975) have more in common with those that Peikoff makes in his article. On the relation between Rand's view and these externalist theories, see n. 87 below and Long 2005b.

35 On free will and the need for morality, see *Atlas* 1013; on self-esteem, see *Atlas* 1020–1021; on philosophy, see "From the Horse's Mouth" (*PWNI* 110); on art, see "The Psycho-Epistemology of Art" and "Philosophy and Sense of Life" (*RM*); on capitalism, see *CUI* vii; on political freedom, see "Man's Rights" (*VOS* 110/*CUI* 369), "What Is Capitalism?" (*CUI* 9), and "Requiem for Man" (*CUI* 358); on property rights, see *Atlas* 1061 and "What Is Capitalism?" (*CUI* 9); and on representative government, see "Representation Without Authorization" (*ARL* 1(1) 91).

36 For man as a tool-maker, see *Atlas* 1043–1044; as a thumb-haver, see *ITOE* 48–49; as a product of chemistry, see *Atlas* 991, 994; as a product of society, see *Atlas* 271; as a product of economic forces, see "What Is Capitalism?" (*CUI* 6).

37 Branden, "Common Fallacies about Capitalism" (*CUI* 73–78) and Greenspan, "Antitrust" (*CUI* 68–70).

38 See esp. the *Critique of Pure Reason* Bxxx. Further references and a good brief discussion can be found in Pasternack and Rossi 2014, §3.4.

39 Cf. 300, below, and Jason Rheins's discussion, 249–251, above.

40 Cf. *ITOE* 29, where she speaks of consciousness as the "faculty of awareness" and the "faculty of perceiving that which exists."

41 This is not to say that every aspect of one's consciousness is transparent to one or that one cannot misidentify one's conscious states – e.g., mistaking fear for anger or an unsupported belief for knowledge. A major theme in Rand's fiction (see esp. *Atlas* 864–868) is that people often hold and act on premises that they cannot articulate, and she discusses the difficulty and fallibility of introspection in several articles (*ITOE* 76, 227, "Philosophical Detection" *PWNI* 20, 23–24, "The Age of Envy" *ROTP* 132; cf. *AON* 3). The present point is simply that one cannot be mistaken in thinking that one is a conscious being.

42 See also Jason Rheins's discussion of the primacy of existence, 258–260, above.

43 A (man-made) illusion of a mountain-top figures in the plot of *Atlas Shrugged* (704). On emotions and intentions as states of consciousness and the possibility of misidentifying them, see *ITOE* 32, 223–229.

44 Rand's discussions of perception in works published during her lifetime are few and brief. The most significant are *Atlas* 1034, 1040–1041, "The Objectivist Ethics" (*VOS* 19–20, *ITOE* 3–4, 5–6, 16), and "Kant vs. Sullivan" (*PWNI* 121). To this we can add several posthumously published or archival sources: *Journals* 654–655, *Letters* 530, and *Workshops* 117–119/*ITOE* 279–282. There are also several lectures that Rand authorized and one that she delivered herself that cover perception in some depth. Nathaniel Branden's *Basic Principles of Objectivism* contained extended discussions of it in lecture 2 (on "Reason") and lecture 3 (on "Logic and mysticism"). Rand sometimes delivered lecture 2, and the Ayn Rand Archives contains a typescript of a version of the lecture written in her voice

THE OBJECTIVIST EPISTEMOLOGY

(*Papers* 109_30x_002; see below, n. 60). The portions of this typescript concerning perception are virtually identical to the corresponding sections of Branden's published version of the course (*VAR* 38–39, 48–50). (There is additional material on perception in lecture 3, *VAR* 85–88.) Lecture 3 of Peikoff's *The Philosophy of Objectivism* (on the authority of which, see 3, above) also discusses perception at length. This discussion forms the basis for *OPAR* 37–54. There is also a significant discussion of perception in Peikoff's *HOP1*, lecture 12. I draw on these lectures in my exposition below. Later elaborations and defenses of Rand's view of perception include Kelley 1986, Gotthelf 2000, 54–57, Ghate 2013a, Salmieri 2013a and 2013b, and Binswanger 2014, 58–96.

45 BonJour 2009, 286–289, n. 1. I take the term "perceptual subjectivism" from BonJour. Perceptual subjectivists have typically thought of the subjective items of which we are immediately aware as sensations, and this is the form of the theory that Rand and her associates addressed. There are more complex versions of the view, which BonJour encompasses by saying that, according to perceptual subjectivism, what we are immediately aware of is "either a kind of object that arguably exists only in relation to the experience of a particular person or else the content of a mental act of sensing or being appeared to" (ibid.).

46 This confusion is possible because our concepts become "automatized" (see below, 288 and 292). A second cause of confusion may be that concepts have an "influence on percepts" (*Papers* 033_15x_002_002). Contemporary philosophers of perception call this phenomenon "cognitive penetration" (see Zeimbekis and Raftopoulos 2015). Whether cognitive penetration is consistent with Rand's view of perception as an inerrant given on which conceptual knowledge is built depends on the extent of the penetration (an issue Rand does not address in her few brief allusions to the phenomenon) and on the details of how conceptual knowledge is built on perception.

47 On the inerrancy of the senses, see *ITOE* 228, where Rand agrees with an associate's statement that the "evidence of the senses" are "incontestable, infallible data."

48 For this reason, most direct realists hold that perception can err. Ghate 2013a and Salmieri 2013b argue that Rand's position on this and related points is superior to that of some other direct realists. These papers form part of a discussion in which Pierre Le Morvan (2013) and Bill Brewer (2013) respond on behalf of the competing theories, and Ben Bayer (2013) replies in defense of Rand's position (as elaborated by Ghate and me).

49 Travis (2004) defends a similar position, taking his inspiration from Austin (1962).

50 This illusion is discussed in Branden's *Basic Principles of Objectivism*, lectures 2 and 3 (cf. *VAR* 47–51, 85–87) and Peikoff's *TPO*, lecture 3 (cf. *OPAR* 39–44). Both lecturers treat the misidentification of the stick as an error that occurs on the rational (or conceptual) level of consciousness, they note that reason (unlike perception) is volitional, and they point out that phenomena such illusions provide important evidence about the nature of light (and of our perceptual apparatus). In all these respects they follow Rand's brief discussion of reflections and mirages (quoted above). In Salmieri 2013a, 50–52, I argue that there are some misidentifications that do not involve concepts or volition but are nonetheless distinct from and posterior to sense perception.

51 See *Papers* 109_30x_002_020–022/*VAR* 48–50; *OPAR* 41–43. For subsequent elaborations on the distinction, see also Kelley 1986, 41–42, 86–95, 130–131, 140–141; Salmieri 2013a, 42–52 and 2013b; Ghate 2013a; Bayer 2013; and Binswanger 2014, 78–85.

52 There will of course be some differences in *what* they perceive as well. For example, the more acute perceivers will perceive more details, the bee will perceive more of the surrounding environment; also, the bat will not perceive color, and, among the perceivers who do, there will be differences in how much of the spectrum they perceive and in how finely they can differentiate between colors. However, the fact remains that there are some things that are perceives by all five and are perceived differently by each.

53 Two more recent authors have attacked this same argument in strikingly similar terms. David Stove (1986; 1991, 151–153, 161–170) identifies "the worst argument in the world" (which he also calls "the Gem") as the argument that "we cannot know things as they are in themselves" because "we can only know things as they are related to us" (or "under our forms of perception and understanding" or "insofar as they fall under our conceptual schemes"). And Olding (1998) writes of "the popular view that the conditions for knowledge prevent it. We have eyes, therefore we cannot see." See Franklin 2002 for helpful elaboration.

54 On this assumption and its role in the history of philosophy, see Kelley 1986, Index s.v. Diaphanous model; Salmieri 2013a, 46–48 and 2013b, 233–236.

55 In *Atlas Shrugged* and some early talks "reason" is defined as the "faculty that perceives, identifies and integrates the material provided by [man's] senses" (*Atlas* 1016, cf. "Faith and Force: The Destroyers of the Modern World" *PWNI* 86, "The Intellectual Bankruptcy of Our Age" *VOR* 89). The earliest occurrence of the definition without "perceives" occurs in "Introducing Objectivism," which was first published on June 17, 1962: "Reason (the faculty that identifies and integrates the material provided by man's senses) is man's only means of perceiving reality, his only source of knowledge, his only guide to action, and his basic means of survival" (*VOR* 4/Column 3). For a few years, Rand evidently used both versions of the definition in different contexts; the earlier definition is included in "The Objectivist Ethics," as it appears in the first (1964) edition of *VOS* (see 20). Rand removed the word "perceives" from the definition in the 1965 edition of *VOS*, and did not include it in the definition thereafter. Allan Gotthelf (McConnell 2010, 338) reports that Rand told him that she eliminated the word "perceives" after Nathaniel Branden pointed out that it could be taken to mean that reason or concepts are involved in processes by which sensations are integrated into percepts – a view that Rand thought implied the idealist position that the world we perceive is a product of consciousness. Branden describes what may be this same exchange between him and Rand in a 1996 talk (Branden 1996, Tape 1), but in his telling, the point he made was not that reason isn't active in sense perception, but that the evidence of the senses are not *objects* of perception but the *means* by which one perceives entities in the world. The two points are related, and it is possible that Branden raised both.

The change in the definition may be evidence of some development in Rand's view of the relation between reason and sense perception, but, if so, the earlier view cannot have been that reason plays a role in the act of sense perception itself, for the idea that reason but not perception is volitional is present in already in *Atlas* (1041), and the idea that percepts are integrated automatically by the brain (rather than rationally and volitionally) is present in the version of "The Objectivist Ethics" that contains the earlier definition. I think the best explanation of the change is that it is only after *Atlas* that Rand came to use the word "perceives" primarily to refer to sense perception. Nearly every occurrence of the word in *Atlas* (including in Galt's speech) has the more general meaning of "apprehends," and she refers to sense perception as "sensory perception" or "direct perception." Thus, taken in its original context, the original definition does not mean that reason engages in sense perception, but rather that it apprehends what has been perceived. But the definition becomes misleading when taken out of that context – especially so when it is included in pieces where "perception" predominantly refers to sense perception. Also, the phrase "the evidence of the senses" refers to the facts of which one is aware by sense perception – facts which one can use as the basis for reasoning. These facts are objects of awareness that figure prominently in reasoning, so there is a sense in which reason can be said to be aware of (i.e., to perceive) them, but this is potentially misleading, since it could be taken to mean that reason is the faculty by means of which we are aware of this evidence, rather than being a faculty that leverages a prior awareness of this evidence to discover further facts. (Thank you to Shoshana Milgram for providing many of the references in this note.)

56 I borrow this term from Linnell 1956.

57 One might wonder about the evidence for attributing such mental processes to young children. Here is what Rand had to say about this in a conversation about a similar example of childhood cognition (for which, see *ITOE* 6): "Now, it isn't that I claim omniscience about the mental processes of an infant, which nobody could really ever demonstrate, but, by the logic of what is involved here, this is the progression as I see it. And the only actual standard of comparison we would have is our own adult processes when we learn a new concept. From that and the logic of what is involved, you can reconstruct the steps by which a child would arrive at this" (*Workshops* 37).

58 Where I have supplied the word "items" Rand uses "unit," in the technical sense discussed below, 286.

59 Rand used the abbreviation CCD herself in such contexts as her workshops on epistemology (transcripts of which have been printed, in an edited form, as an appendix to the second edition of *ITOE*), but not in print. Peikoff uses it in *OPAR* (87, 97) and it has become standard in the secondary literature about Rand's theory. For further discussion, see Gotthelf 2013a, 12–20 and Salmieri 2013a, 52–57.

60 This is the typescript of lecture 2 of the NBI *Basic Principles of Objectivism* written in Rand's own voice for her to use when she delivered the lecture as a guest speaker. (See above, n. 44.) The script indicates that it was prepared in 1967, and it includes some material that must have been composed after 1966, because it references *ITOE*. Much of the text is identical (or nearly so) to the recorded version of the course that Branden released after his break with Rand and to the published transcript of these recordings (*VAR*), but there are also sizable passages that differ, especially in the portion of the talk concerned with concepts. One paragraph from this portion of the typescript is quoted in Branden's released version and attributed to "a lecture given by Miss Rand at NBI on the nature of concept-formation" (*VAR* 42–43; the quoted paragraph can be found on *Papers* 109_30x_002_009–010). Likely the distinctive material in this typescript was written by Rand herself to replace earlier material that had been made obsolete by the publication of *ITOE*. (Rand discusses Branden's "failure to rewrite" the *Basic Principles* course in "To Whom It May Concern" *TO* 7(5) 449–450.)

61 She did not, in the end, write on this subject, but Leonard Peikoff has developed a theory of induction based on her view of concepts. See Peikoff 2003 for his initial presentation of the view and Harriman 2010 for a more formal presentation (endorsed by Peikoff).

62 These facts about the order of learning had already been established in the cognitive psychology literature by the time Rand wrote *ITOE*, and have since been established in greater detail. (See Brown 1958, 14–21, Anglin 1977, which quotes from *ITOE* on page 22, and Rosch 1999.) Robert Campbell (1999) provides a valuable summary of points of contact and discontinuity between Rand's thought and work in cognitive psychology in the 1960s and since. However, part of Campbell's aim in that piece is to show that "Rand's epistemology did not arise in complete isolation from the psychology of her time." It is not clear to me that anyone has ever held the view Campbell refutes. He thinks this view is implied by Rand's statement that "philosophy is not dependent on the discoveries of science" (*ITOE* 289). But that statement only implies this if one assumes an unduly narrow view of the ways in which one field can use material from another. Rand's point is only that, because philosophical questions are fundamental, answering them cannot require "training in physics, or psychology, or special equipment, etc." (*ITOE* 289). This does imply that the proof of an epistemological theory cannot depend on facts that can only be established by research studies utilizing specialized methods of cognitive psychology, but it does not rule out an epistemologist's being inspired by psychological findings to consider certain issues or positions, nor does it rule out her drawing on material from the field to illustrate or elaborate on an epistemological point. Indeed, Rand's general view that a thinker must work to integrate every concept into the whole of his knowledge would mandate that an epistemologist do this sort of thinking, and there is positive evidence in Rand's notes on epistemology that she recognized the need. (See *Papers* 033_15x_014_006/*Journals* 703.)

63 I take the phrase "unit-perspective" from Peikoff (*OPAR* 76). For examples of holding the unit–perspective without forming a concept, see Salmieri 2013a, 54.

64 Rand's talk of "mental files" should not be confused with the subsequent use philosophers (e.g., Grice 1969, 140–44, Strawson 1974, 54–56) have made of this same metaphor in connection with singular terms. Rand's file-folders are concepts, and as such they refer to multiple units. She discusses singular terms (specifically proper names) only in passing (*ITOE* 9–10, 175), and never discusses the Fregean concerns about identity statements that motivate much of the literature on them. However, given her other commitments, she would certainly have held a direct reference theory, and there are parallels between her concept of a "form of awareness" and the Fregean idea of a "sense" or "mode of presentation," as that idea has been interpreted by direct reference theorists (e.g., Evans 1982, John Campbell 2002). This interpretation of "modes of presentation" lies behind much of the recent literature on "mental files" (e.g., Perry 1980, Recanati 1993 and 2013). On the parallels between forms of awareness and modes of presentation, see Salmieri 2013b, 230–232, cf. 2013a, 46 n. 7 and Bayer 2013, 261 n. 8.

65 This is the title of *ITOE*'s Chapter 7.

66 In Objectivist circles, this point is often called "the crow epistemology" (e.g., *ITOE* 172), and the limit on the number of units one can hold in mind is sometimes referred to simply as "the crow." Regarding the experiment itself, Rand describes it as having been "told in a university classroom by a professor

of psychology." Evidently she heard about it from one of the students (possibly Nathaniel Branden). She cautions that she "cannot vouch for the validity of the specific numerical conclusions drawn from [the experiment], since I could not check it first-hand." A reader of *ITOE* informed her in a letter (*Papers* 010_24x_004_001) that the anecdote is recounted in Dantzig (1930), and indeed it can be found on page 3 of that work. However, Dantzig does not give any source for the anecdote. In fact, its origin seems to be Charles Georges Leroy's entry on "instinct" in Diderot's 1791 *Encyclopedia*. The relevant passage can be found in English translation in Leroy 1870, 125–127. This passage is quoted by John Lubbock in an 1855 journal article ("On the Intelligence of The Dog," *Nature* XXXIII), which was in turn quoted in Conant (1896, 3–4). (For further details, see Shedenhelm 2000.) In the late 1950s and early 1960s, the example seems to have sometimes been taught in connection with George Miller's research on the limits on the human ability to process information, though Miller does not himself use the crow example in his classic paper "The Magical Number Seven, Plus or Minus Two: Some Limits on Our Capacity for Processing Information" (*Psychological Review*, 1956, 63).

67 The various kinds of higher-level concepts or "Abstractions from Abstractions" are the subject of *ITOE*'s Chapter 3. Chapter 4 discusses "Concepts of Consciousness" (which can be seen as a special case of concepts of attributes and actions, since consciousness is an attribute and/or activity). For more detailed accounts, based on Rand's, of the several ways in which later concepts depend on earlier ones, see Binswanger 1996, Salmieri 2006, lecture 3, Gotthelf 2013a, 24–29, Salmieri 2013a, 58–60, and Binswanger 2014, 139–170.

68 In contemporary Anglo-American philosophy, the Problem of Universals is most often viewed as a metaphysical problem concerning whether (and in what manner) "universals" or "properties" exist (Blackburn 1994, 387, Landesman 1971, 3–4, Goldstein 1983, Quine 1953, 9–10, Armstrong 1989, 2, Armstrong 1978, 11, Loux 1998, Legg 2001). This way of defining the problem leads to the view that there are only two (broad) solutions to it: realism, according to which such universals exist and anti-realism (often called "nominalism"), according to which they do not, and "everything is particular or concrete" (see, e.g., Rodriguez-Pereyra 2014). On this definition, Rand would qualify as an anti-realist. However, this way of understanding the problem and its possible solutions is superficial. The existence of universals was first posited by Plato (and is still most often defended) as a means to explain "how universal cognition of singular things is possible" (Klima 2013, cf. Salmieri 2008, 38–55). Once we recognize that the question of how and whether universal cognition is possible is the motivation for the posit, we can see that there are no grounds for grouping together all answers to this question that do not involve positing the existence of mind-independent universal objects; for these answers may be no more like one another than they are like realism.

Among philosophers who understand the problem of universals as a strictly metaphysical problem, some (e.g., Aaron 1952, 231–234, Blanshard 1962, 392–421) are concerned with completely determinate universals – for example, an absolutely precise shade of red. They puzzle over how we should understand situations in which two different things are this exact shade of red – whether, for example, we should say that a single item, the shade of red, is simultaneously in two places at once. I mention this only because a few critics who insist parochially that this is the "real" problem of universals fault Rand for failing to address it (Huemer 1996, §4; Ryan 2003, 19–31). In fact, few of the significant figures in the history of thought about universals have puzzled over this issue – Plato and Aristotle, for example, did not, and neither did most of the early moderns. This is because, whatever the merits this puzzle may have, it is not identical (or at least, not *obviously* identical) to the concerns about universals that have loomed largest in the history of philosophy. One's view of how the puzzle is related to these enduring concerns will depend on the position one takes on a whole range of issues. It is for such reasons that different philosophical traditions understand the problem of universals differently.

Huemer and Ryan also allege that Rand presupposes realism (which she claims to reject) by making use of relational properties, like commensurability, which they think are "universals" (in their sense of this word). However, as Badhwar and Long (2012, §2.3) point out, it is open to Rand to consider the relevant commensurability relations "as themselves being relational property-particulars or tropes, rather than universals." Moreover, since Rand is not addressing the metaphysical problem that interests Huemer and Ryan, she is free to speak of characteristics, properties, relations, quantities, etc., using these terms in their ordinary English senses. One of the things that is at issue between realists and anti-realists about "universals" or "properties" (in the relevant senses of these terms) is what sorts of ontological commitments are presupposed by such language, and to accuse Rand of any ontological commitments because she uses these words is to beg this question.

69 The identity of this Jesuit is unknown.

70 Rand must have been familiar with this passage, because it is quoted in Moore (1961, 25) as part of a discussion of universals from which Rand herself quotes in *ITOE*'s foreword.

71 Moore 1961, 27 (quoted in *ITOE* 2).

72 The neo-Thomists attributed this theory of universals to Aristotle and Thomas Aquinas. In Salmieri 2008, 56–122, I argue that the attribution to Aristotle is mistaken. The attribution to Aquinas has been challenged by Geach (1971, 130–131). Rand regarded moderate realism, not as Aristotle's own position, but as an implication from it that departs from the spirit of his philosophy; thus she described him as "unfortunately" the "ancestor" of the moderate realists (*ITOE* 2, cf. 52). Perhaps the clearest case of a moderate realist prior to the neo-Thomists is Locke, though he held this position only with respect to the class of concepts that he called "simple ideas" (see *Essay* II.ii).

73 The ancient Stoics and the medieval philosopher William of Ockham are often cited as exponents of this view. The position was also held by Locke with respect to (what he called) complex ideas. De Wulf (1913) plausibly interprets Kant's view of concepts as a form of conceptualism.

74 Nominalism (in this sense) is sometimes attributed to various medieval thinkers, but its clearest exponents are Berkeley and Hume. In another form, it was held by such twentieth-century philosophers as Ludwig Wittgenstein and W.V.O. Quine.

75 Rand introduced the distinction between the "intrinsic," "subjective," and "objective" in "What Is Capitalism?" (*CUI* 13–16), where she identified them as "three schools of thought on the nature of the good" that differ in the respective roles they assign to mind-independent facts and to human consciousness and choice. *ITOE* presents the three more generally as views of the relation between existence and consciousness. Though "What Is Capitalism?" was not written until 1965, she seems to have had this more general view of the trichotomy as early as 1959, when it appears in her notes for her treatise on Objectivism (*Journals* 701).

76 *ITOE* consistently treats objectivity (in the sense of the term that applies to phenomena of consciousness) as something that arises only at the conceptual level in virtue of the fact that cognition at this level is volitional. (See esp. *ITOE* 82). All of Rand's own usages of the term in print are consistent with this. However, the term was sometimes used more broadly by her associates in the 1960s to denote the status of any form of awareness (even those that are not volitional) by contrast to "intrinsic" features of the objects of awareness and "subjective" mental products. Thus in certain lectures, including his 1967 NBI course on *Objectivism's Theory of Knowledge*, Peikoff described sensory qualities as "objective." (The usage is also in the promotional materials for the course; see *Papers* 117_05B_010_003, cf. 117_05B_004_003.) Peikoff would later describe the application of the objective-subjective-intrinsic trichotomy to sense perception as a "major error," which Rand disabused him of after hearing one of his lectures (Peikoff 1987, session 7, 01:05:03–06:11). The workshops Rand held on *ITOE* between 1969 and 1971 likely occurred before the conversation Peikoff refers to, and they contain a few instances of this broader sense of "objective" and of the application of the trichotomy to sense perception. In all cases the usage originates in questions posed by the other participants. Rand accepts or adopts the usage in answering some questions (*Workshops* 115–117, 46), but she objects to another question posed using this terminology, and she remarks in the ensuing discussion that, though one "could" describe color as objective and light-waves as intrinsic, it is "a dangerous formulation" (*Workshops* 214–216). Peikoff and Binswanger included some of these discussions in the appendix to the second edition of *ITOE* (278–290, 140), but in deference to Rand's preferred usage, they replaced the word "objective" with "epistemological" and "intrinsic" with "metaphysical."

77 Rand's use of the word "integration" is unusual, but not unprecedented. Her earliest uses of the term all pertain to art – most often to an author's intelligent combination of different elements into a unified story (*Journals* 15, 318, 343, 420, *Letters* 125, 160, 231). This sense of "integration" figures prominently in *The Fountainhead*, where Rand draws connections between the artistic integrity of a

building, the biological integrity of an organism, and the integrity of a person's character. In this context, Roark says that "every living thing is integrated," and he describes "an integrating principle" as "the one thought, the single thought that created the thing and every part of it" (*Fountainhead* 606, cf. 12). This idea is further developed in Rand's notes for *Atlas Shrugged* where she discusses the role reason plays in integrating a person's psychology and in integrating his values and actions into a life (*Journals* 477, 480, 531, 564, 648–649, 663). This same idea figures prominently in the notes on psychology she made between 1955 and 1957 (668–677). Rand's view of reason as a faculty that "integrates" the "evidence of the senses" likely arose out of this thinking. As far as I know, her earliest explicit statement of this idea was in a 1953 note for Galt's speech (646), and her first reference to concepts specifically as integrations is in a 1958 note (700–701). However, notes she made sometime in the late 1920s already contain the following ideas: an animal is "utterly illogical" because it "cannot connect together the things it observes"; "man realizes and connects much more than an animal"; "humanity is stumbling helplessly in a chaos of inconsistent ideas, actions, and feelings that can't be put together, without even realizing the contradictions between them or their ultimate logical results"; in the future people can and must "perfect" this ability to connect things, and thereby achieve a "clear vision" (24). A number of nineteenth and early twentieth-century authors from various intellectual traditions draw some of the same connections Rand does between the biological, artistic, psychological, and conceptual integration, but it is not clear which (if any) of these authors Rand had read, and I have found no direct evidence of any influence any of them may have had on her thinking. For additional discussion of integration, see Peikoff 2012b, Chapter 1.

78 See David 2009 (esp. §6) for a useful overview of the "correspondence theory of truth." He notes that the name "correspondence theory" is applied narrowly to the sort of correspondence I describe here, but that it is also applied "more broadly to any view explicitly embracing the idea that truth consists in a relation to reality, i.e., that truth is a relational property involving a characteristic relation (to be specified) to some portion of reality (to be specified)." This broader sense corresponds to the *OED*'s definition 1 of "correspondence": "To answer to something else in respect of fitness; to agree *with*; to be agreeable or conformable *to*; to be congruous or in harmony *with*." The narrower view corresponds to the *OED*'s definition 2a: "To answer *to* in character or function; to be similar or analogous *to* (rarely *with*)."

79 The late Wittgenstein (1953) can be seen as an example here, as can contemporary pragmatists such as Robert Brandom (1998, 2001).

80 John Hospers objected to this definition on the grounds that "there are truths even when nobody knows them and nobody recognizes them" (*Papers* 141_HO2_018_001). Rand replied: "'Truth' is the attribute of an *idea* in somebody's consciousness (the relationship of that idea to the facts of reality) and it cannot exist *apart* from a consciousness" (*Letters* 528). Her view of concepts rules out any view on which propositions exist independent of acts of thought, and so rules out any view on which truth and falsehood are properties of such propositions. (See Salmieri 2013a, 62–65 for more on the implications of Rand's theory of concepts for propositions.) Indeed Rand has a demanding view of what was involved in having a thought that could qualify as true or false: one needs not only to understand the concepts involved, but also to have at least some evidence for the proposition (*TPO* Lecture 6, 30:30–52:00/*OPAR* 163–171, cf. "The Psychology of Psychologizing" *VOR* 24, *AON* 89, and Branden, "Agnosticism" *TON* 2:4). Nonetheless, she would presumably accept that there are beliefs that are true without yet being known – for example, a well-founded, but not yet proven hypothesis. Indeed, in a note to herself, she considered what would follow "If my hypothesis is true" (*Papers* 033_15x_014_006/*Journals* 703). Since she never discussed such cases in connection with her definition of truth; it is unclear to me whether they are counterexamples, or whether she intended "recognition" to be understood widely enough to include them.

81 *Answers* 156–158 is a condensation of *TPO* Lecture 6, 1:57:06–2:08:02, in which Rand (speaking extemporaneously) discusses correspondence in greater depth than in any of her writings. For additional discussion, see Salmieri 2013a, 69 n. 37.

82 For an example of this, see *ITOE* 37–38: "Is there an object in reality corresponding to the word 'and'? No. Is there a fact in reality corresponding to the word 'and'? Yes. The fact is that three men are

walking – and that the word 'and' integrates into one thought a fact which otherwise would have to be expressed by: 'Smith is walking. Jones is walking. Brown is walking.'"

83 There are only two sorts of concepts for which, Rand thought, definition is impossible: axiomatic concepts (on which, see below, 300) and concepts denoting sensations.

84 For the Aristotelian provenance of this rule, see *Topics* VI.4. See also Gotthelf 2013a, 31 n. 46 and the texts cited therein.

85 Since a definition's function is to condense one's knowledge of a concept's units *qua* units, the definition depends logically on their status as units of the concept, therefore a definition is (chronologically and logically) posterior to the concept it defines: the definition depends on the units' status as units, rather than determining whether things are units. This is part of Rand's (and Peikoff's) reason for rejecting any distinction between conceptual truths, which can be known *a priori* by derivation from definitions, and empirical truths, which can only be established based on observation. There can be no distinction between such truths because the definitions themselves are based on (and, when needed, revised in light of) a body of knowledge about the units that derives ultimately from observation. Browne (2001) and Long (2005a, 302–303, 2005b; Badhwar and Long 2012, §2.3) argue that Rand's theory of concepts is compatible with there being a certain class of concepts whose units are determined by their definitions and about which there can be *a priori* knowledge. Their position amounts to a revival of Locke's view, discussed in n. 32, above. Long, following Browne, distinguishes between "Deep-Kind terms" (which Locke had called ideas of substances) and "Shallow-Kind terms" (Locke's ideas of modes). (Browne himself prefers to talk of the kinds themselves rather than the terms, concepts, or ideas for them, but this makes him more difficult to relate directly to Locke or Rand, so, for the sake of brevity, I direct my comments to Long's version of the view.) He thinks that we create "Shallow-Kind terms" arbitrarily (or pragmatically) by simply stipulating a definition that then serves as a criterion for kind membership. Anything that one can then deduce from this definition will qualify as a "conceptual truth" that can be known independent of observation to hold necessarily of any member of the kind. However, as we will see shortly (n. 92, below), Rand's theory of concepts rules out any concept that would satisfy Long's definition of a "Shallow-Kind term." Browne's "Deep Kinds" are no different from "natural kinds" as understood by the neo-essentialist tradition that I discuss below, n. 87. The distinction Browne and Long wish to draw requires regarding the kinds themselves as *intrinsic* (as opposed to objective or subjective) and then viewing concepts as mental items that merely pick them out. (This is why Browne – quite sensibly, given his position – speaks of the kinds themselves rather than of concepts or terms for them.) Rand's epistemology has no room and no use for such a distinction because she regards concepts as *objective*. Though she (naturally, given her view) doesn't speak much of kinds as such, the implication of her view is that kinds too are objective: to be a kind is simply to be a properly conceptualized group, and any discussion about what it is to be a kind (or a kind of a certain sort) will have to make reference to the norms of concept-formation (on which, see below, 295–298).

86 In this respect, Rand differs from theorists like Kuhn and Feyerabend who hold that concepts cannot persist and maintain their meaning across theory changes. On this issue, see Lennox 2013a.

87 In this respect, Rand differs from neo-essentialists like Hilary Putnam (1973, 1975) who also stress that a concept's definition in the context of a mature science will not likely make reference to the observable features that first prompted the formation of the concept. Putnam et al. endorse a variant of realism according to which (at least some) objects are united into "natural kinds" by some *intrinsic* factor such as a common chemical structure or genetic code (Putnam 1975), descent from a common shared ancestor (Griffiths 1999), or being subject to a common "homeostatic mechanism" (Boyd 1991, 141–142). This factor is a metaphysical essence that makes the particulars fall into the kind *intrinsically*, i.e., independently of human consciousness and its methods of cognition. A mature scientific theory would group things in accordance with these metaphysical essences, but long before we are in a position to discover such essences, observation of superficial similarities between the members of a kind may inspire us to form a concept on the hypotheses that these similarities are consequences of an unknown essence. This concept can persist as we accept and reject various hypotheses as to what the underlying essence is. For criticisms from an Objectivist viewpoint of this

neo-essentialism, see Lennox 2013a, 122 n. 18, Norsen 2012, 25–27, and Rheins 2011. On the relation between Rand's view and the literature on "natural kinds," see Griffiths 2013 and Ghate 2013b. On the issue of changing definitions, more generally, see *ITOE* 43–48, 66–67, 230–235, *OPAR* 97–100, Gotthelf 2013a, 33–35, 2013b, and Lennox 2013a, 2013b.

88 See *ITOE* 49, 72, "'Extremism,' or The Art of Smearing" (*CUI* 195), "Thought Control" (*ARL* 3(2) 254), "The Obliteration of Capitalism" (*CUI* 204), and "What Is Romanticism?" (*RM* 97).

89 All of the arguments and explanations mentioned above can be found in *FTNI* 19–21, "Faith and Force" (*PWNI* 90), and *CUI*: "What Is Capitalism?," "The Roots of War," "Notes on the History of American Free Enterprise," Greenspan's "Antitrust," Branden's "Common Fallacies about Capitalism," and Hessen's "The Effects of the Industrial Revolution on Women and Children." For discussion, see 10–11, 199–200, 233–234, 355–357, and 371 in the present volume.

90 On the relation between volition and values, see 63–68, above; on the nature of Romanticism, see Tore Boeckmann's discussion, 428–429, below.

91 On this point, see *RM* vii–viii and "Faith and Force: The Destroyers of the Modern World" (*PWNI* 89–90).

92 The relevant blue-eyed blondes make up precisely the sort of group that Browne (2001) calls a "Shallow-Kind" (see above, n. 85), and the principle that leads Rand to reject as invalid any concept for this group would apply to any "Shallow-Kind term." For the concept to be valid, one has to know enough about the units to know that it is economical to group them together and to regard a certain characteristic as essential. But if one knows this, then the concept and its definition are based on a wealth of knowledge about the units and their relation to the rest of existence. Therefore the kind is not "shallow" (nor is it "deep" in Browne's sense). Long (2005a, Badhwar and Long 2012) thinks that "capitalism," as Rand uses it, is best understood as a "Shallow-Kind term." Because Rand does not think that the political-economic system of any nation has ever satisfied her definition of "capitalism," Long argues, the definition should be understood as stipulating what would count as capitalism. Long is wrong. As I discuss above, Rand thought that the concept "capitalism" integrates a vast body of observation-based knowledge of non-hypothetical countries. That none of them fully satisfied her definition is not surprising. Biological and man-made phenomena always admit of defective cases. Moreover, even if Rand had understood "capitalism" to denote an entirely new social system of her devising, it would no more be a "Shallow-Kind term" than is any concept for a new invention. To invent something is to conceive of a new *kind* of thing – one that is *essentially* different from anything that already exists. And whether some envisioned item qualifies (and, if so, precisely how it is different from other things) is a substantive question the answer to which will depend on relations of similarity and difference and cause and effect. So the definition of the concept denoting this new invention will depend on a wealth of the very sort of observational knowledge on which Rand thinks all definitions depend, and the definition will be revisable as this knowledge grows (for example, as we discover or invent new things).

93 In Rand's notes (*Marginalia* 62–80) on Hospers (1953), *Introduction to Philosophical Analysis*, she identifies other cases of this fallacy and some of the others I discuss in this section. The notes also give one a sense of her take on several issues in the philosophy of language.

94 Aristotle objected on similar grounds to the introduction of new concepts for arbitrary subdivisions of larger wholes. See *Rhetoric* III.13 1414a30–b25, and (for discussion) Salmieri 2008, 257–261.

95 Robert Efron discussed the relevant schools at length in "Biology Without Consciousness and Its Consequences" (*TO* 7(2–5), esp. 7(4) 443–445). See also Rand's "The Stimulus and the Response" (*PWNI*).

96 On "extremism," "isolationism," and "McCarthyism", see "'Extremism,' or The Art of Smearing" (*CUI*), cf. "The Principals..." (*ARL* 2(20) 218). On "polarization," see "Credibility and Polarization" (*ARL* 1(1)). On "rationing," see *Letters* 320–327. On "ethnicity," see "Global Balkanization" (*VOR* 118–120). On "pollution," see "The Left: Old and New" (*ROTP* 165) and "The Anti-Industrial Revolution" (*ROTP* 274, 282–283). On Romanticism, see "What Is Romanticism?" (*RM* 98–99). On "necessity" and "contingency," see "The Metaphysical vs. the Man-Made" (*PWNI* 38–39). On "National Security," see "A Preview" (*ARL* 1(24) 108–109). On "power," see "America's Persecuted Minority: Big Business" (*CUI* 42),

"The Intellectual Bankruptcy of Our Age" (*VOR* 98–99), and *Letters* 580; cf. "An Untitled Letter" (*PWNI* 140–141, 145) on "meritocracy." On "free speech," see "The Cashing In: The Student 'Rebellion'" (*CUI* 293). On "service," see "How *Not* to Fight Against Socialized Medicine" (*VOR* 287–288). On the use of "we" in *Anthem*, see Salmieri 2005, 258–260. On "experience," see *FTNI* 31. On "conservatism," see *Letters* 567. On "libertarianism," see "What Can One Do?" (*ARL* 1(7) 31) and the discussion in the present volume, 381–382, below. On "selfishness" and "egoism," see *VOS* vii, *Letters* 554. Further examples of package-deals can be found in "Of Living Death" (*VOR* 49), "The Cult of Moral Grayness" (*VOS* 88–89), "The Stimulus and the Response" (*PWNI* 189–191), "A Preview" (*ARL* 1(22) 96), "Bootleg Romanticism" (*RM* 131), "An Answer to Readers" (*TO* 6(3) 237), "An Untitled Letter" (*PWNI* 138–139), "The Metaphysical vs. the Man-Made" (*PWNI* 33), *Letters* 540, 557, "Post-Mortem, 1962" (*Column* 65), "Who Will Protect Us From Our Protectors" (*TON* 1(5) 17). In many of the cited passages, Rand describes the term in question explicitly as a "package-deal"; in the other passages she makes the same criticisms without applying that label. Earlier in this chapter, I argued (though not in these words) that certain uses of "empiricism" and "nominalism" are package-deals; see 277–278 and n. 68.

97 Rand thought that most anti-concepts are package-deals, but she seems not to have thought that all were. In particular, she describes "duty" as an anti-concept, and her primary objection to it is not that it packages together essentially different existents, but that it is mystical and denotes a sort of unintelligible obligation that has no basis in reality (*PWNI* 129). This suggests that mysticism may be a source of anti-concepts distinct from package-dealing. And in *Atlas Shrugged*, Galt describes how mystical concepts have no positive meaning and serve to "negate" or "wipe out" knowledge (*Atlas* 1034–1035).

98 See John Lewis's and my discussion of "anti-ideology," 360–361, below.

99 See Allan Gotthelf's discussion of Rand's reasons for thinking that the concepts "ethics" and "morality" apply to her form of egoism, above, 74–76.

100 For discussion of this argument, see above, 63 and 76–78.

101 Of course this is precisely what Russell means to deny. He thinks that an entity, insofar as it "forms part of the experienced world," is nothing more than a "series of appearances and various occurrences." Because the walking is one such occurrence, it has ontological priority over the series of which it is a part, but the walking too is a series made up of more basic occurrences. The ultimate constituents of everything, Russell thinks, are "brief existents" that can only be referred to by such descriptions as "the visual sensation which occupied the centre of my field of vision at noon on January 1, 1919" (Russell 1921, 192–194). Notice the role in his reasoning of the Cartesian-cum-Kantian view of experience that (we have seen) Rand rejects as incoherent.

102 It is worth noting that Rand and her associates were making such arguments in the late 1950s and early 1960s, before "semantic" arguments against skepticism (e.g., Putnam 1981) were commonplace.

103 I discuss how the novel accomplishes this in Salmieri 2009b.

104 Focusing on the integrative nature of Rand's thought and its relation to her political radicalism, Chris Sciabarra (1995) argues that she is a part of a tradition of radical, Russian "dialectical" thinkers, whose methods she learned from N.O. Lossky, a socialist Hegelian who may have taught a college course she took in Ancient Philosophy. (See Shoshana Milgram's discussion of this class, above, 38, n. 9.) Sciabarra is knowledgeable about Rand's corpus, occasionally perceptive about aspects of her thought, and obviously correct that system-building and political radicalism are more characteristic of the Russian thinkers he cites than of mainstream twentieth-century Anglo-American thought. But twentieth-century Anglo-American thought is idiosyncratic in this respect. Historically, almost all philosophers of stature were system-builders, and many took radical political stances that they saw as based on their systems. Certainly this is true of the thinkers of the Enlightenment. (Spinoza is a particularly obvious case, but this is true too of Locke, and of many eighteenth-century French and American thinkers.) Moreover, these facts about historical philosophers are stressed in the histories of philosophy that Rand read by Windelband and Fuller. (See Lennox's discussion, below, 322.) The features Rand has in common with Sciabarra's Russian dialecticians could have been absorbed from any of a number of sources, or (more likely) from the general cultural heritage that all educated people share. It goes without saying that growing up in Russia in the time and place Rand did had

an effect on which works and ideas she was exposed to at which times and that this must have had some influence on her early thought. So a detailed study of how she processed these inputs at different stages in her development would be of great interest. But this is not what Sciabarra provides. His book is long on comparisons between Rand and obscure authors of whom she probably never heard, but it breezes quickly over many thinkers whom she is known to have read or conversed with (e.g., Hugo, Dostoevsky, von Mises, Blanshard, Isabel Paterson, H.L. Mencken, Ortega y Gasset, etc.) and who share at least some of the features that Sciabarra finds in both Rand and the dialecticians. Moreover, Rand lacks the central "dialectical" feature he claims to find in her thought: "a revolt against formal dualism." For as Lennox (1996) observes, though Rand rejects some dichotomies (as do most thinkers of stature), she defends or introduces others.

105 She was especially contemptuous of "linguistic analysis" and other twentieth-century philosophical movements that she saw as disintegrating human knowledge by quibbling sophistically about the meanings of out-of-context terms (*ITOE* 38, 50, 67–69, 77–78, 244–245, *Letters* 510–512, 536–537).

References

Aaron, R.I. 1952. *The Theory of Universals*. Oxford: Clarendon Press.

Allen, James. 2001. *Inference from Signs: Ancient Debates about the Nature of Evidence*. Oxford: Clarendon Press.

Anglin, Jeremy M. 1977. *Word, Object, and Conceptual Development*. New York, NY: Norton.

Armstrong, D. M. 1978. *Nominalism and Realism: Universals and Scientific Realism*, vol. 1. Cambridge: Cambridge University Press.

Armstrong, D. M. 1989. *Universals: An Opinionated Introduction*. Boulder, CO: Westview Press.

Austin, J.L. 1962. *Sense and Sensibilia*. Oxford: Clarendon Press.

Ayers, Michael. 1991. *Locke: Epistemology and Ontology*. London: Routledge.

Badhwar, Neera, and Roderick Long. 2012. "Ayn Rand." Stanford Encyclopedia of Philosophy. http://plato.stanford.edu/entries/ayn-rand/ (accessed May 28, 2015).

Bayer, Benjamin. 2013. "Keeping Up Appearances: Reflections on the Debate Over Perceptual Infallibilism." In Gotthelf and Lennox 2013.

Binswanger, Harry. 1996. "Abstraction from Abstractions." Lecture. Recording available at https://estore.aynrand.org/p/346/ (accessed May 28, 2015).

Binswanger, Harry. 2014. *How We Know: Epistemology on an Objectivist Foundation*. New York, NY: TOF Publications.

Blackburn, Simon. 1994. *The Oxford Dictionary of Philosophy*. Oxford: Oxford University Press.

Blanshard, Brand. 1962. *Reason and Analysis*. London: Allen & Unwin.

BonJour, Laurence. 2007. "Epistemological Problems of Perception." Stanford Encyclopedia of Philosophy. http://plato.stanford.edu/entries/perception-episprob/ (accessed May 28, 2015).

BonJour, Laurence. 2009. *Epistemology: Classic Problems and Contemporary Responses*, 2nd edition. Lanham, MD: Rowman & Littlefield.

Boyd, Richard. 1991. "Realism, Anti-Foundationalism and the Enthusiasm for Natural Kinds." *Philosophical Studies*, 61(1–2).

Branden, Nathaniel. 1996. "Objectivism: Past and Future" [Cassette Tapes]. San Francisco, CA: Laissez Faire Books.

Brandom, Robert. 1998. *Making It Explicit*. Cambridge, MA: Harvard University Press.

Brandom, Robert. 2001. *Articulating Reasons*. Cambridge, MA: Harvard University Press.

Brewer, Bill. 2013. "Direct Perception and Salmieri's 'Forms of Awareness'." In Gotthelf and Lennox 2013.

Brown, Roger. 1958. "How Shall a Thing Be Called?" *Psychological Review*, 65(1).

Browne, Gregory. 2001. *Necessary Factual Truth*. Lanham, MD: University Press of America.

Campbell, John. 2002. *Reference and Consciousness*. Oxford: Oxford University Press.

Campbell, Robert. 1999. "Ayn Rand and the Cognitive Revolution in Psychology." *Journal of Ayn Rand Studies*, 1(1).

Cassirer, Ernst. 2009. *The Philosophy of the Enlightenment*, translated by Fritz Koelln and James Pettegrove. Princeton, NJ: Princeton University Press.

Coffey, Peter. 1938. *The Science of Logic*, Vol. 1. New York, NY: Peter Smith.

Coffey, Peter. 1958. *Epistemology or the Theory of Knowledge: An Introduction to General Metaphysics*, Vol. 1. New York, NY: Peter Smith.

Conant, Levy Leonard. 1896. *The Number Concept: Its Origins and Development*. New York, NY: Macmillan.

d'Alembert, Jean Le Rond. 1995. *Preliminary Discourse to the Encyclopedia of Diderot*, translated by Richard N. Schwab. Chicago, IL: University of Chicago Press.

Dantzig, Tobias. 1930. *Number: The Language of Science*. New York, NY: Macmillan.

David, Marian. 2009. "The Correspondence Theory of Truth." Stanford Encyclopedia of Philosophy. http://plato.stanford.edu/entries/truth-correspondence/ (accessed May 28, 2015).

de Wulf, Maurice. 1913. "Nominalism, Realism, Conceptualism." In *The Catholic Encyclopedia*, Vol. 11, edited by Charles Hernermann, Thomas Joseph Shahan, Conde Benoist Pallen, Edward A. Pace, Andrew Alphonsus MacErlean, and John Joseph Wynne. New York, NY: The Encyclopedia Press.

Edelstein, Ludwig. 1967. "Empiricism and Skepticism in the Teaching of the Greek Empiricist School." In *Ancient Medicine: Selected Papers of Ludwig Edelstein*, edited by O. Tempkin and C.L. Tempkin. Baltimore, MD: Johns Hopkins University Press.

Evans, Gareth. 1982. *The Varieties of Reference*. Edited by John McDowell. Oxford: Clarendon Press.

Ferejohn, Michael. 2009. "Empiricism and Aristotelian Science." In *A Companion to Aristotle*, edited by Georgios Anagnostopoulos. Oxford: Wiley-Blackwell.

Franklin, James. 2002. "Stove's Discovery of the Worst Argument in the World." *Philosophy*, 77.

Frede, Michael. 1988. "The Empiricist Attitude Towards Reason and Theory." In *Method, Medicine and Metaphysics*, edited by Robert Hankinson. Edmonton: Academic Press.

Geach, Peter. 1971. *Mental Acts*. London: Routledge.

Ghate, Onkar. 2013a. "Perceptual Awareness as Presentational." In Gotthelf and Lennox 2013.

Ghate, Onkar. 2013b. "Natural Kinds and Rand's Theory of Concepts" Reflection on Griffiths." In Gotthelf and Lennox 2013.

Goldstein, Laurence. 1983. "Scientific Scotism – The Emperor's New Trousers or Has Armstrong Made Some Real Strides?" *Australasian Journal of Philosophy*, 61(1).

Gotthelf, Allan. 2000. *On Ayn Rand*. Belmont, CA: Wadsworth Publishing.

Gotthelf, Allan. 2013a. "Ayn Rand's Theory of Concepts: Rethinking Abstraction and Essence." In Gotthelf and Lennox 2013.

Gotthelf, Allan. 2013b. "Taking the Measure of a Definition: Response to Bogen." In Gotthelf and Lennox 2013.

Gotthelf, Allan, ed., and James G. Lennox, assoc. ed. 2013. *Concepts and Their Role in Knowledge: Reflections on Objectivist Epistemology*. Ayn Rand Philosophical Studies, vol. 2. Pittsburgh, PA: University of Pittsburgh Press.

Grice, Paul. 1969. "Vacuous Names." In *Words and Objections*, edited by Donald Davidson and Jakko Hintikka. Dordrecht: Reidel.

Griffiths, Paul. 1999. "Squaring the Circle: Natural Kinds with Historical Essences." In *Species: New Interdisciplinary Studies*, edited by R. Wilson. Cambridge, MA: MIT Press.

Griffiths, Paul. 2013. "Rand on Concepts, Definitions, and the Advance of Science: Comments on Gotthelf and Lennox." In Gotthelf and Lennox 2013.

Guyer, Paul. 1987. *Kant and the Claims of Knowledge*. Cambridge: Cambridge University Press.

Guyer, Paul. 2014. *Kant*, 2nd edition. New York, NY: Routledge.

Harriman, David. 2010. *The Logical Leap: Induction in Physics*. New York, NY: New American Library.

Hatfield, Garry. 2003. "Epistemology." In *The Encyclopedia of the Enlightenment*, Vol. 2, edited by Alan Charles Kors. Oxford: Oxford University Press.

Hatfield, Garry. 2014. *The Routledge Guide to Descartes' Meditations*. New York, NY: Routledge.

Heath, Thomas. 1921. *A History of Greek Mathematics, vol. 1, From Thales to Euclid*. Oxford: Clarendon Press.

Helmig, Christoph. 2012. *Forms and Concepts: Concept Formation in the Platonic Tradition.* Berlin: Walter de Gruyter.

Hollinger, Robert. 1984. "Ayn Rand's Epistemology in Historical Perspective." In *The Philosophic Thought of Ayn Rand,* edited by Douglas Den Uyl and Douglas Rasmussen. Urbana, IL: University of Illinois Press.

Hospers, John. 1953. *An Introduction to Philosophical Analysis.* New York, NY: Prentice Hall.

Huemer, Michael. 1996. "Why I'm Not an Objectivist." http://www.owl232.net/rand.htm (accessed May 28, 2015).

Jefferson, Thomas. 1811. Thomas Jefferson to Benjamin Rush, January 16, 1811. National Archives, Founders Online. http://founders.archives.gov/documents/Jefferson/03-03-02-0231 (accessed May 28, 2015).

Kelley, David. 1984. "A Theory of Abstraction." *Cognition and Brain Theory,* 7(3–4).

Kelley, David. 1986. *The Evidence of the Senses.* Baton Rouge, LA: Louisiana State University Press.

Klima, Gyula. 2013. "The Medieval Problem of Universals." Stanford Encyclopedia of Philosophy. http://plato.stanford.edu/entries/universals-medieval/ (accessed May 28, 2015).

Kramnick, Isaac. 1995. *The Portable Enlightenment Reader.* New York, NY: Penguin Books.

Kripke, Saul. 1972. "Naming and Necessity." In *Semantics of Natural Language,* edited by Donald Davidson and Gilbert Harman. Dordrecht: D. Reidel.

Landesman, Charles, ed. 1971. *The Problem of Universals.* New York, NY: Basic Books.

Le Morvan, Pierre. 2004. "Arguments Against Direct Realism and How to Counter Them." *American Philosophical Quarterly,* 41(3).

Le Morvan, Pierre. 2013. "In Defense of the Theory of Appearing: Comments on Ghate and Salmieri." In Gotthelf and Lennox 2013.

Legg, Catherine. 2001. "Predication and the Problem of Universals." *Philosophical Papers,* 30(2).

Lennox, James G. 1996. "Reaching for Roots." *Reason,* February.

Lennox, James G. 2013a. "Rand on Concepts, Context, and the Advance of Science." In Gotthelf and Lennox 2013.

Lennox, James G. 2013b. "Conceptual Development versus Conceptual Change: Response to Burian." In Gotthelf and Lennox 2013.

Leroy, Charles Georges. 1870. *The Intelligence and Perfectibility of Animals From a Philosophic Point of View, With a Few Letters on Man.* London: Chapman and Hall.

Linnell, John. 1956. "Locke's Abstract Ideas." *Philosophy and Phenomenological Research,* 16(3).

Loeb, Louis. 1981. *From Descartes to Hume: Continental Metaphysics and the Development of Modern Philosophy.* Ithaca, NY: Cornell University Press.

Loeb, Louis. 2010. "Locke and the British Empiricists." In *Reflection and the Stability of Belief.* Oxford: Oxford University Press.

Long, Roderick. 2005a. "Praxeology: Who Needs It." *Journal of Ayn Rand Studies,* 6(2).

Long, Roderick. 2005b. "Reference and Necessity: A Rand-Kripke Synthesis?" *Journal of Ayn Rand Studies,* 7(1).

Loux, M.J. 1998. "Nominalism." In *Routledge Encyclopedia of Philosophy,* edited by Edward Craig. London: Routledge.

Maher, Michael. 1900. *Psychology: Empirical and Rational,* 4th edition. London: Longmans, Green, & Co.

Markie, Peter. 2013. "Rationalism vs. Empiricism." Stanford Encyclopedia of Philosophy. http://plato.stanford.edu/entries/rationalism-empiricism/ (accessed May 28, 2015).

Mayhew, Robert, ed. 2009. *Essays on Ayn Rand's* Atlas Shrugged. Lanham, MD: Lexington Books.

McConnell, Scott. 2010. *100 Voices: An Oral History of Ayn Rand.* New York, NY: New American Library.

Moore, Edward C. 1961. *American Pragmatism: Peirce, James and Dewey.* New York, NY: Columbia University Press.

Norsen, Travis. 2012. "Scientific Cumulativity and Conceptual Change: The Case of 'Temperature.'" Paper presented to the Ayn Rand Society at the 2012 Pacific Division Meeting of the American Philosophical Association. Available at http://philsci-archive.pitt.edu/8332/ (accessed May 28, 2015).

Olding, Alan. 1998. "Review of Religious Inventions by Max Charlesworth." *Quadrant,* 42(5).

316

Pasternack, Lawrence, and Philip Rossi. 2014. "Kant's Philosophy of Religion." Stanford Encylopedia of Philosophy. http://plato.stanford.edu/entries/kant-religion/ (accessed May 28, 2015).

Peikoff, Leonard. 1987. "Objectivism: The State of the Art." Lecture series. Recording available from the Ayn Rand Bookstore at https://estore.aynrand.org/p/77 (accessed May 28, 2015).

Peikoff, Leonard. 2003. "Induction in Physics and Philosophy." Lecture series. Recording available from the Ayn Rand Bookstore at https://estore.aynrand.org/p/119 (accessed May 28, 2015).

Peikoff, Leonard. 2012b. *The DIM Hypothesis: Why the Lights of the West Are Going Out*. New York, NY: New American Library.

Pellegrin, Pierre. 2006. "Ancient Medicine and Its Contribution to the Philosophical Tradition." In *A Companion to Ancient Philosophy*, edited by Mary Louise Gill and Pierre Pellegrin. Oxford: Blackwell.

Perry, John. 1980. "A Problem about Continued Belief." *Pacific Philosophical Quarterly*, 61.

Putnam, Hilary. 1973. "Meaning and Reference." *Journal of Philosophy*, 70(19).

Putnam, Hilary. 1975. "The Meaning of Meaning." In *Language, Mind, and Knowledge*, edited by Keith Gunderson. Minneapolis, MN: University of Minnesota Press.

Putnam, Hilary. 1981. "Brains in a Vat." In *Reason, Truth and History*. Cambridge: Cambridge University Press.

Quine, W.V.O. 1951. "Two Dogmas of Empiricism." *Philosophical Review*, 60.

Quine, W.V.O. 1953. *From a Logical Point of View*. Cambridge, MA: Harvard University Press.

Recanati, François. 1993. *Direct Reference: From Language to Thought*. Oxford: Blackwell.

Recanati, François. 2013. *Mental Files*. Oxford: Oxford University Press.

Rheins, Jason. 2011. "Similarity and Species Concepts." In *Carving Nature at Its Joints*, edited by Joseph Keim Campbell, Michael O'Rourke, and Matthew H. Slater. Cambridge, MA: MIT Press.

Rodriguez-Pereyra, Gonzalo. 2014. "Nominalism in Metaphysics." Stanford Encyclopedia of Philosophy. http://plato.stanford.edu/entries/nominalism-metaphysics/ (accessed May 28, 2015).

Rosch, E. (1999). "Principles of Categorization." In *Concepts: Core Readings*, edited by E. Margolis and S. Laurence. Cambridge, MA: MIT Press.

Rossi, Paolo, 2003. "Ants, Spiders, Epistemologists." In *Francis Bacon: Terminologia e fortuna nel XVII secolo*. Rome: Edizioni dell'Ateneo.

Russell, Bertrand. 1921. *The Analysis of Mind*. London: Allen & Unwin.

Ryan, Scott. 2003. *Objectivism and the Corruption of Rationality: A Critique of Ayn Rand's Epistemology*. New York, NY: Writers Club Press.

Salmieri, Gregory. 2005. "Prometheus' Discovery: Individualism and the Meaning of the Concept 'I' in Anthem." In *Essays on Ayn Rand's Anthem*, edited by Robert Mayhew. Lanham, MD: Lexington Books.

Salmieri, Gregory. 2006. "Objectivist Epistemology in Outline." Audio lectures, available at https://estore.aynrand.org/p/181 (accessed May 28, 2015).

Salmieri, Gregory. 2008. *Aristotle and the Problem of Concepts*. PhD dissertation, University of Pittsburgh. Ann Arbor, MI: ProQuest/UMI (Publication No. 3335821).

Salmieri, Gregory. 2009a. "*Atlas Shrugged* on the Role of the Mind in Man's Existence." In Mayhew 2009.

Salmieri, Gregory. 2009b. "Discovering Atlantis: *Atlas Shrugged*'s Demonstration of a New Moral Philosophy." In Mayhew 2009.

Salmieri, Gregory. 2013a. "Conceptualization and Justification." In Gotthelf and Lennox 2013.

Salmieri, Gregory. 2013b. "Forms of Awareness and 'Three Factor' Theories." In Gotthelf and Lennox 2013.

Salmieri, Gregory. 2014. "Aristotelian *Epistēmē* and the Relation Between Knowledge and Understanding." *Metascience*, 23(1).

Sargent, Rose-Mary. 2001. "Baconian Experimentalism: Comments on McMullin's *History of the Philosophy of Science*." *Philosophy of Science*, 68(3).

Sciabarra, Chris. 1995. *Ayn Rand: The Russian Radical*. University Park, PA: Penn State University Press. (2nd edition, 2013.)

Sellars, Wilfrid. 1963. *Science, Perception and Reality*. London: Routledge & Kegan Paul.

Shedenhelm, Richard. 2000. "Where Were the Counting Crows?" *Journal of Ayn Rand Studies*, 2(1).

Snyder, Laura J. 2006. *Reforming Philosophy: A Victorian Debate on Science and Society*. Chicago, IL: University of Chicago Press.

Stove, David. 1986. "Judge's Report on the Competition to Find the Worst Argument in the World." In Stove 1998.

Stove, David. 1991. *The Plato Cult and Other Philosophical Follies*. Oxford: Basil Blackwell.

Stove, David. 1998. *Cricket versus Republicanism*. Sydney: Quakers Hill Press.

Strawson, Peter F. 1974. *Subject and Predicate in Logic and Grammar*. London: Methuen.

Travis, Charles. 2004. "The Silence of the Senses." *Mind*, 113(449).

Wittgenstein, Ludwig. 1953. *Philosophical Investigations*. Edited by G.E.M. Anscombe and R. Rhees. Translated by G.E.M. Anscombe. Oxford: Basil Blackwell.

Woolhouse, R.S. 1988. *The Empiricists*. Oxford: Oxford University Press.

Wright, Darryl. 2008. "Evaluative Concepts and Objective Values: Rand on Moral Objectivity." In *Objectivism, Subjectivism, and Relativism in Ethics*, edited by, Ellen Frankel Paul, Fred D. Miller, and Jeffery Paul. Cambridge: Cambridge University Press.

Wright, Darryl. 2009. "Ayn Rand's Ethics: From *The Fountainhead* to *Atlas Shrugged*." In Mayhew 2009.

Zeimbekis, John, and Athanasios Raftopoulos, eds. 2015. *The Cognitive Penetrability of Perception: New Philosophical Perspectives*. Oxford: Oxford University Press.

Part V

Philosophers and Their Effects

13

"Who Sets the Tone for a Culture?"

Ayn Rand's Approach to the History of Philosophy

JAMES G. LENNOX

It was Ayn Rand's conviction that philosophy is a life and death matter, both for individuals and cultures. Because man's consciousness is conceptual and must be exercised by choice, every value he achieves, even in a simple, agrarian society, requires an active process of thought; this holds all the more so in complex, scientifically-based industrial cultures. But can we trust the results of our thinking? If I put effort into thinking about what things are of value to me as a human being and about how to achieve them, will that effort be rewarded by achievement? Is it morally appropriate to desire such rewards? In Rand's view, whether one seeks answers to these questions and how one proceeds in doing so will make all the difference between a successful, achievement-oriented life and one of self-doubt and passivity. Rand put the point succinctly in her address to the Class of 1974 of the United States Military Academy, West Point, "Philosophy: Who Needs It":

> A philosophical system is an integrated view of existence. As a human being, you have no choice about the fact that you need a philosophy. Your only choice is whether you define your philosophy by a conscious, rational, disciplined process of thought and scrupulously logical deliberation – or let your subconscious accumulate a junk heap of unwarranted conclusions, false generalizations, undefined contradictions, undigested slogans, unidentified wishes, doubts and fears, thrown together by chance, but integrated by your subconscious into a kind of mongrel philosophy and fused into a single, solid weight: *self-doubt*, like a ball and chain in the place where your mind's wings should have grown. ("Philosophy: Who Needs It" *PWNI* 7)

This passage advocates disciplined thought about the nature of reality, our means of acquiring knowledge about it, and the principles that should guide one's life. And as she explains a couple of pages later, a study of the *history* of philosophy, of how philosophers have approached answering these questions in the past, plays an important role in formulating one's own philosophical principles.

A Companion to Ayn Rand, First Edition. Edited by Allan Gotthelf and Gregory Salmieri.
© 2016 John Wiley & Sons, Ltd. Published 2016 by John Wiley & Sons, Ltd.

> Who sets the tone for a culture? A small handful of men: the philosophers. Others follow their lead, either by conviction or by default. For some two hundred years, under the influence of Immanuel Kant, the dominant trend of philosophy has been directed to a single goal: the destruction of man's mind, of his confidence in the power of reason. (*PWNI* 8–9)

She sums up her case for studying the thought of these tone-setters a few paragraphs later: "The battle of philosophers is a battle for man's mind. If you do not understand their theories, you are vulnerable to the worst among them" (*PWNI* 10).[1]

As we will see shortly, Rand realized early that the study of key figures in the history of philosophy, and the grasp of their historical lineage, is an important part of one's own philosophical education; approached in the right way, the history of ideas is a valuable aid in forming your own philosophical principles.

Ayn Rand was not, of course, a historian of philosophy, but a philosopher deeply interested in its history. She did read certain philosophers systematically (at different points in her life we know she read a good deal of Nietzsche, Aristotle, Plato, and Kant). Nevertheless for the broad sweep of philosophy's history she relied on classic presentations, such as B.A.G. Fuller's *A History of Philosophy: Ancient, Medieval and Modern*, which she worked through in the 1940s.[2] Her own style of historical analysis and integration is akin to historians, such as Wilhelm Windelband, who portray philosophical ideas systematically and who focus on identifying the fundamental principles of a philosophical system and tracing the influence of those fundamentals both on other aspects of that philosophy and on the field's subsequent developments.[3]

> The best way to study philosophy is to approach it as one approaches a detective story: follow every trail, clue and implication. ... The criterion of detection is two questions: Why? and How? If a given tenet seems to be true – why? If another seems to be false – why? and how is it being put over? You will not find all the answers immediately, but you will acquire an invaluable characteristic: the ability to think in terms of essentials (*PWNI* 10).

For Rand the primary value of philosophy is that it aids in the development of what she holds to be an invaluable cognitive skill, thinking in terms of essentials. We will consider in some detail what she means by this shortly; but it is clear from the quotation above that she considers the study of the history of philosophy to be of considerable value in developing this skill, enabling one to understand and evaluate a culture in essentials by tracing back different cultural developments to their source, the dominant philosophical trends.

We know from one of the previous quotations that she thinks that much that is wrong with contemporary culture can be traced to the influence of Kant. But she did not think everything about modern culture was bad, and she argued that what is good in the modern world also has a source in philosophy's history:

> ... at the root of every civilized achievement, such as science, technology, progress, freedom – at the root of every value we enjoy today, including the birth of this country [the United States of America] – you will find the achievement of *one man*, who lived over two thousand years ago: Aristotle. (*PWNI* 10)

Ayn Rand was not a scholar of either of the philosophers, Kant and Aristotle, mentioned in these quotations. However, by the time she completed *Atlas Shrugged* she had formed a distinctive view about the philosophical premises that had dominated different periods of human

322

history and about the figures responsible for those premises. The lectures and essays she wrote between 1960 and 1980 and archival materials related to her study of different philosophers and the history of philosophy, provide us with a rich source of information about her motives and her methods for studying various figures in the history of philosophy, as well as about her understanding and assessment of their philosophical views. Many of the lectures and essays I will be drawing on here were originally published in periodicals edited by Rand herself, but there are two important exceptions. The first is the long introductory essay to *For the New Intellectual* published in 1961, which presents, as part of the case for the need for the 'new intellectual' of the title, a highly stylized history of the (largely negative) impact of philosophical ideas on human life, which includes brief discussions of key figures in that history, from Plato to Dewey. The second, from roughly the same time period, and developing a number of the same themes, is "Faith and Force: The Destroyers of the Modern World," a lecture given at Yale University, Brooklyn College, and Columbia University in 1960. The latter was published as Chapter 7 of *Philosophy: Who Needs It*, along with a number of other essays that discuss figures in the history of philosophy. Those essays, along with "For the New Intellectual," and posthumously published material (chiefly *Letters* and *Journals*) will serve as the primary sources for the following discussion.

That discussion will fall into three parts. In the first section, I will discuss the approach Rand took in her exploration of the history of philosophy, and later in writing about that history. This will provide us with the needed framework for looking, in the next section, at a number of distinctive conclusions she derives from her study of the history of philosophy, which lead her to reject some of the standard ways of unifying and distinguishing "schools" of philosophy and locating figures within these schools. Finally, with that background as context, I will return to her provocative claims about the place of Aristotle and Kant in the history of philosophy and culture generally.

Ayn Rand's Approach to the History of Philosophy

In the spring of 1934, at the age of 29, Rand began making notes in a philosophical journal. She identified "thought and reason" as "the only weapons of mankind" and faith as the denial of reason, defended free will as an aspect of reason, extolled individualism and egoism, and reflected on the role of the state in a society (*Papers* 166_04x_001/*Journals* 66–74).

Rand, who had come to America eight years earlier, escaping the tyranny of the Soviet Union, was witnessing American intellectuals praising the collectivism from which she had fled. Her adopted country rested on the Enlightenment philosophical foundations of reason and individualism, and she was certain that embracing the moral principles implied by collectivism would inevitably lead to America's downfall.

These notes engage with an eclectic group of thinkers, including Ortega y Gasset, H.L. Mencken, and Petr Alekseevich Kropotkin, but not with any of the figures whom she would later identify as important philosophers. In what appears to be a later addition to these notes, she commented:

> These are the vague beginnings of an amateur philosopher. To be checked with what I learn when I master philosophy – then see how much of it has already been said, and whether I have anything new to say, or anything old to say better than it has already been said. (*Papers* 166_04x_001_001/*Journals* 66)[4]

Evidently, by "mastering philosophy," Rand meant learning its history, and it is clear that Rand did not view such an historical investigation as an end in itself, but as a way of determining the nature of the battle that lay ahead of her. Would she be required to forge a new philosophical system, or to provide a clearer and stronger defense of ideas that had already been articulated?[5] Three features of her developing philosophical method conditioned the way she approached the study and (later) presentation of the history of philosophy: (1) searching for what is essential to a philosopher's system; (2) insisting on the objectivity of definitions; and (3) insisting on the fundamentality of philosophy in man's life. Before we turn to the lessons Rand draws from her study of philosophy's history, it will be helpful to briefly consider each of these aspects of her approach.

(1) *Going to the philosophical essentials*: In her approach to the history of philosophy, Rand focuses on essentials in three distinct, though related ways: (i) by searching for a philosopher's position on philosophical fundamentals; (ii) by evaluating a philosopher in terms of the hierarchy and consistency of his system; and (iii) by identifying shared foundations that unite different (and sometimes even apparently antithetical) philosophers and philosophical movements. Let me elaborate on each of these aspects of fundamentality.

(i) In studying a particular philosopher she will seek out his views on fundamental questions in metaphysics and epistemology, and trace the impact of his answers to these questions on his less fundamental views (or search for the more basic premises from which the less fundamental views derive). One can see this approach in her essay "Philosophical Detection." The task of the philosophical detective is described in the following terms:

> A philosophical detective must remember that all human knowledge has a hierarchical structure; he must learn to distinguish the *fundamental* from the derivative, and in judging a given philosopher's system, he must look – first and above all else – at its fundamentals. (*PWNI* 16)

She identifies metaphysics and epistemology as fundamental, on grounds that "[o]n the basis of a knowable universe and a rational faculty's competence to grasp it, you can define man's proper ethics, politics and esthetics" (*PWNI* 17).

(ii) But certain philosophers will be more systematic and more consistent than others, and Rand comes to regard these philosophers as fundamental determinants of the history of Western culture generally. In classical Greece, she saw Plato and Aristotle as the most systematic, and thus most influential, defenders of mysticism and reason, respectively; she viewed the thirteenth-century revival of Aristotelian thought as fundamental to the Renaissance, and Thomas Aquinas as its most systematic and consistent exponent. As we will see, she viewed modern philosophy as a turn back toward Platonism that culminated in Kant's attack on reason's efficacy to know a mind-independent reality and his defense of an ethics of pure duty. In Rand's view, Kant's philosophical system, which (in various, superficially different forms) has dominated philosophy since the early nineteenth century, is more consistently mystical and anti-life than Plato's own. Thus her search for essentials leads her to focus on Aristotle and Kant.[6]

(iii) Finally, and as I will demonstrate in the second section of this essay, Rand was able to identify and challenge presuppositions shared by apparently antithetical philosophical systems, presuppositions that in her view had to be challenged before philosophical progress could be made.

(2) *Maintaining the objectivity of definitions*: When discussing figures or schools in the history of philosophy, Rand identified their positions according to what she considered to be the proper, objective definitions of key philosophical concepts. For example, Rand defended the view that

"reason" refers to the cognitive faculty that integrates our perceptual awareness of reality into concepts, links those concepts into propositions, and makes logical inferences on the basis of those concepts and propositions. Reason, so understood, was the standard Rand used in deciding whether someone was a defender of reason or not. Thus when Plato, Kant, and their followers champion in the name of "reason" a faculty that either transcends the perceptual world or is cut off from it, Rand does not hesitate to describe them as mystics and enemies of reason.

This policy flows from a fundamental thesis of her epistemology: that valid concepts are grounded in reality, and thus any properly formed concept has an objective meaning and definition. To adopt a policy, in writing about the history of philosophy, of allowing a term to mean whatever a particular philosopher claims it to mean is implicitly to deny the objectivity of abstract concepts. The appropriate policy, on the premise of the objectivity of concepts, is to define your terms clearly, be prepared to defend those definitions, and to criticize another philosopher who uses the term in a way that divorces it from its basis in reality.[7]

(3) *Stressing the importance of philosophy in human life*: As I noted earlier, it is Rand's view that philosophical ideas are of critical importance for the health and vitality of a person or a culture. A central purpose for her study of the history of philosophy was to trace the historical trends in the development of culture – economic, artistic, political, religious trends – back to their philosophical sources. By doing so Rand was able to integrate features of a culture that, in the absence of an understanding of their philosophical roots, might otherwise appear to be unrelated.[8]

One can see all three aspects of her approach at work in comments she makes about reading she had been doing in the history of philosophy in her correspondence with Isabel Paterson in the 1940s. Consistent with the methodology I've outlined, her primary goals were to identify the fundamentals of different philosophical systems and how those fundamentals shape the philosopher's thinking generally; and to identify which philosophers were the key figures in determining the philosophical direction of European culture.[9] In a letter to Paterson written in late July of 1945, she reports:

> I am reading a long, detailed history of philosophy [by B.A.G. Fuller]. I'm reading Aristotle in person and a lot of other things. At times it makes my hair stand on end – to read the sort of thing those [non-Aristotelian] "sages of the ages" perpetrated. And I think of you all the time – of what you used to say about them. It's actually painful for me to read Plato, for instance. But I must do it. I don't care what the damn fools said – I want to know what made them say it. There is a frightening kind of rationality about the reasons for the mistakes they made, the purposes they wanted to achieve and the practical results that followed in history. (*Letters* 179)[10]

When she says she is reading Aristotle "in person," she is likely referring to *The Basic Works of Aristotle*, a selection of Aristotle's writings made by Richard McKeon from the Oxford English Translation – which was among the things she bought shortly after the publication of *The Fountainhead*.[11]

In a letter dated April 17, 1948, again focused on the fundamental differences between Plato and Aristotle, her methodology is especially clear:

> Since you are interested in philosophy, you have probably heard the statement that every philosopher (and every man) is essentially either a Platonist or an Aristotelian. This is one of the truest statements ever made. Plato and Aristotle *do* represent the basic division of mankind. Aristotle is the father of Individualism and logic, the first and greatest rationalist.[12] I am an Aristotelian.
>
> I would suggest that you study this question thoroughly, if you have not done so. I can give you a helpful hint of what to look for: the crucial difference between Plato and Aristotle lies in their

respective Theories of Knowledge and in their views on the nature of reality. *That* is the root. Their ethics, politics, etc., are the consequences. (*Letters* 394)[13]

In these two paragraphs, Rand identifies Plato and Aristotle as the fundamental antipodes in Greek philosophy, and then points to their epistemologies and metaphysics as fundamental to their opposition. In a letter written to Paterson in August of 1945, Rand stresses the importance of such fundamental premises in thought and action.

But I will mention that the "frightening kind of rationality" I referred to in my [previous] letter – was the discovery I made while reading the philosophers that it is actually impossible for man to be irrational. Let him yelp against reason all he wants. Let him accept the premise that there is no such thing as reason at all. And all his subsequent ideas and actions will follow in perfect logical sequence from that premise. His actions will become irrational and insane – but in perfect agreement with his premise. It was *not* a discovery to me, it was more in the nature of an illustration and a substantiation. (*Letters* 182)[14]

What she has noticed is the way in which, in the case of those philosophers who are consistent, their specific ideas[15] follow logically from their fundamental premises with a "frightening kind of rationality" – frightening, because in most cases, she is coming to realize, the fundamental premises are either implicitly or explicitly denials of the efficacy of reason. She begins by characterizing this as a "discovery," but then corrects herself: her study of the history of philosophy provides illustrations that substantiate the idea that reason is, as she would put it later, man's only absolute. Those philosophers who begin by denying the efficacy of reason will end up affirming it: reaching the conclusions and acting in ways that follow logically from their premise: they will deny that man can or should rationally define and pursue his values, and they will favor authoritarian political systems on grounds that people are irrational and must be controlled for their own good.[16]

Lessons from History

One of Ayn Rand's central reasons for studying the history of ideas, and of philosophy in particular, was her conviction that historical trends in the development of culture – economic, artistic, political, or religious trends – can be traced back to philosophical sources.[17] When did political liberty, individualism, capitalism, or romanticism first begin to emerge, and why in certain places and at certain times rather than others? In Rand's view these questions are to be answered by searching for the philosophical premises that fostered these developments. Conversely, to answer the question why their emergence was so tentative and short-lived, one needs to search for weaknesses in their philosophical defense that undermined them and provided an opening for their opponents. If sound philosophical ideas lie at the source of life-affirming values and unsound ones at the source of the destruction of those values, then nothing can be more important to human life than understanding the connection between fundamental philosophical premises and the day-to-day activities of life.

This premise, of the fundamental role played by philosophical ideas in determining the direction of a culture, had a direct impact on Rand's thinking and writing about the history of philosophy in a number of respects. First, her discussions, in essays and lectures, of the historical impact of philosophical ideas on politics, economics, and art are intended to be object lessons in "philosophical detection." She is advocating for a certain way of reading philosophical texts, one that stresses tracing out the implications for individual lives and for cultures of abstract philosophical principles.[18]

Because she believes that cultures and lives are at stake, her discussions of philosophers and philosophical movements are always impassioned. She does not hesitate to call a philosophical figure evil, based on what she takes to be the consequences for human life of the ideas he advocates. It is her respect for the practical power of philosophical abstractions that leads to the anger of her responses to Kant or the reverence of her responses to Aristotle.

Finally, her views about the practical value of philosophy lead directly to one of her most distinctive critical responses to the history of philosophy: the failure of philosophy to provide an adequate defense for the man of practical reason, the producer. Ayn Rand's concept of "the producer" is, as far as I am aware, unique in the history of philosophy. It groups together the artist, the scientist, the entrepreneur, the farmer, the businessman, along with figures that blend features of these categories, such as architects and engineers, based on one fundamental: the fact that all of them produce things of value to human life by the independent use of their minds.[19] The efficacy of the producer presupposes the efficacy of reason. And yet, Rand argues, philosophers have rarely defended reason as an efficacious tool for both the *acquisition* of knowledge (including moral knowledge) and the *application* of that knowledge to the production of material and spiritual values.

> The producers, so far, have been the forgotten men of history. With the exception of a few brief periods, the producers have not been the leaders or the term-setters of men's societies, although the degree of their influence and freedom was the degree of a society's welfare and progress (*FTNI* 16).[20]

One central aim of "For the New Intellectual" is to provide the outlines of a philosophical defense for the producer.[21] In it one sees clearly what Ayn Rand thinks it takes to change a culture intellectually. The history of philosophy teaches us that it is those philosophers who build consistent systems who have the most significant impact on a culture or period. However, that impact is not direct; it depends on intellectuals in all fields and at all levels, from the professors in the schools of arts and sciences, education, engineering, law, and medicine, to the editorial writers or art critics. Their work will be informed, often without realizing it, by the dominant philosophical ideas of the day. If a new philosophical system is to have an impact, then, it requires "new intellectuals," the target audience for Rand's broad, thematic outline of the history of philosophy.

Readers of standard academic surveys of the history of philosophy will be struck at once by the dramatic style of Rand's essay. Two philosophical archetypes, as Rand calls them, are introduced on page 8, following a lengthy quotation from *Atlas Shrugged*, in which John Galt puts forward the provocative and sweeping claim that throughout most of mankind's history, power has swung back and forth between those who claimed mystic insight as grounds for power over other people and those who simply exercised such power by brute force. Following this quote, Rand writes:

> These two figures – the man of faith and the man of force[22] – are philosophical archetypes, psychological symbols and historical reality. As philosophical archetypes, they embody two variants of a certain view of man and of existence. As psychological symbols, they represent the basic motivation of a great many men who exist in any era, culture, or society. As historical reality, they are the actual rulers of most of mankind's societies, who rise to power whenever men abandon reason (*FTNI* 7–8).[23]

Here I note a point I will return to shortly. The advocates of lives guided by faith and by force, though almost always portrayed as opponents in our culture, are portrayed by Rand as representatives of a shared philosophical vision. These two figures, whom she designates the Witch Doctor and Attila, are – as actual popes and mullahs, or historical monarchs and dictators – responsible for the predominant irrationality (and consequent poverty and brutality) of human societies throughout man's history, and she observes that they only ascend to positions of power when reason is abandoned. That means there ought to be a *third* philosophical archetype, representing the ascendancy of a rational approach to reality – and which ought to be, at a fundamental level, the opponent of both.

This third archetype does not appear in Rand's essay until she has spelled out the implicit metaphysics, epistemology, and morality of Attila and the Witch Doctor, and explained why it is that these superficially quite different figures, one disdainful of the world of ideas, the other disdainful of the material world, so often end up in uneasy alliances (for example, the alliance between church and monarchy in Europe from the twelfth to the nineteenth century, and in much of the Islamic world today). Their alliances are based on an underlying identity in their psycho-epistemologies or "methods of awareness."[24]

> Superficially, these two may appear to be opposites, but observe what they have in common: a consciousness held down to the *perceptual* method of functioning, an awareness that does not choose to extend beyond the automatic, the immediate, the given, the involuntary, which means: an animal's "epistemology" or as near to it as a human consciousness can come. (*FTNI* 8, cf. *FTNI* 13)

Over the next four pages her aim is to characterize the distinctively human form of awareness that Attila and the Witch Doctor choose to evade: reason, the formation of concepts by means of abstraction from the materials provided by perception.

> ... to integrate perceptions into conceptions by a process of abstraction, is a feat that man alone has the power to perform – and he has to perform it *by choice*. The process of abstraction, and of concept-formation is a process of reason, of *thought*: it is not automatic nor instinctive nor involuntary nor infallible. Man has to initiate it, to sustain it and to bear responsibility for its results. (*FTNI* 8)

The expression "has to" in that last sentence is not merely a reference to what man needs to do in order to think – for Rand, recall, reason is man's primary tool of survival: "For an animal, the question of survival is primarily physical; for man, primarily epistemological" (*FTNI* 9). But the reward for a life of sustained rationality, Rand notes, is that we are able to use the knowledge thus acquired to produce an unending stream of material and spiritual values.

What people who choose to live lives governed by force or by faith have in common, on Rand's view, is a desire to live without a sustained commitment to a life of rational productivity. The key to both their souls is their longing for the effortless, irresponsible, automatic consciousness of an animal. Both dread the necessity, the risk and the responsibility of rational cognition. Both dread the fact that "nature, to be commanded, must be obeyed" (*FTNI* 9).

But if productive activity based on reason is man's primary means of survival, how is it that, for most of human history, pharaohs, emperors, kings, dictators, with their priests, popes, archbishops, or astrologers have not only survived, but have lived lives of great wealth and power? "There is only one means of survival for those who do not choose to conquer nature: to conquer those who do" (*FTNI* 9).

So far, then, Attila and the Witch Doctor share a fear and loathing of the life of rational productivity and a solution to the problem that creates for them. Since they do not themselves have the means to produce wealth, they must somehow exploit those who do. Their methods of exploitation, however, differ. Attila, who lives by force, satisfies his needs simply by expropriation and enslavement – his goal is physical conquest. The Witch Doctor, who lives by faith, has a different goal in mind: "*His* method is the conquest of those who conquer those who conquer nature. It is not men's bodies that he seeks to rule, but men's souls" (*FTNI* 11).

Notice that the immediate target of conquest here is *not* the producer, the conqueror of nature, but Attila, the producer's conqueror. This explains the "unholy" alliance that is formed between those who advocate a life of faith and those who live and die by the sword. The Witch Doctor recognizes, and is exploiting for his own ends, the importance of philosophy to human life.

> The secret of the Witch Doctor's power lies in the fact that man needs an integrated view of life, a *philosophy*, whether he is aware of his need or not – and whenever ... men choose not to be aware of it, their chronic sense of guilt, uncertainty and terror makes them feel that the Witch Doctor's philosophy is true.
> The first to feel it is Attila. (*FTNI* 13)[25]

Rand presents the implicit premises behind the Witch Doctor's approach to the world at *FTNI* 12–13:

(1)   This earth is a realm of pain and suffering, inferior to another, "higher," reality.
(2)   Achievement and success on earth are not evidence of virtue but of depravity.
(3)   Reason is deceptive and unreliable, incapable of providing knowledge of reality.
(4)   Man's soul and body are opposed to one another.
(5)   Man's moral values are opposed to his own interest.
(6)   Goodness consists in self-sacrifice, suffering, obedience, humility and faith.

Plato's philosophy is characterized as the source in Western culture of these premises:

> ... with its two realities, with the physical world as a semi-illusory, imperfect, inferior realm, subordinated to a realm of *abstractions* (which means, in fact, though not in Plato's statement: subordinated to man's consciousness), with reason in the position of an inferior but necessary servant that paves the way for the ultimate burst of mystic revelation which discloses a "superior" truth. (*FTNI* 17)[26]

Rand's view of the history of culture, when combined with her idea that philosophical ideas are the driving force behind cultural history, leads to a search for those fundamentals that provide the historical and philosophical foundations for the two archetypes she identifies. She portrays the so-called Dark Ages, beginning with the disintegration of the Roman Empire, as a period dominated by tribal Attilas in search of a new form of mysticism with which to ally themselves – and which they found, in Christianity, under the philosophical influence of the Platonism of Plotinus and Augustine. The recovery of Aristotle's writings and the spread of his influence, especially at the hands of Thomas Aquinas, marks the end of the mysticism-dominated Middle Ages and the beginning of the Renaissance (*FTNI* 19).[27] For the next six pages Rand describes the political and economic consequences of a culture increasingly dominated by a philosophy of reason.

> A society based on and geared to the *conceptual* level of man's consciousness, a society dominated by a philosophy of reason, has no place for the rule of fear and guilt. Reason requires freedom,

self-confidence and self-esteem. It requires the right to think and to act on the guidance of one's thinking – the right to live by one's own independent judgment. *Intellectual* freedom cannot exist without *political* freedom; political freedom cannot exist without *economic* freedom; *a free mind and a free market are corollaries.* (*FTNI* 20–21)

Rand identifies two "twin-motors of progress" in the creation of a truly free and prosperous society: the professional intellectual who "carries the application of philosophical principles to every field of human endeavor" and the businessman who "carries scientific discoveries from the laboratory of the inventor to industrial plants, and transforms them into material products that fill men's physical needs and expand the comfort of men's existence" (*FTNI* 22, 23). But what if the dominant philosophical ideas that the professional intellectuals are purveying to journalists, lawyers, politicians, and artists are undermining "a society based on and geared to the *conceptual* level of man's consciousness?" This, in Rand's view, is what a study of the history of post-Renaissance philosophy demonstrates: rather than building on Aristotle's metaphysics and epistemology, modern philosophers beginning with Descartes rejected Aristotle and progressively undermined man's confidence in the mind's ability to know reality.

> While promising a philosophical system as rational, demonstrable and scientific as mathematics, Descartes began with the basic epistemological premise of every Witch Doctor (a premise he shared explicitly with Augustine): "the prior certainty of consciousness," the belief that the *existence* of the external world is not self-evident, but must be proved by deduction from the contents of one's consciousness. (*FTNI* 24)

Descartes concludes that the only certain basis for knowledge is the principle, *cogito ergo sum,* and he treats the existence and nature of a mind-independent world as an inference from a prior awareness of his own consciousness and its contents. Moreover, he holds that our most certain ideas are abstract and innate, whereas ideas based on perception are subject to doubt and uncertainty.[28] "Empiricists" such as Locke, Berkeley, and Hume are widely thought to present a clear epistemological alternative to the "rationalism" of Descartes. They start by basing our abstract ideas and knowledge on the contents of sense perception, but they take the direct objects of sense perception to be "simple ideas" or "impressions" that are internal to the mind; and so, like Descartes, they hold that we begin with certainty about the contents of consciousness and then need to reason our way to knowledge of the external world.[29] Implicit in this approach is the metaphysical thesis Rand refers to as "The Primacy of Consciousness" – the thesis that consciousness is a primary that can exist independent of external objects for it to be conscious of.[30]

Rand rejects the Primacy of Consciousness as incoherent and takes it as self-evident that we are directly aware in sense perception of a world that exists independently of consciousness. Reason, which is based on this perceptual grasp of reality, enables us to form wider and wider *conceptual* integrations of the objects of perception,[31] and those integrations in turn provide the basis for science, technology, and philosophy. She argues that this conceptual development is guided by three axiomatic concepts that are implicit in every act of perception: consciousness, existence, and identity. Every perception is the *awareness* of an *existent* with an *identity*, and grasping this fact (first implicitly and later explicitly) enables us to direct our consciousness to identifying ever more fully and deeply the existents we observe. Contrary to rationalism, there are no *a priori* concepts; but contrary to empiricism, there are axiomatic concepts about which we can be certain; contrary to both schools, perception is not awareness of images, impressions, or sense data, but of objects that exist independent of our awareness of them. Both rationalism and empiricism in their canonical expressions hold that knowledge based on perception is inherently "uncertain" and "fallible," and there are two reasons for that. The first is that, in both traditions, those things of which we are directly aware are taken to be sensory *representations* of objects rather than objects themselves. The second is that neither has an adequate account of the process of *abstraction*, the process by which concepts (universals) are formed. The rationalists take mathematics as their model of certain knowledge precisely because they deny that it is grounded in perception, while empiricists ground knowledge in perception but lack an adequate account of concepts. Rand characterizes the division in the following terms:

> [T]hose who claimed that man obtains his knowledge of the world by deducing it exclusively from concepts, which come from inside his head and are not derived from the perception of physical facts (the Rationalists) – and those who claimed that man obtains his knowledge from experience, which was held to mean: by direct perception of immediate facts, with no recourse to concepts (the Empiricists). (*FTNI* 27)

She thus identifies the *fundamental* error in post-Renaissance philosophy as its inability "to define the nature and source of abstractions, to determine the relationship of concepts to perceptual data – and to prove the validity of scientific induction" (*FTNI* 26, cf. *ITOE* 2). It is the *fundamental* error because validating conceptual knowledge is philosophy's fundamental task:

> Since man's knowledge is gained and held in conceptual form, the validity of man's knowledge depends on the validity of concepts. But concepts are abstractions or universals, and everything that man perceives is particular, concrete. What is the relationship between abstractions and concretes? To what precisely do concepts refer in reality? (*ITOE* 1)

This fundamental failure of modern philosophy, Rand came to realize, was systematically exploited by Immanuel Kant – and it was her view that, since twentieth-century philosophy consisted fundamentally of variations on Kantian themes, it was a failure that had never been addressed. Long before the recent interest in the common, neo-Kantian source of both "Continental" and "Analytic" philosophy, Rand had made this identification in no uncertain terms. She refers to Logical Positivism, for example, as "a Kantian offshoot" (*PWNI* 108, cf. "The Cashing-In: The Student 'Rebellion'" *CUI* 279–281). André Carus, in a recent historical study of Rudolf Carnap, the central figure in early logical positivism, agrees, devoting two chapters to discussing the pervasive Kantian influence on European culture, and its effect on Carnap. After quoting Kant's famous comparison of his philosophical revolution with the Copernican revolution in astronomy, Carus remarks: "It is fair to regard this 'Copernican revolution' as setting the agenda, in one way or another, for much of philosophy for the next century or two. Certainly it set the agenda for Carnap, as we shall see" (Carus 1992, 69).[32]

In an essay entitled "Kant vs. Sullivan," Rand presents a close analysis and critique of Paul Feyerabend's "Science Without Experience" published in *The Journal of Philosophy* in 1969, arguing that it reveals a swing of the philosophical pendulum back to a specifically Kantian form of rationalism (*PWNI*, esp. 119–120). The following words, written by Ayn Rand more than 50 years ago, continue to be true:

> If one finds the present state of the world unintelligible and inexplicable, one can begin to understand it by realizing that the dominant intellectual influence today is still Kant's – and that all the leading modern schools of philosophy are derived from a Kantian base. (*FTNI* 29)

331

Philosophy's turn toward Kant, Rand argued, was made possible by turning its back on Aristotle "who had not left them a full answer to the problem [of how to validate conceptual knowledge], but had shown the direction and the method by which the answer could be found" (*FTNI* 26). I shall thus close this chapter with a closer look at her discussions of these two towering figures in the history of philosophy.

Ayn Rand on Kant and Aristotle

As we've seen, it was Ayn Rand's view that the failure of early modern philosophy to validate abstract, conceptual knowledge set the stage for Kant's "Copernican revolution" in philosophy. Kant, in essence, performs a devious integration of rationalism and empiricism: reason is limited to the role of providing categorical and causal structure for the phenomenal world of impressions, and it cannot access the noumenal world of things in themselves; thus there is room for faith that there are noumenal grounds for a morality of duty. In a discussion of Friedrich Paulsen's *Immanuel Kant: His Life and Doctrine* (1898),[33] Rand quotes Paulsen on what he sees as Kant's historical achievement.

> ... the critical [Kantian] philosophy solves the old problem of the relation of knowledge and faith. Kant is convinced that by properly fixing the limits of each he has succeeded in furnishing a basis for an honorable and enduring peace between them. Indeed, the significance and vitality of his philosophy rests principally upon this ... it is [his philosophy's] enduring merit to have drawn for the first time, with a firm hand and in clear outline, the dividing line between knowledge and faith. This gives to knowledge what belongs to it – the entire world of phenomena for free investigation; it conserves, on the other hand, to faith its eternal right to the interpretation of life and of the world from the standpoint of value. (Paulsen 1898, 6; quoted in "From the Horse's Mouth" *PWNI* 106–107)

In Kant's more famous words, from the Preface to the second edition of the *Critique*: "I have therefore found it necessary to deny knowledge, in order to make room for faith" (Ak. III, Bxxx, Guyer and Wood 1998).

In her discussion of Kant in *For the New Intellectual*, however, Rand characterized the détente Paulsen hailed as Kant's achievement in terms of the philosophical premises lying behind her archetypes:

> Kant gave *metaphysical* expression to the psycho-epistemology of Attila and the Witch Doctor. ... He surrendered philosophy to Attila – and insured its future delivery back into the power of the Witch Doctor. He turned the world over to Attila, but reserved to the Witch Doctor the realm of morality. Kant's expressly stated purpose was to save the morality of self-abnegation and self-sacrifice. He knew that it could not survive without a mystic base – and what it had to be saved from was *reason*. (*FTNI* 27, cf. "Faith and Force" *PWNI* 87)

She goes on to speak of Kant parceling out reality to her archetypal characters:

> Attila's share of Kant's universe includes this earth, physical reality, man's senses, perceptions, reason and science, all of it labeled the "phenomenal" world. The Witch Doctor's share is another, "higher," reality, labeled the "noumenal" world, and a special manifestation, labeled the "categorical imperative," which dictates to man the rules of morality and which makes itself known by means of a *feeling*, as a special sense of duty. (*FTNI* 27)

Kant characterizes the "critical philosophy" in relation to Hume's skepticism in similar terms: "The sensible world contains merely appearances, which are still not things in themselves, which latter things (noumena) the understanding must therefore assume for the very reason that it cognizes the objects of experience as mere appearances" (*Prolegomena*, Ak. IV, 360, Hatfield 1997). Thus, for Kant, reason directed to the evidence of the senses is restricted to appearances and impotent to know things in themselves. If one thinks that the laws of nature discovered by science seem to refute this claim, Kant, of course, has a reply: "it is, though it sounds strange at first, nonetheless certain, if I say with respect to the universal laws of nature: *the understanding does not derive its (a priori) laws from nature, but prescribes them to it*" (*Prolegomena*, Ak. IV, 360, 320, emphasis in original; cf. *Critique*, Ak. III, A125).

Theism survives Hume's skeptical assault because,

> ... since the transcendental ideas nevertheless make the progression up to these limits necessary for us, and have therefore led us, as it were, up to the contiguity of the filled space (of experience) with empty space (of which we know nothing – the *noumena*), we can also determine the boundaries of pure reason ... (*Prolegomena*, Ak. IV, 354)

And when we stare into the noumenal void, do we see nothing? Not quite:

> We should, then, think for ourselves an immaterial being, a intelligible world, and the highest of all beings (all *noumena*), because only in these things, as things in themselves, does reason find completion and satisfaction, which it can never hope to find in the derivation of the appearances from the homogeneous grounds of those appearances ... (*Prolegomena*, Ak. IV, 354–355; cf. *Critique*, Ak. III, Bxxx)

Rand recognizes that this same "determination of the bounds of pure reason" grounds Kant's Categorical Imperative. In the *Prolegomena*, Kant resolves the seeming contradiction between the necessity apparent in the world of appearance and the freedom required for moral agency by assigning free will to the noumenal realm.

> But if natural necessity is referred only to appearances and freedom only to things in themselves, then no contradiction arises if both kinds of causality are assumed or conceded equally, as difficult or impossible as it may be to make conceivable causality of the latter kind. (*Prolegomena*, Ak. IV, 343)[34]

He thus locates the source of morality in an unknowable realm that stands in an incomprehensible relation to human life:

> ... insofar as we consider a being (the human being) solely as regards this objectively determinable reason, this being cannot be considered as a being of the senses; rather, the aforesaid property is the property of a thing in itself, and the possibility of that property – namely, how the ought, which has never yet happened, can determine the activity of this being and can be the cause of actions whose effect is an appearance in the sensible world—we cannot comprehend at all. (*Prolegomena*, Ak. IV, 345)

In "Causality Versus Duty," Rand discusses Kant's meta-ethics, relying on his *Groundwork of the Metaphysics of Morals*. Kant is the "arch-advocate of duty" as the standard of virtue, in the sense that devotion to duty is an end in itself.

> A deontological (duty-centered) theory of ethics confines moral principles to a list of prescribed "duties" and leaves the rest of man's life without any moral guidance, cutting morality off from any application to the actual problems and concerns of man's existence. (*PWNI* 131)

She cites Kant's discussion of the virtue of honesty as a case in point: "If a man *wants* to be honest, he deserves no moral credit: as Kant would put it, such honesty is 'praiseworthy,' but without 'moral import'" (*PWNI* 131, cf. *FTNI* 28–29).

This is a moral philosophy that stands in stark contrast to Objectivism, according to which, at the level of ethical theory, the question of a standard of value is settled by a rational study of the requirements of human life. "The standard of value of the Objectivist ethics – the standard by which one judges what is good or evil – is man's life, or; that which is required for man's survival qua man." And, "Since everything man needs has to be discovered by his own mind and produced by his own effort, the two essentials of the method of survival proper to a rational being are: thinking and productive work" ("The Objectivist Ethics" *VOS* 25).

Even more fundamentally, Rand argues that despite the Kantian claim that morality lies within the realm of free agency, the only freedom involved is that of giving up on genuine, reality-oriented rationality and submitting to the dictates of pure duty.[35] These dictates, in turn, since their source is in the noumenal realm, are not accepted rationally, but on faith.

> If I were to speak your kind of language, I would say that man's only moral commandment is: Thou shalt think. But a "moral commandment" is a contradiction in terms. The moral is the chosen, not the forced; the understood, not the obeyed. The moral is the rational, and reason accepts no commandments. (*Atlas* 1018)[36]

As in metaphysics and epistemology, so in her opposition to the deontological meta-ethics of Kant, Rand locates her own position within the Aristotelian tradition, in this case in relation to the Aristotelian concepts of conditional necessity and final causality.

> Reality confronts man with a great many "musts," but all of them are conditional; the formula of realistic necessity is: "You must, if–" and the "if" stands for man's choice ... In order to make the choices required to achieve his goals, a man needs the constant, automatized awareness of the principle which the anti-concept "duty" has all but obliterated in his mind: the principle of causality – specifically, of Aristotelian *final causation* (which, in fact, applies only to a conscious being) ... ("Causality Versus Duty" *PWNI* 133)[37]

It is, then, time to turn to her portrayal of Aristotle, his achievements and their consequences, including her identification of errors which later Aristotelians failed to correct, opening the door for Descartes, Hume, Kant, and their lesser modern followers.

Rand sees the emergence of philosophical systems explicitly defended by appeals to reason and evidence in ancient Greece as a monumental turning point in human history.

> ... a comparative degree of political freedom undercut the power of mysticism and, for the first time, man was free to face an unobstructed universe, free to declare that his *mind* was competent to deal with all the problems of existence and that *reason* was his only means of knowledge. (*FTNI* 17)

Nevertheless, Aristotle is the climactic high point in ancient Greek philosophy.

> ... Aristotle's philosophy was the intellect's Declaration of Independence. Aristotle, the father of logic, should be given the title of the world's first *intellectual*, in the purest and noblest sense of that word. (*FTNI* 17)[38]

And with her drive to identify the metaphysical and epistemological fundamentals that lie behind a philosopher's achievements or failures, she immediately provides a summary of those achievements of Aristotle's that set the intellect free.

> ... his incomparable achievement lay in the fact that he defined the *basic* principles of a rational view of existence and of man's consciousness: that there is only *one* reality, the one which man perceives – that it exists as an *objective* absolute (which means: independent of the consciousness, the wishes or the feelings of any perceiver) – that the function of man's consciousness is to *perceive*, not to create, reality – that abstractions are man's means of integrating his sensory material – that man's mind is his only tool of knowledge – that A is A. (*FTNI* 17–18)

This is a remarkably succinct summary of Aristotle's metaphysics and epistemology, identifying five closely related but distinct elements:

(1) Unlike many of his predecessors, such as Parmenides, Democritus, and especially Plato, Aristotle did not divide reality into two realms, a world of "appearances" and a "higher" reality of things as they are in themselves.
(2) The one reality is the one given to us in perception.
(3) It is objective, meaning it exists independently of our consciousness.
(4) Our perception and reason provide knowledge of that objective reality, but play no creative role in shaping it.
(5) Abstractions (universals) are integrations of materials provided by sense perception.[39]

The consequences for human culture of accepting these philosophical fundamentals are, in her view, impossible to overestimate:

> If we consider the fact that to this day everything that makes us civilized beings, every rational value we possess ... is the result of Aristotle's influence, of the degree to which, explicitly or implicitly, men accepted his epistemological principles, we would have to say: never have so many owed so much to one man. (*FTNI* 18, cf. *PWNI* 10, 108)

Aristotle has never, I believe it is fair to say, received higher praise.[40] The consequences of ignoring Aristotle's achievements were inevitably disastrous (the Dark Ages, dominated by religious mysticism aided and abetted by neo-Platonic philosophy), while the rebirth of a world dominated by science and reason was, in her view, a direct result of an Aristotelian rebirth: "The prelude to the Renaissance was the return of Aristotle via Thomas Aquinas" (*FTNI* 19).[41]

The Renaissance, in turn, created the atmosphere of respect for reason as man's tool for understanding, and thereby mastering, reality that were the preconditions for the Scientific Revolution, the Enlightenment, and the Industrial Revolution.[42] However, philosophical fundamentals are, in Rand's view, the ultimate determinants of the direction of a culture, and the philosophical failure to understand abstraction, the relationship between perceptual concretes and conceptual knowledge that climaxes in Kant's Copernican revolution, was well underway during the Enlightenment.

And yet it was Rand's contention that among the producers – the scientists, inventors, businessmen, and artists – Aristotle's influence continued to be felt.

> The men engaged in those activities [science, business, industry, trade] were still riding on the remnants of an Aristotelian influence in philosophy, particularly on an Aristotelian epistemology (more

implicitly than explicitly). But they were like men living on the energy of the light rays of a distant star, who did not know (it was not their primary task to know) that the star had been extinguished. It had been extinguished by those whose primary task was to sustain it. (*FTNI* 24)[43]

That is, it was the philosophers of the seventeenth and eighteenth centuries who, rather than correcting Aristotle's errors and following out his leads, were often openly antagonistic to him. Where he had consistently portrayed universals and abstractions as reached by an inductive process originating with perception, both rationalists and empiricists, in different ways, were driving a wedge between our perceptual awareness of the world and our abstract principles. Logical axioms were either truths derived *a priori* or were true by convention, while for Aristotle they were inescapable truths about being *qua* being. In the climactic radio speech of *Atlas Shrugged*, delivered by John Galt to a bankrupt culture, without mentioning Aristotle by name, Rand both praises him on this point and draws an explicit connection between his philosophy and hers:

> To exist is to be something, as distinguished from the nothing of non-existence, it is to be an entity of a specific nature made of specific attributes. Centuries ago, the man who was – no matter what his errors – the greatest of your philosophers, has stated the formula defining the concept of existence and the rule of all knowledge: *A is A*. A thing is itself. You have never grasped the meaning of his statement. I am here to complete it: Existence is Identity, Consciousness is Identification. (*Atlas* 1016)[44]

As this quote also acknowledges, she did think Aristotle was mistaken on a number of quite fundamental issues, most of which she attributed to lingering Platonic influence. His metaphysics was undermined, in Rand's view, by his failure to clearly distinguish it from his cosmological speculations.[45] In epistemology she interpreted him as defending a "moderate realist" stance, according to which concepts refer to essences that are identical aspects of the concretes subsumed by the concept and are grasped directly (*ITOE* 52–54).[46] She understood Aristotle's *nous* (reason) to be the cognitive faculty that grasps such essences, a view she considered disastrous for his epistemology; and she was also critical of his way of distinguishing theoretical reason from practical reason (*Marginalia* 11; cf. 13–15, 20–21).[47] And in ethics, his remarks about not demanding inappropriate precision and exactness, and the role "the noble and wise man" plays as a standard for virtuous action, come in for criticism.[48] In each case, she identifies elements of his metaphysics, epistemology, and meta-ethics that she believes undermine philosophical principles that are fundamentally sound. Unfortunately, the Aristotelians of the Scholastic and Renaissance periods tended to perpetuate rather than correct these mistakes, involved as many of them were in a project of attempting to reconcile Aristotle with Christianity.

Near the close of her magnum opus, *Atlas Shrugged*, in recognition of Aristotle's explicit defense of the Principle of Non-Contradiction as a *metaphysical* principle, Rand portrays one of the heroes of the book, who had majored in Physics and Philosophy in college and is now preparing to teach philosophy, reading a passage from Aristotle's *Metaphysics*:

> Ragnar Danneskjöld lay stretched out on a couch, reading a volume of the works of Aristotle: "... for these truths hold good for everything that is, and not for some special genus apart from others. And all men use them, because they are true of being *qua* being. ... For a principle which every one must have who understands anything that is, is not a hypothesis. ... Evidently then such a principle is the most certain of all; which principle this is, let us proceed to say. It is, that the same attribute cannot at the same time belong and not belong to the same subject in the same respect." (*Atlas* 1167)[49]

Nor is this the novel's most obvious tribute to Aristotle. *Atlas Shrugged* is divided into three parts. As Rand acknowledged in the "About the Author" page that follows the novel in each edition, her decision to title those parts *Non-Contradiction, Either-Or*, and *A is A* was further recognition of Aristotle's identification of these axioms. As she put it: "his definition of the laws of logic and of the means of human knowledge is so great an achievement that his errors are irrelevant by comparison" (*Atlas* 1171).

Both in the summary of his thought in *For the New Intellectual*, and in these two different forms of recognition in *Atlas Shrugged*, she chooses to emphasize what she sees to be Aristotle's most fundamental metaphysical and epistemological achievements, and those that most fundamentally distinguish Aristotle from other philosophers, and especially from Kant. This is once again illustrative of her approach to the history of philosophy: focus most attention on those philosophers who are philosophically systematic and who represent the most fundamental alternatives, and thus who have had the most far-reaching impact on the history of ideas; characterize their philosophies in terms of broad, abstract principles, with those principles selected in terms of the fundamentals of their philosophical system; and attend to the life and death consequences of accepting those principles.

This focus on the life and death significance of philosophical principles brings us to one last aspect of Rand's approach to the history of philosophy – one that will be taken up in Chapter 15 below: since Rand thinks that philosophers shape the culture, she sees understanding the history of philosophy and correcting its errors as essential to the fight for the type of society in which we can live fully and freely – for America as it might be and ought to be.

What this country needs is a *philosophical* revolution – a rebellion against the Kantian tradition – in the name of the first of our Founding Fathers: Aristotle. This means a reassertion of the supremacy of reason, with its consequences: individualism, freedom, progress, civilization. What political system would it lead to? An untried one: full, laissez-faire capitalism. ("From a Symposium" *ROTP* 175)

Acknowledgments

I would like to take this opportunity to acknowledge the valuable comments I received on earlier drafts of this paper from the editors of this volume, Allan Gotthelf and Greg Salmieri, and from Jason Rheins and Shoshana Milgram. It is a painful truth that Allan Gotthelf, who worked tirelessly on the planning and execution of this volume, is not here to see its publication. I dedicate this paper to his memory.

Notes

1 Cf.: "The philosophical thinking of the twentieth century is the cause of the present state of the world. But what is the cause of the cause? A major part of the answer lies in the history of philosophical thought from Greece to the present; only a knowledge of this history can give one the background, context and perspective required if one is clearly to understand the theories – and therefore the practices – which dominate today's world" (Peikoff, "Books: *A History of Western Philosophy* by W.T. Jones; *Philosophical Classics*, ed. Walter Kaufmann; *A History of Philosophy* by Wilhelm Windelband" *TON* 3(9) 38).

2 I will occasionally note in this discussion books she relied on in this respect. On her reading of Fuller, see n. 10, below.

3 Cf. Windelband 1901. Rand was certainly familiar with Windelband; Allan Gotthelf reports a conversation with her about Windelband's interpretation of Aristotle. She may have studied his *History of Ancient Philosophy* in her Ancient Philosophy class in college; cf. Milgram, above, 38, n. 9.

4 The published transcription of the journal includes a photo replication of the first page of the journal facing the transcription. The quoted remark is squeezed into the upper margin of the first page, above the date and the first entry, and then demarcated from the first sentence of that entry by a line that overwrites some of the words in that sentence.

5 In the biographical interviews, Rand reports that it was just this sort of question that led her to consider writing a systematic presentation of Objectivism. "I began to see that what I took as almost self-evident, was not self-evident at all … Leonard [Peikoff] began to realize the importance of my statement that 'existence is identity,' and he explained to me in what sense no philosopher had claimed it, not in this form. I had thought of it as what I said in Galt's speech, that it's merely clarification of Aristotle. I began to realize in what way it isn't. And it was *that* that was the turning point in my decision. I knew then that I could not write another novel for a long time." For more on this decision, see Milgram, above, 31.

6 Rand's interest in Aristotle began with a philosophy course she took during her first year of college. "That's when I fell in love with him," she later recalled (*Biographical Interviews* 560). She was evidently reading and reflecting on him in 1945 (see *Letters* 179, *Journals* 297 and 306). Her view of Plato as Aristotle's antithesis also dates back to college, but she seems not to have identified Kant's significance until sometime after 1948. See n. 13 below for details.

7 For an explicit defense of this principle, see her correspondence with John Hospers in *Letters* 519–520, 536.

8 John David Lewis and Gregory Salmieri stress this aspect of Rand's political and cultural commentary in Chapter 15, below.

9 It is no coincidence that it is during this same period that Rand systematized her own philosophy, working back from the moral premises she used in structuring a defense of individualism and capitalism, to their grounds and justification in fundamentals about man's nature, and (since reason is essential to man's nature) from there back to fundamentals about man's rational faculty and to its role in acquiring knowledge – and finally, to reason's *volitional* nature, the key to why man needs to define a code of values in conceptual terms. For a perceptive discussion of this development, see Wright 2009.

10 The interpolations were added by the editor of *Letters*. It was reported to one of the editors of this *Companion* by Leonard Peikoff that the history of philosophy she was referring to is Fuller 1945.

11 In a letter dated June 18, 1945 to movie producer Hal Wallis, for whom she had been working as a script writer, Rand writes: "You might like to know what was the first thing I did on regaining my freedom: I went out and bought five dresses by Adrian and the complete works of Aristotle" (*Letters* 227). The evidence from Ayn Rand's personal library indicates that what she purchased was in fact McKeon's (1941) *The Basic Works of Aristotle*.

12 By "rationalist" Rand here means a "defender of reason," not (as she later uses the term) an advocate of the idea that conceptual knowledge is independent of sense perception.

13 I thank Greg Salmieri for drawing my attention to this letter. This letter is interesting in another respect. It identifies "Plato (with Hegel next)" as the philosophers who have done the greatest intellectual and practical harm to mankind – Kant is conspicuously absent. In view of her attitude toward Kant in her non-fiction essays written after 1960, this absence suggests she had not yet identified the distinctive nature of Kant's "Copernican revolution," or its impact on all subsequent philosophy, at this point. Also relevant to dating her views on Kant is a mildly positive reference to "Kant and Nietzsche" in the 1936 *We the Living* which is replaced in the 1958 edition with a reference to Spinoza (*WTL36* 156, *WTL* 122); on this change see Mayhew 2012b, 215. On her view of the relationship of her philosophy to that of Plato and Aristotle in 1945, see the letter to O.W. Kracht, dated March 4, 1945 (*Letters* 222).

14 It should be noted that the context for this remark is a comment in Paterson's letter, that "[t]he "frightening kind of rationality" you find in the philosophers is precisely your own kind." This exchange of letters evidences a growing awareness on the part of both women of deep philosophical disagreements between them, despite their shared political and economic premises.

15 She also mentions "actions," and it is unclear what she means by that. It is unlikely she has in mind the actual actions taken by philosophers. I will interpret her as suggesting that philosophical ideas have inevitable cultural influences that can be observed in the actions of people and institutions in a given culture.

16 As Greg Salmieri pointed out to me, the same point is made to Dagny Taggart by Hugh Akston (*Atlas* 790–791). This theme also runs through her later article "Faith and Force: The Destroyers of the Modern World" (*PWNI* 79–103).

17 In the introductory lectures of courses endorsed by Rand (*HOP1* and *HOP2*), Leonard Peikoff stresses this as the motivation for studying the history of philosophy.

18 One of the most interesting features of posthumously published material such as her letters and journals is what it reveals about her as a lifelong political activist. Not surprisingly, she is constantly stressing in her correspondence with intellectual champions of individualism and political and economic liberty that their political ideas need a moral defense. She becomes increasingly dismayed as she discovers that many of these thinkers, if not entirely aphilosophical, accept the morality of altruism uncritically and attempt to defend individualism and capitalism on its basis. See her letters to Mencken (*Letters* 13), Graves (33–35), Pollock (44–56), and Emery (58–62).

19 A passionate *moral* defense of the producer is already explicit in Howard Roark's testimony in his own defense during the climactic trial in *The Fountainhead*. It is a passionate philosophical defense of creative thinkers, an explicit identification of their role in human progress and their consistent persecution resulting from dominance through most of human history of the morality of altruism. For an illuminating discussion of Ayn Rand's defense of the producer in *Atlas Shrugged*, see Salmieri 2009a, esp. 225–236.

20 In light of her motivation for turning to philosophy and its history, the following comment, in a letter to Tom Girdler, founder of Republic Steel and Vultee Aircraft, written in July of 1943, is significant: "You wished to defend and justify the industrial manager as the true mover of civilization. All through your book one hears a bewildered indignation that society has failed to recognize him as such. May I tell you the reason of that failure? It is because the industrialist has never found the moral principle on which he must stand" (*Letters* 82). More importantly, as she is at this time becoming aware, that moral principle, rational egoism, has never had a proper philosophical defense.

21 One of the more interesting aspects of her concept of "the Producer" is the way in which it unites professions which often are portrayed by today's intellectuals, and by the professionals themselves, as opposites. Artists, for example, often portray themselves as "above" the world of trade and commerce (though few of them turn down wealth if their work acquires value in the marketplace) and with rare exceptions are politically leftist. Rand correctly notes that it was only with the advent of capitalism, with its vast array of profitmaking publishers of books, newspapers, magazines, reviews, concert halls, art galleries, and theatres, that painters, sculptors, writers, composers, and performers had an open marketplace for their products. No longer were they reliant on the patronage of kings or organized religion for their existence. She also correctly notes that a significant number of artists seem to desire a return to a culture of patronage. (See *Atlas* 783–784, *CUI* 165, *RM* 120, *VOR* 241–242.)

22 Rand develops the theme of reason as the common enemy of faith and force in "Faith and Force: The Destroyers of the Modern World" (*PWNI*; see above, 323).

23 In a note appended to this passage she mentions that the names for these archetypes, used in all three senses throughout the rest of the essay, Attila and the Witch Doctor, were coined by Nathaniel Branden.

24 For discussion of Rand's concept of "psycho-epistemology," see Ghate, Chapter 5 in this volume.

25 There is complementary discussion in Galt's speech in *Atlas Shrugged* (1026–1046), in which "the mystics of spirit" and "the mystics of muscle" – and their unholy alliance – are portrayed as twin consequences of accepting the soul-body dichotomy.

26 Note that she is using "reason" here *not* as a translation for Plato's *nous* but as she defines it, as the cognitive faculty that integrates the material provided by the senses into concepts. The very next sentence refers to Aristotle's philosophy as "the intellect's Declaration of Independence." Rand's treatment of Aristotle's place in the history of philosophy will be considered in detail in the next section.

27 That Aristotle's influence is largely responsible for the Renaissance is a much more widely held view today than it was when Rand presented it in *FTNI*. See, e.g., Crombie 1971, Di Liscia, Kessler, and

Methuen 1997, Randall 1961, Schmitt 1983, Wallace 1981. A number of prominent voices, such as Galileo and Francis Bacon, reacting against Scholasticism, typically downplayed the positive influence of Aristotle in the interests of stressing their originality. Moreover, historians of the Scientific Revolution often failed to highlight the difference between the rejection of astronomical and physical theories that Aristotle accepted with the rejection of his epistemological and methodological views: yet adherence to Aristotelian principles would lead one (e.g.) to accept a heliocentric system over a geocentric system, given the availability of the evidence and arguments of Copernicus, Tycho, Kepler, and Galileo.

28 Cottingham, Stoothoff, and Murdoch 1985, 183–185, 193.

29 "It was Attila's soul that spoke when Hume declared that he experienced a flow of fleeting states inside his skull, such as sensations, feelings or memories, but never caught the experience of such a thing as *consciousness* or *self*" (*FTNI* 25).

30 For further discussion, see Rheins on the primacy of existence (ch. 11, above) and Salmieri on rationalism and empiricism (277–279, above).

31 Her theory of concepts and concept formation is presented in *ITOE* and is discussed in detail by Salmieri in Chapter 12, above.

32 Neo-Kantianism as the common source for the strand of philosophy leading to Husserl, Heidegger, and later Phenomenology and Existentialism, on the one hand, and Logical Empiricism and Analytic Philosophy on the other, is discussed in detail in Friedman 2000, and in Parrini, Salmon, and Salmon 2003.

33 Paulsen succeeded Eduard Zeller as Professor of Moral Philosophy at the University of Berlin in 1896.

34 Cf.: "Freedom in this signification is a pure transcendental idea, which, first, contains nothing borrowed from experience, and second, the object of which also cannot be given determinately in experience, because it is a universal law – even of the possibility of all experience – that everything that happens must have a cause" (*Critique* Ak. III A533/B561).

35 Rand is well aware, of course, that Kant portrayed himself as a defender of reason: "He did not, of course, announce himself as a mystic ... He announced himself as a champion of reason – of "pure" reason. ... He did not deny the validity of reason – he merely claimed reason is "limited," that it leads us to impossible contradictions, that everything we perceive is an illusion and that we can never perceive reality or "things as they are" (*PWNI* 87).

36 This line of thought has its origins in her work on *The Moral Basis of Individualism*. See, e.g., these notes for the 1945 draft: "Every living thing exercises a form of choice – to the extent of assimilating those elements which are necessary to its survival. ... To live, a living thing must have a code of values: that which is good for it and that which is not. Its survival is the standard, the measure of value. But for a plant or an animal, the standard, the values, the method of survival and the exercise of that method are automatic; no other choice is possible; no conscious choice is necessary ... Man's method of survival is not automatic. He must establish it by conscious choice based on a rational observation of nature and of himself; he must discover what he is, what he needs, how he must act in order to exist. He must establish his own code of values. Its standard must still be the same: survival. But the values he establishes must be the ones needed by and appropriate to his one and only means of survival – the human means – the rational faculty" (*Papers* 033_13A_004_014–015/*Journals* 298–299).

37 This idea was central to the revival of Aristotelian virtue ethics in recent analytic philosophy, in the form of an influential paper by Philippa Foot entitled "Morality as a System of Hypothetical Imperatives." Foot's argument opens as follows: "it is generally supposed ... that Kant established one thing beyond doubt – namely, the necessity of distinguishing moral judgments from hypothetical imperatives. That moral judgments cannot be hypothetical imperatives has come to seem an unquestionable truth. It will be argued here that it is not" (Foot 1972, 305–316).

38 As noted earlier, she considers Plato's epistemology and metaphysics to be, in essence, mystical, based on the idea that the natural world is an inferior and imperfect reflection of a supernatural world of Forms only accessible via a special kind of insight reserved for a specially trained philosophical elite.

39 The last two clauses – "that man's mind is his only tool of knowledge – that A is A" – are, I take it, drawing out implications of the previous points, specifically that perception and reason, rather than

some non-rational capacity, are our only contact with reality, and that reality is what it is, not what we may wish it to be.

40 Cf.: "If there is a philosophical Atlas who carries the whole of Western civilization on his shoulders, it is Aristotle. He has been opposed, misinterpreted, misrepresented, and – like an axiom – used by his enemies in the very act of denying him" ("Review of Randall's *Aristotle*" *VOR* 6).

41 She is not, of course, claiming that the texts of Aristotle were returned by Aquinas, but that his presentation and defense of Aristotelian philosophy in a form that made it palatable to the Christian tradition brought Aristotle's ideas into the cultural mainstream of Renaissance thought. By the fifteenth century the undergraduate curriculum at almost all European universities was dominated by a core group of Latin translations of Aristotle.

42 In this regard she refers to Francis Bacon's aphorism, "Nature, to be commanded, must be obeyed" as "the best and briefest identification of man's power in regard to nature" (*PWNI* 34).

43 In discussing the progress in material well-being in the nineteenth century, Rand wrote: "People thought they had entered an era of inexhaustible radiance; but it was merely the sunset of Aristotle's influence, which the philosophers were extinguishing" (*PWNI* 106, cf. 108).

44 She explicitly identifies "Existence," "Identity," and "Consciousness" as axiomatic concepts, which can be reformulated as propositional axioms (*ITOE* ch. 6). "A is A," or the Law of Identity, is the propositional form of the axiom of Identity, and Rand regarded the laws of Non-Contradiction and Excluded Middle as corollaries of it (*ITOE* ch. 6). Aristotle explicitly identifies and discusses the Laws of Non-Contradiction and Excluded Middle as axioms in *Metaphysics* IV, but *not* the Law of Identity, which according to William Hamilton (1859–1863) was first explicitly identified as such by Antonius Andreas, a student of Duns Scotus who lived and worked in the late thirteenth and early fourteenth century, in his *Quaestiones super XII libros metaphysicae*, a work that was widely studied in the Renaissance. Hamilton's discussion of Andreas is referenced in Peikoff 1964, ii. Though Aristotle did not in fact defend the axiomatic status of "A is A," there is a strong case for attributing the axiom of identity to him. He defends Non-Contradiction and Excluded Middle on grounds that to deny them amounts to denying that things are "definite," i.e., are just what they are, have identity. But to make any meaningful statement, even one denying Non-Contradiction or Excluded Middle, requires that its words refer to something definite (cf. *Metaphysics* IV 1006a31–b1; 1006b28–35; 1007a20–28; 1008a30–34). Thus, Aristotle's defense of the two axioms he *does* formulate rests on his insistence on the self-evident fact of identity. Rand thought that *Metaphysics* Z.17 1041a14–17 showed that Aristotle "certainly has the concept of 'identity'" (*Workshops* 219). This passage had been brought to her attention by Allan Gotthelf (*Papers* 033_17x_005).

45 On Aristotle's failure to clearly distinguish cosmology from metaphysics, see *Journals* 698–699.

46 Her understanding of Aristotle on this issue is spelled out in more detail in her response to a question about it in the Appendix to the second edition of *ITOE* (137, 141). For a presentation of her views on these issues and some discussion of their relationship to Aristotle's, see Chapters 11 and 12 in this volume.

47 These pages reproduce her fascinating marginal notes on her copy of John Herman Randall Jr.'s *Aristotle*. Her review of Randall's book appeared in *TON* 2(5) and is reprinted in *VOR* 6–12.

48 "The greatest of all philosophers, Aristotle, did not regard ethics as an exact science; he based his ethical system on observations of what the noble and wise men of his time chose to do, leaving unanswered the questions of: *why* they chose to do it and *why* he evaluated them as noble and wise" (*VOS* 14).

49 The quotation is from the W.D. Ross translation of *Metaphysics* Γ.3 1005b19–20.

References

Carus, A.W. 1992. *Carnap and Twentieth-Century Thought*. Cambridge: Cambridge University Press.

Cottingham, John, Robert Stoothoff, and Dugald Murdoch, eds. 1985. *The Philosophical Writings of Descartes*, vol. 1. Cambridge: Cambridge University Press.

Crombie, A.C. 1971. *Robert Grosseteste and the Origins of Experimental Science 1100–1700*. Oxford: Oxford University Press.

Di Liscia, Daniel A., Eckhard Kessler, and Charlotte Methuen, eds. 1997. *Method and Order in Renaissance Philosophy of Nature: The Aristotelian Commentary Tradition*. Aldershot, UK: Ashgate.

Foot, Philippa. 1972. "Morality as a System of Hypothetical Imperatives." *Philosophical Review*, 81(3).

Friedman, Michael. 2000. *A Parting of the Ways: Carnap, Cassirer, Heidegger*. LaSalle, IL: Open Court.

Fuller, B.A.G. 1945. *A History of Philosophy, revised edition*. New York, NY: Henry Holt & Co.

Guyer, Paul, and Allen W. Wood, eds. and trans. 1998. *Immanuel Kant: Critique of Pure Reason*. Cambridge: Cambridge University Press.

Hamilton, William. 1859–1863. *Lectures on Metaphysics and Logic*. Edited by Rev. Henry L. Mansel and John Veitch. Boston, MA: Gould and Lincoln.

Hatfield, Gary, ed. 1997. *Immanuel Kant: Prolegomena to Any Future Metaphysics*. Cambridge: Cambridge University Press.

Mayhew, Robert, ed. 2009. *Essays on Ayn Rand's* Atlas Shrugged. Lanham, MD: Lexington Books.

Mayhew, Robert. 2012b. "*We the Living: '36 and '59.*" In *Essays on Ayn Rand's* We the Living, 2nd edition, edited by Robert Mayhew. Lanham, MD: Lexington Books.

McKeon, Richard, ed. 1941. *The Basic Works of Aristotle*. New York, NY: Random House.

Parrini, Paolo, Wesley C. Salmon, and Merrilee H. Salmon, eds. 2003. *Logical Empiricism: Historical and Contemporary Perspectives*. Pittsburgh, PA: University of Pittsburgh Press.

Paulsen, Friedrich. 1898. *Immanuel Kant: His Life and Doctrine*. New York, NY: F. Ungar.

Peikoff, Leonard. 1964. *The Status of the Law of Contradiction in Classic Logical Ontologism*. PhD dissertation, *New York University*. Ann Arbor, MI: ProQuest/UMI. Publication No. 6501658.

Randall, John H. 1961. *The School of Padua and the Emergence of Modern Science*. Padua, Italy: Antenore.

Salmieri, Gregory. 2009a. "*Atlas Shrugged* on the Role of the Mind in Man's Existence." In Mayhew 2009.

Schmitt, Charles. 1983. *Aristotle in the Renaissance*. Cambridge, MA: Harvard University Press.

Wallace, William. 1981. *Prelude to Galileo: Medieval and Sixteenth Century Sources of Galileo's Thought*. Dordrecht, Netherlands: Reidel.

Windelband, Wilhelm. 1901. *A History of Philosophy*. New York, NY: Macmillan.

Wright, Darryl. 2009. "Ayn Rand's Ethics: From *The Fountainhead* to *Atlas Shrugged*." In Mayhew 2009.

14

Ayn Rand's Evolving View of Friedrich Nietzsche

LESTER H. HUNT

FAVORITE PHILOSOPHER – Nietzsche. His "Thus Spake Zarathustra" is my Bible. I can never commit suicide while I have it.

> Ayn Rand, answering a questionnaire, *circa* 1935[1]

[Y]ou still don't seem to know yourself that your idea is new. It is not Nietzsche or that other goof, ... Max Stirner. ... [Roark] is something, he doesn't even have to say so. You give the logical statement as well, – and at the opposite pole from any Blond Beast super-German. He is an American.

> Isabel Paterson to Ayn Rand, 1943[2]

I am very anxious to separate Objectivism from Nietzsche altogether. ... I don't want to be confused with Nietzsche in any respect.

> Ayn Rand, radio interview, 1964[3]

Friedrich Nietzsche (1844–1900) is no doubt the one philosopher with whom Ayn Rand is most often associated in popular discussions of her ideas. The relationship between her ideas and those of the German writer and thinker are the subject of the wildest misconceptions. The general tendency of these misconceptions is to greatly exaggerate the similarity between the ideas of these two thinkers. Nonetheless, there are connections between them, of a sort, and they are interesting ones.

One thing that can make the relationship between them difficult to understand is the fact that Rand's relation to Nietzsche changes considerably over the years. The history of this relationship can be divided roughly into three different periods. The first begins during her years as a student in Russia and ends with the completion of *The Fountainhead* (approximately 1921–1942). The second period follows upon the completion of *The Fountainhead* and ends with the completion of *Atlas Shrugged* (1942–1957). The third and last period (1957–1982) follows the writing of *Atlas* and ends with her death.

During the first period, it is possible to find ideas, attitudes and even turns of phrase in her writings that readily bring those of Nietzsche to mind. As she matures, those Nietzsche-like elements are typically transformed and rethought, often ingeniously, to suit a point of view

A Companion to Ayn Rand, First Edition. Edited by Allan Gotthelf and Gregory Salmieri.
© 2016 John Wiley & Sons, Ltd. Published 2016 by John Wiley & Sons, Ltd.

that differs from his more and more. In the second period, such echoes of Nietzsche disappear from her work, and her styles – both her style of writing and of thinking – are sharply different from his. During the third period, her activity as a writer takes the form of producing non-fiction essays and books. Explicit references to Nietzsche now reappear in her writings and public statements from time to time, but they are always negative in tone, and sometimes harshly so. Obviously, something has changed over the years: at the very least, her attitude toward Nietzsche has changed. No doubt this change in attitude was brought about by other, deeper developments. In this chapter I will make some suggestions about what those deeper developments were. First, however, I will tell in greater detail the story of Rand's changing attitude toward Nietzsche.

Ayn Rand discovered the works of Nietzsche in Russia, during her first year in college, when she was 15 or 16 years old. As she remembered it years later, an older cousin told her, "not very kindly," that she should read him because "he beat you to all your ideas." She later said that she thought she then read "all his works," or at least all that had been translated into Russian. On coming to America in 1926, the first three books she purchased were the Modern Library edition of *Also sprach Zarathustra* (which the translator Thomas Common rendered as *Thus Spake Zarathustra*), a book that she subsequently read many times, and the Modern Library editions of *Beyond Good and Evil* and *The Antichrist* (*Biographical Interviews* 187).

The years immediately following this were a time of intense interest in Nietzsche. At the age of 23, while living in Los Angeles in 1928, she wrote extensive notes for a novel she was planning at the time to write, titled *The Little Street*.[4] It is beyond doubt the most Nietzschean writing of hers that survives. The Nietzschean themes begin already with the title, which is suggestive of a favorite theory of Nietzsche's, to the effect that the enemy of the ideal is not the bad or the evil, but the small. He believed that the basic traits that enable one to be heroically good also enable one to be evil. It is in terms of such ideas that Rand characterizes the hero of *The Little Street*, a young man "[s]uperior to the mob and intensely, almost painfully conscious of it" (*Journals* 26) – an experience, incidentally, which Nietzsche liked to call "the *pathos* of distance." He also happens to be a murderer. He could, however, have been a great man but for the fact that he lives in a world run by and for suffocatingly boring mediocrity. She quotes from the chapter "The Old and New Tablets," in *Zarathustra*: "Oh, that their best is so very small! Oh, that their worst is so very small!" (41) The story is characterized by unrelenting hostility to Christianity: the villain, and victim of the murder committed by the hero, is a "beloved" clergyman. The real villain of the story, however, is what Rand calls "the mob." In the world of this story, most people have a powerful tendency to bond together with "sympathetic understanding and co-feeling with others" and to react with "subconscious fury" against whatever appears to be above it (42, 39). "To humiliate, to throw down – that is the mob's greatest delight" (39). All this is authentically Nietzschean in terms of its style, sentiment, and ideas as well.[5]

We may have no way of knowing what Rand's whole worldview was like at this stage of her life, and it is extremely doubtful that she ever agreed with all the major tenets of Nietzsche's philosophy. However, the notes for *The Little Street* are full of Nietzschean themes and there is nothing in them that conflicts with Nietzsche's views. The author of these notes is striving to write a work of fiction with a philosophical theme, rather than to originate new philosophical theses, and she is drawing for this purpose on the philosophy of Nietzsche, or on those parts that she finds relevant and congenial.

The earliest concerted attempt at philosophical writing by Rand that we have is a journal entry dated April 9, 1934 (*Papers* 172_43-04 / *Journals* 66–68). This entry expresses attitudes that overlap with those of Nietzsche and yet are sharply distinct from them at the same time. The subject of the note is her opposition to religion: "I want to fight religion," she says at the outset, "as the root of all human lying and the only excuse for suffering." She gives two reasons for her opposition to religion. The first is that religion makes it possible for one to "consider ideals as something quite abstract and detached from one's everyday life." So far, these comments bear some obvious similarities with themes in Nietzsche. He too was critical of various religions (especially Christianity) and he also sought ideals that can be lived here on earth.

However, her tone here is different from the one typical of Nietzsche, and the second reason she gives for rejecting religion suggests a clue as to the reason for this difference: "*Faith is the worst curse of mankind,*" she writes, underscoring the words, "as the exact antithesis and enemy of *thought.*" The reason faith is so bad is that it conflicts with a fundamental and absolute value: "*Thought* and *reason* are the only weapons of mankind, the only possible bond of understanding among them. Anyone who demands that anything be taken *on faith* – or relies on any ... superlogical instinct – denies all reason." This is rather different from the treatment of faith we find in Nietzsche. It is true enough, of course, that he is critical of faith. He says that "faith moves no mountains, but *puts* mountains where there are none." "'Faith,'" he also tells us, "means not *wanting* to know what is true."[6] But his critical comments on faith generally take the form of charging that it is futile or, at worst, a symptom that something *else* is wrong with one's life.

Rand, on the other hand, is charging that faith is actually toxic in and of itself. There is an obvious reason for this difference. Although Nietzsche would agree that faith is inimical to reason, he does not hold reason to be an absolute value. While he later abandoned the complete irrationalism of his first book, *The Birth of Tragedy*, his thinking always contained irrationalist elements, and he certainly never thought that the value of reason is absolute or basic to other values. Consequently, his condemnation of faith does not have the strong, categorical quality that Rand's does. The important point here of course is the difference between Rand and Nietzsche on the question of the value of reason. The later Rand, as is well known, did hold reason to be an absolute value, and she apparently did so at least as early as this 1934 journal entry. Indeed, she made comments in an autobiographical interview decades later to the effect that the vein of irrationalism in Nietzsche's writings was offensive to her from the very beginning. Speaking of *The Birth of Tragedy*, she said: "If before that I thought he was anti-reason, here it was stated specifically that reason is an inferior faculty, and some kind of drunken orgy emotions, the Dionysus principle, were superior. That really finished him for me, in the sense of a serious spiritual ally" (*Biographical Interviews* 190). This difference between her and Nietzsche is a profound one and gives rise to other differences between them, differences that will become increasingly prominent in her work as time goes on.

In another entry in this same journal from 1934, Rand also takes another position that separates her from Nietzsche on a fundamental issue: she defends free will. Nietzsche makes it clear that he is a determinist: it is crucial to his critique of the idea of moral responsibility, and also for his argument for the notion of "the eternal recurrence of the same things." Indeed, this is another point on which, she suggests in the later autobiographical interview, she differed from Nietzsche from the beginning (*Biographical Interviews* 188–189).

However, when people associate Nietzsche with Rand, as they often do, they are not thinking of such metaphysical and epistemological issues as determinism and the validity of reason. They are probably thinking mainly of ethical issues. It is not clear to what extent, by this time in the early 1930s, her ethical position was yet sharply different from that of Nietzsche. There are passages in the first edition of *We the Living* (1936), later cut from or revised in the second edition (1959), that are reminiscent of Nietzschean thoughts and attitudes. They leave the issue of the relation between Rand's ethics and those of Nietzsche rather ambiguous. Asked by Andrei whether we can sacrifice the many for the sake of the few, Kira replies:

> You can! You must. When those few are the best. Deny the best its right to the top – and you have no best left. What *are* your masses but mud to be ground under foot, fuel to be burned for those who deserve it? (*WTL36* 93)

This at least sounds very much like something that the author of *Zarathustra* might say.

Nietzsche's ethical views were focused on matters of character, rather than on issues about what actions one should do. His ideal was a type of person – represented in *Zarathustra* with the trope of the *Übermensch* (which Rand in her journals translates as "superman"). The principal ethical task is to facilitate the existence of these exemplary human beings, and the ideal society for Nietzsche would be one in which those who are not exemplary find meaning in their lives by supporting those who are.[7] This view could be expressed, rather hyperbolically, by saying that the best that most of us can strive for is to serve as "fuel to be burned for those who deserve it." The question of how close Rand is coming in what are sometimes called the "Nietzschean passages" in *We the Living* to accepting this view depends on how one interprets these passages.[8]

If the relation between the ethics of *We the Living* and Nietzsche's is ambiguous, *The Fountainhead* represents a clear, sharp, profound break with Nietzsche.[9] One of the principal issues in the novel is that of the correct understanding of a concept that is fundamental to Nietzsche's philosophy and, in particular, his ethics. This is the nature of power as a value. Two of the novel's principal characters, Howard Roark and Gail Wynand, are contrasted and characterized in terms of the different ways in which they interpret that concept. Rand makes it very clear that power is Wynand's fundamental value. As he says at one point in a conversation with Dominique Francon: "Power, Dominique. The only thing I ever wanted. To know that there's not a man living whom I can't force to do – anything. Anything I choose" (*Fountainhead* 517). On the other hand, Roark is not depicted as someone who would be happy to be powerless. He, too, is interested in power, but it is a completely different sort of power from the one that Wynand seeks. Wynand is interested in power over others, while Roark is interested in having the power to act and, especially, to create.[10] Part of the point of the interaction between these two characters, which results eventually in Wynand's moral ruin, and part of the point of Roark's courtroom speech, is to show that the sort of power that Wynand seeks is not real power. Nietzsche, on the other hand, certainly *would* regard it as real power. This constitutes a profound difference between Rand's values and those of Nietzsche. Obviously, it will lead to deep differences between them regarding the way in which people ought to treat each other.

Though this criticism of Nietzsche will have a profound effect on other differences between Rand and Nietzsche, it is possible to see it as a revision of a central Nietzschean theme, rather than an outright rejection. Power is still an important value, though it is power over nature, and not power over human beings, that represents real power. Indeed, Roark's criticism of Wynandian power in his courtroom speech has an interestingly Nietzschean ring to it: "Rulers of men" he charges, "... exist entirely through the persons of others," in that their "goal is in their subjects, in the activity of enslaving," with the result that they "are as dependent as the beggar, the social worker, the bandit" (*Fountainhead* 714). This is a criticism Nietzsche would have to take seriously, precisely because it is a criticism of him in his own terms: Rand is saying that to pursue power over others is to breach one's own psychological self-sufficiency and this is just the sort of consideration that Nietzsche himself sees as undermining one's own power.[11]

Soon after completing *The Fountainhead*, Rand developed ideas that would make it very clear that her ethics is not merely a radical revision of the Nietzschean one but is actually a diametrically opposed alternative to it. The next major writing project was to be a book-length essay, "The Moral Basis of Individualism," which she eventually abandoned. On the earliest page of the extensive notes and drafts she made for this project, dated August 12, 1943, we find this memorandum: "The proper relationship of man to men, deduced from the moral law. (Traders, *not* servants.)"[12] This is an early appearance in Rand's writings of the idea, later elaborated in *Atlas Shrugged*, of the just society as one in which people are related to each other primarily as *traders*. To see how this indicates a widening rift between her ethics and those of Nietzsche, consider briefly his best-known ethical idea: his account of the difference between "master morality" and "slave morality." Nietzsche used this distinction in order to explain various features of different moral codes that exist today in terms of different psychological reactions that our ancestors had to finding oneself in the position of either a master or a slave. Masters tend to develop one sort of moral code, and slaves tend to create quite a different one. One obvious feature of slavery as a way of dealing with human beings is, of course, that massive amounts of the "over others" sort of power are involved. Another, slightly less obvious feature, which is closely related to this one, is that the relationship between the master and slave is, as game-theorists put it, "zero sum":[13] it is a relationship that benefits one person at the expense of the other. If you take this relationship as a sort of paradigm of what social relations are, then you see the world as one in which "one man's gain is another man's loss." This is indeed how Nietzsche tends to see the world, and it helps to explain why he evaluates power over others very differently from the way Rand does. In a zero-sum world, it will be very important to gain control over others, and to extend it as far and keep it as long as we can. Your neighbors want to live and prosper just as you do and, in such a world, they will not do what is in your interest if they have a choice.

A society of traders is the exact opposite of this sort of world. Trade, unlike slavery, is a relationship based on mutual consent. For that reason, both parties to a trade advance their own goals by means of it, or they would not willingly participate. Acting within the framework of rights that make trade possible, people become positively valuable to one another. The switch from a world of hegemony to a world of trade has implications of breathtaking proportions, extending to one's very sense of life. Nietzsche consistently characterized his view of life as "tragic." Rand's is anything but. One of the likely reasons for this very large sense of life difference between them is the underlying ethical difference.[14]

The introduction of the idea of society as a system of traders brings with it another subtle and basic development. In the same early (1934) philosophical notebook in which Rand declares war on faith, she includes the following comment on political philosophy:

> The new, I hope, conception of the State which I want to defend, is the State as a means, not an end; a means for the convenience of the higher type of man. ... The state, not as a slave of the great numbers, but precisely the contrary, as the individual's defense against great numbers. To free man from the tyranny of numbers. The fault of liberal democracies – giving full rights to quantity – majorities – they forget the rights of quality, which are much higher rights. Prove that differences of quality not only do exist inexorably, but *should exist*. The next step – democracy of superiors only. (*Papers* 172_43-04 / *Journals* 73–74)

Here she is still working on the basis of a Nietzschean premise, according to which superior individuals are so different from others that they do not even have the same rights. This will need to change as she moves to the paradigm of the society of traders. Trade is a relationship of mutual consent, in which neither party can be taken for granted. It also is in a certain way symmetrical: each party gets what it desires from the other only on condition that they meet the conditions, set by the other, for their willing cooperation. At a fundamental level, they must have the same sorts of rights, including most obviously property rights. This is exactly the view that Rand eventually arrives at.[15]

During the years that *Atlas Shrugged* was in preparation, Rand developed her views in the fundamental areas of epistemology and metaphysics, something she had not done before to any great extent. As her thinking on these subjects progressed, the gap between her and Nietzsche widened further. Nietzsche's views on epistemology changed a number of times and are subject to varying interpretations, but on no account could his views be called "objectivist." He often characterized his views as a form of "perspectivism," by which he seems to have meant (at least) that reality is inevitably subject to multiple interpretations, and that, while some of these "perspectives" are better than others, the reasons clearly include pragmatic considerations, and not (or not only) objective truth.[16] In the realm of metaphysics, he eventually sketched, in unpublished notes published posthumously as *The Will to Power*, a view of the universe as a shifting system of "quanta of power." In his view, the world is a Heraclitean flux entirely lacking in the stable substances that populate the sort of metaphysics favored by Rand.[17]

As her thinking became more systematic, she came to see the distance between her thinking and his as enormous. The points of overlap or resemblance were relatively narrow, while the differences concerned very fundamental issues. Eventually, in a radio interview given in 1964, she characterized the relationship between her philosophy and his like this:

> I am very anxious to separate Objectivism from Nietzsche altogether. The reason for the mistaken rapprochement that some people hold between my philosophy and that of Nietzsche is that Nietzsche has certain very attractive, very wise quotations purported to uphold individualism, with which one could agree out of context. But excepting his general "feeling for" individualism, I would not consider Nietzsche an individualist; and above all, he is certainly not an upholder of reason. When you judge a philosophy you must always start by judging its fundamentals. And in all fundamentals – particularly metaphysics, epistemology, and ethics – Objectivism not only differs from Nietzsche but is his opposite. Therefore, I don't want to be confused with Nietzsche in any respect.

When her interviewers asked her to distinguish her treatment of "superior" people such as Howard Roark and Henry Rearden from Nietzsche's discussions of the superior individual, she had this to say:

> [I]t's an equivocation on the word "superior." If you mean "superior" in the sense of excellence – and "superior" is a bad word to use here – if you mean that some men excel, are better, than others, by means of self-developed, self-made virtue, that is a different thing entirely than Nietzsche's concept, which divided men in effect into two species. You see, the word "superior" is more applicable to Nietzsche's philosophy. It is a word which we never use. I never describe my characters as "superior" men, I describe them as ideal men. Now in Nietzsche's concept, a man is superior or inferior by birth: it has nothing to do with morality.

When asked what she thought of Nietzsche's idea that superior people need not follow the rules that apply to inferior people, she said:

A moral code has to be based on man's nature. Men do belong to the same species. ... Since men are all examples of the same species, the fundamental rules of conduct, that which is common to all of them, and applies to all of them, will have to be the same. If some men are better than others, in certain talents or in certain achievements, this is merely a ... difference of degree, not of kind. Therefore you couldn't have different rules for so-called superior or inferior men. ... [T]he basic rules will have to be the same for all men, since they are based on the fundamentals of man's nature, not on degrees of their achievement or of their virtue.[18]

During the last period of her career, Rand leveled several blistering attacks on Nietzsche in print.[19] However, there did remain one surviving debt to Nietzsche, and in a way it was an important one. In the biographical interviews from which I have already quoted, she said of him, "he did do me one service." She explained that it was from her encounter with Nietzsche's works that she came to understand how it is possible to think of "man," as she puts it in the "About the Author" page at the end of *Atlas Shrugged*, "as a heroic being."

She explains that she had earlier thought that in order to think of the human being as heroic, she "had to defend man as the species." That is, the heroic vision of human life seemed to mean that all the people who currently live are somehow heroes. This seems obviously untrue. In addition, the idea that everyone is good would seem to imply, just as much as the idea that everyone is bad, some sort of determinism. This is how she describes how she found her way out of this dilemma:

> And what Nietzsche made me realize is that it doesn't have to be collective. ... [H]e helped me to formulate it in terms of individualism and not of the metaphysical original virtue of mankind as such. So, in a sense, what my attitude could have taken me into would be original virtue determinism. But what I then realized is that the species can be vindicated by one man. And from then on, what my thinking gradually came to in conscious terms: If I am a member of the species then that's what I judge them by. I'm not a freak. (*Biographical Interviews* 201)

Notice that she does not seem to be saying that Nietzsche consciously held the idea that she derived from reading him. What seems to have happened is this. Like Rand, Nietzsche often made some very acerbic judgments about the actions and attainments of actual human beings, while at the same time, again like her, he did seem to see "man" in the abstract as heroic. How is this possible? A full answer to this question would be a long story, but clearly part of it involves taking a heroic individual – perhaps a fictional individual like Zarathustra or Howard Roark – as representing the human type more fully than the far more numerous non-heroic ones do. There is a shared underlying logic, which makes possible the peculiar combination of realism and idealism that characterizes the writings of both these thinkers.

However, as Isabel Paterson pointed out, the natures of the heroes involved are quite different. One is European and aristocratic, while the other is deeply American and adapted to life in a society of producers and traders. One is reason-based and the other is more emotion-based.[20]

Notes

1 Document titled "A Candid Camera of Ayn Rand" (*Papers* 86_18–16). The undated two-page document appears to consist of answers to questions from a publisher to be used to publicize a book, probably *We the Living* (1936). I am indebted to Shoshana Milgram for bringing this document to my attention.
2 Letter postmarked October 14, 1943 (*Papers* 145_33-PAT-B).

3 See n. 18 below.

4 An edited version of these notes can be found at *Journals* 20–48. All references for this manuscript, which is now missing from the Ayn Rand Institute archives, will be to this edition.

5 For statements of these themes in Nietzsche, see the following chapters in *Thus Spoke Zarathustra* in Kaufmann 1959: "The Flies of the Market Place," "On the Tree on the Mountainside," and "On the Love of the Neighbor." On the "pathos of distance," see section 257 of *Beyond Good and Evil*.

6 Sections 51 and 52 of *The Antichrist*, in Kaufmann 1959, 632 and 635.

7 See *The Antichrist*, sect. 57, in Kaufmann 1959.

8 These passages have been discussed very well by Robert Mayhew in his 2012. He discusses a number of different interpretations that may be offered for these passages and points out, among other things, that the more extremely "Nietzschean" interpretations conflict, not only with Rand's later views, but with the themes of *We the Living* itself.

9 I should point out, though, that an early germ of the main idea that separates Rand from Nietzsche in *The Fountainhead* can be found in the 1934 philosophical notebook I discussed above. See *Journals* 71. For evidence of the evolution of Rand's view of Nietzsche during her writing of *The Fountainhead*, see Milgram 2007a, 13–17; cf. Chapter 2 above, 24.

10 Though Roark never characterizes one of his values as a sort of power, he does come close in his courtroom speech: "The creator's concern is the conquest of nature. The parasite's concern is the conquest of men" (*Fountainhead* 712).

11 I explore the critique in *The Fountainhead* of Nietzsche's conception of power in Hunt 2006.

12 *Papers* 36_6-114-A. This material corresponds to *Journals* 244.

13 I owe this way of characterizing the relationship to Stephen Hicks. See Hicks 2009.

14 On the trader principle in Rand's social ethics, see Darryl Wright's discussion in Chapter 7 above, 160–172.

15 On the place of rights – and, in particular, property rights – in Rand's mature political thought, see further Chapters 7 and 8 above, 172–177 and 188–199.

16 For Rand's views on the nature of objectivity, see Chapter 12 in this volume, 290–292.

17 See Chapter 11 in this volume.

18 The Ayn Rand Program, WKCR-FM Radio, December 13, 1964 (cf. *VOS* xi). I am indebted to Allan Gotthelf for bringing this material to my attention and supplying me with a recording of the interview.

19 See the following passages: *FTNI* 34; "Introduction to the 25th Anniversary Edition" (*Fountainhead* xii); and "Apollo and Dionysus" (*ROTP*).

20 On Rand's view of man as a heroic being, see in this volume, 4, 96–97, and 459–460.

References

Hicks, Stephen. 2009. "Egoism in Nietzsche and Rand." *Journal of Ayn Rand Studies*, 10(2).

Hunt, Lester H. 2006. "Thus Spake Howard Roark: Nietzschean Ideas in *The Fountainhead*." *Philosophy and Literature*, 30(1).

Kaufmann, Walter, ed. 1959. *The Portable Nietzsche*. New York, NY: Viking Penguin.

Mayhew, Robert, ed. 2012a. *Essays on Ayn Rand's* We the Living, 2nd edition. Lanham, MD: Lexington Books.

Milgram, Shoshana. 2007a. "*The Fountainhead* from Notebook to Novel: The Composition of Ayn Rand's First Ideal Man." In *Essays on Ayn Rand's* The Fountainhead, edited by Robert Mayhew. Lanham, MD: Lexington Books.

15

A Philosopher on Her Times

Ayn Rand's Political and Cultural Commentary

JOHN DAVID LEWIS AND GREGORY SALMIERI[1]

Between the publication of Atlas Shrugged (in 1957) and the end of her life (in 1982), Rand's literary output consisted almost entirely of non-fiction articles and talks, most of them published in the periodicals she (co-)edited. Some of these pieces were abstract, theoretical essays, but most of them focus on current events or trends. She characterized such pieces as belonging to a "middle range" that falls "somewhere between theoretical and journalistic articles" because they "consist of the application of abstractions to concretes." Middle-range pieces "accept a theoretical proposition and analyze some current event or some aspect of the culture from that viewpoint" (AON 4–5). Rand's viewpoint was the philosophy she called "Objectivism," and her purpose in these pieces was "to explain today's trends by identifying their philosophical roots and meaning and to present the Objectivist alternative" ("A Last Survey" ARL 4(24) 381.)

Our subject in this chapter is Rand's distinctive view of the philosophical roots and meaning of the events of her time – especially the events of the 1960s and 1970s when she was most active as a commentator on current events. In addition to the "middle-range" pieces written in the decades after Atlas, we will look at her (comparatively few) earlier writings on current events, at the remarks she made in interviews and question-and-answer periods, and at the positions taken in pieces written under her editorship.[2]

In broad strokes, she viewed the period in which she lived as one when a philosophy of irrationalism, altruism, and statism was on the ascendency around the world. The American people valued reason, individual achievement, and freedom, but they were unable to articulate or defend these values, so they were vulnerable to intellectuals and politicians who sold them statism by degrees and under different names. These intellectuals and politicians were primarily (though not exclusively) liberals, but the conservatives were at least as responsible for America's movement toward statism, because rather than offering an alternative to the liberal's statist policies, they accepted and implemented moderated versions of the same policies.

The chapter is organized thematically with sections devoted to issues, trends, or figures on which Rand commented. These sections are ordered chronologically, by the period in which

A Companion to Ayn Rand, First Edition. Edited by Allan Gotthelf and Gregory Salmieri.
© 2016 John Wiley & Sons, Ltd. Published 2016 by John Wiley & Sons, Ltd.

their subjects were most prominent in her writings. We begin with a section on Rand's political writings and activism in the 1930s and (especially) 1940s, when Rand attempted to promote a philosophy of individualism as the principled alternative to the New Deal and the Communist influence in American culture. In the late 1940s Rand withdrew from such activism to focus on *Atlas Shrugged*. The subject of our second section is a series of talks and essays written in the few years after that novel's publication, in which Rand provides a broad philosophical and historical context for the issues facing the world. With the founding of *The Objectivist Newsletter* in 1962 Rand began to comment in more detail on current events. In the first issue she named antitrust and censorship as the two most pressing political issues of the day, and she went on to discuss each often in the years that followed. These two topics are the subject of our third section.

Our fourth section deals with the Kennedy administration, which Rand thought represented a more naked form of statism than the country had yet seen, and with the 1964 election, which she interpreted as a referendum on Kennedy's policies. She saw the Republicans' failure to take a principled stand and Johnson's landslide victory as unleashing a flood of negative developments that we discuss in subsequent sections. One result is that it was generally accepted that policy decisions were a matter, not of applying political principles, but of brokering deals between pressure groups. Our fifth section discusses this phenomenon in connection with the domestic policies of the Johnson and Nixon administrations, and our sixth section discusses the unprincipled nature of American foreign policy, especially during the "Cold War." In our seventh section, we discuss the perverting influence Rand thought that this anti-principle, pressure-group mindset had on the civil rights and feminist movements.

In our next three sections we consider Rand's view of the "New Left," a movement that purported to be the voice of the younger generation. The first of these sections deals with the rise of civil disobedience and politically motivated violence; the second with the educational establishment and its effects on America's youth. The third covers the distinctive ideas of the movement (chiefly environmentalism and egalitarianism). In this section we also discuss the 1972 presidential election, which Rand saw as a referendum on these ideas. She interpreted George McGovern's spectacular defeat as a reassertion of America's inarticulate individualism, and as an end to the worst of the disasters caused by the 1964 election.

The American people had rejected the left, Rand thought, because there was a visceral conflict between the new leftists and American values. But the people lacked a positive ideology that articulated and defended the values that had made America great. In our next two sections we discuss Rand's harsh criticisms of Libertarianism and Conservatism, two movements that are often thought to be based on such an ideology and with which Rand is often associated. We close with a discussion of what Rand called "The American Sense of Life," the inarticulate embrace of reason, egoism, and individualism that she thought had protected America from the worst effects of some of the trends discussed in earlier sections.

Early Individualist and Anti-Communist Writing and Activism (1936–1946)

Rand's earliest published writing to deal with contemporary events is her first novel, *We the Living*.[3] In letters to her agent, she explained that the novel was intended as the "*Uncle Tom's Cabin* of Soviet Russia" – "the *first* story by a Russian who knows the living conditions of the new Russia and who has actually lived under the Soviets in the period described" (*Letters* 19, 4).[4] However, she was adamant that her book "is *not* a novel about Russia"; its subject is "the problem of the individual versus the mass" which she described as "the most tremendous problem of the world today." The story is set in Russia, "merely because that problem stands out in Russia more sharply, more tragically than anywhere on earth" (*Letters* 12, 13, cf. *WTL* ix–xiii). In what would become a hallmark of Rand's fiction and non-fiction, she treated concretes as embodying philosophical principles.

Russia embodies the principle of *collectivism* (or *statism*) which Rand went on to define (in a 1944 essay) as "the subjugation of the individual to a group – whether to a race, class or state does not matter. Collectivism holds that man must be chained to collective action and collective thought for the sake of what is called 'the common good'" ("The Only Path to Tomorrow" *Column* 114).[5] She regarded "Fascism, Nazism, Communism and Socialism" as "only superficial variations" of this "same monstrous theme" (*Letters* 127).[6]

By contrast to the collectivism of Russia, Rand revered America as "the country of individualism" (*Letters* 79). So she was alarmed to discover in the 1930s that collectivists (including many Communists) dominated the nation's intellectual life, obstructing the publications of individualistic or anti-Soviet works (including *We the Living*), and propagating their ideology with no serious intellectual opposition.[7] She was alarmed also by Franklin Delano Roosevelt's "New Deal," which entrenched collectivism into American domestic policy, and especially by his attempt to "reorganize" the Supreme Court, which she saw as an attempt to subvert the separation of powers established by the Constitution.[8] In a 1937 letter to the editor of the *New York Herald Tribune* (which was not published at the time), she argued that it was this separation of powers that distinguished America from Soviet Russia and Nazi Germany, which had constitutions and elections but lacked any "independent organ to watch that the constitution be obeyed" and "to check on the polls." She described the reorganization of the court as one of a series of measures by which tyranny was being established, and said that "the vast majority of the people would rush to arms against it – if they understood what it really means and how it can affect their personal lives." She called for "a committee, an organization, or headquarters created at once to lead and centralize the activity of all those who are eager to join their efforts in protest" and she urged readers to write their congressmen (*TIA* 10(2) 6–9, *Papers* 099_05x_003).

No such organization was established in time to influence the 1938 mid-term elections, as Rand had hoped, but in 1940 a series of regional clubs sprung up to support the presidential campaign of Wendell Willkie, who had been a prominent critic of several New Deal programs. Rand regarded the election as so crucial that she volunteered to work full-time for the New York Willkie Club. There she organized a research department that provided "intellectual ammunition" for clubs across the country, and she lectured publicly on issues related to the campaign.

Rand attributed Willkie's electoral defeat to his failure to challenge the collectivist principles behind the New Deal (indeed, he endorsed them).[9] This failure was not unique to Willkie, as she explains in a 1941 letter to conservative writer Channing Pollock:

> Evasion and compromise have killed all pro-capitalist movements so far. I think the tragedy of Capitalism from the beginning has been the lack of a consistent ideology of its own. It moved on the strangest mixture of Collectivist-Christian-Equalitarian-Humanitarian concepts, the worst mental hodgepodge in history. (*Letters* 46)

Rand persuaded Pollock to help her address this lack by forming an organization of uncompromising individualists that would "*formulate and propagate* a basic ideology of Individualism and Capitalism" and offer members "a concrete program of personal, individual *activity*" (*Letters* 47, 54–55). Toward this end, she drafted an open letter "To All Innocent Fifth Columnists" and an "Individualist Manifesto."[10] Both documents argue that totalitarian regimes are the result of a collectivist ideology, and that a small minority of revolutionaries were propagating this ideology in America in the form of insidious slogans and policy proposals that were subtle enough to be unwittingly spread and advocated by people who would reject this ideology out of hand if it were presented to them outright. Rand called on defenders of America to articulate and consistently defend individualism – the doctrine that "man is an independent entity with an inalienable right to the pursuit of his own happiness in a society where men deal with one another as equals in voluntary, unregulated exchange" – and to "learn to reject as total evil the conception that 'the common good' is superior to individual rights."[11]

Though the organization for which Rand wrote these documents never materialized, she remained politically active during the 1940s. Of particular note is her work with the Motion Picture Alliance for the Preservation of American Ideals (MPA), a group formed to combat the "perversion" of the film industry by "Communist, Fascist, and other totalitarian-minded groups" seeking to use films as "an instrument for the dissemination of un-American ideas and beliefs."[12] As a member of the organization's board, Rand argued that they should focus on educating filmmakers about the nature of propaganda so that they could identify and stop attempts to smuggle it into their films (Mayhew 2005c, 78–80, Burns 2009, 100). Toward this end, she wrote a "Screen Guide for Americans" that was published and widely distributed by the Alliance.[13]

The guide contains Rand's first published comments on an issue that would loom large in her later writings: the injustice and the ideological meaning of the popular attitudes toward businessmen:

> Too often industrialists, bankers, and businessmen are presented on the screen as villains, crooks, chiselers or exploiters. One such picture may be taken as non-political or accidental. A constant stream of such pictures becomes pernicious political propaganda: it creates hatred for all businessmen in the mind of the audience, and makes people receptive to the cause of Communism. (*Journals* 358)

As with members of any other "class or profession," Rand argued, if an individual businessman is presented as a villain, it should be made clear that his evil is a personal characteristic, rather than something inherent in his profession. In particular, filmmakers should avoid depicting "a desire to make money," which is essential to business, "as a sign of villainy" (*Journals* 359–360).

Rand's "Screen Guide" brought her to the attention of the House Committee on Un-American Activities (HUAC), which was holding hearings on Communist activities in Hollywood. She appeared in October of 1946 as an expert witness on identifying propaganda in films. Her testimony was not, as she had hoped, an opportunity to educate Americans about the subtle collectivist propaganda in popular films. She was asked only about *Song of Russia* (MGM 1944), a crudely pro-Soviet, wartime film that "wouldn't fool anybody" (Mayhew 2005c, 96–97). In private notes and interviews, Rand was critical of the Committee, but she defended the government's authority to investigate the Communist Party because it was a treasonous, criminal conspiracy that "not merely preaches, but actually engages in acts of violence, murder, sabotage, and spying in the interests of a foreign government" (*Papers* 097_01x_007_001/*Journals* 382).[14]

354

The HUAC hearings are controversial in part because they led to the blacklisting of some Hollywood Communists, and this is widely regarded as a violation of their freedom of speech. Rand had addressed this issue in her "Screen Guide": "The principle of freedom of speech" requires that "we do not *pass laws* forbidding them to speak," but it "*does not* imply that we owe them jobs and support to advocate our own destruction at our own expense" (*Journals* 366). In later years, she would add that the true victims of Hollywood blacklists were not the Communists (most of whom, she said, continued to work under assumed names), but anti-Communists who never found work again after testifying before the HUAC (*Letters* 433–434, 435–436, *Answers* 80–85).[15]

Though Rand thought that it was appropriate to expose and boycott individual members of the Communist Party, she did not think that this was the central means by which Communism should be fought, because she did not think that Communist conspiracies were the cause of America's growing statism.[16] The cause was, rather, that "most people today, of all classes, all stages of education and all political parties" accept "the ideal of collectivism" (*Letters* 258; cf. 296–298). What was "desperately needed," Rand wrote in a 1946 letter, was "*EDUCATION IN INDIVIDUALISM*, in every aspect of it: philosophical, moral, political, economic – in *that* order" (*Letters* 260).[17]

"An Age of Moral Crisis": 1959–1961 Pieces on the State of the Culture

As the 1940s drew to a close, Rand withdrew from activism, focusing instead on *Atlas Shrugged*.[18] The novel, published in 1957, dramatizes her philosophy and depicts a world in the final stages of a collapse due to its acceptance of an opposite philosophy of mysticism, altruism, and collectivism. The ideas presented in *Atlas* inform all of her subsequent writings on politics and culture, and many of her articles liken real-world characters, events, or trends to the concretes in the novel.[19]

In a series of talks and articles written between the publication of *Atlas* and the founding of *The Objectivist Newsletter* in 1962, Rand presented an interpretation of American history and culture that set the context for her subsequent analysis of political events and figures.[20]

As James Lennox explains in Chapter 13 of the present volume, Rand saw America as the product of the Enlightenment, a period in which the leading intellectuals venerated reason and the inalienable right of each individual to pursue his own happiness.[21] Capitalism, in her view, was the political and economic system that implemented these ideals. Its "fundamental principle," as Rand understood it, is "*the separation of State and Economics* – that is: the liberation of men's economic activities, of production and trade, from any form of intervention, coercion, compulsion, regulation, or control by the government" ("The Intellectual Bankruptcy of Our Age" *VOR* 90–91).[22] Only under such a system is each individual free to use his own reason to discover and produce the values he needs to survive and flourish, interacting with others when it serves this purpose, but never being forced to sacrifice his life or happiness for the sake of others.

The freedom that is the essence of capitalism was never made explicit or consistently implemented, but Rand thought that it was approximated in the nineteenth century by the northern United States and by England, and that its influence spread across Europe displacing the feudal system.[23] The new freedom people enjoyed, especially in the United States and England, made possible a new profession: the businessman, who by intelligently organizing human effort and applying the discoveries of science, was able to produce wealth on a scale never before imagined (*FTNI* 22–23). The result was the Industrial Revolution and "a level ... of prosperity, of human happiness, unmatched in all the other systems and centuries combined" ("Conservatism: An Obituary" *CUI* 217).[24]

Rand thought that these advances were fragile, however, because the essence of capitalism was not understood, and because it is incompatible with the altruist morality that was an un-challenged legacy from Christianity. Rand identified the essence of altruism as the demand that the individual sacrifice for the sake of others.[25] Under capitalism, by contrast, people deal with one another as traders who each expect to benefit from the transaction. The task of resolving this contradiction fell to the intellectuals of the nineteenth century. But instead of challenging altruism and championing reason and freedom, these intellectuals adopted Immanuel Kant's philosophy which, Rand argued, undercut reason in order to preserve altruism. (On Kant and his influence, see 332–334, above, and Peikoff's detailed discussion in *Parallels* and *HOP2*.)

The nineteenth-century intellectuals were predominantly liberals at a time when "the term 'liberal' meant an advocate of individual rights" and "an opponent of the authoritarian state" (*VOR* 87). But, Rand argued, their acceptance of altruism blinded them to the nature and possibility of the ideal system that was within reach. This blindness caused two errors that transformed liberalism into a movement advocating "greater government control over the economy" (*VOR* 86). First, the intellectuals likened successful industrialists to feudal barons, because both were wealthy and had many people working for them. This was an error because unlike the barons' fortunes, which were based on conquest and the exploitation of serfs, the businessmen's fortunes were earned through production and trade to mutual advantage. In Rand's view, the ultimate source of both the businessman's unprecedented wealth and the general rise in the standard of living was the businessmen's *ideas* for new forms of produc-tion and trade, which they were free to implement under capitalism. But the liberals did not recognize this, and so, though they saw themselves as champions of "freedom of the mind," they opposed the economic freedom needed by "the most active exponents of creative intel-ligence, the businessmen" (*VOR* 95, cf. Branden *WIAR* 43). The liberals' second error was to embrace the use of force by the government to compel unwilling individuals to sacrifice (as altruism demands) in order to achieve what the intellectuals deemed to be "the public good" (*VOR* 95–96). Thus a movement that had been dedicated to the rights of the individual be-came increasingly collectivist.[26]

In the ninetenth century, Rand observed, "conservative" had referred to "an advocate of the state's authority, of tradition, of the established political order, of the status quo, and an opponent of individual rights" (*VOR* 87). In the early twentieth century, however, the term came to refer to those who opposed the new liberals' policies. As Rand understood these twentieth-century conservatives, what they sought to conserve was capitalism, but they were "paralyzed by the profound conflict between capitalism and the morality that dominates our culture." Lacking the courage to challenge this morality, they projected a "non-intellectual, non-philosophical attitude." Thus collectivism faced no intellectual opposition and was em-braced (in various forms) as a "moral ideal" the world over ("Conservatism: An Obituary" *CUI* 217–218). In continental Europe this led to the rise of dictatorships. England became social-ist, and America (which has the strongest Enlightenment heritage) developed into a "mixed economy" in which the principle of freedom was diluted by ever-greater controls.

By 1960, Rand thought, the ideal of collectivism had been widely discredited by the hor-rors of Nazi Germany and Soviet Russia, and by England's decline from a mostly capitalistic world power to a mostly socialistic mediocrity ("Faith and Force" *PWNI* 93–95).[27] As a result, the liberals had become as "feeble, futile, and evasive" in their advocacy of statism as the conservatives were in their advocacy of capitalism (*PWNI* 94). Since neither party dared to identify (especially to itself) the nature of the system it was advocating, political discourse was reduced to "single, isolated, superficial concretes," without reference to principles. As an example, Rand observed that, in the 1960 presidential election, instead of debating "socialized medicine," Kennedy and Nixon quibbled over "the cost and the procedure of medical aid to the aged" (*VOR* 88).

Rand thought that, under the continued influence of altruism, the world was still drifting toward statism despite the demise of collectivism as an ideal. Soviet Russia (now acting with "the plain aggressiveness of a thug") was gaining influence on the world stage, and government controls were rapidly multiplying in America (*PWNI* 95). The conservatives were worse than ineffective at stopping this trend: rather than advocating for the Enlightenment ideals on which capitalism depends, they appealed to faith, tradition, and the religious notion that man is "depraved." The term "conservative" was reverting to its nineteenth-century sense of "an advocate of authority" (*VOR* 87).

Thus, in the period when Rand began to write regularly about current events, she viewed the culture as "bankrupt" and headed toward the sort of collapse she had depicted in *Atlas*. To avert this fate, she thought, the "intellectual vacuum" would need to be filled by "a new type of intellectual" who would reject altruism and fight for capitalism on the basis of a philosophy of reason and egoism (*VOR* 99). Having presented such a philosophy in *Atlas Shrugged*, Rand would now focus on applying it to the concrete events and trends of the 1960s and 1970s.

"Choose Your Issues": The Menaces of Antitrust and Censorship

The first issue of *The Objectivist Newsletter* (January 1962) began with an article, "Choose Your Issues," in which Rand argued that "a *cultural* movement is the precondition of a *political* movement" ("Choose Your Issues" *TON* 1(1)). She concludes by identifying antitrust and censorship as the two issues "with which the 'practical' fight for freedom should begin" because "they involve the fundamental principles of our culture." She took these issues up (respectively) in the next two issues of *Newsletter* and in other talks and writings from this period.

In February of 1961, 29 manufacturers of electrical equipment, including General Electric and Westinghouse, were convicted under the Sherman Antitrust Act of conspiring to fix prices, and 7 executives were sentenced to jail (Bowden 2005, 111–112). "The Great Price Fixing Scandal," as the papers dubbed it, remained in the news for several years, while civil actions against the convicted companies made their way through the courts. Rand described the affair as the "ultimate climax" of the "sordid record" of antitrust law, and she pursued the topic in a series of talks and articles in the early 1960s.[28]

Rand's primary objection to the antitrust laws was that "they are an accumulation of non-objective, undefinable, unjudicable statutes, so contradictory and inconsistent that no two jurists can agree on their meaning, and any business practice can be construed as illegal" ("Government by Intimidation" *Column* 21).[29] She saw it as significant that this injustice was perpetuated specifically against successful businessmen.[30] Her first piece on antitrust, "America's Persecuted Minority: Big Business" (*CUI*), expands on the point (first made in her "Screen Guide") that businessmen are victims of prejudice:

> If a small group of men were always regarded as guilty, in any clash with any other group, regard-less of the issues or circumstances involved, would you call it persecution? If this group were always made to pay for the sins, errors, or failures of any other group, would you call that persecution? If this group had to live under a silent reign of terror, under special laws, from which all other people were immune, laws which the accused could not grasp or define in advance and which the ac-cuser could interpret in any way he pleased – would you call that persecution? If this group were penalized, not for its faults, but for its virtues, not for its incompetence, but for its ability, not for its failures, but for its achievements, and the greater the achievement, the greater the penalty – would you call *that* persecution? (*CUI* 40)

Anti-business prejudice was one of the two errors that Rand thought transformed nineteenth-century liberalism into an anti-freedom movement. The other was the failure to reject the use of force and to recognize that all the interactions among private individuals in a capitalist system are voluntary. She saw a version of this second error in the rationale for the antitrust laws. They were thought to be necessary to restrain the power of businesses, but under capitalism the only power any private individual or institution has is "the power to produce and to trade what one has produced." This power is no threat to anyone because it is "achieved only by ... the voluntary choice and agreement of all those who participate in the process of production and trade" (*CUI* 44) and is "exercised by means of a *positive*, by offering men a reward, an incentive, a pay-ment, a value." Rand called this sort of power "economic power" and contrasted it with *political power* – "the power to force obedience under threat of physical injury – the threat of property expropriation, imprisonment, or death" (*CUI* 43). A government by definition has a monopoly on political power, and in the capitalist system, it exercises this power only against those who attempt to use force on others. In nineteenth-century America, when the world came nearest to this system, innovative businessmen created unprecedented wealth "by free trade on a free market." But the nation did not have pure capitalism, and during this same period there were other businessmen "with political pull" who grew rich not by producing wealth, but "by means of special privileges granted to them by the government ... It was the political power behind their activities – the power of forced, unearned, economically unjustified privileges – that caused dislocations in the country's economy, hardships, depressions, and mounting public protests" (*CUI* 46).

Because the distinction between economic and political power was not clearly drawn, "it was the free market and the free businessmen that took the blame," and so further controls were placed on the economy enabling bureaucrats to wield ever greater political power over innocent businessmen.

To address this persecution, Rand called for the establishment of a Civil Liberties Union for businessmen that would seek the repeal of the antitrust laws as its "ultimate goal," and the abolition of jail penalties as a "first step" (*CUI* 61).

Rand took on censorship with "Have Gun, Will Nudge" in the second issue of *The Objectivist Newsletter* (March 1962) and in several other articles written over the next two years.[31] Several of these articles were prompted by the policies of Newton N. Minow (President John F. Kennedy's chairman of the Federal Communications Commission (FCC)), who famously described televi-sion as "a vast wasteland" and warned broadcasters that their licenses would not be renewed unless their programming served the "public interest" (as determined by FCC hearings) (Minow 1961). Rand saw Minow's "open threats and ultimatums" as making explicit the regime of "censorship-by-displeasure" under which broadcasters had operated since the 1927 Radio Act, which nationalized the airwaves and empowered the FCC to issue broadcast licenses by the undefinable standard of "the public interest" ("The Property Status of Airwaves" *CUI* 135, *Speaking* 74–76). She argued that the FCC should be abolished and the broadcast frequencies auctioned to the highest bidders, who would then own them outright (*CUI* 139).

Regulation of the airwaves was sometimes advocated in the name of "free speech." Minow, for example, claimed to be fighting against "censorship by ratings, by advertisers, by networks, by affiliates which reject programming offered to their area." Many similar uses of the terms "censorship" and "free speech" were heard in 1962 during the controversy over a documentary about Richard Nixon that featured an interview with Alger Hiss. The documentary was an ABC program, but some of the network's affiliates refused to air it, and some sponsors canceled their contracts.[32] Returning to a theme from her 1946 "Screen Guide," Rand argued that it is only by "evading" the difference between political and economic power that one can believe that members of the media are censored by their voluntary economic relationships and that governmental intrusion into these relationships is not a means of censorship ("Have Gun, Will Nudge" *TON* 1(2) 9).

In *Atlas Shrugged* statist officials "make sure that nothing dangerous gets printed or heard" by enacting economic regulations concerning "paper, ink and printing presses" (*Atlas* 546). Thus Rand was especially alarmed in July of 1962 when the *New York Times* reported that "an antitrust panel of the House Judiciary Committee is preparing a broad inquiry on the press and other news media."[33] The inquiry sought to determine whether owners of multiple news outlets were slanting the news in accordance with their own political views. Rand argued that newspaper owners have a right to express their opinions, and she observed that the only newspaper chains named by the committee's chair were critical of the Kennedy administration. Because the antitrust laws are non-objective, Rand warned, they could be used by an administration to intimidate the press and to prevent any critics from achieving or maintaining a national voice. She urged her readers, and especially members of the press, to speak up against what she saw as an assault by the Kennedy administration on freedom of speech.

Taken together, Rand thought that the FCC and the antitrust laws gave the government "the legal weapons it needs to transform this country into a totalitarian state" ("Choose Your Issues" *TON* 1(1) 1). She warned that the Kennedy administration was sending up statist "trial balloons" with "growing frequency," but she pointed out that the key laws that made Kennedy's policies possible had all been advocated or passed by Republicans.[34] The threat to liberty stemmed not from the specific agenda of either party, but from deeper premises shared by both. Thus the solution was philosophical rather than political. Her analysis went beyond the concrete controversies debated among politicians to identify underlying philosophical problems, and the concrete policy proposals she advocated were intended as components of a broader movement aimed at larger-scale change.

"The Last Ideological Administration": Kennedy's Presidency and the 1964 Election

Rand saw Kennedy's policies concerning antitrust and censorship as parts of a campaign to push America across the frontier into statism – specifically, into *fascism*. The feature that distinguishes fascism from other forms of statism is that "men retain the semblance or pretense of private property," though "the government holds total power over its use and disposal" ("The Fascist New Frontier" *Column* 98). America had been headed in this direction, Rand thought, since the New Deal ("The New Fascism: Rule by Consensus" *CUI* 245–246), and Kennedy was a would-be Mussolini or Franco who sought to complete the process.[35] As evidence, she cited his rhetoric, which she likened to Göring's. When accepting the Democratic Party's nomination for president, Kennedy promised "more sacrifice, instead of more security," he called on Americans to "match the Russian sacrifice of the present for the future," he described this future vaguely in terms of "national greatness," and he accused the Republicans of representing "private comfort," "security," "normalcy," and "mediocrity" (Kennedy 1960). Rand commented:

> His is not the line or the style of a liberal, nor of a middle-of-the-road'er, nor even a naive, old-fashioned Socialist – all of whom profess to hold the *welfare*, the *comfort*, the *security* of their citizens as the standard of the nation's greatness.
> When a man extols "*leadership*" – leadership without direction – leadership without any stated purpose, program or ideal – leadership for the sake of leadership – you may be sure that you are hearing the voice of a man motivated by power-lust. ("JFK: High Class Beatnik?" Bibliography #21)

In *The Objectivist Newsletter*, Rand and her associates accused Kennedy of attempting to gain control over the medical, food, and drug industries by advocating (what became) Medicare and the Kefauver–Harris Amendment to the Federal Food, Drug, and Cosmetic Act.[36] She was particularly alarmed by his press conference on April 11, 1962 in which he railed against several steel companies for raising prices in defiance of his earlier declaration that doing so would be contrary to the "national interest":

> Mr. Kennedy was threatening the steel companies with retaliation by means of: Antitrust prosecutions, grand jury investigation, Senate and House Committees investigations, Department of Justice investigation, Federal Trade Commission investigation, the "reconsidering" of tax legislation favorable to industry, etc., etc. – including, for full scare effect, the melodramatic touch of F.B.I. agents awakening newspaper reporters in the middle of the night to question them about the public statement of one of the steel industrialists. No, Mr. Kennedy was not afraid of creating in the public mind the connotations of a totalitarian state: he was *seeking* to create them. ("The National Interest, *c'est moi*" TON 1(6) 22, cf. *Column* 104–105)

When the stock market crashed on May 28, Rand blamed the president's bullying of industry, and she warned that unless the nation started decontrolling, a larger crash would come in the future. Statist politicians would blame the future crash on capitalism and use it as a pretext to "impose on us an emergency system of totalitarian controls" ("Account Overdrawn" *TON* 1(7) 30).[37]

Rand saw Kennedy's speeches as attempts to prepare freedom-loving Americans to accept increasingly fascist policies. She singled out his 1962 commencement address at Yale, in which he complained that "stale phrases," "stereotypes," "illusions," "platitudes," "myths," "clichés," "traditional labels," and "warn-out slogans" were preventing Americans from realizing that, unlike "the basic clashes of philosophy or ideology" that the country faced in the nineteenth and early twentieth century, "the differences today are mainly matters of degree" concerning "the practical management of a modern economy" (Kennedy 1962). Rand saw the speech as an attack "against ideology as such." While the whole world was engaged in a "life and death struggle" between "freedom and statism," the president was effectively claiming "that, for us, the conflict is over, and statism – a government-managed economy – has won." Instead of claiming this openly, however, he was attempting to undermine the concepts needed to differentiate between the two systems. "If we don't use any 'labels' – which means: if we never identify the nature of different political systems – we will not discover that we are accepting statism, or notice how the switch is pulled on us" (*Column* 100–102, cf. "Who Will Protect Us From Our Protectors" *TON* (1)5).

A related tactic of which Rand accused the administration was perverting the meaning of established terms. One example of this in Minow's use of "censorship," which we have already discussed. Another is Kennedy's talk of a "partnership" between business and government. Rand described this as "an indecent euphemism for 'government control'" ("An Intellectual Coup d'Etat" *Column* 16–17, "The Fascist New Frontier" *Column* 102).

Rand would later coin the term "anti-ideology" for the approach to ideas that the Kennedy administration practiced.

> Anti-ideology consists of the attempts to shrink men's minds down to the range of the immediate moment, without regard to past or future, without context or memory – above all, without memory, so that contradictions cannot be detected, and errors or disasters can be blamed on the victims.
>
> In anti-ideological practice, principles are used implicitly and are relied upon to disarm the opposition, but are never acknowledged, and are switched at will, when it suits the purpose of the moment. ("The Wreckage of the Consensus" *CUI* 251)

Anti-ideology was not unique to Kennedy. Rand found instances of it in his predecessors and successors, and she identified Kant as its fountainhead, but she thought that Kennedy and his "New Frontiersmen" were distinctive in how consistently and purposefully anti-ideological they were.[38] Rand thought the country desperately needed the sort of principled political debate that the administration was working to forestall, so she took a special interest in the 1964 presidential election. Seven of the articles she produced between October of 1963 and December of 1964 addressed the election.[39] By the time of the general election, of course, Kennedy had been assassinated and Johnson had assumed office, but (by Rand's lights, at least) the election remained a referendum on Kennedy's policies, which Johnson continued.[40]

By 1963 many conservatives saw little difference between the Republican Party leadership and the Democrats. In search of a genuine alternative, these conservatives drafted Barry Goldwater into the race for the Republican presidential nomination. Nelson Rockefeller, who was seeking the nomination with the support of the party leadership, responded by denouncing "extremist groups" that he claimed were trying to take over the party. He listed several of the "extremists'" positions: opposition to the income tax and the United Nations (UN), support for racial segregation, and the view that Earl Warren and President Eisenhower were "crypto-communists."[41] Rand, who did oppose the income tax and the UN, wrote that Rockefeller had "slapped [the] face" of advocates of capitalism by "lumping all opponents of the welfare state with actual crackpots and smearing them as 'the radical right lunatic fringe.'" As "the most effective and direct form of protest," she urged her readers to register Republican and vote for Goldwater in the primary ("A Suggestion" *TON* 2(10)).

This was Rand's first mention in print of Goldwater, though she had made favorable public statements about him as early as 1960, and the two had exchanged letters in which he expressed his appreciation of *Atlas Shrugged* and she described him as "the man who might bring the American Conservatives back to life, by means of a clear-cut, unequivocal stand."[42] In March of 1964 she gave him a more full-throated public endorsement as "the best candidate in the field today." She was especially impressed with his foreign policy, describing him as "a candidate who, with profound pride, asserts America's self-interest and self-esteem." ("How to Judge a Political Candidate" *TON* 3(3) 10).[43] She had the following to say of his domestic policy:

JOHN DAVID LEWIS AND GREGORY SALMIERI

> Like all of today's political figures, he is the advocate of a mixed economy. But the difference between him and the others is this: they believe that some (undefined) element of freedom is compatible with government controls; he believes that some (undefined) government controls are compatible with freedom. (*TON* 3(3) 9)

In this same piece, Rand warned that the election would be difficult for Goldwater. Because the culture lacked an "intellectual base" for capitalism, he would have to rely on the individualistic "subconscious basic premises" (or "sense of life") shared by most Americans. Since subconscious premises are not a reliable guide to action and may "seek expression in their own opposite," Goldwater would be vulnerable to "smears and misrepresentations" by his opponents (in both the primary and the general election). Several of her articles from the period contain discussions of such smear tactics.[44] And in a private July letter to Goldwater, she put herself "at your disposal, if you think that my services can be useful to you in your great battle."

Throughout the campaign she expressed concern in her *Newsletter* that Goldwater was "helping his enemies whenever he softens his stand" ("The Argument from Intimidation" *TON* (3)7 28), and in October she predicted that he would be defeated if he continued to speak in "vague generalities" rather than making the case for capitalism and against the "statist-socialist trend of his opponents." She asked readers who "are active in the campaign" to "urge him to raise some essential issues" ("Special Note" *TON* 3(10)). Also in October, she sent his campaign a "Suggested Speech" (*Papers* 043_05A_01) that she had written for his use. Goldwater did not deliver the speech, but from it we can get a sense of the campaign Rand thought he could have and should have run. The speech develops ideas from her 1962 article, "War and Peace" (*Column/TON* 1(10)), and she later repurposed some of its text and many of its arguments for her 1966 article "The Roots of War" (*CUI* 31–32).[45] Readers can get a sense of the (unpublished) speech's content from these two sources.

The Johnson campaign had portrayed Goldwater as "trigger happy" for his willingness to consider using tactical nuclear weapons in Vietnam, so Rand's speech begins by discussing the horrors of nuclear war and then moves quickly to the issue of why wars occur. They are inevitable results, she writes, of the principle that also lies behind dictatorships: the idea that "some men have the right to rule others *by force*." She then identifies the hypocrisy of peace advocates who oppose violence between nations but are indifferent to the violence totalitarian states visit on their own citizens. The essence of the American system of government is the principle of individual rights, which demands that "the use of force must be banned from human relationships." There will be no peace among or within nations until this principle is understood and accepted. The speech goes on to discuss how this principle leads to "the system of *free enterprise*" and material prosperity, whereas statism leads to internal strife, economic stagnation, and aggression against neighboring nations in an attempt to seize their resources. The speech advocated eliminating the growing statist elements in America's own government. With regard to foreign policy, the speech advocated setting an example for the rest of the world by proudly asserting the moral superiority of the American system and by standing firm in the face of statist aggression against American interests, so that statist regimes would know that they could not solve their domestic problems by attacking America and its allies. Such a policy would leave the statist regimes with no choice but to gradually liberate their countries so as to avoid total economic collapse.

In her initial piece endorsing Goldwater, Rand had written that his candidacy represented "the first, somewhat experimental, step in the direction of [capitalism's] return" ("How to

Judge a Political Candidate" *TON* 3(3) 12). Her interpretation of the experiment's result is summarized by the title of her article analyzing Goldwater's landslide defeat: "It Is Earlier Than You Think" (*TON* 3(12)). Unlike previous, "me-tooing" Republican candidates, Goldwater had moral courage and integrity, but he had "nothing to say." He had been thrust into prominence by an inchoate movement of people disturbed by the nation's direction, and he needed to translate the concerns of this movement into a coherent position for which he could lead a crusade. He was unable to do this because he lacked "*intellectual* courage – a quality one cannot acquire except from a set of firm philosophical convictions." It was too early, Rand concluded, "to fight for capitalism on the level of practical politics," and she rededicated herself to the task of fighting for it on "*moral-intellectual* grounds" and fostering the *cultural* movement that is needed for the "the advocates of freedom" to be "heard or understood at the polls" (*TON* 3(12) 49–50).[46]

Looking back on the 1964 election seven years later, she identified the Republicans' "miserably poor intellectual showing" as a "turning point" that "marked a perceptible change in this county's culture and an acceleration of its decadence."

> It proved to the collectivists that no matter what they attempted to get away with, they would encounter no *intellectual* opposition in the immediate future. The result was President Johnson, his "consensus," and the student rebellion at Berkeley – i.e., an open break with reason, an explicit proclamation of gang (pressure-group) warfare as a way of life, and the introduction of brute physical force as a means of solving social issues. ("Brief Summary" *TO* 10(9) 1090–1091, cf. *Speaking* 219)

Though (as we will see) Rand continued to comment on the specific policies of later administrations, her focus shifted to broader cultural movements in the years after 1964.

Pragmatist Politics: The Johnson and Nixon Administrations and the Mixed Economy

In a 1978 talk, Rand described Kennedy's as the "last ideological administration of modern times" – i.e., the last administration with "a program of long-range action, with the principles serving to unify and integrate particular steps into a consistent course" ("Cultural Update" Bibliography #30, "The Wreckage of the Consensus" *CUI* 251). The administration's program was "the destruction of ideology as such" in order to ready the American people to accept totalitarian rule ("Cultural Update"). She thought that the 1964 election revealed that Kennedy had removed the last traces of ideology from American political discourse. Subsequent presidents and other prominent politicians were pragmatists acting on the expediency of the moment, with no coherent long-range goals. They continued to employ anti-ideology in an ad hoc manner to blind themselves and others to the nature and consequence of their actions, but not as part of a sustained effort to transform the nation.

Though Rand thought that Kennedy had succeeded in ideologically disarming America, she did not think the result was a population ready to accept statism. Americans remained opposed to it on an emotional (or "sense of life") level. Rand saw evidence of this in the Republican victories in the 1966, 1968, and 1972 elections, which she interpreted as popular rejections of the Democrats' statist policies.[47] However, since the nature of these policies and the ideas that led to them were never explicitly identified and rejected, and since the Republicans shared less-virulent versions of the same ideas, the elections could not reverse the nation's course. They only slowed its progression. America continued to "drift" toward "a tired, worn, cynical fascism" – "fascism by default, not like a flaming disaster, but more like the quiet collapse of a lethargic body slowly eaten by internal corruption" ("The New Fascism: Rule by Consensus" *CUI* 247).

Rand described Lyndon Johnson's presidency as "a ludicrous kind of period when all the Kennedy plans were put into effect, but were accompanied by an old ward-heeler's notion of inspirational propaganda" ("Cultural Update").[48] She did not view him as a fascist or an adherent to any political philosophy, but as a shrewd political operator who enjoyed wielding power and "whose vision does not extend beyond the range of the next election" (*CUI* 240). His approach to politics was widely described as "government by consensus."[49] Rand saw this phrase as a piece of anti-ideology meant to provide "a semblance of justification" for "the brute facts of a mixed economy." In a mixed economy, anyone's interests can be sacrificed to whatever the faction in power claims to be the public good. As a result the country breaks up "into an ever-growing number of enemy camps, into economic groups fighting one another for self-preservation in an indeterminate mixture of *defense and offense*, as the nature of such a jungle demands." A mixed economy retains "a semblance of law and order" politically, in that leaders are elected and laws are passed and enforced through a civilized process, but economically the society is the equivalent of anarchy: "a chaos of robber gangs looting – and draining – the productive elements of the country."

> A mixed economy is rule by pressure groups. It is an amoral, institutionalized civil war of special interests and lobbies, all fighting to seize a momentary control of the legislative machinery, to extort some special privilege at one another's expense by an act of government – i.e., by force. In the absence of individual rights, in the absence of any moral or legal principles, a mixed economy's only hope to preserve its precarious semblance of order, to restrain the savage, desperately rapacious groups it itself has created, and to prevent the legalized plunder from running over into plain, unlegalized looting of all by all – is *compromise*; compromise on everything and in every realm – material, spiritual, intellectual – so that no group would step over the line by demanding too much and topple the whole rotted structure. (*CUI* 232)

In a society that rejects political principles limiting the use of governmental force, what it means to come to consensus is for various interest groups to jockey and negotiate for the privilege of using this force for their particular ends. The specific policies of such a government change frequently as different groups gain and lose influence, but since all the groups desire "a strong government" that is "unconstrained by any ideology," there is a consistent trend in the flux of shifting policies: the government "hoards an ever-growing power ... for the sake and use of any 'major' gang who might seize it momentarily to ram their particular piece of legislation down the country's throat" (*CUI* 233, cf. "Our Cultural Value Deprivation" *VOR* 107–108).

Rand had dramatized this process of pressure-group warfare in *Atlas Shrugged*, and had discussed it in some articles during Kennedy's presidency, but it became a more prominent theme in her political writing during the Johnson presidency, and remained so into the 1970s.[50] Throughout, she spoke against calls for "consensus" or "unity." "It is not unity, but intellectual coherence that a country needs. That coherence can be achieved only by fundamental principles, not by compromises among groups of men – by the primacy of ideas, not of gangs" ("The Wreckage of the Consensus" *CUI* 250).

Attempts at consensus in the absence of such an ideology amount to attempts by temporarily powerful factions to forcibly impose their will on others, and this inevitably breeds resentment. Rand saw this as the cause of Johnson's rapid descent "from the height of a popular landslide [in 1964] to the status of a liability to his own party [in 1966]" (*CUI* 250, cf. "The Dead End" *ARL* 1(20) 85). His policies had "disintegrated and atomized the country to such an extent that no communication, let alone agreement, is possible" (*CUI* 265).

The ideological change that Rand thought the country needed "is not the province of politicians and is not accomplished at election time" (*CUI* 266). Accordingly, she took little interest in the 1968 election, addressing it in a single article published in October of that year ("The Presidential Candidates, 1968" *TO* 7(6)). "It should be obvious," she wrote, "that the man to vote for this year is Richard M. Nixon." In the early 1960s Rand had criticized Nixon as a compromising moderate, but by 1968 she thought he had "grown and improved" ("How To Judge a Political Candidate" *TO* 3(3), *Speaking* 19).[51] She summed him up as "an advocate of the mixed economy, but on the free enterprise side of the mixture." Though not "an ideal candidate" he "took the proper stand" on a number of issues that she had identified as crucial to individual rights: he opposed the "street violence" of the student activists (on which, see 374–375, below) and the growing power of Federal regulatory agencies such as the FCC and Securities and Exchange Commission. With regard to foreign policy, Rand applauded his policy goal of maintaining nuclear supremacy over Russia and China.

By comparison to his opponents, Rand wrote, Nixon "appears to be the voice of sanity and civilization." She described the Democratic nominee Hubert Humphrey as a "somewhat seedy apostle of the status quo, who postures as a revolutionary," and said that the Democrat-turned-independent George Wallace "represents the emergence of open fascism in this country – or, more exactly, the crude elements from which an explicit fascism is to come." She saw it as "enormously significant" that Wallace attracted many of Robert Kennedy's followers after the latter's death. These two politicians appealed to many of the same voters, despite being on opposite sides of the main issues of the day, because they presented themselves as "activists" who would "take direct action, *action by the use of physical force*, to solve problems or to achieve (unspecified) goals" ("The Presidential Candidates, 1968" *TO* 7(6) 465).

Rand observed that, after assuming office, Nixon discarded "every approximate principle he was approximately believed to stand for" and "accelerated the march to statism" ("Credibility and Polarization" *ARL* 1(1) 3, "The Moratorium on Brains" *ARL* 1(2) 5). She was especially appalled by Executive Order 11615, which was signed on 15 August, 1971 and is often referred to as "The Nixon Shock." The order ended the Bretton Woods system under which dollars were convertible into gold at a fixed rate, and it imposed a 90-day freeze on prices and wages. Rand likened the order to *Atlas Shrugged*'s Directive 10-289, which completes the establishment of a dictatorship by exerting total control over the economy and attempting to enforce stability.[52] Nixon did not recognize the dictatorial nature of his freeze, she explained, because "as a pragmatist, he believes that anything is 'free enterprise' if we believe it is, and nothing is 'dictatorship' if we don't use that name" ("The Moratorium on Brains" *ARL* 1(2) 6).

She opposed many of Nixon's other policies including his endorsement of a guaranteed minimum income (as part of his, defeated, 1969 Family Assistance Plan), his foreign policy (on which, see below 370), and his institution (during his second term) of a "windfall tax" on oil companies during the energy crisis of 1973.[53] She praised him however for keeping "one promise of his 1968 campaign – perhaps, the most important one: the appointment to the Supreme Court of men who respect the Constitution."[54] "The Supreme Court," she wrote, "is the last remnant of a *philosophical* influence in this country" ("The American Spirit" *ARL* 2(4) 136). Even here, Nixon was not an unalloyed positive. She criticized the justices he appointed for their pragmatist opinions on several obscenity cases.[55]

As bad as Rand thought Nixon was, she urged readers to vote for him in 1972 "as a matter of national emergency" because of what his opponent, George McGovern, represented. (We will discuss that election below, 379–380.)

The defining event of Nixon's second term was the Watergate scandal. Rand wrote several pieces about it, all focused on the role of pragmatism in different aspects of the scandal.[56] Nixon's lack of a coherent campaign policy left his subordinates to try to anticipate and manipulate his "indeterminate views"; because these subordinates were contemptuous of political principles, they saw the election in terms of personalities and factions rather than ideas; so they sought dirt on their opponents and, unfettered by principle, some of them stooped to "bugging, spying, and burglary to get it." Similar motives led senators of both parties to stage public hearings, "running their future campaigns from the green pastures of the committee table." And liberal pedants were suddenly zealous to uncover and prosecute conspiracies, though they had ignored evidence of cover-ups and voter fraud connected to Kennedy and had excused the "politically motivated" crimes of leftist groups. The hearings exposed the sordid nature of politics in an increasingly controlled economy, the smallness of the men who rise to power in such a system, and the senselessness of the policies that their negotiations produce.

> You have seen the Watergate hearings on television. As I have suggested, multiply the chaos of those hearings over and over again, and you will have some idea of what it means to do business in a controlled economy. It is controlled by everyone and anyone, and no one: by dozens of government departments, agencies, bureaus, commissions, committees, by hundreds of pressure groups, with their lobbyists, their publicists, their special interests, their manipulators, their climbers. As indicated on television, none of the bureaucrats knows or cares to know what the others are doing. Each of them is clinging ferociously to his own square foot of territory and scrambling to enlarge it, flaunting his power, throwing his weight about, making decisions, and passing the buck when necessary. ("The Energy Crisis" *ARL* 3(3) 258)

Foreign Policy: The "Cold War," Vietnam, and the Draft

The central foreign policy issue in the 1960s and 1970s was the Cold War – specifically the War in Vietnam, which Rand described in a 1967 speech as "the consequence of fifty years of a suicidal foreign policy" ("Wreckage of the Consensus" *CUI* 255). The policy to which she was referring began with America's (1917) entrance into World War I, and continued through World War II and Korea. In a 1960 article, she summarized the rationale for and results of the World Wars:

> Now remember that Woodrow Wilson's policy plunged the United States into World War I and, instead of "making the world safe for democracy," as promised, it brought into existence three *new* "economic and political frameworks": Communist Russia, Fascist Italy, Nazi Germany. Franklin Roosevelt's policy plunged the United States into World War II and, instead of achieving the "Four Freedoms," as promised, it surrendered one-third of the world's population into slavery to Communist Russia. In both cases, the results were the exact opposite of the promises. ("JFK: High Class Beatnik?" Bibliography #21)[57]

Rand's opposition to America's involvement in these wars was not based on pacifism, on sympathy for the nations with which America was at war, or on any concerns about their alleged rights. "Dictatorship nations," she wrote in a 1963 essay, "are outlaws. Any free nation had the *right* to invade Nazi Germany and today, has the *right* to invade Soviet Russia, Cuba or any other slave pen," provided that the "conquerors" proceed to "establish a *free* social system, that is, a system based on the recognition of individual rights" ("Collectivized Rights" *VOS* 122). This is what the United States did after World War II in Japan and (with the Western allies) in West Germany. Rand defended America against charges of "imperialism" on the grounds that the nation "never engaged in military conquest and has never profited from the two world wars, which she did not initiate, but entered and won" ("Philosophy: Who Needs It?" *PWNI* 11–12). Her objection was that the wars represented "a foolishly overgenerous policy, which made this country waste her wealth on helping both her allies and her former enemies" (*PWNI* 12).

A proper foreign policy would be "explicitly and proudly dedicated to the defense of America's rights and national self-interests, repudiating foreign aid and all forms of international self-immolation" ("Wreckage of the Consensus" *CUI* 255).[58] Such a policy would mean identifying Soviet Russia and its allies as dictatorships that were hostile to the US and had no legitimate claim to sovereignty. But it would not require or lead to war with the Soviets. Their "alleged power was a giant bluff," she wrote; like any bully, they would retreat before firm opposition ("The Cuban Crisis" *Column* 62).[59] A central thesis of *Atlas Shrugged* is that evil is impotent and can survive only through the support of good people.[60] The Soviet government in Russia was able to persist despite impoverishing the country only because of aid they received from the free world – for example, the lend-lease equipment that the Soviets had received from the United States during World War II and the resources they had been allowed to plunder from conquered countries after the war. All that was necessary to defeat the Soviets, Rand thought, was an economic boycott by free nations and the removal of the moral sanction that these nations granted Russia by maintaining diplomatic relations with it ("*Playboy* Interview" 42, *Letters* 435–436).[61]

The chief vehicle of this sanction was the UN: "an institution allegedly dedicated to peace, freedom, and human rights, which includes Soviet Russia – the most brutal aggressor, the bloodiest dictatorship, the largest-scale mass-murderer and mass-enslaver in all history – among its charter members" ("The Anatomy of Compromise" *CUI* 161). Rand thought that the UN was largely responsible for the spread of Communism after the Second World War, because it hamstrung Western responses to Soviet aggression (including Soviet-sponsored coups). For example, she observed that the UN did not intervene to stop Russia's 1956 invasion of Hungary, but did deploy troops in 1960 to prevent Katanga from seceding from the (Communist) Democratic Republic of Congo (*CUI* 162).[62]

During the Cuban Missile Crisis of 1962, Rand urged "an uncompromising policy" toward Russia. She wrote that this could result in "the return of the United States to dignity, efficacy and national self-esteem – and, consequently, the eventual return of the world to a civilized state of existence" (*Column* 62).[63] She applauded Kennedy for standing up to Khrushchev and asserting America's interests. However, she wrote that Kennedy later "negated the moral base of his own stand" by submitting the matter to UN mediation, and she regarded the weak verification measures of the negotiated settlement as a compromise on American security to appease the Russians ("The Munich of World War III?" *Column* 72).[64]

Rand's first public statements on the Vietnam War came in a 1966 talk when she spoke contemptuously of the idea "that young men must be drafted and sent to die in jungle swamps, in order that the South Vietnamese may hold a 'democratic' election and vote themselves into communism, if they so choose" ("Our Cultural Value Deprivation" *VOR* 109, cf. "The Roots of War" *CUI* 36). Her main pieces on the subject are the 1967 talk "The Wreckage of the

Consensus" (*CUI*) and a 1975 article, "The Lessons of Vietnam" (*VOR*).[65] In both pieces, she argues that the war was "shameful because it was a war which the US had no *selfish* reason to fight, because it served no national interest, because we had nothing to gain from it, because the lives and the heroism of thousands of American soldiers (and the billions of American wealth) were sacrificed in pure compliance with the ethics of altruism, i.e., selflessly and sense-lessly" (*VOR* 140).

> None of us knows *why* we are in that war, *how* we got in, or *what* will take us out. Whenever our public leaders attempt to explain it to us, they make the mystery greater. They tell us simultaneously that we are fighting for the interests of the United States – and that the United States has no "self-ish" interests in that war. They tell us that communism is the enemy – and they attack, denounce, and smear any anti-communists in this country. They tell us that the spread of communism must be contained in Asia – but not in Africa. They tell us that communist aggression must be resisted in Vietnam – but not in Europe. They tell us that we must defend the freedom of South Vietnam – but not the freedom of East Germany, Poland, Hungary, Latvia, Czechoslovakia, Yugoslavia, Katanga, etc. They tell us that North Vietnam is a threat to our national security – but Cuba is not. ("The Wreckage of the Consensus" *CUI* 253)

America was clearly not acting on a coherent foreign policy grounded in any political ideology. Rather, it was acting in the typical short-range manner of a mixed economy in which politicians scramble to satisfy the shifting demands of various gangs. For example, liberal groups who had smeared conservatives as "isolationists" for holding "that the internal affairs of other countries are not the responsibility of the United States" were now "screaming that the United States has no right to interfere in the internal affairs of Vietnam" (*CUI* 254, cf. *VOR* 142).[66] Some of these same liberal groups were beginning to oppose the draft on the grounds of "individual rights," while many conservatives who posed as defenders of such rights were now defending the draft.

Such inconsistent positions would not be able to persist, Rand argued, without anti-ideology, and this same anti-ideology led the nation to conduct the war in an incoherent manner. In particular, the term "cold war," which Rand described as "a typically Hegelian term," enabled policy makers to treat Vietnam as both a "war" and a "non-war" (*CUI* 251, cf. *VOR* 140–141). Thus the nation attempted to "fight and non-fight at the same time"; it "sent its soldiers to die as cannon fodder," while "forbidding them to win"; it tolerated pro-Viet Cong propaganda that would have been deemed treasonous if the conflict were treated unambiguously as a war; and it engaged in cultural exchanges with the enemy and built "*trade* bridges to bolster the enemy's economy and enable it to produce the planes and guns which are killing our own soldiers" (*CUI* 252, cf. *VOR* 141).

Rand thought that the incoherence of the policy that led America into Vietnam left the na-tion in an impossible position: continuing to fight would be self-sacrificial, but to withdraw for pragmatic reasons would be yet another act of "appeasement."[67] In the absence of a principled foreign policy based on the defense of American interests, she said, "the only alternative is to fight that war and win it as fast as possible – and thus gain time to develop new statesmen with a new foreign policy, before the old one pushes us into another 'cold war,' just as the 'cold war' in Korea pushed us into Vietnam" ("The Wreckage of the Consensus" *CUI* 255, cf. *Answers* 86–87, 91–94).[68]

In "The Wreckage of the Consensus," Rand observes that sacrificial wars like Vietnam and Korea would not be possible without the military draft.[69] She discusses the draft at length, describing it as "the worst" of "all the statist violations of rights in a mixed economy." Her view of the draft and the steps taken by her and her students to oppose it are discussed ably by Fred Miller and Adam Mossoff in Chapter 8 of this volume.[70] For our present purposes, we will add only that Rand thought the evil of the draft is compounded when a country's incoherent foreign policy makes it impossible to predict when a war might break out, or to understand the cause for the sake of which one might be compelled to risk one's life.

> The years from about fifteen to twenty-five are the crucial formative years of a man's life. This is the time when he confirms his impressions of the world, of other men, of the society in which he is to live, when he acquires conscious convictions, defines his moral values, chooses his goals, and plans his future, developing or renouncing ambition. These are the years that mark him for life. And it is *these* years that an allegedly humanitarian society forces him to spend in terror – the terror of knowing that he can plan nothing and count on nothing, that any road he takes can be blocked at any moment by an unpredictable power, that, barring his vision of the future, there stands the gray shape of the barracks, and, perhaps, beyond it, death for some unknown reason in some alien jungle. ("The Wreckage of the Consensus" *CUI* 259, cf. "The Left: Old and New" *ROTP* 165)

This terror can lead one to the "conviction that existence is hopeless" and that one's "life is in the hands of some enormous, incomprehensible evil." Rand regarded this as one cause of an attitude that (as we will see) she thought was prevalent among the youth of the late 1960s and 1970s: "a helpless, searing contempt for the hypocrisy of his elders, and a profound hatred for all mankind" (*CUI* 259).

At the time that Rand was making these statements, it was only groups on the far political left that were voicing opposition to the draft and the Vietnam War. Rand thought that this was shameful and indicative of the unprincipled nature of American politics that the conservatives, who presented themselves as defenders of rights and of a pro-American foreign policy, supported such blatant rights violations and national sacrifice. And she observed that the opposition of the leftists was not based on the principle of rights, for many of the leftists were in favor of conscription for non-military service and objected to the war because they sympathized with the Viet Cong (*CUI* 256).

South Vietnam fell to the Communist North in 1975, two years after America's withdrawal from the war. Rand likened the defeat to the Russian White Army's defeat by the Communists, which she had witnessed as a teenager. In both cases the Communists "had an allegedly intellectual program, Marxism, and an allegedly moral justification: altruism, the sacrifice of all to some 'higher' cause," whereas their anti-Communist opponents had no positive program behind which to rally support (*VOR* 138, 141). She saw this same pattern in the defeat of the anti-Communists in China, Hungary, Czechoslovakia, and Poland, and in the American conservatives' failure (despite electoral victories) to oppose the statist policies of the left. As in so many other issues, Rand called on Americans to look into the philosophical causes that lie behind the disaster of Vietnam, and to articulate a coherent alternative to them – a rational foreign policy.

If this is not done, she warned, "the American people's legitimate weariness, confusion and anger over Vietnam" could be used by statist intellectuals to prevent the US from protecting its legitimate international interests. Rand identified Israel and Taiwan as "the two countries that need and deserve U.S. help – not in the name of international altruism, but by reason of actual U.S. national interests in the Mediterranean and the Pacific" (*VOR* 142).

> Of all the various refugee groups that escaped from the mass slaughter conducted by totalitarian regimes in their native lands, only two – the Chinese Nationalists [i.e., the Taiwanese] and the Israelis – had a chance not to vanish into the resigned futility of "ethnic" memories, rituals and prayers, and have built a new life for themselves against tremendous odds. Are we – the United States of America, the country that had proudly stood as an asylum for victims of tyranny – are we to betray men of that caliber and deliver them into the hands of their executioners? ("The Shanghai Gesture" *ARL* 1(15) 66)[71]

She did not think it necessary or proper to go to war to defend either country, but she thought that the United States should send "technology and military weapons" to Israel during the 1973 Arab–Israeli War, and she encouraged people to donate money privately to this cause, as she herself had done (*Answers* 96). With regard to Taiwan, she wrote in 1972 that America's "token military presence" had protected the Taiwanese since 1950.[72] She thought the withdrawal of these forces that began under the Nixon administration violated America's obligation (under the Sino-American Mutual Defense Treaty of 1955) to defend the island from Communist China, and she warned that the withdrawal could "precipitate a war involving the entire Pacific" by emboldening the Chinese Communists as "the Allies' withdrawal from the Sudetenland and the Ruhr" had emboldened the Nazis.[73]

The withdrawal of troops from Taiwan was part of Nixon's broader policy of establishing diplomatic relations with Communist China – a policy that culminated in his 1972 visit. Rand discussed this visit in depth in a 1972 article "The Shanghai Gesture" (*ARL* 1(13–15)).[74] Because of the rift that had developed between Russia and China, Rand thought that, so long as the US (immorally) maintained diplomatic relations with Russia, it was wise to seek rapprochement with China. Such a rapprochement could prevent a war between China and Russia, by making it clear that the US would not take Russia's side in such a conflict. However, Rand argued that, because of Nixon's pragmatism, he was unequipped to negotiate with opponents committed to the evil ideology of Communism. She thought his visit resulted in a senseless betrayal of Taiwan and an enormous propaganda victory for the Communists.

To our knowledge, there are only two instances in which Rand spoke publicly in favor of sending American forces into battle.[75] First, she praised President Ford for his swift military response to the (1975) seizure of the USS. *Mayaguez* by the Khmer Rouge, writing "when a foreign county initiates the use of armed force against us, it is our moral obligation to answer by force – as promptly and unequivocally as is necessary to make it clear that the matter is nonnegotiable" (*VOR* 145). The second instance is an application of this same principle. When asked about the Iranian Hostage crisis in a 1980 question period, she said the following: "If we didn't march with force on the first or second day after the hostages were taken [i.e., on November 5 or 6 of 1979], nothing we do after that will be any good, and it will take us years to live it down" (*Answers* 97).[76]

Rand saw a common cause behind America's failure to respond forcefully to the Iranians, Nixon's appeasement of the Chinese Communists, and America's involvement in the Vietnam War (and indeed in all the wars of the twentieth century). All were due to the lack of an *ideology* that would enable the nation to define its interests. In the place of such an ideology stood the altruistic doctrine that it is wrong for the nation to protect its own interests and right for it to sacrifice these interests to serve others around the globe. And since the nation was neither willing to implement this policy consistently, nor to reject it, America acted pragmatically on the world stage, with no coherent goals and no sense of direction.

Racism, Sexism, and The Civil Rights and Women's Liberation Movements

One of the major developments of the second half of the twentieth century was the changing societal attitudes and governmental policies concerning race and gender and the movements that arose from and contributed to these changes. Rand discussed racial issues in several pieces, most prominently her 1963 article "Racism" (*VOS*). The article was written in the context of the debate over (what would become) the Civil Rights Act of 1964, but its scope extends beyond the then-current controversies surrounding political solutions to the racism against blacks in America. Her subject is the nature and causes of, and solutions to, racism in general. The article begins as follows:

> Racism is the lowest, most crudely primitive form of collectivism. It is the notion of ascribing moral, social or political significance to a man's genetic lineage – the notion that a man's intellectual and characterological traits are produced and transmitted by his internal body chemistry. Which means, in practice, that a man is to be judged, not by his own character and actions, but by the characters and actions of a collective of ancestors. (*VOS* 147)

Racism is a form of collectivism because it regards human beings not as individuals but as members of collectives. It is more primitive than other forms of collectivism (e.g., Marxism) because the collectives are defined in terms of perceptually obvious, physiological features. Rand writes that it reflects "a mentality that differentiates between various breeds of animals, but not between animals and men," because it ignores the fundamental difference between human beings and animals that gives rise to the need for moral evaluation: the fact that human beings are *rational* beings with *free will* (*VOS* 147).[77]

Thus the essence of racism, in Rand's view, is not the persecution of racial minorities, but a broader evil from which this persecution stems: regarding people (oneself included) primarily as members of ancestral groups. We can see Rand's attitude toward this way of regarding oneself and others in her personal life. She was raised in a (largely non-observant) Jewish family in Russia, where Jews were persecuted and pogroms were a regular occurrence. As an adult, she did not normally self-identify as Jewish, and (speaking privately to friends in the early 1960s) she described certain American Jews as racist because they self-identified primarily as Jewish and associated exclusively with other Jews (*Biographical Interviews* 249, cf. McConnell 2010, 535–536). However, she did assert that she was Jewish when she encountered anti-Semitic remarks – for example, when one friend disparaged "Jewish intellectuals" (*Biographical Interviews* 516), or when another friend expressed approval of Hitler's final solution (McConnell 2010, 36).

Rand's 1963 article goes on to discuss racism's connections to other forms of collectivism, writing that during the nineteenth century "persecution of racial and religious minorities" waned in Europe's more capitalist countries such as England, but persisted or increased in more statist countries such as Russia and (20th Century) Germany. She saw the same pattern in America. Slavery in various forms was practiced worldwide, often with a racist rationale, until Capitalism displaced it in the nineteenth century, and in America, it was "the capitalist North that destroyed the slavery of the agrarian-feudal South." She thought it was to America's credit that the country was willing to fight a civil war to "give individual rights to every human being regardless of race" (*VOS* 151, *Answers* 105).[78]

Rand did not regard twentieth-century America as racist, by comparison to other nations and periods. However she recognized that prejudice against blacks was a significant evil. She

371

wrote that it was "originated and perpetuated by the non-capitalist South, though not confined to its boundaries." In the rest of the country such prejudice was "was slowly giving way under the pressure of enlightenment and of the white men's own economic interests" (*VOS* 152). But she did not think this excused such instances of the evil as remained, and she condemned anti-black prejudice when she saw it and praised some works of art (such as the film *In the Heat of the Night* and the TV series *Roots*) for their anti-racist themes and strong black heroes.[79]

She thought that the evil of racial discrimination was greatly compounded when enforced by the government, and that such enforcement in the South was retarding the process by which racist attitudes were giving way in the rest of the country.

> The policy of the Southern states toward Negroes was and is a shameful contradiction of this country's basic principles. Racial discrimination, imposed and enforced by law, is so blatantly inexcusable an infringement of individual rights that the racist statutes of the South should have been declared unconstitutional long ago. (*VOS* 153)[80]

Thus, she wrote that "right, justice and morality" were on the side of "Negro leaders" in their fight against such laws. However, she opposed the Civil Rights Act of 1964 because (in addition to provisions forbidding discrimination by the state governments) it included provisions outlawing segregation in privately owned businesses. "Private racism," Rand wrote, "is not a legal, but a moral issue – and can be fought only by private means, such as economic boycott or social ostracism" (*VOS* 156). Just as the law must protect a communist's freedom of speech, she argued, it must protect a racist's right to the use and disposal of his property.

Rand saw the Act as a sign that the Civil Rights movement had lost its way. Rather than fighting for "'color-blindness' in social and economic issues," she wrote, the movement's leaders were arguing that "'color' should be made a primary consideration," and "instead of fighting for equal rights, they are demanding special race privileges."[81] This was an instance of a broader phenomenon: "In the absence of any coherent political philosophy, every economic group has been acting as its own destroyer, selling out its future for some momentary privilege." She identified such fighting among pressure-groups (organized along racial and other lines) as a symptom of the growing collectivism in America – a theme she revisited in several articles from the 1970s about the movement that is now known as "multiculturalism."[82] The primary victims of this movement, Rand thought, were the more ambitious members of the minority groups whom the movement purports to help. As examples she cited "the self-respecting small home owners and shop owners" who "are the unprotected and undefended victims of every race riot" and successful black men who are "attacked as 'Uncle Toms'" ("The Age of Envy" *ROTP* 143).

For the same reasons that Rand objected to the direction the Civil Rights movement took in late 1960s, she opposed the Women's Liberation movement of the 1970s (which has come to be called "second-wave feminism"). She saw this movement as "a vicious parasitical pressure group" that "rides on the historical prestige of women who fought for individual rights against government power, and struggles to get special privileges by means of government power" (*Answers* 106, "The Age of Envy" *ROTP* 147).

It is obvious from Rand's own life and from the heroines of her novels that she rejected contemptuously "the notion that a woman's place is in the home" – a view that she described as "an ancient, primitive evil, supported and perpetuated by women as much as, or more than, by men" (*ROTP* 147–148).[83] We can see her opposition to this view and its attendant attitudes in her mention of "the subtle injustice an intellectual girl has to suffer while she grows up" in a 1950 letter (*Letters* 473), and in her publication (in 1963) of a glowing review (by Edith Efron) of Betty Friedan's *The Feminine Mystique* (*TON* 2(7)). The review endorses Friedan's conclusions and prescriptions, with one significant exception: the creation of a federal program to send housewives to college at public expense. By Rand's lights, women who wanted educations and careers should earn them as men did. The prejudices such women faced must be combated by voluntary means, rather than through (private or governmental) force, and individuals who wanted to support the efforts of career women should do so with their own money.[84]

The call for governmental coercion was incidental to Friedan's book, but it was essential to the movement that the book helped to spark. The primary activity of most chapters of the National Organization for Women in the early 1970s was filing complaints to the Equal Employment Opportunity Commission, which had been established by the Civil Rights Act of 1964 (Staggenborg 1994, 39). Rand commented:

> Women's Lib proclaims that success should not have to be achieved, but should be guaranteed as a right. Women, it claims, should be pushed by law into any job, club, saloon or executive position they choose – and let the employer prove in court that he failed to promote a woman because she is a slob and *not* because she is a woman. (*ROTP* 148)

We can see this same call for governmental assistance in the three "principal demands" of the Women's Liberation "Strike" (on August 26, 1970): "free abortion on demand, the establishment of community-controlled 24-hour day-care centers for the children of working mothers and equality of educational and employment opportunity."[85] Rand (who was an adamant supporter of abortion rights – see 383–384, below) saw such demands as a *reductio ad absurdum*:

> Proclaiming women's independence from and equality with men, Women's Lib demands liberation from the consequences of whatever sex life a woman might choose, such consequences to be borne by others: it demands free abortions and free day-nurseries. To be paid for – by whom? By men. (*ROTP* 148)

Even worse than such demands, from Rand's perspective, was the attitude toward men projected by many of the marchers. She focused especially on a placard reading: "OPPRESSED WOMEN: DON'T COOK DINNER! STARVE A RAT TODAY!!"[86] In such slogans she saw the soul of "the aggressive, embittered, self-righteous and envious housewife," who "is the greatest enemy of the career woman. Women's Lib pounces upon this aggressiveness, bitterness, self-righteousness, envy – and directs it toward men." Thus Rand saw the movement as an attempt "to surpass the futile sordidness of a class war by instituting a sex war" (*ROTP* 148).[87]

Civil Disobedience and the Rise of Political Violence

Even when she agreed with the aims of the Civil Rights movement, Rand sometimes disagreed with its methods – in particular, its use of civil disobedience. She thought it was justifiable when an individual or group "disobeys a law in order to bring an issue to court, as a test case," because this "involves respect for legality and a protest directed only at a particular law which the individual seeks an opportunity to prove to be unjust." This is what Roark had done at the climax of *The Fountainhead* (648, 706–718), and it is what Rosa Parks did in her famous refusal to comply with Montgomery, Alabama's segregation law. However, Rand opposed civil disobedience when it "involves the violation of the rights of others – regardless of whether the demonstrators' goal is good or evil."

> The forcible occupation of another man's property or the obstruction of a public thoroughfare is so blatant a violation of rights that an attempt to justify it becomes an abrogation of morality. An individual has no right to do a "sit-in" in the home or office of a person he disagrees with – and he does not acquire such a right by joining a gang. Rights are not a matter of numbers – and there can be no such thing, in law or in morality, as actions forbidden to an individual, but permitted to a mob.
>
> The only power of a mob, as against an individual, is greater muscular strength – i.e., plain, brute physical force. The attempt to solve social problems by means of physical force is what a civilized society is established to prevent. ("The Cashing-In: The Student 'Rebellion'" *CUI* 291/*ROTP* 26)

One can infer from this that Rand was opposed to the Greensboro sit-ins of 1960 and the marches from Selma to Montgomery in 1965, though she did not comment on either event specifically, and only began writing on civil disobedience when the tactic was taken up by other groups.[88] In the case of the Civil Rights movement, she wrote, "the issue was confused by the fact that the Negroes *were* the victims of legalized injustice and, therefore, the matter of breaching legality did not become unequivocally clear" (*CUI* 291/*ROTP* 26).

Rand's first article on civil disobedience focuses on the "Free Speech Movement" that had begun in the fall of 1964 at The University of California, Berkeley. Students who objected in the name of "free speech" to university regulations restricting political activities on university grounds had surrounded a police car and later staged a "sit-in." Rand argued that the university was within its rights to set limits on the activities that could be engaged in on its property, and that the activists were violating rights with their sit-ins and "other acts of physical force, such as assaults on the police and the seizure of a police car for use as a rostrum" (*CUI* 267/*ROTP* 5). In a 1978 discussion of a neo-Nazi march, Rand explains succinctly why such actions are not instances of "freedom of speech":

> There is no such thing as "symbolic speech." You do not have the right to parade through the public streets or to obstruct public thoroughfares. You have the right of assembly, yes, on your own property, and on the property of your adherents or your friends. But nobody has the "right" to clog the streets. The streets are only for passage. The hippies in the 1960s, should have been forbidden to lie down on city pavements. (They used to lie down across a street and cause dreadful traffic snarls, in order to display their views, to attract attention, to register a protest.) If they were permitted to do it, the Nazis should be permitted as well. Properly, both should have been forbidden. They may speak, yes. They may not take action at whim on public property. ("The First Amendment and Symbolic Speech" *Column* 117)[89]

Rand saw the (1965) Free Speech movement as an attempt to obliterate this distinction between speech and action and "to condition the country to accept force as the means of settling political controversies." Over the years that followed, she praised certain college administrators and politicians (including Ronald Reagan and Richard Nixon) for standing up to students' uses of force, but she thought that the dominant response was to appease such students, and that as a result they were becoming more violent.[90] Writing in 1970, in the wake of a string of bombings in Chicago by "The Weathermen" (a faction of Students for a Democratic Society), she decried "the unspeakable little drugged monstrosities who resort to violence – and who have progressed, without significant opposition, from campus sit-ins to arson and to such an atrocity as mass terrorization and the bombing of public places" ("Political Crimes" *ROTP* 177, cf. "The Left: Old and New" *ROTP* 171). Rand thought that calls for "special leniency" for "criminals who claim to be motivated by political goals" were part of the effort to subvert the distinction between speech and action. "Since an individual has the right to hold and propagate any ideas he chooses," she wrote, the government "may not take any judicial cognizance whatever of his ideology." "If the government assumes the power to exonerate a man on the grounds of his political ideas, it has assumed the power to prosecute and condemn him on these same grounds" ("Political Crimes" *ROTP* 176, 178).

With regard to the ideas motivating the Free Speech movement at Berkeley, Rand noted that, though the students railed against what they called "The Establishment" and agitated for and against various concrete policies, they did not put forward a holistic positive program: indeed, they were "militantly opposed to all 'labels,' definitions, and theories." Their "central theme and basic ideology," she wrote, was "*anti-ideology*." This is the same term she was using in connection with the Johnson administration and the pressure-group warfare among lobbyists ("The Cashing-In: The Student 'Rebellion'" *CUI* 273/*ROTP* 11). Far from "rebelling" against established ideas, she argued, the students were simply "cashing in" on the premises of the older generation – that is, they were applying these same premises more consistently and more brazenly. The students simply dropped the pressure-groups' veneer of civility and brought the use of force into the open. Years later, Rand wrote of the youth movement more generally that they "are the embodied symbols and protégés of the Establishment they are going through the motions of defying" ("The Inexplicable Personal Alchemy" *ROTP* 126, cf. "Apollo and Dionysus" *ROTP* 115–116).[91]

The Intellectual Establishment and its Products

The Establishment that Rand thought produced the student activists was a philosophical one, rooted in the ideas of Kant (on whom see 332–334, above). He had "divorced reason from reality," and "his intellectual descendants have been diligently widening the breach."[92] As a result, "the philosophical 'mainstream' that seeps into every classroom, subject, and brain in today's universities is: epistemological agnosticism, avowed irrationalism, ethical subjectivism" ("The Cashing-In: The Student 'Rebellion'" *CUI* 279/*ROTP* 15). In a number of essays written between 1970 and 1972, she examined the form in which this anti-ideology shaped American education and the institutional factors that enabled it to become so entrenched, and she proposed some reforms that could help alternative approaches to arise and survive.

"The Comprachicos" (*ROTP*) discusses the impact of pragmatism (one variation of Kantianism) on American education.[93] The essay's title is a reference to Victor Hugo's description (in *The Man Who Laughs*) of the practitioners of an ancient art by which a child's developing bones were twisted to mold him into a freak. Similarly, Rand thought, modern educators twist the developing minds of their students through a process of socialization that punishes thinking and rewards emotionalism and conformity. As a result the development of the rational faculty is stifled, creating a "concrete-bound pragmatist mentality," that has no abstract ideas or conceptual values and so relies uncritically on emotions and on social groups for guidance.

Rand saw the pragmatist politicians who were running the country in the 1960s as the products of an early, less comprehensive version of this same approach to education, but she thought that the comprachicos' "most successful products" were the rioting student activists.

375

> They act in packs, with the will of the pack as their only guide. The scramble for power among their pack leaders and among different packs does not make them question their premises: they are incapable of questioning anything. So they cling to the belief that mankind can be united into one happily, harmoniously unanimous pack – by force. Brute, physical force is, to them, a natural form of action. (*ROTP* 90)

Rand meant this description to apply only to "a small minority" of students, but she thought that this minority was very effective because they were surrounded by "a helpless, confused, demoralized majority" whose minds had been less completely destroyed by the same educational system. Among this majority, Rand identified "the hippies" as "the activists' fellow travelers and prospective converts."

Unlike the activists, who she thought were thugs, she saw the hippies as essentially bums who "live down to [the progressive nursery school's] essential demand: non-effort."

> If they are not provided with brightly furnished rooms and toys, they live in dank basements, they sleep on floors, they eat what they find in garbage cans, they breed stomach ulcers and spread venereal diseases – anything rather than confront that implacable enemy of whims: reality. (*ROTP* 91)

As the prime example of this phenomenon, she cited the famous Woodstock Music and Art Fair, which she described as "300,000 people wallowing in the mud on an excrement-strewn hillside" ("Apollo and Dionysus" *ROTP* 109). Quoting liberally from newspaper accounts, she portrayed the event as the epitome of mindlessness: because the concert's promoters and its attendees had failed to plan for needs and contingencies that could easily have been anticipated, hundreds of thousands of young people found themselves stranded in the rain without adequate provisions; rather than dealing with the situation in a civilized manner, they looted what they could from the townspeople, shouted at the rain to stop, and, when it did not comply, embraced the muck.

Another prominent aspect of Woodstock, and of the hippie culture generally, was drugs. Rand cited "the phenomenon of an entire generation turning to drugs" as a proof of the failure of the establishment ("The Comprachicos" *ROTP* 92). In part, she thought, drug use was a response to the terror (discussed above) of being drafted to fight an unintelligible war ("The Wreckage of the Consensus" *CUI* 259–260), but she thought that the main cause was a school system that had presented the world as a frightening chaos, devalued reason in favor of allegedly superior forms of consciousness, and trained young people to be obedient to peer pressure (*ROTP* 92–93).[94]

The hippies, by their own statement, were a Dionysian movement – one that embraced emotionalism, mysticism, and intoxication over reason. Rand argued that (as with the violent student activists) they were not a departure from the generally accepted cultural ideals, but a more consistent and overt embodiment of these ideals. In a series of articles she connected the hippies' practices and statements with the pronouncements of various cultural leaders or heroes, all of whom professed allegiance to something allegedly higher than reason.[95] And behind these cultural leaders was Kant, whom Rand with deliberate irony described as "the first hippie in history" ("Apollo and Dionysus" *ROTP* 105).

If America were to reverse course, the anti-ideology that dominated its educational instructions would need to be supplanted by rational ideas. In both "The Cashing-In" and "The Comprachicos," Rand calls upon college students to expose the bankruptcy of their peers and professors and to "boldly [proclaim] a full, consistent and radical alternative" (*CUI* 306/*ROTP*

39, cf. *ROTP* 94–95).[96] In other articles she (and her associates) praise the Montessori Method of early education as a rational alternative to progressive nursery schools and public elementary schools.[97]

Rand thought the chief obstacle to the spread of such alternative ideas and methods was university departments' unwillingness to give a hearing to views that pose fundamental challenges to the orthodoxies in their fields. "The Establishing of an Establishment" (*PWNI*), written in the spring of 1972, describes how governmental support for research creates this dogmatic intellectual establishment by entrenching the opinions of the most prestigious researchers in the field. Two of Rand's other articles from that same period suggest ways in which the monopoly of this establishment could be broken.

In "Fairness Doctrine for Education" (*PWNI*), she writes that an ad hoc movement could pressure (or sue) universities into adopting an equivalent of the Fairness Doctrine – an FCC policy that required broadcasters to present contrasting positions on controversial issues. Rand held that the FCC policy could not be objectively interpreted or implemented and that its result was only a vague approximation of intellectual freedom, but this was the best that was possible in a nation that regulated the airwaves as public property, and so long as the universities were being funded (and so controlled) by the government, the public had every right to demand that they adopt a similar policy.

In "Tax Credits For Education" (*VOR*), she argued that allowing people to pay for (their own or others') education with money saved from their taxes "would give private schools a chance to survive (which they do not have at present)" and "bring their tuition fees within the reach of the majority of people." By doing so, it would "break up the government's stranglehold, decentralize education" and so enable a "free marketplace of ideas" (*VOR* 250).

Neither the Fairness Doctrine nor the tax credits would be possible or necessary under the capitalist system Rand advocated, but she endorsed them as a means to mitigating the worst effects of the mixed economy. She thought that both proposals could win popular support in the present culture, and that they would create or preserve the conditions needed for the robust cultural change that was needed to reverse the country's statist trend and, ultimately, establish capitalism.

The Envious New Left: Environmentalism, Egalitarianism, and the 1972 Election

During the 1965 protests at Berkeley, the press began to use the phrase "New Left" to denote the groups (chiefly Students for a Democratic Society) behind the protests and similar demonstrations in the years that followed.[98] By 1970, the phrase had come to denote a broader, vaguely defined movement, which one sympathetic scholar describes as "a flamboyant upsurge against the new, affluent suburban way of life in postwar America" (Gosse 2005, 6).[99] Various New Left groups blamed this affluent middle-class lifestyle for (alleged) evils ranging from the oppression of minorities and women in America, to the subjection of third world nations, and the destruction of the environment. The Old Left (i.e., early twentieth-century Marxists and liberals) had presented themselves as champions of the American worker and were steadfast allies of organized labor, but the New Left was often at odds with labor unions and the middle-class workers they represented.[100] And where the Old Left had seen industrialization as the means to widespread prosperity, the New Left was often hostile to industry, idealizing a more agrarian lifestyle.

377

This New Left became a prominent subject in Rand's writing between 1970 and 1972, and she collected her most relevant essays (including several discussed above on the student "rebels" and education) into *The New Left: The Anti-Industrial Revolution*.[101] This collection, published in 1971 with an expanded edition in 1975, is her only book wholly devoted to contemporary culture and politics.[102] (The book is no longer in print in its original form, but all of the essays in it are included in *The Return of the Primitive*.)

Rand saw the New Left as a consequence of the discrediting of many of the claims that had been made on behalf of collectivism prior to World War II. She observed that "Old-line Marxists" had claimed that Soviet technology would quickly surpass that of the United States, that central planning was necessary to bring the benefits of industrialization to the masses, and that the leaders of capitalist countries were keeping these masses complacent by promoting religion and drug dependency. However, by the mid-sixties everyone could see the superiority of American industry and the American standard of living over that of the Communist countries (and even of "socialist Britain"). It was now clear that mankind faced "the choice of an industrial civilization or collectivism," and the New Left represented the liberals' choice to "discard" industrial civilization. It was now the leftists who were asking people to sacrifice material comforts for alleged "spiritual" benefits and who were promoting drug use.

> The old-line Marxists used to claim that a single modern factory could produce enough shoes to provide for the whole population of the world and that nothing but capitalism prevented it. When they discovered the facts of reality involved, they declared that going barefoot is superior to wearing shoes. ("The Left: Old and New" *ROTP* 168–169)[103]

Rand saw this rejection of technology as the essence of "the ecology movement" – the precursor of present-day Environmentalism. She argued that the Ecologists' aim was not to protect the human environment (e.g., human beings' supply of clean air or water), but to protect nature as an end in itself from human beings. This meant reversing the Industrial Revolution. But since human beings survive by altering their environment, rather than adjusting to it as animals do, Rand saw any attack on industry as an attack on human life as such. Thus, in her view, the movement amounts to a call to self-sacrifice for the sake of non-human organisms and inanimate matter ("The Anti-Industrial Revolution" *ROTP*). Rand recognized that pollution could be a genuine threat to human health, and she held that laws prohibiting direct and provable physical nuisances should be enforced.[104] But concerns about pollution could never justify abandoning technological growth, because "we must remember that life in nature, without technology, is wholesale death" (*ROTP* 283).

The Ecology movement made it clear, Rand thought, that opposition to capitalism was not driven by "concern with poverty and with the improvement of human life on earth" ("The Left: Old and New" *ROTP* 169). What motivated the most zealous adherents to all collectivist movements, she maintained, was an emotion that she called "envy" for short, but which is far worse than the ordinary meaning of that term. Most accurately described as "hatred of the good for being the good" ("The Age of Envy" *ROTP* 130), it is the desire to destroy someone else because one sees his abilities, virtues, and accomplishments as a reproach to oneself. This is the motive that drives the most evil characters in Rand's fiction, and in *Atlas Shrugged*, she argues that the felt need to rationalize this ugly motive is the psychological root of mysticism, altruism, and collectivism.[105] It is only "a small, depraved minority in any age or culture" who are primarily motivated by this hatred, but Rand thought such people and their doctrines attain cultural prominence by pandering to the worst elements in ordinary people.[106] This occurs to some extent in all cultures, but Rand thought that the culture of her own time was dominated by this hatred – a point she made by characterizing the period (in the title of a 1971 article) as "The Age of Envy" (*ROTP*).[107]

Appeals to envy always have to be disguised in seemingly noble terms, such as the Marxists' alleged concern for the poor, but Rand thought that such appeals were becoming more overt in the 1970s. She interpreted the concept of "egalitarianism" as "the last fig leaf of academic pretentiousness" used to "disguise" the nature of the left. Rand was an advocate of "political equality" (i.e., "equality under the law"), but this is not what she understood egalitarians to mean by "equality":

> They turn the word into an anti-concept: they use it to mean, not *political*, but *metaphysical* equality – the equality of personal attributes and virtues, regardless of natural endowment or individual choice, performance and character. It is not man-made institutions, but nature, i.e., *reality*, that they propose to fight – by means of man-made institutions. ("The Age of Envy" *ROTP* 140)[108]

It is an unalterable and unevaluable fact, Rand argued, that human beings differ in their abilities, their values, and their choices, and therefore that they will differ in their accomplishments – including in the wealth and opportunities that they produce. Any attempt to judge these facts as fair or unfair can only be based on a mystical fantasy.[109] And any attempt to make people more equal can only proceed by preventing the more able people from achieving, or by destroying or appropriating their achievements. Thus, Rand argued that equality is not a legitimate value for anyone – including for those who are inferior in ability, accomplishment, or any other respect. Rational people benefit from one another's successes, and no one's rational interests are harmed by anyone else's greater achievements. The crusade for equality, Rand concluded, is simply a thinly veiled expression of envy – of hatred for the people one regards as superior to oneself.[110]

Rand saw George McGovern's 1972 presidential campaign as embodying the egalitarian ideas she opposed, and she described him as "the first to offer full-fledged statism to the American people" (Bibliography #27). This description was based on an unpopular plan he had endorsed in January 1972. The plan included a new tax policy and an annual $1,000 grant to every American, which would replace the welfare system.[111] Rand described the grant as an egalitarian attempt to "wipe out the difference between an earned income and an unearned one" and so to "place everyone, on principle, on the level of welfare recipients."[112] She noted that Nixon had earlier endorsed a similar proposal on pragmatic grounds; what was new about McGovern was his explicit endorsement of the principle inherent in such programs and in the welfare state as a whole. He described his aim as the "redistribution of income" away from the top 20 percent of earners.[113] Rand saw this as an attempt "to establish a claim to the total income of the nation."

> If a man proposes to *redistribute* wealth it means that the wealth is his to distribute. If he proposes it in the name of the government, then the wealth belongs to the government. No one did or could establish a difference between that proposal and the basic principle of communism. ("McGovern is the First to Offer Full-Fledged Statism to the American People")

"McGovern's candidacy," Rand wrote, "represents a declaration of war on the American people by the intellectuals of the New Left" (ibid).

All but two of the 11 issues of the *Ayn Rand Letter* published between July and November of 1972 were devoted to issues directly connected with the election.[114] The most detailed of these articles, "A Preview" (*ARL* 1(22–24)), places the campaign in the context of the development of American liberalism across the twentieth century. The New Deal, which had transformed America into a welfare state, was sold to Americans largely as a means to protect workers from (allegedly) unfair treatment by industrialists. It consisted of a set of welfare programs that purported to benefit the average American, and a series of laws granting special privileges to labor unions. These laws tied the hands of industry and were unfair to the most able workers, but because American workers were essentially producers who sought to earn their livings, rather than to live as parasites on others, the effects of the statist measures were limited. The labor unions were not natural allies for power-lusting intellectuals and politicians, and by the 1960s organized labor was the primary force standing in the way of many of the leftists' ambitions. Rand had pointed this out in 1962, in connection with the AFL-CIO's (American Federation of Labor and Congress of Industrial Organizations) objection to an attempt by the Kennedy administration to intervene in labor-contract negotiations in the steel industry.[115] In order for the leftist intellectuals to further advance their statist agenda, they would need to find some new, allegedly mistreated group for whose sake they could demand that the American workforce make sacrifices. Thus the intellectuals of the New Left were trying to stir up envy against the upwardly mobile middle class by encouraging people to think of themselves as members of various disadvantaged groups, defined in terms of race, sex, age, and economic status. McGovern, in Rand's view, was simply an unscrupulous politician who took on the mantle of this movement hoping that it would sweep him into power. But, she argued, he had miscalculated: Americans were not an envious people, and the negative public response to the 1968 Democratic Convention showed that they felt contempt for the intellectuals and hippies who were McGovern's power base.

Rand interpreted McGovern's landslide defeat as an assertion of America's individualistic "sense of life" and an unequivocal public rejection of the New Left. It exposed the fact that the envy-ridden intellectuals do not speak for the American people ("The American Spirit" *ARL* 2(4)). Reflecting on the election six years later, she wrote that it "was the first time that the American people had a chance to grasp the nature of statism, and they voted accordingly" ("Cultural Update"). It put an end to the most virulent manifestations of the New Left, such as the hippies, who, she wrote, "are dead, at least as an alleged subculture or as a major public nuisance." The country was finally turning to the right "in the sense of a strong anti-statist, anti-collectivist trend" ("Cultural Update"). And by the time of the 1976 election, she thought that "the country has gone so much towards capitalism that Carter was 'me-tooing' Ford and the Republicans throughout the campaign" (*Answers* 71). She noted that Carter's initial lead (due largely to disillusionment over the Watergate scandal) was lost when he took actions that were perceived as "too liberal" and that he was able to win in the end only because the public saw little difference between his position and Ford's.[116]

Thus, though she had contempt for Carter, whom she characterized as an "unspeakable, cheap, small-town peanut power luster" (*Answers* 70), she did not see him as a significant long-term threat to America. The dominant factor in American politics remained an anti-statist trend. The situation was "precarious," however, because "a trend against something is not enough" to reverse the damage that had been done by decades of statism; "intellectual leadership" would be needed to transform the trend into an explicitly pro-capitalist movement. The greatest danger to the incipient movement (and to the nation) was that instead it would be "perverted" by anti-capitalist ideas. ("Cultural Update") In the next two sections, we discuss two developments that she thought threatened to do just this.

The Libertarian Movement

The early 1970s saw the birth of the self-styled "New Right" or "Libertarian" movement, which cited Rand as one of its primary inspirations. Many readers find Rand's vehement disavowal of this movement difficult to understand, because Libertarians seem to share many of her political goals. It will be clarifying, therefore, to look briefly at the history of this movement and Rand's view of it.

The term "libertarian" and Rand's (occasional) use of it dates at least back to the early 1960s, when she observed in a radio interview that that word is often applied to those conservatives who are "defenders of capitalism on a non-mystical, scientific basis" and "do not advocate a mixed economy." She cited Ludwig von Mises and Henry Hazlitt as the "best exponents" of this position (*Speaking* 16). Rand criticized Hazlitt and von Mises for lacking "a philosophic framework," but she was personal friends with both, and she recommended their books (published in some cases by "the Libertarian Press") in the bibliography of *Capitalism: The Unknown Ideal*. It is significant, however, that she did not use the term "libertarian" publicly in her own voice, and she expressed concern that it was "loosely defined" (*Speaking* 17).[117]

In 1969, Rand elaborated on this concern, saying that though "some people today use the word 'libertarian' to designate the pro-free enterprise position," the term also has "undefined connotations," which would make it easily co-opted (as "liberal" and "conservative" had been) by opponents of capitalism who could then assume the mantle of its defenders and obscure the fundamental issues at stake (*AON* 120, cf. *Speaking* 16–20).[118] This is just what she thought went on to happen in the early 1970s, when the Libertarian movement coalesced under the leadership of anarchists such as Murray Rothbard and Karl Hess.[119]

A sign of this development was the cover story of the July 10, 1971 issue of *The New York Times* magazine: "The New Right Credo – Libertarianism," a manifesto by two Columbia students. The piece names Rand as Libertarianism's "key philosopher," but the quotations and arguments used to lay out the Libertarian position are all drawn from Rothbard and Hess.[120] It intimates that Libertarians are sympathetic to the tactics of the New Left activists and that they are "not all that opposed – in principle at any rate – to shaking up or even overthrowing the liberal state." Worse, the piece trivialized the disagreements between violent anarchist revolutionaries and peaceful defenders of limited government:

> At present the only areas of disagreement within the libertarian movement are whether the movement should strive for anarchy or for limited government, and whether it should work through revolution or within the system. While "only" may sound like an understatement, and ends and means seem to be major rather than minor areas of disagreement, the conflict is really more apparent than actual. Limited government and anarchy are really not as far apart as they seem [...] Those who call for limited government and those who call for anarchy would be content to live in one another's systems if either were instituted.

Rand, who had denounced the violent tactics of the New Left and who would not have been "content to live in" anarchy was outraged by such "attempts to cash in on my name and mislead my readers into the exact opposite of my views" (*Letters* 664).[121] She probably had the

Times piece in mind later that year, when she responded to a question about "libertarianism" as follows:

> All kinds of people today call themselves "libertarians," especially something calling itself the New Right, which consists of hippies who are anarchists instead of leftist collectivists; but anarchists *are* collectivists. Capitalism is the one system that requires absolute objective law, yet libertarians combine capitalism and anarchism ... Anarchism is a logical outgrowth of the anti-intellectual side of collectivism. I could deal with a Marxist with a greater chance of reaching some kind of understanding, and with much greater respect. Anarchists are the scum of the intellectual world of the Left, which has given them up. So the Right picks up another leftist discard. That's the libertarian movement. (*Answers* 72)[122]

By comparison with the fundamental difference between limited government and anarchism, Rand regarded any seeming agreements between her and the anarchists as insignificant or illusory, and she rejected any movement (or concept) that sought to embrace both.

> Above all, do not join the wrong *ideological* groups or movements, in order to "do something." By "ideological" (in this context), I mean groups or movements proclaiming some vaguely generalized, undefined (and, usually, contradictory) *political* goals. (E.g., the Conservative Party, which subordinates reason to faith, and substitutes theocracy for capitalism; or the "libertarian" hippies, who subordinate reason to whims, and substitute anarchism for capitalism.) To join such groups means to reverse the philosophical hierarchy and to sell out fundamental principles for the sake of some superficial political action which is bound to fail. It means that you help the defeat of *your* ideas and the victory of your enemies. ("What Can One Do?" *PWNI* 277)[123]

Thus she viewed the Libertarian movement as essentially anti-intellectual – a product of the same cultural forces that had bred the New Left.[124]

The Religious Right and the Right to Abortion

In a 1960 letter to Barry Goldwater, Rand warned of a "pressure group" that sought "to tie Conservatism to religion, and thus to take over the American Conservatives":

> When a political movement lacks a firm, consistent set of principles, it can be taken over by any minority that knows what it wants. In the nineteen-thirties, the Liberals were thus taken over by the Communists ... In any group of men, those who formulate basic principles will direct those who don't, and will determine the practical policy of the group. I am convinced that what the Communists did to the Liberals, the professional religionists are now attempting to do to the Conservatives. (*Letters* 571)[125]

Any attempt to justify capitalism on religious grounds, Rand argued, is disastrous, because it amounts to a false admission that the statists have science and reason on their side. She saw the reliance on such arguments since World War II as the source of "the growing apathy, lifelessness, ineffectuality and general feebleness of the so-called Conservative side" (*Letters* 571).[126] Rand's principal objection to the religionists, however, was not their ineptness at defending capitalism. As the comparison to Communists indicates, she viewed them as insidious proponents of an evil agenda. She would later describe these same "religious conservatives" as "pure fascists": "They are not for free enterprise; they want controls – spiritual, moral, and intellectual controls" (*Answers* 68).[127]

The last quote comes from 1976, by which time the religious conservative agenda had crystallized, with opposition to abortion as one of it its central planks. Rand regarded the legality of abortion as "a fundamental *moral* issue of enlightened respect for individual rights versus savagely primitive superstition" ("A Suggestion" *TO* 8(2) 596). In her December 1968 talk, "Of Living Death," she had argued that "Abortion is a moral right – which should be left to the sole discretion of the woman involved; morally, nothing other than her wish in the matter is to be considered" (*VOR* 58–59)[128] Accordingly, the following year, she urged her New York readers to write to their state legislators in support of a law that would legalize abortion "when the pregnancy endangers a woman's physical or *mental* health" (*TO* 8(2) 596),[129] and in 1973 she praised the US Supreme Court decision in *Roe v. Wade* as "a great contribution to justice and to the protection of individual rights" ("Censorship: Local And Express" *PWNI* 235). She attributed the opposition to abortion and other forms of birth control to the same nihilism that she thought animated the New Left – a point she made by comparing two seemingly discordant encyclicals by Pope Paul VI.

> The so-called conservatives (speaking in religious, not political, terms) were dismayed by the encyclical *Populorum Progressio* (*On the Development of Peoples*) – which advocated global statism – while the so-called liberals hailed it as a progressive document. Now the conservatives are hailing the encyclical *Humanae Vitae* (*Of Human Life*) – which forbids the use of contraceptives – while the liberals are dismayed by it. Both sides seem to find the two documents inconsistent. But the inconsistency is theirs, not the pontiff's. The two encyclicals are strictly, flawlessly consistent in respect to their basic philosophy and ultimate goal: both come from the same view of man's nature and are aimed at establishing the same conditions for his life on earth. The first of these two encyclicals forbade ambition, the second forbids enjoyment; the first enslaved man to the physical needs of others, the second enslaves him to the physical capacities of his own body; the first damned achievement, the second damns love. (*VOR* 46–47)[130]

In Rand's analysis, each encyclical expressed a desire to reduce human beings to a pre-industrial level of existence, by tying each person to the biological actions of his own body (thus the opposition to contraception and abortion) and to a subsistence level of existence (thus the opposition to capitalism).[131] Rand's discussion highlighted an emotional parallel between the two encyclicals, which she saw as a profound hatred for human life and a longing for the Dark Ages. Her view of the motive for anti-abortionism explains the great importance she placed on the issue when judging politicians.

> Not every wrong idea is an indication of a fundamental philosophical evil in a person's convictions; the anti-abortion stand *is* such an indication. There is no room for an error of knowledge in this issue and no venal excuse: the anti-abortion stand is horrifying *because* it is non-venal – because no one has anything to gain from it and, therefore, its motive is pure ill will toward mankind." ("A Last Survey" *ARL* 4(2) 383)[132]

This last passage was written in response to Ronald Reagan's challenge to Ford for the 1976 Republican presidential nomination. Ten years earlier, Rand had regarded Reagan as a "promising public figure" who projected "consistency, clarity, and moral self-confidence" ("The Wreckage of the Consensus" *CUI* 265). She praised his strong stand against the student activists at Berkeley and, earlier, his 1964 speech endorsing Goldwater, which she cited as a model for how the latter's campaign should have been run ("It Is Earlier Than You Think" *TON* 3(12)).[133] By 1976, she objected to Reagan on several counts: she thought that he engaged in scaremongering by greatly exaggerating the Soviet Union's military capabilities, and she described his domestic policy as "a mixed economy with government controls slanted in favor of business rather than labor" ("The Moral Factor," "A Last Survey" *ARL* 4(2) 382).[134] But her strongest objection was to his stand on abortion: "A man who takes it upon himself to prescribe how others should dispose of their own lives ... has no right to pose as a defender of rights" (*ARL* 4(2) 383).[135] Responding to the "vicious nonsense of claiming that an embryo has a 'right to life'," she continued, "a piece of protoplasm has no rights – and no life in the human sense of the term ... To equate a *potential* with an *actual*, is vicious; to advocate the sacrifice of the latter to the former, is unspeakable" (*ARL* 4(2) 383).[136]

Rand was vehement in her opposition to Reagan, and to other such conservatives.[137] For example, in October of 1980, she declined an invitation to take part in a television series on conservatism, writing that "[t]his year in particular, I would be ashamed to be connected with the so-called Conservatives in any way. Their anti-abortion stand is outrageous – and so is their mixture of politics with religion" (*Letters* 666).

In an interview with *The Atlanta Journal-Constitution* from that same month, she explained that the mixing of religion with politics amounts to "forcing religion on people at the point of a gun and destroying the intellectual freedom of your citizens."[138] She went on to describe the horrors of past theocracies and of the theocratic regime that had recently risen in Iran. The difference between these dictators and the conservatives' injection of religion into politics, she argued, is "only a matter of degree," and America is protected from the "savage" religiosity of such regimes only by rapidly eroding "remnants" of its founding philosophy.

Rather than voting for Reagan or Carter, Rand sat out the election (something she had not done since 1956). "There is a limit to the notion of voting for the lesser of two evils," she explained in "The Age of Mediocrity," her 1981 talk about the Reagan administration (*TOF* 2(3) 1).[139] Though the talk is overwhelmingly negative, she said that Reagan's economic and foreign policies would probably be an improvement over Carter's. In particular, she expressed generalized agreement with his stand that government spending and taxes needed to be cut, she agreed strongly with his increase of the defense budget, and she applauded his strong statements against the Soviets (though, she cautioned that so far they were only statements). But these positive aspects of Reagan's presidency were "short-term" gains; viewed from a long-term perspective, she argued, Reagan was a catastrophe.

The problem was that he had no philosophy of his own (hence "mediocrity"). Rand's contemptuous (1976) description of him as a "cheap Hollywood ham" indicates that she thought he was even less intellectual and more venal than Nixon, and on a par with Carter. But Reagan was worse than Carter both because he was thought to represent capitalism, and because of the influences that were able to prevail on the right due to his lack of intellectual leadership. During Reagan's presidency "Halloween-like creatures" who ordinarily are consigned to "the dark, unventilated corners of history" were "crawling out in the full, open moonlight," and exerting a growing influence on policy. These "creatures" were the "Moral Majority" and those who claimed to be "pro-life" on abortion. (She put both terms in scare quotes because she thought that the "Moral Majority" was neither moral nor a majority and that the "pro-life" movement hated life.)

Rand compared such conservatives to Ayatollah Khomeini, "the man who has succeeded in uniting religion with politics and establishing a religious dictatorship" (*TOF* 2(3) 2). In addition

POLITICAL AND CULTURAL COMMENTARY

to their anti-abortion stand, she criticized the conservatives for their attempts to equate religion (in the form of creationism) with science and to turn "family" into "some sort of political value or goal." She described the latter as "un-American" and a form of "mini-racism," since it amounted to placing special significance on one's lineage (*TOF* 2(3) 5).[140]

She noted that, on the issues where the conservatives were motivated by religion, they exhibited a militant self-righteousness that had previously been characteristic of the left, and their liberal opponents "argue in terms of uninspiring nonessentials" (*TOF* 2(3) 3–4, cf. 6–7). Each side, Rand thought, was most vigorous with respect to the issues on which it was (by her lights) worst, because these were the issues on which its position was most consistent with the philosophy of irrationalism and self-sacrifice to which both sides (in one form or another) subscribed. The logical consequence of this philosophy is dictatorship, and Rand saw the "militant mystics" on the right and their equivalents on the left as hastening the country's movement in that direction.

If one is to defend freedom, Rand had always argued, one must begin by defending reason, and she predicted that Reagan's legacy would be to make the fight for freedom harder by associating the advocacy of capitalism with the anti-intellectuality of religion (*TOF* 2(3)).

The American Sense of Life

As we have seen, Rand held that political trends are determined by philosophical ideas, and that America's intellectuals espoused evil ideas that were leading the nation toward dictatorship. Yet the nation did not descend into dictatorship, and Rand did not expect it to do so ("Don't Let it Go" *PWNI* 290). The force saving America, she thought, was its "Sense of Life." Onkar Ghate discusses the concept of a "sense of life" as it pertains to an individual in Chapter 8; for our present purposes it is sufficient to say that it is the equivalent of an inarticulate philosophy held in emotional terms as a characteristic response to (and way of approaching) the world. Each individual has a unique sense of life – "the individual style of a unique, unrepeatable, irreplaceable consciousness" ("Philosophy and Sense of Life" *RM* 22) – but there are commonalities between individuals' senses of life that enable us to speak of groups of people sharing a more generic sense of life. The sense of life of a nation is the worldview that is embodied in and transmitted through a people's characteristic lifestyle (as distinct from its intellectual culture), and it is "the source of what we observe as 'national characteristics'" (*PWNI* 281). It is shared by the majority of the members of a nation, though (of course) not by everyone, nor by everyone to the same degree.

Rand's most detailed discussion of the American sense of life is in her 1971 article, "Don't Let It Go."[141] There she explains it by contrasting Americans and Europeans. Whereas a typical European regards himself as a servant of the state, a typical American sees himself as "an independent entity" and will not tolerate "being pushed around." Europeans are class conscious, venerating aristocrats and political leaders and looking down on working people who are regarded (by themselves and others) as "the masses."[142] Americans, by contrast, view themselves and one another as individuals. They strive to improve their lives through productive achievement, and they admire such achievements in others. Thus, when they "feel respect for their public figures, it is the respect of equals; they feel that a government official is a human being, just as they are, who has chosen this particular line of work and has earned a certain distinction" (*PWNI* 283). Whereas a typical European keeps to his prescribed place, seeing the course

385

of his life as determined by forces beyond his control, a typical American has an optimistic, can-do, self-determining approach to life; he takes the initiative, assuming new responsibilities and charting new courses. As a result Americans are characteristically happy, benevolent, and proud. Europeans, by contrast, feel helpless, resigned, and guilty, and many of them are prone to the emotion of envy, which is uncommon in America.

The event that she thought most crystalized the American sense of life was the public reaction to the Apollo missions. Rand saw the missions as presenting "the concretized abstraction of man's greatness" ("Apollo 11" VOR 166).[143] Rand observed that the American people reacted with their characteristic pride, benevolence, and optimism. But she noted that this reaction was not unanimous: many prominent intellectuals characterized this enthusiasm for science and technology as hubris ("Apollo and Dionysus" ROTP 102–104, cf. "Epitaph for a Culture" VOR 157–158). Rand thought these differing responses to a stupendous illustration of reason's power revealed the fundamental gulf between the American people and American intellectuals: the people valued and were inspired by reason and achievement, but the intellectuals held that reason was impotent and saw human beings as sacrificial objects. This fundamentally un-American philosophy had dominated the universities and cultural institutions of the world across the twentieth century, and had caused the growth of statism.

Unlike the European people (especially the Eastern Europeans) who had accepted dictatorship, the American people rejected statism whenever they were presented with an unambiguous choice. It was the American sense of life that Rand thought had turned most Americans against the authoritarian Democrats by the late 1960s. It led the country to be horrified by the violence of the New Left and to vehemently reject McGovern in 1972.[144] She argued that the American sense of life made it impossible for a dictatorship to take hold in the near future; and she predicted that, in the decades to come, it would lead Americans to reject demands by Environmentalists to give up "progress, technology, the automobile, and their standard of living" (PWNI 289).

But the American sense of life could not prevent Americans from embracing more subtly anti-American ideas and from accepting statism in small increments, which is just what Rand thought the country had done across the twentieth century. Emotional, sense-of-life reactions are insufficient guides for a person or a nation, and intellectual leadership would be needed to reverse the course along which the nation was headed. Without such leadership, this sense of life would erode as Americans were bombarded by a hostile intellectual culture and became acclimated to an ever less-free way of life.

What Americans desperately needed, in Rand's view, was "the words to name their achievement, the concepts to identify it, the principles to guide it" (PWNI 285). These are the words that Rand herself sought to give to her adopted country and to people everywhere in the world who share the values America represents. In her novels she dramatized the "concept of man as a heroic being, with his own happiness as the moral purpose of his life, with productive achievement as his noblest activity, and reason as his only absolute" (Atlas 1171–1172). In these same novels and in her theoretical essays, she articulated the philosophical principles required for such a life. And in the many pieces we discussed in this chapter, she applied these principles to the political concretes of her time. Rand saw herself as the first of the "new intellectuals" America needed to correct its course and live up to its potential, and she was alert to signs of her own influence in the culture.

In her (1968) introduction to the 25th Anniversary edition of The Fountainhead, she cited as one cause of the novel's "lasting appeal" that it is one of the "very few guideposts" for young people seeking "a noble vision of man's nature and of life's potential" (*Fountainhead* xiii). She thought that the novel had become a classic in part because it was one of the few forces in a hostile culture that reinforced the American sense of life and helped young people to understand and appreciate the best within themselves. Undoubtedly she thought the same of *Atlas Shrugged*.

Rand's most explicit statement of her own contribution to the political and cultural developments of her time comes at the end of "Cultural Update," a 1978 talk in which she revisits each of the topics that she had addressed at the Ford Hall Forum since her first appearance there in 1961. Her conclusion to the talk will also serve as a fitting conclusion for our survey of her topical writings.

> Well, that's my record at the Ford Hall Forum.
>
> What conclusions do I draw from it? First, a confirmation of what I knew before I started: that the heart of the battle lies in philosophy. Observe the variety of the issues I discussed; observe that they varied only in journalistic detail; in essence, they remained the same. Whether you fight the New Deal or the New Frontier or the hippies or the ecologists, the enemy is still mysticism-altruism-collectivism-statism; and you must know how to recognize them. The only cause worth living and fighting for is reason-egoism-individualism-capitalism. Nothing less can win.
>
> Second, seventeen years is a long time in the life of a person, but it's only a moment – a very brief moment in history. So I am happy to be able to see the reassertion and, possibly, the rebirth of the American spirit. Historically, it was a very rapid development.
>
> Third, do I take any credit for it? Yes, some. Objectivism is the only philosophy that gives a clear, theoretical direction out of today's vacuum.
>
> Fourth, what do we do next? I don't think it is up to me any longer. It is up to you. ("Cultural Update")[145]

Notes

1 [Note by Gregory Salmieri: John David Lewis passed away in January of 2012. He had completed two substantial drafts of this chapter. Shortly before his death, he and I agreed that I would either do the necessary work to complete the chapter myself or select someone else to do so, and that I would decide how best to credit the chapter. I had initially hoped to revise the chapter only lightly and to publish it under John's name alone, but as work proceeded on the other chapters in this volume, it became clear that, because of the paucity of secondary literature on Rand's topical articles and the close connections between these articles and the topics treated elsewhere in this volume, the book would profit from a lengthier treatment of Rand's topical writing than Allan Gotthelf and I had initially commissioned from John, so Allan and I decided that it was best for me to expand and reorganize the piece, and to list myself as a second-author. The present version is approximately twice the length of John's draft. Accordingly much of the chapter did not have the benefit of his direct input, and I should be held solely responsible for any errors or shortcomings it may have. However, John's initial drafts and his research deserve much of the credit for the strengths of this chapter – including those portions of it which John did not himself compose. Benjamin Bayer also deserves a great deal of credit for additional research, suggestions as to the chapter's structure, and many formulations that I have incorporated into the present version. Shoshana Milgram, with her encyclopedic knowledge of Rand's life, was invaluable in supplying biographical context for some of Rand's topical knowledge. If John were still with us, I am sure he would join me in thanking Ben, Shoshana, and several other mutual friends whose input (in one form or another) has improved this chapter: Allan Gotthelf, Onkar Ghate, Mike Berliner, Gena Gorlin, David Hayes, Mike Mazza, Robert Mayhew, and Karen Salmieri.]

2 On the editorial policy of Rand's periodicals see pages 3 and 32 in this volume. In addition to recommending particular books and articles, Rand recommended three periodicals edited by students of her philosophy that dealt with political subjects. See "A Recommendation" *TON* 4(12); cf. *CUI* 266 for

her recommendation of *Persuasion* (edited by Joan Kennedy Taylor) based on the contents of its 1965 issues, and see "The Sanction of the Victim" *VOR* 156–157 for her recommendations of *The Objectivist Forum* (edited by Harry Binswanger, with Rand and then Leonard Peikoff serving as philosophical consultants) and *The Intellectual Activist* (edited by Peter Schwartz). We occasionally reference articles from these works below because they provide some indirect evidence for Rand's opinions on certain issues, but unlike articles written under her editorship, they should not be regarded as authoritative sources for her views.

3 Regarding pre-Soviet Russia, Rand would later write: "the Czarist regime was a rotten form of absolutism which was falling apart and Russia was moving slowly in the direction of Capitalism and freedom. The Communists threw it back in the form of slavery and savagery infinitely more vicious than any known in recorded history" (*Letters* 462–463). On the state of life in the USSR, see (in addition to the novel) *Speaking* 3–7. See also Rand's discussion of the White Army in "The Lessons of Vietnam" *VOR* 138–140. The state of Russia in this period is also discussed at length in the *Biographical Interviews*.

4 The description of the novel as the "*Uncle Tom's Cabin* of Soviet Russia" originated with her friend Gouverneur Morris; but Rand quotes it approvingly as expressing her intention.

5 Peikoff distinguishes between collectivism and statism, defining "collectivism" as "the theory that ... the collective ... is *the unit of reality and the standard of value*" (*Parallels* 17, cf. *OPAR* 362) and statism as the "concentration of power in the state at the expense of individual liberty" (*Parallels* 16, cf. *OPAR* 369). Rand's usage of the terms generally reflects this distinction, but since she thought that collectivism (on a societal scale) invariably leads to statism, she often uses the terms interchangeably. (See, e.g., "Introducing Objectivism" *Column* 4, and *Letters* 126.)

6 Her view that these ideologies are interchangeable is illustrated by a revision she made in the 1950s to her play *Think Twice* (*Plays*). The original version (*Papers* 56_01A_01), written durring World War II, features a character, Emil Reiner, who is revealed to be a Nazi spy. Since that would have no longer been contemporary in the 1950s, Reiner is replaced in the revised version by Serge Sookin, a Russian who is revealed to be a Soviet spy. The two characters' actions and motives are identical.

7 On Rand's difficulties finding a publisher for *We the Living*, see Ralston 2012. On the role of Communists in this, see esp. 163–165; Britting 2004, 47; and Burns 2009, 34–37. See also Ralston 2007, esp. 66. For Rand's analysis in 1940 of the contemporary intellectual and literary establishment, including its antipathy to the "the mind" and why "most of our editors and literary authorities are Red," see *Letters* 48–51 (cf. 55). This analysis is dramatized by Ellsworth Toohey's activities throughout *The Fountainhead*.

8 For some of Rand's comments on Roosevelt's domestic policy, see "Man's Rights," *VOS/CUI*; cf. B. Branden's review of *The Roosevelt Myth*, *TON* 1(12) 54. On his foreign policy, see "The Chickens' Homecoming" *ROTP* 41–50, and "Preview" *ARL* 1(23) 102. Rand later wrote that Herbert Hoover had "opened the way for the welfare-state policies of President Roosevelt" ("The Dead End" *ARL* 1(21) 85; cf. "The Property Status of Airwaves" *CUI* 135–136, "It Is Earlier Than You Think" *TON* 3(12) 52). It is worth noting that Rand was not opposed to Roosevelt when he first ran in 1932; in fact she voted for him in that election, because of his stand against prohibition (*Biographical Interviews* 487 on which, cf. n. 117, below).

9 Willkie objected to the New Deal's "excesses" while endorsing such measures as collective bargaining laws, minimum wages, and social security (Barnard 1966, 206). After losing the election he disavowed his more pro-capitalist statements (Willkie 1943). For Rand's view of him, see *Letters* 308–309, 326, 328–329, 472, and *Answers* 57–58. For her (more positive) view of the Willkie Clubs, see *Letters* 102, 154–155.

10 For more on "The Individualist Manifesto," see *Letters* 45; Britting 2005, 70–80; and Burns 2009, 60–64. Part of this piece was published in *Reader's Digest* (Jan. 1944) as "The Only Path to Tomorrow" and can now be found under that title in *Column*. (The version in *Column* removes some alterations made by the editors of *Reader's Digest*.)

11 "The Only Path to Tomorrow" *Column* 114, cf. "The Only Path to Tomorrow" *Journals* 154–155.

12 The quoted material is from the MPA's "Statement of Principles," which was widely disseminated at the time (Mayhew 2005c, 82; Critchlow 2009, 145). Prominent members of the MPA included "Gary

Cooper, Barbara Stanwyck, Adolphe Menjou, Ward Bond, King Vidor, Clark Gable, Irene Dunne, Spencer Tracy, John Wayne, and Walt Disney" (Watts 2001, 240).

13 The "Screen Guide" was published by the MPA as a pamphlet without Rand's byline in 1947. It is now available in *Journals* (356–367). On the subtle ways in which films can convey ideological messages, see also "An Analysis of the Proper Approach to a Picture on the Atomic Bomb" (*Journals* 312–326) and her letters to Cecil B. DeMille and Walt Disney concerning the value of a film adaptation of *Anthem* (*Letters* 316–317).

14 On the criminal activities of the Communist Party of the USA and its members, see Klehr and Haynes 1998.

15 Cf. Mayhew 2005c, 84–93. On private blacklists and government investigation of subversion; see also "The Disenfranchisement of the Right" *ARL* 1(6) 27.

16 In later years Rand was contemptuous of conservative groups, such as the John Birch Society, which held such conspiratorial views. See "Bootleg Romanticism" *TON* 4(1) 3, "Brothers, You Asked For It!" *ARL* 2(15) 191, "The Energy Crisis" *ARL* 3(4) 261, *Letters* 621–622, and *Speaking* 24. Cf. Joyce Jones "Where's the Mainstream?" *Persuasion* 1(2); Elenore Boddy "Who and What is the John Birch Society?" and Joan Kennedy Taylor "How Not to Write a Book" *Persuasion* 2(3); David J. Dawson "A Red Under Every Bed" *Persuasion* 2(9).

17 Rand was writing to Leonard Read about his new organization, the Foundation for Economic Education (FEE). Rand served as an informal advisor for FEE during much of its first year, but broke with the organization in September after it published *Roofs* or *Ceilings*, a pamphlet by Milton Friedman and George Stigler, which Rand described (at the time) as "the most pernicious thing ever issued by an avowedly conservative organization" (*Letters* 320). See Onkar Ghate's treatment of this issue, 238, above.

18 As a result of this withdrawal from political activity, she said and wrote very little about the Truman and Eisenhower administrations. However, her notes (*Journals* 407) reveal that Truman was the model for "Mr. Thompson," the vicious, mealy-mouthed "Head of State" in *Atlas Shrugged*. Her assessment of Eisenhower is revealed by her statement (in a 1976 question period) that she abstained from the 1952 and 1956 elections, on the grounds both candidates were evil (*Answers* 69). Her statements about him in the *Biographical Interviews* (545–546) make clear that she regarded him as a compromiser whose nomination "destroyed the possibility of an opposition" to government controls on the economy.

19 Rand's regular column in *The Objectivist Newsletter* was titled "Check Your Premises," after a piece of advice given by Hugh Akston and Francisco d'Anconia in *Atlas* (199, 331, 489, 618, 737, 807). Francisco is also the source for the titles "Account Overdrawn" *TON* 1(7), "The Moratorium on Brains" *ARL* 1(2-3), and "Brothers, You Asked For It!" *ARL* 2(14–15) (see *Atlas* 413, 496, 551, 567, 925). Other articles with Atlas-based titles include: "The Pull Peddlers" *TON* 1(9) (*Atlas* 9912) and "The Sanction of the Victims" *TOF* 3(2) (*Atlas* 454, 461). For further examples, see nn. 101 and 141, below.

20 "Faith and Force: The Destroyers of the Modern World" (*PWNI*), "Conservatism: An Obituary" (*CUI*), "The Intellectual Bankruptcy of Our Age" (*VOR*), and "For the New Intellectual" (*FNTI*). See also the opening paragraphs of "The Objectivist Ethics" (*VOS*), which was written in this same period, and "Notes on The History of American Free Enterprise" (*CUI*), which were written during her work on *Atlas*. In addition to these readily available sources, Rand gave a series of four talks (jointly titled "Our Cultural Vacuum") on WBAI radio in 1960: "The Moral Vacuum," "The Philosophical Vacuum," "The Esthetic Vacuum," and "The New Intellectual." Manuscripts or typescripts for all four talks can be found in *Papers* 103_01x, 104_08a, 104_08b and 105_15a.

21 On Rand's relation to the Enlightenment, see also 273–278, above.

22 Cf. *Speaking* 172–173, "Notes on the History of American Free Enterprise" *CUI*. On Rand's understanding of capitalism, see Chapters 8 and 10 above.

23 When Rand speaks of the capitalism of nineteenth-century America, she always has in mind the Northern states and not "the agrarian, non-industrial, *non-capitalist* states of the South, where the state governments upheld the institution of slavery" ("The Intellectual Bankruptcy of Our Age" *VOR* 96). On the extent to which nineteenth-century Europe was capitalist, see *Letters* 464.

24 See Robert Hessen's "The Effects of the Industrial Revolution on Women and Children" *CUI* for Rand's position on the common charge that the Industrial Revolution led to miserable living conditions for workers.

25 For elaboration, see Chapter 6, above, especially 136–141.

26 On the causes of decline of nineteenth-century liberalism, see also *Marginalia* 148.

27 Cf. "The Monument Builders" *VOS* and "The Left: Old and New" *ROTP* 168. By "socialist England" Rand refers to the Labor Party government which came to power after World War II and proceeded to nationalize England's major industries and utilities, centrally control its economy, and establish a range of welfare programs including the National Health Service.

28 "America's Persecuted Minority: Big Business" *CUI* 57, "Antitrust: The Rule of Unreason" *TON* 1(2), and her reviews of Harold Fleming's *Ten Thousand Commandments TON* 1(4) and Lowell Mason's *The Language of Dissent TON* 2(8). Cf. Joan Kennedy Taylor "The Emperor Must Sell His New Clothes" *Persuasion* 2(7).

29 On Rand's view of objective and non-objective law, see Chapter 9.

30 "America's Persecuted Minority: Big Business" *CUI* 61, "Antitrust: The Rule of Unreason" *TON* 1(2) 6. (The content of the two pieces overlaps considerably.)

31 "Freedom of Speech" and "Government by Intimidation" *Column*; "The New Enemies of the Untouchables" *TON* 1(8), "Vast Quicksands" *TON* 2(7), "The Property Status of Airwaves" *TON* 3(4). Cf. "Man's Rights" (*VOS/CUI*) and "The Fascist New Frontier" *Column* 105–109. Censorship and related issues again became a prominent topic in Rand's writings in the 1970s. See: "Censorship: Local and Express" *ARL* 2(23–25), "Thought Control" *ARL* 2(26)–3(2), "Ideas vs. Goods" *ARL* 3(11), "Ideas vs. Men" *ARL* 3(15). There are also several pieces on censorship in periodicals Rand recommended: "Deregulation Comes to Broadcasting" *TIA* 1(1); "New Frontier for the FCC" *TIA* 1(6); "FCC Shows Its Powers" *TIA* 1(9); "The First Amendment and the SEC" *TIA* 1(16); "Minds and Guns" *TIA* 2(1); "Airwave Deregulation" *TIA* 2(1)3.

32 Ronald Sullivan, "Hagerty Defends Hiss TV Interview" *New York Times*, Nov. 16, 1962; cf. Murray Illson, "Network Rejects Protest Over Hiss" *New York Times*, Nov. 15, 1962; "Sponsor Drops Ads on A.B.C. Over Hiss" *New York Times*, Dec. 1, 1962. Rand briefly discussed this incident in "Freedom of Speech" *Column* 70.

33 C.P. Trussell, "House Prepares Inquiry on Press; Groundwork Is Being Laid to Cover Broad Field" *New York Times*, July 15, 1962, 27 (Quoted in "Government By Intimidation" *Column*).

34 On the passage of the Sherman Act by a Republican Congress, see "America's Persecuted Minority" *CUI* 51 and "The Fascist New Frontier" *Column* 109–110. Rand attributed the Radio Act largely to the influence of Herbert Hoover, who fought for it in his capacity as Secretary of Commerce under Calvin Coolidge ("The Property Status of Airwaves" *CUI* 135–136).

35 Sometimes Rand was more specific, describing the system toward which America was heading as "guild socialism" – i.e., the control of industry by government-empowered guilds or interest groups (*CUI* 245–246; cf. "The Cashing-in" *CUI* 297–298/*ROTP* 32–33). This system was briefly promoted under this name in early twentieth-century England by the Fabian socialists. Rand, following von Mises (1951 II.III.15.6 and 1949 XXXIII.4), held that this was the same system that had been implemented in Italy by Mussolini, who called it "corporatism" or "corporativism." Cf. Avis Brick "Review: The Democrat's Dilemma" *Persuasion* 1(5) and "Review: Reason, Irrationality, and Kennedy's Method" *Persuasion* 2(8).

36 On Medicare, see: "How Not to Fight against Socialized Medicine" *TON* 2(3) and Peikoff's "Doctors and the Police State" *TON* 1(6) Special Supplement. See also Judith Kroeger's interview with Bruce Henricksen in *Persuasion* 2(4) 1–8. On the Kefauver–Harris Amendment, see: "Who Will Protect Us from Our Protectors?" *TON* 1(5). Articles on healthcare in periodicals Rand recommended include: "Vital Statistics" *Persuasion* 2(2); "Further Notes on Medicare" *Persuasion* 2(7); Judith Kroeger, R.N. "Health Care" *Persuasion* 2(12); Aubrey T. Robinson "The Role of the Government in Public Health" *Persuasion* 4(10); Llewellyn Rockwell "The Health Hazard of Government-Controlled Medicine" *TIA* 1(8), 1(10); "The New Health Planners" *TIA* 1(19).

37 "Account Overdrawn," Rand's article on the crash, shares its title with *Atlas* Part II, Ch. 5. The titular phrase first appears earlier in the novel, in a speech on "the meaning of money" that Francisco d'Anconia makes before instigating a panic that causes a stock market crash (413).

38 On anti-ideology and the related idea of an "anti-concept," see, in this volume 298. On Kant, see 11, 294, and 332–334. For mentions of anti-ideology in Johnson and Nixon, respectively, see "The New Fascism: Rule by Consensus" *CUI* 228 and "The Moratorium on Brains" *ARL* 1(3) 13. For mentions of pre-Kennedy anti-concepts see her discussions of "isolationism" in "'Extremism,' or The Art of Smearing" *CUI* 193–194 and "The Lessons of Vietnam" *ARL* 3(24) 364, and of "McCarthyism," also in "'Extremism,' or The Art of Smearing" *CUI* 194–195.

39 "How To Judge a Political Candidate" *TON* 3(3), "The Argument From Intimidation" *TON* 3(7), "'Extremism,' or the Art of Smearing" *TON* 3(9), "Special Note" *TON* 3(10), and "It's Earlier Than You Think" *TON* 3(12). To these we can add two pieces that do not mention the election as such but address the issues that she saw as essential to it: "The Anatomy of Compromise" *TON* 3(1) and "The Cult of Moral Grayness" *TON* 3(6). See also *Speaking* 18–19, 23–29.

40 Rand did not write on Kennedy's assassination as such, but in an interview she referred to Lee Harvey Oswald as "a monstrous criminal" (*Speaking* 71), and she is reported to have responded as follows to a questioner who implied that, given her view of the president, she should not be upset about his assassination: "This is America. This is not the way we do away with presidents. We vote. We do not kill people" (McConnell 2010, 177).

41 Rockefeller's remarks were made in a speech ("Call For a Unified Republican Party in the 1964 Election") at the Republican National Convention on July, 21 1963 and in a television interview on *Meet The Press* on September 15 of the same year. The claim that the "extremists" supported segregation was largely based on "The Southern strategy" – the idea that a conservative candidate could win the presidency by carrying the South (which had been consistently Democratic for decades), even if he loses in the Northeast and California (which no Republican was likely to carry). Rockefeller characterized the strategy as an attempt to "erect political power on the outlawed and immoral base of segregation." It was widely thought that Goldwater would appeal to Southern segregationists because he objected (on constitutional grounds) to some of the measures taken by the federal government to promote integration – most notably the Civil Rights Act of 1964. (See, e.g., Stewart Alsop, "Can Goldwater Win in 64?" *The Saturday Evening Post*, Aug. 24, 1963, 19–25.) Supporters of the strategy argued that it was not resentment over integration but a growing middle class that made the South a potential base for conservatives, and they argued that the lack of a serious Republican challenge in the South made it easy for the Democrats to avoid dealing with the disagreement over segregation within their party. (See, for example, William Rusher, "Crossroads for the GOP," *National Review*, February 12, 1963, 110.) We discuss Rand's view of these racial issues below, 371–373.

42 The exchange began with a letter (dated May 11, 1960) in which Goldwater thanked her for defending "my conservative position" on a recent episode of the Mike Wallace show. An episode featuring Rand did air in the first week of May, and no tape of it survives, but a script of Wallace's questions for the interview indicates that he asked her about contemporary conservatives (Mike Wallace Papers, Box 8, Syracuse University Library). Burns (2009, 190), who describes this interview as Rand's "network television debut" and writes that "Rand had not mentioned the senator by name," has evidently confused this interview with Rand's 1959 appearance on Wallace's show (footage of which is widely available).

Rand's favorable opinion of Goldwater is also reported in the August 4, 1960 edition of *Human Events* (324). And she answered some questions about him after a 1961 lecture (*Answers* 58–59) and encouraged people to support his nomination in a radio interview (*Speaking* 18–19) that must have been recorded sometime between September 19, 1963 (when Goldwater made a speech before Congress on the Nuclear Test Ban Treaty) and July 16, 1964 (when the Republican convention was held).

43 In an earlier piece ("A Suggestion" *TON* 2(10)), she was more specific in her praise of his foreign policy, singling out his speech opposing the Nuclear Test Ban Treaty (Goldwater 1963, cf. *Playboy Interview* 42) and his stance on Cuba, by which she presumably meant his view that the US should train Cuban exiles who sought to overthrow Castro, but that the US should not commit troops to any such effort ("Goldwater Urges Aid to Cuba Exiles: Says U.S. Should Support Efforts to Oust the Reds" *New York Times*, Sept. 9, 1963, L23).

44 "How to Judge a Political Candidate" *TON* 3(3) 12, "'Extremism,' or The Art of Smearing" *TON* 3(9) 39–40, and "The Argument from Intimidation" *TON* 3(7). See also *Speaking* 23–29.

JOHN DAVID LEWIS AND GREGORY SALMIERI

45 The key ideas were also part of a "confidential" essay Rand wrote for Hal Wallis concerning "The Proper Approach to a Picture on the Atomic Bomb" (*Journals* 312–326, esp. 315–316).

46 There are several pieces on Goldwater and the 1964 election in periodicals Rand recommended: "Goldwater's Record on Labor" *Persuasion* 1(2); and "It Makes Sense" and Lois Roberts "Review: The Goldwater Girls" *Persuasion* 1(3), "The Republican Dilemma" *Persuasion* 1(5); Avis Brick "The Making of a Loser" *Persuasion* 2(5); and "Price Controls" *TIA* (1)10.

47 "Cultural Update," "The Wreckage of the Consensus" *CUI*, "The American Spirit" *ARL* 2(4). See also Harry Binswanger "The Swing to the Right" *TOF* 1(1), published alongside Rand's recommendation of the periodical.

48 For Rand's view of some of the particular programs that constituted Johnson's "War on Poverty," see her review of Shirley Scheibla's *Poverty Is Where the Money Is* in *TO* 7(8). Cf. the following pieces in periodicals Rand recommended: "Alice in Johnsonland," Joyce Jones "Where's the Mainstream?" and Avis Brick "Reviews: Why Not Defeat?" *Persuasion* 1(2); "New Deal, Fair Deal, and Now, Big Deal" and "Here We Go Round the Government Bush" *Persuasion* 1(3); "How to Build the Great Society (Or, Let the Government Do It) New York Edition" and "We, the Industrious" *Persuasion* 1(5); "Give Till It Hurts" *Persuasion* 2(1).

49 See, for example, Louis Koenig "The Hard Limits," *New York Times*, March 7, 1965, 193, 309, 352, 353.

50 See: "The Pull Peddlers" *CUI*, "The New Fascism: Rule by Consensus" *CUI* 231–232, "Credibility and Polarization" *ARL* 1(1) 3, "… and the Principles" *ARL* 2(21) 221–222, "A Nation's Unity" *ARL* 2(4) 132, "Fairness Doctrine for Education" *PWNI* 258–259, and "The Age of Envy" *ROTP* 142. Cf. Avis Brick's "Cultural Trends" *TO* 7(6) 476. Related pieces in publications Rand recommended include: "Guilty Until Proven Guilty," and Lois Roberts "Labor Legislation: The Shop That Government Built" *Persuasion* 2(8), Joan Kennedy Taylor "Right to Work Revisited" *Persuasion* 2(10) and "An Interview with Lowell B. Mason" *Persuasion* 3(6), Joyce Jones "Was Free Enterprise Ever Free?" *Persuasion* 3(7) and 3(9); also, "Cutting Down the FTC," "Standing Up to the FTC," and "Paternalism at the FTC" *TIA* 1(2), 1(5), and 1(10). For discussions of the effects of a mixed economy on the energy markets, see "Oil, Profits, and Demagoguery" and "Demagoguery, Part 2" *TIA* 1(3); "Energy Mobilization Board" *TIA* 1(6); "Gasoline Rationing" *TIA* 1(7); "Oil and Inflation" *TIA* 1(13); "Businessmen and Capitalism" *TIA* 1(14); George Reisman "An Open Letter to President Carter" *TIA* 1(1), 1(3), 1(5); and Herb Schmertz "An Energy Story the Press Hasn't Told" along with the editor's "A Reply to Herb Smertz" *TIA* 1(4) and "Postscript to Herb Schmertz" *TIA* 1(5).

51 For some of Rand's early criticism of Nixon, see *Playboy Interview* 42. As context for Rand's more positive view of Nixon in 1968, see "The Wreckage of the Consensus" *CUI* 250, where she describes George Romney (father of Mitt) as "an unformed, soft-shelled thing" whom some Republicans favored as a 1968 presidential candidate – on Romney, cf. her 1965 article, "The Obliteration of Capitalism" *CUI*.

52 Her article on the freeze, "The Moratorium on Brains" *ARL* 1(2–3), takes its name from Francisco d'Anconia's description of the Directive (*Atlas* 551). The phrase is also used as the title of *Atlas* Part II, Ch. 7, where Rand discusses "what such a system does to men's psychology" ("The Moratorium on Brains" *ARL* 1(3) 14). See Onkar Ghate's discussion in Chapter 10, above, on Rand's view that economic regulation stifles the mind. See "… and the Principles" *ARL* 2(21) 222 for Rand's discussion of the specific effects of Nixon's freeze.

53 On the guaranteed minimum income see "Fairness Doctrine for Education" *PWNI* 276 and "The Dead End" *ARL* 1(20) 85; on foreign policy, see "The Shanghai Gesture" *ARL* 1(13–15), "Hunger and Freedom" *ARL* 3(22), and *Answers* 99, where she responds to a question about her discussion of Henry Kissinger; on the energy crisis, see "The Energy Crisis" *ARL* 3(4–5).

54 On Nixon's appointment of William Rehnquist and the controversy surrounding it, see "The Disenfranchisement of the Right" *ARL* 1(6).

55 See "Censorship: Local and Express" *ARL* 2(23–25), "Thought Control" *ARL* 2(26)–3(2) and "Ideas v. Goods" *ARL* 3(11).

56 "Brothers, You Asked for It!" *ARL* 2(14–15); "The Principals …" and "… and the Principles" *ARL* 2(19–21), and "Postscript" to Peikoff's "Pragmatism vs. America" *ARL* 3(17).

57 Rand's few comments about World War I can be found in "The Roots of War" (CUI 33), "The Wreckage of the Consensus" (CUI 257), "The Intellectual Bankruptcy of Our Age" (VOR 97-98), and "What is Romanticism" (RM 112). She had more to say on World War II, though she wrote little about it. Her position at the time of the 1940 election (though she did not voice it publicly at the time) was that America should not even send aid to the Allies, because doing so would draw the nation into the war, and she faulted Willkie for not taking this stand, which, she thought, would have been enormously popular with voters (*Biographical Interviews* 494-496, cf. 350-351) She later held that the primary beneficiaries of America's involvement in the war were the Soviets. (See the sources cited in n. 61, below.) For an indication of how and why Rand thought Roosevelt's policies caused the Japanese attack on Pearl Harbor (and so America's entry into the war), see Peikoff's brief discussion of this issue in *Parallels* (272-273). Other comments on World War II can be found in "The Shanghai Gesture" *ARL* 1(13) 57, "The Lessons of Vietnam" *VOR* 142, "The Roots of War" *CUI*, Rand's testimony before the HUAC (*Journals* 378-381), and her notes for the film project *Top Secret* (*Journals* 311-344).

58 Rand was also naturally opposed to the commitment to global altruism implied by America's foreign aid policies (*Answers* 92-93). Interestingly she also saw the "idealistic" altruistic justification for foreign aid merging with pragmatic "realist" justification for the policy based on appeasing likely targets for Communist takeovers. Her article "The Pull Peddlers" (*CUI*) is an exposé of the role of the pragmatically defined concept of "the public interest" in foreign lobby for American aid money. See "Hunger and Freedom" *ARL* 3(22) and "Cashing In On Hunger" *ARL* 3(23) for a discussion of these issues in the context of the foreign policy of the 1970s.

59 Rand maintained that the only two nations that needed and deserved foreign aid were Israel and Taiwan, in order to protect US interests in the Middle East and the Pacific ("The Shanghai Gesture" *ARL* 1(14)). And though she thought the Soviet threat was exaggerated, she still advocated advanced military preparedness in the face of it (*Answers* 88-89).

60 Rand elaborates on this point in the abstract and in connection to foreign policy in "The Anatomy of Compromise" *TON* 3(1) 4.

61 On Russia's dependence on American aid and diplomatic support, see Keller 1962 (which was recommended by Rand in "Let Us Alone!" *CUI* 155 and positively reviewed by Edith Efron in *TON* 1(11)), Crocker 1961 (reviewed by Beatrice Hessen in *TON* 3(1)), Sutton 1968 (reviewed by Robert Hessen in *TO* 9(1)), and von Mises 1951, 555-556 (which is included in *CUI*'s bibliography of recommended readings). See "Ayn Rand Comments" *TIA* 1(8) for her advocacy of a boycott of the 1980 Olympics, which were held in Moscow; see also, in that issue, Peter Schwartz's "Moscow Olympics."

62 On the UN, see: "Don't Let It Go" *ARL* 1(5) 20, "The Anatomy of Compromise" *CUI* 161-162, and "The Shanghai Gesture" *ARL* 1(14), where Rand also condemned the UN for the expulsion of Nationalist China, a "Charter Member" and "friend of the United States," in favor of Red China, which gained power by force and held it by terror. Cf. Joyce Jones "Black is White and Red All Over" *Persuasion* 2(1).

63 Dated November 11, 1962.

64 Dated December 9, 1962. Cf. *Answers* 86.

65 See also "The Chickens' Homecoming" *ROTP* and *Speaking* 70-71, 195-197. Cf. Joan Kennedy Taylor "Vietnam: The Past," "Vietnam: Part II Communists and Communist Fronts," and "Vietnam: Part III Uncle Sam Knows Best" *Persuasion* 4(11-12), 5(1).

66 On the term "isolationism," see "'Extremism,' Or the Art of Smearing" *CUI* 193-194.

67 *Answers* 92-93; "The Chickens' Homecoming" *ROTP* 148-149, "Brothers, You Asked for It!" *ARL* 2(15) 194, and "The Lessons of Vietnam" *VOR* 148.

68 In a (never published) "Open Letter to President Truman" (*Papers* 081_03x_008), written sometime shortly after Truman's dismissal of MacArthur (on April 11, 1951), Rand argues against the Korean War via a series of 20 rhetorical questions that include all of the major objections that she would later make against the American involvement in Vietnam. Among the questions are: "Why should we fight to protect an inch in Korea, while we gave away hundreds of miles in China?" "If our military commander is not permitted to destroy the bases, the supply lines and the reinforcements of the enemy in Red China – then does this not mean that our soldiers are sent to Korea merely to stand under fire,

without the right to shoot back, in the hopes that the enemy will eventually get tired of shooting at them?" "In view of the millions of Red Chinese and Red Russians, which are regarded as mere cannon fodder by their rulers – how many American boys do you propose to sacrifice in this game, as helpless targets for these hordes?"

69 On the draft, see also "The Roots of War" *CUI* 36, and *Playboy Interview* 42.

70 In addition to the sources cited therein, see Henry Mark Holzer and Phyllis Holzer's "The Constitution and the Draft" *TO* 6(10–11). There were additional anti-draft writings in periodicals Rand recommended: "Heads I Win, Tails You Lose" *Persuasion* 3(7); "Persuasion Goes to a Party" *Persuasion* 4(7), esp. 6–7 and 10–11, 13; "The Draft" *TIA* 1(11).

71 On Taiwan, see also *Letters* 652.

72 Specifically she wrote in 1972: "Our token military presence has kept Taiwan peacefully safe for twenty-two years." In the context of the Korean War, 22 years earlier President Truman ordered the 7th Fleet to the area in order to "prevent any attack on Formosa" (as Taiwan was then called) and to "see that" the (non-communist) "Chinese Government on Formosa" complied with his "call" to "cease all air and sea operations against the mainland" (Truman, Statement of June 27, 1950). In her "open letter" to Truman the following year, Rand objected to this second role for the fleet: "Why does our fleet hold the Chinese Nationalists imprisoned on Formosa and prevent them from fighting for their own country against an imperialistic aggression?" (*Papers* 081_03x_008).

73 Rand evidently regarded this stand as an application of the same principled approach to foreign policy that lead her to oppose aid to the Allies in World War II, but since her only comments on foreign aid in 1930s and 1940s are in brief remarks not intended for publication, one can only speculate as to why she thought that America's interests required aiding these allies in the 1970s, but not aiding the British in 1940. It is probably relevant that, unlike any of the dictatorships of the 1940s, the USSR of the 1970s was armed with intercontinental ballistic missiles, and therefore was more of a credible threat to America.

74 The article's title is presumably an allusion to the 1918 Broadway play of the same name and/or the 1941 movie that was made from the play. Rand mentions the play in the *Biographical Interviews* (322), which were conducted in 1960 and 1961.

75 We do not count under this heading her view that so long as America was involved (which it should not be) in the wars in Korea or Vietnam, it ought to fight aggressively to win the war, rather than engaging in a defensive war of attrition.

76 On the Iranian revolution and hostage crisis, see also the following writings in periodicals Rand recommended: "Appeasement in Iran" *TIA* 1(8); "The US and the Shah ..." "...and the Ayatollah ...," and "... and the President" *TIA* 1(12); "America and Iran, Cont'd" *TIA* 1(15); "The Hostage Surrender" *TIA* 1(22); and M. Northrup Buechner's "The Root of Terrorism" *TOF* 2(5).

77 For an earlier discussion of collectivism as "the foundation for racial hatred," see the "Screen Guide for Americans" (*Journals* 362–363). For a later discussion of the primitive "anti-conceptual" character of racism, see "The Missing Link" *PWNI* 56–57. Discussions of racism in periodicals Rand recommended include: Joan Kennedy Taylor "The New Racism" *Persuasion* 1(3), Aubrey Thornton Robinson "'My Name is Ishmael': Some Thoughts on Racial Collectivism" *Persuasion* 3(12), esp. 170; "Tests and Racism" *TIA* 1(9), and George Reisman "Capitalism: The Cure for Racism" *TIA* 2(15–17).

78 On the Civil War, see also "Moral Inflation" *ARL* 3(14) 313 and "Theory and Practice" *CUI* 136.

Slavery is one of several features of America's history that are often cited as large-scale examples of racism, and it is the only one that Rand addressed in print. However, in a question and answer period, she was asked how she reconciled her positive view of America with "the cultural genocide of native Americans, the enslavement of black men in this country, and the relocation of Japanese Americans during World War II." Her long and wide-ranging answer can be heard at: "Philosophy: Who Needs It?" Bibliography #28, 00:50:19–01:03:56; a truncated version is in *Answers* 102–104. Her answer begins as follows: "To begin with, there is much more to America than the issue of racism. I do not believe that the issue of races, or even the persecution of a particular race, is as important as the persecution of *individuals*, because when you deprive individuals of rights – if you deprive any small group – all individuals lose their rights. Therefore, look at it fundamentally: if you are concerned with minorities, the smallest minority on Earth is an individual. If you do not respect individual rights, you will sacrifice or persecute all minorities, and then you'll get the same treatment given to a majority, which you can observe today in Soviet Russia."

Rand went on to address each of the issues in turn. We pass over what she said about slavery, since she discussed it in print (and her views are discussed above). The internment of Japanese-Americans was done by Roosevelt, whom Rand regarded as an opponent of Americanism, so she did not think that action should be held against America as such. (Incidentally, Rand employed and was friendly with a Japanese-American family that had been in the internment camps; see McConnell 2010, 87–107.)

Rand thought that Native American tribes were primitive and unjust societies that did not respect rights. Consequently, she held that anyone had the right to come in, as the European settlers had done, and set up a civilized society (just as she believed that anyone had the right to invade Communist dictatorships). "It would be wrong to attack any country (or tribe for that matter) that respects individual rights, because, if they do, you are an aggressor and you are morally wrong, if you attack them. But, if a country does not protect rights – if a given tribe is the slave of its own tribal chief, why should you respect the rights they do not have – or any country which has a dictatorship. The citizens still have individual rights, but the country does not have any rights." She held that it was primarily the Native American tribes that had violated earlier agreements with the settlers (rather than the reverse), and argued that those Native Americans who fought the settlers (rather than assimilating or living side by side with them) were fighting to continue a primitive existence of "brute stagnation and superstition."

79 Examples of Rand's condemnation of racism against blacks include her remarks on George Wallace "The Presidential Candidates, 1968" *TO* 7(6), and her response to a black fan, who wrote to her that the actions of the black leadership made him ashamed to be black (*Letters* 653–654). See also McConnell 2010, 491 on her response to an ethnic slur. On *In the Heat of the Night*, see B. Branden's review ("Cultural Barometer" *TO* 7(1) 391–395). On *Roots*, see *Answers* 208–110. Interestingly, Rand's own fiction includes few if any members of persecuted racial or ethnic minorities, even when set in environments in which such persecution was common. For example, no Jews (and so no persecution of Jews) are portrayed in *We The Living*, even though many of the characters were based on Rand's family and acquaintances, most of whom were Jewish and did suffer such persecution. (On these characters and their models see McConnell 2012 and Federman 2012). Similarly (as has often been observed), *The Fountainhead* and *Atlas Shrugged* do not contain any black characters or members of other persecuted racial minorities. The reason for this is probably that Rand thought racial distinctions and the related prejudices would distract from her themes, which were meant to be universally applicable. The race of the protagonist in *Anthem* is never indicated, and when asked about it, Rand wrote that he could be "any race – since he represents the best possible to all races of men" ("Questions and Answers on *Anthem*" *Column* 122).

80 Rand condemned "so-called 'conservatives'" who advocate racism or defend racist laws on the grounds of "states' rights" (a concept Rand rejected as a "contradiction in terms").

81 Examples of race-conscious policies that some Civil Rights leaders advocated and that Rand opposed as racist are: racial hiring quotas (on which see *VOS* 154 and *Answers* 105) and busing children to schools outside of their neighborhoods to create greater racial diversity (on which, see *Answers* 24–25). For a contemporaneous account by a student of Objectivism, see "Will Someone Please Decide?" *Persuasion* 1(3).

82 See: "The Age of Envy" *ROTP* 142–143, "Credibility and Polarization" *ARL* 1(1), "Fairness Doctrine for Education" *PWNI* 269, "Representation without Authorization *ARL* 1(21), "Moral Inflation" *ARL* 3(14) 309–310, "A Preview" *ARL* 1(23) 100, "A Nation's Unity" *ARL* 2(1), "Global Balkanization" *ROTP*.

83 Rejecting this view does not necessarily mean rejecting all aspects of traditional gender identities, and there are aspects of these identities that Rand thought were valid and valuable. In particular, she thought that, though woman and men are morally and intellectual equal, the biological differences between the sexes and the nature of the sex act lead to an asymmetry within a healthy romantic relationship. There is a sense in which the man is "dominant" and the woman "worships" him. The capacity and desire for this emotional response gives rise to femininity as a distinctive "sexual identity."

The principal published source for Rand's views on femininity is "About a Woman President" (*VOR*), in which she explains her view that a rational woman would find the job of president intolerable because it would prevent her from having any relationship with a man over whom she was not in authority. See also Nathaniel Branden's discussion of sexual identity in "Self-Esteem and Romantic Love" *TO* 7(1) 385–387. Branden and Allan Blumenthal both elaborated on these issues in lecture courses offered under Rand's auspices, but which are not generally available.

84 In this connection, it is worth mentioning that Rand's relation to the Hollywood Studio Club, an organization operated by the YWCA that provided low-cost housing and other support to young women starting careers in the motion picture industry. Rand lived at the club during her time in Hollywood, and subsequently contributed money to the organization and wrote an endorsement letter that they used in their fundraising literature (*Letters* 28, 31–33).

85 The quote is attributed to Bella Abzug in a *New York Times* article (Aug. 27, 1970, 30 L+). Rand marked it on her copy of the article.

86 The sign (part of which is quoted in *ROTP* 147) is pictured in "It Was a Great Day For Women On the March" *New York Times*, Aug. 30, 1970. For more on sex and gender by a student of Objectivism, see "The Wages of Sex" and "Neuterism: The Ultimate Egalitarianism" *TIA* 2(29).

87 Rand's objection to the misandry of Woman's Lib sets the context for two disparaging comments she made about lesbians. She criticized Woman's Lib for "proclaim[ing] spiritual sisterhood with lesbians" ("The Age of Envy" *ROTP* 149) and "join[ing] common front with lesbians and prostitutes" ("The Disenfranchisement of the Right *ARL* 1(6) 26). These are her only two comments in her own voice about homosexuality that were intended for publication (but see "Our Cultural Value Deprivation" *VOR* 111, "The Cashing In" *CUI* 270, Nathaniel Branden's "The Psychology of Pleasure" *VOS* 76, and Peikoff *Parallels* 163–164 and 291). When asked about homosexuality in a 1971 question period (some months after her first reference to lesbians), she responded: "there is a psychological immorality at the root of homosexuality," because it "it involves psychological flaws, corruptions, errors, or unfortunate premises" ("The Moratorium on Brains" Bibliography #26, starting at 1:03:30). When Rand made these remarks, the view that homosexuality was a mental disorder was the consensus among psychologists (though this would change by 1973), and it was generally assumed to be immoral.

Given Rand's moral theory, for homosexuality to be immoral it would have to be both a result of choice and detrimental to an individual's own life and happiness. She would probably have thought that a homosexual orientation was detrimental because romantic love is a crucial life-sustaining value (see 88–89, above) and she thought that an opposite-sex partner is necessary to fully realize this value. Nathaniel Branden argues briefly for this point in "Self-Esteem and Romantic Love" *TO* 7(1) 387. As for the role of choice in homosexuality, Rand held that one's thinking is under one's volitional control, and her 1971 remarks attribute homosexuality to mistakes in one's thinking. She may have thought that the relevant mistakes were sustained and perpetuated by further choices including, perhaps, the choice to act on one's homosexual desires. For an indication of the sort of initial mistakes Rand may have thought generated homosexuality, see Branden's mention of an "adolescent who flees into homosexuality because he has been taught that sex is evil and that women are to be worshipped, but not desired" ("Mental Health vs. Mysticism and Self-Sacrifice" *VOS* 47). Despite her view that homosexuality was pathological and immoral, she explained in the 1971 question period that it should be legal between "consenting adults"; she had voiced this same opinion in another question period three years earlier (*Answers* 18). Her view that homosexuality is immoral and pathological should not be taken to imply that she thought that all gays were fundamentally immoral or unhealthy. Especially in her private notes, Rand sometimes used morally condemnatory language for traits, actions, or ideas that she took to be flaws of people that (the context makes clear) she held in high regard. That she regarded homosexuality in this way is suggested by Leonard Peikoff's (2009) recollection that Rand had several friends whom she knew to be gay and some of whom she regarded as Objectivists. (Other associates of Rand's with whom we have spoken, have also mentioned these friendships.)

Sciabarra 2003, 6–44 contains some useful documentation of the attitudes within the Objectivist movement toward homosexuality, both in Rand's time and thereafter. The prevailing current view within the movement is best represented by Leonard Peikoff's (2009) statement that a homosexual relationship can be "something chosen by two people that hurts no other person, that's compatible with a rational life and that gives them both pleasure." Sex, he explains, is "one of the most crucial pleasures of life," "the premises that would lead to homosexuality or heterosexuality are formed in early childhood subconsciously" and "we have no means whatever of changing sexuality," so it would be a "monstrous position" to hold that gays "should refrain from sex for the rest of their lives."

88 A much earlier example of Rand's opposition to civil disobedience can found in her 1937 letter to the *News Herald Tribune*, which contains the sentence "Look at Michigan to see what an organized minority of unscrupulous but determined law-breakers can do" (*TIA* 10(2) 6–9/*Papers* 099_05x_003). She is almost certainly referring to the General Motors Sit-Down Strike, which was taking place while Rand wrote.

89 It should be noted that Rand was opposed to the institution of public property. Under the capitalist system she advocated, universities and roadways would be privately owned and operated, so assemblies that were not welcome by their owners would be trespasses. Because of the "contradictions" inherent in the "collectivist institution of 'public property,'" whatever policies the government adopts for its universities and roads will violate someone's rights. However, Rand held that these rights violations have to be fought through the political process, and that as a student on the campus of a public school or a traveler on a public road (rather than as a voter), one has the same sort of relationship with the school or road that one would have with a private school or road and the same obligations to respect its policies and its property (*CUI* 295/*ROTP* 29–30).

90 On Nixon, see "The Presidential Candidates, 1968" *TO* 7(6) 466 and "Brief Comments" *TO* 8(3) 609. The latter article concerns Nixon's support for the President of The University of Notre Dame in his decision to expel "anyone or any group that substitutes force for rational persuasion, be it violent or nonviolent." On Reagan, see "The Wreckage of the Consensus" *TO* 6(5) 263, where she references (though not by name) his (May 12, 1966) speech "The Morality Gap at Berkeley" (in Reagan 1968, 125–129). In a radio address delivered in May of 1968 ("The Rebellion at Columbia" Bibliography #25), Rand commended the *New York Times* (April 25, 1968) for describing student activists as hoodlums and she praised the Committee for Defense of Property Rights, a campus group organized by Columbia University students. (The group included Allan Gotthelf and Harry Binswanger, both contributors to this volume.)

91 By contrast to the anti-ideological activism of the conformist "rebels," Rand praised dissidents living abroad under dictatorships, who risked their lives to speak in opposition to government. Commenting on seven Soviet students who staged a protest in Red Square in 1968 against the USSR's invasion of Czechoslovakia, Rand wrote that the students were motivated by "an independent mind dedicated to the supremacy of ideas, i.e., of truth" ("The 'Inexplicable Personal Alchemy'" *ROTP* 123).

92 Rand commented, in this connection, on several of the movements of mid-twentieth-century philosophy. The linguistic analysts were heirs to the logical positivist tradition and claimed to be defenders of scientific reason. But Rand saw their obsession with linguistic trivia and their skeptical abandonment of substantive theory-building in philosophy as disconnected from reality. She understood the rival existentialist camp as reacting to the heirs of the positivists, proclaiming, in effect, "Since *this* is reason, to hell with it!" (33). She thought that the student activists were most sympathetic with the practical, political orientation of the second faction, but that they were empowered by the skeptical arguments of the first. On these issues, see also "The Philosophical Vacuum" Bibliography #24, "Our Cultural Value-Deprivation" *TO* 5(4) 49–56, esp. 52–54, and "The Chickens' Homecoming" *TO* 9(6) 849–856, and George Walsh, "Herbert Marcuse, Philosopher of the New Left" *TO* 9(9–12) 903–912, 920–928, 936–944, and 950–957.

93 On the relationship of pragmatism to Kant from an Objectivist perspective, see "The Philosophical Vacuum" and Peikoff *Parallels* 125–35, and esp. 130–132 on progressive education. For a contemporary pragmatist's account of the relation, see Brandom 2011.

94 On drug use and its causes, see also "Our Cultural Value Deprivation" *VOR* 112–113, "Apollo and Dionysus" *ROTP*, "A Nation's Unity" *ARL* 2(2) 125. See also *Answers* 13–15, for Rand's view that, though immoral, the use and sale of drugs should be legal.

95 See "Apollo and Dionysus" *ROTP*, "The Left: Old and New" *ROTP* 163–164, "From a Symposium" *ROTP* 173–174, and George Walsh "Herbert Marcuse, Philosopher of the New Left" *TO* 9(9–12).

96 In some issues of *TO*, she acknowledged students who had taken up this advice. See: "A Statement of Policy" *TO* 7(6) 472 and the other issues cited therein.

97 "The Comprachicos" *ROTP* 54, 58–59, "Don't Let It Go" *PWNI* 291, "Fairness Doctrine for Education" *PWNI* 271, "The Age of Envy" *ROTP* 145, "Tax Credits for Education" *VOR* 252, Beatrice Hessen's "The Montessori Method" *TO* 9(5–7) and review of Elizabeth G. Hainstock's *Teaching Montessori in the Home TO* 10(7). On education and child raising generally, see also Joyce Jones "The Playground: Testing Ground for the Future of America" *Persuasion* 4(6).

98 The *New York Times* first used the phrase in the relevant sense on November 7, 1965 in a piece by Thomas Brooks called "Voice of the New Campus 'Underclass,'" and the phrase appeared with increasing frequency in its pages over the next several years.

99 There is some controversy among scholars as to how widely to define this movement. Some (e.g., McMillian et. al. 2003) limit the term "New Left" to a movement of radicalized white men, and see it as independent of the Black Power and Women's Liberation movements from the same period; others (e.g., Gosse 2005) see it as a broader "movement of movements" that embraces all of these related movements.

100 See Levy's (1994, 3–6) discussion of the competing views of the extent and causes of this rift.

101 In addition to being the subtitle of the book, "The Anti-Industrial Revolution" is the title of one of the included essays. It comes from *Atlas Shrugged* (544) where the phrase is used by the leader of a labor union to characterize Directive 10-289 (on which, see above, 365).

102 It was not, however, the first time Rand planned such a collection. In 1963 she was working on a collection of her essays on the Kennedy Administration, to be titled *The Fascist New Frontier*, but this project transformed into *VOS* and *CUI*, neither of which is essentially topical (see Chapter 2, 33). Of course Kennedy's death would have made a book on his specific policies no longer timely, but the dominant cause of the change in orientation from topical books to ones that feature more theoretical material is probably Rand's interpretation of the 1964 election.

103 See also, Joyce Jones "Automation Part I – Modern Luddites" *Persuasion* 2(6) and Harry Binswanger "Philosophy and Nuclear Power" *TOF* 1(5–6).

104 However, Rand also called into question the scientific merit of some Environmentalist claims (*Speaking* 210–211).

105 For this motivation in *Atlas* see especially the characterization of James Taggart and Lillian Rearden, (especially in Part III, Ch. 4), on the relation between this form of motivation and altruism and mysticism, see especially 1034–1047. For non-fiction treatments of these issues in the early 1960s, see "For the New Intellectual" *FTNI* with special attention to the archetypes of the Witch Doctor and (to a lesser extent) Attila. See also "Through Your Most Grievous Fault" *VOR*.

106 For a fictional example of this process, see *Atlas* 668. For an earlier example see the story of Ellsworth Toohey in *The Fountainhead*, especially Part II, Ch. 9.

107 See also her 1962 attribution of Marilyn Monroe's suicide to the actress's inability to understand or cope with the envy directed at her ("Through Your Most Grievous Fault" *VOR*) and her criticism of various social and artistic movements as "nihilistic" ("Our Cultural Value Deprivation" *VOR* 114).

108 Rand wrote (in 1971) that a "crusade" for "the belief in the equality of all men" in a political sense "is dated by about a century or more" (*ROTP* 140). This statement is surprising for a number of reasons. Universal woman's suffrage was not granted in the United States until 1920, the Jim Crow laws, which Rand opposed (see above, 372) remained in effect into the mid-1960s, and Rand held that the antitrust laws treated businessmen as a "persecuted minority" deprived of due process (see above, 357–358). Perhaps her position was that political equality was established as a principle of American law by the 14th Amendment and that, even when this principle was violated, it was not rejected. Segregation laws, for example, were defended, not on the grounds that unequal treatment under the law was acceptable, but on the grounds that the treatment afforded by the law was "separate but equal." It is doubtful, however, that absence of (and opposition to) woman's suffrage between 1868 and 1920 can be understood along these same lines.

109 Rand makes this point most fully in "An Untitled Letter" *PWNI*, where she criticizes John Rawls's (1971, 17–22) famous "original position" thought experiment.

110 Rand also discussed the role of egalitarianism in antitrust ("The Age of Envy" *ROTP* 144–146) and in the inflation that America was experiencing in the 1970s ("Egalitarianism and Inflation" *PWNI*). Cf. *Atlas* 911 on the consequences of eating one's "stock seed."

111 McGovern proposed different versions of this plan and there was some disagreement about the specific income threshold above which the plan would be more burdensome than the system it sought to replace. A *Time Magazine* analysis of an early version of the plan estimated the threshold to be $12,000 per year for a family of four ("What McGovern Would Mean to the Country" *Time Magazine*, June 26, 1972). A *New York Times* analysis of a later version of the plan placed the threshold at $20,000 (Leonard Silk, "McGovern's Proposals" *New York Times*, Sept. 6, 1972). See also: "McGovern Calls for Tax Reform" *New York Times*, Jan. 14, 1972 and Jack Rosenthal, "Growth of an Issue: McGovern Dilemma" *New York Times*, July 8, 1972.

112 Rand, "McGovern is the first to offer full-fledged statism to the American People" Bibliography #27.

113 Leonard Silk, "McGovern's Proposals" *New York Times*, Sept. 6, 1972.

114 "The Dead End" *ARL* 1(20) discusses McGovern in the context of the Democratic primaries. "Representation without Authorization" *ARL* 1(21) concerns the system of race-, sex-, and age-based quotas that the Democratic Party adopted in 1972 to select delegates for its national convention; McGovern was co-chair (with Fred Harris) of the commission that developed the system. "A Preview" *ARL* 1(22–24) focuses on the convention itself and what it portends for the future of the party and the country. On the convention, see also Rand's postscript to Peikoff's "Altruism, Pragmatism And Brutality" *ARL* 2(6). "A Nation's Unity" *ARL* 2(1–3) and "The American Spirit" *ARL* 2(4) are about the aftermath of the election and its broader implications.

115 See "The National Interest, *c'est moi*" *TON* 1(6). Similarly, she would later credit both labor and the National Association for the Advancement of Colored People for protests that were holding back Environmentalist measures that would sacrifice "desperately needed industries" to "protect the survival of endangered, inch-long fishes" ("Cultural Update").

116 For Rand's generally positive view of Ford, see "A Last Survey" *ARL* 4(2–3) and *Answers* 69–70.

117 The only instance we know of where she does use the term in her own voice without qualification is in the (private) *Biographical Interviews* (488) when she describes Roosevelt as having "what was probably the most libertarian platform of anyone" in the 1932 election, because in addition to opposing prohibition, "he criticized Hoover for too much bureaucracy and ... the taxes being too high and the national budget being too high."

118 The people Rand cites as calling themselves "libertarians" included von Mises and Hazlitt (see *Speaking* 16–20), on whom, see 30 and 237–239, above.

119 See 30, above, for Milgram's discussion of the personal history between Rand and Rothbard.

120 Miller and Mossoff discuss Rand's objections to "anarcho-capitalism" above, 193–194.

121 Cf. Rand's letter to the editor in the *New York Times Magazine* (Aug. 11, 1976, L, reprinted in *TIA* 10(2) 14).

122 On Rand's view of anarchism see Miller and Mossoff's discussion, 193–194, above. Cf. Binswanger's recollections in McConnell 2010, 597–598.

123 For a detailed criticism of Libertarianism from the perspective of Rand's philosophy (and why many Objectivists consider Libertarianism to be anathema), see Peter Schwartz "Libertarianism: The Perversion of Liberty" *VOR*. Today, the stronghold of the movement Rand denounced is the Ludwig von Mises Institute. Other "libertarian" groups (such as the Cato Institute and the Institute for Humane Studies), though they grew out of this same movement, have become more eclectic. And, in general usage, the term "libertarian" seems to be reverting to something nearer to its early 1960s meaning. Whether and in what ways to associate with various, self-proclaimed "libertarian" groups (including those named here), continues to be a controversial issue among Objectivists.

124 See "The Missing Link" *PWNI* 59–60.

125 Rand named as one "manifestation" of this pressure group *The National Review*, which had published a review denouncing *Atlas Shrugged* for its "aggressive atheism." Rand's warning to Goldwater was prompted by passages she objected to in his *Conscience of a Conservative*. She attributed the passages

to a ghostwriter. Though Rand may not have known this at the time, the book was ghostwritten by L. Brent Bozell Jr., an associate and brother-in-law of the *National Review*'s editor, William F. Buckley Jr. (Kelly 2014, 50–51 and index, s.v. Buckley Jr., William F. and Bozell, Patricia Buckley).

126 See also "Conservatism: An Obituary" *CUI* and "The Age of Mediocrity" *TOF* 2(3). Related writings in periodicals recommended by Rand include: Joan Kennedy Taylor "Review: Church, State, and Economics" *Persuasion* 4(7), Harry Binswanger "Swing to the Right" *TOF* 1(1), and Schwartz "The New Right" *TIA* 1(21) d.

127 These remarks were made in the course of a discussion of the 1976 senate race between Daniel Patrick Moynihan and then-incumbent Senator James L. Buckley, brother of William F. While conceding that Buckley would vote against various statist economic measures, Rand found his position against abortion rights to be intolerable and recommended voting for Moynihan (whom she considered to be good on foreign policy and otherwise "semi-decent").

128 To our knowledge, this is the first instance of Rand publicly advocating the right to abortion; however, a minor character in *We The Living* has an abortion (*WTL36* 216/*WTL* 168) and, in *Ideal*, a husband urges his wife to terminate a pregnancy (*Early* 268–269). In both cases the characters are mixed morally, but their motive in seeking the abortion is portrayed sympathetically. Cf. James G. Lennox "The 1980 Abortion Plank: The GOP's Attack on the Right to Life" *TIA* 1(19).

129 The italics are Rand's: "A clause including the protection of a woman's mental health, is essential to a meaningful abortion-law reform. Without it, any reform passed would be worse than none: it would be a pretense that might delay actual reform for another 86 years." The bill was defeated, but in 1970 a more permissive bill was passed allowing abortions even when the mother's health was not in jeopardy.

130 On *Populorum Progressio*, see "Requiem for Man" *CUI*. Some of the points Rand makes in these articles about the political philosophy of the Catholic Church date back to a correspondence she carried on with Isabel Paterson in 1948 about the political views of the Church and of such affiliated thinkers as Bishop Fulton J. Sheen; see *Letters* 204–217 for Rand's side of this correspondence.

131 Thus Rand's title "Of Living Death," which may be an allusion to Galt's description of "the state of living death" in which a person exists if he chooses not to live as a man and so is reduced to "a thing that knows nothing but pain and drags itself through its span of years in the agony of unthinking self-destruction" (*Atlas* 1015).

132 For a pointed criticism of the religious right and advocates of anti-abortion laws, as well as Rand's views of when life begins, see "The Age of Mediocrity" *TOF* 2(3).

133 Reagan's speech, "A Time For Choosing," was delivered on October 27, 1964, as part of the television program *Rendezvous with Destiny*. The speech is reprinted in Harrison and Gilbert 2004.

134 See also *Answers* 69–71. Rand also blamed Reagan, who had failed to campaign for Ford in the general election, for Ford's loss against Carter.

135 Ford, whom Rand favored in the 1976 election, also opposed abortion rights. Rand called this stand a "disgrace," but said that "you have to vote for Ford because the opposition is hopeless" (*Answers* 69).

136 In a later speech, she dismissed the idea that opposition to abortion could be based on "love for the embryos," describing this as "a piece of nonsense no one could experience" and noting that opponents of abortion are not typically advocates for contraception ("The Age of Mediocrity" *TOF* 2(3) 3).

137 It is worth noting that, by this time, Rand was in possession of a 1966 letter from Reagan in which he expresses his "great admiration" of her, and a 1972 letter in which he praises the "depth and correctness" of Rand's analysis (in "The Dead End" *ARL* 1(3)) of McGovern and says that he plans to draw on it in his own speeches on the subject (*Papers* 100_13B_013 and 022_07A_003). Both letters were written by Reagan to acquaintances of Rand's who had sent him articles of hers.

138 Jerry Schwartz, "Interview with Ayn Rand" *The Atlanta Journal-Constitution*, April 27, 1980. Reprinted in *TOF* 1(3–4), quote from 1(3) 2.

139 For Rand's account of the election she previously sat out, see *Answers* 69.

140 Also see "The Sanction of the Victims" *VOR*. Cf. Michael S. Berliner "Creationism and the Intellectuals" *TOF* 2(2).

141 The title comes from *Atlas Shrugged*: "Don't let it go!" is the soundless cry of Dagny Taggart, as she contemplated the withering of industrial civilization and the middle-class standard of living; Eddie Willers echoes it as he struggles to restart a train stranded in an encroaching wilderness (*Atlas* 655, 1166).

142 For Rand's view on this failing of European culture, see (in addition to "Don't Let it Go") "The Missing Link" *PWNI* 57–58, "Global Balkanization" (*VOR/ROTP*), and "What is Capitalism" (*CUI* 3).

143 Rand did not think that the space program was a proper function of the government (except insofar as it has a military purpose), and she regarded President Kennedy's "notion of a space competition between the United States and Soviet Russia" as "shameful," but she regarded the Space Program as a productive and inspiring achievement that made manifest the power of the human mind. See "Apollo 11" *VOR*, "Apollo and Dionysus" *ROTP*, and "Epitaph for a Culture" *ARL* 2(8).

144 See, especially, "The American Spirit" *ARL* 2(4).

145 For Rand's view of the influence of her philosophy on contemporary politics, see also "A Last Survey" *ARL* 4(3) 385–387.

References

Barnard, E. 1966. *Wendell Willkie, Fighter for Freedom*. Amherst, MA: University of Massachusetts Press.

Bowden, Thomas. 2005. "Antitrust: The War Against Contract." In *The Abolition of Antitrust*, edited by Gary Hull. New Brunswick, NJ: Transaction.

Brandom, Robert. 2011. *Perspectives on Pragmatism: Classical, Recent, and Contemporary*. Cambridge, MA: Harvard University Press.

Britting, Jeff. 2004. *Ayn Rand*. New York, NY: Overlook Duckworth.

Britting, Jeff. 2005. "*Anthem* and 'The Individualist Manifesto'." In *Essays on Ayn Rand's* Anthem, edited by Robert Mayhew. Lanham, MD: Lexington Books.

Burns, Jennifer. 2009. *Goddess of the Market*. Oxford: Oxford University Press.

Critchlow, Donald T. 2009. *Hollywood and Politics: A Sourcebook*. London: Routledge.

Crocker, George. 1961. *Roosevelt's Road to Russia*. Washington, DC: Henry Regnery Co.

Federman, Dina. 2012. "*We the Living* and the Rosenbaum Family Letters." In Mayhew 2012a.

Goldwater, Barry. 1963. "The Test Ban Treaty: Only an Illusion of Peace." *Vital Speeches of the Day*, 29(24), 767.

Gosse, Van. 2005. *Rethinking the New Left: An Interpretative History*. New York, NY: Palgrave Macmillan.

Harrison, Maureen and Steve Gilbert. Eds. 2004. *The Speeches of Ronald Reagan*. Santa Cruz, CA: Excellent Books.

Keller, Werner. 1962. *East Minus West = Zero*. New York, NY: Putnam.

Kelly, Daniel. 2014. *Living on Fire: The Life of L. Brent Bozell Jr.* Wilmington, DE: Intercollegiate Studies Institute.

Kennedy, John F. 1960. "Democratic Nomination Acceptance Speech" (speech, Los Angeles, CA, July 14), http://www.presidency.ucsb.edu/ws/?pid=25966 (accessed July 3, 2015).

Kennedy, John F. 1962. "Commencement Address at Yale University" (speech, New Haven, CT, June 11), http://www.presidency.ucsb.edu/ws/?pid=29661 (accessed July 3, 2015).

Klehr, Harvey and John Earl Haynes. 1998. *The Soviet World of American Communism*. New Haven, CT: Yale University Press.

Levy, Peter B. 1994. *The New Left and Labor in the 1960s*. Champaign, IL: University of Illinois Press.

Mayhew, Robert, 2005c. *Ayn Rand and Song of Russia: Communism and Anti-Communism in 1940s Hollywood*. Lanham, MD: Rowman and Littlefield.

Mayhew, Robert, ed. 2012a. *Essays on Ayn Rand's* We The Living, 2nd edition. Lanham, MD: Lexington Books.

McConnell, Scott. 2010. *100 Voices: An Oral History of Ayn Rand*. New York, NY: New American Library.

McConnell, Scott. 2012. "Parallel Lives: Models and Inspirations for Characters in *We the Living*." In Mayhew 2012a.

McMillian, John Campbell and Paul Buhle. 2003. *The New Left Revisited*. Philadelphia, PA: Temple University Press.

Minow, Newton N. 1961. "Television and the Public Interest," speech delivered 9 May to the National Association of Broadcasters in Washington, DC. Available online at http://www.americanrhetoric.com/speeches/newtonminow.htm (accessed July 3, 2015).

Peikoff, Leonard. 2009. "Is Homosexuality Immoral?" Podcast. Available at: http://www.peikoff.com/2009/05/25/is-homosexuality-immoral/ (accessed July 3, 2015).

Ralston, Richard. 2007. "Publishing *The Fountainhead*." In *Essays on Ayn Rand's* The Fountainhead, edited by Robert Mayhew. Lanham, MD: Lexington Books.

Ralston, Richard. 2012. "Publishing *We the Living*." In Mayhew 2012a.

Rawls, John. 1971. *A Theory of Justice*. Cambridge, MA: Belknap Press of Harvard University.

Reagan, Ronald. 1968. *The Creative Society: Some Problems Facing America*. New York, NY: The Devin-Adair Publishing Co.

Sciabarra, Chris. 2003. *Ayn Rand, Homosexuality, and Human Liberation*. Cape Town, South Africa: RSA Litho.

Staggenborg, Suzanne. 1994. *The Pro-Choice Movement: Organization and Activism in the Abortion Conflict*. Oxford,: Oxford University Press.

Sutton, Antony C. 1968. *Western Technology and Soviet Economic Development, 1917 to 1930*. Stanford, CA: Hoover Institution Publications.

von Mises, Ludwig. 1949. *Human Action: A Treatise on Economics*. New Haven, CT: Yale University Press.

von Mises, Ludwig. 1951. *Socialism: An Economic and Sociological Analysis*. New Haven, CT: Yale University Press.

Watts, Steven. 2001. *The Magic Kingdom: Walt Disney and the American Way of Life*. Columbia, MO: University of Missouri Press.

Willkie, Wendell. 1943. *One World*. New York, NY: Simon & Schuster.

Part VI

Art

16

The Objectivist Esthetics

Art and the Needs of a Conceptual Consciousness

HARRY BINSWANGER

Ayn Rand was both an artist and an esthetic theorist. Her experience with artistic creation was extensive. She began creating stories at age 8, and went on to write not only the four novels for which she is renowned, but also four plays – one of which, "Night of January 16th," had a successful run on Broadway – and several screenplays, including the screenplay for the 1949 movie version of *The Fountainhead*. Her experience was not limited to literature. In high school in Russia, she took a class in drawing, at which she became fairly skilled. Her sister studied piano, and her husband, Frank O'Connor, was an actor and in later life became a painter. After the publication of her last novel, *Atlas Shrugged*, she gave a small class for aspiring writers on how to write fiction (published posthumously in edited form as *The Art of Fiction*).

In *The Romantic Manifesto*, her main work on esthetics, Rand deals with a wide range of issues, but the fundamental question she addresses is: what is the nature and function of art? Art, she notes, has no utilitarian function. Paintings, music, poems, sculptures, and the like offer no practical aid in meeting life's material needs. Art is said to exist for its own sake – *ars gratia artis* – and some have concluded that art is detached from the needs and practical concerns of life.[1] Many have regarded art as mysterious and unanalyzable, as something *sui generis*, not subject to rational explanation, and have regarded artistic creation as an inexplicable, non-rational process.[2] In contrast, Rand developed a theory of art that recognizes art's non-utilitarian nature but accords it a non-mystical, this-worldly function. She held that the esthetic response, though importantly different from other emotional responses, is yet amenable to rational analysis:

> No human emotion can be causeless, nor can so intense an emotion be causeless, irreducible and unrelated to the source of emotions (and of values): to the needs of a living entity's survival. Art *does* have a purpose and *does* serve a human need; only it is not a material need, but a need of man's consciousness. Art *is* inextricably tied to man's survival – not to his physical survival, but to that on which his physical survival depends: to the preservation and survival of his consciousness. ("The Psycho-Epistemology of Art" *RM* 5)

A Companion to Ayn Rand, First Edition. Edited by Allan Gotthelf and Gregory Salmieri.
© 2016 John Wiley & Sons, Ltd. Published 2016 by John Wiley & Sons, Ltd.

As this passage suggests, Rand opposed not only the mystical but also the subjectivist view of art, according to which art has no objective definition, and anything presented as a work of art must be accepted as such.[3] Based on her understanding of what art is and does for man, she argued that we must exclude from the realm of art modern non-objective works, such as Jackson Pollock's "action paintings," James Joyce's deliberately ungrammatical and largely unintelligible later writings, and their equivalents in every field of art (or non-art, in her view).[4]

Rand conceived of esthetics, the philosophy of art, as a broad field addressing not only the question of what art is and does but also a range of other questions, including: How is art's function achieved in the various forms of art (painting, sculpture, literature, etc.)? What are the possible forms of art, and why? What are the standards for judging artistic merit? Note, however, that her esthetics is not a theory of "beauty" as such (though her theory may have implications for that), but of the *meaning* of artworks.

Art as the Voice of Philosophy

The essence of Rand's view of art is that an artwork presents a philosophy – that is, a basic view of life. "What an artwork expresses, fundamentally, under all of its lesser aspects is: '*This* is life as *I* see it'" ("Art and Sense of Life" *RM* 25).

She held that a philosophy is a theory of "the *fundamental* nature of existence, of man, and of man's relationship to existence."[5] It is philosophy as a worldview, not as a technical academic pursuit, that she has in mind when she describes art as "the voice of philosophy" ("The Psycho-Epistemology of Art" *RM* 12).

An artwork will express the artist's personal outlook, she held, and his outlook will typically reflect the philosophy of his era: Classical Greek sculptors can be expected to hold the Classical Greek worldview, medieval sculptors can be expected to hold the (quite different) Christian one. An individual artist need not conform to the views prevailing in his culture, Rand maintained; but she also remarked on the rarity of an artist being a philosophic originator, questioning the basic assumptions of his era and formulating his own philosophy. Consequently, she held that the great majority of artworks do express the philosophy dominant in the artist's culture. This, on Rand's view, is the truth behind the commonplace that art expresses culture; it is the culture's philosophic views – rather than its crafts, cuisine, manners, and so on – that art conveys. What sets art apart from other cultural expressions is that art is devoted to expressing not the journalistic concretes of a given culture but its fundamental outlook on man and existence.

For instance, she regarded the typical statuary of the ancient Egyptians, with its rigid, symmetrical poses and impassive faces, as expressing a preoccupation with a static eternity, the afterlife; and the sculpture of Classical Greece as conveying the serene self-command of an active, confident, hero; and the bas-relief of the Middle Ages as typically depicting man as a fallen, sinful creature helpless before an omnipotent God. As the philosophy of these cultures differs, so does its expression in art, she holds.[6]

In a journal edited by Rand, esthetician Mary Ann Sures described how the sculpture of Egypt, Ancient Greece, and the Middle Ages conveyed their differing philosophy. On the sculpture of the Greek Classical period, she writes:

> The history of Greek sculpture from the seventh to the fifth century BC is a record in marble of the gradual development of the concept of man as a self-confident being, able to live ... It was

man's body that they glorified, and it was an affirmative view of the human spirit that their statues projected ... Sculptors ... featured only those physical attributes which contributed to the image of a healthy, perfect and sensuous body.

The potentiality of movement is evident in all Greek sculpture. Sculptors carefully articulated the joints and musculature, in recognition of the fact that no body can move without them. They distributed the body's weight so that the figures were balanced, but not frozen into rigid positions ... Sculptors created the illusion of flesh that was both firm and soft, emphasizing the subtle rise and fall of the skin as it moves over the complexity of the underlying skeletal and muscular structure. In this way, they stressed the sensuous aspect of the body ...

Few of the heads of classical Greek statutes have survived; but those that have, convey one quality: serene awareness. A calm face with a smooth brow – a face with no sign of inner conflict – was the Greek ideal. ("Metaphysics in Marble" *TO* 8(2) 605–606)

As this example of the abstract meaning of sculptures indicates, an artwork need not be *explicitly* philosophical in order to express and embody a deeply philosophical message. Dealing with ideas explicitly, as Rand's own novels do, is possible only in literature, and is not common even there. The usual way that philosophy is expressed in artworks is by implication – by presenting concretes in a way that guides the viewer to the abstract meaning. Rand maintains that even so "mute" a work as a still-life painting conveys the artist's view of existence. To view a still life by Cezanne, with its flattened, inaccurate perspective and rough-hewn fruit, is to enter a universe very different from that of a still life by a Dutch master, like Willem Kalf, with its profuse, crowded display of carefully rendered, dramatically lit objects of luxury. Still another universe is conveyed by the smoothly lit harmonies of color among clearly rendered, glowing pears, plums, and drapery in a still life by the contemporary painter Paul S. Brown.[7]

Or, in theater and film, the familiar storyline "Boy meets girl, boy loses girl, boy gets girl," still carries a deeper, philosophical message: success is the norm, personal values are important, happiness is achievable. For, consider the effect of changing the ending to "boy gets cancer and dies."

Rand's view of art reflects her distinctive view of philosophy's fundamental role in life. Philosophy, she held, provides the general framework integrating all of one's goals, values, and daily concerns.[8]

In order to live, man must act; in order to act, he must make choices; in order to make choices, he must define a code of values; in order to define a code of values, he must know *what* he is and *where* he is – i.e., he must know his own nature (including his means of knowledge) and the nature of the universe in which he acts – i.e., he needs metaphysics, epistemology, ethics, which means: *philosophy*. He cannot escape from this need; his only alternative is whether the philosophy guiding him is to be chosen by his mind or by chance. ("Philosophy and Sense of Life" *RM* 19–20)

The final sentence indicates her view that philosophy is inescapable: everyone has a philosophy of life, one that shapes his choices and the course of his life. Forming generalizations about life is unavoidable, she held, and the only issue is whether a person uses his conceptual faculty actively and logically, to deal with his life-experiences consciously and rationally, or lets himself "drift in a semiconscious daze, merely reacting to any chance stimulus of the immediate moment" ("The Objectivist Ethics" *VOS* 22). In either case, he will generalize from his experiences, she holds, to form conclusions, explicit or implicit, about what is normal, what is possible, and what matters most deeply to him.

The development of an implicit philosophy, she says, begins in childhood, as the child acquires increasingly abstract concepts. The terms a 7-year-old uses in beginning to draw conclusions about life obviously cannot correspond to the terms one finds in academic journals. Even the adolescent or young man normally holds his philosophical conclusions in informal, unsystematized concepts, not in the language used in the formal discipline of philosophy, but Rand views his conclusions as being no less philosophical for that. Rand gives examples of the informal terms in which alternative philosophical conclusions might be held:

> "It is important to understand things" – "It is important to obey my parents" – "It is important to act on my own" – "It is important to please other people" – "It is important to fight for what I want" – "It is important not to make enemies" – "My life is important" – "Who am I to stick my neck out?" (*RM* 18)

These examples concern a certain category of philosophical conclusions, those that Rand calls "metaphysical value-judgments" (which have direct significance for art, as we shall see), but similarly homespun conclusions could be given for the entire gamut of philosophy, from metaphysics and epistemology through politics. For example: "Facts are facts," "What's true for you is not true for me," "There's an explanation for everything," "Some things will forever remain mysteries," "If I work at it, I can understand things," "It's safest to follow others – I can't be certain on my own," "I'm in charge of my own life," "People are as society makes them," "What's mine is mine," "It's right to share with others who are less fortunate," "I have a right to my own life," "We're all in it together, no man is an island," "I need to be free to pursue my own goals," "I need to be taken care of."

No one is born with a view on such subjects, or even with the concepts necessary to have such a view. Rand holds that even before one has the required concepts, one develops an emotional equivalent of a philosophy, which she calls a "sense of life." Her definition is: "A sense of life is a preconceptual equivalent of metaphysics, an emotional, subconsciously integrated appraisal of man and of existence."

"A sense of life is formed by a process of emotional generalization which may be described as a subconscious counterpart of a process of abstraction, since it is a method of classifying and integrating. But it is a process of *emotional* abstraction: it consists of classifying things *according to the emotions they evoke*" (*RM* 16). Thus, a series of emotional generalizations becomes a "sense of life." And that sense of life amounts to an *implicit* philosophy, consisting of attitudes that can be expressed in terms of philosophic ideas, such as realism versus subjectivism, reason versus mysticism, determinism versus free will, individualism versus collectivism, and so on.

In adolescence, a person has the cognitive equipment to take a further step: to "translate his incoherent sense of life into conscious terms" (*RM* 18). Whether or not one takes this last step to consciously examine and check one's implicit conclusions about life, these conclusions, explicit or implicit, form one's basic outlook and shape all of one's choices, Rand maintains. Philosophic conclusions are fundamental to one's identity and serve as the background framework conditioning all one's more concrete judgments and decisions. Accordingly, Rand holds that, far from being a castle in the air or just a technical pursuit for professional academics, philosophy goes to the core of who one is and directs the course of one's life ("The Psycho-Epistemology of Art" *RM* 12).[9]

Art's Function

The question then arises, what is the function of art? Why does an artist care to present his philosophy of life and why does its audience respond to it? How does the artistic expression of a philosophy fulfill a need of man's consciousness, as Rand maintains it does?

Rand sees two needs that are fulfilled by art (or two corollary aspects of the overall need for objectifying philosophic abstractions). One need pertains to cognition – how an artwork helps one hold and use philosophy; the other need pertains to motivation – how being inspired by an artwork provides what she calls emotional "fuel."

Rand titled the main presentation of her esthetic theory "The Psycho-Epistemology of Art," "psycho-epistemology" being a term she used to denote a field that lies, in effect, at the intersection of psychology and epistemology.[10] In this context, Rand is referring specifically to the psychological mechanics of cognition. From this standpoint, let us look at what cognitive function she sees as being performed by the artistic presentation of a philosophy.

Philosophic concepts and judgments are highly abstract. Although based, ultimately, on perceptual concretes, philosophic ideas are reached only by a long chain of intermediate ideas moving progressively farther from the perceptual level. Even my "homespun" examples, such as "I'm in charge of my own life," summarize an immense complexity of abstract material – for example, such large and multifaceted issues as being responsible to decide for oneself what career to pursue, whom to associate with, where to live, whether or not to marry, to have children, even what kind of person to become. The contrary premise, "I am a social product," holds that such issues are decided for one by one's social environment.

What Rand says about concepts generally applies most markedly to philosophic ideas:

> Concepts represent a system of mental filing and cross-filing, so complex that the largest electronic computer is a child's toy by comparison. This system serves as the context, the frame-of-reference, by means of which man grasps and classifies (and studies further) every existent he encounters and every aspect of reality. (*ITOE* 69)

And there is another, even more complex, aspect involved in abstract concepts:

> The other part consists of *applying* his knowledge – i.e., evaluating the facts of reality, choosing his goals and guiding his actions accordingly. To do that, man needs another chain of concepts, derived from and dependent on the first [on cognitive abstractions], yet separate and, in a sense, more complex: a chain of *normative* abstractions. (*RM* 6)

The upshot is: to consciously hold in mind and apply a philosophy is a difficult, complex matter. One's philosophy of life is not automatically consistent; nor is it self-evident how one's philosophy applies to any given choice one confronts. Suppose that one holds the premise, implicitly or explicitly, that one is in charge of one's own life. One may yet fail to realize that "taking charge of one's life" is what is involved in a given issue one faces, or one may fail to see clearly what "taking charge" would require in a given case.

The same is true of any of one's ideals and philosophic convictions: their concrete meaning and practical application in any given case is not self-evident or automatically, effortlessly available to one. It is in this regard that Rand sees art as performing a vital "psycho-epistemological" function. Art lets one hold the vast, crucially important, complexity of one's philosophy, including its application to one's life, as a single, clear, integrated, condensed totality.

> Art brings man's concepts to the perceptual level of his consciousness and allows him to grasp them directly, as if they were percepts ... *This* is the psycho-epistemological function of art and the reason of its importance in man's life (and the crux of the Objectivist esthetics). (*RM* 8)

The immense value of "bringing concepts to the perceptual level," she suggests, applies in at least two ways. First, the power of art to condense philosophy into a unitary whole helps a man hold and apply his philosophy to guide his choices and actions. Second, to the extent that the philosophy expressed by an artwork matches and resonates with one's own implicit philosophy, or "sense of life," it affirms the rightness of one's deepest conclusions and confirms one's mind's efficacy.[11]

Art *objectifies* philosophy, Rand holds, giving a sense of reality to the philosophy it expresses. To achieve this objectification, the artwork presents *concretes* open to direct perception (or, in the case of literature, uses language that describes *concrete* men and concrete events). In informal lectures on the art of fiction-writing, she spoke of the Aristotelian metaphysics involved here:

> [E]very artist properly is an Aristotelian. Abstractions don't exist. Abstractions are only a name for concretes. All that exists is concretes. If you want to present your view of what is valuable to man, what is man, what is his existence, or what should it be, you have to present it in concrete form, because that's the only thing that really exists.[12]

Thus, for Rand, *concretization* is the essential process by which the artist conveys his philosophy of life. Concretization objectifies the artist's philosophy of life and makes it perceptually real. "To acquire the full, persuasive, irresistible power of reality, man's metaphysical abstractions have to confront him in the form of concretes – i.e., in the form of art" (*RM* 12). How does this concretization work?

Concretization is the process of clarifying the meaning of an abstraction by presenting concrete examples selected to isolate the referent class, highlighting the distinction drawn by a given abstraction.

Of course, concretization is used much more widely than in artistic concretization; any abstraction can be concretized. A physics teacher can use the collision of billiard balls to concretize the law of conservation of momentum, or, to concretize a friend's cleverness, one may recount some of his witticisms. And in this opening passage from "Art and Sense of Life," Rand juxtaposes two hypothetical concretes to concretize artistic concretization itself – that is, what it is to be a concrete carrying an abstract, philosophic meaning:

> If one saw, in real life, a beautiful woman wearing an exquisite evening gown, with a cold sore on her lips, the blemish would mean nothing but a minor affliction, and one would ignore it.
>
> But a painting of such a woman would be a corrupt, obscenely vicious attack on man, on beauty, on all values – and one would experience a feeling of immense disgust and indignation at the artist. ("Art and Sense of Life" *RM* 24)

The painter didn't have to include the cold sore. His inclusion of it was a choice he made. And by making that choice, by creating a painting to freeze that moment forever and hold it up for contemplation, he is implying that the temporary blemish is significant, important – that "such is life."

> The cold sore on the lips of a beautiful woman, which would be insignificant in real life, acquires a monstrous metaphysical significance by virtue of being included in a painting. It declares that a woman's beauty and her efforts to achieve glamour (the beautiful evening gown) are a futile illusion undercut by a seed of corruption which can mar and destroy them at any moment – that this is reality's mockery of man – that all of man's values and efforts are impotent against the power, not even of some great cataclysm, but of a miserable little physical infection. (*RM* 27)

410

Such a painting says "Sic transit gloria mundi," and says it with a snicker.

> The naturalistic type of argument – to the effect that, in real life, a beautiful woman *might* get a cold sore – is irrelevant esthetically. Art is not concerned with actual occurrences or events as such, but with their metaphysical significance to man. (*RM* 27)

Rand explains how the concretization leads the viewer to the abstract message of the work:

> The psycho-epistemological process of communication between an artist and a viewer or reader goes as follows: the artist starts with a broad abstraction which he has to concretize, to bring into reality by means of the appropriate particulars; the viewer perceives the particulars, integrates them and grasps the abstraction from which they came, thus completing the circle. Speaking metaphorically, the creative process resembles a process of deduction; the viewing process resembles a process of induction. (*RM* 25)

The success of an artistic concretization, on this account, depends upon the artist selecting the right concretes to use and on the selection of which aspects of those concretes to emphasize, in a process Rand calls "stylization":

> An artist does not fake reality – he *stylizes* it. He selects those aspects of existence which he regards as metaphysically significant – and by isolating and stressing them, by omitting the insignificant and accidental, he presents *his* view of existence. (*RM* 26)

To identify what an artwork concretizes, Rand introduces her concept of "metaphysical value-judgments." By a "metaphysical value-judgment," Rand does not mean an evaluation of facts of nature as being "right" or "wrong," which would make no sense, since there is, she holds, no alternative to "the metaphysically given."[13] Rather, "metaphysical value-judgments" are the kind of conclusions about man and existence that underlie and condition all one's value-judgments. Her list of examples of alternative metaphysical value-judgments makes this clear:

> Is the universe intelligible to man, or unintelligible and unknowable? Can man find happiness on earth, or is he doomed to frustration and despair? Does man have the power of *choice*, the power to choose his goals and to achieve them, the power to direct the course of his life – or is he the helpless plaything of forces beyond his control, which determine his fate? Is man, by nature, to be valued as good, or to be despised as evil? ("The Psycho-Epistemology of Art" *RM* 7)

One's answers to these questions would clearly influence one's choice of values, underlie one's sense of personal identity, and produce certain expectations about what life has to offer.

Reviewing her examples of alternative metaphysical value-judgments (which she does not present as an exhaustive list), it appears that they all describe judgments affecting, and affected by, one's basic sense of efficacy and moral worth – that is, by "self-esteem," which she holds to be a basic psychological need. Peikoff describes her view:

> "Self-esteem" is a fundamental, positive moral appraisal of oneself – of the process by which one lives and of the person one thereby creates. It is the union of two (inseparable) conclusions, neither of which is innate: I am right and I am good – I can achieve the best and I deserve the best I can achieve – I am *able* to live and I am *worthy* of living. (*OPAR* 306)

411

In order to feel *able* to cope with life, a person must be convinced that the universe is intelligible (and intelligible *to him*), that he can succeed in achieving goals, that he can direct the course of his life, and so on. To feel *worthy* of living, that his happiness is worth fighting to achieve, a person must be convinced that he is capable of making the right choices, that man is not depraved by nature (*Atlas* 1057). Such convictions arise *prior* to the specifically normative question of what are the right values for man to pursue, and hence metaphysical value-judgments, as Rand conceives them, precede and condition one's conclusions about values and morality. (Clearly, however, there is a "feedback" involved here: if one accepts a moral code that is impossible to practice with consistency, one cannot consistently hold that happiness is possible, man is good, or even that existence is fully intelligible; but, acknowledging this reciprocal influence, the primary influence runs from metaphysical value-judgments to ethics.)[14]

An interesting question here is why one needs to see one's metaphysical value-judgments objectified and confirmed in works of art. Why isn't it sufficient to have reached these conclusions, explicitly or implicitly, over the course of one's development? After all, an artwork is an invented artifact, so it cannot *prove* the validity of a philosophy. What, then, is the nature of the confirmation and inspiration one derives from art that objectifies one's metaphysical value-judgments?

I have already presented part of Rand's answer in terms of the psycho-epistemological function of art: the condensation provided by art facilitates the application of one's convictions to concrete issues in his life, and the objectification provided by art affirms the rightness of these convictions. But I am now turning to the emotional side of art – which is, in effect, the personal, emotional value of the affirmation – and, more widely, of being able to contemplate one's own values and view of life. What, in other words, is the emotional-motivational function of art?

The motivational power of art follows from its psycho-epistemological function. In essence, Rand's point is that inspiring art helps one keep focused on what truly *matters* in life. Or, as she puts it, on what is *important* – important, "metaphysically." An artist, as she indicated in a passage quoted earlier, "selects those aspects of existence which he regards as metaphysically significant" ("Art and Sense of Life" *RM* 26).

What does Rand mean by something being "metaphysically significant"? The key to understanding this issue seems to be the difference between the long-range and the short-range. The short-range can be governed by accidental contingencies, but Rand holds that the long-range, in nature and in man's life, is governed by *fundamentals*.

As illustration of how this distinction applies in regard to nature, consider Brownian motion. A dust mote in the air is subject to random collisions with the molecules in the air, moving it in an erratic, unpredictable path in the short term; but the pull of gravity is a constant amidst the randomness, so the long-term, net movement is downward.[15]

As to the role in man's life of focusing on the long-range, consider this passage:

> Amidst the incalculable number and complexity of choices that confront a man in his day-by-day existence, with the frequently bewildering torrent of events, with the alternation of successes and failures, of joys that seem too rare and suffering that lasts too long – he is often in danger of losing his perspective and the reality of his own convictions. ("The Psycho-Epistemology of Art" *RM* 11–12)

The "perspective" that can be lost, but that one has to keep, is, I take it, the perspective of the long range – the long-range consequences of alternative choices, especially the long-range prospects for success.

Suppose a man has been struggling to solve, at work, a baffling problem that has for months resisted all his efforts. Discouragement, frustration, and depression will not be obviated by the mere fact that he holds such metaphysical value-judgments as that "the universe is intelligible." To hold onto that conviction, to have it motivate his renewed efforts, it is immensely valuable to have a vision of a world in which answers are reached, obstacles have been overcome, and the struggle for values has been joyously rewarded. He needs to be reminded, in a concretely real form, not only that answers exist but also that the struggle to find them is worth it. (This is a theme frequently sounded in Ayn Rand's fiction. For instance, in the memorable scene that opens Part IV of *The Fountainhead*, a young man is given "the courage to face a lifetime" by contemplating the splendor of an architectural work by Howard Roark.)[16]

One's sense of life does not provide an emotional armor-plating against the barrage of tedious, discouraging, or painful events of daily life. And one's intellectual understanding of philosophy, Rand holds, is far too abstract and complex to easily activate one's motivational mechanism, which she sees as being geared to respond primarily to concretes. As Rand has one of her characters say, "A spirit, too, needs fuel. It can run dry" ("Ideal" *Plays* 177). By holding up a vision of one's metaphysical value-judgments, and one's basic values, art provides emotional "fuel."

Rand's summary description of the inspirational power of art is too eloquent not to quote at length:

> It is not journalistic information or scientific education or moral guidance that man seeks from a work of art (though these may be involved as secondary consequences), but the fulfillment of a more profound need: a confirmation of his view of existence – a confirmation, not in the sense of resolving cognitive doubts, but in the sense of permitting him to contemplate his abstractions outside his own mind, in the form of existential concretes.
>
> Since man lives by reshaping his physical background to serve his purpose, since he must first define and then create his values – a rational man needs a concretized projection of these values, an image in whose likeness he will re-shape the world and himself. Art gives him that image; it gives him the experience of seeing the full, immediate, concrete reality of his distant goals.
>
> Since a rational man's ambition is unlimited, since his pursuit and achievement of values is a lifelong process – and the higher the values, the harder the struggle – he needs a moment, an hour or some period of time in which he can experience the sense of his completed task, the sense of living in a universe where his values have been successfully achieved. It is like a moment of rest, a moment to gain fuel to move farther. Art gives him that fuel; the pleasure of contemplating the objectified reality of one's own sense of life is the pleasure of feeling what it would be like to live in one's ideal world. ("Art and Sense of Life" *RM* 28–29)

The Definition of Art

We are now in a position to consider Rand's definition of "art." First, a preliminary about her theory of definition. She holds that a definition states the essential distinguishing characteristic of the concept's referents, and is thus objective, rather than being either a stipulation or a report on usage.[17] The determination of what characteristic(s) is essential – that is, explains the greatest number of the referents' other distinguishing characteristics – can be made only after one

413

has formed the concept (and has gained a certain amount of knowledge of its referents and what distinguishes them from things in the same genus). Accordingly, the definition of "art" she offers is to be taken not as something merely "laid down," but as a solidifying and deepening of the preceding analysis of art. Her definition is:

> Art is a selective re-creation of reality according to an artist's metaphysical value-judgments. ("The Psycho-Epistemology of Art" *RM* 8)[18]

Why a "re-creation of reality"? Because to perform its function – to objectify metaphysical value-judgments – an artwork has to provide concrete entities open to perception. Objectivism, as we have seen, holds an entity-centered view in metaphysics.

> The concept "entity" is (implicitly) the start of man's conceptual development and the building-block of his entire conceptual structure. It is by perceiving entities that man perceives the universe. *And in order to concretize his view of existence, it is by means of concepts (language) or by means of his entity-perceiving senses (sight and touch) that he has to do it.* ("Art and Cognition" *RM* 36–37)

She notes, immediately following this passage, that music is a special case (of which she gives a separate discussion – which I cover below, 416–417).

This brings us to Rand's objection to non-objective or "abstract" art. Such works cannot convey anything philosophical, she holds, because they do not present an intelligible, meaningful subject matter from which any theme or message could be induced. For instance, take the non-objective paintings of Piet Mondrian or Mark Rothko. The sensory qualities involved in vision are: color, shape, and texture. If a canvas contains only non-representational daubs and smears of pigment, it cannot present anything more than those sensory qualities – for instance, greenness, roundness, and smoothness. Whether neat, like a Mondrian, or messy, like a Pollock, these canvases represent *design*, she held, not fine art, because they do not provide the concretes from which one can draw a meaning.[19] They cannot objectify even simple journalistic judgments, like "New York is a busy place," or "That man is exhausted," let alone objectify metaphysical value-judgments.

To objectify or communicate anything beyond the sensory qualities of the pigment, Rand maintains, an artist must re-create entities, entities that are perspicuous examples of the work's theme. She gives a similar argument against non-objective sculpture, "music" that lacks musical tones, and books that lack grammar.[20] The issue for her is that there are definite requirements of grasping the nature and meaning of what one is viewing, whether one is viewing objects in real life or an artwork. Objective art, in her view, respects and fulfills the requirements of making objective a message about what life has to offer.

If pigment smears, random noises, heaps of clay, and Joycean word-salads *could* succeed in concretizing a philosophy, they would on Rand's view be art. But lacking such content, she holds, they are *fundamentally different* from the paintings, music, sculptures, and literature traditionally classed as art.[21] The non-objective productions differ, not merely in their attributes, but more crucially in what they do for us, cognitively and motivationally: only objective art, she argues, can convey a philosophy of life and thus resonate with one's deepest values.[22]

Thus, Rand's exclusion of non-objective works from the realm of art does not proceed from her definition of art (which would be a question-begging approach), but from her view that the differences between non-objective works and (traditional) art are *fundamental*: she holds that the works traditionally considered as art concretize philosophic abstractions while non-objective works do not. In opposing the inclusion of non-objective works in the category of art, she is applying her general epistemological thesis that we should form our classifications in a way that captures fundamental similarities and differences, avoiding what she regards as cognitively destructive "intellectual package-deals."[23]

Rand says that artistic re-creation is *selective*. A certain selectivity would seem to be inherent in any re-creation of reality – for example, a news report, a scale model of an airplane, or a mannequin for fashion display. The re-creator in most cases simply could not include every detail, and to do so would interfere with the purpose of making the re-creation. Art is distinctive, in Rand's view, by virtue of the standard of selection involved. In artworks, the standard of selection is the metaphysical value-judgments to be concretized. Thus, the genus of her definition is "re-creation of reality," and the differentia is "selected according to an artist's metaphysical value-judgments."

The selection involved guides the viewer to make, in effect, an induction. For instance, in *The Fountainhead*, the characters of Howard Roark and Peter Keating are alike in many ways that are non-essential in relation to the theme – they are both architects, they are almost the same age, they attend the same school, they even live in the same house (Roark as a boarder) – but they stand sharply opposed in their basic approach toward life: Roark is a man of unshakeable independence, Keating is dependent through and through. By setting up such a "laboratory experiment," the novel draws the reader's attention to the way in which Roark and Keating differ: the issue of independence versus dependence. Their similarities serve as background pushing that difference into the foreground of attention. (The cognitive need of differentiation in the process of concept-formation, and more widely in conceptual functioning, is essential to Rand's theory of knowledge, and illustrates once more the role of her general epistemology in grounding her artistic theory and practice.)

In summary, Rand's definition reflects her essential position that art concretizes a view of man's relationship to existence.

Two Special Cases: Architecture and Music

Rand's esthetic theory, being reached inductively rather than being deductively imposed on phenomena, allows for special cases which differ in certain respects, such that the same general principles apply in a somewhat different way. Architecture and music are such cases.

Architecture, Rand notes, "is in a class by itself, because it combines art with a utilitarian purpose and does not re-create reality, but creates a structure for man's habitation or use, expressing man's values ... (Architecture, qua art, is close to sculpture: its field is three-dimensional, i.e., sight and touch, but transposed to a grand spatial scale)" (*RM* 36).[24]

Since architecture does not seem to represent anything, it is not obvious how it can be a "re-creation of reality" or express metaphysical value-judgments. Rand did not give a non-fiction presentation of her views on the esthetics of architecture, since she considered the subject to be covered in *The Fountainhead*.[25] Let's consider, then, some passages from the novel.

> The Temple was to be a small building of gray limestone. Its lines were horizontal, not the lines reaching to heaven, but the lines of the earth. It seemed to spread over the ground like arms outstretched at shoulder-height, palms down, in great, silent acceptance. It did not cling to the soil and

415

it did not crouch under the sky. It seemed to lift the earth, and its few vertical shafts pulled the sky down. It was scaled to human height in such a manner that it did not dwarf man, but stood as a setting that made his figure the only absolute, the gauge of perfection by which all dimensions were to be judged. When a man entered this temple, he would feel space molded around him, for him, as if it had waited for his entrance, to be completed. It was a joyous place, with the joy of exaltation that must be quiet. It was a place where one would come to feel sinless and strong, to find the peace of spirit never granted save by one's own glory. (*Fountainhead* 343)

Howard Roark built a temple to the human spirit. He saw man as strong, proud, clean, wise and fearless. He saw man as a heroic being. And he built a temple to that. A temple is a place where man is to experience exaltation. He thought that exaltation comes from the consciousness of being guiltless, of seeing the truth and achieving it, of living up to one's highest possibility, of knowing no shame and having no cause for shame, of being able to stand naked in full sunlight. He thought that exaltation means joy and that joy is man's birthright. He thought that a place built as a setting for man is a sacred place. (*Fountainhead* 365)

If architecture has the ability to convey content of this depth and impact, then architecture does seem more similar to sculpture and painting than to, say, furniture design.

But how can a building concretize metaphysical value-judgments, such as "man as a heroic being" and "joy is man's birthright"? Rand's writings do not directly address that question, but it is relevant to note the crucial role of the fact that a building is to be entered, dwelled in, inhabited. Thus, a building creates an environment, a small world of its own. In contrast, a small scale-model of a building may be esthetically pleasing but it does not carry a metaphysical meaning (if viewed only as an object in itself, not as representing a larger structure). As one architect and architectural esthetician adhering to Rand's views puts it:

All other art forms recreate some portion of the world – a single human figure, or a two-dimensional scene on a canvas. Only architecture can create a total environment, one that literally surrounds the viewer. Architecture creates a man-made, idealized world – an environment created by the architect to fit the kind of life he sees as proper to man. Architecture conveys a view of man *indirectly*, not by projecting an image of man himself [as sculpture, painting and literature do] but by projecting the proper environment for man to live in. (Sherri Tracinski "Architecture and Sense of Life" *TIA* 12(4) 10–11)

As to music, Rand devotes over 14 pages of "Art and Cognition" to a discussion of how music, though operating very differently from the other art forms, fits in with her general theory of art. Here, I will only summarize a few points from that discussion.

Music, Rand writes, "employs the sounds produced by the *periodic* vibrations of a sonorous body, and evokes man's sense-of-life emotions" (*RM* 36).[26]

She finds an introspectible difference between music and the other arts in terms of how the esthetic response is generated. In other arts, she writes, the process proceeds "from perception – to conceptual understanding – to appraisal – to emotion." But in responding to music, she sees the sequence as being "from perception – to emotion – to appraisal – to conceptual understanding" (*RM* 41).

Since the appraisal follows upon the emotion, this suggests that the emotions evoked by the music are what are being evaluated. The emotional content of a piece of music, she holds, plays essentially the same role as do the concretes represented in a painting, sculpture, or story.[27] She notes that music is not, in this sense, representational:

Music cannot tell a story, it cannot deal with concretes, it cannot convey a specific existential phenomenon, such as a peaceful countryside or a stormy sea. The theme of a composition entitled "Spring Song," is not spring, but the *emotions* which spring evoked in a composer. Even concepts ... such as "peace," "revolution," "religion," are too specific, too *concrete* to be expressed in music. All that music can do with such themes is to convey the emotions of serenity, or defiance, or exaltation. (*RM* 42)[28]

In what sense does Rand hold that a listener evaluates an emotion? The emotion evoked by the music, she maintains, is evaluated in terms of its congruence with one's own emotions – particularly, with one's sense of life: "Music communicates emotions, which one grasps, but does not actually feel; what one feels is a suggestion, a kind of distant, dissociated, depersonalized emotion – until and unless it unites with one's own sense of life" (*RM* 42).

Rand holds that, as a matter of observation, people agree about the emotional content of works of music, even when they have opposite reactions to it. There is generally agreement about what pieces are gay or melancholy, pensive or exuberant, languid or defiant. She cites friends who reported, in regard to the same piece: "I felt exalted because this music is so light-heartedly happy," and "I felt irritated because this music is so light-heartedly happy and, therefore, superficial" (*RM* 43).[29]

Rand regards as "the great, unanswered question" *why* and *how* music evokes emotions.[30] She offers an interesting hypothesis about the process involved, suggesting that the cause may lie in the nature of how the brain integrates a series of musical tones into a melody, as an entity-like whole. "Music offers man the singular opportunity to reenact, on the adult level, the primary process of his method of cognition: the automatic integration of sense data into an intelligible, meaningful entity. To a conceptual consciousness, it is a unique form of rest and reward" (*RM* 50).

But, however music evokes emotions, Rand's essential theory is that music's content is emotions, and that the listeners' response depends upon "how they feel about these feelings" (*RM* 43).

As an arch-defender of objectivity, Rand is careful to place us on notice that there is at present no objective esthetics of music. Until we have a firmly established understanding of how music evokes emotions, such that we can distinguish, objectively, which aspects of a given person's experience of a piece of music are due to features of the music itself and which are due to his particular psychology, "No one ... can claim the *objective* superiority of his choices over the choices of others. Where no objective proof is available, it's every man for himself – and *only* for himself" (*RM* 46).

The Esthetic Response

For Rand, the esthetic response is a natural, this-worldly emotion, to be understood in the same basic terms as any other emotion. This sharply distinguishes her view from those previous theorists of art who have taken the esthetic response as "disinterested" (Kant), or treat it as an undefined primitive (Neo-Wittgensteinians/conventionalists). In contrast, Rand holds that the esthetic response, like any other emotion, is a value-response – in this case, a response to the "metaphysical values" subconsciously integrated into a "sense of life."[31] The viewer responds to a given artwork, she holds, according to whether it matches or clashes with his own sense of life. This sense-of-life response is produced automatically, not by a conscious analysis but by a subconscious process of relating the perceived artwork to one's own deeply ingrained conclusions.

417

Suppose that two people view Edvard Munch's *The Scream*. The first man experiences an immediate resonance with his core sense of anxiety and alienation, and his instantaneous response amounts to, "Yes! – that's the nightmare that life is," and he is held transfixed. The second person, holding opposite metaphysical premises, reacts with a feeling amounting to: "What the hell is that?" giving a slight shudder of revulsion and moving quickly on.[32] Such sense-of-life reactions, Rand states, are not a matter of one's avowed philosophic conclusions, but of one's most deeply ingrained, automatized outlook on life.

In explaining her concept of "sense of life," Rand calls our attention to its manifestation in issues wider than one's response to artworks. She holds, for instance, that sense of life also supplies a basis for one's sense of kinship, estrangement, or neutrality in reacting to another person. Sense of life, she writes, "is involved in everything about that person, in his every thought, emotion, action, in his every response, in his every choice and value, in his every spontaneous gesture, in his manner of moving, talking, smiling, in the total of his personality. It is that which makes him a 'personality'" ("Philosophy and Sense of Life" *RM* 21).

In discussing the role of sense of life in romantic love, Rand describes a person's sense of life as:

> that essential sum, that fundamental stand or way of facing existence, which is the essence of a personality ... the *style* of his soul – the individual style of a unique, unrepeatable, irreplaceable consciousness. (*RM* 22)[33]

Rand views sense of life as a background emotion or "feel," underlying one's more concrete emotions. As a constant background, sense of life is hard to isolate and identify, whether in one's self or others:

> Introspectively, one's own sense of life is experienced as an absolute and an irreducible primary – as that which one never questions, because *the thought of questioning it never arises*. Extrospectively, the sense of life of another person strikes one as an immediate, yet undefinable, impression – on very short acquaintance – an impression which often feels like certainty, yet is exasperatingly elusive, if one attempts to verify it. (*RM* 21)

Sense of life, Rand holds, is not exactly an emotion, but it is an affective state, and as such she treats it in accordance with her general theory of such states. As with her distinction in the realm of cognition between physiologically produced perception and volitionally controllable conceptual processes, so in the realm of affective responses she distinguishes between physiologically produced affective states, such as physical pleasure and pain, and higher affective states, such as emotions of fear and joy. These emotions, she holds, depend upon *acquired* evaluations, which have become automatized – in contrast to bodily sensations, based on physiology. In general, Rand holds that emotions, as opposed to bodily sensations, are explainable in terms of ideational content, applied automatically to the object of the emotion.

> Emotions are the automatic results of man's value judgments integrated by his subconscious; emotions are estimates of that which furthers man's values or threatens them, that which is *for* him or *against* him – lightning calculators giving him the sum of his profit or loss. (*VOS* 30)

Though sense of life is a generalized affective state rather than a concrete emotion, Rand holds that it is also the product of an estimate – in this case, of metaphysical value-judgments. Again, it is not a matter of one's explicit, avowed conclusions, but of one's ingrained core beliefs about man, reality, and one's fundamental prospects for success or failure in life.

Sense of life is also the phenomenon that Rand calls upon to explain the process of artistic creation. However much the artist calls upon his conscious knowledge to conceive and edit or refine his product, in the basic act of creation, the artist is necessarily guided by his sense of life, Rand holds, because the number of esthetic considerations he deals with are too great to be subject to conscious calculation.[34]

Rand's explanation of the psychological process of artistic creation eschews any mystical source of "inspiration," seeing the process as explainable in terms of stored ideational content, activated by a "subconscious integration." She viewed artistic creation as an expression of reason – conscious thought in the past by which the artist acquires his (literal or metaphorical) vocabulary, conscious thought to master his means of expression, conscious thought to conceive, organize, and select his subject, and conscious thought to edit and/or critically refine a particular artistic product.

Rand distinguishes a response to subject from a response to style, with "style" defined as "a particular, distinctive or characteristic mode of execution." One's response to an artwork's style, she says, is based on one's psycho-epistemology (here meaning one's own characteristic method of thinking).

> The subject of an artwork expresses a view of man's existence, while the style expresses a view of man's consciousness. The subject reveals an artist's *metaphysics*, the style reveals his *psycho-epistemology* ... An artist's style is the product of his own psycho-epistemology – and, by implication, a projection of his view of man's consciousness, of its efficacy or impotence, of its proper method and level of functioning.
>
> Predominantly (though not exclusively), a man whose normal mental state is a state of full focus will create and respond to a style of radiant clarity and ruthless precision – a style that projects sharp outlines, cleanliness, purpose, an intransigent commitment to full awareness and clear-cut identity – a level of awareness appropriate to a universe where A is A, where everything is open to man's consciousness and demands its constant functioning.
>
> A man who is moved by the fog of his feelings and spends most of his time out of focus will create and respond to a style of blurred, "mysterious" murk, where outlines dissolve and entities flow into one another, where words connote anything and denote nothing, where colors float without objects, and objects float without weight – a level of awareness appropriate to a universe where A can be any non-A one chooses, where nothing can be known with certainty and nothing much is demanded of one's consciousness. ("Art and Sense of Life" *RM* 30–31)

Although it is clear from this passage what Rand's moral assessment is of the two archetypes she presents, she is equally insistent on distinguishing clearly between esthetic judgment and other types of judgment, a topic to which we now turn.

Esthetic Judgment

Esthetic theory has the task of defining standards for judging works of art. Rand's own critiques of artworks are wide-ranging. She wrote introductory essays for three of her favorite novels, *Ninety-Three* and *The Man Who Laughs*, by Victor Hugo, and *Calumet K*, by Samuel Merwin and Henry Kitchell Webster, and reviewed or commented on many novels, television series, paintings, and plays.[35]

Rand stresses that esthetic judgment is judgment of an artwork qua artwork: it concerns how well a work fulfills its artistic goal – that is, how consistently, clearly and powerfully it

419

expresses *its* philosophic viewpoint, as opposed to being a judgment about the validity of that viewpoint. "The fact that one agrees or disagrees with an artist's philosophy is irrelevant to an *esthetic* appraisal of his work qua art. One does not have to agree with an artist (nor even to enjoy him) in order to evaluate his work" (*RM* 32).[36]

On what basis, then, does Rand think that esthetic judgments can be made *objectively*? What Aristotle said about judging excellence in any human activity applies here: playing the flute *well* means full realization of the function of flute-playing, and "in general, for all things that have a function or activity, the good and the 'well' is thought to reside in the function."[37] If the purpose of an artwork is to concretize a given theme, the standards of esthetic judgment pertain to how well that theme is concretized in the work.[38]

> In essence, an objective evaluation requires that one identify the artist's theme, the abstract meaning of his work (exclusively by identifying the evidence contained in the work and allowing no other, outside considerations), then evaluate the means by which he conveys it – i.e., taking *his* theme as criterion, evaluate the purely esthetic elements of the work, the technical mastery (or lack of it) with which he projects (or fails to project) *his* view of life. (*RM* 32–33)

Though she explicitly reserved the task of giving detailed criteria for judging this "technical mastery" to professional estheticians working in each of the branches of art, she did cite in a lecture "certain basic criteria of [esthetic] value" that she held to be "applicable to all the arts," and briefly outlined "a few of them" ("The Esthetics of Literature" *Papers* 109_33x_002_029).[39]

The first is the requirement that the artist obey the nature of the medium in which he works:

> Since every category of art is defined and delimited by the medium it employs, the first and foremost esthetic criterion is that *a work of art must not violate its appropriate medium* – that is, must not depart from it or step outside its limits. This is a precondition of classifying a work as a work of art.
>
> A writer must achieve all his effects by means of language, a painter by means of color, etc. A writer may not, for instance, describe a character's appearance by writing: "She looked like this – " and then drawing a picture on the page ... A painter may not do a landscape and write across its blank upper part: "Here there is a sunset." (109_33x_002_029 emphasis in the original)

The second requirement she lists is: intelligibility. She held that "a work of art should be potentially *understandable* to a rational consciousness ... the artist should be able to define – to himself, not necessarily to an audience – in objective, conceptual terms, the essence of what his work is saying and the means by which he expects it to be understood" (109_33x_002_030).

The limits of intelligibility, as has been discussed above, are reached when there is no longer any recognizable subject-matter represented. "A work of art that does not present intelligible objects (or integrated sounds) is not a re-creation of reality, cannot convey any values and ceases to be a work of art" (109_33x_002_030).

Integration is the next "cardinal requirement" she cites.

> Every aspect and attribute of a work of art must be ruled by one central idea, by a central principle which constitutes its theme, determines the artist's choices and unites the work into a non-contradictory sum. Contradictions destroy one of the essential, defining characteristics of a work of art: the perspective of a single viewpoint, a single set of values, without which a work becomes a random collection of accidents. (109_33x_002_030, cf. *Fountainhead* 12, 121)

Integration implies not only the absence of inconsistency, but, more positively, the mutually reinforcing coherence of elements, to form a unified whole. Rand's emphasis on integration, which she calls "the hallmark of art" ("Art and Cognition" *RM* 56), reflects the crucial role she assigns to integration in epistemology:

> The different branches of art serve to unify man's consciousness and offer him a coherent view of existence. Whether that view is true or false is not an esthetic matter. The crucially esthetic matter is psycho-epistemological: *the integration of a conceptual consciousness* … *[I]ntegration* is the psycho-epistemological key to reason. (*RM* 64 and 68)

The esthetic judgment of a work of art, she holds, considers the extent to which every aspect of the work, every choice the artist made (consciously or by sense of life), integrates with its theme. The obvious method of the esthetician in this regard is to ask, "what if this element were changed?": would the work be more expressive of its theme or less so? In a painting, what if the color of this item were different? what if this item were placed in a different location or rotated? what if the brushstroke were more apparent? what if the man presented were noticeably older, or younger? what if the light in the background were brighter? And so on. The greatness of a work of art depends on the extent to which every choice is as it had to be, the extent to which every imagined change would render the work less expressive of its theme.

Rand viewed integration as implied by the essential characteristic of art: that it is *selective*.[40] "The *accidental*," she stated, "has no place in art" (*Papers* 109_33x_002_030). Selectivity in regard to *what* is included – including all and only that which enhances the work's effect – is the fundamental form of exercising selectivity, Rand holds. "The subject is not the only attribute of art, but it is the fundamental one, it is the end to which all the others are the means" ("The Goal of My Writing" *RM* 159). Selectivity regarding style she held to be "a corollary" of the requirement of integration, giving rise to what she termed the requirement of *stylization*.

> It is by means of stylization – by means of what he emphasizes or omits, what he features or ignores – that an artist projects his values and his view of existence.
>
> For example, an artist may choose to emphasize the slenderness, the lightness, the long-lined elegance possible to the human body – and produce stylized figures of women who look like Greta Garbo, as in the paintings of the pre-Raphaelites. Or an artist may choose to emphasize the brute muscular crudeness, the awkwardness possible to the human body – and produce figures of the modern "beef-trust" style of sculpture. (*Papers* 109_33x_002_031)

Although her own preferences are apparent from the passage, her point is that the stylization must be appropriate to the *artist's* theme. But this does not imply subjectivism, as she writes: "The degree and the kind of stylization that an artist chooses are not matters of his arbitrary whim, but must be determined and logically justified by the nature of his theme, of the meaning he intends to convey" (109_33x_002_031).

Stylization should be adapted, as means to end, to the requirements of the subject: "There is no dichotomy, no necessary conflict between ends and means. The end does *not* justify the means – neither in ethics nor in esthetics. And neither do the means justify the end: there is no esthetic justification for the spectacle of Rembrandt's great artistic skill employed to portray a side of beef" (*RM* 159).[41]

421

The emphasis on selectivity reflects Rand's principle of "unit-economy" in epistemology.[42] Of two artworks presenting the same message and otherwise similar, she would maintain that the work doing it more economically deserves more esthetic credit. The less economical artwork, Rand would argue, takes up more of the viewer's "mental space" on material unnecessary to its theme, thereby diffusing attention rather than concentrating it, resulting in a less forceful expression of that theme.

In the case of art, everything that is included, Rand writes, "acquires metaphysical significance by the mere fact of being included, of being thought *important* enough to include" ("Art and Sense of Life" *RM* 27). She cites, with approval, the statement posted in the office of director Fritz Lang during the filming of *Siegfried*: "Nothing in this film is accidental." "*This*," she writes, "is the motto of great art" ("Art and Cognition" *RM* 63).

Romanticism

As the title *The Romantic Manifesto* indicates, Rand was a champion of the Romantic school of art, which she regarded as the highest form of art.[43] In regard to literature, it is the one school devoted to integrating every aspect of a work: theme, plot, characterization, and style. Contrasting Romanticism with the "Naturalist" school (e.g., of Flaubert, Tolstoy, Sinclair Lewis, and most writers of that era), she argues that Naturalism abandons selectivity in regard to subject-matter, instead slavishly reproducing "a slice of life," and restricts selectivity to style and characterization ("The Goal of My Writing" *RM* 157). This she sees as an arbitrary restriction, opposed to the very nature of art, and limiting the power of these works. Naturalist works don't get lower marks from her because of what she regards as their philosophic error (the doctrine of psychological determinism), but for their self-imposed esthetic limitation ("The Psycho-Epistemology of Art" *RM* 11). She wrote, "The philosophical and esthetic contradictions of determinism are irrelevant in this context, just as the truth or falsehood of an artist's metaphysical views is irrelevant to the nature of art as such" (*RM* 11).[44]

Romanticism she saw as based on the opposite of determinism, the premise that man has free will, which means he freely chooses the values he pursues and which makes him, through the accumulated effect of such choices, the author of his own character. It is the premise of volition, she wrote, that is the fundamental giving rise to the manifestations of Romanticism that are widely recognized: plot structure, emotional intensity, heroes and villains, dramatic conflicts, and "color."[45]

Rand's championing of Romanticism is thus one more case in which she applies the principle that underlies her entire esthetics: that art serves a fundamental need of man's consciousness by "bringing [his] concepts to the perceptual level of his consciousness and allowing him to grasp them directly, as if they were percepts," thereby "unify[ing] man's consciousness and offer[ing] him a coherent view of existence" ("Art and Cognition" *RM* 64).

Notes

1 E.g., Clive Bell, in his influential book, *Art*, writes: "the rapt philosopher, and he who contemplates a work of art, inhabit a world with an intense and peculiar significance of its own; that significance is unrelated to the significance of life. In this world the emotions of life find no place. It is a world with emotions of its own" (1914, 27).

2 In regard to artistic content, Hans-Georg Gadamer states that art "cannot be satisfactorily translated in terms of conceptual knowledge" (1986, 69). In regard to artistic creation, Michael Swan writes that "[T]he sources of artistic creation are always invisible and inexplicable" (1975, 48), and Cooper et. al., in their introduction to the first edition of their 1995, tell us that Plato and Kant both held that "artistic creation is a mystery."

3 E.g., the "institutional" approach of George Dickie 2007, defining art as whatever the elite authorities (members of the "artworld") say is art. In the 1950s, Moritz Weitz argued on Wittgensteinian lines that art simply cannot be defined (1956, 27–35).

4 For the grounds for her exclusion of non-objective works from the field, see above 414–415.

5 On art as voice of philosophy, see *RM* 24. On philosophy's subject-matter, see "Philosophy: Who Needs It" *PWNI* 2–3. For a fuller discussion of Rand's conception of philosophy, see 7–9, 106, and 321 in the present volume.

6 Compare these three sculptures at: http://www.hblist.com/sculpture (accessed July 4, 2015).

7 Compare these three still lifes at: http://www.hblist.com/Still_life (accessed July 4, 2015).

8 Her view of how an individual forms his philosophy and of its fundamental role in man's life is discussed more fully by Onkar Ghate 105–106, above.

9 See also Chapter 5 above (esp. 118–123) for a further discussion of "sense of life."

10 See 123–125 above for a discussion of psycho-epistemology, which I draw on in what follows.

11 Even if the philosophy expressed is illogical or invalid, one still *feels* this affirmation when the view an artwork expresses matches one's own implicit philosophy.

12 From a transcription of Rand's 1958 class on the art of fiction-writing, lecture 2 (This material was not included in *AOF*, the edited book version of that course). Rand here is concerned to deny the "Realist" view of concepts, but her own view is equally opposed to nominalism (which the quote might seem to endorse). Her own theory of concepts (see ch. 12 283–292) is a "third way" that is neither realist nor nominalist.

13 See Jason Rheins's discussion, 262–265, above, of Rand's distinction between the metaphysically given and the man-made.

14 For more on metaphysical value-judgments, including their relation to self-esteem, see Onkar Ghate's discussion, 119 above.

15 See also, Tore Boeckmann's excellent discussion of metaphysical significance in his 2009, 161ff.

16 "... he wanted to decide whether life was worth living. He did not know that this was the question in his mind. He did not think of dying. He thought only that he wished to find joy and reason and meaning in life – and that none had been offered to him anywhere ... Let me see that in one single act of man on earth. Let me see it made real" (*Fountainhead* 527–528).

17 See Gregory Salmieri's discussion of Rand's view of definition, 292–295, above.

18 Traditional definitions have used the term "representation" or the Greek "mimesis" (imitation). Either, however, would suggest something more akin to copying than to the creative element conveyed by "re-creation." (And, for this reason, Rand excludes photography as such from art, regarding it as reproduction, not re-creation.) Further, it is essential to Rand's view that what is re-created be not just a particular concrete but a portrayed or implied world – i.e., be of "reality."

19 I heard her opine (during a discussion with art students at Pratt Institute, in the Fall of 1965) that Mondrians might make good patterns for drapery or linoleum floor coverings.

20 Rand did not write extensively on "modern art," but for her most extensive, and scathing, discussion, see "Art and Cognition" *RM* 67–70. An extended defense of Rand's position here, though laden with self-congratulatory and studied carping on details, is given in Torres and Kamhi 2000.

21 The "traditional" concept of art (or "fine art") is said to date only from the eighteenth century. And it is not uncommon for the growth of knowledge and/or practice to require expanding a definition to accommodate new referents – provided they retain a fundamental similarity to the old. (Rand discusses the need to revise definitions in this manner in Chapter 5 of *ITOE*, considering three broad categories of cases.) In the case of new *objective* forms, such as motion pictures, it was a simple matter to give convincing evidence that they, like older forms, objectified clear, communicable themes concerning

life as such; but 100 years after the advent of the non-objective, no such evidence has been presented for broadening the scope of "art" to include them. To fill the void, the promoters of the non-objective offer the "they laughed at Columbus" argument, the answer to which was provided by Carl Sagan: "the fact that some geniuses were laughed at does not imply that all who are laughed at are geniuses. They laughed at Columbus, they laughed at Fulton, they laughed at the Wright Brothers. But they also laughed at Bozo the Clown" (1986, 75).

22 It is worth bearing in mind that non-objective works are a recent phenomenon, historically speaking. From prehistoric times until the onset of World War I, it was only to selective re-creations of reality that men turned for esthetic contemplation and inspiration. Moreover, the "avant-garde" emerged as a self-conscious, intellectually led form of nose-thumbing at traditional art, not as a natural progression toward some means of fuller expression of esthetic values. And despite 90 years of self-righteous agitation on its behalf by the entire intellectual establishment, non-objective art has signally failed to gain any popular audience (with the possible exception of abstract painting used as wall decoration).

23 For her account of this cognitive error, see 297–298 above.

24 Regarding the "grand spatial scale," note that a small-scale model of a building, taken as an object in itself, however decorative, presumably would not qualify as art for Rand; the fact that one enters inside of a building, and moves around within its contrived spaces, seems to endow it with the quality of a mini-world.

25 For which she is, strangely, upbraided by Torres and Kamhi 2000. Rand once commented that the views she expressed in *The Fountainhead* were largely a re-statement of the ideas of the "form follows function" school of architecture (personal conversation, circa 1980).

26 The non-periodic vibrations of percussion instruments, such as drums, presumably would be understood as playing an ancillary role. But aperiodic sounds as such are noise, which Rand opposes to music.

27 She is careful, however, not to say that the music "represents" or "denotes" emotions, instead saying the music "evokes" or "expresses" emotions, or "induces an emotional state."

28 An interesting question here would be what role one's cultural experience plays in grasping the emotional content of music. Plausibly, people raised in India find Indian music more emotional and/ or more intelligible than Westerners who lack familiarity with, and perhaps exposure in childhood to, the "vocabulary" of Indian music.

29 She does not claim to be reporting the exact words used.

30 She regarded Helmholtz's *On the Sensations of Tone as a Physiological Basis for the Theory of Music* as making the first steps in this direction (see "Art and Cognition" *RM* 46–47).

31 For more on "sense of life" see 118–123.

32 In saying "moving quickly on" I am speaking only of one possible response; it may, of course, be the case that a viewer who is repelled by the painting's sense of life is yet fascinated, in an impersonal way, by the vivid depiction of a world so alien to him and may devote considerable time to pondering or studying the work; or he may decide to analyze the painting from an esthetic standpoint – e.g., to determine *how* it accomplishes its effect. The point is, rather, that one's sense of life determines whether or not one feels a personal, emotional kinship with the work.

33 For more on Rand's view of romantic love, see 88–89 above.

34 Here she clearly speaks from her own experience as a novelist, and reports from literary acquaintances; also, as mentioned above, her husband, Frank O'Connor, was a painter.

35 The three introductions were: "Introduction to *Ninety-Three*" *RM*; repr. from Hugo 1962 (cf. her review of the novel in *TON* 1(8)); "An Introductory Note to *The Man Who Laughs*" *TO* 6(12), repr. from Hugo 1967; and "Introduction to *Calumet 'K'*" *TO* 6(10), repr. from Merwin and Webster 1967. Comments on specific works of art are scattered throughout *RM*. See also "The New Enemies of 'The Untouchables'" *TON* 1(8), and her reviews of the painter Capuletti (*TO* 5(12)), of a 1962 television production of *Cyrano de Bergerac* ("Vandalism" *Column*), and of Mickey Spillane's *The Girl Hunters* (*TON* 1(10)) and *Day of the Guns* (*TON* 3(10)).

36 Interestingly, Rand holds that the more an artwork relies on mystical or contradictory ideas, the less successful and convincing will be its attempt to concretize and objectify its message. She comments, for instance, on the failure of Romantic writers to present a convincing hero of altruism: "altruism

introduced an insolvable conflict into Romantic literature from the start. The altruist morality cannot be practiced (except in the form of self-destruction) and, therefore, cannot be projected or dramatized convincingly in terms of man's life on earth (particularly in the realm of psychological motivation)" ("What is Romanticism?" *RM* 106). For her critique of altruism, see *Atlas* 1031–1032 and 141–144 above.

37 *Nicomachean Ethics* 1097b25–27, trans. Ross and Urmson (quoted from Barnes 1984).

38 For Rand, this presupposes that one is dealing with a work of *art* rather than non-objective works; see 414–415 above for her reasons for excluding these from the category of art.

39 This lecture, likely written by Rand in 1963, was sometimes delivered by her as part of the Nathaniel Branden Institute's *Basic Principles of Objectivism* series (on which, see 13 and 32, above).

40 Accordingly, Peikoff lists "selectivity" as one of the standards of esthetic judgment for the Objectivist esthetics; see *OPAR* 440–443.

41 Rand is presumably referring to Rembrandt's *Carcass of Beef* (1657), an image of which can be found at: http://www.rembrandtpainting.net/complete_catalogue/landscape/ox.htm (accessed July 4, 2015).

42 See above, 288–289.

43 Rand discusses Romanticism almost exclusively in regard to literature, the subtitle of *RM* being: "A Philosophy of Literature."

44 Rand herself was an admirer of Sinclair Lewis's novels.

45 For much more on Rand's view of Romanticism see the following chapter by Tore Boeckmann.

References

Barnes, Jonathan, ed. 1984. *The Revised Oxford Translation of the Complete Works of Aristotle*, 2 vols. Princeton, NJ: Princeton University Press.

Bell, Clive. 1914. *Art*. London: Chatto & Windus.

Boeckmann, Tore. 2009. "*Atlas Shrugged* and the Metaphysics of Values." In *Essays on Ayn Rand's Atlas Shrugged*, edited by Robert Mayhew. Lanham, MD: Lexington Books.

Cooper, David E., Joseph Margolis, and Crispin Sartwell, eds. 1995. *A Companion to Aesthetics*. Oxford: Blackwell.

Dickie, George. 2007. "What is Art?" In *Philosophical Inquiry*, edited by J.E. Adler and C.Z. Elgin. Indianapolis, IN: Hackett Publishing.

Gadamer, Hans-Georg. 1986. *The Relevance of the Beautiful*. Cambridge: Cambridge University Press.

Hugo, Victor. 1962. *Ninety-Three*, translated by Lowell Bair. New York, NY: Bantam Books.

Hugo, Victor. 1967. *The Man Who Laughs*, translated by Joseph Blamire. New York, NY: NBI Press.

Merwin, Samuel and Henry Kitchell Webster. 1967. *Calumet 'K.'* New York, NY: NBI Press.

Sagan, Carl. 1986. *Broca's Brain: Reflections on the Romance of Science*. New York, NY: Random House.

Swan, Michael. 1975. *Inside Meaning*. Cambridge: Cambridge University Press.

Torres, Louis and Michelle M. Kamhi. 2000. *What Art Is: The Esthetic Theory of Ayn Rand*. Chicago, IL: Open Court.

Weitz, Moritz. 1956. "The Role of Theory in Aesthetics." *Journal of Aesthetics and Art Criticism*, 15.

17

Rand's Literary Romanticism

TORE BOECKMANN

"The literature of the past was a shallow fraud," says the writer Balph Eubank, a minor villain in *Atlas Shrugged*. "It whitewashed life in order to please the money tycoons whom it served. Morality, free will, achievement, happy endings, and man as some sort of heroic being – all that stuff is laughable to us" (*Atlas* 133).

Eubank may be taken as representative of Ayn Rand's own critics: objections like his had met *The Fountainhead*, and would meet *Atlas Shrugged* itself. Yet through this character, Rand not only satirizes her enemies but says something important about her own art. Her novels do emphasize precisely those aspects of life that Eubank dislikes: morality, free will, achievement, heroism – and this fact does make the novels seem as if they belong to a bygone age.

Speaking in her own voice, Rand would put the point more directly. Her novels, she said (in her introduction to the 25th Anniversary Edition of *The Fountainhead*), belong to "a literary school which is virtually non-existent today: Romanticism."

> Romanticism is the *conceptual* school of art. It deals, not with the random trivia of the day, but with the timeless, fundamental, universal problems and *values* of human existence. It does not record or photograph; it creates and projects. It is concerned – in the words of Aristotle – not with things as they are, but with things as they might be and ought to be (*Fountainhead* vii).[1]

Rand admired Victor Hugo above all other Romantic writers; and in her introduction to his novel *Ninety-Three*, she observes that "a first encounter with Hugo might be shocking to [the young]: it is like emerging from a murky underground ... into a blinding burst of sunlight." Her introduction, she notes, provides "an intellectual first-aid kit" ("Introduction to *Ninety-Three*" RM 147).[2]

The present chapter has a similar purpose: to provide a first-aid kit for readers of Ayn Rand. I draw on her esthetic discourse, especially her essay collection *The Romantic Manifesto: A Philosophy of Literature* and her lecture course on fiction-writing, edited and published as *The Art of Fiction: A Guide for Writers and Readers*.[3] Noting Rand's linkage of Romanticism with plot, I first discuss how plot enables a writer to show the events of a story as following logically from the values and premises of the characters, and how this method implies a specific approach to characterization. Then I look at plot in relation to a story's *theme*; to the author's projection of his own unique values and personality; and to the distinctive use of imagination typical of Romantic art. Finally, I address the question of how Rand's advocacy of plot relates to her concept of objectivity. The overall theme of the chapter is the role of plot in showing "what might be and ought to be" both in Ayn Rand's theoretical esthetics and in her artistic practice.

First, however, I want to look briefly at Romanticism in its historical context. This will help one understand not only Romanticism itself, but more widely, the nature of a *school* of art with a credo and a methodology of its own.

Romanticism, Classicism, and Naturalism

The Romantic movement in art flourished in the early nineteenth century. Among its famous representatives were Walter Scott and Victor Hugo in literature, Caspar David Friedrich in painting, Chopin and Liszt in music. In Rand's words, "the Romanticists were the great [esthetic] rebels and innovators of the nineteenth century," who "saw their cause primarily as a battle for their right to individuality" ("What is Romanticism?" *RM* 96 and 97).

Romanticism was originally defined in contradistinction to Classicism, the school it came to replace as the dominant esthetic force in Western culture. Rand describes Classicism as "a school that had devised a set of arbitrary, *concretely* detailed rules purporting to represent the final and absolute criteria of esthetic value" (*RM* 96) – rules that were justified, not by independent, first-hand argument, but by the "appeal to tradition, to scholarship and to the prestige of antiquity" (*RM* 96). (The word "Classicism" signifies a return to the values of ancient Greece and Rome.) A subdivision of this school was "French Classicism," a form of drama modeled on Greek tragedy and best represented by the playwrights Pierre Corneille and Jean Racine. Of the rules of French Classicism, the best known are the so-called "unities" of time and place: the action of a play could span no more than 24 hours and must be set in a single location.[4] Among the many lesser rules, a typical one is the ban on violent deaths being shown on stage, although "[a] character could come to breathe his last on the stage if the blow had already been struck behind the scenes" (Wright 1920, 136).

The architectural equivalent of such rules was the parts and proportions of the Five Orders, derived from Greek and Roman models.[5] In *The Fountainhead*, Howard Roark's Dean at the Stanton Institute of Technology represents the Classicist approach. He tells Roark that "everything beautiful in architecture has been done already." For this reason, "[w]e can only choose from the great masters. Who are we to improve upon them? We can only attempt, respectfully, to repeat" (*Fountainhead* 11).

Roark asks "Why?" – and so did artists at the height of the Romantic era.

In the famous preface to his play *Cromwell* (1827) – a preface that became the manifesto of the Romantic movement – Hugo declared that writers "should be judged, not according to rules" (the Classicist way) "but according to the immutable principles of the art of composition, and the special laws of their individual temperaments" (Hugo 1910, 405). By "the art of composition," Hugo means plot construction;[6] and the question of how the "immutable principles" of plot differ from Classicist rules is one I shall address in the final section of this chapter. What is important at present is Hugo's emphasis on the artist's individual "temperament," that is, values.

This emphasis is quintessentially Romantic. Expressing the same sentiment, Caspar David Friedrich warned the Classicists to

> take great care not to impose your theories and rules on everyone in tyrannical fashion [or else] you could easily crush the most delicate flowers, destroy the temple of individuality, without which

427

man can accomplish nothing great. You cannot construct anything better; no matter how much you think of yourselves, the individual in man reveals itself in its own fashion, to each in a different way according to his inner nature. (Quoted in Schmied 1995, 45)

Or take Liszt's (mild) criticism of Chopin in the following passage:

Not content with success in the field in which he was free to design, with such perfect grace, the contours chosen by himself, Chopin also wished to fetter his ideal thoughts with classic chains. His Concertos and Sonatas are beautiful indeed, but we may discern in them more effort than inspiration ... His beauties were only manifested fully in entire freedom. We believe he offered violence to the character of his genius whenever he sought to subject it to rules, to classifications, to regulations not his own, and which he could not force into harmony with the exactions of his own mind. (Liszt 2005, 20)

Howard Roark voices the same sentiment of creative freedom in conversation with the Dean – "I set my own standards. I inherit nothing" (*Fountainhead* 13) – and he carries out the Romanticist program in his architectural drawings (for which the Dean expels him):

It was as if the buildings had sprung from the earth and from some living force, complete, unalterably right ... No laws had dictated a single detail. The buildings were not Classical, they were not Gothic, they were not Renaissance. They were only Howard Roark. (*Fountainhead* 7)[7]

In Rand's words, the Romanticists brought to art "*the primacy of values*, an element that had been missing in the stale, arid, third- and fourth-hand (and rate) repetitions of the Classicists' formula-copying" ("What is Romanticism?" *RM* 97). This does not mean that the Classicists dispensed with all values; but what they could not feature was any major value breaking with tradition and distinctive to the individual artist. As one scholar sums it up:

The work of the classical artist is to give individual expression, the beauty of form, to a body of common sentiments and thoughts which he shares with his audience, thoughts and views which have for his generation the validity of universal truths. (Herbert Grierson, quoted in Praz 1970, 7)

The stress on personal values is the prerogative of the Romanticist, and the source of the Romantic school's individualism and creative freedom. In Rand's words, "the essential attribute of Romanticism" is "the independent, creative projection of an individual writer's values" (*RM* 103).[8]

Just as Romanticism replaced Classicism as the leading art movement, so it was itself replaced – in the mid-nineteenth century – by Naturalism. This latter school still retained some cultural force in Rand's time; and it was mostly with Naturalism that she compared Romanticism in her writings on literary esthetics. In the quoted passage from her introduction to *The Fountainhead*, Rand has Naturalism in mind when she alludes to art that is concerned with "things as they are," as opposed to "things as they might be and ought to be" (the concern of Romanticism).

These are eloquent slogans; but in her analysis of the two schools, Rand goes deeper. She defines Romanticism as "a category of art based on the recognition of the principle that man possesses the faculty of volition." Naturalism she defines as a category of art which denies the existence of human volition (*RM* 91).[9] (By "volition," Rand means the ability to choose one's own values and actions rather than having them determined by antecedent or external causes. See Chapters 5 and 11 above.)

Rand's definition of Romanticism is not generally accepted. "There is no generally accepted definition of Romanticism," she observed, "(nor of any key element in art, nor of art itself)" (*RM*

95). Yet as historian Jacques Barzun notes: "If one consults the accepted sources of information about romanticism, one is likely to be told that its outstanding feature is individualism" (Barzun 1961, 6). And the Romantic emphasis on an individual vision of what ought to be – as opposed for instance to the tradition-bound vision imposed by Classicism – does imply that human beings are free agents in the realm of evaluation. To have values of one's own implies the power to choose one's values (see below, 442).

Rand's definition of Naturalism is less innovative; one of the school's foremost representatives, the novelist Émile Zola, actively promulgated its determinist basis. "Determinism dominates everything" (1893, 18) he wrote, and the Naturalistic novel, accordingly, is "the study of the natural man, governed by physical and chemical laws, and modified by the influences of his surroundings" (23). It follows that a Naturalist is no more engaged in self-expression than is a chemist or a physicist. Zola thus rejected the proposed definition of an artist as one "who realizes in a work of art an idea or a sentiment which is personal to him." His comment: "On this basis if I represented a man as walking on his head, I should have made a work of art, if such happened to be my personal sentiments. But in that case I should be a fool and nothing else" (50–51).

(Rand did not say where Classicism stands on the issue of volition, but it can be regarded as a mixed case. A Classicist presents and admires values – in traditional forms and as defined by traditional standards. But he does not, qua Classicist, perform independent evaluations; human values are what they are and must be accepted as the given. As it were, the Classicist can choose *to value*, but not *what* to value.)

It is not only Romanticism that is virtually non-existent today; Classicism and Naturalism are equally dead, at least in the sense of grand-scale, methodologically self-conscious movements. Why, then, is it important to know about these schools? One answer is that each of them encompasses some of the greatest artworks in history. Yet precisely because these works are based on out-of-favor intellectual presuppositions, modern audiences may have difficulty grasping them on their own terms and enjoying them fully. Knowledge of the schools helps one overcome this difficulty.

Such knowledge also helps one judge artworks objectively, avoiding parochialism – the attitude of regarding one's own standards of judgment as not merely superior to other standards, but as the only *possible* ones. Balph Eubank exemplifies esthetic parochialism when he declares that "the literature of the past" (he means Romanticism) is not merely deficient in some specified way, but just "laughable."

While Rand often speaks dismissively of Classicism and Naturalism, she does acknowledge the literary merit of at least the greatest works of these schools. She speaks of the "array of genius ... supported by the court of Louis XIV," mentioning specifically Corneille and Racine ("Let Us Alone!" *CUI* 156). In her lectures on fiction-writing, she compares her novels to those of Sinclair Lewis (*AOF* 59–83); and while she regards her own method as better, she is respectful of Lewis' aims and standards as a Naturalist.

Let us now turn to a closer study of literary Romanticism and Rand's novels.

Plot and the Projection of Values

Rand calls plot "the essential element" of literary Romanticism ("What is Romanticism?" *RM* 111). She acknowledges that some pre-Romantic stories have plots,[10] and even that some Romantic stories do not (*Answers* 199–200, cf. *AOF* 36–37);[11] but in the context of comparing

Romanticism and Naturalism, she holds that "the attribute of plot or plotlessness ... serves as the main distinguishing characteristic" (*RM* 93).

Rand does not use the term "plot" in the colloquial sense of simply a coherent storyline. Her precise, technical definition is: "a purposeful progression of logically connected events leading to the resolution of a climax" ("Basic Principles of Literature" *RM* 73). A close analysis of this definition will help one understand the role of plot in the projection of values. (To "project," in this context, means to give something mental a perceptible form.)

To begin with, a "purposeful progression of events" implies that "the main characters of the novel are engaged in the pursuit of some purpose – [that] they are motivated by some goals that direct their actions" (*RM* 73). Now, it might seem that this would be true of any story. For instance, a writer might present a drunkard who renounces drink and puts away his bottle, only to take it out again three hours later and have a shot. Both actions are purposeful, and they are characteristic of a certain type of person. However, in defining plot, Rand has in mind not goal-directedness in this minimal sense, but the kind of long-range purposes and values proper to human beings. As Gregory Salmieri puts it, "[a] purpose conceived and pursued over time is a *value* in the sense in which that term is properly applicable to man" (2009a, 237). Such values may be concrete, as in the case of a person or a career that one loves, or abstract, as in the case of a moral virtue which shapes one's character and guides one's pursuit of concrete values.

To see a character who has long-range values, read the scene in *Atlas Shrugged* where the owners and workers of the Twentieth Century Motor Company vote for a plan deciding that everybody will work according to ability but be paid according to need.

> "This is a crucial moment in the history of mankind!" Gerald Starnes yelled through the noise. "Remember that none of us may now leave this place, for each of us belongs to all the others by the moral law which we all accept!" "I don't," said one man and stood up ... He stood like a man who knew that he was right. "I will put an end to this, once and for all," he said. His voice was clear and without any feeling. That was all he said and started to walk out. He walked down the length of the place, in the white light, not hurrying and not noticing any of us. Nobody moved to stop him. Gerald Starnes cried suddenly after him, "How?" He turned and answered, "I will stop the motor of the world." Then he walked out. (*Atlas* 671)

John Galt, the hero of *Atlas Shrugged*, "walks out" in more than the literal sense. He calls a strike of the men of the mind against the altruist-collectivist ideas that dominate not only a single motor company, but (in one form or another) all of society.

What *values* make Galt walk out?

First, he upholds the morality of rational self-interest – a code of values originated by himself (in the novel) and by his creator Ayn Rand (in real life). Second, he values his own concrete life and happiness (values sanctioned by his abstract code). Third, his inviolate self-esteem makes him unable to accept that he is an object of sacrifice for the benefit of others. These values not only make Galt go on strike, but in combination with his love for Dagny Taggart, direct his actions throughout the novel.

His values are part of the reason why *Atlas Shrugged* has a purposeful progression of events – but only part. Rand writes that the word "purposeful" in the definition of plot

> has two applications: it applies to the author and to the characters of a novel. It demands that the author devise a logical structure of events, a sequence in which every major event is connected with, determined by and proceeds from the preceding events of the story. (*RM* 73)

As Rand states in her definition, plot is a progression of "logically connected" events.

Though it may seem paradoxical, the method of having every major event proceed from the preceding ones highlights human volition. It is a means of showing actions that follow from values – or more precisely, of showing them *as* following from values. Take Galt, who values the pursuit of rational self-interest, his own concrete life and happiness, and his self-esteem. It is not true that if a man holds these values, he will quit his job and make others quit theirs. Speaking generally, no particular action follows logically from a moral premise or other long-range value, apart from context. For instance, a brave man might logically draw his sword, but only because he is attacked. To show the connection between values and action, a writer must therefore establish both the relevant values and the requisite contexts; and the context for a literary event is: the preceding events of the story.

This is the reason why Galt quits only when the voters at the motor company – and more broadly, the intellectuals and politicians setting the terms of society – demand that he sacrifice himself. Given this circumstance, quitting and calling the strike is the only way he can preserve his values – but what causes his action is not these values in isolation, but his values in combination with the immediate story context.

It is no coincidence that Galt's context is a *conflict* with society. "Before you construct a story," Rand said, "you must decide on the central conflict, which will then serve as the standard telling you what you have to include in order to fully develop this conflict, and what is superfluous" (*AOF* 36). A plot progression leads "to the resolution of a climax" because it is based on a conflict that must be resolved for the story to end. In her lectures on fiction-writing, Rand gives detailed practical advice on how to use conflict in storytelling. Here I want to make a theoretical point which she does not make explicitly, but which I believe is implicit in her analysis.

Plot shows particular actions as following logically from values – in the context of a story's events. But in most real-life cases, the context directing someone's actions is a complex combination of knowledge, circumstances, and hierarchically ranked values – little of which can be explained by means of a few "preceding events." However, if a man confronts a *threat* to an important value, one may readily grasp the logic of his effort to counter the threat, irrespective of contextual complexities.

Take the simplest of examples. If a man goes hunting for tigers, one may grasp his short-range goal – to enjoy the thrill of the hunt – but it is hard to grasp his action as a logical function of long-range, life-encompassing values. Why does he not instead choose to enjoy the thrill of a card game? However, if a tiger starts hunting *him*, and he runs, his running is immediately seen as following from his wish to live.

A plot conflict, which is an enduring clash of values between human beings, produces in a more complex form the same effect as does the preying tiger. Until resolved, it continually faces everyone concerned with threats to their values, generating a chain of contexts in which their actions may be grasped as logical.[12] In this manner, plot conflict reveals a profound philosophical truth. As Rand writes: "The events of men's lives follow the logic of men's premises and values – as one can observe if one looks past the range of the immediate moment, past the trivial irrelevancies, repetitions and routines of daily living" (*RM* 74). Plot action is what allows one to look past the irrelevancies – and to see how events follow the logic of premises.

Conversely, the Naturalist school denies the role of the mind in human motivation, and so has no use for plot. It conceives of human character as dominated by concrete and mostly short-range desires – usually inculcated by the social environment.[13] This view makes Naturalists object to every important feature of Romantic fiction. For instance, some say that Rand's

431

(and Dostoevsky's) dialogue is unrealistic because real people do not give philosophical reasons for their actions. Rand disagrees, and explains why.[14] It is also said that real people do not state their motives with the exactness and coherence of Rand's heroes, and this is true – but then, Rand's goal is to present things as they ought to be, not as they are. However, it is the element of plot that Naturalists most object to.

Often describing plot structures as "contrived," Naturalists point out (in Rand's summation) that

> the events of men's lives are inconclusive, diffuse and seldom fall into the clear-cut, dramatic situations required by a plot structure. This is predominantly true – and this is the chief esthetic argument *against* the Naturalist position ... To isolate and bring into clear focus, into a single issue or a single scene, the essence of a conflict which, in "real life," might be atomized and scattered over a lifetime ... is the highest, hardest and most demanding function of art. (*RM* 74–75)

An example is the scene in *The Fountainhead* where Howard Roark meets with the officers of a bank company. Roark has run out of money and soon will have to close his office. He has submitted drawings for the bank's new building, in his own style; and he is told that the commission is his – if he agrees to add a Classical motif on the façade.

> "You understand the situation, Mr. Roark?"
> "Yes," said Roark. His eyes were lowered. He was looking down at the drawings.
> "Well?"
> Roark did not answer.
> "Yes or no, Mr. Roark?"
> Roark's head leaned back. He closed his eyes.
> "No," said Roark.
> After a while the chairman asked:
> "Do you realize what you're doing?"
> "Quite," said Roark.
> "Good God!" Weidler cried suddenly. "Don't you know how big a commission this is? You're a young man, you won't get another chance like this. And ... all right, damn it all, I'll say it! You need this! I know how badly you need it!"
> Roark gathered the drawings from the table, rolled them together and put them under his arm.
> "It's sheer insanity!" Weidler moaned. "I want you. We want your building. You need the commission. Do you have to be quite so fanatical and selfless about it?"
> "What?" Roark asked incredulously.
> "Fanatical and selfless."
> Roark smiled. He looked down at his drawings. His elbow moved a little, pressing them to his body. He said:
> "That was the most selfish thing you've ever seen a man do." (*Fountainhead* 196)

Like Galt's going on strike, Roark's turning down the bank commission is an act of loyalty to abstract values: moral absolutism in the pursuit of rational, long-term self-interest. And like Galt's action, Roark's follows logically from his character only in the context of a value-threat: the bank's demand that he subordinate himself to majority standards (which would harm him if he accepted it).

Note that a "Naturalistic," non-plot action also is understood in a context: for example, a man becomes sentimental and then belligerent after drinking too much. But here the pattern of behavior is intelligible because it is familiar; we are meeting a recognizable type: the alcoholic. By contrast, in a story with an original plot, the author constructs unique combinations of

432

action and context. The intelligibility of such action depends on an abstract ethical motive – that is, on a value which can direct different actions in different contexts, and the particular plot action in the particular plot context.

The ethical motive involved does not have to be virtuous. Dostoevsky is a master of plot; but he presents his characters' actions as following from dishonest premises and rationalizations. Still, his approach is ethics-oriented; and for this reason Rand considers him fundamentally a Romantic writer – although an atypical one.

The primary focus of the Romantic school, and certainly of her own fiction, she holds to be the good, not the evil. "That one should wish to enjoy the contemplation of *values*, of the *good* ... is self-explanatory. It is the contemplation of the *evil* that requires explanation and justification" ("The Goal of My Writing" *RM* 160). Rand holds that "negatives are worth re-creating only in relation to some positive, as a foil, as a contrast, as a means of stressing the positive" (*RM* 160). For instance, Galt's walking out and Roark's turning down the bank commission are virtuous actions. The actions of the factory voters and the bank officers are, as Rand sees it, immoral; but by introducing conflict, they help projecting the good.

Just as a Romantic work can present both good and evil, so it can present characters of varying degree of moral ideality. The Romantic method is a means of projecting *some* values, however minimal, but not necessarily exalted ones. At one extreme of this range is the avowedly anti-heroic Joseph Conrad.[15] Somewhere in the middle is a writer like Terence Rattigan.[16] And at the other extreme is Ayn Rand.

"The motive and purpose of my writing," she stated,

> is *the projection of an ideal man*. The portrayal of a moral ideal, as my ultimate literary goal, as an end in itself – to which any didactic, intellectual or philosophical values contained in a novel are only the means. (*RM* 155)

Perhaps Edmond Rostand, author of *Cyrano de Bergerac*, is the one writer who projects an equivalent spirit of ethical hero-worship.

Rand formed her basic literary outlook at a young age.

> I decided to be a writer at the age of nine ... I did not start by trying to describe the folks next door – but by inventing people who did things the folks next door would never do. I could summon no interest or enthusiasm for "people as they are" – when I had in my mind a blinding picture of people as they could be. (*Letters* 669)

Later, Rand would perceive her own attitude as mirrored in Aristotle's statement, in the *Poetics*, that a fiction-writer's function is "to speak not of events which have occurred, but of the kind of events which *could* occur, and are possible by the standards of probability or necessity."[17] Rand often quotes a less accurate translation of this statement, which has "might be and ought to be" instead of "could occur."[18] For this she has been criticized by several commentators. Torres and Kamhi write that she "misquotes Aristotle and misrepresents his intent" by "suggesting that Aristotle was advocating idealization in literature" (Torres and Kamhi 2000, 63). But this is to look at the issue superficially.[19]

Though Aristotle does not advocate "idealization" in the *Poetics*, he does advocate an ethics-oriented approach to fiction. He holds that the "first and foremost" aim of characterization is "that the characters be good,"[20] and he advocates what is in fact the *means* of ethical

433

characterization: a plot structure. The events of a story, he writes, should follow "by either ne- cessity or probability from the preceding events: for it makes a great difference whether things happen because of one another, or only *after* one another."[21]

It would be anachronistic to call Aristotle, or any author he knew, a Romanticist. But he was the first to identify the method of plot, which Romantic writers would later use to present their vision of things as they might be and ought to be.

"The place of ethics in any given work of art," writes Rand, "depends on the metaphysical views of the artist" ("The Psycho-Epistemology of Art" *RM* 11).

Art is a concretization of metaphysical value-judgments – judgments like "the universe is intelligible to man" or "man is doomed to frustration and despair." Such judgments and their role in art are discussed in the preceding chapter. For the present, note simply that a metaphysi- cal value-judgment is *metaphysical* because it judges values not as good or evil (which would be a *moral* judgment) but, in effect, as possible or impossible to achieve, by the nature of existence. As Leonard Peikoff writes, the issue raised by metaphysical value-judgments "is not: 'By what rules should a man live?' but, in effect, 'Can man live?'" (*OPAR* 415). Metaphysical value-judg- ments come at this central issue from various angles; for instance, the view that "the universe is intelligible to man" is, in effect, a judgment that knowledge is an achievable human value.

An artist's view of what is metaphysically possible in the realm of human values will direct ev- erything in his work, including whether that work has an ethics-orientation. Take Roark's refusal to compromise his artistic integrity. Why does Rand consider an action like this important enough to include in a novel? Only because she holds that the achievement of moral values is possible for man. If one held the premise of Original Sin – if one regarded a virtue as metaphysically impossible – one would have to regard Roark's seemingly virtuous action as an illusion or a fluke; and one would not feature it in a novel. But Rand does feature it, because she has given the opposite an- swer to the question: "Is man, by nature, to be valued as good, or to be despised as evil?" (*RM* 7)

Thus an ethics-orientation in literature depends on, implies, and *projects* a metaphysical viewpoint: the recognition of the human potential for moral goodness.

Romantic Characterization

Rand holds that "in order to understand a man's character, it is the motivation behind his actions that we must understand." She also holds that "a man's basic premises and values ... form his character and move him to action" ("Basic Principles of Literature" *RM* 79). Consequently, liter- ary characterization is for Rand fundamentally an issue of establishing the characters' abstract value-premises. This is done primarily through the plot actions – which follow logically from the given premises and so demonstrate both their existence and their motivational efficacy.[22]

This form of characterization, when practiced by Rand as well as other Romanticists, com- monly meets with two interrelated objections. Characters moved by abstract convictions are said to lack individuality, being stereotypes, and to lack depth and subtlety, being "cardboard figures." Rand disagrees that such flaws are inherent in the Romantic method; but she indicates that they are dangers an author must look out for. With regard to individuality, she writes that a literary figure "has to be an abstraction, yet look like a concrete; [the figure] has to have the universality of an abstraction and, simultaneously, the unrepeatable uniqueness of a *person*" (*RM* 78). To see how she herself achieves this effect, note some touches in the scenes I have discussed.

434

When Roark turns down the bank commission, he gathers his drawings, rolls them together, and puts them under his arm. Then he is called selfless. He smiles. "He looked down at his drawings. His elbow moved a little, pressing them to his body." This kind of sensuously expressed love for his own creative work is typical of Roark. The same touch is shown when he walks through the construction site of his first building, feeling a sense of ecstasy. "He did not stop. He went on calmly. But his hands betrayed what he wanted to hide. His hands reached out, ran slowly down the beams and joints" (*Fountainhead* 130). Or take his looking at the unfinished Aquitania Hotel, on which construction has been suspended. "His hands would move as they had moved over the clay model; at that distance, a broken projection could be covered by the palm of his hand; but the instinctive completing motion met nothing but air" (*Fountainhead* 346).

Like Rand's other heroes, Roark wants to change, as he puts it, "the shape of things on this earth" (*Fountainhead* 39). Unlike her other heroes, he is an architect, who deals directly with the attributes of shape and texture, adapting materials to appeal to one's sight and touch.[23] His tactile sensuousness – a contrast to his usual austere demeanor – fits his profession and his passion for it. In other words, Roark's sensuousness integrates with Rand's overall conception of the character. But at the same time, this touch is not merely an aspect of Roark's abstract premises; it is an individualizing trait, part of what makes Roark's personality unique.

Now observe that Roark, in confronting the bank's ultimatum, gives some evidence of inner tension. When asked for a response, he first does not answer. When asked directly "Yes or no?" he leans his head back and closes his eyes; then says "No." This momentary struggle for control of his emotions underscores the importance of the decision Roark faces. But Galt, too, walks away from something he has valued highly (not only his job but also his innovative new motor). Yet in his scene, there is no equivalent of Roark's struggle. On the contrary, his voice is clear and without any feeling. He walks out "not hurrying and not noticing any of us."

The same absolute emotional serenity is evident at the end of *Atlas Shrugged*, when Galt is rescued from the cellar where he has been tortured. "'I'll find them some day, whoever they were ...' said Francisco [d'Anconia]; the tone of his voice, flat, dead and barely audible, said the rest." Galt answers: "If you do, you'll find that there's nothing left of them to kill" (*Atlas* 1155).[24] Galt's serenity fits his abstract characterization as a man who has defined a new philosophy of reason, and who is convinced that evil, on its own, is impotent. But his serenity is not merely an aspect of the abstractions "rationality" or "impotence of evil"; it is an individualizing trait, part of what makes his personality unique.[25]

Although Galt's serenity differentiates him both from people commonly observable in real life and from other literary heroes, not everybody regards it as a successful touch of characterization. For instance, some readers subscribe to the rule, popular in Hollywood's version of Classicism, that inner conflicts are the indispensable means of characterization and that a protagonist therefore *must* have them. Such readers often regard Galt's serenity as a *lack* of characterization. This is a case of smuggling in the standards of one esthetic approach in judging the works of another.

Other readers are influenced by Naturalism and do not see Galt's serenity as an individualizing trait precisely because of its consonance with his overall characterization. The Naturalist method is to make characters concretely real by giving them *accidental* attributes, such as being bald, or lactose intolerant, or a middle child. A reader who views this as the only valid form of characterization will tend to perceive a Romantic character as a stereotype regardless of how many non-accidental touches are provided. Thus, since Roark has no regional accent, since Galt does not stutter, since Dagny Taggart does not use words like "Gosh," some readers think they all "sound alike."

435

But consider the subtle difference in the ways Galt and Francisco speak.

It is characteristic of Galt to respond to a non-philosophical statement by broadening the context to basic philosophy, often in a playful or slightly enigmatic form. His dialogue with Dagny Taggart when she crashes in the strikers' hideaway valley is rich in examples. She asks: "What is this valley?" and he answers: "The Taggart Terminal" (*Atlas* 702–703). Galt is saying that the valley represents, in actual fact, what Dagny (wrongly) thinks her railroad represents: the achievement of her highest values.

When Dagny is reminded that she named a railroad line after Galt, she says: "But I named it after an enemy." He says: "That's the contradiction you had to resolve." She says: "It was you ... wasn't it ... who destroyed my Line ..." He replies: "Why, no. It was the contradiction" (*Atlas* 710). Galt's point is that he and Dagny are enemies because she thinks she can achieve her values (such as the John Galt Line) by making terms with the destroyers of achievement. This premise is a contradiction, as Galt recognizes; and any achievement based on it is ultimately futile.[26]

By contrast, Francisco d'Anconia's speaking style is less philosophical and often takes the form of wit undercutting the pretensions of the morally corrupt.[27] For instance, he attends a party where Balph Eubank says: "We need a national subsidy for literature. It is disgraceful that artists are treated like peddlers and that art works have to be sold like soap." Francisco replies: "You mean, your complaint is that they *don't* sell like soap?" (*Atlas* 141).

Another guest at the same party is Dr Pritchett, head of the philosophy department at a once great university. "We were just discussing a most interesting subject," an earnest matron informs Francisco. "Dr. Pritchett was telling us that nothing is anything." Francisco answers gravely: "He should, undoubtedly, know more than anyone else about that" (*Atlas* 141).

By puncturing these villains' pretensions to martyred genius (Eubank) or intellectual stature (Pritchett), Francisco's wit projects a strong aspect of avenging justice. And this aspect of his character fits one of his main actions in the plot: his systematic destruction of the wealth of looters, like James Taggart, who have invested in his copper company. Of course, Galt, too, is just; but his role specifically as avenger is not stressed in his personality. This differentiates him as a character from Francisco, an effect achieved partly by the two men's ways of talking (but see also their reactions, quoted earlier, when Galt is rescued from the torture chamber).

In addition to their supposed lack of individuality, Romantic characters are often said to lack depth and subtlety. And the presence or absence of these qualities are indeed interrelated. It is the subtle touches that one hardly thinks about, like Galt's style of speech, that create the most authentic individuality. And it is the subtlety with which characters grasp and apply their premises that gives them depth of motivation (since their going beyond the obvious conveys a sense that their premises are not just superficial slogans).

With these factors in mind, let us judge the depth of Rand's characterization by means of one scene between Dagny, Francisco, and Galt. Dagny has one week left to spend in the valley, where she works as Galt's live-in cook and housemaid. Francisco, who used to be in a love relationship with Dagny but left her to join Galt's strike, does not know that she and Galt are now in love. Each of these characters holds selfishness as a virtue; but Dagny is afraid that Galt "might throw the three of them into the hopeless waste of self-sacrifice" (*Atlas* 795), by stepping aside to let Francisco have her. It is at this point that Francisco tells her: "I'd like you to spend this last week with me. I'd like you to move to my house. As my guest, nothing else, for no reason, except that I'd like you to."

> "But I'm an employee," she said, with an odd smile, looking at Galt, "I have a job to finish."
> "I won't hold you to it," said Galt ... "You can quit the job any time you wish. It's up to you."

"No, it isn't. I'm a prisoner here. Don't you remember? I'm to take orders. I have no preferences to follow, no wishes to express, no decisions to make. I want the decision to be yours."

"You want it to be mine?"

"Yes!" ...

He smiled, as at a child's complex scheming which he had long since seen through. "Very well." But he did not smile, as he said, turning to Francisco, "Then – no." (*Atlas* 796)

Why does Dagny not herself say no to Francisco? This action would seem to follow from her premise of selfishness, since Dagny presumably would rather spend her remaining week with Galt, whom she loves, than with anyone else. So why does she insist on making Galt decide?

The reason is that Dagny sees beyond the most obvious application of her moral philosophy. What is at stake for her is not where she will spend the next week, but how she will spend the rest of her life – which depends on *Galt's* character (and her own view of it). After Galt gives his answer, Dagny reflects on the stakes.

Part of the intensity of her relief – she thought, as she walked silently by his side – was the shock of a contrast: she had seen, with the sudden, immediate vividness of sensory perception, an exact picture of what the code of self-sacrifice would have meant, if enacted by the three of them. Galt, giving up the woman he wanted, for the sake of his friend, faking his greatest feeling out of existence and himself out of her life, no matter what the cost to him and to her, then dragging the rest of his years through the waste of the unreached and unfulfilled – she, turning for consolation to a second choice, faking a love she did not feel, being willing to fake, since her will to self-deceit was the essential required for Galt's self-sacrifice, then living out her years in hopeless longing, accepting, as relief for an unhealing wound, some moments of weary affection, plus the tenet that love is futile and happiness is not to be found on earth – Francisco, struggling in the elusive fog of a counterfeit reality, his life a fraud staged by the two who were dearest to him and most trusted, struggling to grasp what was missing from his happiness, struggling down the brittle scaffold of a lie over the abyss of the discovery that he was not the man she loved, but only a resented substitute, half-charity-patient, half-crutch, his perceptiveness becoming his danger and only his surrender to lethargic stupidity protecting the shoddy structure of his joy, struggling and giving up and settling into the dreary routine of the conviction that fulfillment is impossible to man – the three of them, who had had all the gifts of existence spread out before them, ending up as embittered hulks, who cry in despair that life is frustration – the frustration of not being able to make unreality real. (*Atlas* 797–798)

Such are the considerations that underlie Dagny's emotions and actions.

This kind of characterizational depth is rare in Romantic literature, much of which, as Rand acknowledges, does have cardboard heroes. But she does not blame this flaw on the Romantic method as such. "The archenemy and destroyer of Romanticism," she writes, "was the altruist morality."

Since Romanticism's essential characteristic is the projection of values, particularly *moral* values, altruism introduced an insolvable conflict into Romantic literature from the start. The altruist morality cannot be practiced (except in the form of self-destruction) and, therefore, cannot be projected or dramatized convincingly in terms of man's life on earth (particularly in the realm of psychological motivation). ("What is Romanticism?" *RM* 106)

A serious presentation of altruism, I take Rand to be implying, would have to deal with the kind of issues that Dagny deals with in her projection of the future – including how the requirement to sacrifice one's most precious values makes one evade their existence, nature, and importance. In the absence of such treatment, one gets cardboard altruist heroes. Rand's example is Vinicius in Henryk Sienkiewicz's *Quo Vadis* (*RM* 106–108).

It is telling that perhaps the most psychologically perceptive novelist of the Romantic tradition, Dostoevsky, is perceptive specifically about evil, not about the altruism he regards as the good (*RM* 107). But Rand brings her perceptiveness to bear on both good and evil, egoism and altruism, Roark's turning down the bank commission and Dagny's projection of the future if Galt had answered "Yes."

Plot and Theme

The theme of a novel is "the core of its abstract meaning" ("Basic Principles of Literature" *RM* 76).[28] The theme, Rand writes, "sets the writer's standard of selection, directing the innumerable choices he has to make and serving as the integrator of the novel" (*RM* 72). For instance, she identifies the theme of *Atlas Shrugged* as "the role of the mind in man's existence – and, as corollary, the demonstration of a new moral philosophy: the morality of rational self-interest" (*FTNI* 97). The scenes I have discussed pertain to this theme. Galt's walking out is the protest of a man of the mind against the altruist creed that demands the mind's sacrifice. When he says "No" to Dagny's staying with Francisco, Galt acts as a rational egoist. Similarly, in Roark's bank scene, an individualist confronts majority standards, which act pertains to the theme of *The Fountainhead*: individualism versus collectivism (*FTNI* 73).

The twin functions of a theme, selectivity and integration, are key features of any artwork (see Harry Binswanger's discussion of these in the preceding chapter).

Consider the role of the theme in the following scene from *Atlas Shrugged*. A young Dagny Taggart wakes up next to the man she loves, Francisco d'Anconia, and sees that he holds "his mouth closed like a man lying in resignation in unbearable pain, bearing it, making no attempt to hide it."

> She was too frightened to move. He felt her glance and turned to her. He shuddered suddenly, he threw off the blanket, he looked at her naked body, then he fell forward and buried his face between her breasts. He held her shoulders, hanging onto her convulsively. She heard the words, muffled, his mouth pressed to her skin:
> "I can't give it up! I can't!"
> "What?" she whispered.
> "You."
> "Why should – "
> "And everything."
> "Why should you give it up?"
> "Dagny! Help me to remain. To refuse. Even though he's right!"
> She asked evenly, "To refuse what, Francisco?"
> He did not answer, only pressed his face harder against her ...
> He moaned, "It's right, but it's so hard to do! Oh God, it's so hard!"
> After a while, he raised his head. He sat up. He had stopped trembling. (*Atlas* 114–115)

At issue here is whether Francisco will go on strike, giving up both his business career and (for an indefinite future) Dagny, who he knows is not ready to quit. His values and context are similar to Galt's – he is a man of the mind who is being bled dry by altruist-collectivist politicians – and so the abstract meaning of his going on strike is similar to that of Galt's doing so. The above scene, showing Francisco's mental struggle and final decision, is thus united with the scene where Galt quits (and with the novel's other events) under the thematic abstraction.

438

But there is another way in which the events of a novel form a unity, a way that concerns not primarily the theme, but the plot progression. Francisco refers to going on strike not only by the words "it's right" but also by the words "he's right." This last is an allusion to the immediate story context of Galt's recruiting his friends to the strike he has just initiated. It is this context, not just his values in isolation, that makes Francisco quit.

Although they can be isolated conceptually, the concrete unity of plot and the abstract unity of theme are not independent story attributes. Rand regards it as a "cardinal principle of good fiction" that the theme and the plot "*must be integrated* – as thoroughly integrated as mind and body or thought and action in a rational view of man" (*RM* 76 emphasis in original).[29] And the means of theme–plot integration is the element Rand calls the *plot-theme*. The plot-theme

> is the first step of the translation of an abstract theme into a story, without which the construction of a plot would be impossible. A "plot-theme" is the central conflict or "situation" of a story – a conflict in terms of action, corresponding to the theme and complex enough to create a purposeful progression of events. (*RM* 76)

The simplest statement of the plot-theme of *Atlas Shrugged* is "the men of the mind going on strike against an altruist-collectivist society" (*RM* 77).[30] To add complexity, the plot-theme or central situation sets in opposition the story's major characters. Galt and Francisco are in conflict not just with society, but with Dagny, who is not yet ready to strike. This latter conflict, too, "corresponds to the theme," since Dagny's lack of readiness is caused by her conviction that the altruist-collectivists ultimately do respect the mind and their own self-interest: she "cannot believe that men can ... remain blind and deaf to us forever, when the truth is ours and their lives depend on accepting it" (*Atlas* 807).

I have quoted Rand's statement to aspiring fiction-writers that the central conflict serves "as the standard telling you what you have to include in order to fully develop this conflict, and what is superfluous" (*AOF* 36). She also made the point that

> when you begin to construct a plot ... *the plot comes above your message.* I do not mean that you can ever decide on a plot which contradicts your message – if it does, you must select a different plot. I mean only that the plot must be your sole consideration *while you are constructing it.* (*AOF* 31)

The reason for this apparent demotion of the theme's creative role is simple: the thematic standard on its own yields only abstract unity. Suppose Rand had written *The Fountainhead* with the theme as her only standard. She might have ended the novel with a young woman trying to escape Soviet Russia across the Latvian border. But instead, that particular concrete under the abstraction "individualism versus collectivism" belonged in a different novel with a different plot-theme – *We the Living*.

The plot-theme – which corresponds to the theme and in effect incorporates it as a standard of selection – yields both abstract and concrete unity, and integrates plot and theme. Observe that the compound conflict of Galt and Francisco versus both society and Dagny logically unfolds into events like Francisco's leaving Dagny – events that are part of a single unity of plot and theme. (And since the plot-theme must correspond to it, the theme remains the ultimate standard.)

As an added element of integration, a plot structure conveys abstract meaning not only through its separate events, but also as a totality – a totality which includes the climax. For instance, the triumph of Rand's heroes, after a long struggle, projects that human beings have volition not only in the realm of consciousness, in their choice of values, but also in the realm of existential action, where they can achieve their values.[31] Such triumph is a testament to the power of one's chosen values to govern one's existential fate. (This implication is presumably what Balph Eubank is really opposing when he derides "happy endings.")

The Projection of a Self-Made Soul

Authors who deal with abstract moral themes are often accused of didacticism. They are, it is said, out to preach a message, not to create art as an end in itself. Thus Victor Hugo is supposedly concerned only with protesting society's injustice to the poor and weak (*Les Misérables*), Rand with protesting its injustice to the rich and able (*Atlas Shrugged*).

Leaving aside this overly narrow conception of Rand's theme, what these critics miss is a theme's *artistic* function. The theme is a means to the selectivity and integration required by the objectification of values. An author will naturally choose as a theme some idea that he regards as important, that is, that reflects his values. Note as evidence that Rand's themes all center on a single characteristic concern: the sanctity of the individual, the ego, the sovereign mind. But the basic purpose of her novels is to objectify her values, not to spread them. As she wrote:

> My basic test for any story is: Would I want to meet these characters and observe these events in real life? Is this story an experience worth living through for its own sake? Is the pleasure of contemplating these characters an end in itself? ("The Goal of My Writing" *RM* 156)

That the heroes of Rand's novels objectify her values does not mean that she agrees with all of their premises, only that she finds some element of "what ought to be" in their actions. Consider Dominique Francon in *The Fountainhead*. After rejecting the bank commission, Roark takes a job in a granite quarry. There he meets Dominique, and they fall in love. Later, when his career is progressing, Dominique stops him from getting an important commission. Then she comes to his apartment.

> You know that I hate you, Roark. I hate you for what you are, for wanting you, for having to want you. I'm going to fight you – and I'm going to destroy you – and I tell you this as calmly as I told you that I'm a begging animal. I'm going to pray that you can't be destroyed – I tell you this, too – even though I believe in nothing and have nothing to pray to. But I will fight to block every step you take. I will fight to tear every chance you want away from you. I will hurt you through the only thing that can hurt you – through your work. I will fight to starve you, to strangle you on the things you won't be able to reach. (*Fountainhead* 279)

The world is run, Dominique believes, by men like the bank officers who wanted Roark to conform to tradition – and who in effect sent him to the quarry. An independent man like Roark can either conform or get crushed – or he can choose to pursue no serious values at all. This last is what Dominique has done in her own life, which is why she tells Roark she hates him. He is so much her kind of hero that she cannot help loving him – which ties her to the world she despises. Now she has a serious value, Roark, who is under threat from the forces of social conformity, but who will not give up his career voluntarily. Dominique can protect him only by stopping his career at the outset, forestalling the harsher blows of society.

Rand does not share Dominique's malevolent view of the world (which Dominique herself abandons after observing the events of the novel). But she does share the passionate idealism that makes Dominique act to protect her highest value. And even if she does not share it, Rand is in *sympathy* with Dominique's particular form of malevolence. "Dominique," Rand is reported to have said, "is myself in a bad mood."

Dominique's malevolent view of the majority's power to crush the individual – the view that puts her in conflict with Roark – pertains to the theme of *The Fountainhead*: individualism versus collectivism.[32] However, the Roark–Dominique conflict projects an additional meaning, one that has nothing to do with the theme. Dominique tells Roark:

> "I have hurt you today. I'll do it again. I'll come to you whenever I have beaten you – whenever I know that I have hurt you – and I'll let you own me. I want to be owned, not by a lover, but by an adversary who will destroy my victory over him, not with honorable blows, but with the touch of his body on mine. That is what I want of you, Roark. That is what I am. You wanted to hear it all. You've heard it. What do you wish to say now?"
>
> "Take your clothes off." (*Fountainhead* 279)

To Rand, masculinity is strength, while femininity is hero worship – the desire to look up to man. A woman is not an inferior human being; intellectually and morally, she ought to be the equal of the man she worships. What she seeks to admire is specifically his masculinity – his strength, physical and mental ("About a Woman President" *VOR* 268). And since the heroine of an Ayn Rand novel expects to look up to a lover's superior strength, she expects of a potential lover that he demonstrate his strength in some appropriate way, which makes her pose a challenge to him. This is why Dominique, in her conflict with Roark, tells him both "I'm going to destroy you" and "I'm going to pray that you can't be destroyed."

In other words, beyond the theme of *The Fountainhead*, the Roark–Dominique conflict expresses Rand's values in the realm of love and sex.[33]

Just as a literary character must have both "the universality of an abstraction" and "the unrepeatable uniqueness of a *person*," so must a story as a whole ("Basic Principles of Literature" *RM* 78). Take an example from *Atlas Shrugged*: Hank Rearden's invention of a new alloy that is to be "to steel what steel had been to iron." The metal is described as having "an odd tinge, it was greenish-blue" (*Atlas* 30, 36). Knowing no more than this, we can already see that Rearden Metal expresses Rand's values on two levels: thematic and personal. She regarded industrial production as a noble product of the mind, and green-blue was her favorite color.

Any theme subsumes an incalculable number of concretes with all kinds of attributes which in and of themselves have no connection to that theme. For instance, the theme of *The Fountainhead* is individualism versus collectivism, and Howard Roark, as a hero of individualism, embodies the first half of this abstraction. But the hard consonants of his name (Roark), his nationality (American), his hair color (red), the long lines of his body, his tactile sensuousness, his lack of facial hair – none of these are what makes Roark an individualist. They do, however, have "Ayn Rand" written all over them. These were her personal preferences, which she projects by means of her novel.

The projection of values beyond the theme does not violate the selectivity or integration of an artwork, since the *means* of projection are attributes of the material concretizing the theme. The Roark–Dominique test of strength is an attribute of their intellectual conflict, which is part of Rand's concretization of the theme of collectivism versus individualism. The greenish-blue of Rearden Metal is an attribute of an alloy whose primary story function is to concretize the mind's role in human existence.

"Like God," says Hugo, "the true poet is present in every part of his work at once" (Hugo 1910, 388). So is Rand in hers. Her personal values and premises are projected in every attribute of her fiction.

Any human being, and thus any artist, has some values unique to himself; and every artist, of whatever school, projects his own distinct personality in his work (unless he is a hack). For instance, Corneille is more of a hero-worshiper than is Racine. But what leads an artist to *feature* his personal values, or to relegate them to a secondary role, is his answer to the question: "Does man have the power of *choice*, the power to choose his goals and to achieve them, the power to direct the course of his life – or is he the helpless plaything of forces beyond his control, which determine his fate?" ("The Psycho-Epistemology of Art" *RM* 7). Whether one answers that man can choose, or that he cannot, one is making a metaphysical value-judgment – a judgment (this time) not merely of the possibility of achieving values, but of the possibility of having them in the first place.

Rand considers her unique view of the sanctity of the individual, her conception of ideal femininity, and her favorite color as important enough to project in a novel only because she holds that the individual forms his values by choice. If one held the premise of determinism – if one regarded human values as set by tradition or society – one would have to regard any seemingly unique and personal value as a delusion or a fluke; and one would not feature it in a novel.

"Man is a being of self-made soul," writes Rand, "which means that his character is formed by his basic premises, particularly by his basic value-premises" ("Art and Moral Treason" *RM* 138). For Rand, this is true of any person and thus of all artists – Naturalists and Classicists as well as Romanticists. But only a Romanticist holds such a view of human nature *as* a character-forming premise, allowing it to shape his values and actions.

One acts consistently with the premise that one is a being of self-made soul by taking responsibility for the making of that soul. This means, above all, forming one's values and basic premises by independently *evaluating* every aspect of reality, including the values of others, as opposed to simply accepting whatever values others hold.

One can tell that someone else has formed his character in this way by the extent to which he *has* values of his own which direct and color whatever he does. A Romantic artwork's abundance of individual values is what projects the spirit in which those values were formed: the spirit of a self-made soul embracing its own autonomous nature.

Romantic Art as a Product of Imagination

"Man's imagination," Rand writes, "is nothing more than the ability to rearrange the things he has observed in reality" ("The Metaphysical versus the Man-Made" *PWNI* 34). All artists use this ability – but the Romantic artist does so in a distinctively self-assertive manner.

Compare the Naturalistic and Romantic standards. "The value of a Naturalist's work," Rand writes, "depends on the specific characters, choices and actions of the men he reproduces – and he is judged by the fidelity with which he reproduces them." "The value of a Romanticist's work has to be created by its author; he owes no allegiance to men (only to man), only to the metaphysical nature of reality and to his own values" ("What is Romanticism?" *RM* 110).

Particular works of Naturalism or Romanticism adhere to the fundamental standards of their respective schools in different degrees. After the publication of *Atlas Shrugged*, Rand said that "*The Fountainhead* now, to me, seems a little too realistic." But *Atlas Shrugged* is "completely my kind of universe, primarily for two reasons." First, "it is built on an unusual plot device which is not Naturalistic in any sense. It's not even realistic." Second, "it is completely detached from any journalistic reality."

> The form of literature in which I personally feel most at home, which represents my literary sense of life, [is] where everything is made by me – everything except the metaphysical human abstraction. In other words, it has to be things as they might be, but from then on I want them to be as they ought to be – as I want to make them. I don't like being tied to the choices of other people. That is what it amounts to when you go into cultural issues; it's really the choices of others. And I want to be in my own universe of my own abstractions. (*Biographical Interviews* 565)

The Naturalist's fundamental standard is "things as they are," in real life. The Classicist's fundamental standard is things as they ought to be – according to tradition. These standards tie an artist to the choices of other people. By contrast, the Romanticist is not supplied with ready-made standards by others. As Roark tells the Dean, "I set my own standards." To be precise, the Romanticist creates, through an act of imagination, the standard that governs the further steps of the creative process.[34] This is the nature and function of a plot-theme, like "the mind on strike" (which is what Rand refers to when she says that *Atlas Shrugged* is built on an unusual plot device).

Zola gives essentially the same analysis of literary Romanticism and Naturalism – with an opposite evaluation. Naturalism, he writes approvingly, represents the "fall of the imagination" (1893, 209). The interest "no longer lies in the strangeness of the story; on the contrary, the more commonplace and general it is the more typical it becomes" (212). The Naturalistic novelist "invents a plan, a drama; only it is a scrap of drama, the first story he comes across and which daily life furnishes him with always. Then in the arrangement of the work this invention is only of very slight importance" (210).

In a Romantic story, the central dramatic invention is not a "scrap" furnished by daily life, but is a creative and characteristic product of the writer's imagination. And rather than being of "slight importance" in the further arrangement of the work, it is the standard of selection that determines everything else. Thus the work comes to be made fully in accordance with the writer's own values and independently of journalistic reality.

The nature of Romantic imagination is illuminated by the irrelevance of a certain kind of objection raised against particular Romantic works, to the effect that the author has deviated from some convention or other of literary form. I have mentioned the charge that Galt "has no inner conflicts." A related objection is that he "does not change." Yet another objection in the same Classicist category is that Galt's climactic speech to the world is long. (The historical Classicists did in fact have rules about the length at which any character could speak in a scene.) All these things are true, but they would be esthetic flaws only on the Classicist premise that the proper method of art is subordination to traditional rules.

If the above facts about *Atlas Shrugged* and its hero were judged on Romantic grounds – respecting the plot-theme as the standard of selection and determinant of subsidiary features – one's evaluation would be different. The novel's plot premise is that Galt calls a strike of the men of the mind and so "stops the motor of the world." In other words, he brings about the collapse of civilization. This is not an action that a moral man could take without explaining himself to the world, and especially to any innocently confused victims of the world's collapse. Nor can the explanation be perfunctory; it must be thorough and detailed and go all the way down to the philosophical foundations that justify and make necessary the strike. Given Galt's central plot action, nothing less than his 60-page radio address will do.[35]

443

Similarly, a moral man cannot bring down civilization if he is racked with inner conflict or is less than fully convinced, from the beginning, of the rightness of his course. The reasons that Galt gives in his speech at the end of the novel must have been fully known to him throughout; given Galt's central action, nothing less than a monolithic certainty could possibly suffice. There is no room in the story for a Galt that doubts, or "changes."

Had Rand jettisoned Galt's constancy and the length of his speech in conformity to conventional rules of drama, she would have breached the integrity of her self-created standard of selection, just as much as if Roark had agreed to add a Classical façade to the bank building. Rand is not a Classicist, conforming to rules. She is a Romanticist – and so upholds her freedom of imagination in the context of the standards she, like Roark, sets for herself.

Deeper than these particular Classicist objections to Romantic imagination is the Naturalistic objection to the very use of imagination itself (beyond the trivial sense in which any artistic selection is imagined). As Zola implies, Romantic characters and events are not commonplace but "strange." Men like Galt and Roark, Cyrano de Bergerac and Jean Valjean, it is often claimed, do not exist. But the Romantic ear is deaf to this objection: the goal of Romanticism is not to describe existing people, but to project what is possible to human beings. Conversely, Naturalism has been criticized by Rand (and by many others in Naturalism's youth, when there were still many Romanticists around) for presenting "commonplace" events and characters – which is precisely the goal of Naturalism. Both of these objections (to Romanticism and Naturalism, respectively) are based on a standard opposed to that by which the works being criticized were created.

Such judgments are not in and of themselves parochial, so long as the different standards involved are identified. However, a less direct charge against Romanticism equates the school's penchant for "strangeness" (or unfamiliarity) with a psychological flaw: "escapism." Romantic writers and readers allegedly seek escape from unpleasant realities by mental refuge in worlds of imagination. Rand dismisses this accusation: "If the projection of value-goals – the projection of an improvement on the given, the known, the immediately available – is an 'escape,' then medicine is an 'escape' from disease" ("The Goal of My Writing" *RM* 161).

However, Rand does hold that much Romantic literature *is* an escape, not by the essence of the school, but as a historical fact. She wrote that

> the impossibility of applying altruism to reality, to men's actual existence, led many Romantic writers to avoid the problem by escaping into history, i.e., by choosing to place their stories in some distant past (such as the Middle Ages). ("What is Romanticism?" *RM* 108)

As a champion of egoism, Rand needed no escape from the problem of dramatizing altruism as a virtue, and she mostly chose contemporary settings for her novels. "I am a Romantic Realist," she said, "distinguished from the Romantic tradition in that the values I deal with pertain to this earth and to the basic problems of this era" (*WTL* xi).

In what sense of the word is Rand a "realist"?

Note that literature can vary in degree of realism according to how radical the author's rearrangement of reality is: the more radical, the less reality-based the fabric of the story. In this regard, Rand's major novels became progressively *less* realistic, moving from *We the Living*, which has autobiographical elements, to *The Fountainhead*, which is based partly on the real-life struggle for modern architecture, to *Atlas Shrugged*, "where everything is made by me." As Rand made clear, this last characteristic, not realism, is what represents most fully her literary values. Within the metaphysical confines of what "might be," she seeks the greatest freedom to project her vision of what "ought to be."[36]

So when Rand calls herself a realist, she has in mind something else than how radically she rearranges reality according to her values. She is referring to the nature of those values – to the fact that they "pertain to this earth and to the basic problems of [her] era" and are dramatized through appropriate contemporary subject-matter. The theme of *We the Living* is the evil of totalitarianism, and the novel is set in Soviet Russia at the birth of this first modern totalitarian state – a birth Rand witnessed personally. The theme of *The Fountainhead*, individualism versus collectivism, Rand considered the central issue of her time, touching every field of endeavor, including contemporary architecture. The theme of *Atlas Shrugged*, the role of the mind in human existence, pertains to – and, in fact, explains – the post-industrial revolution era in which the novel is set, since industry for Rand rests on the mind.

Is *Atlas Shrugged* "realistic"? No, insofar as its events do not resemble those of real life. Yes, insofar as its theme and its values can be applied to – and, in the novel, *have been* applied to – the facts and issues of contemporary human existence.

The Objectivity of the Romantic Method

In Romanticism's youth, Victor Hugo opposed the Classicists' rule-mongering, but he also added a word of caution for would-be Romanticists. He championed, he said,

> the freedom of art against the despotism of systems, codes and rules. It is his [i.e., Hugo's own] habit to follow at all risks whatever he takes for his inspiration, and to change moulds as often as he changes metals. Dogmatism in the arts is what he shuns before everything. God forbid that he should aspire to be numbered among those men, be they romanticists or classicists, who compose *works according to their own systems*, who condemn themselves to have but one form in their minds, to be forever *proving* something, to follow other laws than those of their temperaments, and their natures. The artificial work of these men, however talented they may be, has no existence so far as art is concerned. (1910, 395, cf. *Answers* 199–200)

As noted above, the same Hugo who here proscribes other laws than those of a writer's temperament also spoke of "the immutable principles of the art of composition," that is, of plot. Is he contradicting himself? Should not an artist who upholds free self-expression cast aside all method and do whatever he feels like? Or to put the question in more fundamental terms: Is not subjectivism the only alternative to dogmatism?

Observe that Romanticism often *has* been viewed as a form of subjectivism (and not only by the school's detractors). This charge is directed either at *what* is expressed in Romantic works, or at *how* it is expressed (or both).

With regard to expressive content, a typical critic is Zola, who dismisses adherents of Romanticism as people who "regard art as the burden of personal error which the artist has put into his study of nature" (1893, 51). Romanticists, he is saying, are not engaged in the objective study of existence but distort nature by indulging in the expression of subjective personal values. Rand's philosophy gives her a ready answer to this objection. Human beings are not determined, and their lives are shaped by their chosen premises and values, whether true or false. It follows that the artist who explores the values of the individual is the one who does study the true nature of human existence.

445

With regard to Romanticism's creative method, or the alleged lack of such, literary scholar Irving Babbitt may represent the critics. He sees Romanticism encapsulated in a sentence of Edgar Allan Poe's: "Imagination, feeling herself for once unshackled, roamed at will among the ever-changing wonders of a shadowy and unstable land." Babbitt comments: "To take seriously the creations of this type of imagination is to be on the way towards madness" (1955, 269).[37] Babbitt also quotes Byron's statement that "The best of life is but intoxication," and drawing a comparison to Romantic creativity, writes: "The subrational and impulsive self of the man who has got drunk is not only released from the surveillance of reason in any sense of the word, but his imagination is at the same time set free from the limitations of the real" (147).[38]

Rand would not agree with this characterization of Romanticism; but I think she would hold the following: absent a standard so constituted as to enable the projection of individual values in a unified whole with an intelligible theme, an attempt at expressing such values *would* amount to subjectivism. The artist would be rearranging reality at random, as he felt like, vainly trying to capture an unintelligible "what ought to be" severed from "what might be." In *Atlas Shrugged*, composer Richard Halley speaks for Rand when he says about such an artist:

> he's the vehicle of higher mysteries, he doesn't know how he created his work or why, it just came out of him spontaneously, like vomit out of a drunkard, he did not think, he wouldn't stoop to thinking, he just *felt* it, [the] uncongealed bastard! (*Atlas* 783)

The opposite of such an artist is Howard Roark. To quote further from the description of his early architectural drawings: "The structures were austere and simple, until one looked at them and realized what work, what complexity of method, what tension of thought had achieved the simplicity." Interestingly, Roark's way of working is differentiated from two alternatives: "It was not as if the draftsman had [pieced] together doors, windows and columns, as his whim dictated and as the books prescribed" (*Fountainhead* 7). Roark is neither a subjectivist nor a dogmatist.

Instead, his own account of his method is in effect a description of working with a self-created standard. He says:

> I want to make [my work] real, living, functioning, built. But every living thing is integrated. Do you know what that means? Whole, pure, complete, unbroken. Do you know what constitutes an integrating principle? A thought. The one thought, the single thought that created the thing and every part of it. (*Fountainhead* 606)

Like Roark, the Romantic plot-writer has an integrating principle and standard: the particular plot-theme of his story. As with Roark, in his creation and use of such a standard, there is nothing mad, drunken, or subjective. And neither does such a standard amount to a "despotic system" of prescribed rules.

Plot is not imposed on a writer's material without regard for his individual values – it is a *means* of expressing precisely such values. Furthermore, leaving aside the (metaphysical) premise of volition implicit in the stress on individual values and abstract motivation, the method of plot is normatively non-restrictive; it can be used to objectify almost any values or value-premises that people do – or could – hold.

In her ethics and epistemology, Rand opposed both subjectivism and what she called "intrinsicism" – the view that one is obliged to adhere to certain standards regardless of one's personal values (see Chapters 3 and 12 above). Instead she argued that standards should be *objective* – determined by the facts of reality that make it necessary to proceed in a certain way *if one is to attain one's values*. The "immutable principles of composition" are objective in Rand's sense.[39]

It is in the nature of literature that a storyteller objectifies his own values through the values and actions of his characters. It is a fact of reality that the premises and value-hierarchy which lead to other people's actions are hard to grasp – except when they confront threats to their values. These facts give rise to a method of storytelling: plot conflict. One can use this method if it suits one's particular purpose; but there is no rule *demanding* that one use it regardless of one's purpose. Plot is the most important method of literary Romanticism, but the school does not uphold it as a Classicist absolute – as Rand noted,[40] and as her fiction demonstrates.

Indeed, one of her characteristics as a writer is the delight she seems to take in the imaginative experimentation with literary forms. For instance, her play *Night of January 16th* is a courtroom drama with alternative endings where the jury is drawn from the audience. This device allows Rand to project the opposition between independence and conformity – the two outlooks on life which would psychologically lead to either a Not Guilty or a Guilty verdict. The alternative-endings device is part of a self-created standard which governs Rand's selection; for instance, she has to calibrate the factual evidence so as not to favor one verdict or another, thus making the ending depend on where the audience-jurors fall in regard to the thematically opposed worldviews.

Rand's play *Ideal* is also based on a story idea which demands a structure that varies from a plot progression. The play confronts, consecutively, six characters with essentially *the same* context or "preceding events," in order to test how their true values – as these relate to their self-professed idealism – will lead them to act.

The best example of Rand's "changing moulds" as often as she "changes metals" is her novelette *Anthem*, a psychological fantasy about a man who lacks the word "I" and his discovery of this concept through the steps he takes to reinvent the electric light (which has similarly been lost to mankind in a collectivist future). As Rand observed, this story has no plot, no logical sequence of existential actions. Since its central device is the idea of an inner condition (lacking a concept of self) and progression (toward acquiring one), what unifies the events is not an external conflict but a sustained mental quest.[41]

In her fiction, Rand keeps to the basic methodology of Romanticism: selection by self-created standards. By this means, she achieves the projection of her values – without any element of a subjectivist revolt against objectivity on the one hand, or, on the other, any dogmatic subordination to intrinsicist rules. If one considers the wider tenets of her philosophy, Objectivism, it should be no mystery that she chose, as her artistic home and source of inspiration, the school of Romanticism.

Acknowledgment

I am grateful to The Ayn Rand Institute for a grant which supported the writing of this chapter, and to Kristi Boeckmann, Robert Mayhew, and Harry Binswanger for astute comments on earlier drafts. Above all, thanks to the editors, Allan Gotthelf and Gregory Salmieri, whose staunch commitment to perfection improved every page.

Notes

1 Regarding the accuracy of the quote from Aristotle, see below, 433–434.
2 Originally published in Hugo 1962.
3 All quotes from this course will be from the book version. A recording of the course is available from AynRandBookstore.com.
4 See Wright 1920, 98–115.
5 See Tzonis and Lefaivre 1986, 35–115.
6 One principle he has in mind is "unity of plot." He allows subplots only so long as they "shall tend constantly toward the central plot" (Hugo 1910, 379).
7 For a discussion of Roark's kind of architecture as Romantic, see my 2007a.
8 Her basic point is true of Romanticism in any form of art (as I believe she would have agreed).
9 I take it that Rand is here defining Romanticism and Naturalism in any form of art, not just in literature, which was the focus of her esthetic writings.
10 Question period of "Our Esthetic Vacuum" Bibliography #22.
11 See below 447.
12 I discuss the dramatic role of value-threats and conflict in my 2007b.
13 I discuss Romantic vs. Naturalistic characterization, in terms of abstraction-guided vs. emotion-driven motivation, in my 1993. For Rand's discussion of this issue, see *Answers* 215–216, and Chapter 7 of *AOF*.
14 See "Philosophy: Who Needs It" and "Philosophical Detection" in *PWNI*.
15 Like Rand, Conrad was a self-described Romantic realist. See below, 444.
16 For Rand's take on Rattigan, see *Answers* 198–199, and also Kay Nolte Smith "Terence Rattigan" *TO* 10(3) 1001.
17 *Poetics* 1451a36–38 (trans. Halliwell 1987, 40).
18 Her source was probably Nock 1943, 191. In her copy of this book, Rand had marked Aristotle's statement, translated by Nock in the form Rand would later use. (Reported by Jeff Britting of the Ayn Rand Archives.)
19 See my 2007b, and also Mayhew 2005d.
20 *Poetics* 1454a16–17 (trans. Halliwell 1987, 47). See also my 2007b and Halliwell 1986, 150–151, as well as Halliwell's commentary accompanying his 1987 translation (75–76).
21 *Poetics* 1452a19–21 (trans. Halliwell 1987, 42).
22 Rand discusses characterization at length in Chapter 7 of *AOF*.
23 Regarding these aspects of architecture, see "Art and Cognition" *RM* 36, 40.
24 I owe this example to Robert Mayhew.
25 Galt is serene, but not repressed; and he does experience emotional tension in scenes relating to his romantic conflict with Dagny Taggart.
26 For an extensive analysis of Dagny's contradiction, see Salmieri 2009b, 420–436.
27 Of relevance to this discussion is Rand's view of humor. See WKCR Interview on "The Nature of Humor" *Speaking*, and Mayhew 2002.
28 Rand sometimes uses the word "theme" more broadly to include the widest metaphysical meaning of an artwork.
29 For a discussion of Rand's view on mind–body unity, see Peikoff OPAR *passim*, and also Salmieri 2009a, 239–245.
30 In what follows I rely on a somewhat wider conception of the novel's plot-theme.
31 Rand comments on the reverse, "Byronic" premise that human beings must struggle heroically in the face of inevitable defeat, possessing volition in regard to consciousness but not to existence ("What is Romanticism?" *RM* 101–102).
32 See Ghate 2007, 253–257.
33 I discuss such "extra-thematic" values in my 2008, and also in my 2009, 149–66.
34 I discuss self-created standards in Romantic art in my 2007a and 2008.
35 See Ghate 2009b.
36 Rand did not write metaphysical fantasy, but she regarded it as a valid form if used to project a theme applicable to and therefore in some manner consistent with reality. Thus, in the widest sense,

allegiance to "what might be" concerns the abstract intelligibility of a work of art. See *AOF* 169–172, and *Answers* 181.

37 The Poe quote is from the story "The Unparalleled Adventure of One Hans Pfaall."
38 The Byron quote is from *Don Juan.*
39 Gregory Salmieri helped me clarify this point.
40 See *Answers* 212–215.
41 See AOF 36–37, and my 2005, 83–118.

References

Babbitt, Irving. 1955. *Rousseau and Romanticism.* New York, NY: Meridian Books.

Barzun, Jacques. 1961. *Classic, Romantic, and Modern.* Chicago, IL: The University of Chicago Press.

Boeckmann, Tore. 1993. "Conscious vs. Subconscious Motivation in Literature." *The Intellectual Activist* 7(4–5).

Boeckmann, Tore. 2005. "*Anthem* as a Psychological Fantasy." In *Essays on Ayn Rand's* Anthem, edited by Robert Mayhew. Lanham, MD: Lexington Books.

Boeckmann, Tore. 2007a. "*The Fountainhead* as a Romantic Novel." In Mayhew 2007a.

Boeckmann, Tore. 2007b. "What Might Be and Ought to Be: Aristotle's *Poetics* and *The Fountainhead.*" In Mayhew 2007a.

Boeckmann, Tore. 2008. "Caspar David Friedrich and Visual Romanticism." *The Objective Standard*, 3(1).

Boeckmann, Tore. 2009. "*Atlas Shrugged* and the Metaphysics of Values." In Mayhew 2009.

Ghate, Onkar. 2007. "The Basic Motivation of the Creators and the Masses in *The Fountainhead.*" In Mayhew 2007a.

Ghate, Onkar. 2009b. "The Role of Galt's Speech in *Atlas Shrugged.*" In Mayhew 2009.

Halliwell, Stephen. 1986. *Aristotle's Poetics.* London: Duckworth. Reprinted 1998 with new introduction, Chicago, IL: The University of Chicago Press.

Halliwell, Stephen. 1987. *The Poetics of Aristotle: Translation and Commentary.* London: Duckworth.

Hugo, Victor. 1910. "*Preface to Cromwell.*" In *Prefaces and Prologues to Famous Books*, edited by Charles W.Eliot. New York, NY: P.F. Collier & Son Company.

Hugo, Victor. 1962. *Ninety-Three*, translated by Lowell Bair. New York, NY: Bantam Books.

Liszt, Franz. 2005. *Life of Chopin*, trans. Martha Walker Cook. New York, NY: Dover. Reprinted from Boston, MA: Oliver Ditson & Co., 1880.

Mayhew, Robert. 2002. "Ayn Rand Laughed: Ayn Rand on the Role of Humor in Literature and in Life." *The Intellectual Activist* 16(1).

Mayhew, Robert. 2005d. "Ayn Rand as Aristotelian: Literary Esthetics." Paper presented to the Ayn Rand Society at the December 2005 Eastern Division Meeting of the American Philosophical Association.

Mayhew, Robert, ed. 2007a. *Essays on Ayn Rand's* The Fountainhead. Lanham, MD: Lexington Books.

Mayhew, Robert, ed. 2009. *Essays on Ayn Rand's* Atlas Shrugged. Lanham, MD: Lexington Books.

Nock, Albert Jay. 1943. *Memoirs of a Superfluous Man.* New York, NY: Harper and Brothers.

Praz, Mario. 1970. *The Romantic Agony.* Oxford: Oxford University Press.

Salmieri, Gregory. 2009a. "*Atlas Shrugged* on the Role of the Mind in Man's Existence." In Mayhew 2009.

Salmieri, Gregory. 2009b. "Discovering Atlantis: *Atlas Shrugged*'s Demonstration of a New Moral Philosophy." In Mayhew 2009.

Schmied, Wieland. 1995. *Caspar David Friedrich.* New York, NY: Harry N. Abrams, Inc.

Torres, Louis and Michelle M. Kamhi. 2000. *What Art Is: The Esthetic Theory of Ayn Rand.* Chicago, IL: Open Court.

Tzonis, Alexander and Liane Lefaivre. 1986. *Classical Architecture: The Poetics of Order.* Cambridge, MA: The MIT Press.

Wright, C.H.C. 1920. *French Classicism.* Cambridge, MA: Harvard University Press.

Zola, Émile. 1893. *The Experimental Novel and Other Essays.* New York, NY: Cassell Publishing Company.

Coda

18

Hallmarks of Objectivism

The Benevolent Universe Premise and The Heroic View of Man

ALLAN GOTTHELF AND GREGORY SALMIERI[1]

In London, England, in the year 1478, workers in gold were required for the first time to bring their wares to the Goldsmiths' Company for stamping, to certify their gold content. The Goldsmiths' Company place of business was called "Goldsmiths' Hall," and the mark of certification came to be called a hall-mark. In time the term "hallmark" came to be used more generally, for any sign of authenticity or quality, and then for any distinctive characteristic that was a striking sign of its possessor. In this chapter, we discuss a pair of interrelated theses that are hallmarks of Objectivism: the benevolent universe premise and the heroic view of man.

These theses are dramatic consequences of the defining essentials of the philosophy, and they are central to the sense of life conveyed by Ayn Rand's novels. They are key to understanding the tremendous emotional resonance these novels have for people who share this sense of life, and the visceral hatred that many readers with a contrary sense of life feel for Rand's work. In Chapter 5, above, Onkar Ghate discusses the role that such premises play in an individual's psychology, and in Chapter 16, Harry Binswanger discusses their role in art and in esthetic responses. Our focus here is on the meaning of these propositions themselves.

Because Rand's conception of heroism has been discussed at length in other chapters, we will spend most of our time on the benevolent universe premise. We will look at some of the passages that express it, offer an explicit characterization of it, indicate the history of Rand's use of the relevant terminology, and show how it depends on the fundamentals of Objectivism. This will enable us to see how it is a hallmark of her philosophy. We will then turn briefly to the heroic view of man, looking not at the content of Rand's view of heroism (which is covered in Chapter 4), but at how this view of heroism colored her view of humanity and of specific human beings.

Before we turn to Rand's benevolent universe, however, let us consider two passages – one from philosopher Bertrand Russell, one from the poet, A.E. Housman – that project a very different sense of life.[2]

> The life of man is a long march through the night, surrounded by invisible foes, tortured by weariness and pain, towards a goal that few can hope to reach, and where none may tarry long … Let us not

weigh in grudging scales [our fellow men's] merits and demerits, but let us think only of their need – of the sorrows, the difficulties, perhaps the blindnesses, that make the misery of their lives; let us remember that they are fellow-sufferers in the same darkness, actors in the same tragedy as ourselves ...

Brief and powerless is man's life; on him and all his race the slow, sure doom falls pitiless and dark. Blind to good and evil, reckless of destruction, omnipotent matter rolls on its relentless way; for Man, condemned to-day to lose his dearest, to-morrow himself to pass through the gate of darkness, it remains only to cherish, ere yet the blow falls, the lofty thoughts that ennoble his little day; disdaining the coward terrors of the slave of Fate, to worship at the shrine that his own hands have built; undismayed by the empire of chance, to preserve a mind free from the wanton tyranny that rules his outward life; proudly defiant of the irresistible forces that tolerate, for a moment, his knowledge and his condemnation, to sustain alone, a weary but unyielding Atlas, the world that his own ideals have fashioned despite the trampling march of unconscious power. (Russell 1903, 423–424)

And how am I to face the odds
of man's bedevilment and God's?
I, a stranger and afraid
in a world I never made.
(Housman, 1922)

This is a world, say Russell and Housman, full of suffering – a world of tragedy in which man cannot ultimately succeed, achieve happiness, or rationally celebrate his existence. In contrast, consider now the following passages from *Atlas Shrugged*. First, an exchange between Dagny Taggart and Ragnar Danneskjöld, in the valley, when she learns he is married to Kay Ludlow:

"How can" – she [Dagny] tried to stop, but the words burst involuntarily, in helpless indignant protest, whether against him, fate or the outer world, she could not tell – "how can she live through eleven months of thinking that you, at any moment, might be ...?" She did not finish.

He was smiling, but she saw the enormous solemnity of that which he and his wife had needed to earn their right to this kind of smile. "She can live through it, Miss Taggart, because we do not hold the belief that this earth is a realm of misery where man is doomed to destruction. We do not think that tragedy is our natural fate and we do not live in chronic dread of disaster. We do not expect disaster until we have specific reason to expect it – and when we encounter it, we are free to fight it. It is not happiness, but suffering that we consider unnatural. It is not success, but calamity that we regard as the abnormal exception in human life." (*Atlas* 759)

Second, listen to what John Galt says to Dagny, in the tunnels of Taggart Transcontinental, after they consummate their relationship, about his reaction to learning earlier that Dagny (with whom he was already in love) was romantically involved with another man:

Dagny, it's not that I don't suffer, it's that I know the unimportance of suffering, I know that pain is to be fought and thrown aside, not to be accepted as part of one's soul and as a permanent scar across one's view of existence. Don't feel sorry for me. It was gone right then. (*Atlas* 959–960)

It is this view of life that Ayn Rand called "the benevolent universe premise." It is the view that the universe is open to man's achievement and success – that the achievement of values and the enjoyment of happiness are, as Ragnar says, the natural state, the norm, the to-be-expected. It is the view that suffering and tragedy are the accidental, "to be fought and thrown aside," as Galt says, "not to be accepted as part of one's soul and as a permanent scar across one's view of existence."

Rand held this view all her life and struggled to hold on to it in her worst moments. Reflecting on her adolescence in Soviet Russia, she stressed the salvation provided her by the vision of "abroad" she got from operetta and from American movies (*Biographical Interviews* 203–209); and in her introduction to the 25th anniversary edition of *The Fountainhead* (viii–ix), she describes how the person, and sometimes the words, of her husband, Frank O'Connor, helped her to preserve this view of life.

The benevolent universe premise permeates all her novels, and much of her non-fiction, but it seems that she first conceptualized this view under this name sometime in the 1940s. Her earliest recorded uses of the phrase "benevolent universe" are in notes she wrote while planning *Atlas Shrugged*. The first of these, dated April 18, 1946, is part of a reflection on the character who will become Dagny Taggart: "it is proper for a creator to be optimistic, in the deepest, most basic sense, since the creator believes in a benevolent universe and functions on that premise" (*Papers* 159_13x_005_003/*Journals* 425). The second occurrence of the phrase is in notes dated March 8, 1947, in which Rand speaks of a person's need to articulate and be consciously convinced of the validity of several convictions that are implicit in the knowledge and values he formed at earlier stages in his psychological development. Among these convictions is that he lives in "a *benevolent universe* in which he can achieve happiness" (*Papers* 159_09D_009_005/*Journals* 555).

The contrary expression, "malevolent universe," is used twice in notes from 1946, in dialogue sketched for an exchange between Galt and a potential striker (*Papers* 158_09B_002_013/*Journals* 402). Rand uses both expressions again in letters to Isabel Paterson in 1948 (*Letters* 199, 202, 215).

In all of these cases, Rand uses the expressions as if they are already familiar to her. She seems to assume that "benevolent universe" is familiar to Paterson as well, but some of Paterson's apparent confusion about the idea of a malevolent universe suggests that Rand may be introducing her to that expression.

In fact, both expressions can be found in print prior to the exchange between Rand and Paterson, but "benevolent universe" seems to have been more common.[3] We are not certain of the origins of the phrase, but the earliest usage we have found is in an 1887 translation of an 1878 work by the German theologian Otto Pfleiderer. Commenting on David Friedrich Strauss's (1872) *Der alte und der neue Glaube*, he writes of the "flagrant inconsistency" between Strauss's materialistic, Darwinian worldview and his "reverence for a 'reasonable and benevolent universe'" (1887, 133). In Pfleiderer's original German edition, the phrase he attributes to Strauss is: "*vernünftigen und gütigen Universums*" (1883, 460). This phrase does not itself appear in Strauss's book, but Strauss does often conjoin forms of the words "*vernünftig*" ("rational," "reasonable") and "*gütig*" ("benevolent," "good"), and he says that these traits are inherent in the universe itself, rather than being products of divine craftsmanship, as is usually thought. (See Strauss 1872, §44.) The phrase "vernünftiges und gütiges Universum" begins to appear in German theological and philosophical works in 1873 – often attributed to Strauss, and often in the context of claims (like Pfleiderer's) that such a universe would require a God.[4] It may be that the phrase "benevolent universe" entered English from this German literature. In any case, most of the nineteenth- and early twentieth-century sources we found containing the English phrase are concerned (as is the German literature) with questions about the relation between religious and scientific worldviews. One example will suffice. Here is a passage from a 1926 *New York Times* article describing the opinions of physicist Robert A. Millikan:

> The discoveries of modern science tend in general to corroborate the religious idea of a benevolent universe, a world in which everything acts according to intelligent law and one which is ready to be used for and by mankind as soon as it is understood. ("Millikan Reviews Stages of Religion," *New York Times*, April 20, 1926, 13)

It is not clear exactly where Rand and Paterson encountered the phrase "benevolent universe" or how much of its history they knew, but since Paterson was religious, it is easy to imagine her and Rand arguing about whether there needs to be a God in order for the universe to be benevolent to man. However it was that Rand came by the terminology, it captures something that she had always held implicitly and that was coming explicitly to occupy a central place in her thought.

Pfleiderer thought that it was absurd for an atheist to attribute benevolence to the universe, because benevolence is an attribute of consciousness – a certain attitude that one person can feel toward another. This is not what Rand meant by the term in this context. She meant, rather, that the universe is such that happiness is achievable for human beings, and that an individual can rationally expect to achieve it if he forms rational values and works consistently to discover and implement the means to them. We can see this in how Rand elaborates on the "benevolent universe" premise in the 1947 notes quoted above:

> if [a man's] desires are derived from and based on reality correctly observed – they *will be achievable* in this universe. All his desires come from reality – but the wrong ones are due to his mistakes in judgment; if he realizes the mistake, a contradiction, or an inherent impossibility, he will *not* continue to desire these objects; he won't damn the universe for not giving him the irrational or impossible. (*Papers* 159_09D_009_005/*Journals* 555–556, cf. *Atlas* 1054)

As an example of damning the universe for not accommodating an irrational desire, consider the longing for immortality that is implicit in the passages from Russell quoted earlier. In Rand's view, absent some evidence that immortality is achievable, it is irrational to desire it, and it is certainly irrational to bemoan the brevity of human life, as Russell does. If, unlike Russell, our desires are informed by an understanding of what is possible and how it can be achieved, then all our desires will be necessarily achievable.

We can see here some philosophical theses on which Rand's benevolent universe premise rests. One is that our values and desires are not innate, but results of our reasoning. (On this point, see above 68, 82, and 114–116.) We could not grasp what is possible and how it can be achieved if reality did not behave in a consistent and law-like fashion, and unless our minds were capable of identifying the relevant laws, so the benevolent universe premise presupposes also the laws of identity and of causality (on which, see Jason Rheins's discussion, above, 249 and 255–256) and the potency of human reason (on which, see Chapter 12).

The benevolent universe premise is what Rand calls a "metaphysical value-judgment." It is metaphysical in that it answers a question about the nature of the universe (including human nature). And it qualifies as a value-judgment because a person's answer to this question is a fundamental factor in his selection of goals.[5] Someone who believes, with Russell and Housman, that the universe is inhospitable to human beings, that suffering is our natural fate, and that great efforts are doomed to failure, will reject ambitious existential goals as unattainable and will not value his own happiness (which he will also regard as unattainable). But someone who, like Ragnar and Galt, is convinced that misery is unnatural and that success is the to-be-expected result of the rational pursuit of rationally chosen values, will be motivated to pursue happiness by forming values and working to realize them.

Rand recognized that success and happiness are not guaranteed, even to a rational, moral man. There are many factors that can prevent or destroy one's achievements. But Rand thought that all such factors are *journalistic*, rather than *metaphysical* – that is, they are due to the details of specific circumstances, rather than being inherent in the nature of existence as such.

Of the factors that can imperil values, the one that most concerned Rand was the immorality of other people. Dominique Francon holds the malevolent universe premise throughout most of *The Fountainhead* because she mistakenly regards this factor as metaphysical. We can see this in a thought she has late in the novel, once the mistake has been corrected.

> I have never been able to enjoy it before, the sight of the earth, it's such a great background, but it has no meaning except as a background, and I thought of those who owned it and then it hurt me too much. I can love it now. They don't own it. They own nothing. They've never won. I have seen the life of Gail Wynand, and now I know. One cannot hate the earth in their name. The earth is beautiful. And it is a background, but not theirs. (*Fountainhead* 697)

The root of Dominique's error is the premise that the world is "owned" by contemptible people – that is, that the depravity of others is a fundamental and insurmountable force opposed to great achievements (such as Howard Roark's buildings).[6] What she discovers by observing Wynand is the true nature of the force she had feared. Evil people (such as Ellsworth Toohey), who wish to destroy achievement, are fundamentally impotent. When they are able to cause grand-scale damage, it is only because an achiever like Wynand has put his creations at their disposal. (In Wynand's case, this was motivated by an error similar to Dominique's own.[7]) However prevalent the errors and compromises that empower evil may be at a particular place and time, they are not an inherent feature of the universe to which we must resign ourselves. Evil can always be fought, and understanding its nature enables one to fight it effectively and to protect one's values from its effects. This is a central theme in *Atlas Shrugged*, and much of Rand's non-fiction is about identifying and fighting the evil in our own culture. (See, especially Chapters 13 and 15, above, for discussion.)

This does not mean that a person can make himself invulnerable to the effects of evil (any more than he can make himself invulnerable to accidents). When a good person's values are destroyed or jeopardized by the evil of others, he will (properly) feel pain and anger. But, if he is on the benevolent universe premise, it will be a delimited emotion pertaining to the specific loss, rather than a holistic response to a hostile world. We can see this in something Roark says to Dominique, earlier in *The Fountainhead*, when a temple he designed is about to be destroyed and Dominique looks at him "as if she knew his worst suffering":

> What you're thinking is much worse than the truth ... I'm not capable of suffering completely. I never have. It goes only down to a certain point and then it stops. As long as there is that untouched point, it's not really pain. You mustn't look like that. (*Fountainhead* 354; cf. 499, 513, 650)

"That untouched point" is Roark's perspective, not on his specific circumstances, but on the universe as such and his relation to it. From this perspective, the facts that he designed and built the temple are what stand out, and "nothing else can seem very important."

We can see this same perspective in Dagny's first words to Galt.[8] "We never had to take any of it seriously, did we?" she asks, referring to a series of senseless evils that had brought her to the brink of despair. Galt responds, "No, we never had to" (*Atlas* 702).[9] In this context, to take an evil seriously would mean to regard it as metaphysical, rather than journalistic – to "take it as the essence and meaning of life" (*Letters* 584). This is something that Rand's heroes do not do, even when faced with the most horrific evils and overwhelming pain.

Over the course of *We the Living*, the Soviet system thwarts all of Kira Argounova's plans and destroys everyone she loves, but at the end of the novel she sees the world not as a realm of futility and despair but as "an endless earth where so much had been possible." What she regards as metaphysically significant is the fact that profound values are achievable by human beings, and she recognizes that maintaining this perspective in the face of great horrors is itself a profound achievement. Here are her last thoughts, as she lies in snow, shot in an attempt to cross the Latvian border to freedom:

> She smiled. She knew she was dying. But it did not matter any longer. She had known something which no human words could ever tell and she knew it now. She had been awaiting it and she felt it, as if it had been, as if she had lived it. Life had been, if only because she had known it could be, and she felt it now as a hymn without sound, deep under the little hole that dripped red drops into the snow, deeper than that from which the red drops came. A moment or an eternity – did it matter? Life, undefeated, existed and could exist.
> *She smiled, her last smile, to so much that had been possible.* (*WTL36* 570/*WTL* 443)

This conviction that *so much is possible to man on earth* is the benevolent universe premise. Let us now review how it follows from some of the central theses of Objectivism, discussed in earlier chapters:

- "A is A" (*Atlas* 1016). Everything that exists has an identity – it is what it is and acts in accordance with its nature. That is, things have definite causes and effects, which, once learned, can be used to predict and control outcomes. (See Chapter 11, above.)
- "Man is a rational being" ("Representation Without Authorization" *VOR* 91). This means that all of a human being's actions and the course of his life as a whole are determined by the faculty of reason. Reason, as Rand understands it, is a *powerful* faculty that enables us to understand in fundamental terms *what* things are and *why* they act as they do. Because of this, we can attain the knowledge we need to transform the world to serve our needs and values. (See Chapter 12, above.)
- "Man is a being of volitional consciousness" (*Atlas* 1012). The volitional nature of reason means that we are not pawns whose lives are determined by factors outside of our control. We can *choose* values consistent with one another and with the facts of reality, and we can forge a character that enables us to achieve these values and to experience their emotional concomitant, "a state of non-contradictory joy" (*Atlas* 1022). (See Chapters 3 and 5, above.)
- "There *is* a morality of reason, a morality proper to man, and *Man's Life* is its standard of value" (*Atlas* 1014). Far from being the enemy of personal happiness, morality is the means to it. It consists of rational principles that tell us how to form and achieve the sort of values in which human life and happiness consist. (See Chapter 4, above.)
- "There are no conflicts of interest among rational men" (*Atlas* 1022), so the happiness of some individuals does not require (and cannot be achieved by) the sacrifice of others, and it is possible to implement "an ideal social system" (*CUI* viii) that secures for all individuals the freedom each needs to realize fully his potential. Thus the strife and injustices of any given society are not reasons to think that the world is inhospitable to human happiness; they are simply problems that (like any others) one must work to solve (by reforming one's

society, escaping it, or finding a way to minimize the effects of its injustices on one's values). (See Chapters 7 through 10 and 15.)

If all these theses are true, then the universe is benevolent: a profound happiness is possible to us, and each of us can rationally expect to attain this happiness, even in adverse (journalistic) conditions, if he commits himself to realizing his highest potential as a rational being. But this is a very demanding achievement, which brings us to our second hallmark: Rand's *heroic view of man*.

We can treat this topic briefly because the content of Rand's view of moral heroism has been discussed at great length in Chapter 4. What we would like to consider here is what it means to ascribe this heroism to *man* rather than some specific man. Let us begin by examining two passages. The first is a description of Francisco d'Anconia. The second is Hugh Akston's statement about his three students, Francisco, Galt, and Ragnar.

His tall, slender figure had an air of distinction, too authentic to be modern, and he moved as if he had a cape floating behind him in the wind. People explained him by saying that he had the vitality of a healthy animal, but they knew dimly that that was not correct. He had the vitality of a healthy human being, a thing so rare that no one could identify it. He had the power of certainty. (*Atlas* 117)

Don't be astonished, Miss Taggart, and don't make the mistake of thinking that these three pupils of mine are some sort of superhuman creatures. They're something much greater and more astounding than that: they're normal men – a thing the world has never seen – and their feat is that they managed to survive as such. It does take an exceptional mind and a still more exceptional integrity to remain untouched by the brain-destroying influences of the world's doctrines, the accumulated evil of centuries – to remain human, since the human is the rational. (1071)

These passages stress both the normalcy and unusualness of the heroes. They are normal in the sense of being the human analog to a healthy animal of other species. That is, they have developed their natural capacities and are fully and consistently *living*, rather than acting (even part-time) as their own destroyers. Such a life is *in accordance with the nature* of any living thing, and for all living things other than man, such a life comes naturally – automatically. But since man is the rational animal, and reason is a volitional faculty, human beings have no automatic course of action – no way of life that comes naturally to them. As Galt puts the point:

Man has to be man – by choice; he has to hold his life as a value – by choice; he has to learn to sustain it – by choice; he has to discover the values it requires and practice his virtues – by choice. (*Atlas* 1013)

Because of this, achieving and maintaining the natural, healthy, and normal state for a human being is an accomplishment. This accomplishment is especially difficult if one is living at a time when the relevant values and virtues have not yet been identified explicitly, or if one is living in a culture that is dominated by opposite ideas that are poisonous to the human potential. Thus healthy human beings are vanishingly rare and it is a great "feat" to attain and retain fully one's stature as a human being. In particular, it requires a strong mind and great endurance.

Nonetheless, Rand's view is that the ideal that her heroes represent is open to all human beings by nature. This means that, with the possible tragic exceptions of people with extreme mental illness (including those who have grown up in environments deleterious enough to destroy entirely their rational capacity), any person in any circumstance is capable of developing into the moral equivalent of John Galt. In some circumstances this will be much more difficult than others, but because the ideal is demanding, even in the most favorable circumstances, living up to it remains a difficult and profound accomplishment – something deserving of reverence and emulation.

Like the benevolent universe premise, the heroic view of man is a metaphysical value judgment. It is not just the belief that human beings have the potential to achieve a heroic stature; it is regarding this potential as what is *important* about oneself and others. This is the perspective that Rand's novels convey, and it is why millions of readers find them so compelling. It is a perspective that can be difficult to maintain amidst the minutiae of daily life, especially in a culture that (Rand thought) is hostile to this sense of life. But, she maintained that this perspective represents a grasp of a profound truth – one for which she offered an articulation and defense in the form of a philosophical system. We hope that the chapters of this volume have served to orient you to that system and to the rich and varied body of works in which she develops, expounds, and applies it.

We leave you with Rand's description of a rare real-life event – the Apollo 11 launch – that she thought embodied her heroic vision of what human beings might be and ought to be.

> What we had seen, in naked essentials – but in reality, not in a work of art – was the concretized abstraction of man's greatness.
>
> The meaning of the sight lay in the fact that when those dark red wings of fire flared open, one knew that one was not looking at a normal occurrence, but at a cataclysm which, if unleashed by nature, would have wiped man out of existence – and one knew also that this cataclysm was planned, unleashed, and *controlled* by man, that this unimaginable power was ruled by *his power* and, obediently serving his purpose, was making way for a slender, rising craft. One knew that this spectacle was not the product of inanimate nature, like some aurora borealis, or of chance, or of luck, that it was unmistakably human – with "human," for once, meaning *grandeur* – that a purpose and a long, sustained, disciplined effort had gone to achieve this series of moments, and that man was succeeding, succeeding, succeeding! For once, if only for seven minutes, the worst among those who saw it had to feel – not "How small is man by the side of the Grand Canyon!" – but "How great is man and how safe is nature when he conquers it!" ("Apollo 11" *VOR* 166–167)

Notes

1 [Note by Gregory Salmieri: When Allan Gotthelf passed away, approximately half of this chapter was written and there were notes for parts of the uncompleted portion. I finished the chapter, as I did with Chapter 4, above, but in this case, I took more liberty in the use of my own ideas and research, so I present it as a jointly authored piece.]

2 Both passages were familiar to Rand. Parts of each were both quoted and discussed by Nathaniel Branden in his *Basic Principles of Objectivism* course, which she endorsed. (The relevant material can be found in *VAR* on pages, 326–328 and 425, respectively; on the relation between this book and the course Rand endorsed, see entry #51 in the annotated bibliography.) Branden also quotes the Housman stanza at the beginning of "Alienation" (*CUI* 308), and Rand quotes a phrase from it in "The 'Conflicts' of Men's Interests" (*VOS* 61).

3 The earliest use of "malevolent universe" we have found so far is a comment on the closing paragraph (quoted above) of Russell's "A Free Man's Worship." Warner Fite (1914, 182) remarks: "Shameful to relate, throughout this really noble passage, I find myself obsessed by the vision of a Platonic realist

shaking his fist at a cigar-shop Indian. I can grasp what is meant by a rational attitude towards a benevolent or an accommodating universe, or toward a malevolent universe. But what would be a rational attitude towards a universe that is simply bloodless and inscrutable strikes me as a most perplexing problem, and a problem which realism has yet to solve." Other examples include Bernard 1924, 227, and Boveri 1939, 88.

4 See: Nippold 1873, 156, Wutzdorff 1873, 43, and Holtzendorff 1882, 38. (Thank you to Sascha Settegast for his help in researching these German theologians.)

5 See Onkar Ghate's discussion 119, above, and Harry Binswanger's 408.

6 Rand described Dominique as "in effect, myself in a bad mood" (*Biographical Interviews* 363). Rand's notes for *The Little Street* (*Journals* 20–48) reveal her at her most Dominique-like. See Ghate 2007 on the relation between these notes and Rand's mature position (as expressed in *The Fountainhead* and subsequent writings).

7 On the impotence of evil, see also: *Journals* 264–265. On how errors about this point can lead to a malevolent universe premise, see *Atlas* 812–813.

8 There is an interesting parallel between this passage and the passage (quoted above) from *The Fountainhead* in which Dominique rejects the malevolent universe premise. The heroine of each novel is lying on her back looking up at (among other things) the sunlight and green leaves. For obvious reasons, this image of sunlight filtering through leaves evokes the vitality of life (a point highlighted in the *Fountainhead* passage); evidently, for Rand, it was also strongly associated with the recognition that the world is hospitable for human life and achievement.

9 On this passage and the different senses in which evil should and should not be "taken seriously," see *Answers* 166 and *Letters* 583–584. On Dagny's struggle, see Salmieri 2009b, 420–436.

References

Bernard, Luther Lee. 1924. *Instinct: A Study in Social Psychology*. New York, NY: Holt.

Boveri, Margret. 1939. *Minaret and Pipe-Line*. Oxford: Oxford University Press.

Fite, Warner. 1914. "The Philosophy of Bertrand Russell," *The Nation*, 98(2538).

Ghate, Onkar. 2007. "The Basic Motivation of the Creators and the Masses in *The Fountainhead*." In *Essays on Ayn Rand's* The Fountainhead, edited by Robert Mayhew. Lanham, MD: Lexington Books.

Holtzendorff, Franz von. 1882. *Die Verantwortlichkeit der Schule nach Seiten der gesundheitlichen Volksinteressen*. Berlin: Carl Habel.

Housman, A.E. 1922. "No. 12: The laws of God, the laws of man," In *Last Poems*. New York, NY: Henry Holt and Co.

Nippold, Friedrich. 1873. "Die literarischen Ergebnisse der neuen Straußischen Kontroverse. Kritische Studie." In Lodwijk Willem Ernst Rauwenhoff and Friedrich Nippold, *D. Fr. Strauß' alter und neuer Glaube und seine literarischen Ergebnisse. Zwei kritische Abhandlungen*. Leipzig, GE: Richter & Harrassowitz/ Leiden: von Doesburgh.

Pfleiderer, Otto. 1883. *Religionsphilosophie auf geschichtlicher Grundlage*, 2nd, augmented edition. Berlin: G. Reimer.

Pfleiderer, Otto. 1887. *The Philosophy of Religion on the Basis of its History, vol. II, Schelling to the Present Day*. London: Williams and Norgate.

Russell, Bertrand. 1903. "The Free Man's Worship." *Independent Review*, 1(3).

Salmieri, Gregory. 2009b. "Discovering Atlantis: *Atlas Shrugged*'s Demonstration of a New Moral Philosophy." In *Essays on Ayn Rand's Atlas Shrugged*, edited by Robert Mayhew. Lanham, MD: Lexington Books.

Strauss, David Friedrich. 1872. *Der alte und der neue Glaube. Ein Bekenntnis*. Leipzig: S. Hirzel.

Wutzdorff. 1873 "Ueber Freiheit und Nothwendigkeit." In *Neues Lausitzisches Magazin*, edited by E.E. Struve. Görlitz: E. Remer.

Annotated Bibliography of Primary and Quasi-Primary Sources

GREGORY SALMIERI

This bibliography includes all of the works referenced in this volume that were either written by Rand or endorsed by her as accurate statements of her views. It also includes works that are of special interest because they are derived from works that were so authorized, and posthumously published or archival materials by Rand.

Each numbered entry denotes the earliest edition of a work. Such entries are ordered by category and subcategory and, within these, by date of publication. Unnumbered subentries are given for later editions of each work, including the edition cited in this volume and any intervening editions that introduced significant revisions or new material.

Entries for the editions cited in this volume include the abbreviations by which the works are cited (as listed in "A Note on Abbreviations and References" in the front of the book). Absent some indication to the contrary, all citations are to the most readily available editions of Rand's works. In cases where there are multiple editions in print, citations are given to the quality (hardcover or trade paperback) editions, rather than to the Signet mass market paperbacks, because the pagination in the latter sometimes varies without warning from one printing to the next. Unfortunately, several books are only readily available in these inconstant Signet editions; the bibliography entries for these books include the printing number of the version against which we have checked the quotes.

I. Rand's Works and the Objectivist Corpus

By the "Objectivist corpus," I mean works by Rand published under her own name during her lifetime, and works by others that she endorsed as expressions of her philosophy. This section includes the most widely available sources of material in the corpus. Some of these sources also contain material that is not part of the corpus, and this is indicated in the relevant entries.

A. Fiction

1 1936. *We the Living*. London, UK: Macmillan. **[WTL36]**
  1959. New York, NY: Random House. (This edition was revised and includes a new introduction by Rand.)
  2011. 75th anniversary deluxe edition. New York, NY: New American Library. **[WTL]**

A Companion to Ayn Rand, First Edition. Edited by Allan Gotthelf and Gregory Salmieri.
© 2016 John Wiley & Sons, Ltd. Published 2016 by John Wiley & Sons, Ltd.

2 1936. *Night of January 16th: A Comedy-Drama in Three Acts*. Nathaniel Edward Reeid, editor. New York, NY: Longmans, Green and Co. (This version of the play was edited contrary to Rand's wishes, and she did not consider it to be part of her corpus. For her repudiation of it, see *Plays* 13.)

1968. Final definitive version. New York, NY: World Publishing.

1987. Final revised version. New York, NY: Plume. (This edition includes changes Rand made for a 1973 production. This same version of the play is included in *Plays*.)

3 1938. *Anthem*. London, UK: Cassell. **[*Anthem38*]**

1946. Los Angeles, CA: Pamphleteers. (This edition was revised and includes a new introduction by Rand.)

2005. Centennial edition. New York, NY: Dutton. **[*Anthem*]**

4 1943. *The Fountainhead*. Indianapolis, IN: Bobbs-Merrill.

1968. 25th anniversary edition with a special introduction by the author. Indianapolis, IN: Bobbs-Merrill.

1994. New York, NY: Plume. **[*Fountainhead*]**

5 1957. *Atlas Shrugged*. New York, NY: Random House.

2005. Centennial edition. New York, NY: Dutton. **[*Atlas*]**

B. Non-fiction volumes first published during Rand's lifetime

Most of the material published in the following books had been previously published, usually in Rand's own periodicals (see section I.D, below). In some cases, Rand revised the pieces for inclusion in the books. Since the books are much more widely available than the periodicals, citations in this volume are always to the books, except in cases where the passage being referenced appears only in the version of a piece published in the periodical.

6 1961. *For the New Intellectual: The Philosophy of Ayn Rand*. New York, NY: Random House.

2005. Centennial edition. Printing 50. New York, NY: Signet. **[*FTNI*]**

7 1964. *The Virtue of Selfishness: A New Concept of Egoism*. New York, NY: Signet (New American Library).

1965. Hard cover edition. (This is the first version to include an index.)

2005. Centennial edition. Printing 70. New York, NY: Signet. **[*VOS*]**

8 1966. *Capitalism: The Unknown Ideal*. New York, NY: New American Library.

1967. Revised edition.

2005. Centennial edition. Printing 50. New York, NY: Signet. **[*CUI*]**

9 1967. *Introduction to Objectivist Epistemology*. New York, NY: The Objectivist.

1979. New York, NY: New American Library. (This edition is the first to include Leonard Peikoff's "The Analytic–Synthetic Dichotomy.")

1990. Expanded second edition. Harry Binswanger and Leonard Peikoff, editors. New York, NY: Meridian. (This edition includes as an appendix, substantial material selected and edited by Peikoff and Binswanger, from workshops Rand conducted on epistemology; cf. #50, below. This material should be considered with the works listed in section II.C, below.) **[*ITOE*]**

10 1969. *The Romantic Manifesto: A Philosophy of Literature*. New York, NY: New American Library.

1975. Revised edition.

2005. Centennial edition. Printing 30. New York, NY: Signet. **[*RM*]**

11 1971. *The New Left: The Anti-Industrial Revolution*. New York, NY: New American Library.

1975. Revised edition.

1999. See #15, below.

C. Posthumously published collections of earlier published material

12 1982. *Philosophy: Who Needs It*. Indianapolis, IN: Bobbs-Merrill. (This collection was planned by Rand, who made revisions to some of the articles, but final editorial decisions were made by Peikoff after her death. The few editorial interpolations by Peikoff are indicated by brackets.)
1982. Centennial edition. Printing 30. New York: Signet. **[PWNI]**

13 1990. *The Voice of Reason: Essays in Objectivist Thought*. Leonard Peikoff, editor. New York, NY: Meridian. (In addition to pieces by Rand, this book includes six pieces written after her death, five by Leonard Peikoff and one by Peter Schwartz.) **[VOR]**

14 1991. *The Ayn Rand Column*. Peter Schwartz, editor. New Milford, CT: Second Renaissance Books. 1998. Revised edition. **[Column]**

15 1999. *Return of the Primitive: The Anti-Industrial Revolution*. New expanded edition of *The New Left: The Anti-Industrial Revolution*. Peter Schwartz, editor. New York, NY: Meridian. (This book includes all of the articles from #11, but they have been re-sequenced and interspersed with five additional articles, two by Rand and three written by Schwartz after her death. The result is essentially a new book with a new title.) **[ROTP]**

D. Periodicals edited by Rand

Rand endorsed the material in these periodicals as "authentic sources of information on Objectivism" ("A Statement of Policy" *TO* 7(6) 471).

16 1962–1965. *The Objectivist Newsletter*, volumes 1–4.
1990. Bound edition. New Milford, CT: Second Renaissance Books. **[TON]**

17 1965–1971. *The Objectivist*, volumes 5–10.
1990. Bound edition. New Milford, CT: Second Renaissance Books. **[TO]**

18 1971–1976. *The Ayn Rand Letter*, volumes 1–4.
1990. Bound edition. New Milford, CT: Second Renaissance Books. **[ARL]**

E. Periodicals recommended by Rand that contain material by her

It is only the material in these periodicals that Rand herself wrote or specifically endorsed that qualifies as part of the Objectivist corpus.

19 1979–1991. *The Intellectual Activist*, volumes 1–5. Edited by Peter Schwartz.
2005. Bound edition. Louisa, VA: Tracinski Publishing Company. **[TIA]**

20 1980–1987. *The Objectivist Forum*, volumes 1–8. Edited by Harry Binswanger.
1993. Bound edition. TOF Publications, Inc. **[TOF]**

F. Cited works by Rand not available in the above sources

21 1960. "JFK, High Class Beatnik?" *Human Events*, 17(35), September 1, 393–394.

22 1962. "The Esthetic Vacuum" (or "Our Esthetic Vacuum"). Radio address, available at http://estore.aynrand.org/p/58 (accessed May 22, 2015).

23 1964. "Playboy Interview: Ayn Rand," by Alvin Toffler. *Playboy*, March, 35–43. (Rand had the opportunity to edit the text of her answers; so, unlike the sources, listed in II.C, below, the answers in this interview are not extemporaneous or adapted by another editor.) **[*Playboy Interview*]**

24 1966. "The Philosophical Vacuum." Radio address, published in *The Exacting Ear*, Eleanor McKinney, editor. New York, NY: Pantheon.

25 1968. "The Rebellion at Columbia." Radio address, available at https://estore.aynrand.org/p/62 (accessed May 22, 2015).

26 1971. "The Moratorium on Brains." Lecture, available at https://estore.aynrand.org/p/21 (accessed May 22, 2015).

27 1972. "McGovern is the First to Offer Full-Fledged Statism to the American People." *Saturday Review of the Society*, October 21, 50.

28 1974. "Philosophy: Who Needs It." Lecture, available at https://estore.aynrand.org/p/42 (accessed May 22, 2015).

29 1976. "The Moral Factor." Lecture, available at http://aynrandlexicon.com/ayn-rand-works/moral-factor.html (accessed May 22, 2015).

30 1978. "Cultural Update." Lecture, published in small quantities as a pamphlet by Palo Alto Book Services. Recording available at http://estore.aynrand.org/p/15 (accessed May 22, 2015).

G. Cited works endorsed by Rand that are not included in the above sources

31 Branden, Nathaniel, and Barbara Branden. 1962. *Who Is Ayn Rand?* New York, NY: Random House. (Rand listed this book among the "authentic sources of information on Objectivism" ["A Statement of Policy" *TO* 7(6) 471].) **[*WIAR*]**

32 Peikoff, Leonard. 1970. *Founders of Western Philosophy: Thales to Hume*. Lecture course. Recording available at https://estore.aynrand.org/p/95 (accessed May 22, 2015). (This and #34, among other lecture series, are endorsed in *ARL* 4(3) 389.) **[*HOP1*]**

33 Peikoff, Leonard. 1970. *Modern Philosophy: Kant to the Present*. Lecture course. Recording available at https://estore.aynrand.org/p/96 (accessed May 22, 2015). **[*HOP2*]**

34 Peikoff, Leonard. 1976. *The Philosophy of Objectivism*. Lecture course. Recording available at https://estore.aynrand.org/p/6 (accessed May 22, 2015). (Rand attended this course, participated in some of the question periods, and endorsed it as "the only *authorized* presentation of the entire theoretical structure of Objectivism, i.e., the only one that I know of my own knowledge to be fully accurate" ["A Last Survey" *ARL* 4(3) 387].) **[*TPO*]**

35 Peikoff, Leonard. 1982. *The Ominous Parallels: The End of Freedom in America*. New York, NY: Stein and Day. (The book, published shortly after Rand's death, includes an introduction written by her two years earlier, in which she describes it as "a great, new, crucial achievement" and "the first book by an Objectivist philosopher other than myself.") **[*Parallels*]**

II. Posthumously Published Materials

Rand's posthumously published material cannot be considered part of her corpus, both because much of it consists in notes or informal statements that she may not have considered exact and because it has been edited by other hands. However, these sources provide important evidence concerning her thought and development, and they contain many valuable ideas that she did not express in print, so they are referenced frequently in this book.

A. Fiction

36 1985. *The Early Ayn Rand.* Leonard Peikoff, editor. New York, NY: New American Library. 2005. Revised edition. Printing 10. New York, NY: Signet. **[*Early*]**

37 2005. *Three Plays.* Printing 10. New York, NY: Signet. **[*Plays*]**

38 2014. *The Unconquered* with another, earlier adaptation of *We The Living*. Robert Mayhew, editor. New York, NY: Palgrave Macmillan. **[*Unconquered*]**

39 2015. *Ideal: The Novel and the Play.* Richard Ralston and Leonard Peikoff, editors. New York, NY: New American Library. **[*Ideal*]**

B. Other writings

40 1995. *Ayn Rand's Marginalia: Her Critical Comments on the Writings of over 20 Authors.* Robert Mayhew, editor. New Milford, CT: Second Renaissance Books. **[Marginalia]**

41 1997. *Letters of Ayn Rand.* Michael S. Berliner, editor. New York, NY: Dutton. **[Letters]**

42 1999. *Journals of Ayn Rand.* David Harriman, editor. New York, NY: Dutton. **[Journals]**

43 1999. *Russian Writings on Hollywood.* Michael S. Berliner, editor. Dina Garmong, translator. Irvine, CA: Ayn Rand Institute Press. (Much of the contents of this book were first published during Rand's lifetime, but only in Russian and anonymously or under her given name, A. Rozenbaum.) **[Russian Writings]**

C. Adaptations of spoken material

Adapting spoken material to written form necessarily involves more editing than does preparing written material for publication. This should be kept in mind when referring to the sources listed below. In most cases the original recordings are available and scholars should consult them before relying on a particular statement. *AOF* and *AON*, in particular, are adaptations of courses Rand delivered extemporaneously and required considerable reorganization (as explained in their introductions). Since *Answers* is a "best of," its editor, Robert Mayhew, had to exercise considerable judgment as to which of Rand's answers (or parts of longer answers) are her best. In my view, his judgment is usually sound, given the aims of the book. The volume presents a lot of fascinating material by Rand in an easily digestible form. This makes it perfect for fans who want a sampling of her Q&A. It is also a godsend for scholars, because it makes it easy to access Rand's comments on a wide range of issues that she did not address in print. Of course, once they have found the relevant answers, scholars will want to listen to them in their original form and context, rather than relying on Mayhew's edited versions.

44 2000. *The Art of Fiction: A Guide for Writers and Readers.* Tore Boeckmann, editor. New York, NY: Plume. **[AOF]**

45 2001. *The Art of Nonfiction: A Guide for Writers and Readers.* Robert Mayhew, editor. New York, NY: Plume. **[AON]**

46 2005. *Ayn Rand Answers: The Best of Her Q&A.* Robert Mayhew, editor. New York, NY: New American Library. **[Answers]**

47 2009. *Objectively Speaking: Ayn Rand Interviewed.* Marlene Podritske and Peter Schwartz, editors. Lanham, MD: Lexington Books. **[Speaking]**

III. Unpublished Archival Materials

The materials listed below are in the Ayn Rand Archives, which "makes its holdings and services available to all serious scholars, researchers, and general writers on equal terms of access." Information on the Archives can be found at https://www.aynrand.org/~/media/pdf/archives.ashx (accessed May 22, 2015), or by writing to archives@aynrand.org.

48 *The Ayn Rand Papers*, Ayn Rand Archives, Ayn Rand Institute, Irvine, CA. (Materials in this collection are cited by their reference number.) **[Papers]**

49 *Ayn Rand Biographical Interviews, 1960–1961.* Transcriptions of the biographical interviews of Ayn Rand by Barbara and Nathaniel Branden, New York, NY, December 1960–May 1961. Ayn Rand Archives, Ayn Rand Institute, Irvine, CA. **[Biographical Interviews]**

50 *The Objectivist Workshops Transcript with Previously Omitted Sections.* Benjamin Bayer, transcriber. Ayn Rand Archives, Ayn Rand Institute, Irvine, CA. (Portions of an earlier version of this transcript have been published, in an edited form, as an appendix to the expanded second edition of *ITOE*; see #9, above.) **[Workshops]**

IV. Works Based on Courses Authorized by Rand

51 Branden, Nathaniel. 1969. *Basic Principles of Objectivism.* Recorded Lectures. Los Angeles: Academic Associates. (These recordings, which have since been re-released on several media, purport to be the original *Basic Principles of Objectivism* course offered by NBI with Rand's endorsement. However the provenance of the recordings is uncertain, and they were released after Rand's denunciation of Branden and despite her strenuous objections; see *TO* 8[4] 656. [On this break and the related concerns about Branden's credibility as a source on Rand, see above, 13, 33–34, and 36.] During the years that NBI was active, the *Basic Principles* course was delivered numerous times in New York City and elsewhere; sometimes it was recorded, and these recordings were made available by "tape transcription" to groups of students in other cities. Presumably at least some of the material released by Academic Associates derives from these recordings, but since no complete set of original recordings is available, it is impossible to determine exactly how the released material relates to them. Internal evidence suggests that some of the released lectures, or parts thereof, were recorded early in the NBI period. Other parts cannot have been recorded earlier than 1967 and may postdate Rand's break with Branden in 1968. The editing of the earlier and later material together may have been done to produce tapes for the transcription series, or it may have been done by Branden post-break. Given the uncertainties, the recordings cannot be relied upon as an accurate representation of the course Rand authorized. However, they are evidence as to the contents of the original course; and my own preliminary comparison between the recordings and the limited materials available in the Ayn Rand Archives has not revealed any positive evidence of changes made after the break.)

2009. *The Vision of Ayn Rand: The Basic Principles of Objectivism – The original, never-before published NBI Lecture series*. Gilbert, AZ: Cobden Press. (This book is a transcript of taped lectures of uncertain provenance, with a new introduction by Barbara Branden and an additional essay by Nathaniel Branden, criticizing Rand.) **[VAR]**

52 Peikoff, Leonard. 1991. *Objectivism: The Philosophy of Ayn Rand*. New York, NY: Dutton. (This book, written after Rand's death, is based on #34, above. Since those recordings are available, it is possible to compare Peikoff's later formulations to the ones in the course Rand formally endorsed.) **[OPAR]**

Index

All unattributed titles in the index are by Rand. Sub-headings for such works occasionally include numbers in parentheses; these refer to page numbers in the referenced works, rather than page numbers in this volume.

Page references in bold represent the most fruitful places to start when researching a much-discussed topic.

A Companion to Ayn Rand, First Edition. Edited by Allan Gotthelf and Gregory Salmieri.
© 2016 John Wiley & Sons, Ltd. Published 2016 by John Wiley & Sons, Ltd.

J

O